FRUIT GROWING

FRUIT GROWING

DR. J.S. BAL
Ph.D. (Hort.)
Ex. Professor of Horticulture
Department of Fruit Science
Punjab Agricultural University
Ludhiana

KALYANI PUBLISHERS
LUDHIANA – NEW DELHI – NOIDA (U.P.) – HYDERABAD - CHENNAI
KOLKATA – CUTTACK – GUWAHATI – KOCHI - BANGALORE

KALYANI PUBLISHERS

Head Office :
B-I/1292, Rajinder Nagar, **Ludhiana**-141 008
e-mail : kalyanibooks@yahoo.co.in

Administrative Office :
4779, Ansari Road,
23, Daryaganj, **New Delhi**-110 002

Works :
B-16, Sector 8, **Noida** (U.P.)

Branches :
1, Mahalakshmi Street,
T. Nagar, **Chennai**-600 017

110/111, Bharatia Towers Badambadi
Cuttack-753 009 (Odisha)

3-5-1108, Narayanaguda, **Hyderabad**-500 029 (A.P.)

10/2B, Ramanath Mazumdar Street,
Kolkata-700 009

1st Floor, Saraswati Road, Pan Bazar,
Guwahati-781 001

Convent Road, **Kochi**-682 035

No. 24 & 25, Ist Floor, Hameed Shah Complex,
Banpet Main Road, **Bangalore**-560 002

Third Revised Edition, 2014
Reprinted, 2019

P-30142 2

Typesetting & Diagrams by :
(Fruit-14)
Datalink Computer
213-Sangam Complex, Milap Chowk,
Jalandhar-144001

ISBN 978-93-272-3980-5

PRINTED IN INDIA
at Diamond Agencies Pvt. Ltd., B-125, Sec. 63, NOIDA

Dedicated to

My Respected Mother
who inspired me to
fulfil this commitment

FOREWORD

Third Edition

Climate of India is quite favourable for the production of vast variety of fruits ranging from tropical to temperate fruits. Still our per capita production and consumption of fruits are minuscule of that in the developed countries. In total however, India is the second largest producer of fruits in the world with the production of 76 million tons of fruits from 6.7 million hectares of land and accounts for 12percent of total world production of fruits. The country leads in the production of mango, banana, sapota, pomegranate, lime and aonla. This level of production of fruits has been achieved through adoption of better yielding verities as well as improved production and protection technologies.

Mango, banana, citrus, guava and apple are the major fruits grown in india. Sapota, grapes, pomegranate, Papaya, pineapple, litchi, ber, aonla, pear, peach, plum, almond, apricot, walnut, cherry and strawberry are also grown on sizeable area. Maharashtra is the leading fruit growing state in India, which accounts for 14 percent of the fruit production in country. Also the economic returns per unit of land from most of the fruits, compares better with the returns from other traditional crops like wheat, rice, cotton etc. Some fruits like pineapple, papaya, banana and grapes have very high productivity ensuring much better returns.

The existing area under fruits in Punjab is only 1 percent of the total cultivated area in the state. The area under the fruits in the state can be increased substantially and can be easily doubled or even trebled. There is similar scope in other states of the country also. The demand for fruit consumption is increasing very fast in the country due to increasing incomes, changing consumption pattern towards protective foods and increasing population in the country. Extent situation is that fruits are getting out of reach of the middle and low income classes of the society due to unprecedented increase in the prices of the fruits. Yet the area under fruit crops is not expanding upto the desire extent

The culprit is the market, especially the retail market, which does not allow more than 20 to 25 percent of what the consumer pays, flow to the producers of fruits and vegetables. There is also a dire need for creating modern cold storage, cold chains and processing in order to minimize the post harvest losses which have been varied estimated between 20 to 30 percent of the produce.

Further, wheat and rice crop rotation is fast depleting the underground water table and is vitiating the water balance of the state along with soil, water and air pollution creating environmental hazard for the state. There is an urgent need for diversification of cropping pattern of the state and reducing the area under rice and even wheat. Horticulture crops are one of the most suited alternatives to this rotation.

The book, "Fruit Growing" is a very comprehensive work containing all the detailed information for orcharding on scientific lines. The students of horticulture in colleges and universities, fruit growers, scientist and technical experts and nurserymen will be considerably benefited because quite exhaustive details are incorporated on various aspects of fruit production.

I appreciate the efforts made by Dr. J.S. Bal in coming out with such a useful work, sharing his vast experience in this third revised version of his book.

26 January, 2014

Dr. S.S. Johal
Chancellor
Central University of Punjab

PREFACE

(Third Revised Edition)

Fruits are nature's gift to mankind. They are not only delicious and refreshing but are also the chief source of vitamins, minerals and proteins. It may not be exaggeration to say that 80- 90 per cent of problems arising from under nutrition or malnutrition can be well managed with indigenous medicines and fruits are an important part of these.

The basic chapter in this book on selection of site and soil for planting an orchard, preparation of land and layout of an orchard, orchard cultural practices with special reference to soil and plant management practices and flowering and fruiting are specially dealt with in the light of recent recommendations. The chapter on propagation and nursery management provides fundamental information necessary for raising a fruit nursery. The methods of vegetative propagation including division, cutting, layering, budding, grafting and micro-propagation are considered in comprehensive form. Modifications of standard practices and accepted methods for the commercial propagation of specific fruit plants are also given in detail. The exhaustive information on tropical, sub-tropical and temperate fruits grown commercially in various agro-climatic condition of India, is incorporated.

The book is primarily meant for the students of graduate and post-graduate in the field of Horticulture of all Agricultural Universities in India and neighbouring countries. The information included in this book is considered to be of utmost value to students of horticulture, fruit growers, nurserymen, gardeners, subject matter specialists and extension workers engaged in the field of horticulture. As a guide in practical work, the book deals with recent practices that have been introduced by research workers. In addition, I have also shared my personnel experience on fruit crops acquired during last thirty six years.

The book will prove boon for students contesting Indian Council of Agricultural Research, Junior and Senior Research fellowship, Agricultural Research Services examination, NET and various other fellowships in the field of horticulture. Teachers in the field of horticulture find themselves handicapped as they recommend foreign books to the students as only few Indian books are available. I have tried to make this book as up-to-date as possible, although I do not claim any originality of approach as I have followed the generally accepted literature.

I am highly thankful to the University Grants Commission, New Delhi for providing me assistance in writing of this book under University text book writing scheme.

I acknowledge with pride that successful completion of this work owes to my wife Dr. Kanwaljit Kaur for her inspiration and encouragement during the writing of this book.

Last, but not the least, I can never forget the nice cooperation rendered by my son Dr. Naveet Singh Bal and and daughter Dr. Harit K. Bal whose patience made this work less difficult.

15 January 2014 **Dr. J.S. Bal**

CONTENTS

Ch. No.	Chapters	Page No.

A. FUNDAMENTAL HORTICULTURE

1. **Fruits : Their Importance and Scope** 3–13
   Horticulture
   Branches of Horticulture
   Nutritive value of fruits
   Area and production of fruits in India
   – Main fruit producing countries
   – Export of fruits
   – Major markets of fruits in India
   Scope of fruit growing
   Problems of fruit cultivation
2. **Selection of Site and Soil** 14–20
   Locality and site
   Climate
   Classification of fruit trees according to climatic requirement
   Adverse effects of high temperature
   Protection against hot weather
   Adverse effects of low temperature
   Protection against cold
   Choice of soil
   Soil testing
3. **Preparation of Land and Layout of Orchard** 21–27
   Preparation of land
   Systems of layout
   Methods of planting fruit plants
   Planting distance of fruit plants
   High density planting
   Planting season
   Purchasing fruit plants from nursery
4. **Propagation and Nursery Management** 28–55
   Sexual propagation: Advantages and disadvantages
   Vegetative propagation: Advantages and disadvantages
   Propagation by seed
   Asexual propagation methods
   (*i*) Division
   (*ii*) Cutting
   (*iii*) Layering

Ch. No.	Chapters	Pages
	(*iv*) Budding	
	(*v*) Grafting	
	(vi) Micro propagation	
	Micro propagation techniques	
	Preparation of tissue culture media	
	Mist propagation technique	
	Green houses for propagation	
	Factors for successful graftage	
	Progeny trees	
	Raising of rootstock and propagation techniques	
	Care of nursery plants	
	Weeding and hoeing	
	Plant protection measures	
5.	**Orchard Cultural Practices**	**56–72**
	(*a*) **Soil management practices**	
	Soil culture	
	Inter culture	
	Manuring and fertilization	
	Deficiency symptoms of some essential elements	
	Leaf sampling in fruit crops	
	Irrigation systems	
	Proper use of drip system	
	(*b*) **Fruit plant management practices**	
	Training of fruit plants	
	Pruning of fruit plants	
	Ringing of fruit trees	
	Fruit thinning	
	Spraying	
	Harvesting and fruit handling	
	Marketing of fruits	
6.	**Flowering and Fruiting**	**73–79**
	Bearing habit of fruits	
	Type of inflorescences	
	Blooming period	
	Forms of flower	
	Mode of pollination	
	Agencies of pollination	
	Pollen viability	

B. TROPICAL FRUITS

7.	**Mango**	**83–106**
8.	**Banana**	**107–121**

Ch. No.	Chapters	Pages
9.	Papaya	122–131
10.	Pineapple	132–140
11.	Guava	141–150
12.	Sapota	151–159
13.	Cashewnut	160–169
14.	Custard Apples	170–177
	C. SUB-TROPICAL FRUITS	
15.	Citrus	181–212
16.	Grapes	213–242
17.	Litchi	243–255
18.	Ber	256–271
19.	Loquat	272–279
20.	Date-Palm	280–288
21.	Pomegranate	289–297
22.	Jamun	298–303
23.	Phalsa	304–309
24.	Avocado	310–315
25.	Aonla	316–324
	D. TEMPERATE FRUITS	
26.	Apple	327–346
27.	Pear	347–360
28.	Peach	361–373
29.	Plum	374–385
30.	Almond	386–394
31.	Apricot	395–402
32.	Walnut	403–412
33.	Cherry	413–421
34.	Strawberry	422–431
	References	432–434

A. FUNDAMENTAL HORTICULTURE

1. Fruits, their Importance and Scope
2. Selection of Site and Soil
3. Preparation of Land and Layout of Orchard
4. Propagation and Nursery Management
5. Orchard Cultural Practices
6. Flowering and Fruiting

CHAPTER 1

Fruits : Their Importance and Scope

WHAT IS HORTICULTURE

Modern horticulture may be defined as an agricultural science which treats of the production, utilization and improvements of fruits, vegetables and ornamental plants. The term is derived from the Latin word hortus 'garden' and cultura 'cultivation'.

BRANCHES OF HORTICULTURE

The general subject of horticulture is made up of four branches i.e. 1. Pomology, 2. Olericulture, 3. Floriculture and 4. Landscape gardening.

Pomology: Pomology is regarded as that phase of horticulture which treats of fruits. The word pomology, when given a liberal and flexible translation , means the science of fruits. The term is derived from the Latin word pomum 'fruits' and the Greek term logy 'science'.

Olericulture: Olericulture is that branch of horticulture which deals with vegetables. Basically olericulture is the art and science of the so called truck-crops. The word olericulture is derived from the Latin word oleris 'pot herb' and the English word culture 'the culture of succulent vegetables'.

Floriculture: Floriculture treats of flowers. It deals with all the operation and practices incident to the care of all such plants as are cultivated exclusively for their flowers or foliage.

Landscape Gardening: Landscape gardening deals with landscape architecture and such plant materials as are essential to landscape development. In the practical sense, the identification of plants, planning, planting and maintenance of home grounds, city and rural parks, school grounds, municipal estates are phases of landscape gardening.

NUTRITIVE VALUE OF FRUITS

Fruits are nature's gift to mankind. These are not only delicious and refreshing but are also the chief source of vitamins, minerals and proteins. These constituents are essential for the normal physiological well being and help in maintaining healthy state through development of resistance against pathogens. The fruits also contain mineral salts, the deficiency of which can lead to disturbance of metabolism resulting in ill-health. Carbohydrates and fats are the chief source of energy and, therefore, are essential for keeping good health. Their pectin and cellulose contents help in stimulating the intestinal activity. Certain extract like **Badam Roghan** obtained from almonds possess specific medicinal value that makes the use of fruits in our daily diet imperative. It may not be an exaggeration to say that 80-90 per cent of problems arising from under nutrition or malnutrition can be well managed with indigenous medicines and fruits are an important part of these.

DIETIC REQUIREMENTS

According to nutrition experts, an individual should consume at least 85 g . fruits per day in addition to vegetables, pulses, milk, meat, eggs etc, to maintain proper health. The consumption of fruits as part and parcel of balanced diet acts as a catalyst and therefore, has a special significance. The suitable composition of balanced diet is given in Table 1.

Table 1. Suitable composition of balanced diet

Food	Quantity (gms)
Cereals	400
Milk and milk products	284
Green leafy vegetables	114
Fruits	85
Pulses, nuts and oilseeds	85
Root vegetables	85
Other vegetables	85
Fish and meat	85
Sugar and jaggery	57
Vegetable oil and Ghee	57
Eggs	40 (1 egg)

The approximate nutritive value of this diet is calories 3000, protein 90g, carbohydrates 450 g, calcium 1.4 g, phosphorus 3 g, iron 47 mg, nicotine acid 22 mg and vitamin C 240 mg.

FRUITS AS ESSENTIAL DIET

Vitamins

These are the most important constituent of fruits and are indispensable part of human diet. Although required in very minute quantities, they are absolutely essential for the maintenance of health. The deficiency of any vitamins from the diet for considerable period may lead to diseased state or disorder conditions.

Vitamin A (Carotene) : The deficiency of vitamin A in our daily diet leads to the disorders like night blindness, cessation of growth in young ones, drying up of lachrymal glands in the eyes, eruption of skin, bitterness of teeth and susceptibility to various diseases. Carotene is a precursor of vitamin A which is found in most fruits in varying quantities. Fruits like mango, papaya, jackfruit, persimmon, cashewnut, fig and ber are the chief sources of vitamin A.

Vitamin B_1 (Thiamine) : The absence of this vitamin in the daily diet causes beri-beri, paralysis, loss of sensitivity of skin, enlargement of heart, loss of appetite, loss of weight and fall in body temperature. Fruits like cashewnut, walnut, almond, banana, apricot, apple, pear and plum are the chief sources of thiamine.

Vitamin B_2 (Riboflavin): Riboflavin is important for growth and health of skin. The deficiency of this vitamin causes sore throat, cataract, loss of body weight, anorexia and development of swollen nose. The fruits which are major sources of this vitamin are : bael (bil), litchi, papaya, pineapple, pomegranate and pear.

Other B-complex Vitamins: The deficiency of these vitamins (B_6B_{12}) in human diet cause megaloblastic (macrocytic) anaemia.

Nicotinic acid has a specific curative agent for human pellagra which occurs because of its deficiency. Pantothenic acid deficiency causes dermatitis. The fruits like peach, plum, apricot, apple, pear, guava, grapes, bael, litchi, pineapple, pomegranate, almond, walnut, and cashewnut are the good sources of vitamins B_6, nicotinic acid and pentothenic acid.

Vitamin C (Ascorbic Acid) : This vitamin is essential for the formation of normal teeth and bones. It improves the resistance of vascular walls. This vitamin has a significant role in the assimilation of proteins obtained from other sources. Absence of vitamin C is responsible for the condition called scurvy which is characterised by pain in the joints and swelling of limbs (rheumatism), bleeding of gums, tooth decay etc. Aonla (Amla) is the richest sources of vitamin C followed by guava, ber, citrus fruits (orange, mandarin, grapefruit, lime and lemon), strawberry and pineapple.

Minerals

A large number of minerals are present in human body. Bones and teeth are mainly made up of calcium, magnesium and phosphorus. Iron is an important constituent of blood whereas iodine regulates the functioning of hormones (thyroxine). Minerals like zinc, molybednum and manganese are activators of certain enzymes. In addition to these, many other elements are also required for adequate growth of tissues. Minerals are found in varying concentrations in fruits. For example, karonda is rich in iron and walnut and almond are rich in phosphorus and calcium and blue-berry and banana in potassium, respectively. Calcium, phosphorus and iron contents of selected fruits is given in Table 2.

Table 2. Mineral composition of selected fruits

Fruits	Calcium (%)	Phosphorus (%)	Iron (%)
Almond	0.23	0.39	3.47
Aonla	0.05	0.02	1.20
Apple	0.01	0.01	1.68
Ber	0.03	0.04	1.14
Cashewnut	0.05	0.45	5.00
Dates	0.07	0.08	10.60
Grapes	0.005	0.02	0.40
Guava	0.01	0.04	1.04
Karonda	0.16	0.06	39.70
Mango	0.007	0.02	0.25
Papaya	0.01	0.01	0.27
Peach	0.006	0.03	1.70
Raisins	0.10	0.08	4.00
Walnut	0.10	0.38	4.80

Carbohydrates, Fats and Protein

Carbohydrates and fats provide energy to the human body while protein builds up the body tissues. Some fruits are important source of carbohydrates, protein and fat which are essential for proper growth and development of the human being.

Fruits are the best coprescription. A patient with night blindness is advised to take mango and papaya and those suffering from scurvy diseases should take amla and guava. The children deficient with protein energy malnutrition (PEM) are coprescriped with fruits rich in protein and carbohydrates like almond, cashewnut, walnut, apricot (dry), banana, bael, dates, karonda and raisins. Similarly, citrus fruits are mandatory coprescription to diuretic. Bael is a useful tranquiliser. Its aquous extract, (sharbat) has a cooling effect, therefore, it is useful in

Table 3. Carbohydrates, fat and protein content of selected fruits

Fruits	Carbohydrate (%)	Fat (%)	Protein (%)
Almond	10.5	58.7	20.8
Apricot (dry)	72.8	0.7	1.7
Avocado	0.8	22.8	1.7
Banana	36.4	0.2	1.3
Bael	30.6	0.2	1.3
Ber	13.6	0.1	0.9
Cashewnut	22.3	46.9	21.2
Dates	67.3	0.2	3.0
Karonda	67.1	9.6	2.3
Raisins (dried grapes)	77.3	0.2	2.0
Walnut	11.0	64.5	15.6

hot summer days. Almond oil extract is useful in malnourished as well as bronchy asthma cases in winter. Dried powder of amla in combination with Harad and Bahera is commonly dispensed as useful remedy for constipation. Banana is a useful coprescription in diarrhoea.

AREA AND PRODUCTION OF FRUITS

India is the second largest producer of fruits after China, with a production of 76.4 million tonnes of fruits from an area of 6.7 million hectares (Table 5). It is almost 29 per cent of the area under horticulture in India. The production has increased to manifold in the last five decades from 6.8 million tonnes to 76.4 million tonnes. In the year 2005-06, the area under fruits was 5.3 million hectares with annual production of 55.4 million metric tonnes (Table 4). A continuous increase in area and production was registered every year but a brief lull in area was observed between the year 2009-10 and 2010-11. In recent year of 2011-12, there was considerable increase in area under fruits which was recorded 6.7 million hectares.

Table 4. Area and Production of Fruits in India (2005-06 to 2011-12)*

Year	Area (000, ha)	Production (000, mt)	Productivity (mt/ha)
2005-06	5324	55356	10.4
2006-07	5554	59563	10.7
2007-08	5857	65587	11.2
2008-09	6101	68466	11.2
2009-10	6329	71516	11.3
2010-11	6383	74878	11.7
2011-12	6705	76424	11.4

* India Horticulture Database 2012.

India accounts for 12 per cent of total world production of fruits and leads the world in producing mango, banana, papaya, sapota, pomegranate, lime and aonla. This increase in production is accounted for enhanced productivity owing to the adoption of high yielding cultivars and improved production and protection technologies. Most of the fruits are grown on wide range of agro-climatic conditions with varied production.

A large variety of fruits are grown in India, of which banana, mango, citrus, guava and apple are the major ones. Apart from these, sapota, grapes, pomegranate, papaya, pineapple, litchi, ber and aonla in tropical and sub-tropical group and pear, peach, plum, almond, apricot, walnut and strawaberry in the temperate group are grown in sizeable area. The fruits are grown throughout the country, however, the major fruit growing states area wise are Maharashtra, Andhra Pradesh, Jammu & Kashmir, Karnataka, Gujarat, Uttar Pradesh, Tamil Nadu, Odisha, Bihar, Kerala, West Bengal, Himachal Pradesh and Uttarakhand. The major fruit producing states on the basis of fruit prodction are Maharashtra, Andhra Pradesh, Tamil Nadu, Gujarat, Karnataka, Uttar Pradesh, Bihar, Madhya Pradesh, West Bengal, Kerala, Jammu and Kashmir and Odisha.

Table 5. Area and Production of Fruits in India 2011-12*

Fruits	Area (000′ ha)	Production (000′ mt)	Per cent		Productivity (mt./ha)
			Area	Production	
Mango	2378	16196	35.5	21.2	6.8
Citrus	915	7922	13.6	10.4	8.7
Banana	797	28455	11.9	37.2	35.7
Apple	322	2203	4.8	2.9	6.8
Guava	220	2510	3.3	3.3	11.4
Sapota	163	1426	2.4	1.9	8.7
Walnut	150	284	2.2	0.4	1.9
Papaya	117	4457	1.8	5.8	38.1
Grape	116	2221	1.7	2.9	19.1
Pomegranate	112	772	1.7	1.0	6.9
Pineapple	102	1500	1.5	2.0	14.7
Litchi	80	538	1.2	0.7	6.7
Others	1233	7940	18.4	10.3	6.4
Total	6705	76424	100.0	100.0	11.4

* India Horticulture Database 2012.

Mango is the most important fruit covering 35.5 percent of area and accounting for 21.2 per cent of total production in the country, which is 40 per cent of global mango production. The productivity varies from 3.6 to 14.9 tonnes per hectare in different mango growing states. Major mango growing states are Uttar Pradesh, Andhra Pradesh, Karnataka, Bihar, Gujarat, Tamil Nadu, Odisha, West Bengal, Jharkhand and Maharashtra.

Citrus fruits are grown in 9.15 lakh hectares with total production of 79.22 lakh metric tonnes annually. Productivity of citrus varies from 4.4 to 21.9 metric tonnes per hectare depending upon agro-climatic regions. Mandarin, sweet oranges (Mosambi), lime and lemons cover bulk of the area under citrus fruits. These fruits are grown mainly in Maharashtra, Andhra Pradesh, Punjab, Madhya Pradesh, Gujarat, Karnataka, Rajasthan, Assam, Odisha, Haryana and Uttarakhand. Limes and lemons producing states are Andhra Pradesh, Gujarat, Maharahstra, Karnataka, Bihar, Madhya Pradesh, Assam and Chhattisgarh. The higher production of limes and lemons to the tune of 31 per cent is recorded in Andhra Pradesh followed by 19 per cent in Gujarat. Mosambi (Sweet Orange) is cultivated only in few states like Maharashtra, Andhra Pradesh, Karnataka and Punjab. Andhra Pradesh is the leading Mosambi producing state with a share of 46.8 percent. In Mandarin, Nagpur Sangtra and Kinnow are the two important cultivars grown in India. Maharashtra, Madhya Pradesh, Andhra Pradesh, Punjab, Assam and Rajasthan states have largest area under mandarin cultivation. Punjab is the leading state in kinnow production where average productivity is highest *i.e.* 21.4 metric tonnes per hectare.

Banana rank second in area and occupying 13.6 percent of the total area and accounting for 37.2 percent of the total production in India. India has first position in the world in banana production. Tamil Nadu leads other states in area with a share of about 23.7 per cent. Gujarat has highest productivity of 62.3 metric tonnes against India's average of 35.7 metric tonnes per hectare. The major banana growing states are Tamil Nadu, Maharashtra, Gujarat, Andhra Pradesh, Karnataka, Bihar, Madhya Pradesh, Uttar Pradesh, West Bengal and Assam.

Apple is the fourth most important fruit crop in India. The fruit is grown in 3.22 lakh hectares having annual production of 22.03 lakh metric tonnes accounting for 4.8 and 2.9 per cent of area and production, respectively. Apple is largely grown in Jammu and Kashmir, Himachal Pradesh, Uttarakhand and Arunchal Pradesh. The production of fruit is the highest in Jammu and Kashmir which is 80.6 per cent of the total production in India. The average productivity in the state is 10.4 metric tonnes per hectare.

Guava is the fifth most widely grown fruit crop in India. The area under guava is 2.20 lakh ha yielding annual production of 25.1 lakh metric tonnes accounting for 3.3 per cent each of area and production. Maharashtra is the leading state in guava production with a share of 12.8 per cent of total production in India. Madhya Pradesh (10.2%), Uttar Pradesh (10.0%) and Bihar (9.8%) are other leading guava producing states. Guava is also grown widely in West Bengal, Punjab, Gujarat, Karnataka, Andhra Pradesh, Chhattisgarh and Odisha.

Sapota emerged as sixth important fruit crop on the basis of area under cultivation. Major sapota producng states are Karnataka, Gujarat, Maharashtra, Tamil Nadu and Andhra Pradesh. Karnataka is the leading state producing 26.5 per cent of total produce in India. It is followed by 21.7 per cent in Gujarat and 20.9 per cent in Maharashtra.

Walnut is grown in 1.5 lakh hectares with annual production of 284 lakh metric tonnes. Papaya is grown on 1.17 lakh hectares with annual production of 44.57 lakh metric tonnes. Productivity of papaya is the highest among the fruit crops. Major Papaya producing states are Andhra Pradesh, Gujarat, Karnataka, West Bengal, Madhya Pradesh and Maharashtra. Andhra Pradesh and Gujarat area producing major share of 26.7 and 23.8 per cent, respectively of the total production in the country.

Grapes occupy 1.16 lakh hectares area producing 22.21 lakh metric tonnes annually. Maharahstra occupies the first position in production of grapes with a total share of 81.5 per cent. The other grape growing states are Karnataka, Tamil Nadu, Andhra Pradesh and Mizoram.

Pomegranate is cultivated in 1.12 lakh hectates accounting for 1.7 per cent of the area. Maharahstra state has maximum area of 82000 hectares under pomegranate with annual production of 4.7 lakh metric tonnes. But, the productivity is the highest (26.4 mt/ha) in Tamil Nadu. Pomegranate growing states in Indian are Maharashtra, Karanataka, Gujarat, Andhra Pradesh, Madhya Pradesh, Tamil Nadu and Rajasthan.

Pineapple is cultivated on 1.02 lakh hectares with annual production of 15 lakh metric tonnes. The highest productivity of 58.2 metric tonnes per hactare was recorded in Karnataka. The overall production of fruit is the highest in West Bengal and area is maximum in Assam state. The other pineapple growing states are Tripura, Bihar, Manipur, Meghalaya, Nagaland, Kerala and Arunachal Pradesh.

Aonla occupies 95000 hectares area producing 9.6 lakh metric tonnes annually. Litchi is cultivated in 80000 hectares accounting for 1.2 per cent of area and 0.7 per cent of fruit production. Bihar is the leading litchi producing state in country with a total share of 43.9 percent. The states growing litchi are West Bengal, Jharkhand, Assam, Punjab, Chhattisgarh, Odisha, Uttarakhand and Tripura.

Ber is also coming up as future fruit crop of India. The area under ber is about one lakh hectare producing approx 10 lakh metric tonnes fruits annually. Maharashtra, Gujarat, Uttar Pradesh, Tamil Nadu, Jammu and Kashmir, West Bengal, Chhattisgarh, Haryana, Rajasthan, Madhya Pradesh, Punjab, Karnataka, Bihar and Andhra Pradesh states are producing ber crop.

Cashewnut is grown in the west coast, east coast and in Karnataka and Madhya Pradesh. The highest productivity is observed in Maharashtra. The total area under this crop is

9.79 lakh hectares with annual production of 7.25 lakh metric tonnes. Major cashewnut growing states are Andhra Pradesh, Chhattisgarh, Goa, Gujarat, Jharkhand, Karnataka, Kerala, Maharashtra, Meghalya, Puducherry, Odisha, Tamil Nadu, Tripura and West Bengal.

Area under different temperate fruits is quite limited. Pear is grown in 4800 hectares, peach on 36400 hectares, plum on 26000 hectares and almond on 23810 hectares with corresponding production of 2.94 lakh metric tonnes, 2.86 lakh metric tonnes, 72000 metric tonnes and 17230 metric tonnes, respectively.

The leading fruit growing state in India is Maharashtra which accounts for 14 percent of production followed by Andhra Pradesh (13%), Tamil Nadu (11%), Gujarat (10%), Karnataka (9%), Uttar Pradesh (8%) and Bihar (5%).

Banana is the major fruit crop accounting for 37 per cent of total production followed by mango 21 per cent, citrus 10.4 per cent, papaya 5.8 per cent and guava 3.3 percent.

Table 6. Area and Production Estimate for Fruits in India 2012-13*

Fruits	Area (000′ ha)	Production (000′ mt)	Per cent		Productivity (mt/ha)
			Area	Production	
Mango	2500	18002	35.8	22.1	7.2
Citrus	1042	10090	14.9	12.4	9.7
Banana	776	26509	11.1	32.6	34.2
Apple	312	1915	4.5	2.4	6.1
Guava	236	3198	3.4	3.9	13.6
Sapota	164	1495	2.3	1.8	9.1
Walnut	123	233	1.8	0.3	1.9
Papaya	132	5382	1.9	6.6	40.8
Grape	118	2483	1.7	3.1	21.0
Pomegranate	113	745	1.6	0.9	6.6
Pineapple	105	1571	1.5	2.0	15.0
Litchi	83	580	1.2	0.7	7.0
Others	1278	9082	18.3	11.2	7.1
Total	6982	81285	100.0	100.0	11.6

* National Horticulture Board 2013.

Main Fruit Producing Countries

China ranks first in area and production of fruits in the world. It occupies 12.3 million hectares area with annual fruit production of 135 million metric tonnes. India is the second largest country in area and production of fruits. China is producing 21 per cent and India producing 12 per cent share of fruits in the world. Brazil is placed at third position growing fruits on 2.45 million hectares which is producing 27 million metric tonnes. The average productivity of fruits is the highest (23.9 mt/ha) in USA. The other important fruit producing countries are Italy, Philippines, Mexico, Spain, Indonesia and Turkey. The average productivity in Philippines is 22.9 metric tonnes per hectare which is also quite high only after USA. The total area under fruits in the world is 57.5 million hectares with annual production of 639 million metric tonnes.

Export of Fruits

The annual production of fruits in India is 76.4 million tonnes and offer good opportunities for export. India exported fruit worth Rs. 2503.7 crores during 2012-13. Mango, walnut, grapes, banana and pomegranate account for larger portion of fruits exported from India.

The major importing countries are United Arab Emirates, Bangladesh, Malaysia, United Kingdom, Netherland, Pakistan, Saudi Arabia, Sri Lanka and Nepal. This export of fruits has been achieved due to estabilishment of cold chain infrastructure and quality assurance measures. Large investment has been done by the public and private sectors. In several centres for perishable Cargo and post-harvest handling facilities have been set up with the assistance of APEDA. Capacity building initiatives at the growers, processors and exporter's levels has also contributed towards this gole.

Major Markets of Fruits in India

Azadpur Fruit Market Delhi is the major market in India. Chandigarh, Amritsar, Jaipur, Patna, Kolkata, Lucknow, Kanpur, Agra, Varanasi, Mumbai, Pune, Bangalore, Indore, Hyderabad and Chennai are the other important fruit markets in India.

SCOPE OF FRUIT GROWING

Cultivation of fruits contributes to the health, happiness and prosperity of the people. The standard of living of the people can be judged by production and consumption of fruits per capita. Inspite of the fact that India is climatically favourable for production of a variety of a tropical, sub-tropical and temperate fruits, our per capita per day consumption of fruits is the lowest (60 g) relative to developed (250-450g) countries like Switzerland, France, Sweeden, Australia, Netherland, USA and Canada and even developing countries (100-200 g) like Hungary, Germany, Philippines, Pakistan and Japan. Present availability of fruits in India is less than the minimum dietary requirement of 85 g. So, there is great need to increase the area and production of fruits to meet the minimum dietary requirements at a reasonable cost.

The fruits in India occupy only 6.7 million hectares area. There is good scope to increase the area under fruit crop.With growing urbanization, requirements for fruits in the cities is increasing tremendously and there is need to boost fruit production. Presently, the fruits are available at very high cost in the markets and are not within the reach of common people. The production has to be increased till the country becomes self-sufficient in the fruit and the price of the fruit falls to a level at which all people, rich and poor can afford to buy it. This can be only achieved by increasing the area under fruits and by rajuvenating the existing orchards.

Earlier the fruit production was confined to the pleasure gardens of kings and nobles. However, the commercial fruit production emerged in a real sense, after the end of second world war and it was adopted as a profession by many enterprising farmers. Fruit cultivation is labour intensive industry and it is ideally suited to over populated countries of the world like India and China, where per capita cultivated land holding is less than one hectare. Like all other branches of horticulture, the fruit production involves certain specialised skills in production, harvesting, marketing and canning and processing and many intricacies of the trade require a touch of professionalism. The involvement and commitment of small and medium level enterpreneurs is highly desirable and prerequisite for increasing the level of production and the profitable marketing of the fruit what has been produced.

The economic productivity of the fruit plants per unit area is no less than any of the agricultural crops. Some of the fruit plants have a very high and encouraging production. The production of 45 tons of pineapple, 40 tons of papaya, 30 tons of banana and 25 tons of grapes from a hectare of land per annum is obtained and these may compete with any other agricultural crop enterprises. It has been reported that the horticultural crops with their meagre share of 2-3 per cent of land area in most of the countries, contribute 5-7 per cent of gross food production and 10-35 per cent of the national income from the crop enterprise.The high productivity of fruit trees gives higher economic return per unit area. This also provides higher caloric return from the the same area of land.

The mulitiple cropping system in the orchards also generate more avenues for employment apart from giving additional income. The intensive horticultural practices may accommodate skilled and trained personnels where unemployment is a serious problem. Mango, litchi and pear are the permanent fruit crops and comes into bearing late. The filler trees like kinnow, peach, plum, papaya and phalsa can be intercropped in the permanent trees during pre-bearing period. Vegetables can be intercropped between the tree rows in the orchard.

With our rapid increasing population, the pressure on land is likely to continue and size of holding will remain small in the foreseable future. Moreover, fruit crops give much more production per unit of area and are certainly more paying than ordinary farm crops. The growers can net an income of Rs. 1,00,000 lakh to Rs. 2,00,000 lakhs per hectare by growing fruit crops which is much more than field crops. Keeping in view the above facts, there is an enormous scope for expanding area under fruits in the country.

The fruit production has a great possibility in trade and industrial development. A large number of ancillary industries and trade sectors are also developed. Processing units, garden tools, CFB boxes and wooden crates, baskets, spray pumps, insecticides and pesticides, fungicides, cold storage and refrigerated vans are the important areas of trade.

In addition,the fruit crop may fit well in crop diversification programmes in various scales, ranging from organised large orchards to a few trees in the waste land or backyard of home or elsewhere. Wheat - rice rotation is not profitable. Water table is going deep. Rice crop should be replaced slowly with fruit crops.

PROBLEMS OF FRUIT CULTIVATION

In fruits, some of the national problems like malformation, alternate bearing and spongy tissue in mango, wilt in guava and bunchy top and wilt in banana are still defying solution. Yet no headway has been achieved in production of superior quality planting materials and nurserymen are following the age old practices. No precise information is available on water requirement of fruit crops. There is lack of suitable varieties resistant to biotic and abiotic stresses. The suitable rootstocks have not been indentified for high density planting to increase the production. Appropriate horticulture-based cropping systems for different agroclimatic areas particularly in dryland, arid, coastal and hilly areas need to be developed. Due emphasis needs attention on integerated control of pests and diseases and pesticide residue. However, the most important problems being faced in the way of profitable fruit growing are discussed below :

(*i*) **High initial orchard investment :** The initial investment on establishment of new orchard is very high. It includes cost of plants, expenditure on layout, digging and refilling of pits, farmyard manures and insecticides and pesticides. The basic expenditure on planting of new orchard in different fruit plants is Rs. 25,000 to 50,000 per hectare. It is still more in grapes where erection cost of training structure touches to Rs. 2.0-3.0 lakhs per hectare. The ordinary farmer having small land holding can t afford to establish an orchard. There is strong need to implement schemes to provide liberal loan facility at lower interest rate for establishment of new orchards.

(*ii*) **Long juvenile period of fruit plant :** The major constraint in the way of increasing the area under fruit crop is long waiting period stretching upto 10 years in many cases, before a fruit grower can expect any income from an orchard. The permanent fruit crops like mango, pear and litchi comes into bearing very late and a small or middle level farmer can not wait such a long period without substantial income.However, by planting filler trees like kinnow, plum, peach, papaya, phalsa and guava in the permanent trees like mango, litchi and pear, the economic loss of pre-bearing period can be compensated.

(*iii*) **Lack of high quality fruit plants :** A healthy nursery plant is the foundation of an orchard and adequate availability of healthy plants is essential for a fruit industry.Use of poor planting meterial is the major constraint limiting higher production in most of the orchards. In number of government, as well as private nurseries proper care is not exercised in the selection of outstanding mother plants free of diseases. The poor grade plants propagated from these mother trees are distributed in large number. These inferior trees become permanent liabilities to the growers as any package of intensive cultural practices would not be able to change their inherent poor production potential. The fruit plants purchased from private nurseries and footpath sellers, prove to be a very expensive investment in the long run because these plants are generally from poor strains. The growers come to know about the yield and quality of the fruit after several years when the plants start bearing.

Citrus plants supplied to the growers are very often infested with citrus canker, citrus scab, leaf miner and citrus psylla, mango with vegetative malformation, peach with root-knot nematode. The citrus plants which can be infected with virus and virus like diseases through insect vectors in the nurseries are propagated by the Governent as well as the private nurseries without adequate checks.

Regular and uniformly bearing disease - free plant meterial should replace the existing ones. Trees of outstanding merits of all the popular varieties of important fruit crops should be indentified for large scale clonal propagation and distribution to the growers.

(*iv*) **Faulty marketing system :** The marketing of fruits in India is the most sorry aspect of fruit industry. The lack of marketing facilities is a big hurdle in the expansion of horticulture. The fruit crop is auctioned by the growers to the middle man who earn better profit from this produce. The whole process of marketing of fruit is outlined below.

To produce and to market fruit are very different and yet less understood aspects. Usually our farmers are good producers but they are ill adept at marketing methods. The most common way is to sell the fruit crop as given in the Fig. to the fruit contractors who are financed by the commission agents located in big city markets. Contractor generally does not pay to the farmer more than 35 per cent of the crop value. Thus about 65 per cent of the crop value is shared by the middlemen. Wholesalers purchase the fruit from commission agents and finally the fruit is given to the retailers for selling it to the consumers. It is a very lengthy procedure and cost much more to the consumer.

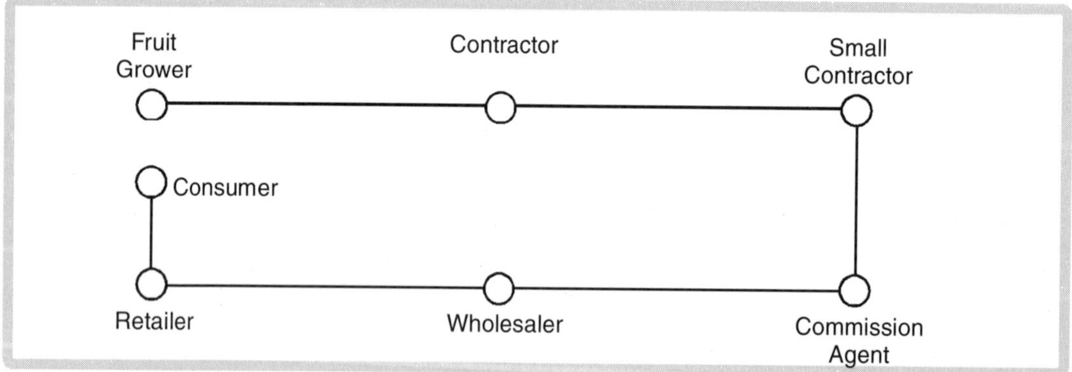

It would seem very simple to suggest that grower should bring his produce to the market and sell it himself and increase his margin of profit. A few individual who might have or may try this approach have to struggle very hard against a well entrenched system which has been exploiting the horticultural producers for very long time. So, considering this, there is need to develop **Apni Mandi** or Cooperative system of marketing.

(*v*) **Lack of storage and transportation facilities :** The post- harvest losses occure 20-30 per cent in most of the fruits. These losses take place due to poor availability of eliminating field heat facilities. After harvest, the fruits need to be transferred to cooling units within half-an hour. Due to poor cold storage and controlled atmospheric storage facilities, the losses further increase.

The present system of transporting fruits in India is in-efficient and highly injurious to the fruit trade. Roads connecting the orchards with the terminal markets are poor, vehicles operating on roads are multipurpose conveyances and do not protect the fruit adequately from damage. Railways have so far taken a negligible part in the development of fruit transportation. There is strong need to introduce fleet of refrigerated carriers.

Many cooling units have come up in Maharashtra, Gujarat and Andhra Pradesh. Cold chambers and ripening chambers has been established in few fruit markets in big cities by Mandi Board, Punjab to cater the need of the fruit growers. Still there is need to establish more cooling and ripening facilities in various fruit markets and fruit zones. In addition to these, the growers' cooperatives have set up their own cold storage units. The availability of refrigerated containers and their accessability have helped to maintain the cold chain. The State Govt. should set more cooling units to enhance the shelf life of the fruits for considerable length of time.

(*vi*) **Lack of processing units :** No worth while industry can be developed without creating adequate processing facilities. The world over fruits are either consumed fresh or they are processed into various products. In certain fruit crops like grapes and peach about 90 per cent of the total produce is processed. For every fruit the list of processed products is long. The processing industry for horticultural crops is the need of the day. Thus horticultural development cannot be conceived without active participation of processing industry. In sub-tropical and tropical climate 20-30 per cent of the fruits produced are wasted. If there were industries to process this waste, it would generate many useful byproducts. Available varieties of citrus, mango, litchi, grapes, guava, papaya, pineapple, banana, pear, peach, plum, ber and aonla can be processed into various forms for which there is an insatiable domestic and foreign market.

At present, the fruits are processed at very limited scale in India. Only a few number of processing units are working in different states. The processing industry may preferably be established in the public and private sectors with proper safeguards for the interests of the producers.

(*vii*) **Perishable nature of fruits :** Most of the horticultural produce is highly perishable because of high water content. In spite of very heavy losses, very little work has been done on post-harvest technology of horticultural crops.There is an urgent need to develop appropriate on-farm post-harvest handling and storage systems suitable for different commodities and agro-climatic situations and to standardize packaging, transportation and handling systems, development of new processed and economic utilization of processing wastes.

(*viii*) **Low purchasing power of the people :** The fruits are sold at very high cost in the markets. Low income and middle income group has low purchasing power and do not purchase the fruits regularly. The different fruits are available at very high rates *e.g.* apple Rs. 80-150/kg, grapes Rs. 80-100/kg, Musambi Rs. 60-100/dozen, Mandarin Rs. 50-80/kg, banana Rs. 50-60/dozen, pomegranate Rs. 100-150/kg, mango Rs. 50-80/kg, sapota Rs. 50-70/kg, soft pear Rs. 60-80/kg and papaya Rs. 30-40/kg. Under such circumstances, the fruits are not within the range of ordinary consumer. The marketing system of the fruit is defective and middleman is getting more profit out of the growers produce. There is a strong need for developing the co-operative system of marketing, so that the fruit growers get decent return of their investment. Also, the production of fruits has to be increased by putting more area under fruits with a view that the fruit should be available at reasonable prize in the market.

CHAPTER 2

Selection of Site and Soil

Orcharding is a long-term investment. Mistakes committed initially on selection of site and soil reduce the returns greatly from the investment, besides wastage of time and energy. Thus, one should give atmost attention and care, while planning a new orchard.

LOCALITY AND SITE

One has to take into consideration a number of factors while making choice of kinds of fruits and their varieties. Market demand would be one of the most important factor. A fruit which is more popular or is being supplied from a distant market offers a favourable opportunity. If fruit gardening is already being practised in the locality, it will be an additional advantage as one can make use of previous experience and expertise of the growers of that particular locality. Other factors, which have an important bearing on the success of an orchard in a particular locality, are nearness to the market, railway station, transport, easy accessibility by road, storage facilities, water supply, nearness to processing plant, etc. which will facilitate expeditious disposal of fruits and involve less expense on marketing. Most of the fruits being highly perishable, their speedy marketing is extremely desirable for getting decent returns.

Selection of proper site for an orchard is the most important aspect of fruit industry. Fruits that can be marketed in dried form may be grown in areas away from consumer market or where quick transport facilities are lacking. However, perishable fruits need quick transport facilities and their production centres should be near to the market. While considering the site for orchard, emphasis should be given to factors like climate, soil, market and transport facilities. Availability of trained labour, other inputs like fertilizers, insecticides, pesticides, etc. could be of added advantage.

The climate and soils of the zone are the chief natural factors, a favourable combination of which governs the success of fruit growing. All fruits cannot be grown successfully in every type of climate and soil. Therefore, the selection of suitable kinds and varieties of fruits for a particular region should be made on the basis of their performance.

CLIMATE

Climate may be defined as the weather changing in a certain manner during the course of a year. This includes several basic environmental factors such as temperature, atmospheric humidity, rainfall, wind and hail.

Temperature: It plays an important role in determining the success or failure of a fruit crop in a particular locality. Every type of fruit needs a certain range of temperature. The deciduous fruits like apple, pear, peach and plum can grow only on sites having sufficiently cool climate (45-55° F) to induce the trees to shed leaves during winter and after a specific period of rest come into flowering and leafing again.The fruits like mango and banana require a long-growing season and high temperature (65-75° F) without any frost or snowfall. However, different varieties of fruit may differ in their tolerance or adaptability. Banana, a tropical fruit crop, suffers heavily if the temperature falls below 50° F. The vital temperature for plant growth and development of different fruits varies from 45-75° F.

High temperature may promote high sugar contents whereas low temperature cause delayed blossoming and also inhibit the activity of pollinators.

Sunshine plays important role in fruit growing because of its influence on pollination and on the development and colouring of fruit. The same temperature acts differently on the shaded buds as against those receiving sunshine. Intensity and quality of light influence the formation of carbohydrates. Sunshine also influences the formation of flower bud.

Atmospheric humidity : The fruits like banana, papaya and sapota require high atmospheric humidity while others like mango and ber require less humidity. If the fruits of high atmospheric humidity requirements are grown in arid zones, they will not survive. Humid conditions are conducive for fungal and bacterial growth *e.g.* powdery mildew in mango and ber, scab in apple, black-rot and downy mildew in grapes and brownrot in peaches. In certain fruit crops, high humidity affects adversely on the fruit colour and keeping quality.

Rainfall: The amount of rainfall and its distribution in a particular region is very important in deciding the kind of fruits and varieties which can be grown successfully. Rainfall affects plant growth and development in many ways. Generally, heavy rainfall is unfavourable to fruit trees grown in the plains, as it leads to waterlogging and affects adversely the flowers and fruits. At the time of blossoming, rain washes away the stigmatic fluid and pollen from the stigma. Due to the heavy rains, activities of pollinators are greatly reduced. On the other hand light rainfall needs to be supplemented by additional irrigation to meet the growth and fruiting requirements of plants and thus increase the expenditure. Rains before harvesting cause softening of fruits in banana and date palm and induce infection of fruit-fly in guava and peaches.

Wind: High velocity and hot winds cause heavy damage to fruit trees. They cause breakage of limbs of fruit trees. High velocity winds also cause shedding of flowers and dropping of immature fruits. The increasing wind velocity retards the activity of pollinators. Bee activity is maximum when wind is still, gets little reduced when wind is 2-3 km per hour, gets greately reduced when wind velocity is 25 km per hour and their activity is altogether ceased when the wind velocity is 40 km per hour.

For successful cultivation of fruit crops, raising of dense windbreak rows around the orchard is necessary. The trees like Euclyptus, shisham, mulberry, seedling mango, jamun, ber and karonda may be used as windbreak.

Hail: The hail-storm causes great damage to the fruit crops. Occurrence of hail at the time of fruit maturity is very disastrous because fruit drop is heavy and the growers get poor return of their produce. For successful cultivation of fruit crops, only those areas where hail storms do not occur should be selected.

CLASSIFICATION OF FRUIT TREES ACCORDING TO CLIMATIC REQUIREMENTS OF INDIA

On the basis of climate, India can be divided into temperate, north western sub-tropical, north eastern sub-tropical, central tropical, southern and coastal tropical humid zones.

1. Temperate zone : These fruits grow successfully in cold regions where temperature falls below freezing point during winter. During the cold season, the trees shed their leaves and enter into rest period. A definite chilling period is needed for breaking this rest period. Temperate regions are further sub- divided into two groups *i.e.* higher and lower elevations.

(*a*) Higher elevation 1500-2500 metres above sea level : In this region, the fruits like apple, pear, walnut, almond and cherry can be successfully grown.

(*b*) Lower elevation 1200-1500 metres above sea level : The fruits like peach, plum, apricot and strawberry can be grown successfully.

The important regions where these fruits are grown are Kashmir valley, Kullu, Kangra, Kotgarh and Nahan in Himachal Pradesh and Kumaon hills in Uttarakhand.

2. North Western Sub-tropical zone. In this zone, the temperature occasionally goes below the freezine point, but not as a rule below 25°F. The sub tropical fruits grow mostly in the plains where the climate is hot and comparatively dry and the winter is dry and less cold. The types of fruits grown in this zone are citrus, mango, guava, litchi, ber, grape, pear, peach, plum, phalsa, loquat, aonla, datepalm and pomegranate.

The chief regions of this zone are Punjab, Haryana, Rajasthan, Uttar Pradesh and parts of Madhya Pradesh and Uttarakhand.

3. North Eastern Sub-tropical zone. The temperature is high, slightly humid during summer. The winter is less cold. The fruits like citrus, mango, guava, fig and litchi can be grown successfully. The tropical fruits like pineapple and avocado can also be grown in this zone. Some varieties of pear, peach, plum and apple of temperate zone can also be grown on commercial scale in this zone.

The chief regions of north eastern sub-tropical zone are eastern Uttar Pradesh, Bihar, parts of Madhya Pradesh, West Bengal, Jharkhand, parts of Chhattisgarh, Assam, Meghalaya, Nagaland and Manipur.

4. Central Tropical zone. The temperature of this zone is hot during summer with humid conditions during rainy season. The winter is mild and less humid. The fruits like mango, grape, guava, citrus, pomegranate, ber, aonla, papaya, sapota and banana can be grown successfully.

This zone includes the regions of Gujarat, parts of Madhya Pradesh, Odisha, Maharashtra, Chhattisgarh and parts of Karnataka and Andhra Pradesh.

5. Southern Tropical zone. The climate of this zone is hot and humid during summer. The winter is mild. The fruits like mango, banana, cashewnut, guava, citrus, grape, sapota, pineapple and papaya are grown on commercial scale.

The chief regions of southern tropical zone are Karnataka, Andhra Pradesh and Tamil Nadu.

6. Coastal Tropical Humid zone. The climate is hot and high humid during summer and mild in winter. The types of fruits grown in this zone are mango, banana, cashewnut, guava, pineapple and papaya.

The important regions of this zone are Kerala, Goa and Coastal belt of Maharashtra, Andhra Pradesh, Karnataka, Tamil Nadu, Odisha and West Bengal.

ADVERSE CLIMATIC EFFECTS ON FRUIT PLANTS

A. Adverse effects of high temperature

The fruit trees, especially the young plants, need much more attention and adequate protection against the hot and scorching weather in May-June. The tolerance of the fruit plants to withstand high temperature varies greatly with species. The fruit plants like those of mango, litchi, citrus, etc. are liable to damage from hot weather as compared with other fruit plants. High temperature during the growing and rest period cause injuries like sunburn and sunscald.

1. Sunburn: The excessive heat during the growing season often results in the burning of leaves and fruits. During the day, branches, leaves, fruits and stem portions which are exposed to the sun become much hotter than the atmosphere and are subjected to sunburn injuries. The transpiration losses are also much higher at that time.The bark of the affected trunks and branches may crack or peel off in long strips in extreme cases. Such damage to the bark may result in the eventual death of trees or they may get crippled.

2. Sunscald: The hot intense sun rays fall on the exposed parts of the tree facing south-west side, resulting into sunscald injuries. The hot sun also scorches the developing fruits, especially those of citrus. The affected portions of the fruits first turn yellow, then brown on further scorching and later even turn black. Such fruits cease to grow from the affected side, whereas the growth on the other side continues as usual. The fruits thus become malformed and misshappen. The peel of such fruits clings to the segments, which becomes woody and dry. Such defective cull and deformed fruits do not fetch good prices in the market, as their quality is very poor.

Protection against hot weather

The following measures should be adopted to save the fruit trees from sun injuries and adverse effects of hot weather.

White-washing: This is the most practical method for saving the trunks of fruit trees from sun injury. The lower bare trunck portions of the fruit trees should be white-washed during April. White-washing may have to be repeated in June-July if it gets faded or is washed out by rains. In the white-wash meterial, little amount of copper sulphate should be added as it helps in warding off the fungal diseases. The effective white-wash can be prepared as follows.

Lime slaked	25 kg
Copper sulphate	500 g
Gum suresh	500 g
Water	100 litres

Providing shelters: Young fruit plants of tender type can be conveniently protected by erecting thatches or *Kullies* made of *Sarkanda, parali* (Rice straw) or Khajoor leaves (Date- palm) over them. Quick-growing temporary shade plants like those of *Jantar* and *Arhar* planted around the basins provide shade and thus minimise sunburn injury.

Wrapping of bare trunks: Wrapping of lower portions of the trunks of fruit trees with old gunny bags or some other farmwaste materials like *parali* (Rice straw) or sugarcane trash (Khori) is also very desirable practice, especially in case of young fruit plants of tender type.

Low-headed trees: The plants trained to low-headed framework escape the ill-effects of the hot sun better than the high headed trees.It is, therefore, desirable that the fruit trees should be trained to develop low heads, especially in the hot and arid tracts.

Windbreaks: By growing windbreaks on the western side of the orchards, damage by hot winds can be avoided. The windbreaks should be planted before the planting of the fruit trees. Euclyptus, mango seedlings, jamun seedlings, arjan, shisham, mulberry, etc. are suitable windbreaks.

Frequent irrigation: Irrigation at regular intervals is quite effective against the hot weather and sun injury. The frequency of irrigation should be increased during the hot period (May-June) when desiccating winds generally blow, especially in the arid and hot regions.

B. Adverse effects of low temperature

December and January are the coolest months in Northern plains when the frosts are commonly experienced. Sometimes frost may also occur in February. Both early and late frosts are more dangerous and inflict heavy damages in killing foliage, twigs, branches, flowers, etc, especially in the orchards which are not properly protected against this hazard. The evergreen fruit trees like papaya, mango, litchi, citrus, guava, atc. are highly susceptible to cold injury under North Indian conditions. Sometimes even grown-up trees may be affected badly, when the incidence of frost is severe, especially in the frost-prone localities.

The newly planted evergreen fruit plants and young plants are much more susceptible to frost damage than the old and well-established fruit trees.The old and well-established fruit trees in healthy condition may, however, escape frost damage. Weak and sickly plants and those suffering from malnutrition are more prone to frost injury than healthy and vigorous plants. The fruit trees which continue their growth during the winter season due to continued watering and late application of nitrogenous fertilizers, suffer much more from frost than those which have ceased their growth and have entered into dormancy.Due to the adverse effect of low temperature, different types of injuries have been reported.

Black heart: In this injury the inner wood is darkened while the cambium and the bark remain alive.The growth of the tree continues and recovers from the injury. Mostly the nursery plants are susceptible to black heart injury.

Collar injury: In this injury the damage by frost is usually caused at the ground level. The bark of stem of young trees is killed and cracks appear at the ground level. The inner sap carrying tissues are ruptured through freezing. The injury may also extend down to the roots. Under such conditions, dead bark should be removed and wounds painted to prevent entrance of water or fungi. Bridge grafting is followed to keep the plants healthy.

Crotch injury: The injury is specified when tissues are killed in the crotches or fork of both large and small branches.

Splitting of bark: It is caused by severe occurrence of frost. The injury may extend to the entire length of the trunk or branches under severe conditions.

Killing back of shoot and young branches: The sub-tropical and tropical fruit trees may be damaged by frost in early spring.The bark along the cambium layer become discoloured or killed very often. In such cases, normal growth can not be resumed for a considerable time. With this injury the flowers in mango may be killed and even fruits may be injured in papaya and citrus.

Protection against cold

The following measures of permanent and temporary nature should be adopted for protecting the orchards from the frost injury.

1. Permanent measures

Planting frost-tolerant kinds: In the localities, where frost incidence is more common, plant only those kinds and varieties of fruits which can withstand frost damage. It is advisable to plant frost-resistant deciduous fruits in such localities like pears, peaches, almond, plums, grapes, etc. or plant relatively more tolerant evergreen plants like kinnow, loquat, ber, guava, etc. Among the citrus fruits the tolerance is in the following descending order: mandarin, sour orange, sweet orange, grapefruit, *galgal,* sweet lime and *Kagzi* lime. Therefore, **kagzi** lime needs greater protection from cold than the other citrus species.

Planting windbreak: Always plant windbreaks on the north-western sides of the orchard, which afford protection from the cold waves during the winter season. The ideal windbreak plants are Euclyptus, mango seedling, ber, arjan, shisham, mulberry and karonda etc.

Healthy trees: Healthy trees can withstand frost damage much more effectively than weak and sickly plants.The fruit trees may be kept healthy by adopting proper cultural practices and plant protection measures.

2. Temporary measures

Training of plants: Well-trained, low-headed trees withstand cold better than tall and improperly trained trees. So, it is very important to train young fruit trees properly.

Covering with thatches: The young trees, as well as the newly planted fruit trees, should be covered with thatches or *Kullies* made of *sarkanda* and farmwaste materials like sugarcane trash, rice parali, maize stalk, etc. The south-west side should be left open to allow sufficient sunlight.

Wrapping of trunk: The exposed portions of the lower trunk of the young plants should be wrapped with old gunny cloth to avoid damage to bark by cold injury.

Providing smoke screens: The heaps of dry leaves, grass or trash should be kept ready in the orchard at several places. As and when a frost is threatened or imminent, these heaps should be ignited and allowed to burn slowly. The fire and smoke raises the atmospheric temperature of the orchard by a few degrees and thus the fruit trees are saved from the frost injury.

Irrigation: By irrigating the orchards during winter, it is possible to raise the temperature by 1°-2°C. This is one of the most easy and the most practical method to ward off frost. It is, therefore, desirable to irrigate the orchard during cold spell period.

In horticulturally advanced countries, oil lamps are installed at several places and these are ignited when there is a foecast of the occurrence of frost.Wind machines have also been installed.These are commissioned as and when needed. Violent movement of wind, helps to keep away the frost.

Above all, the growers should remain alert and vigilent and keep in touch with the weather forecasts or frost warnings by Radio and TV. The growers should instal thermometers in their orchards for knowing fall in temperature. When the temperature falls around 0°C and the atmosphere is still and sky is clear, the frost is sure to occur. At that time, measures like light watering, burning farmwaste materials, etc, may be resorted-to promptly.

SOILS

Soils play a significant role in the success of fruit growing. The roots of the fruit trees generally penetrate into the soil to a much greater depth than the field crops. So, the nature of the sub-soil plays an important role in the growth of the fruit plant. Both soil and sub-soil should be suitable for orchard plantation.

Suitable soil : The soil for growing fruit plants should be deep, well-drained, loamy and fertile. There should be no hard-pan within two metres of its depth. The water table should be below three metres and it should not be fluctuating. Water-logged, marshy, salinic or acidic soils should be avoided for fruit- growing.

Most fruit trees do well in soil with pH ranging between 6.5 to 7.5. The maximum availability of primary nutrients like nitrogen, phosphorus and potassium and of secondary nutrients like sulphur, calcium and magnesium lies within this range. The availablity of micro-nutrients like iron, manganese, boron, copper and zinc is more in acid range. There are fruit trees like date-palm, ber and guava which have been found to grow successfully even in soil above pH 8.5 and even up to pH 9.5. Normally when pH is higher than 8.7, application of gypsum is recommended for successful cultivation of fruit trees.

Fruits trees vary in their tolerance to salt present in the soil.Only the fruits which are able to tolerate salt may be planted in such soils. In response to salt tolerance the fruit trees are grouped as follows:

High-salt tolerant fruits : Date-palm,guava, ber, aonla, bael and coconut.

Medium salt tolerant fruits : Pomegranate, fig, olive, phalsa, jamun, cashewnut, grapes, almond and oranges.

Low salt tolerant fruits: Pear, peach, apple, mango, grapefruit, lemon, mandarin, plum, apricot, strawberry and avocado.

Soil testing : Since the nutritional status and other conditions of the sub-soil are also important for the growth of fruit trees, land for orchard plantation should be sampled to the depth of two metres. It is better to get the soil tested from a soil-testing laboratory before planting an orchard. The soil samples from different soil layers should be collected separately, *i.e.* from the top 15 cm, 15 to 30 cm, 30 to 60 cm, 60 to 90 cm, 90 to 120 cm, 120- to 150 cm and 150 to 200 cm. Each sample should be labelled separately indicating the depth of layer from which it has been taken. Pack them separately in clean cloth bags avoiding any contamination and send the samples to the nearest Soil Testing Laboratory.

Suitability limits for orchard plantation :

	*Character	Citrus and peach	Other fruit plants
(*i*)	Conductivity (mmhos/cm)	< 0.5	< 1.0
(*ii*)	Calcium carbonate (%)	< 5	< 10
(*iii*)	Lime concretion (%)	< 10	< 20
(*iv*)	pH	< 8.5	Upto 8.7 if EC is below 0.5 mmhos/cm.

*Concerns all soils horizons upto the depth of 2 metres.

CHAPTER 3

Preparation of Land and Layout of Orchard

Orcharding is a long term investment and needs lot of planning and expertise. While planning and planting a new orchard, one should give utmost attention and care to various aspects like selection of location and site, nature of soil and subsoil, planting of suitable kinds and varieties of fruits, proper planting distance and purchasing of fruit plants from reliable nurseries. Mistakes committed initially on any aspect reduce the returns greatly from the investment, besides wastage of time and energy. Thus one should give utmost attention and care, while planning a new orchard. As orcharding is highly specialized vocation, the intending grower should avail of expert advice on the establishment of new orchards and their proper maintenance.

PREPARATION OF LAND

The land should be cleaned properly for free movement of man and machinery. All the trees, bushes and creepers should be removed. The stubbles should be uprooted to avoid regeneration of growth and obstruction for movement of machines. The soil of the area destined for growing fruit plants needs thorough preparation. A virgin land requires a deep ploughing and harrowing. The land should be repeatedly ploughed and bring the soil to a fine tilth and pulverise the weeds or other undesirable herbs under the soil. The land should be thoroughly harrowed and levelled. While preparing the land, the subsoil which is usually less fertile than the surface soil, should not be disturbed as far as possible. If possible, green manuring crop like daincha, sunhemp, cowpea etc, may be raised and ploughed down during land preparation to enrich the orchard soil and improve its physical condition. In the hills, terraces should be made along the contours.

LAYOUT PLAN

Layout: The marking of position of the plant in the field is referred as to layout.

The layout plan of the orchard should be prepared carefully, preferably in consulation with horticultural experts. The orchard layout plan includues the system of planting, provision for orchard paths, roads, water channels and farm building. A sketch of the proposed orchard should be prepared on a paper before the actual planting is taken in hand.

SYSTEMS OF PLANTING

The following are the important systems of planting generallly followed on the basis of agro-climatic conditions.

1. Square system: It is the most commonly used method and easy to layout in the field. In this system, plant to plant and row to row distance is the same. The plants are at the right angle to each other, every unit of four plants forming a square. This system facilitates the interculture in two directions after the orchard is planted.

2. Hexagonal system. In hexagonal system, the trees are planted in the corners of equilateral triangles. Six trees thus form a hexagon with another tree at its centre.This system, though a little difficult for execution but accommodates 15 per cent more plants.Cultivation of land between the tree rows is possible in three directions with this system. This system is generally followed where the land is costly and very fertile with ample provision of irrigation water.

3. Rectangular system: In this system, the plot is divided into rectangles instead of squares and trees are planted at the four corners of the rectangle in straight rows running at right angles. Like square system, this system also facilitiates the interculture in two directions. The only difference is that in this system more plants can be accommodated in the row keeping more space between the rows.

4. Triangular or Alternate system: In this sytem, trees are planted as in the square system but the plants in the 2nd, 4 th, 6 th, and such other alternate rows are planted midway between the Ist, 3rd, 5th, and such other alternate rows. This system provides more open space for the trees and for intercrops. However, it becomes difficult to carry out intercultural operations.

5. Quincunx or diagonal system: This system is exactly like the square system but one additional tree is planted in the centre of each square. The number of plants per acre by this system is almost doubled than the square system. Fruit trees like peach, plum, papaya, kinnow, phalsa and guava can be planted as fillers in the permanent orchard of mango, litchi and pear. The planting of filler trees provides an additional income to the grower in the early life of the orchard. The filler trees are uprooted when the main orchard trees start commercial fruiting.

6. Contour system: This system is usually followed in the hilly areas with high slopes but it is very much similar to the square/rectangular system. Under such circumstances, the trees may be well planted in lines following the contour of the soil with only a slight slope. Irrigation and cultivation are then practised only across the slope of the land as this practice reduces the chances of soil erosion.In this system layout is done as in square/rectangular system, first by establishing the base line at the lowest level and then marking for the trees should be done from the base to the top. Bench terraces are used where the slope is greater than 10 per cent.

7. Hedgerow system: In this system, the distance between the trees in a row is half to one third the distance between rows. This system of planting is followed in Italy where dwarf apple trees are planted in double offset rows due to higher intensity of light.

8. Adjacent planting: In this system, two plants are placed closely keeping a double space between the rows and the next set of plants. This system is followed in the arid zone where moisture supply is limited as well as in the less fertile soils where both moisture and nutrients are not easily available to the plants. This system provides large areas between rows for intercropping.

METHOD OF LAYOUT

For laying out an orchard, according to square system, a base line is first established and the position of the trees is marked along this line putting wooden stakes in the ground. Another base line at right to the first base line, is then marked along with the other edge of the field with the help of a carpenter square or a cross staff.

The right angle can also be drawn with the help of measuring tape. One end of this tape is fixed at 3 metre distance from the corner along the first line and the tape is then stretched along the second base line for a distance of 4 metre. The diagonal distance between these two points should be 5 metre. The wooden stakes are put in the ground at the desired distance along the second line. All the four rows are thus established and staked. Three men, one putting the pegs in the field and other correcting alignment while moving along the base line, can easily stake the whole field.

For laying out of an orchard according to the triangular system, a base line is set on one side of the field as in the square system. A large triangle with a ring in each corner is used. The sides of this triangle are equal to the distance to be kept of the plants in the orchard. Two of these rings are placed on the stakes of the base line. The position of the third ring indicates the position of the plant in the second row. This row is then used as a base line. The whole area is laid out in a similar manner.

DIGGING AND FILLING OF PITS

Marking of pits and planting should always be done with the help of planting board. The guide pegs are installed at both the ends.One metre deep pits of one metre diameter should be dug. Top 30 cm soil should be kept on one side which is used for refilling the pits as it is considered the fertile soil. Bottom 70 cm soil should be kept on other side which is discarded. The pits should be left exposed for a few days before actual planting. These pits should be refilled with a mixture of top soil, 2-3 baskets of silt and 2-3 baskets of well-rotten farmyard manure. To each pit, add 15 ml of Chlorpyriphos 20 EC mixed in about 2 kg soil against white ants. The refilled pits should be watered a few days before planting the tree.

METHOD OF PLANTING

Bore holes of suitable size in the centre of the filled pits with the help of planting board. Place the earth ball of a plant in it in such a way that the upper surface has the same level as the ground. Fill loose earth around the ball and press it firmly with the handle of a spade or khurpa. Apply irrigation soon after setting the plants in the pits.

PLANTING DISTANCE OF FRUIT PLANTS

The spacing given to the fruit trees is generally governed by the different factors like climate and soil, choice of varieties, growth habit of tree, rootstock used, nature of irrigation and pruning technique followed. The spacing may vary according to different systems of planting. Provision of optimum spacing to fruit trees is one of the most important aspect of successful fruit culture. The fruit plants grow poorly in close spacing, thus, produce small quantity of fruits of inferior quality and suffer heavily from insect-pests and diseases. In case of widerly spaced plantation, there is wastage of valuable orchard land without having any direct benefit on ultimate yield of the orchard. Therefore, optimum spacing is required so that the fruit trees may grow and bear crop properly. Optimum spacing regulates the proper utilization of sunlight, avoids competition in the uptake of nutrients caused by the collision of root systems, and facilitates proper irrigation. The latest technology on high density plantation system where trees are planted at critical spacings for maximum utilization of space is becoming popular.

It will be very difficult to suggest exact spacing for fruit trees which will suit every locality or soil.

Given below is the spacing of some important fruit plants which serve the basic guideline for establishing a new orchard.

Normal Density Planting

Name of fruit t]ree	Planting distance (M)	Number of plants/ha (square system)
Mango	9	123
Citrus, pomegranate, Soft Pear, Guava, Plum, Apricot	6	275
Grapes (*i*) Head system	2.0 × 1.5	3300
(*ii*) Kniffin system	3.0 × 3.0	1100
(*iii*) Bower system	3.0 × 3.0	1100
Loquat, Peach	6.5	225
Litchi. Sapota, Walnut	7.5-9.0	180-123
Ber, Sarid Pear/Aonla	7.5	180
Date-palm, Almond	6-7	275-202
Jamun	10-12	105-75
Phalsa, Papaya	1.5	4400
Banana (*i*) Tall varieties	2.7 × 3.0	1210
(*ii*) Dwarf varieties	1.8 × 1.8	3052
Pineapple	30 × 60 × 90 cm	43500
Cashewnut	7-8	202-140
Custard Apple	5	390
Avocado	10	105
Apple	3.0-7.5	1100-180
Cherry	9-12	123-75

High Density Planting

Fruit Plant	Planting distance (m)	Actual Plants (per ha)
Kinnow	6 × 3	550
Grapes	4 × 1.5	1650
Guava	6 × 5	330
Ber	6 × 6	275
Peach and Plum	6 × 1.5	1100
Sand Pear (Patharnakh)	8 × 4	300
Pineapple	0.25 × 0.35 × 0.75	72727

High density planting (6 × 3m) in kinnow mandarin is recommended for better economic returns. Plantation is widened by uprooting alternate trees at fifteen year of the tree age and distance is left (6 × 6m). The purpose of uprooting alternate tree is to prolong the life expectancy of kinnow orchards.

PLANTING SEASON

The planting season of different fruit crops vary on the basis of their evergreen or deciduous nature.

Evergreen fruit plants : There are two planting times for evergreen fruits viz. February-March (spring) and August- September (rainy season). The fruit plants such as citrus, mango and litchi should preferably be planted during September or in the beginning of October when the weather becomes mild and more favourable and there is enough moisture in the soil. Kinnow and ber plants can be transplanted bare rooted during December to February. Guava can also be planted bare-rooted during February-March or August- September. The plants should be defoliated and the roots covered with moist material.

Most of the sub-tropical and tropical evergreen fruit plants are suitably transplanted during the rainy season when the atmospheric humidity is high and sufficient supply of soil mositure is obtained.During this active period of growth, the plants easily penetrate their roots in the soil and get established. High atmospheric humidity during the rainy season helps them to minimise the transpirational loss.

The evergreen plants can also be transplanted during the onset of spring with equal success provided an ample quantity of irrigation water is available. Early regeneration of rootlets due to high temperature and available mositure during this period helps in early establishment of the plants in most of the cases.

Deciduous fruit plants: The deciduous fruit plants are planted during winter when they are dormant. Their planting must be completed before the start of new growth *i.e.* upto middle January is case of peach and plum and upto middle of February in case of pear and grapes. The bare rooted **ber** can also be planted during January and up to middle of February.

It would be wise, if the planting operation in deciduous fruit plants could be done well before the dormancy is broken and the plants start their growth afresh during the subsequent period.

Planting should be avoided during hot and dry spells of weather. The fruit trees should preferably be planted in the afternoon and on cloudy and humid days rather than in bright sunshine and dry weather.

PURCHASING FRUIT PLANTS FROM NURSERY

The fruit trees, unlike annual crops, are expected to remain in the field for many years. The choice of kind of fruit shall, however, depend largely on the location of orchard. The varieties, of course, must be selected depending upon the consumer's preference. Since the poor selection of trees may often lead to headaches, heartaches and bankruptcy. The following points need to be kept in view while purchasing fruit plants.

(*i*) **Health of plant**

- The fruit plants should be healthy, vigorous and free from diseases and insect-pests.
- True-to-type of plants on suitable rootstocks should be purchased.
- They must have been propagated from progeny trees of proven merit in regard to yield and quality.

(*ii*) **Age of plants**

- The age of the plant is usually reckoned from the age of scion but it does not imply that these should have been buddeed on old stock.
- One or two year old fruit plants are ideal for planting.
- Older plants should not be purchased as they do not establish easily, particularly the evergreen fruit plants where the shock of transplanting is greater as compared to the young plants. The prolonged stay in the nursery beds or pots reduces their vigour. The roots become pot bound, especially in the older plants and thus they have a poor transplanting success.

(*iii*) **Size of plants**

- The trunk size of one or two years old citrus plants should be 1.5 to 2.5 cm in diameter.
- The budded or grafted plants with weak stock scion union should also be rejected.

(*iv*) **Source of supply**

- Never purchase the fruit plants from private nurseries and footpath sellers as they proves to be a very expensive investment in the long run because these plants are generally from poor strains. The growers come to know about the yield and quality of the fruit after several years when the plants start bearing.
- The fruit growers should always purchase plants from a nursery of known repute and honesty, preferably the nurseries of the State Agricultural University, State Department of Horticulture and Government approved nurseries.
- The plants should be reserved well in advance of the actual planting.
- Always purchase 10-20 per cent more plants than the actual requirement.These plants should be kept in nursery to fill up gaps which may develop subsequently due to the death of plants.
- The plants should preferably be purchased from nearest nursery as it greatly facilitates their transport, avoids delay in transit and reduces the transport charges.

HANDLING AND TRANSPORTATION OF NURSERY PLANTS

Plants should be carefully handled during transportation to avoid breakage of earth balls, as the plants with broken earth balls are likely to dry up. Before loading the plants (with earth ball) in the vehicle a layer of cushioning material such as **parali** (rice straw), dried grass or sand should be spread at the bottom. Then place the plants carefully in the vehicle. During long transportation sprinkle water on the foliage to keep these turgid.

Bare rooted plants may be packed in small bundles. The root portion of these bundles should be given mud coating and then wrapped with moist material such as wet gunny bags, **parali** (rice straw) or polythene sheet to avoid dehydration of feeder roots during transit.

CARE OF PLANTS ON ARRIVAL

The plants should be given utmost care when received. The shock of digging from the nursery is rather severe and they must not be further exposed to the hot sun or the wind.The packing of the plants should be opened or loosened as soon as they are received, otherwise they may be injured due to heating within these packages. The plants should be placed in shade and sprinkled with water until they are planted in the field.

AFTER CARE OF YOUNG PLANTS

The newly planted young fruit plants, being very tender need lot of care and attention for their better survival and growth.

The plants should be watered at frequent intervals. However, heavy irrigation should be avoided as stagnation of water in their basins may do more harm than good.

The young plants need staking so as to make them grow upright and straight. The support should be strong, preferably of bamboo or other wooden logs and should be well fixed in the soil.

Keep examining the young plants and remove all the growth which has taken place below the bud-union. The tying materials still tied at the graft union may also be removed carefully.

Training of the young plants should be given utmost attention for developing proper framework and shape. Remove dead and diseased portions by careful pruning.

The young plants should always be protected against diseases and insects by proper and timely sprays of suitable fungicides/insecticides. The white ant attack if noted, should be checked by applying chlorpyriphos @ half liter per acre followed by light irrigation.

Nitrogenous fertilizers which are required for growth, should always be given in small split doses to young fruit trees.

Provide adequate protection against vagaries of summer and winter season.

HEDGES/WINDBREAKS FOR PROTECTION

A good windbreak should be provided on the windward side of orchard well before the orchard is established. Eucalyptus, Arjuna, Jamun, Seedling mango, Mulbery etc. and good windbreak plants. In the spaces between windbreak trees, a hedge may also be planted. *Inga dulcis* (Jungli julebi), *Lawsonia alba* (Mehndi), Bouganvillea, Jatti khatti, Galgal, Karonda, etc. are a few good hedges. Never plant a hedge of citrus species around the citrus orchard.

CHAPTER 4

Propagation and Nursery Management

Healthy and good quality fruit plants are the foundation of successful and remunerative fruit production. There are scores of nurserymen in different fruit belts who multilpy fruit plants for supplying to the fruit growers. Majority of them are still producing these plants on traditional lines. Therefore, the need for modernising our fruit nurseries become more urgent with rising demand of pedigree plants.Moreover, the plant propagation has become a vastly specialised industry involving a large outlay of certified and highly develped skill and technology. The propagation of plants has long been recognised as a fundamental practice in the field of horticulture. The methods of vegetative propagation are considered in comprehensive form in this chapter.

PROPAGATION

Plant propagation is defined as the multiplication of plants by both sexual and asexual means.

Sexual propagation: Plants are raised from seeds and such plants are known as seedlings.

Advantages

1. Seedlings are long lived, hardy, bear more heavily and are easier to propagate.
2. This is the only method of propagation in phalsa and papaya where other methods are not possible.
3. In-breeding for evolution of new varieties, the hydrids are first raised from seed.
4. Chance seedlings of very superior quality may result. Such seedlings have been of great benefit to the fruit industry.
5. Rootstocks are usually obtained by means of sexual propagation because they are hardy and develop better root system.
6. Mostly the seedlings are free from virus diseases.
7. Properly stored seeds can be kept for longer duration for future use.
8. Seeds of some fruits like citrus and mango varieties ae capable of giving out more than one seedling from one seed. They arise from the cells of the nucellus and are called polyembryonic. These nucellar seedlings can be utilized for raising uniform plants, if they can be carefully detected at the nursery stage.

Disadvantages

1. Multiplication of these plants by sexual means results into segregation of characters and the resultant plants are never true- to-type.
2. Plants are not always uniform in growth, quality of fruit and yield as compared to asexually raised plants.
3. Plants come into bearing later than grafted ones.
4. Larger trees are uneconomical to handle, *i.e* cost of harvesting, pruning and spraying is more.
5. The exact characters of any superior selection can not be perpetuated through seed.

Asexual or Vegetative propagation : A vegetative part of a plant such as leaf, stem or root is placed in such an environment that it develops into a new plant. The new plant being a portion of the parent plant, possess all its characteristics.

Advantages

1. The plants are generally true-to-type, uniform in growth, yielding capacity and fruit quality.
2. Most of the fruit plants like Apple, mango, citrus, guava, litchi, etc. are cross pollinated and heterozygous in nature and the genetic architecture of the offsprings can only be maintained true-to-type through vegetative propagation.
3. Picking or harvesting of fruits becomes easy due to the restricted growth.
4. Plants in some cases bear seedless fruits *i.e.* Banana, pineapple, some varieties of grapes, guava and lemon.
5. Such plants come into bearing earlier than the seedling trees.
6. The plants can be produced disease free by budding or grafting on resistant rootsocks.
7. Rootstock regulate tree size and fruit quality *e.g.* Apple trees remain dwarf on M_9, M_{26} and M_{27} rootstocks.
8. Cross-pollination can be affected by grafting shoots of other suitable varieties on some of the branches of the self- unfruitful varieties *e.g.* some varieties of Almond which are self-unfruitful can be made to bear crops if pollinising varieties are grafted on some of the branches of these trees.
9. By asexual method, we can correct to some extent the initial mistakes of planting inferior varieties in the orchard by doing top-working.

Disadvantages

1. Such plants are not so vigorous and long-lived as the seedling trees.
2. New variety cannot be evolved by this method.
3. Sometimes it is expensive as it requires special techniques.

PROPAGATION BY SEED

The fruits like papaya, phalsa, kaghzilime, *jamun* and guava are usually propagated from seed. Similarly, the rootsocks for citrus, ber, loquat, mango, pear, peach, plum, etc. are usually raised from seed. Propagation from seed has been responsible for the production of chance seedlings of highly superior merit and has contributed towards evolution of new varieties. The man made hybrids are first raised from seed. It is the usual means of commercial reproduction in papaya, phalsa and karonda where other methods of vegetative propagation are not satisfactory.

Selection of fruits and seed extraction : Always select mature, uniform and healthy fruits of a known rootstock species\variety. Discard under and oversized and diseased fruit. Extract seeds by removing pulp in the case of mango, guava, loquat, peach, kainth (pear), ber, plum, papaya, etc. In case of citrus, cut the fruit into two halves, squeeze out the seeds alongwith the juice in non-metallic container. Make the seeds free from pulp-juice, wash with water and dry under shade for 2-3 days. Seeds of mango, citrus, guava, ber, etc. should be sown within a week.

Storage of seeds : The seeds generally lose viability when allowed to dry for a long period. If the seeds are to be stored for several months, they should be surface dried quickly after thorough washing and then mixed with equal parts of powdered charcoal, packed in a tight wooden box or tin container and kept in a dry cool place at a temperature of 3 to 12°C.

Dormancy in seeds : The dormancy in seeds might be imposed by the hardness of the seed coat, impermeability to water and gases, physiological immaturity of embryo, deficiency of some endogenous growth promoters or exess of endogenous growth inhibitors. Different methods like scarification, acid scarification, chemical treatment,soaking seeds in water, stratification are used for breaking dormancy in seed to improve seed germination.

Testing seed viability : The conventional methods for testing the germination capacity of seeds in petri dishes or in sand are time consuming and laborious. Most of the non dormant fruit seeds require 7-21 days and the dormant seeds require few months to carry out germination tests. Citrus seeds lose their viability within a short period and are stored under special storage conditions. The tetrazolium test makes it possible to determine the seed viability within 4-24 hours. It's special advantage over other biochemical tests is that it can be performed on individual seed organs and tissues vital to growth. The embryo of seed capable of normal germination and growth contain reducing enzymes which convert the almost colourless triphenyle tetrazolium bromide solution into a clearly visible red stain upon the cut surfaces of the embryo tissue.

SOWING OF SEEDS

The seeds of fruit like papaya, phalsa, citrus, mango, jamun and loquat do not require any special treatment before sowing. In ber, the germination of seed is quite difficult on account of stony endocarp which contains the seed. Before sowing, seeds should be dipped into 17-18% salt solution for 24 hours. The seeds can also be sown by cracking the hard shell. The seeds of guava should be soaked in water for about two weeks before sowing. Placing the seeds in the boiling water for about five minutes also reduces the time required for germination. The seeds of pear, peach and plum need stratification before they are sown in the field or on raised nursery beds.

The seeds of citrus, guava, phalsa and kainth (pear rootstock) are sown in carefully prepared 15-20 cm raised beds to facilitate drainage. The soil of the seed beds should be well pulverised and mixed with well rotten farmyard manure. Seeds beds usually 1.2 to 1.5 meter wide and 2.0 to 2.5 meter long alternated with 60 cm wide irrigation furrows are prepared with spade and khurpa. The seeds are sown in lines at a distance of 10-15 cm and 2-3 cm deep. Seed is covered with a thick layer of sand or leaf mould mixture to prevent crust formation.In the beginning the beds are watered with watering Can and after germination light and frequent irrigation is applied through furrows. The seed beds should be covered with *Sarkanda* to preserve moisture.

Germination starts in about 2-3 weeks and thereafter *Sarkanda* is removed. When the seedlings are 10-15 cm in height, they are transplanted in well prepared nursery plots at 30 × 30 cm spacing in plants and rows. The seedlings of evergreen fruit plants are transplanted in February-March and August-September and deciduous fruit plants in December-January. The seeds of mango, ber, loquat and jamun are sown in flat beds.

RAISING THE SEEDLINGS IN POLYTHENE BAGS

The seedlings of sexually propagated plants raised in polythene bags can stand transplanting better than those raised in seed beds. Perforated polythene bags of 22.5 × 15 cm size with 100 gauge thickness can be used for sowing the seed. These bags are filled with a mixture of farmyard manure, soil and sand in equal proportion. The rooting media of equal proportion should be treated with Brassicol 75 WP. Two or three seeds are sown in one bag and after germination only one seedling is retained. These seedlings in the polythene bags should be treated with Captan (0.2 per cent) after their emergence.

INDENTIFICATION OF NUCELLAR SEEDLINGS IN CITRUS NURSERY

Seeds of most citrus species are endowed with the ability to produce more than one embryo. One of the embryos arises from the union of male and female gametes and is called gametic or sexual embryo whereas the others are produced by simple mitotic division of cells of the nucellus without the male gamete taking part in their formation are known as nucellar embryo. Since these nucellar embryos arise from the tissue of the mother parent alone, they are genetically alike and exhibit the same characteristics as their mother parent.

The phenomenon of nucellar embryo is of common occurrence in the genus citrus. Most citrus fruits of commercial importance like sweet orange, loose skined organges, grapefruit,lime, lemons and some of the species used as rootstocks like rough lemon, kharna khatta, Rangpur lime etc. exhibit a high percentage of nucellar embryony. In some citrus varieties like Troyer citrange, tangelos and Unshiu mandarin, even the gametic embryo aborts after a cetain stage of development and the seed is left with only the vegetative or a sexual embryos that are capable of producing cent per cent nucellar seedlings.

SELECTION OF NUCELLAR SEEDLINGS

In a mixed population of gametic and nucellar seedlings of a particular variety, it will be observed that whereas a large majority of seedlings fall within one vigour group and are more or less of the same size, others will be either too small or too tall than the commonly prevailing type. The small proportion of seedlings that differ from prevailing type in regard to vigour may on careful examination, also show differences in other characters like internodal length, branching habit, shape and size of foliage, serration on leaf margin and development of wings etc. These variants are apparently seedlings produced from the sexual embryos. Roguing out of these variants at different stages in the nursery will ensure the availability of nucellar seedlings. In actual practice, roguing out of gametic seedlings is mostly done on the basis of vigour differences.

First roguing to eliminate gemetic seedlings should be done when they are about 10 to 12 cm tall and ready for transplanting in the nursery. All small sized, slow growing and weak seedlings should be discarded at this stage. Likewise some of the seedlings which manifest extra vigour and are very tall should also be discarded. Only seedlings of uniform vigour should be transplanted in the nursery rows and allowed to grow there till they are ready for budding. At the time of budding again, all such seedlings which have been lagging behind in growth and exhibit morphological differences should be discarded. Some of the gametic seedlings which might have escaped notice at the time of first roguing will show vigour differences in the nursery rows when they are allowed to grow for a longer period and should be eliminated. In this way a very large population of gametic seedlings shall have been discarded and the remaining seedlings will largely consist of nucellars which should be budded with appropriate scion variety during budding season.

A third and final roguing should be done at the time of selecting budlings for transplanting in the field. Experience has shown that even the growth of scion buds on gametic seedlings is not quite as good as on nucellar seedlings. In case,therfore, some gametic seedlings which escaped notice at eailer stages of roguing were budded, the scion buds on them will make relatively less growth. Budlings which have made poor growth, therefore, should not be transplanted in the field. If after conducting roguing at three different stages, budlings showing uniform growth are selected for transplating, then the grower can safely assume, that he has eliminated practically all the gametic seedlings. The resultant plant material will be of a very good quality and will not give rise to heterozygosity in orchard trees. Nucellar embryo thus provides the citrus nurserymen valuable tool, producing superior quality of uniform genetic make up.

ASEXUAL PROPAGATION METHODS

Asexual propagation involves no change in genetic make-up of the new plant. All the characteristics of the parent plant are reproduced in the daughter plant due to exact duplication of chromosome system that takes place during cell division. Thus, the plants are true-to-type in growth, ripening, yield and fruit quality. There are different methods which can be used for multiplication of various fruit plants commercially. These include division, cutting, layering, budding and grafting.

1. Division

It is a method of asexual propagation by which vegetative part that separate naturally from the parent plant or may be readily separated from it, is used. These include rhizomes, suckers, offsets, crowns, runners, etc.

(*i*) **Rhizomes :** Botanically, a rhizome is an elongated, horizontal fleshy underground stem having nodes and internodes bearing buds in the axils of reduced scale leaves *e.g.* banana. The rhizomes are cut into pieces, each with one or two viable bud and planted in favourable atmospheric conditions. Adventitous roots and shoots develop from the nodes.

(*ii*) **Suckers :** A shoot arising on an old stem or underground part of the stem or on horizontal root systems is known as sucker *e.g.* datepalm, pear, banana and pineapple. These shoots, when separated from the mother plant and transplanted produce adventitious roots. In banana, sword suckers are commonly used for propagation of plants.

(*iii*) **Offsets:** An offset is a characteristic type of lateral shoot or branch that develops from the base of the main stem in certain plants *e.g.* pineapple, datepalm. Offsets are removed by cutting them close to the main stem with a sharp knife.

(*iv*) **Crowns:** It is a very short condensed part of plant at the surface of the ground which gives rise to new shoots. The crown is principally a point of location near the ground surface making the general transition zone between stem and root. Crown grown on top of the pineapple fruit is a vegetative growth attached to the central core of the fruit which is used as planting material. Splitted crown into four to eight pieces, can also be used but they take longer duration to bear fruits.

(*v*) **Runners :** A runner is a specialized stem that develops from the axil of a leaf at the crown of a plant, grows horizontally along the ground and forms a new plant at one of the nodes *e.g.* strawberry. The runner production is favoured by long day and high temperature. The daughter plants are separated and used as new planting material.

(*vi*) **Slips :** Slips are shoots just arising below the crown but above the ground. Pineapple is generally propagated through slips.

2. Cutting

Cutting is the method of propagating fruit plants by the use of detached plant parts which when placed under favourable conditions develop into a complete plant resembling in all characteristics to the parent from which it was taken. This method is commonly used in plants which root easily and readily, thus, multiplication of plants is very quick and cheap. Some fruit plants such as grape, plum, pear, pomegranate, fig, baramasi lemon, sweet lime and hill lemon (galgal) are commercially propagated by cuttings.Cuttings are broadly classifield into four groups *i.e.* stem cuttings, leaf cutting, leaf bud cutting and root cutting.

(*i*) **Stem cuttings :** Stem cuttings can be divided into four types *i.e.* hardwood, semi-hardwood, softwood and herbaceous cuttings.

Hardwood cuttings : Hard wood cuttings are prepared from the trees when the tissues are fully mature. The shoots of about one-year- old or more can easily be used for preparing hard wood cuttings. In case of deciduous fruit plants such as grape, pomegranate, plum, pear, phalsa and fig, the cuttings are made after pruning (December-January). The pruned wood can be used for preparing such cuttings.In sweet lime, hill lemon (Galgal) and baramasi lemon, the cuttings can be prepared during the spring (February- March) and rainy season (August-September).

Generally, the cuttings of 15-20 cm length and having 3-5 buds are made. The lower cut is given in a slanting manner just below the bud to increase the absorption of nutrients. The upper cut is given at a right angle (round) to reduce the size of the wound and as far as possible away from the upper bud to avoid its drying. After the cuttings are prepared they should not be allowed to dry. These cuttings are usually tied in small bundles (20-25 cuttings) and buried in moist soil/sand for a certain period for healing of wounds which is known as callusing.

Rooting Media: The rooting media for planting cuttings should be loose and easily workable to facilitate planting of cuttings and particularly the lifting of the plants with little damage to the roots. It should be well drained , free from fungi and bacteria and available at reasonable cost. Generally the sand alone and a mixture of sand and farmyard manure are used for planting the cuttings.

(*i*) **Sand :** Sand is most widely used media for propagating plants from cuttings. It is well aerated and useful for extensive root growth. It is low in water holding capacity and cuttings planted in it must be watered frequently. Since sand contains little or no organic matter, it does not harbour disease organisms. Since it is low in nutrition, plants should be supplied with nutrients for better growth. For better results, sand should be sterilised before use.

(*ii*) **Mixture :** Mixture of sand and well-rotten farmyard manure (1 : 1) is also commonly used for propagation of plants by cuttings. It is well drained and also holds sufficient moisture for root development. It is rich in nutrients. The mixture should be treated with 5 ml of chlorphyriphos 20 EC mixed in about 2 kg soil to avoid the attack of termites to cuttings.

Planting of cuttings : The cuttings are usually planted 10-15 cm apart in the well prepared nursery fields. The dormant cuttings should be planted during January, while best time of planting the evergreen cuttings is February-March and August-September. Usually, 2/3rd portion of the cutting be placed in the soil taking care that the lower buds should not get damaged. The soil is throughtly pressed around the cutting and watered regularly to keep it moist. Weeding and hoeing should regularly be done. However, the cuttings should not be disturbed before they have made sufficient growth. Similarly, the nursery where cuttings have been planted should be kept free from insect pests and diseases for healthy plant growth. Generally, the cuttings are kept in the nursery for one year. The rooted cuttings of deciduous fruit plants are lifted from the nursery as bare-rooted during December-January, while those of evergreen plants with earth- balls during February-March and August-September.

Semi-hardwood cuttings: Semi-hardwood cuttings are prepared from partially mature but tender woody shoots. Citrus and olive can be propagated in this manner. The cuttings are made 7.5 to 15 cm long with leaves retained at the upper end. The shoot terminals are often used in making cuttings but the basal parts of the stem will usually root also. The cutting wood should be obtained in the cool, early morning hours when the stems are turgid. Intermittent moist sprays of water and treatment with auxins have been reported to be beneficial.

Softwood cuttings: Cuttings are prepared from the soft, succulent terminal portion of woody perennials. Although fruit tree species are not commonly propagated by softwood cuttings, those of apple, peach, pear, plum, apricot and cherry will root, especially under mist. It is desirable to retain some leaves on the cuttings for photosynthesis. Large leaves should be reduced in size to lower the transpiration rate and to occupy less space in the propagating bed. Soft wood cuttings are 7.5 to 12.5 cm long. The basal cut is given just below the node. The leaves on the lower portion of the cuttings are removed, while those on upper part retained. Cuttings should be taken from slightly mature but flexible, moderately vigorous shoots in March-April in deciduous plants and May-September in evergreen plants. Cuttings put forth roots within 15-30 days if temperature is between 20-25°C and humidity is at 80 per cent. The exogenous application of auxin helps in better rooting in softwood cuttings.

Herbaceous cuttings : Harbaceous cuttings are the tender succulent special leafy part of the stems of herbaceous plants. The terminal 7.5 to 12.5 cm of a healthy shoot is cut and the basal leaves are removed leaving the upper leaves undisturbed. They are rooted under the same conditions as shoftwood cuttings, requiring high humidity. Herbaceous cuttings of some plants that exude a sticky sap such as pineapple do better if the basal ends are allowed to dry for a few hours under low light conditions before they are inserted in the rooting medium. The application of auxin promots the regeneration of adventituous roots.

(*ii*) **Leaf cuttings :** In leaf cuttiings, the fleshy leaf or leaf blade and petioles are used as propagating materials. Adventitious roots and an adventitious shoot form at the base of the leaf and develop into the new plant, the original leaf does not become a part of the new plant. New plants arise at the point where the veins are cut. High humid condition is essential for better success in leaf cutting. Leaf cuttings has very little application on fruit crops.

(*iii*) **Leaf-bud cuttings :** A leaf-bud cutting consists of a leaf blade, petiole and a short piece of the stem with the attached axillary bud. This method is practised in black raspberry, blackberry, lemon, etc. Leaf-bud cuttings are best made from material having well developed buds and healthy, actively growing leaves. The adventitious roots are found at the base while the dormant bud develops into new shoot system. High humidity is essential and bottom heat is desirable for rapid rooting.

(*iv*) **Root cuttings :** The root cutting method is followed in apple, pear, cherry, guava, wood apple etc. The root cuttings should be taken from root pieces of young stock plants in late winter or early spring when the roots are well supplied with stored foods but before new growth starts. It is important with root cuttings to maintain the correct polarity when planting as the new shoot develops from the proximal end *i.e.* from the part close to the crown. The proximal end of the root piece should always be up.

3. Layering

Layering is a method of vegetative propagation which can very easily be used for the multiplication of fruit plants, especially those which do not root readily from cuttings or graft easily. In layering, the roots are induced on the shoots while they are still attached to the mother plants. Like other methods of vegetative propagation, such as cutting, budding and grafting, the plants propagated by layering also are true-to-type in growth, yield and fruit quality. Moreover, much larger and mature plants can be obtained by layering as compared with other methods of vegetative propagation. Most commonly used methods of layering are ground, mound and air layering.

(*i*) **Ground layering :** This type of layering is also known as simple layering. It is commonly know as *Dab*. In this method, a branch of plant is drawn to the soil. This is then fastened firmly with a wooden hook. A ring of bark about 2.5 cm in diameter is removed just below the bud to encourage rooting. This portion of the branch is covered with moist soil, keeping the terminal portion of the branch uncovered. The soil is regularly watered to keep it moist. Within a few weeks, the roots are formed and the new plant is separated from the mother plant. Separation should be done in such a way that the rooting goes along with the new plant. These new plants should preferably be planted in pots or nursery rows for develpment of better root system and shoot system before planting in the fields.

Several new plants can be prepared from a single tree, depending upon the vigour of mother tree and the number of branches available for burying in the soil. Lemon and limes can easily be multiplied by this method.

(*ii*) **Mound layering :** This method is also known as stool layering. It can be used for the clonal propagation of pear, ber, apple and guava.

In this method of layering, the parent plants are first established in the nursery. In pear, these plants are then cut down to ground level when they are dormant during December-January. The stubs or the stools are earthed up so that the new stools coming out in spring (February-March) are about 1/3 to 1/2 covered with soil. Just before covering, a ring of bark about 2.5 cm in diameter is removed just below the bud from that portion of the stools which is to be covered with the moist soil. These shoots develop roots at ringed portion. These are then detached from the mother plants during the next winter and are planted in the nursery rows for budding or grafting with the desired scion.

In guava the heading back can be done either in February or in July. These stools which come out during April and September, respectively are similarly treated (removal of ring of bark) and covered with moist soil as done in case of pear. The rooted stools of April stooling are separated during rainy season and those of August are removed in the following spring. These stools, after separating from the parent plant are planted in the nursery fields.

This method of layering can also be used for the clonal propagation of ber rootstocks. The heading back of mother plants is done during May and the mounds are made in the similar manner as in case of pear and guava. The rooted stools are separated during August-September and planted in the nursery field.

(*iii*) **Air layering :** This is also known as goottee or hawaii dab. In this method one-year-old, healthy and straight shoot is selected and a ring of bark measuring about 2.5 cm just below a bud is removed. Moist sphagnum moss is placed around this portion and is wrapped with a polythene strip. It is light in weight, and has a very high water-holding capacity being able to absorb 10 to 20 times its weight of water. If moist sphagnum moss is not available, then a mixture of clay soil and cow dung (1 : 1) can be used to cover that portion of the shoot from where the ring of bark has been removed. This is then wrapped with a moist piece of gunny bag which, in turn, is covered with a polythene sheet. The clay cow dung mixture along with moist gunny bag also retain sufficient moisture for root development. The polythene covering does not allow the moisture to come out but permits gas exchange. Moreover, the layers need not to be watered afterwards which saves considerable labour.

Air layering can be practised during February-March and July-August in guava, litchi, sapota, loquat, etc. After a few weeks the roots are developed, which are visible, through the polythene covering. Then a half way cut should be given to the rooted layers on the parent branch at least 15 days prior to their permanent removal from the mother plant. At the time of separation, a few leaves or small shoots should be removed from the rooted layers to keep an optimum balance of root and shoot. It is also advisable to plant these rooted layers in the nursery for close attention than to plant them directly in the field. These layers can be planted in the fields during the following year in February or September-October.

(*iv*) **Tip leayering :** It is generally followed in plants which have trailing type of shoots. In this type of layering, tips are burried to a depth of about 7.5 cm or they may be burried in pots filled with rooting medium leaving a few cm of the shoot tip above ground. The covered portion strikes roots within 2-3 weeks. The rooted layer is then removed and transplanted either in the nursery bed or in a pot. This method of propagation is used usually in black berries, raspberries, and gooseberries.

(*v*) **Trench layering :** Trench layering consists of growing a plant or a branch of a plant in a horizontal position in the base of a trench. The soil is earthed up around the new shoots as they develop so that shoot bases are etiolated. For the establishment of mother tree one year old budded/grafted plants are transplanted in 45-75 cm apart on an angle of 30-45° down a row. The rows should be 1.2 to 1.5 metres apart wide enough to allow the cultivation. The plants are then cut back to uniform height of 45-60 cm and are left to grow for one season. In case of walnut, plants can be placed horizontally in the trench and the developing shoots are layered in the first year.

Before the beginning of the growth in the spring the parent plant/branches of the plant are bent over into a shallow trench of 5-7 cm and the tip and internodes are usually pegged to hold the stem in place. All part of the plant/branch should be completely flat on the floor of the trench. Before the buds swell, the entire layer is covered with 2.5- 5.0 cm fine soil or other rooting medium. When the developing shoots have pushed through the first layer of soil then add another layer of soil which is gradually increased as the shoots grow till basal 5-8 cm portion of the shoots are etiolated. By mid summer, process of adding the soil is repeated until the layered branches are covered to depth of about 15 cm. In late autumn or early spring the soil is removed from around the layered shoots and each rooted layer is cut off from the original mother plant very close to the base. These layers are planted under shade. Every year new shoots arising from adventitous buds of mother plants can be pegged down to produce new supply of rooted layers.

This method is primarily used for propagating certain fruit tree rootstocks difficult to propagate by other methods. Clonal rootstocks of pear, cherry, some Malling rootstock of apple and various types of quince are generally propagated by this method.

(*vi*) **Compound or Serpentine layering :** It is essentially the same as simple layering except that the branch is alternately covered and exposed along its length. The branch to be layered by this method is usually long and flexible. The exposed part of the branch should have at least one bud on it develop new shoots. The etiolated part gives rise to roots underneath. After rooting takes place, the branch is cut in section made up of the new shoots and the portion containing roots. Several new plants are thus possible from a single branch. The portion desired to form roots may also be treated with root promoting hormones. This method is used for propagating Muscadine grapes.

4. Budding

Budding is a form of grafting in which only one bud is inserted in the rootstock. This method is very easy and fast. In budding, the bud wood is greatly economised as compared to grafting. Budding is done in citrus, peach, ber, almond, pear and plum. This method is generally employed during spring and rainy season. As soon as the bark starts slipping both on the stock and scion, this is considered to be the optimum time for budding. This shows that the combium which is the tissue responsible for union is active.

Selection of scion : The mother plant from which the bud-wood is obtained for budding should be true-to-type, healthy, vigorous, free from insect-pests and diseases. The round bud-wood should only be selected because it sets perfectly on the stock, whereas the angular wood does not make a satisfactory union. The scion wood should be from mature shoot of atleast one year old. A scion wood of diameter 0.6 – 1.2 cm is satisfactory for better bud wood. Water sprouts or long shoots in the centre of a tree which bear light crops of poor quality fruit should not be used for taking bud- wood. Bud-wood should be obtained only a short time before the actual budding operation is performed and is usually cut into pieces having about 8 to 10 buds. Care should be taken to avoid the bud-wood from drying. This can be done by keeping the sticks in polythene bags containing damp saw-dust or wrapping the bud- sticks in moist gunny bag pieces.

Selection of rootstock : The rootstock should be prepared well before budding is started. This can be done by removing the leaves and thorns around the place where the bud is to be inserted. The stock should be uniform, healthy and of a diameter equal to that of a pencil (1 cm). The stock should be actively growing so that the bark will separate readily from the wood. The rootstock should have a proper vigour and growth and have wide range of edaphic adaptability habits. It should be resistant to soil borne diseases and other pests. The age of the rootstock should be one and half year and not more than two years.

Selection of Interstock. Interstock is a piece of stem inserted by means of two graft unions between the stock and scion. It is used to avoid incompatibility between the stock and scion and to make use of winter hardy trunk. The advantage of dwarfing rootstock can be availed off eg. apple. To restore tree size and improve rooting in apple *e.g.* MM111 rootstook with M9 interstock, MM106 rootstock with M9 interstock.

(*i*) **'T'-budding :** This is also known as shield budding. This is the most common method of budding used in most of the commercial fruits like citrus, apple, pear, peach, almond, ber, aonla etc. First a horizontal cut about 1/3rd the distance around the stock is given on the stock 15-20 cm above the ground level. Another vertical cut 2-3 cm in length is made down from the middle of the horizontal cut and the flaps of the bark are eased with the ivory end of the budding knife to receive the bud. After the 'T' has been made in the stock, the bud is removed from the bud stick. To remove the shield of bark containing the bud, a slicing cut is started at a point on the bud-stick about 1.25 cm below the bud, continuing underneath about 2.5 cm above the bud. A second horizontal cut is then made 1.25 to 2 cm above the bud, thus permitting the removal of the shield piece. The shield is removed along with a very thin slice of wood. The shield is, then, pushed under the two raised flaps of bark until its upper horizontal cut matches the same cut on the stock. The shield should fit properly in place, well covered by the two flaps of bark, but the bud itself exposed. The bud union should be wrapped with polythene strip to hold the two components firmly together until the union is completed. T-budding can be performed at any time of the year provided cell-sap flows freely. In most fruit trees it is performed either in the spring (March-April) or in the rainy season (July-September) period.

(*ii*) **Patch budding :** This type of budding is quite successful in guava and it gives 60 to 70 per cent success during May and June. Freshly cut angular bud-wood from current season's growth should be used as scion. A rectangular or square patch or piece of bark about 1.5 cm broad and 2.5 cm long is removed from the rootstock at about 15 to 20 cm from ground level. A similar patch with a bud on it is removed from the bud stick taking care not to split the bark beneath the bud. This patch is then transferred to the rootstock and fixed smoothly at its new position and tied immediately with polythene strip.

Improved patch budding in guava is quite successful and gives 75-80 per cent success during May - June. A semi-circular or a rectangular patch of bark (2.5 × 1.0 cm) with two buds is removed from the scion stick taking care that the bark does not split. It is then fixed on the exposed portion of the rootstock and tied immediately with the polythene strip leaving both the buds uncovered. The polythene is removed after a weak or so when the bud-take has occurred. When the shoot developing from the buds have attained a length of 15–20 cm, retain the vigorusly grown shoot and remove the weaker one.

Aonla is commercially propagated through patch budding from June to September

(*iii*) **Inverted T-budding :** This is another method of budding which is commonly used at places where rainfall is heavy. In this case the horizontal cut is first made at the desired height on the stock and the vertical cut is given at top rather than below as in the case of T-budding. It is generally seen that the insertion of the bud shield is much easier and faster in inverted T as compared to straight T-budding.

(*iv*) **Ring budding :** This method is commonly used for budding peaches, almond, ber and mulberry. This is a tedious and time consuming method and the plants in which this method is usually practised can easily be T-budded.

Ring budding is similar to patch budding, the only difference being that cylindrical portion of bark about 1.5 cm in thickness is removed instead of a rectangular or square patch. The ring of bark containing the scion bud is placed smoothly into the cylindrical slot made by removing the bark from the rootstock. The bud wood is then tied with a plastic tape. In ring budding, when the scion bud fails to grow the top portion of the rootstock also dies because it is girdled. This method is followed when bark slips freely.

(*v*) **Chip budding :** This method is usually employed when the stock and scion are still dormant, that is just before the start of new growth. For this, 2.5 - 2.8 cm long slanting cut is given into the wood or stock. Another cut at the lower end of this first cut is given at an angle of 45° and the chip of bark is removed from the stock. The bud from the scion wood is removed in the same way so that it matches the cuts given in the rootstock. This chip with a bud on it is fitted smoothly into the cut made in the rootstock taking care that the cambium layers of the stock and the scion unite at least on one side. The bud is then tied and paraffin wax is applied to prevent drying up of the bud.

The plants budded by this method have a long growing season and make bigger trees in the nursery. When the chip budding fails on certain stocks, ordinary T-budding is then practised in the normal budding season.

(*vi*) **Forkert budding :** In this, a transverse cut about 1.25 cm long is given on the rootstock at an appropriate height. Two vertical cuts, one from each end, are made to a length of about 1.5 cm. The bark so demarcated is carefully peeled out but it remains attached with the rootstock on the lower side. The scion-bud of a size corresponding to the size of cut made on the rootstock is removed and fitted into the exposed part of the rootstock. This bud is covered with the bark flap of the rootstock and tied with polythene strip. After about 4 weeks when the union between the bud and the stock has occurred, polythene wrapping is removed and flap is also cut off. As the bud starts growing, rootstock top is also cut off. This method is followed for propagation of mango and aoula plants.

(*vi*) **I-budding :** In I-budding two transverse cuts are given on the bark of the stock which are connected by one vertical cut at their centres. The flaps are then loosened with the spatula of the budding knife. The scion bud is prepared correspondingly and inserted into the I-cut, followed by tying. I-budding is practised where the bark of stock plant is thicker than scion.

(*vii*) **Flute budding :** It is just like ring budding except with the difference that while removing the patch of bark encircling the rootstock, a narrow strip of bark is left on the rootstock. While removing the bud from the bud stick, two transverse cuts, one below the bud and the other above the bud are made around the budstick. Then a vertical cut is made to connect the horizontal cuts and the patch with a bud (flute) is removed. After placing this flute on the stock, it is tied with a polythene tape. When the union between the bud and the rootstock has been completed and the bud shows signs of sprouting, the tape is removed and top of the rootstock is cut back.

5. Grafting

Grafting is a method of vegetative propagation where two plant parts are joined together in such a manner that they unite and continue their growth as one plant. In this method, the scion twig has more than two buds on it. Grafting is commonly done in pear, peach, plum, almond, mango, guava, loquat, sapota, etc. In temperate fruits like peach, plum and almond grafting is done when the plants are dorment but in mango, guava, loquat and sapota, the operation is carried out when the trees are in active growth. The following methods of grafting are commercially followed in these fruit plants.

(*i*) **Tongue grafting :** This method is very useful for grafting nursery stock. Top working with tongue can also be done when the plants to be top-worked are quite young with branches only one centimeter in thickness. In this method, stock and scion should be of equal diameter. First, a long, smooth, slanting cut of about 4 to 5 cm long is made on the rootstock but if the top growth is quite heavy then it is better to remove the top with the secateur before making the slanting cut. Another downword cut is given starting approximately 1/3 from the top and about a centimeter in length. Similar cuts are made in the scion wood exactly matching the cuts given in the rootstock. The scion having 2 to 3 buds is then tightly fitted with the rootstock taking care that the cambium layer of at least one side of the stock and scion unites together. This is then wrapped with polythene strip.

(*ii*) **Cleft grafting :** This is also known as wedge grafting. This method is useful in the nursery where the rootstock is quite thicker than scion and tongue grafting cannot be employed successfully. The stock upto 8 cm in thickness can be grafted with this method.

The rootstock to be grafted is cut smoothly with a secateur or saw. It is then split in the middle down to about 4 cm. The bud stick having 3 to 4 buds is trimmed like a wedge at the lower end with outer side slightly broader than the inner side. The lower bud on the scion should be located just where the wedge starts. The scion is than fitted well into the stock making sure that the cambium layers of both the stock and the scion are perfectly matched. Tongue and cleft grafting are performed in pear, peach, plum and almond during dormant period *i.e.* December-January.

(*iii*) **Inarching :** This is also called approach grafting as the scion remains attached to the parent tree till the union is completed and the stock plants are raised in pots and placed on raised platforms are brought in contact with the scion shoots. Alternatively, the mother plants are trained to be low headed and the stock is sown under their canopy. When these rootstock plants become ready for grafting, the inarching is done right there.

In this method, the diameter of the rootstock and scion should be approximately the same about 1.25 to 1.5 cm. A slice of bark along with a thin piece of wood about 4 cm long is removed from matching portions of both the stock and the scion. They are then brought together making sure that their cambium layers make contact at least on one side. These grafts are then tied firmly with polythene strip or any other tying material. The stock and scion plants are watered regularly to hasten the union.

The union is complete in about 2 to 3 months. A cut is then given to the scion shoot about half way through its thickness. If the shoot does not show any sign of wilting for a week or so, it is completely detached from the mother plant. In case the scion starts wilting, it shows that the union is not complete. In such cases the scions are detached from the mother plants after some days when the union is complete. This method is commonly followed in mango, guava, loquat, sapota and aonla. Last week of July or the first week of August is the best period for inarching.

(*iv*) **Side grafting :** This method is very successful for propagation of mango and it has replaced veneer grafting in the commercial multiplication of mango plants. This method is more efficient and cheaper than even inarching.

A three-sided rectangular cut about 4 × 1.25 cm is made on the rootstock at a height of about 15-20 cm from the ground level and the bark of the damarcated portion is lifted away from the rootstock. A matching cut is also made on the base of the scion to expose cambium. The length of the scion should not be more than 7.5 cm otherwise considerable breakage of the grafted plants in the nursery may occur. The scion should be prepared well before the actual grafting is done. The healthy scion shoots from the last mature flush are selected for this purpose. The selected scion shoots should have plump terminal buds. Those with swollen, protuded auxillary buds should be avoided as the use of such shoots has been found to produce malformed plants. After the selection of the scion shoots, remove the leaf blades, leaving petioles intact. In about 7 to 10 days, the petioles shall drop and terminal buds become swollen. At this stage the scion stick should be detached from the mother tree and grafted on the stock. The prepared scion is inserted under the bark flap of the rootstock so that the exposed cambia of the two components are in close contact with each other. The bark flap of the rootstock is resorted in its position. The graft union is then tied firmly with polythene strip. After the completion of the grafting operation, a part of the top of rootstock is lopped to encourage growth of the scion. When the scion has sprouted and its leaves turned green, the rootstock portion above the graft union should be cut away. Side grafting can be carried out successfully from March to October but July to September is the best time.

(*v*) **Veneer grafting :** Mango can also be propagated through this method. A shallow downward cut of about 4 cm long is given on the rootstock at a height of about 15-20 cm from the ground level. At the base of this cut, a second short downward and inward cut is made to join the first cut, so as to remove a piece of wood and bark. The scion is prepared exactly as in side grafting. The cuts on the rootstock and the scion shoot should be of the same length and width so that the cambial layers of both components match each other. Then, the prepared scion is inserted into the rootstock and tied securely with polythene strip. After the union is complete the stock is cut back, leaving the scion to grow. July-September is the best time for doing veneer grafting.

(*vi*) **Whip or splice grafting :** This method is useful for grafting for relatively thin material *i.e.* 0.8-1.2 cm diameter and is highly successful due to considerable cambial contact. It heals quickly and makes a strong union. The diameter of stock and scion should be uniform. The scion should contain two or three buds with the graft made in the smooth internode area below the lower bud. The cut made at the top of the stock should be exactly the same as those made at the bottom of the scion. The length of the cut is kept 2.5-5.0 cm and cut is given with the single stroke of the knife. Then they are tied and whole union is covered with grafting wax. This type of grafting is done in early spring.

(*vii*) **Saddle grafting :** Diagonal cuts of equal length are made on the scion and stocks of equal girth in the form of saddle to match each other. The cuts are brought together facing cambium layers, tied securely and coated with grafting wax.

(*viii*) **Bridge grafting :** Sometime the rodents or other animals eat away the bark of the tree trunk, thus girdling the tree. Some fungal diseases also cause girdling of orchard trees. Such trees can be saved by bridge grafting.

Bridge grafting is done when the sap is flowing in the tree but the scion is still dormant. First, the injured bark is cut away to healthy tissue on both sides of the girdle. Scion sticks are prepared in such a way that they not only cover the girdled area but also extend into the healthy bark at both ends at least 3-4 cm.

Sloping cuts, 5-6 cm long are made on the same side of the both ends of the scion. This side is to be put in contact with the healthy tissue across the girdle. Slanting cuts about 2-5 cm long are also made on the opposite side of the scion exposing additional cambium for a better union. The bark on both sides of the girdle is lifted and the scion which has been prepared as above is inserted there. The scion is nailed down firmly on both ends and wax is applied. Three or four such grafts are made to bridge the girdled stem.

(*ix*) **Bark grafting :** This method is rapid, simple, rapidly performed and highly successful. It can be easily performed on branches ranging from 2.5 - 3.0 cm diameter. Healing of thicker branches is difficult. Two or three or more scions are inserted per stub depending upon the thickness of the branch. The scions should be dormant 10-15 cm long containing 3-4 buds and of 0.75 to 1.25 cm diameter. One cut of about 5 cm long is made along one side at the base of the scion. In the stock, for each scion, a vertical cut about 5 cm long is made at the top end of the stub through bark to the wood. The bark is lifted and scions are placed. Then they are waxed.

(*x*) **Epicotyl or Stone grafting :** The method is commonly practised in mango. Stones are sown in moist sand bed and covered with 5-7 cm layer of leaf mould for germination. When the seedlings are of 15 days old they are taken out and grafted indoor. The top of the seedling is removed by giving a slanting cut at height of 5 cm from the stone. The scion shoot of 8-10 cm long from current season's growth is prepared by giving a slanting cut at the base in one side so as to match with the cut end of stock. It is then placed on the stock and tied with polythene tape. The grafted seedling is then planted in a polythene bag containing sand, soil and farmyard manure at a ratio of 1 : 1 : 1 and watered immediately. The polythene bags are kept in a partial shade condition and watered daily. When the scion produces four true leaves, they are transplanted in the nursery bed.

MICRO-PROPAGATION

The term micropropagation is used specifically to refer to the application of tissue culture techniques to the propagation of plants starting with very small plant parts grown aseptically in a test tube or other container.

Tissue culture helps in rapid multiplication of true-to-type plants throughout the year. Large number of plants can be produced in culture tubes in small space with uniform growth and productivity instead of growing them in large areas in nursery. Tissue culture plants especially raised through meristem are free from any diseases. Tissue culture coupled with somatic hybridization helps in evolving new cultivars in a short time.

The meristem explant used for micropropgation is about 0.1 – 0.5 mm size having one or two leaf primordia.

Advantages of micro propagation. This method has many advantages over the conventional propagation methods.

(*i*) The plants can be produced round the year irrespective of seasonal constraints.

(*ii*) Little space is required to maintain and multiply large number of plants.

(*iii*) A small tissue is required as an explant, thus saves the scion wood to great extent.

(*iv*) Such produced plants exhibit vigorous growth and higher yield.

(*v*) The plants are usually free from virus.

(*vi*) It is highly beneficial in dioecious fruit plants like date palm and papaya, where large production of female plants is possible.

(*vii*) This method helps in reducing the breeding cycle.

(*viii*) It is very usefully in plants in which vegetative propagation is not possible *e.g.* papaya and date palm.

(*ix*) It is possible to produce homozygous plants under *in vitro* conditions.

PATHWAY OF REGENERATION

There are number of pathways for the regeneration of whole plantlet from excised plant parts. The three main pathways are :

1. Regeneration from existing meristems : This is also known an axillary shoot proliferation. The existing meristems such as shoot tip or nodal bud is cultured on the medium, containing cytokinins. The shoot proliferation depends on the cytokinin used. The commonly used cytokinins are Benzyl aminopurine (BAP) and Kinetin. The regenerants are considered to be genetically stable, as compared to regeneration from adventitious meristems.

2. Regeneration from adventitious meristems : Shoot multiplication either directly or by callus formation can be obtained by inducing adventitious shoots on mature plant organs such as leaves, stems and roots. For initiation of adventitious meristems, a proper balance of auxin and cytokinin is needed in culture medium. In general, shoots are formed when a high ratio of cytokinin to auxin is present and reverse is true for root formation. The plants regenerated via this method are not always genetically stable, due to accumulation of aneuploid and polyploid cells with continuous subculturing of callus causing mixoploids. The repeated subculture of callus also reduces its morphogenetic potential/regenerative capacity.

3. Regeneration by somatic embryogenesis : The induction of somatic embryos is the best technique for rapid and true to type multiplication of plants. The somatic embryos originate from somatic or vegetative cells, and are bipolar structures, which possess both shoot and root meristem. The induction of embryo requires a high level of auxin in culture medium, followed by low auxin and cytokinin medium. Somatic embryos may arise in culture directly on explants or via callus formation or liquid suspension cultures. The somatic embryos can be encapsulated, thus producing artificial or synthetic seeds, which is an attractive alternative for propagation of plants.

Among two methods *i.e.* hydrated or dessicated, for artificial seed production, the production of hydrated seeds is more popular. In this method, the individual somatic embryo is encapsulated in a water based gel (hydragel such as calcium alginate). Embryos developed through tissue culture technique are mixed with sodium alginate and dropped with pipette into a calcium chloride solution to form calcium alginate capsules. The capsules are washed in water and then placed on culture medium for germination. Artificial seeds have been produced in Banana, mango, citrus, apple, olive and kiwi.

TECHNIQUE OF MICROPROPAGATION

Four main stages are involved in micropropagation of plants, such as explant establishment, shoot proliferation, rooting of shoots, hardening and transfer to soil/field.

Table 1. Commonly used disinfectants for sterilizing explants.

Disinfectant	Concentration (%)	Duration* treatment (min.)
Mercuric chloride	0.1–1	2–10
Silver nitrate	1	5–30
Bromine water	1–2	2–10
Sodium hypochlorite	0.5–5	5–30
Calcium hypochlorite	9–10	5–30
Hydrogen peroxide	3–12	5–15
Ethyl alcohol	70–95	0.5

*Duration is just a range, which need to be standardized for each spp/explant.

1. Explant establishment : The establishment of explant depends on several factors such as the source of explant/genotype, type of explant such as leaf, root, surface sterilants (Table 1) and the *in vitro* culture conditions such as culture media composition, temp, humidity, light etc. The explants showing growth are considered established.

2. Shoot multiplication : The established explants are subcultured after 2-3 weeks, on shoot multiplication medium. The medium is designed in such a way to avoid the formation of callus, which is undesirable for true to type multiplication of plants. Thus, the careful use of auxins like NAA, 2, 4-D and cytokinins like BAP, Kinetin is done in culture medium. It is well-established fact that cytokinins enhance shoot multiplication.

3. Rooting of shoots : The *in vitro* regenerated shoots are rooted in the medium containing auxins like NAA, IBA. The rooting can also be induced when *in vitro* shoots are exposed to stress conditions. The rooting should also be preferably without formation of callus, thus avoiding somaclonal variants.

Table 2. List of media used for hardening of tissue culture raised plants.

Sr. No.	Media*	Purpose	Remarks
1.	Garden soil	Source of natural nutrients	To enhance water holding capacity of sand
2.	Sand	To enhance aeration	Need frequent watering and mineral nutrients
3.	Peat	High water holding capacity and source of Nitrogen	Partially decomposed water vegetation
4.	Perlite	To enhance aeration	Grey/white material, contain no mineral nutrients
5.	Vermiculite	Good source of magnesium and potassium	Magnesium-aluminium-iron silicate (Hydrated)
6.	Soilrite mix	Good water holding capacity and enhance aeration.	Mixture of peat, perlite and vermiculte

* The listed media are generally used in different combinations, so as to have uniform aeration and nutrition to the plants.

Table 3. Protocols available for fruit crops commercially micropropagated in India.

Fruit Crop	Company	State
Apple	Agrigene International	Himachal Pradesh
Banana	Harrison Malayalam Ltd.	Karnataka
	Indo-American Hybrid Seeds	
	Godrej Plant Biotech	Andhra Pradesh
	Nath Seeds, Microplantae	Maharashtra
	Kumar Gene Tech, Maharashtra	Maharashtra
	State Seed Corporation	
	SPIC Biotech	Tamil Nadu
	A.V. Thomas & Co.	Kerala
Papaya	Harrison malayalam Ltd.	Karnataka
	Spic Biotech	Tamil Nadu
Strawberry	Microplantae	Maharashtra
	Indriyani Biotech	Maharashtra
	Godrej Plant Biotech	Andhra Pradesh
	Harrison Malayam Ltd.	Karnataka
	M and M Micropropagation	Chandigarh (U.T.)

4. Hardening and transfer to soil/field : The *in vitro* obtained plants are hardened/acclimatized before transfer to the field. The hardening is necessary as the tissue culture derived plants grow under high humidity conditions, have open stomata, lower epicuticular wax, thus leading to increased transpiration losses and resulting in mortality of plants.

MICROPAGATION TECHNIQUES

Meristem culture and micrografting techniques have been standardized in different fruit plants to produce virus free plants. The success varies with the plant species, variety and the culture environment.

(1) Meristem tip culture. This technique is widely used in carnation, dahlia, orchids and in potato. The meristem tip consisting of one or two pairs of leaf primordia are cultured in a medium. The plantlets are regenerated after a few weeks. After hardening of plantlets, these are transplanted in the soil under natural environmental conditions. Meristem tip cultured plants give rise to polyploid plants instead of diploid plants. This tip culture method is very useful for the elimination of viruses from infected plant material. Rapid multiplication of plants is possible through meristem culture. The plants produced are free from pathogens and can be stored for longer period.

(2) Micrografting. The various steps in micrografting include scion preparation, rootstock preparation, *in vitro grafting* and acclimitization/hardening of the plants. The *in vitro* raised nucelear seedlings are used as rootstocks. The scion (meristem 0.1 – 0.4 mm) is obtained either from young growth of field grown trees, defoliated glass house grown plants or *in vitro* proliferated nodal segments obtained from mature trees. The grafting is done with the help of stereomicroscope, under aseptic conditions. Many virus have been eliminated via micrografting in fruit plants *e.g.* citrus tristeza virus, peach latent mosaic viroid, pear vein yellow virus.

Micropropagation have been successfully adopted in many horticultural crops. Strawberry was the first fruit to be propagated commercially by this technique. The tissue culture technique has been used in banana, grape and papaya in India. In banana, shoot tip excised from rhizomes of wood sucker are suitable explants and MS medium supplemented with 3 per cent sucrose, gelite (0.25%) is the best. In grapes, shoot tips and two nodel micro cuttings are highly suitable explants for faster and disease free production of plants through tissue culture. In papaya, shoot tip culture technique has been demonstrated to produce female plants in the desired ratio

PROBLEMS ENCOUNTERED DURING MICROPROPAGATION

The success of micropropagation in several instances is hampered by the following problems.

1. Microbial contamination : Bacterial/fungal contamination in the culture do not allow the propagules to grow. This problem can be overcome by growing donor plants in growth chambers, systemic fungicide spray prior to explant removal, effective sterilization of explants, performing inoculations in laminar air flow cabinets fitted with HEPA filters (0.2 μm) and using sterilized surgical instruments. Fumigation of inoculation room using dilute formaldehyde solution also helps to minimize this problem.

2. Browning of cultures : The cultured explants of certain plant species secrete phenolic substances into the medium, which cause browning due to oxidation of phenols and formation of quinones, the toxins which effect the growth of cultured explants. The use of antioxidants such as activated charcoal (1-2%), citric acid or ascorbic acid (50-100 mg/1) and polyvinylpyrrolidone (PVP), polyvinylpolypyrrolidone (PVPP) in the culture medium helps to check the browning.

3. Variability in Tissue Cultured regenerated plants : Variability is highly indesirable in the micropropagated plants. It may occur due to callusing and regeneration of plants from callus instead of direct shoot induction and prolifiration. Moreover, the plants regenerated through adventitious meristems as compared to axillary meristem are suseptible to mutations, as it is derived from either a single cell or a small group of cells. This leads to variation in regenerated plants. The variation occurred due to callusing can be overcome by addition of growth substances which inhibit callusing such as TIBA (triidobenzoic acid), phloroglucinol and phloridzin and also by reduction of inorganic salt concentration in the culture medium.

4. Hardening of plants : Apart from these problems the tissue culture regenerated plants have abnormal leaf morphology, poor photosynthetic efficiency, malfunctioning of stomata (open), reduced epicuticular waxes and thus are amenable to transplantation shock. Hardening of such plants is thus must before transplantation under field conditions. Transplanting of tissue culture derived plants on appropriate soil media (Table 2), the conservation of moisture by creating high humidity around the plants, partial defoliation and application of antitranspirants are useful for hardening of *in vitro* raised plants. To prevent mortality, it is must to harden or acclimatize tissue cultured plants.

Limitations in Micropropagation

The following are the main limitations in micropropagation of plants.

(i) The facilities required for micropropagation are usally costly.

(ii) Technical skill is required to carry out different procedures in the laboratory.

(iii) Pathogens once appeared in the system, they multiply at a faster rate in a short time.

(iv) The plants having high level of phenols, usually do not respond to this propagation technique.

(v) Establishment of plants (hardening) in the field conditions is very difficult.

Success in Hardening of Plants

To have success in hardening of microprogated plants, the following approaches are needed to be adopted.

(*a*) Balanced proportion of roots and shoots in micropropagated plantlets.

(*b*) There should be appropriate rooting media for establishment of plants *ex vitro*.

(*c*) Balanced nutrition for survival of rooted plantlets.

(*d*) Simultaneous rooting and acclimatization is required.

(*e*) Cleaning of gelling agents from roots before transfer of rooting media.

(*f*) Moisture content or humidity around transferred plantlets.

PREPARATION OF TISSUE CULTURE MEDIA

The technique of culturing cells, tissues and organs under aseptic conditions on a synthetic nutrient medium is known as tissue culture. The type of culture media used in tissue culture vary with the plant species, varieties and even among the different plant parts such as shoot tip, nodal/internodal segments, leaf and roots. To start with there has to be a medium (basal medium), which can support a wide range of plant tissues and that can be modified according to the requirement of cultured tissue. The basal nutrient medium is one, which is a constituent of major elements, minor elements, vitamins, amino acids and carbohydrates. To achieve an optimal rate of micropropagation, this basal medium is modified with the addition of plant growth regulators such as auxins, cytokinins and gibberellins. Among the various basal media developed till date, the MS (Murashige and Skoog, 1962) medium is the most commonly used for *in vitro* propagation of horticultural plants.

Preparation of MS medium : For micropropagation of horticultural plants, the MS basal medium is modified by the addition of plant growth regulators. To precisely add the medium constituents and required growth regulators, there is a need to prepare stock solutions.

Preparation of MS medium stock solution : To prepare the stock solution (number 1–5) for MS medium (Table 4) add the required quantity (g) of the constituent salt according to the needed strength (X) of the stock solution *e.g.*, to prepare 1/2 litre of X–50 calcium chloride stock solution (number 2), dissolve 11 g of calcium chloride in distilled water and then make the final volume to 1/2 litre. To prepare 1 litre MS basal medium, 20 ml of this stock solution is used.

Preparation of growth regulator stock solution : The growth regulators (Table 5) in tissue culture regulate the growth and development of cultured tissues. Auxins have a role in cell elongation and rooting, cytokinins are used for cell division and shoot proliferation. The gibberellins help in elongation of shoots.

Auxin stock solution : Take 50 mg of auxin in a clean/dry test tube. Add in it 2–3 ml ethanol. Shake to dissolve and then slowly (to avoid precipitation) add more distilled water to make final volume to 100 ml. The final concentration of stock will be 0.5 mg/ml.

Table 4. Composition of Murashige and Skoog (1962) medium stock solutions.

Stock Sol. (no.)	Strength	Constituent salts	Quantity (g)	Use (ml/l)	Actual amount (mg/l)
			2 litre		
1.	X 20	Ammonium nitrate ($NH_4.NO_3$)	66.0	50	1650
		Potassium nitrate (KNO_3)	76.0		1900
		Potassium dihydrogen phosphate ($KH_2.PO_4$)	6.800		170
		Boric acid (H_3BO_3)	0.248		6.2
		Manganese sulphate ($MNSO_47H_2O$)	0.892		22.3
		Zinc sulphate ($ZNSO_4.7H_2O$)	0.344		0.825
		Potassium iodide (Kl)	0.033		0.025
		Copper sulphate * ($CuSO_4.5H_2O$)	1.0 ml		0.025
		Cobalt chloride ** ($CoCl_2.6H_2O$)	1.0 ml		0.250
		Sodium molybdate *** ($Na_2MoO_4.2H_2O$)	1.0 ml		
To avoid precipitation of stock solution no 1 add 1 ml HCl.					
			1/2 litre		
2.	X 50	Calcium chloride ($CaCl_2.2H_2O$)	11.0	20	440
			1/2 litre		
3.	X 50	Magnesium sulphate ($MgSO_4.7H_2O$)	9.250	20	370
			1 litre		
4.	X 100	Ferrous sulphate ($FeSO_4.7H_2O$)	2.780	10	27.80
		Ethylene diamine tetra acetic acid disodium salt (Na_2EDTA)	3.728		37.28
Heat slightly stock solution no. 4, to avoid precipitation					
			1 litre		
5.	X 100	Thiamine HCl	0.010	10	0.1
		Nicotinic acid	0.050		0.5
		Pyridoxine HCl	0.050		0.5
		Glycine	0.200		2.0

Sucrose (30 g) and myo inositol (100 mg) are also added in the medium. Agar (7 g) is added as solidifying agent.

* Dissolve 100 mg copper sulphate in 100 ml distilled water. ** Dissolve 100 mg cobalt chloride in 100 ml distilled water. *** Dissolve 1 g Sodium molybdate in 100 ml distilled water.

Table 5. List of growth regulators used in tissue culture media.

Growth regulator	Abbreviation	Solvent	Working concentration (mg/l)
Auxins			
2, 4-Dichlorophenoxy acetic acid	2, 4-D	Ethanol/1N NaOH	0.1–5.0
Napthalene acetic acid	NAA	lN NaOH	0.1–10.0
Indole-3-butyric acid	IBA	Ethanol/1N NaOH	0.1–10.0
Indole-3-acetic acid	IAA	Ethanol/1N NaOH	0.01–3.0
Cytokinins			
Adenine	Adenine	Water	0.1–5.0
6-Benzyl amino purine	BAP	1N NaOH	0.1–10.0
6-Dimethyl allyl amino purine	2-ip	1N NaOH	1–30
Kinetin	Kinetin	1N NaOH	0.1–5.0
1-Phenyl-3-(1,2,3-thiadiazol-5 yl) urea	Thdiazuron	DMSO/Ethanol	0.001–0.05
Zeatin	Zeatin	1N NaOH	0.01–5.0
Others			
Gibberellic acid	GA_3	Ethanol	0.01–5.0
Maleic acid hydrazide	MH	1 N NaOH	0.01–10.0
Phloroglycinol	Phloroglucinol	Water	50–150

Precautions : Always store the stock solution in refrigerator. Never use precipitated stock solutions for media preparation. IAA stock solution should be kept in dark coloured bottles to avoid oxidation.

CYTOKININ STOCK SOLUTION

Take 50 mg of cytokinin in a clean dry test tube. Dissolve in 1–2 ml of 1N NaOH. Slightly warm it and then add more distilled water volume to 100 ml. The final concentration of this stock will be 0.5 mg/ml.

Steps involved in medium preparation (MS 1 litre medium)

1. Take 1 litre capacity flask.
2. Add 50 ml of stock solution number 1.
3. Add 20 ml each of stock solutions number 2 and 3.
4. Add 10 ml each of stock solutions number 4 and 5.
5. Add 100 mg of myo inositol.
6. Add 30 g of sucrose.
7. Add distilled water to make volume to 900 ml.
8. Dissolve sucrose and myo inositol by continuous stirring/shaking the flask.
9. Add required concentration of growth regulator.
10. Adjust the pH of the medium to 5.8 with 1 N NaOH/HCl.
11. Add 7 g of agar (solidifying agent).
12. Make final volume to 1 litre with distilled water.
13. Boil the medium and stir while boiling to dissolve the agar.
14. Pour the boiled medium (15–20 ml) in the test tube/jars and plug with cotton plug/ caps, respectively.

15. Autoclave the media at 121°C, at 15 lbs/square inch pressure for 20–25 minutes.
16. Store the media after autoclaving at room temperature for 2–3 days, before inoculations.

Precautions : To avoid precipitation due to mixing of mono and divalent salts, prepare stock solutions (no. 1–5) as recommended. Store stock solutions in dark coloured bottles. Stock solutions should be properly labeled and stored in refrigerator. Never use precipitated stock solutions for media preparation. Adjust the pH of the media carefully otherwise media may not solidfy after autoclaving. For inoculations, always use the media at least 3 days after autoclaving.

MIST PROPAGATION TECHNIQUE

In the propagation of plants by soft wood herbaceous cuttings and leaf cuttings, one of the main problem is the loss by wilting due to desiccation before the cuttings have produced roots. In some other situations, when atmospheric temperature rises suddenly after rooting, the young roots are unable to absorb moisture from the soil at a rate, at which it is being lost by the transpiring surface of the young leaves. The result in such situations is again desiccation and death of the young rooted cuttings. Even for the rooting of hardwood cuttings, they should also be maintained in fully turgid condition during the rooting period for a high rooting success. This can be accomplished by keeping the relative humidity of the air surrounding the cuttings at a high level (usually 90-95 per cent) by manual sprinkling of water on the foliage several times a day during the rooting period. Such procedures are difficult and costly and they usually fail to avoid heat build up in the propagation chambers.

Mist chamber

To achieve this end water can be added to the air of propagation chamber by a number of mechanical means. Usually water is let into the chamber air through suitably designed nozzles under pressure (150-500 lbs per square inch, a high pressure system or 30-70 1bs per square inch a low pressure system) to form a fog or mist in the propagation chamber. This type of mechanism creates and maintains a thin layer of water on the leaf surface. It lowers the transpiration rate as well respiration rate and thus prevents wilting, desiccation and death of soft leafy cuttings and helps in promoting rooting and subsequent vigorous growth of the roots. The mist system consists of a regular water source, water strainers, electrically operated Day-Night timer, time interval cyclic timer, magnetic solenoid valve, mist nozzles and provision for bottom heat in the rooting beds. This type of intermittent mist operates automatically and maintains the chamber air at proper humidity and temperature to facilitate rooting. The quality of irrigation water used in the mist system is very important. It should be very low in salts to avoid salt deposition on leaves of cuttings and also to prevent clogging of the nozzles and the lines. This is particularly important in arid regions when salts are usually high in the water.

Different kinds of nozzles are available in the market to regulate the delivery of water into the propagation chamber air. Oil burner nozzles operate best at pressure higher than 150 1b/m^2, the others operate at pressure less than 100 1b/m^2 and are usually employed for mist formation where excessive watering is required. High pressure nozzles are more costly than the low pressure nozzels. The arrangement on nozzles in the chamber will depend upon objective, local conditions, and arrangement of benches and greenhouse structure. Above propagation benches, nozzles spaced every 3-4 feet will be satisfactory. The length to which a mist line can be extended shall depend upon the pressure of water source. But usually, the length of mist chamber is 100 feet or lesser.

GREEN HOUSES FOR PROPAGATION

To propagate plants around the year and to produce off season fruits the green houses are used. Their use is also essential for mass multiplication of plants through tissue culture.

The optimum growth in green houses is promoted by maintaining high relative humidity and temperature control, adequate day length and light intensity. Good light conditions are essential for the sturdy growth of the seedlings. The green house runs from east to west are the best for better light penetration in winter and early spring.

Greenhouses can be constructed by using plastic polyethylene or fibreglass or other appropriate covering material. The greenhouse should be well equipped with elaborate structures and have percise control temperature, light intensity and humidity. The size and type of greenhouse primarily depends upon the need. Glass covered greenhouses are expensive but they have long life. For quick and short term need plastic covered green houses can be constructed. Several types of sheets are available like UV stabilized polyethylene, polycarbonate and fibreglass which are light in weight and comparatively inexpensive. Plastic covered greenhouses are lighter than the glass covered ones. The proper ventilation should be made in plastic covered greenhouses to avoid undesirable water drops on the plants.

Polyvinyl chloride (PVC) has also been used in construction of green houses but it tends to darken pre-maturely in sunlight. In India, low cost green houses are constructed either of wood or metal framework and one covered with polyethlene sheet of 0.10 to 0.15 mm thickness which is resistant to ultra-violet rays. Such houses are equipped with thermostat, cooler or an conditioner or humidifier etc. for rigid control on temperature and humidity.

In green houses, two types of beds are used for growing seedlings. The beds may either by prepared on ground itself or raised beds or bench type beds are used.

FACTORS FOR SUCCESSFUL GRAFTAGE

The different factors to be taken into consideration for success in vegetative propagation through budding and grafting are as follows :

(*i*) The stock and scion should preferably belong to the same species or genus of the family.

(*ii*) The rootstock to be selected should be well suitable and compatible with different scion varieties.

(*iii*) The budding and grafting should be performed when the stocks are in active state of growth and there is sufficient flow of sap.

(*iv*) The thickness of stock and scion should preferably be the same *i.e.,* of lead pencil thickness.

(*v*) The air must be excluded from the point of union and there must be very close contact between the cambia of both stock and scion. This contact at the graft joint may be effected by fastening them securely.

(*vi*) The budding or grafting joints should be well protected from the direct sun rays and rains until union is complete.

(*vii*) The stock and scion should be of appropriate age. Never use too old stock for grafting operation.

(*viii*) The bandage should be removed after successful union has taken place. Avoid girdling at the grafting joint by removing bandage at appropriate stage.

(*ix*) To keep the stock plants in active stage of growth, maintain sufficient moisture in the soil or in pots.

(*x*) A given budding or grafting method is not equally successful in all kinds of fruit plants *e.g.* T-budding is best method in citrus but it is failure in mango. Skilled workers, smoothness of cuts, tying and waxing also affect budding/grafting success.

(*xi*) The environmental factors like temperature, humidity and light have direct influence on stock-scion relationship.

- Temperature have a profound effect on cell division and finally on callus formation. Callus formation is best at 26 – 29°C.

- Low humidity in the atmosphere reduced budding/grafting success *e.g.* stone grafting in mango. Success in stone grafting is improved by keeping graft union in warm and moist conditions due to better callus formation.
- Excess exposure to light also reduce grafting success as it cause dessication of the scion.

(*xii*) Certain insect - pests and diseases play negative role in budding/grafting success. Stem borer, bacteria or fungi cause damage to graft union. Virus free bud wood result into greater success.

NURSERY PRODUCTION

PROGENY TREES

The bud-sticks/graft wood should always be taken from healthy and true-to-type progeny trees, free from viruses diseases and insect-pests. The past history and the performance of these trees must also be known. Suitable fruit crops should be selected to meet the demand of the customers. There should be a collection of good number of promising varieties of popular crops to make a wide choice. A nurserymen should have progeny trees of all the commercial cultivars of fruits that can be grown in that particular area.

RAISING OF ROOTSTOCKS AND PROPAGATION TECHNIQUES

The rootstocks are known to have a profound effect on the vigour, productivity, precocity, fruit quality and tree longevity of scion varieties grafted or budded into them. They also influence the susceptibility of scion trees to various diseases and pests. It is now well recognised that optimum performance of scion cultivar depends on the proper selection of rootstocks for a given set of agroclimatic conditions. In order to achieve success in orcharding, not only it is important to select a right type of stock for the particular fruit or cultivar, but it is equally important to raise the stock seedlings in a proper manner so that there is good germination and the stock seedlings are ready for budding/grafting in the shortest possible time. There should be adequate arrangement for the supply of rootstock seeds of desired kinds and varieties. It will be desirable to have rootstock trees in the nursery itself.

The information with regard to raising of rootstocks and using different propagation techniques are discussed in detail under individual fruit.

CARE OF YOUNG NURSERY PLANTS

The young nursery plants need intensive care to make them grow well and to save them from vagaries of weather. They must be provided protection against intense heat and cold.

(A) Protection against hot weather

In North India, the temperature during May and June is very high. The nursery plants need much more attention and adequate protection against the hot sun. The tolerance of the fruit plants to withstand high temperature varies greatly with species. Fruit plants, such as those of mango, litchi, citrus, papaya, etc. are more liable to damage from hot weather as compared with other fruit plants. The following measures should be adopted to save the fruit plants from sun injury and adverse effects of hot weather.

Erection of thatches : The young nursery plants can be conveniently protected by erecting thatches made of sarkanda, *parali* (rice straw) or *Khajoor* (date palm) leaves over them. Sowing of Jantar around nursery beds during February-March affords good protection against severe heat and loo, (hot winds). in the hot months of April-June. Arhar can also be planted in the nursery rows which provide shade and minimise the sunburn injury.

Windbreaks : The windbreaks should be planted before establishing of fruit nursery. Eucalyptus, Mango seedling, Shisham (Tahli), Jaman, Mulberry, Arjan, Karonda etc., are the most effective windbreaks.

Irrigation : The frequency of irrigation should be increased during the hot period of May-June, when desiccating winds generally blow and cause higher losses due to evaporation and transpiration.

(B) Protection from cold

December and January are the coolest months in North India when the occurrence of frost is quite common. Sometimes, late frost may also occur in February. Both early and late frosts are more dangerous and inflict heavy damages to the nursery plants. Weak and sickly plants and those suffering from malnutrition are more prone to frost injury than healthy and vigorous plants. The following protection measures should be adopted.

Frost tolerant plants : In localities, where frost incidence is more common, raise only those nursery plants which can withstand frost damage. In such localities, raise deciduous plants like Apple, peaches, plums, pears, almond, apricot, grapes, etc., or raise relatively more tolerant evergreen plants like sweet orange, loquat, ber, etc.

Planting windbreak : Always plant windbreaks on the northern and western sides of the nursery which afford protection from the cold waves during the winter season.

Covering with thatches : The nursery beds of Jatti Khatti as well as susceptible plants like those of mango, litchi, citrus, papaya, etc., should be covered with Sarkanda thatches. The other farmwaste materials like sugarcane trash, rice straw (*parali*), maize stalks, etc., can be used for the preparation of thatches. The south-west side should be left open to allow sufficient sunlight.

Providing smoke screens : The nurserymen should keep ready heaps of dry leaves, grass or trash in the nursery at several places. As and when a frost is threatened or imminent, these heaps should be ignited and allowed to burn slowly. The fire and smoke raises the atmospheric temperature of the nursery by a few degree and thus the young fruit plants are saved from the frost injury.

Irrigation : An easy and more practical method to ward off frost is to irrigate the nursery as and when frost is threatened. Irrigation during cold spell period is most necessary.

WEEDING AND HOEING

The weeds grow frequently in the nursery, water-channels, roads and paths. They compete with young and tender nursery plants for water and nutrients. Eradication of these weeds should be done from time to time. The weeds on the paths and roadside should also be destroyed, so that they do not shed their seeds into the orchard soil. For the destruction of weeds like 'baru', 'kahi', 'Motha', etc. special efforts would be needed to clean the area of these obnoxious and hardy weeds. The nursery area should be kept scrupulously clean. The weeds can be effectively controlled with chemicals. Diuron as pre-emergence herbicide and glyphosate or gramoxone as post-emergence herbicides can be tried in fruit nursery with good success.

PLANT PROTECTION MEASURES

There are many insect-pests and diseases which attack the young nursery plants and if timely control measures are not adopted, these plants suffer from the serious damage. The growth of such plants is restricted and the plants look sickly and pale. Such plants take more time to become saleable. The reputation of a nursery supplying unhealthy fruit plants is spoiled and the fruit growers avoid buying fruit plants from such nurseries. Therefore, the fruit nursery has to be kept free of insect-pests and diseases by regular sprays. Thus, good arrangements for sprays pumps, insecticides, fungicides, etc. should exist with the nurserymen. A brief description and control measures of important pests and diseases of different fruit plants are given below:

Pests, diseases and symptoms of attack	Control measures
(A) DECIDUOUS FRUIT PLANTS **Pear, peach, plum, almond and apricot**	
(*a*) **Insect pests :**	
(*i*) **Peach-leaf-curl aphis :** Leaves infested with aphis acquire a characteristic curly appearance generally from March to May.	Spray 800 ml of Rogor 30 EC (Dimethoate) in 500 litres of water. Repeat the spraying after 15 days, if necessary.
(*ii*) **Leaf hoppers and aphids.** Cause serious damage to the plants by sucking the cell-sap from the leaves and tender fruits. Aphids are active from last weak of February to first week of April.	Spray 1 kg Hexavin 50 WP (carbaryl) or 800 ml Rogor 30EC (dimethoate) in 500 litres of water.
(*iii*) **Hairy-caterpiller :** They also feed on leaves.	(*i*) Collect and destroy the gregariously feeding young caterpillars. (*ii*) Spray 700 ml of Thiodan 35 EC (Endosulfan in 500 litres of water.
(*iv*) **Mites :** Mites attack in April-May. As a result of their feeding, brownish spots appear on the leaves. If the incidence is high, the whole of leaf becomes pale. Later, it dries and falls down.	Spray 500 ml of Rogor 30 EC (Diamethoate) or 1000 ml Kelthane 18.5 EC (dicofol) or 500 ml Fosmite 50 EC (ethion) in 500 ml of water.
(*v*) **Chaffer and other defoliating beetles.** They destroy the foliage.	Spray in the evening 1 kg of carbaryl (Sevin 50% W.P.) in 500 litres of water as soon as the damage starts. Repeat the spraying after 5 or 6 days if the damage continues or the insecticidal deposit is washed away by rain.
(*b*) **Diseases :**	
(*i*) **Pear scab :** Olive-dark mouldy spots appear especially on the underside of the leaf. Later, the spots turn gray and necrotic	(*i*) Apply bulky organic manures to nursery plants (*ii*) Spray 0.2% Captan (*iii*) Collect and burn the fallen leaves.
(*ii*) **Shot hole :** Dark brown, scattered lesions appear on the leaves of peach-plum which enlarge rapidly. Abscission of the diseased parts result in shot holes.	Spray with Captan, Ziram or Thiram (0.2%).
Grapes	
(*a*) **Insect-pests :**	
(*i*) **Grapevine thrips :** Minute slender-bodied yellowish insects cause yellowing and bronzing of leaves. Jassid is also serious after rainy season and causes stippling of leaves.	Spray 500 ml of Malathion 50 EC in 500 litres of water.
(*b*) **Diseases :**	
(*i*) **Anthracnose and cercospora leaf spot:** Dark brown circular spots on leaves	(*i*) Spray Bordeaux mixture 2 : 2 : 250 in last week of March, last week of May and middle of August.

around the mid-rib and main veins. Dark brown sunken spots with dark purple raised margins on the shoots. In cercospora, necrotic small areas appear on leaves with straw coloured centre and reddish brown margins.	(*ii*) Spray Bavistin 50 WP @ 1 g/litre of water during last week of April, middle of July and first week of September.
(B) EVERGREEN FRUIT PLANTS Citrus	
(*a*) **Insect-pests**	
(*i*) **Citrus Psylla :** Cause serious damage to citrus nursery throughout the country. Orange yellow nymphs of citrus psylla are found on new foliage.	Spray 1250 ml Rogor 30 EC (dimethoate) or 200 ml Imidacloprid 200 SL in 500 litres of water per acre during March with the appearance of the pest and again in the first week of September.
(*ii*) **Leaf-Minor :** The leaf minor makes zigzag silver white galleries on new leaves which get twisted.	Spray 500 ml Sumicidin 20 EC (fenvalerate) or 1000 ml Ripcord 10 EC (Cypermethrin) or 1250 ml Hostathion 40 EC (triazolphos) or 200 ml Imidacloprid 200 SL in 500 litres of water during. April-May and August - September.
(*iii*) **White Fly :** The nymphs and pupae are found on the under surface of the leaves and cause serious damage by sucking of sap.	Spray 1000 ml Fosmite 50 EC (ethion) or 1250 ml Hostathion 40 EC (triazophos) in 500 litres of water per acre during April – May and again during September - October.
(*iv*) **Leaf Folder.** This pest is active in the nursery and young plantations from May to October. The larvae feed inside the leaves by webbing them together and starts feeding from top to downwards. The plants become stunted.	Spray 1250 ml Dursban 20 EC (chlorpyriphos) or 1000 ml Ekalux 25 EC (quinalphos) in 500 litres of water per acre.
(*v*) **Mites :** Sometimes become serious in August–September. The leaves have minute white specks left by the feeding. Leaves are generally covered with dust.	Spray 670 ml of Rogor 30 EC (Dimethoate) in 500 litres of water per acre during August–September.
(*b*) **Diseases :**	
(*i*) **Canker :** Dark brown, rough and raised areas on leaves and twigs.	Give the sprayings of 50 g streptocycline in October, December and February. Prepare the solution by mixing 50 g streptocycline in 500 litres of water. Also add 25 g copper sulphate to increase the potency of antibiotic in the mixture. Bordeaux mixture 2:2:250 or 50% copper oxychloride (0.3%) can also be sprayed.
(*ii*) **Scab :** Small, dark brown, rough, irregular raised lesions on leaves and twigs	Clipping of infected leaves in July and apply three sprays of Ziram 27 SC (0.25%) or Dithane M-45 (0.25%) or Bordeaux mixture (2 : 2 : 250) or 50% copper oxychloride (0.3%) during last week of June to August at 20 days interval.

(*iii*) **Wither-tip or die-back** (Anthracnose): Drying of tips and branches; necrotics, circular areas on leaves.	Remove the infected branches and then spray with Bordeaux mixture and copper oxychloride as above during March, July and September.
Virus and Virus-like diseases	
(*i*) **Greening :** Stiff, upright, multiple twigs and buds ;small chlorotic or mottled leaves, premature defoliation, die-back of branches.	(*i*) Use disease free budwood and tolerant rootstocks such as Rough lemon. (*ii*) Control vector citrus psylla.
(*ii*) **Tristeza :** Veinlets clearing in young leaves, necrosis of sieve tubes at bud union, honey combing (inverse-pits), decline of top.	(*i*) Use disease free bud-wood and tolerant rootstocks such as Rough lemon. (*ii*) Control vector aphids
(*iii*) **Exocortis :** Cracking and scaling of bark of trifoliates, citranges and Rangpur lime, epinasty and curling of leaves, yellow blotches and cracks on shoots of some citrus; stunting of trees.	(*i*) Use disease free bud-wood. (*ii*) Avoid susceptible rootstocks. (*iii*) Sterilize budding knife and other tools.
(*iv*) **Ring Spot.** The disease appear as yellow rings on mature leaves. The ring number varies from one to several per leaf with variable diameter. These ring may coalesce to form bigger patches by covering the entire leaf.	(*i*) Use virus free bud wood. (*ii*) Sterilize budding knife and other tools.
(*v*) **Damping off :** Both pre and post emergence death of seedlings in nursery beds	(*i*) Treat the seed with 3 g of Captan or Thiram per kg of seed before sowing. (*ii*) Drench the nursery beds with 0.4% Captan or Thiram solution (4g in 1 litre water) 5-7 days after germination. Repeat the drenching after 7-10 days if necessary.
Mango	
(*a*) **Insect-pests :**	
(*i*) **Mango hopper :** It is very active during February-March. The nymphs and adults suck the sap from the tender leaves.	Spray two times *i.e.,* in the end of February and end of March with 1 kg Sevin or Hexavin 50 WP end of (Carbaryl) or 800 ml of Malathion 50 EC in 500 litres of water per acre.
(*b*) **Diseases :**	
(*i*) **Mango malformation (Bunchy top) :** On seedlings over three months old, swellings appear in the axils of leaves. Small clustered leafy shoots are produced at the apx, on the main shoots or laterals.	Remove the affected seedlings and destroy them.

Ber	
(*a*) **Insect-pests :**	
(*i*) **Leaf-eating caterpillars :** Feed on leaves and cause huge damage.	Spray 750 g Sevin 50% (Carbaryl) in 250 litres of water per acre as soon as the damage is noticed.
(*b*) **Diseases :**	
(*i*) **Leaf mould and leaf-spot :** The underside of the leaves shows a blackish and sooty appearance. Leaves turn yellow and drop prematurely. Necrotic, small to medium spots appear on the affected leaves.	Spray with Bordeaux mixture 2 : 2 : 250 or with 0.3% copper oxychloride 50% (300 g in 100 litres of water).

CHAPTER 5

Orchard Cultural Practices

When the orchard is layed out and planting is done, then the fruit grower is interested in the optimum growth of the trees and the maximum production of fruit. Soil management, cultivation of intercrops, manuring and fertilization, irrigation and training and pruning are some of the important factors which have to be taken into consideration for getting the economic returns and maintaining the vigour of fruit trees. Given below are the important cultural practices being followed in the orchard.

A. SOIL MANAGEMENT PRACTICES

1. Soil culture

(*i*) **Tillage :** It means ploughing and hoeing of the soil. The objective of the tillage is to loosen and pulverize the soil so that the roots of fruit plants may penetrate in the soil easily. It facilitate circulation of air and absorption of water. Tillage removes the weeds and helps in mixing manures and fertilizers. It releases the locked up plant food material through the activity of the micro organisms.

(*ii*) **Clean cultivation :** It means keeping the land of the orchard always free from grasses or any other vegetation. It controls the weed growth and improve moisture retention in soil. Clean cultivation also improves the soil aeration and increases the nutrient availability. However, it causes soil compaction and deteriorates the soil structure. Soil becomes depleted of nutrients under continuous clean cultivation without the addition of organic matter or growing any leguminous crop.

(*iii*) **Sod culture :** It means the fruit plants are grown in permanent grasses without tillage and addition of any litter. This practice is common in hilly areas. Sod culture checks erosion. There is less damage to the fallen fruits. The disadvantage of sod culture is that water and available nitrogen is taken by the weeds. Hazards of fire are involved due to dry grass. Attack of rats and insect-pests is there.

(*iv*) **Mulching :** Mulching is a system of soil management in which hay, straw, or cut grass is placed on the soil between the tree rows to conserve the soil moisture by checking surface evaporation. It is considered that cultivation and the maintenance of a soil mulch are important as means of preventing the evaporation of moisture. If weeds are removed without disturbing the surface of the soil, very little water is lost by evaporation. Mulching checks germination of weeds. However, mulching is susceptible to fire outbreak. Mulch also facilitates the hibernation of rodents.

(*v*) **Clean basin management :** This practice is carried out manually by keeping the basin free of all weeds. It is the most common method of orchard floor management in apple. In this system 4-6 cultivations are given throughout the year to control weeds. The cultivation of basins after harvest facilitates the application of fertilizers in winter. It is recommended for young apple trees to develop deeper root system and to avoid any compitition for nutrition or water by weeds with the plants. However, this system is not recommended for bearing trees due to its effect on feeding root system and soil moisture levels.

The chief objective of orchard soil culture is to provide the necessary conditions for the fruit plant to grow satisfactorily, utilising the moisture and nutrient supply in the soil to the best advantage. Manures can also be well incorporated into the soil only when the soil is loosened. This is also necessary to incorporate green manures and residues of cover, intercrops and mulches to help the process of decomposition. On sloping land, the culture of the orchard soil is specially harmful. Growing of permanent cover crops on such land or planting of strips of grass between the narrow strips of clean tilled rows of fruit trees on the contours, are the usual practices which are aimed to prevent the soil from erosion.

The orchard cultural practices depend both on the kind of fruit and environments. In mango, soil culture is mostly done in the pre bearing age of the orchard. Raising of green manure, inter or cover crops is the common practice. As the trees grow and cover much of the ground, only an annual tillage is generally done, normally a month or two before flowering. In citrus, few shallow ploughings especially during June-July and October to December are necessary to keep down the weeds and mend the irrigation channels.

2. Inter culture

(*i*) **Intercrops :** Intercrops are raised in an orchard during pre-bearing period for increasing the income from land such as through raising of vegetables, pulses and short duration fruit crops.

When the new plants are set in the orchard, there is considerable area between the rows and trees which is not used by the fruit plants at that stage as the roots of the young plants are not spread to the whole vacant area around them but are limited to a short circular area extending not more than a few feet. The space which is lying vacant can be utilized for planting for a few years, till the root system of the permanent tree is spread almost in the entire area. When the fruit tree in the orchard are young and have not started bearing fruits as yet, they may not be using all the area under them and as such the farmers can intercrop the orchard to supplement their income.

In mango orchard, pear, plum, phalsa and papaya may be planted as filler trees. They come into bearing quite early and yield good income before the permanent mango plants start bearing commercial crop. These temporary plants are kept well away from the permanent tree so that their roots do not compete with one another. When the permanent trees grow and occupy more space and their root system extend towards the filler trees, these should be removed.

Vegetables and some of the leguminous crops are also preferred as intercrops. The cereals are not grown because they are quite exhaustive thereby harming the fruit plants. The truck crops can be grown successfully as annual cash crops. If the orchards are situated near towns and cities, the vegetables as intercrops are best suited. In the orchards which are far from the market, intercrop only those vegetables/crops which can be transported to distant markets, or stored for some period. When the fruit plants do not start bearing good commercial crop, the vegetables grown as intercrops should be fertilized adequately so that the fruit trees are not adversely affected for want of nutrients needed by them for their proper growth.

Gram and dwarf peas are the best intercrops for orchards where the trees have been budded on a rootstock requiring a well drained soil. The gram can be grown successfully as intercrop for the first 3-4 years after planting the orchard. It not only gives good return but also enriches the soil. Gram and peas intercropped in rabi season are harvested by the first week of April and thereafter in kharif season for a short duration, legume crop like Moong should be grown. Being a leguminous crop, it also enriches the soil. Guara grown for seed has also proved a good intercrop.

The following intercrops can be grown successfully in the fruit crops.

Interplanting of fruit plants in orchards

Fruit crops		**Fillers**
Mango, litchi, pear	:	Peach, plum, phalsa, papaya and kinnow mandarin.

Intercropping of vegetables

Near the cities	:	Cauliflower, cabbage, radish, carrot and tomato.
Far from the market	:	Onion, potato, chilli, and peas
Intercropping with leguminous crops	:	Gram, cowpeas, peas, guara, etc.
Intercropping pulses	:	Mung, mash, gram, cowpeas, etc.

Crops like barseem which require lot of irrigation should be grown in guava and pear orchards because these trees can tolerate wet soil condition to a greater extent. Avoid creeper type vegetables in the orchard. Tall and exhaustive crops like cotton, bajra, maize, chari and bhindi should be avoided in the orchard.

(*ii*) **Cover crops :** These crops are raised mainly in the beginning or in advance of the rainy season, so that these may provide the necessary protection to the soil when damage by soil erosion is the greatest *e.g.*, cowpeas, moong and soyabean. Cover crops help to improve the physical condition of the soil by adding the organic matter to the soil. Retention of cover crops during summer months is undesirable as it will compete with the main fruit trees for soil moisture. Cover crops may also serve to draw off surplus moisture during monsoon.

(*iii*) **Green manuring crops :** These crops are raised during the rainy season and burried into the soil after a few months of growth for incorporation of the organic matter. e.g., guara, senzi, daincha and cowpeas. To facilitate rapid decomposition of all green matter, it is necessary to plough down the same while still tender or succulent. The green manure crops are generally cut down and incorporated into the soil just when they reach the blooming stage. Green manuring crops also help to improve the physical condition of the soil by adding the organic matter to the soil.

When leguminous crops are used as inter, cover or green manuring crops, these are able to fix nitrogen from the atmosphere. Regular use of green manure may also help to reduce the expenditure on manuring and fertilization in the orchard.

3. Weed Management

The weeds should be eradicated from the orchards as they compete with fruit trees for water and nutrient. Bathu, pohli, piazi, pit papra etc. are the commonly found growing winter weeds. Motha, kahi and baru are the common weeds found growing during the rainy season. Cultivation of orchard land can help to kill weeds. Cultivation with tractor or ploughing rather helps their further spread. The orchard infested with such obnoxious weeds should be dug up and all rhizomes/bulbs collected with a rake/fork should be burnt.

The weeds in orchards can be best controlled by spraying pre-emergence herbicide like Hexuron 80 WP (diuron) or post-emergence herbicide like Glycel 41 SL (glyphosate) or Gramoxone 24 WSC (paraquat).

4. Manuring and Fertilization

Application of manures and fertilizers to the fruit trees constitutes a very important cultural practice. For successful orcharding, one has to apply organic manures as well as chemical fertilizers at the right time, in proper dose and in a right manner. Fruit trees remove large amount of nutrients from the soil than most other farm crops. The manurial requirements of a fruit trees are governed by multiplicity of factors like age of the fruit tree, type of soil, climatic conditions, cultural practices being followed etc. An orchard can be maintained in commercial bearing only by adding adequate manuring. Plants require N, P, K, Ca, Mg, S and traces of Mn, Bo, Cu, Fe, Zn and Mo from the soil for its normal growth. Orchards are manured both by organic manures and inorganic fertilizers.

(*i*) **Organic manures :** Farmyard manure, poultry manure, compost, oil cakes and green leaves are the chief organic manures. Organic manures improve the physical condition of the soil and also add some quantity of nutrients to the soil. The percentage of nitrogen contained in common organic manures ranges from 0.5 per cent in the low grade fresh cattle manure to a little over 2.5 per cent in the poultry manure. Farmyard manure is the most popular manure and is widely used in orchards. If properly maintained, it may contain about 1.5 per cent nitrogen, 0.9 per cent phosphorus and 1.3 per cent potash. The farmyard manure to be used in the orchard, should always be well-rotten as otherwise its application may attract white ants.

Poultry manure is also very rich in nitrogen which ranges from 1.0 to 1.8 per cent. Its phosphorus content is 1.4 to 1.8 per cent and potash is 0.8 - 0.9 per cent. Green manure or ploughing in a cover crop is another form of organic manuring and is better done during a dormant or semi-dormant period of the trees. Oil cake is a rich source of nitrogen and is being used chiefly for its nitrogen content. Daincha, guara and sanhemp are also good source of nitrogen and contains 0.62, 0.34 and 0.75 per cent nitrogen, respectively. Sanhemp also contains 0.12 per cent phosphorus and 0.51 per cent potash.

(*ii*) **Inorganic manures :** Use of fertilizers in the present agriculture is indespensable. To achieve the desired goal, the farmers have to use varying amounts of a variety of fertilizers supplying nutrients essential for successful fruit production. It is, therefore, important that the growers are well familiar with the different fertilizer materials they use in their orchard.

Urea : It is available in the form of white round pills which are free flowing. It is highly hygroscopic because of which it has to be packed in moisture proof bags. It can be mixed with phosphatic and potassic fertilizers provided the mixture has to be used immediately after preparation. It contains 46 per cent nitrogen in amide form. It is highly soluble in water. Therefore, if applied under extensively wet conditions, it may be leached to deeper layers of the soil. As such it is desirable to apply it to soil under moderately wet conditions followed by mixing it thoroughly with soil. It has highly acidic reaction in soil. It is also suitable for foliar application in the form of a solution in many fruit crops.

Ammonium Sulphate : It is available in the form of white or grey coloured crystalline salt. It absorbs very little moisture from air i.e. non-hygroscopic and possess excellent physical properties owing to which it can be easily mixed with phosphate and potassic fertilizers while applying to soil. It keeps well during storage and transport. It has 20.6 per cent nitrogen in ammonical form. It is quickly soluble in water. It is not susceptible to leaching. In addition to N, it contains 24 per cent sulphur also and thus supplies sulphur in the sulphur deficient fields. It has an acidic residual effect in soil.

Calcium Ammonium Nitrate (CAN) : It is available in the form of grey or light brown granules which are free flowing. Because of being highly hygroscopic in nature, it has to be stored in moisture proof bags like urea. It can be mixed with phosphatic and potassic fertilizers provided the mixture has been used immediately after it is ready. It contains 25 per cent nitrogen, half of which is in ammonical and half in nitrate form. It has neither acidic nor alkaline residual effect on soil.

Diammonium Phosphate (DAP) : It is available in the form of granules of light grey colour and contains both nitrogen (18%) and phosphours (46-48% P_2O_5). It is totally water soluble in nature. Diammonium phosphate is non hygroscopic and slightly hard in nature. Its physical properties are the best among most of the fertilizers and can be mixed with nitrogen and potassic fertilizers before application. The quality of this fertilizer does not deteriorate much on storage but it tends to caking with prolonged storage in airy and humid stores. It is neutral in reaction.

Superphosphate : Superphosphate is available both in powder and granulated form. Single superphosphate contains 16% P_2O_5, double superphosphate contains 32% P_2O_5 and triple superphosphate contains 46% P_2O_5. Whole of phosphorus in these fertilizers is water soluble. It is prepared by adding sulphuric acid to rock phosphate and gypsum is added as a filler in it. It is greyish in colour. It does not absorb moisture from soil and had little tendency to caking. It is acidic in nature. Superphosphate has best physical conditions and can be mixed with other fertilizers before adding.

Muriate of Potash : It is available in the form of pinkish crystalline salt and absorb very little moisture from air i.e. non-hygroscopic in nature. It possess excellent physical properties and can be mixed with other nitrogenous and phosphatic fertilizers while adding to soil. Muriate of potash contains 60% K_2O. It keeps well during transportation and storage. It is highly water soluble and is neutral in reaction.

Applications of Fertilizers and Manures

In order to obtain maximum benefits and to minimise possibilities of any adverse effects it is important that fertilization should be done at appropriate time in a suitable manner.

Time of application : In north India where summer and winter seasons are well marked, there are definite periods of growth and dormancy or rest for the fruit trees. From February to April the fruit trees have the highest requirements of nutrients for vegetation, flowering and fruit setting. To be effective, the nutrients must be readily available at a time when these are needed the most.

The best time for applying N fertilizers is about two weeks prior to the initiation of growth and flowering. If the quantity is small, the application can be made in a single dose. However, if it is large, split the quantity in two equal doses i.e. one before the initiation of growth and second after fruit set. The P fertilizer should be applied along the N fertilizers. The K fertilizer should be applied in spring or in some fruit trees about 4-5 weeks prior to the fruit maturity as it improves fruit quality.

Organic manures should be applied about 3 months ahead of the spring flush so that by that time nutrients are converted into readily available form.

The time of application of micronutrients depends upon the kind of fruit tree and the severity of deficiency. If the deficiency is mild, one spray in April may be enough, but if it is acute 4-5 repeated sprays at monthly intervals may be needed to correct the deficiency. Usually the sprays are more effective than soil applications. However, in soils with neutral pH, soil application may be attempted either with pure chemicals or with chelated compounds. The time of soil applications is same as for other fertilizers.

Method of application : The method of application should be appropriate taking into consideration the age of trees, their root extensibility, type of orchard management, kind and amount of fertilizers to be applied. The different methods are as follows :

Broadcasting : It consists of spreading the fertilizer uniformly over the entire field. This is applicable in full bearing or closely planted orchards.

Band/Strip placement : This placement can be made either in bands or in trenches around the trees or fertilizers are drilled or injected into the soil. This method is commonly used when fertilizers are applied in small quantities to young trees and when P and K fertilizers need to be incorporated into the root zone or in case of plants with poorly developed root systems.

Foliar application : The spraying entails applications either with manually operated or with power sprayers. Generally foliar sprays include micronutrients application or nutrient which cannot easily be supplied through soils. This is followed as a means of fertilizer application in fruit trees, which must be sprayed at regular intervals to affect the growth and fruit quality.

This fertilizer may also be applied either as injections to tree trunks or as dabs to cover the pruning wounds as is done in grapes. Applications of concentrated fertilizers should not be applied too close to the trunks. Each fertilizer application should be followed by a copious irrigation.

Fertigation : Fertigation involves the application of fertilizers with irrigation water at a slow and controlled rate to meet nutritional requirements at different stages of crop growth. Under fertigation, the fertilizers can be applied in ten splits as compared to one-two splits. Such applications result in increased crop yields with substantial savings in fertilizer and irrigation water. The application of liquid fertilizers makes the nutrients continuously available to the plants. Fertilizers containing one or more elements can also be applied by injecting them through suction side of the pump or by injecting under pressure in the irrigation pipes or by injecting in the irrigation pipes through a ventury. Easily soluble fertilizers should be applied to avoid precipitation, clogging and damage to the components of the system.

Deficiency Symptoms of some Essential Elements

The major essential elements include C, H, O, N, P, K, Ca, Mg, S. The minor elements comprises of Fe, Mn, B, Zn, Cu, Mo required in smaller quantity. In addition, some elements are also essential, although they are required in traces by some of the fruit plants. The trace elements like N, Cl, Al, Si, Co, etc. are required by some plants in a very minute quantity. Nutrients deficiency symptoms are one of the criteria of judging the nutritional status of the plant. The given below information describes the nutrient deficiency symptoms on the foliage of fruit plant alongwith the carriers.

Element	Deficiency symptoms	Carriers
Nitrogen (N)	Stunted plant. In early stages pale yellowish colour of older leaves. In acute condition younger leaves also become pale and older leaves start falling	**Ammonical-N** — Ammonium nitrate — Ammonium phosphate — Ammonium sulphate and urea. **Nitrate - N** — Calcium nitrate — Calcium ammonium nitrate and — Sodium nitrate
Phosphorus (P)	Dwarfing and abnormally dark green plant, leaf erect and usually narrow. In acute cases purple pigmentation, bronzing on back side of leaf. Blossoming poor, delays fruit maturity and poor yield.	— Mono calcium phosphate — Dicalcium phosphate
Potassium (K)	Yellowing of tips and margins of older leaves. In acute cases cupping of leaves, marginal necrosis.	— Potassium chloride — Potassium sulphate

		– Potassium nitrate
Magnesium (Mg)	Chlorosis starting from tips and margins with no dead spots, main vein green. In acute conditions-leaf base necrosis, leaves curling upward, become brittle and easy to detach.	– Magnesium sulphate – Calcium magnesium carbonate (Dolomite)
Sulphur (S)	Uniform yellowing of young leaves along with veins, stunted growth.	– Ammonium sulphate – Calcium sulphate (gypsum).
Calcium (Ca)	Young buds become chlorotic, hooks and die-back at tip margins,, death of terminal bud. Rest of the plant remains dark green. Fruit exhibit water soaked lesions at blossom end.	– Calcium nitrate – Calcium sulphate (gypsum)
Zinc (Zn)	Interveinal chlorosis of young leaves, shortening of internodes, leaves small and erect (Rosette). In acute cases die-back of twigs, fruit small, pale rind at maturity.	– Zinc sulphate – Zinc chloride.
Iron (Fe)	Young leaves chlorotic, no spots (lime-induced chlorosis)	– Ferrous chelate – Ferrous sulphate – Ferric citrate
Manganese (Mn)	Leaf chlorotic, main and small veins green, no marked reduction in leaf size.	– Manganese sulphate – Manganese chloride.
Copper (Cu)	New leaves wilt, chlorotic, then necrotic, shoot tips show dieback in summer, multiple bud formation below the dead growing points, gumming in citrus fruits. Fruits become misshapen.	– Copper sulphate – Chelated copper
Boron (B)	Young expanding leaves necrotic or distorted, death of growing points. Stems may be rough, cracked or split along the vascular bundles. Fruits small, hard, cracked, central regions of the fruit corky.	– Boric acid – Calcium or Magnesium borates.
Molybdenum (Mo)	In early symptom older leaves chlorotic resembling Nitrogen deficiency symptoms and then necrotic spots leaving holes in leaves. In later stages symptoms develop on young leaves.	– Ammonium molybdate
Chloride	Browning and shrinking of leaves, Leaf margins turn necrotic.	– Sodium chloride (common salt)

Leaf Sampling in Fruit Crops

Leaf sampling in fruit crops is an essential tool for manipulation of manurial requirement of the plants. Plant analysis is the second criteria after soil testing that is critical to improving crop nutrition and yield. The plant analysis identifies how will the plants utilized the soil and applied nutrient. It allows the plant to tell us what nutrients it needs for proper growth. Leaf analysis can be used to diagnose nutrient problems after symptoms are found. This is achieved by identifying nutritional shortage or excesses before symptoms are developed and resulting in a more economical fertilizer schedule.

Sampling Procedure : Collect 4-8 leaves per tree from each direction (North, East, South and West) at working height of one to two metres by taking one leaf per shoot. Sample along diagonals (X pattern) from about 10-20 per cent trees from selected blocks in the orchard. Collect leaf samples in polythene bags. Keep the bags in the ice-box and immediately send to the Leaf Analysis Laboratory.

In order to diagnose or confirm nutrient deficiencies or toxicities and to determine nutrient status of fruit trees, following leaf sampling procedures should be adopted.

Name of the fruit	Leaf age (Months)	Sample size (Number of leaves/ petioles)	Season	Remarks
Citrus	4-8	100 leaves	July - October	Immediately behind the fruit
Mango	5-7	30 leaves	March - April	Non-flushing and non-fruting twigs
Guava	5-7	50 leaves	August - October	Midshoot leaves from non-fruiting terminals
Ber	5-7	70 leaves	November - January	From middle of the shoot
Apple	4-5	100 leaves + petioles	August	Mid shoot leaves with petioles on current season extension growth
Pear	4-6	50 leaves	July - September	Mid shoot leaves from current season growth
Peach	3-5	100 leaves	Mid-May to Mid-July	Mid shoot leaves from current season growth
Plum	3-4	100 leaves	May - July	Mid shoot leaves from current season growth
Litchi	6	50 leaves	March	leaflets from 3 to 5 position on the shoot
Grape	1-2	100-200 petioles	March (one month after bud burst)	Collect 1-2 petioles per vine from the leaf opposite of the shoot during full bloom stage
Sapota	9	50 leaves	December	Leaves from middle portion of shoot
Papaya	6 months after planting	20 leaves	February - March	Mature leaf petioles are taken

5. Irrigation Systems

Irrigation is very important in fruit crops as sufficient moisture must be maintained in the soil for obtaining the optimum yield of good quality fruits. The aim of irrigating a fruit tree should be to wet the entire root zone without allowing any wastage of water beyond the root zone. The irrigation system have to be properly devised so that the water requirements of the trees are met at the minimum expenditure without any wastage of water.

System of irrigation of fruit plants vary with the age of trees. Several methods are employed for the irrigation of fruit trees depending on the age of the tree, the soil topography and the availability of irrigation water. Thus the system of irrigation must be decided in relation to the varying orchard conditions. Different systems of irrigation commonly adopted are as follows :

(*i*) **Flood system :** In this system whole of the area is irrigated through one head *i.e.* without sub-division of the unit area into small plots. Irrigation water used in this case is excessive as the entire field is to be wetted to meet the need of the excessive root system. It provides fully saturation of root zone. The system is useful where intercrops or green manuring crops are grown in an orchard. In this system, the wastage of water is more and this also leads to excessive weed growth. There is a risk of bark diseases like collar rot or foot rot because the tree trunks remain in contact with water for long time. This system is suitable for orchards of more than 8-10 years old.

(*ii*) **Furrow system :** This system is suitable in areas where the orchards are planted in slopy land. In this system the water moves slowly in furrows in the area between tree rows. The trees are fed through the lateral movement of water. The consumption of water is less in this system and there is no risk of bark diseases. Saturation of root zone is comparatively less. Intercropping or green manuring is not possible in furrow system. This system is suitable for old orchard.

(*iii*) **Basin system :** In this method, a small circular basin is provided around the tree trunk. These basins are linked directly with one another through straight channel. There is less wastage of water and it checks weed growth. Water passing through the channel touches the tree trunk directly and hence risk of bark diseases is involved. The water flow also draws away the manure from the tree basins and deposits it at the end of the channel. This system is suitable for young fruit plants below 1- 2 years of age.

(*iv*) **Modified basin system :** This system is an improvement over the basin system. In this system, main channel runs in between the tree lines and the basins are linked with it independently through small sub-channels. The only drawback of this system is that this needs more attention to block the sub channels after the basin has received adequate water. The size of the basin is increased with the extension of the leaf drip of each tree every year. Intercropping is not possible in this system. This is a good system of irrigation for the young orchard upto 6-8 years of age and also for the arid-irrigated areas where there is a shortage of water.

In improved modified basin system, the basins are linked with the channel passing through along the side of these basins. This system avoids the risk of bark diseases and intercropping is possible.

(*v*) **Sprinkler system :** This system is used where water supply is not adequate. The water is pumped with pressure through the sprinklers attached to pipes and these sprinklers are adjusted in such a manner to overlap upto one fourth area covered by the other sprinklers. These are then moved to the next point after sufficient percolation has taken place. This system is very costly and is suitable in areas where the sub surface water is not fit and the soil is uneven or sloppy and the water supply is not regular from the canals. It is suitable for the full grown orchards.

(*vi*) **Drip system :** The water is supplied with pressure after filtering it through the pipes with attached hoses designed to supply water in drops. These small hoses are placed around the tree in a circular pattern and the percolating water moves down and side ways wetting the root zone. This system of irrigation is very costly and most useful in areas with scanty rainfall for high density plantation. This system requires regular water supply. In this system, the loss of water due to evaporation and erosion of soil are nil but percolation and seepage losses are appreciable. The pipelines and the sprouts are occasionally damaged due to growth of the root zone and unprudent operation of machinery. The advantage of application of liquid fertilizer to the root system is available. High cost of operation, damage to pipelines and infestation of diseases to the underground parts of the plants starting from collar regions are the disadvantages of this system.

Proper Use of Drip System in Orchards

The drip irrigation system has great potential to use irrigation water judiciously and efficiently alongwith improvement in the yield. Drip system supplies water near the root zone of the plants through dripper/emitters @ 2-10 litres per hour at a low pressure from 0.20 to

1.5 kg/ cm^2, to meet daily crop consumptive use. Micro sprinklers are also used in place of drippers, which supply 20 to 40 litres water per hour depending upon the nozzle size and the working pressure. It is reported that drip systems allow irrigation of 50 to 200 per cent additional area enabling it to give additional produce.

The water for drip system may be available from canal, stored rainfall or tubewell. In case of tubewell irrigation, the water can be directly pumped through mesh filter into the drip system. In case of canal water, the water should be first stored in the storage tank and then pumped into drip system through sand filter and mesh filter. The storage tank should be lined. Its capacity should be according to the command area and availability of canal water. Water storage tank of 800 m^3 capacity is sufficient for 10 acres of command area. The floating inlet should be adopted to reduce the sucking of silt load.

Components : It includes (1) Control unit *i.e.* pumping, filteration and fertilizer application unit (2) The distribution network *i.e.* a network of main, sub main, lateral and emitters/micro sprinklers (3) The miscellaneous components *i.e.* joints, flow and pressure regulating valves and water meters.

Working of the system : The diameter of the main and submain (PVC) lines (25-75 mm) should be selected very carefully according to the size of the area to be irrigated. The mains and submains are laid 45-60 cm below the soil surface to avoid damage during interculture and deterioration due to ultraviolet radiation. The lateral lines (12-16 mm) are spread along the lines of trees and length of each line depending on length of the plant row. These laterals are joined with the main/submain line with the help of adopters. The discharge of the dippers may not vary more than 10 per cent of the specified one during working of the system.

When the system is to be operated in big orchard, the command area should be divided into two or four sub-units so that each sub-unit is not more than 10 to 15 acres. This will results in proper, judicious and economical utilization of irrigation water. The planting distance can be kept closer in drip irrigated orchard due to less spread of the trees. Initial cost of drip system is more but is compensated through coverage of more command area under irrigation and thereby increasing the productivity.

Precautions : In canal water supply, sand filter should be cleaned after every two to three weeks depending upon the silt load by back washing. Mesh filter should be closed everyday. The emitter discharge should be measured periodically to check any clogging. After 3-6 months any algae or bacterial formation should be removed from the drip pipes using one litre hydrochloric acid in 1000 litres of water. Pump this solution in the pipes by injection, keep it for 15-20 hours in pipes and then flush it out.

B. FRUIT PLANT MANAGEMENT PRACTICES

Canopy management is the most important fruit plant management practice. In temperate fruits, a regular annual pruning is essential to induce a good and healthy growth which will provide a maximum fruit bearing area on the tree as well as to improve fruit size and quality.

1. Training and Pruning of Fruit Trees

Training and pruning of fruit trees are the specialised horticultural operations. Training of the fruit trees should be done in such a manner that sufficient air and light gets penetrated inside the foliage to facilitate proper colouration and development of fruit of superior quality. Sufficient attention must, therefore, be given to training of young fruit trees to an appropriate system of training.

The deciduous fruit trees like apple, pear, peach, plum, almond, apricot, grapes and phalsa need annual pruning, in order to keep them in proper vigour and for obtaining good fruit yields of superior quality over the years. Pruning is an important horticultural practice, which is not properly understood and often neglected by the growers. The purpose of pruning, at any specific time, depends upon the age and kind of the fruit plant, vigour of the plant and whether it is bearing or non-bearing.

(*a*) **Training :** When a plant is staked or tied or supported over a trellis or pergola in certain fashion or some of its parts are removed or trimmed with a view to giving the plant a particular shape, the operation is called training.

Objectives of training : The main objectives of training are as follows :

(*i*) To admit more light and air to the centre of the tree.

(*ii*) To expose maximum leaf surface to the sun.

(*iii*) To direct the growth of the tree so that various cultural operations such as spraying and harvesting are performed at the lowest cost.

(*iv*) To protect the tree from wind damage.

(*v*) To secure a balanced distribution of fruit bearing parts on the main limbs of the tree.

Training Systems : The following training systems are in vogue in different kinds of fruit trees.

(*i*) **Central leader system :** The main trunk is allowed to grow and smaller side branches grow in various directions. This system approaches the natural type of growth of most trees. It provides a strong trunk with well-spaced and well-distributed bracnches with strong crotch angles. The trees under this system grow too tall and are less spreading. It is rather difficult to spray, prune, thin and harvest from trees trained to this system. The system is found most suitable for pear.

(*ii*) **Open-Centre system :** The main trunk is allowed to grow upto 75 cm by cutting within a year of planting. All side branches are headed back. This system lacks strong crotches and provides weak frame work and as such is less satisfactory. However, it may be favoured in fruits like peaches and plums for admitting more sunlight for better colouration of the inside fruits. But under sub-tropical conditions where sunshine is plenty and there are strong winds during summer, this system is not suitable in view of the weak frame-work and other obvious defects.

(*iii*) **Modified leader system :** It is first trained like central leader by allowing stem to grow for the first two years, then headed back at 75 cm height. Lateral branches are allowed to grow and cut back as in open centre system. With this system, the height of the tree is lowered as the length of main trunk is reduced. The scaffold branches are encouraged to become larger and grow to greater length. The trees possess strong crotches and a durable frame-work. The system suits most of the commercial fruit trees because the height of the tree is comparatively less, which facilitates operation like spraying, pruning, harvesting, etc.

(*b*) **Pruning :** Pruning may be defined as the removal of any excess or undesirable branches, shoots, roots or any other parts of a plant so as to allow the remaining parts to grow normally or according to the desire of the pruner.

Objectives of pruning : The chief objectives of pruning are as follows :

(*i*) To remove the non-productive parts

(*ii*) To remove diseased, dried and broken branches

(*iii*) To remove the criss-crossed branches

(*iv*) To divert the energy into those parts that are capable of bearing fruits

(*v*) To allow the light to enter the interior of the tree.

(*vi*) To control the size of the plant

(*vii*) To regulate the fruit crop.

Pruning Methods : Generally, the trees are pruned annually in two ways.

(*i*) **Heading back :** When only one-third to one-half terminal portions of the branches, having their basal portions intact, are removed. Thus, the apical dominance of the twig, shoot or branch is destroyed and the lateral buds are stimulated to growth.

(*ii*) **Thinning out :** When the shoots or branches which are considered undesirable are removed entirely from the base or point of attachment with the main trunk or branches without leaving any stub. It encourages longer growth of the remaining terminals and net result is reduction of laterals. Sometimes this practice is used for the rejuvenation of older trees.

Time of pruning : The best time for pruning of deciduous fruit is winter when the trees become completely dormant after shedding their leaves. Pruning of pear, peach, plum and phalsa should be carried out during January, whereas in case of grapes the pruning should be initiated in the second forthnight of January and completed by first week of February.

2. Bending of Scaffold

It has been found that main branches with wide crotch angles come into bearing earlier than those growing upright. These scaffolds also give out secondary branches and help in the fast spread of trees. The scaffold bending if carried out manually helps in the reduction of juvenile period. So fruit plants like pear, mango which come into bearing late can be trained by bending the scaffolds downward. Bending of branches in pear enhances spur formation and plants come into bearing at the age of four years only.

3. Ringing of Fruit Trees

The method of increasing fruit bud formation is termed as ringing. This practice is commonly followed in mango and grapevine. Ringing interrupts the downward passage of carbohydrates through the phloem causes them to accumulate in the part of the tree above the ring. When a ring is made on a small branch just below a flower or flower cluster, fruits will be unusually big. Large amount of downward moving carbohydrates which collected above the ring, pass into the developing fruits or flowers.

Principles of ringing : The main principles of ringing are as follows :

(*i*) Ring of bark removed should be such as not to injure the cambium layer.

(*ii*) The healing of ring and complete restoration of new bark on the ringed portion is highly imperative after fruits have set.

(*iii*) Ringing should be practised only on the trees which are vigorous in vegetative growth.

(*iv*) The week and exhausted trees should not be ringed.

(*v*) Ringing is employed to check vigour of the plant.

(*vi*) Ring should be done in early growing period so as to encourage blossom bud formation.

Method of Ringing

Ringing is a specialized operation which need a good skill. It is important to know that removal of girdle or bark is a drastic treatment. The width of the girdle should not be exceeded 1.0 - 1.5 cm. In big trees with stem of 25 cm or more diameter, ring may be made 2 cm wider. Always ring on stem should be made where bark is smooth and free from knots. While doing ringing, press the point of a sharp knife up to required depth and should be pulled round the trunk until a circle is described by which time point of knife will have reached the starting position once again. Same operation is repeated at desired distance and in-between strip is peeled off.

Sometimes two half girdles can be removed instead of removing one complete girdle. These are less drastic than a single girdle. Instead of whole tree, few branches making excessive growth can be girdled. The girdled portion should be treated immediately and adhesive tape of same width may serve the purpose. A little neglect in treatment may result into death of the plant.

Ringing increase fruit set and berry size in grapevines due to increase in supply of carbohydrates above the ring. In mango, ringing of branches improve fruit yield during "off" year.

4. Fruit Thinning

Fruit thinning refers to the removal of some portion of fruit crop from the tree before its maturity in order to improve the general size and quality of the remaining crop.

Objectives of thinning : The broad objectives of thinning are as follows :

(*i*) Fruit thinning is necessary where uniform fruit is required for processing and canning or for table purpose or fancy trade.

(*ii*) It improves the size of remaining fruits on the tree and increases the marketable yield.

(*iii*) It helps in maintaining the vigour and productivity of the tree over a longer period.

(*iv*) It reduces the cost of picking and handling of the crop at harvest, by reducing the number of pickings of fruits from the tree.

(*v*) It improves the final colour, eating and keeping quality of fruits.

(*vi*) It reduce limb breakage of the tree.

Methods of Thinning : Normally two methods are followed for thinning of fruits.

(*i*) **Hand thinning :** In this operation, start thinning first by shaking the branches lightly to dislodge some of the fruits which are likely to drop off naturally. If there is still surplus fruit, then start thinning from top to the bottom of the branches. Hold the stem, (Dandi) of the fruit to be removed between thumb and second finger and pull it off gently. The main point to be kept in mind while thinning is to remove all the small, undersized, misshapen, insect or disease attacked fruits.

The job of thinning by hands can be done more efficiently by employing women or young boys and girls with a little training and supervision as compared with the stiff fingered persons engaged in hardwork.

(*ii*) **Chemical thinning :** Ethephon, Naphthalene acetic acid and sevin are used as chemicals for thinning in different fruits. These chemicals are applied at full bloom stage. In the use of chemicals, the time and rate of application are very critical. In peach, ethephon @ 200-300 ppm is applied 30-40 days after full bloom, whereas Naphthalene acetic acid @ 25-50 ppm is applied 15-20 days after full bloom. Planofix sprayed at full bloom period (75% flowering) of peach @ 25 ppm is effective in flower thinning in Flordasun and Shan-i-Punjab varieties. Information about chemical thinning in different fruit is meagre and thus, not reveiwed here in detail.

5. Spraying

Spraying the fruit plants against timely control of insect-pests and diseases is the important horticultural practice. Widely used method of application of fungicides is spraying on leaves. By spraying a thin film of fungicide adhered to leaf surface, it destory fungal spores present on it. Some phenyl/mercury fungicides enter into the host tissues and eradicate the pathogen already invaded. In these days, systematic fungicides are widely used for spraying which enter into the host tissues, persist in the host protoplasm and provide resistance to host against any fungal infection.

Fungicide suspension does not adhere to leaf surface. It remains in small droplets and subsequently it may be larger in size with other droplets and ultimately they may be shreded off. To overcome this problem, some wetting agents are mixed with the suspension. Similarly, spreaders and stickers are also used to have long term and better efficiency of the fungicides.

Spraying is done with the help of knapsac sprayer, foot sprayer and power sprayer. The operational principles of sprayer are that a pump generates pressure in the spray-fluid and releases it through a nozzle along with small droplets of the spray-fluid.

Precautions : Spraying should be undertaken immediately as the first signs of a disease or a pest appear on the trees. Tree and bush spraying requires high pressure to ensure good coverage of the foliage. Both the lower and the upper surfaces of the leaves should be covered with sprays. The spray concentrations should in no case exceed the recommendation. Leaves can be sprayed when they are dry, stems and roots are sprayed when the ground is damp. If possible, spraying must be done after irrigation. Spraying should not be done in the middle of the day during hot, dry periods. During high wind, spraying should be avoided.

6. Harvesting and Fruit Handling

Utmost care needs to be taken while harvesting and handling of fruits. The fruits should be picked only at a proper stage of maturity. Sorting and grading should be regularly practiced before the fruits are marketed so that they sell at a premium. The fruits should be sent immediately to markets after packing them properly. The low grade and cull fruits may be used profitably for the preparation of preserved products.

It is a common experience to find the contractors and even some growers harvesting the fruits while still immature and dumping those in the markets. This practice causes ill-effects on the human health.

Harvesting indices : Good quality of fruits is obtained when harvesting is done at the proper stage of maturity. Immature fruits when harvested will give poor quality and erratic ripening. On the other hand, delayed harvesting of fruits may increase their susceptibility to decay, resulting in poor quality and hence low market value. Moreover, if the produce is to be shipped to distant markets or stored to wait for a better price, it should be picked in the mature but unripe state.

The degree of maturity for harvest is of prime importance which depends on whether the fruit is meant for long distance transport or local consumption. Maturity indices differ considerably among fruits and their varieties. Fruits like mango and banana are harvested when they are mature, others like citrus, pineapple and grapes are ripened on the plant itself. Several parameters have been suggested to judge and harvest maturity of different fruits such as firmness, total soluble solids, (TSS), acid-sugar ratio, flesh colour, starch content, pulp/peel ratio, days after fruit set etc. But non of these appear to be adopted in practice. Traditionally, maturity is determined by the shape, colour, size, development of aroma, disappearance of astringency etc,

Harvesting : In general, manual harvesting is followed. Fruits require different methods of harvesting which vary according to the type of fruits. Green and mature mangoes are harvested manually with the help of bamboo pole with a net attached and lowered to the ground in a basket with the help of a rope. Mature banana bunches are cut at the stalk end retaining 30 cm length with the help of a sharp sickle. Citrus fruits are plucked or clipped manually and are collected in baskets. Grape bunches are clipped with scissors. Papaya is harvested by twisting the fruit till it snaps off. Pineapple is picked by giving a downward bend until the peduncle breaks off. Apple, peaches and plums are harvested by skilled labour. Litchi and dates are harvested by their stalks. Ber is harvested by shaking the branches.

Harvesing methods : Two methods are followed for harvesting of fruits. The factors which should be taken into consideration are the perishability of the fruit, economy of labour and market requirements.

(*i*) Hand harvesting : This is commonly followed method of harvesting of fruits. The fruits like strawberries and raspberries are very soft which are borne on low growing plants, harvesting is done by simply removing them from the plant and putting them into a suitable containers. The fruits like mango, citrus and avocados are difficult to harvest. Ladder is used to reach the fruit. This is time consuming process. Picking platforms which can be raised and lowered are used by the harvesters.

(*ii*) Mechanical harvesting : Very little fruit required for fresh market is harvested by machines because the likely damage could result in rapid deterioration in quality during marketing chain. The fruits required for processing may be harvested mechanically. The oranges for juice extraction may be removed from the trees by powerful wind machines being dragged through the orchards followed by a device for collecting the oranges from ground.

Tree shakers can also be used which are attached to the tree trunk and violently shake the tree to dislodge the fruits.

Chemical sprays are used in certain fruits for the formation of natural abscission layer on the fruit stalk and should be applied a few days prior to harvesting. Ethrel, Abscisic acid and cycloheximide are effective chemicals for this purpose.

Grapes and soft fruits for processing may be harvested by tractor mounted machines with combing fingers which are run up the stems, pulling of the fruit branches as well as a high proportion of the leaves.

Mango harvesters is developed at Konkan Krishi Vidyapeeth, Dapoli (Maharashtra) and CISH, Lucknow. These harvesters harvest the fruits with 1-2 cm long pedical and harvesting capacity is 50-177 kg fruit per hour.

Handling of fruits : The fruits like mango, banana, papaya, sapota, guava, apple, avocado, apricot, peach, pear, and plum are climacteric in nature and, therefore, require careful handling. The fruits like citrus, grape, ber, pomegranate, litchi, pineapple and cherry are non-climacteric in nature

Grading of fruits should be regularly practised. Systematic grading is a pre-requisite for efficient marketing system and raising the quality of fruits. Grading is a critically important process because produce presentation is judged on the basis of uniformity.

Grading prescribed for many fruits is based on physical characteristics like weight, size, colour, shape and free from diseases which vary depending on the agroclimatic conditions.

Grading of fruits is done with different methods as follows :

(*i*) Manual grading (*ii*) Partly mechanical and partly manual grading (*iii*) Mechanical grading (*iv*) Optical methods of grading-colour grading, spectrophotometric techniques, delayed light emission and colour meters.

The proper grade standards prescribed for each fruit should be followed.

Proper packaging helps in efficient marketing of fruits as it protects from mechanical damage, moisture loss, pilferage and dirt. Wooden crates, carrugated fibre board cartons, gunny bags, jute and plastic pack and polynets are now used for packing of different fruits. Mango, banana, pineapple fruits are transported as free load in trucks. Paper shavings, dry grass, saw dust, pulp trays, honey-comb partition, cell pack etc. are being used as cushion materials. The use of corrugated fibre board cartons for storage and transport of apples and grapes have proved successful in reducing spoilage.

The usual transport for marketing of fruits, is by headload, bullock cart, trucks and rail. Refrigerated and insulated wagons/trucks are used worldwide for transportation of perishable fruits. Atmospheric control and in-transit control of levels of oxygen, carbon-dioxide and removal of ethylene and other volatiles from the cargo space could be helpful.

Storage losses of fresh produce are high in India due to high temperature and humidity. Storage at low temperature immediately after harvest reduces the rate of respiration resulting in reduction of build up of the respiration heat, thermal decomposition, microbial spoilage and also helps in retention of quality and freshness for a long period. The storage life, however, is governed by variety, stage of maturity, infection at the time of harvest, harvest interval, rate of cooling, storage temperature, RH, rate of accumulation of carbon dioxide, pre-packing, air distribution system and utilization of storage space, etc. Storage of fruits in controlled or modified atmosphere is an important practice. Combined with low temperature, it markedly retards respiratory activity and delays softening, senescence and changes in quality and colour of the stored fruits.

7. Marketing of Fruits

Marketing plays a key role in the post-harvest operation of fruit. A perfect and efficient marketing system covers all aspects of handling from the stage of harvesting till the commodity reaches the consumer. Marketing of perishable fruits presents more problems as compared to other agricultural commodities. The interest of the producers as well as consumers are poorly served. The growers always gets less return of his produce and consumer pays more than is necessary. Due to the presence of the middleman the price of fruits is 50-100 per cent higher in terminal market (mandis) than in growing areas. The middle men are also known to manipulate the situation by artificially creating gluts and offering low price to the growers. They falsely reject the fruits as substandard and indulge in other malpractices. The cooperative systems can play a very important role in the marketing of fresh fruits.

The growers are facing some other problems in the way of marketing the fruits which are as follow :

(a) Inadequate post-harvest infrastructure

- The inadequate post-harvest infrastructure leads to 20-30 percent post harvest losses.
- The growth in cold storage facilities meant for fruits only and processing industry is not keeping pace with the increased production of fruits thus facing the growers to dispose off their produce at throw away prices.
- After harvest, fruits need to be transferred to cooling units within half an hour. Due to poor cold storage and CA storage facilities, losses further increased.

(b) Imperfect competition

- Because of perishable nature of the fruits, it is difficult to create time and space utilities.
- Imperfect competition is prevailing in the fruit trade. Only few influential traders are involved in this business.

(c) Insufficient information

- Growers get insufficient information of limited markets regarding prices of their produce which shows large variation in daily prices. Thus, growers have to face problems in getting the best price for their produce.

Steps for Better Marketing of Fruits

- Fruit markets need to be properly regulated. There should be fixed commission-monitory system to save the growers from exploitation. Modern methods should be used in these markets.
- There is an urgent need to set up an efficient market information network so that growers can get timely and adequate market related information which will help to them to get better price of their produce. Thus, growers can negotiate with the traders with strength.
- Creation of marketing organisations near fruit growing areas is needed. Such organisations should provide facilities to growers like credit at lower rate of interests,

supply various inputs, transport and make arrangement for speedy pick up of produce from orchard to markets so that post-harvest losses can be minimized.

- A system should be developed where the growers can sell the fruits directly to the consumers at retail outlets without the involvement of middlemen.
- Cold storage with variable temperature set up as per fruit need should be established so that the growers can save the perishable product from the losses occurring due to glut during peak marketing season to earn better profit during lean period.
- Refrigerated transport facility (cold chain system) should be strengthened to facilitate efficient marketing of fruits to reduce post-harvest losses.
- Processing units in fruit growing areas should be established where the growers can sell the surplus fruits conveniently. Contact farming system should be encouraged in this regard.
- Producers need to be organized into cooperate marketing societies, which should take care of marketing of the fruits. These societies can effectively replace the middlemen.
- Foreign markets should be tapped. Improved varieties of fruits should be developed for ready acceptance in the foreign markets.
- Support price of the commercial fruits grown in the state should be fixed.
- Fruit crops should be covered under comprehensive crop insurance scheme to save the growers from losses occurred due to natural calamities.

CHAPTER 6

Flowering and Fruiting

In many fruit plants the time of flower opening depends on the environmental conditions. The length of flowering period is also dependent upon the temperature and atmospheric humidity. The type and morphological features of flower are very important from horticultural point of view. It is very important that one should be thoroughly familier about the bearing habit of the fruit trees. The position of the flower on the inflorescence is a criteria determining fruit set in many species. Mode of pollination and agencies of pollination are important aspects of flower that helps the breeder in making desired crosses. Pollen viability particularly when immediate pollination is not possible, in storage for short time or long duration is also an important consideration in fruit breeding. In fruits, there are three sex type of flowers. All the three sex type of flowers are found in different fruits. Hence, this chapter includes brief information about bearing habit of fruits, type of inflorescence, blooming period, mode of pollination, agencies of pollination and pollen viability.

1. BEARING HABIT OF FRUITS

In every kind of plant, most of the flower buds are found in a certain definite position. In the developing buds, a stage is finally reached when such a differentiation cannot take place except when bud unfolds into a leafy structure and the subsequent formation of a fruit bud at a new growing point. The position of flower or inflorescence on the shoot, relative to the growth of current season, is characteristics of the species or the variety and is subject to little change. Flower bearing shoots may arise from either terminal or lateral bud, either on long or short growths (spurs) or they may arise from adventitious buds. The position of the flower bud is different in different varieties. Buds having the potential to flower are formed either terminally, laterally or adventitiously. The terminal buds may be formed on long or short growth, laterally on current or past season growth and adventitiously from any point on the trunk or root.

Classification of plants according to bearing habit

There are six main types of fruiting and nine distinct bearing habits. The classification being based upon the location of the fruit buds and the type of flower bearing structure to which they give rise.

Group I : Fruit buds borne terminally, containing flower parts only and giving rise to inflorescence with leaves *e.g.,* Mango, litchi, loquat.

Group II : Fruit buds borne terminally, unfolding to produce leafy shoots that terminate to flower clusters as in apple and pear. The fruit buds are mixed and invariably give rise to very short growth and a few short internodes, leaves of ordinary size and a lateral branch arising in the axil of one of the leaves. This branch may bear fruit in the following season *e.g.,* **citrus.**

Group III : Fruit buds borne terminally, unfolding to produce leafy shoots with flowers or flower clusters in the leaf axils.

This might be called as an incomplete 'terminal bearing habit' for the fruit bud itself is not borne terminally, but it is lateral to the growth upon which it appears. However, the flower buds are terminal. The terminal buds of the flowering shoots may differentiate flower parts for the following year's production or new buds may develop from lateral leaf buds. It is found in pomegrenate, guava etc.

Group IV : Fruit buds borne laterally, containing flower parts only and giving rise to inflorescences without leaves. If leaves are present, they are much reduced in size *e.g.,* **peach, plum, almond, citrus, datepalm.**

The sweet cherries and the domestica and institia groups of plum form their buds for the most part laterally on spurs. These come from lateral buds on the shoots of the preceding season, and their new shoots form both terminal and lateral buds on shoot or on older wood.

Group V : Fruit buds borne laterally, unfolding to produce leafy shoots that terminate in flower clusters *e.g.,* **blackberry, raspberry, grape.**

Group VI : Fruit buds adventitious since these are necessarily lateral, the plants included here might readily be classed with those of Group IV and V. However, this bearing habit is more or less distinct and these fruits may well be placed in a separate class *e.g.,* the Cacao bears in the same way. The flower buds appear first on the trunk as the trees grow and then on the branches.

Group VII : This is an another group of plants which have fruit buds in the axils of the leaves and in which these buds unfold and develop their flowers and fruits very soon after the flower parts are differentiated. However, it is not possible to draw clear line between their fruiting habit and that described for group IV *e.g.,* **in papaya.**

In the unopened flower bud of the grape, the inflorescence is terminal to a leafy shoot also within the bud. As the bud opens, however, the bud in the axil of the top most leaf of this developing shoot unfolds and continues the growth of the shoot. This results in pushing the flower cluster to one side so that inflorescence is lateral and opposite a leaf.

Group VIII : Fruit buds borne laterally (or pseudoterminally), unfold to produce leafy shoots with flower clusters in the leaf axils *e.g.,* **fig, mulberry, ber, avocado, persimmon.**

Group IX : Fruit buds borne both terminally and laterally, inflorescences generally terminal *e.g.,* Walnut, pecan etc. The terminal bud may give rise to a short leafy shoot ending in a female inflorescence. The male flower are borne on leafless inflorescence arising from lateral buds not far below the terminal.

Table 1. Main Types of Bearing Habit for Fruit Plants

	Terminal fruit plants	Lateral fruit buds
Fruit bud containing	1 Mango Loquat	4 Peach Plum (domestica) Almond Apricot Cherry, Detepalm Citrus, Walnut (Staminate catkins) Pecan (Staminate catkins)

Flower bud mixed Flowering shoot with terminal inflorescence	2 Apple (Principally) Pear (Principally) Walnut (Pistillate flowers) Pecan (Pistillate flowers)	5 Grape Cashewnut Raspberry Apple (Occasionally) Pear (Occasionally)
Flower bud mixed Flowering shoot with lateral inflorescence	3 Guava Pomegranate Olive (partly)	6 Fig. Mulberry Ber Avocado Persimmon

2. TYPES OF INFLORESCENCE

The knowledge of different types of inflorescence is very essential for successful orcharding. Flowers may occur singly or in closely associated clusters. The arrangement of flowers on stem or axil is known as inflorescence. Morphologically the inflorescence is a flower bearing shoot, either determinate or indeterminate in growth. The inflorescence may terminate in a shoot or it may be borne in the axil of the leaf. The branched inflorescence usually but not always bear bracts or modified leaves.

Kinds of Inflorescence

There are several kinds of inflorescence or arrangements of flowers in a cluster.

1. Solitary flower : A flower may be borne singly in the axil of a foliage at the terminus shoot or on a specialized stalk e.g., trifoliate orange, quince, guava, peach, **apricot, almond etc.**

2. The Racemose inflorescence : In this case, the penduncle continues to grow and new flower buds with their subtanding brackets continue to form near the growing points, thus, producing a succession of new flowers. The lowest flowers, being the oldest are first to open and blossoming proceeds upward. This indeterminate type of inflorescence is by far the most common. There are various types of inflorescence in this class.

(*a*) **Raceme :** Flowers are borne on the pedicels which are about equal in length. This type is found in the wild cherry, currents, gooseberry, blackberry, blueberry, Raspberry, etc.

(*b*) **Catkin :** A spike or raceme with a slender rachis, bearing many unisexual apepetalous flowers, which falls as a whole when the fruit is mature *e.g.,* **mulberry, chestnut, walnut, pecannut etc.**

(*c*) **Corymb :** The main axis is elongated and the pedicels are of unequal length in such a way that the lower ones are the longest and the upper ones or central ones are shortest resulting in flowers lying in a horizontal plane *e.g.,* Pear.

3. The cymose inflorescence : In this type at the growing point, a flower bud is produced so that the floral axis can not elongate further. The other flower buds are produced below this point on the axis towards the base. Thus this becomes determinate growth and the opening of the flower is basipetal or centrifugal. The solitary flower is in a sense, a cymose type *e.g.,* citrus, phalsa, sapota, strawberry, persimmon, etc. The cymose inflorescence is further of two types and these are :

(*a*) **Fasicle :** A cyme with flowers closely crowded on a very shorter penduncle and with pedicels of about equal length e.g., cherry (sweet and sour), plum, ber.

(*b*) **Panicles :** In this case main axis is indeterminate but the secondary and ultimate axis is a cymose *e.g.,* **grapes, mango, litchi, loquat, pistachio, etc.**

4. Anomalous types of inflorescence : Some types of inflorescence are also observed which do not fit into the conventional types *e.g.,* in apple. Terminal flowers open first which suggest a cyme but then the basal ones open next and then the anthesis of individual flowers proceed more or less upward to the apex which suggests a racemose type.

5. Special types of inflorescence

1. Spadix : It is a large, boat shape structure (spathe) enclosing an inflorescence *e.g.,* **datepalm, banana.**

2. Hypanthodium : It is the modification of capitulum in which the receptacle is hollowed into a flask. It opens to the outside by the apical pore which is borne on the innerside of the receptacle in which the male flowers lie towards the apical pore and female flowers towards the base *e.g.,* **Fig.**

3. BLOOMING PERIOD

The blooming period of different fruit plants varies due to prevailing agro-climatic conditions in different regions of India. Broadly, blooming time of various fruit plants grown in North and South India is divided into three periods.

(*a*) **February to May :** Apple, pear, peach, plum, apricot, almond, walnut, mango, citrus, grape, litchi pomegranate and datepalm flowers in North India.

Banana, papaya, pineapple, sapota and fig flowers during this period in South India.

(*b*) **June to September :** Guava, ber and papaya bloom during this time in North India. Pomegranate and citrus gives flower in South India at this time.

(*c*) **October-January :** Guava, sapota, ber and loquat flowers in North India. Sapota, guava, mango, ber flowers during this time in South India.

Flowering period in different fruits : The mango flowers late in January or in the beginning of February or even as late as March in many parts of North India. The flowering in citrus takes place mostly in spring. In lime and lemons, flowering takes place almost throughout the year. In kinnow, flowering takes place during end February to early March in North India. Flowers in grapes mostly develop in Spring. Guava tree normally produces as many as three crops in a year. In northern India, three distinct flowering seasons *i.e.,* summer, rainy and autumn have been observed. The flowering in litchi takes place in February. The flowering period in ber lasts for about two and a half months from September to November. The blooming period of loquat is very long, lasting from mid July to January or sometimes even up to May. The flowering in date palm takes place during end February to early March. In evergreen promegranate, the flower buds of the spring flush are borne on mature wood of one year old shoot, where as the flowers which appear during July-August are borne on current year's growth. In deciduous cultivars, the flowers are borne on current year's growth between July and August. The flowering in Jamun starts in the first week of March and continues upto middle of April. In phalsa, flowering starts from February-March and continues till May. The papaya is found to flower throughout the year.

Sapota flowers throughout the year with main two flowering seasons *i.e.,* July to November and again in February-March. Normally, there are three growth flushes in cashew and in South India, the flower bud emergence commences by the middle of September and continues till the end of February, the main season being October-November. The flowering period of custard apple is very long commencing from March-April, continues upto July-August. The peak flowering is observed in April and May. In the climate of Poona, the avocado produces flowers from November to January in three main flushes.

In apple, flowering takes place in April in Himachal Pradesh. The flowering in pear starts in last week of February and continues upto third week of March. In peach, flowering starts in the first week of February and continues till end of February. Flowering in Japanese plum starts in the second fortnight of February and last up to first week of March. Almond is one of the first tree to bloom in spring. Flowering takes place in very early season occuring between January to April. In Himachal Pradesh, the flowering in apricot cultivars mostly occurs in the month of March. The peak flowering period of walnut is mid-April which is prolonged till the first week of May in late blooming cultivars under Shimla conditions.

4. FORMS OF FLOWER

There are three sex types of flowers *i.e.,* hermaphrodite or perfect, staminate and pistillate flowers. Hermaphrodite flowers are called perfect or complete in which both the stamens and pistils are functional. Pistillate flowers are devoid of anthors. Staminate flowers are ones with non-functional pistils.

(*i*) **Perfect flower :** Apple, peach, plum, grape, mango, avocado, cashewnut, papaya, citrus, sapota, guava, etc.

(*ii*) **Staminate flowers :** Papaya, mango, litchi, grape, date, cashewnut, pomegranate, walnut, etc.

(*iii*) **Pistillate flowers :** Papaya, walnut, grape, pecan, etc.

(*iv*) **Teratological flowers :** Papaya, mango, grape, pomegranate, etc.

5. MODE OF POLLINATION

Pollination means the transference of the pollen from the anther to the receptive stigma whether of the same flower or of a different flower. As the pollen is not capable of locomotion, this act either involves some agent for this transference or the anther must be placed in the flower right above the stigma so that pollens may drop directly on the stigma by sheer gravity.

I. Autogamy or self pollination : If a stigma be pollinated by the pollen of the same flower.

(*i*) **Cleistogamy :** In these cases the flowers never open as opposed to most flowers which show chasmogamy (*i.e.,* flowers open normally during anthesis). In cleistogamous flowers the pollens are shed within the closed flowers so that self- pollination is obligatory *e.g.,* Grape, sapota and papaya.

(*ii*) **Homogamy :** The stamens and carpels of a flower mature at the same time. So, there is a greater chance of self- pollination although that is not obligatory. Some homogamous flowers, however, show special mechanism for self-pollination *e.g.,* **citrus, peach, apricot, etc.**

II. Allogamy or cross pollination : When the pollen of a flower pollinates the stigma of another flower located on a different plant, whether of the same kind or not, it is called allogamy. Special contrivances ensuring cross-pollination as noted below are very conspicuous.

(*i*) **Dicliny or unisexuality :** Cross pollination is the rule among diclinous plants *i.e.,* those bearing unisexual flowers.

(*a*) **Monoecious :** Occurrence of male and female flowers on different locations on a single tree e.g. walnut, pecan, chestnut.

(*b*) **Dioecious :** Male and female flowers borne on difficult plants of same species e.g. papaya, date palm, pistachio, fig, strawberry

(*ii*) **Self incompatibility :** This is the condition when a flower cannot be fertilized by the pollen of the same flower or sometimes, from any flower of the same strain of plants. Cross pollination is obligatory in such plants. *e.g.,* almond, apple, mango, pear, pineapple, cherry, apricot.

(*iii*) **Dichogamy :** When stamens and carpels of a bisexual flower mature at different times, pollination between them becomes ineffective. Sometimes, however, it is found that self- pollination may take place at a later stage if cross-pollination fails. Dichogamy may be of two types.

(*a*) **Protandry :** When the anthers ripen first. As a result when the anthers bursts, it pollinates stigma of other flowers but not its own stigma which is not yet ripe *e.g.*, walnut, coconut.

(*b*) **Protogyny :** The carpel matures first as in many members of Annonaceae. When the stigma is receptive, its own pollen is not ripe so that it has to depend on foreign pollens *e.g.*, fig, annona, banana, plum, pomegranate and avocado.

(*iv*) **Heterostyly :** In certain plants there are flowers of two (dimorphic) or three (trimorphic) different forms with anthers and stigmas at different levels. This dimorphism or trimorphism usually involves heterostyly (Styles of different lengths). In diamorphic heterostyly, the flowers have short styles and long filaments and other flowers on the same tree have long style and short filaments/stamens. In trimorphic heterostyly, stamens and styles are of three different length *e.g.* Pomegranate, litchi, sapota and almond.

(*a*) **Pin type :** Sapota, pomegranate

(*b*) **Thrum type :** Almond

6. AGENCIES OF POLLINATION

When the anthers are mature, the pollen grains are shed from the pollen sacs and are disseminated by various agencies like insects, wind, birds and human being. Some of the pollen grains may, by one agency or another finally reach the stigma of the flower. Depending upon the type of agency which is instrumental for the transference of the pollen from the anthers to the stigma, various terms are used to indicate the type of the pollination using a particular type of agency e.g.

(*i*) Pollination by wind or anemophily

(*ii*) Pollination by animals or zoophily :

The zoophily may include

(*a*) Pollination by insects or entomophily

(*b*) Pollination by birds or ornithophily

Given below is the information about different fruit plants pollinated through insect, wind and bird and human being.

(*a*) **Insect pollinated fruits :** Apple, pear, peach, plum, almond, walnut, mango, guava, ber, litchi, citrus and annona.

(*b*) **Wind pollinated fruits :** Papaya, datepalm, cashewnut, pomegranate and coconut.

(*c*) **Bird pollinated fruits :** Banana and pineapple

(*d*) **Human being pollinated fruits :** Data palm.

7. POLLEN VIABILITY

Initial fruit set depends upon pollination and fertilization of egg cell. For fertilization of egg cell, besides the compatibility factors, pollen should be viable and should have capacity to germinate on stigmatic surface so that pollen tube elongates sufficiently and fertilize the egg cell. Therefore, to obtain higher fruit yield, the knowledge of pollen viability and germinability is very important.

Pollen viability : Pollen viability is found out through acetocarmine test. In this test, pollen grains are taken on cavity slide and stained with 1-2 per cent acetocarmine. The pollen grains which get stained are considered viable whereas the unstained pollen grains are considered non-viable. The living protoplasm gets the stain. The percentage of viable pollen is calculated by counting viable and non-viable pollen under microscope.

Pollen germination : The germination of pollen grains is studied in cavity slides in different concentration of sugar solution viz. 15, 20 and 25 per cent. Other media like agar and Boron can also be used to enhance pollen germination. For this purpose, sugar solutions of different concentrations are prepared and pollen grains are incubated in sugar solution for varying times. Pollen grains can also be germinated in distilled water but to enhance the pollen tube growth sugar is added. The cavity slides are then seen under microscope repeatedly and number of germinated pollen grains is counted and calculation of percentage of germination is made. The size of pollen tube is also measured with micrometer.

Pollen viability and germinability of fruits : In ber, pollen grains are highly viable, the viability ranging between 87 to 91 per cent in different cultivars. The pollen grains in pomegranate that germinated was over 90 per cent. In sapota, the highest pollen viability of 95.8 to 97.6 per cent was noted in cultivar Kalipatti. The pollen germination was observed maximum *i.e.,* 45.4 -57.5 per cent in 15 per cent sucrose solution. Poor pollen grain germination has been reported in all the species of Annona. In Japanese plum, pollen viability and germinability ranged from 30 to 90 per cent and 30 to 70 per cent respectively. In aonla pollen viability and pollen grain germinability varies from 82-96 and 16.7 to 37 per cent, respectively.

B. TROPICAL FRUITS

7. Mango
8. Banana
9. Papaya
10. Pineapple
11. Guava
12. Sapota
13. Cashewnut
14. Custard apples

CHAPTER 7

Mango

The mango (***Mangifera indica*** L.) is considered to be the king of fruits. It is, undoubtedly, one of the choicest and most ancient fruits known to mankind. In India, it has always been a prized and favourite fruit throughout the recorded history of this country. The fruit not only finds a prominent mention in the old Sanskrit literature but almost all the foreigners, right from the Chinese pilgrims who travelled here in Seventh Century A.D. down to the modern writers, have spoken in glowing terms about this fruit. During the Mughal rule, mango was honoured with a real patronage. The well-known **Lakh Bagh**, known to be stocked with 1,00,000 mango trees, was planted near Darbhanga in Bihar state by Akbar. Some mango orchards planted during that period notably the Shalimar Garden of Lahore and Mughal Gardens at Pinjore near Chandigarh are still preserved and bear testimony to the high esteem this fruit enjoyed in the past. The mango occupies the same position in the tropical and sub-tropical regions, which is enjoyed by the Apple in temperate region.

ORIGIN, HISTORY AND DISTRIBUTION

Several authorities have testified to the origin of mango in the Indo Burma region, where it has been in cultivation for atleast 4000 years. This fruit has become deeply interwoven with religious rites and folklore of the inhabitants of this country due to its antiquity, popularity, and usefulness. It is a fruit par excellence for millions of people in the Orient, especially those in India. The mango which combine utility with beauty has the status of the national tree of India and is very rightly considered 'King' among fruits grown in the country.

The mango spread quite early in eastern part. Some Chinese travellers who came in India in seventh century, they described that mango is very sweet and delicious fruit. Even earlier than that in the Budhist and Hindu temples their is life like images of mango. Mango travelled to the west only after the sea-route was discovered. Alexander saw first mango tree in Indus Valley, which proves that it did not travel towards the Western countries before Alexander. Portuguese people took mango fruit to South Africa and Brazil in about 1700 A.D. Spanish people introduced in Philippines. Mango was introduced in Jamica around 1782. From Maxico, it was introduced in Florida during 1833. In 1869 grafted mango trees were taken to Florida from India. Mango was introduced in Israel in 1929 through seeds brought from Egypt. This fruit is grown on commercial scale in India and neighbouring countries.

AREA AND PRODUCTION

The leading mango producing countries are India, China, Thialand, Pakistan, Mexico, Indonesia, Brazil, Bangladesh, Philippines and Nigeria.

India is leading at the top with mango production of 16.2 million tonnes per year. In India, mango occupies 35.5 per cent of the total area under fruits comprising of 2.38 million hectares. The mango growing states in India are Uttar Pradesh, Andhra Pradesh, Karnataka, Bihar, Gujarat, Tamil Nadu, Odisha, West Bengal, Jharkhand, Maharashtra and Kerala. Uttar Pradesh is the leading mango producing state with a share of 23.71 per cent in production.

Of the various States Maharashtra and Andhra Pradesh has the largest area accounting for nearly 20.3 and 17.2 per cent, respectives of the total area in the country, followed by Uttar Pradesh (10.8%). In Punjab, the total area under mango is approximately 6664 hectares with the annual production of 105921 tonnes. The production is far too low, with the result that this State has to import a bulk of fruit particularly of grafted varieties, from other States every year.

The mango grows and prosperous in almost all parts of the Punjab, barring very hot and dried zones of the south-west Punjab, where it fails to thrive. However, the best zones for the commercial cultivation of mango in Punjab are the sub-montane tracts of Gurdaspur, Hoshiarpur, Ropar, SAS Nagar and Patiala districts. The sub-montane belt has numerous seedling mango trees, many of which are of enormous size and some of them over 100 years old.

Export potential : India is the largest mango producing country, accounting for 42 per cent of world production. There are bright prospects of building up a flourishing trade for the export of this fruit to other countries as well as of its products like 'Canned mango slices' and 'bottled mango juice'. Already mangoes are exported to nearly 20 countries, whereas its products are sent to over 40 countries. However, the present turn out of export of mango from India to different countries during the year 2012-13 is Rs. 264.76 crores. India is exporting mango to United Arab Emirates, Bangladesh, United Kingdom, Saudi Arabia, Nepal, Kuwait, Singapore, Qatar, Bahrain, USA etc. The commodity share of mango from India to UAE is to the tune of 67.8 percent of the total export. Mango can thus earn for India a handsome foreign exchange, through the export of fresh mangoes and mango products. There are vast stretches of areas where the cultivation of this choice fruit could be developed and expanded usefully and profitably.

IMPORTANCE AND USES

Mango possess unique nutritional and medicinal qualities apart from being a rich source of vitamins A (4000 IU) and C. Besides its attractive form and appearance, delicious taste and appetising flavour; the ripe mango fruit, according to nutritional experts, is also highly invigorating, fattening, laxative and diuretic.

Every part of mango, from root to top, is used in a variety of ways. The fruit itself, in the various stages of its development, is used in many ways. In its raw stage, the fruit is used for extraction of tannin and other astringent products as well as for the preparation of delightful chutneys, curries and pickles. Ripe fruits are a delicacy for the table, while the unmarketable and inferior ones can be converted into delicious squashes, juices, nectars, syrups, jams and jellies. Canned mango slices and pulp are indeed very popular. The stones, besides their use for propagation, can serve as a good stockfeed for cattle. The inside kernel of the stone, being rich in carbohydrates, calcium and fat, can be used as a source of food for certain industrial purposes. Thus the mango is a unique fruit, and possesses all the endearing qualities which justifiably lend to it a universal appeal.

BOTANY

Mango belongs to the family Anacardiaceae and genus **Mangifera.** The genus has 69 species, out of which only a few have edible fruits. In India only 3 species are found i.e.

Mangifera indica, Mangifera sylvatica and ***Mangifera coloneura***. The species ***Mangifera indica*** bears edible fruit.

Mangifera sylvatica is a wild species, grown in north east parts of India and fruit is not edible.

Mangifera indica : It is a cultivated species of India. The tree is a medium in size, ranging from 10-13 metres in height. The tree top is oval or dome shaped. The trunk of the tree is mostly straight, cylindrical, 75-100 cm in diameter. Mango is a evergreen tree bearing numerous branches. In the upper portion the branches ascend gradually but in the centre the branches are nearly erect type. The mango has simple, alternate, thick, leathery and short pointed leaves which may be either oblong, elliptical and lanceolate in shape. Leaves have short petiole, swollen at the base and irregularly placed around the twigs. The leaves are dark shinning, green from above and yellow green from below. Inflorescence of mango is large panicles which is known terminally. Sometimes inflorescence is axillary also. These panicles may be 6-40 cm long and 3-25 cm in diameter. Flowers are small in the inflorescence and both side of male and female flowers are borne in the same flower *i.e.* hermaphrodite. These flowers may be 6-8 mm in diameter. There are 4-5 stamens which are unequal in length. Only one or two are fertile ; the others are reduced to very minute purple or yellow white structure called staminodes which are infertile. The ovary is one celled structure, oblique and slightly compressed. Sometimes there may be a 3 carpels in a flower.

Mango fruit is drupe and mesocarp is the edible portion. Fruit size, shape, colour, flavour and taste vary according to variety. In many varieties beak is very prominent especially in Langra. Skin of the fruit has many glands with dots. The colour of skin varies from green yellow, red or any shade of the colour. Pulp also varies from green yellow to orange in colour.

The number of panicles in mango varies from 200-300 per tree. The panicles may have 300-1000 flowers in each panicles. Out of these flowers only few fruits are formed depends upon the season and variety. The panicles of male and hermaphrodite flowers varies 1:4, 1:1, 2:1. In Punjab, it was found that Dusehari and Langra varieties had on an average 77.9 and 66.8 per cent perfect flowers, respectively. This shows that the grafted plant has more hermaphrodite flowers than the seedling mango.

FLOWERING AND FRUITING

During the first year of planting, the young mango grafts may begin to flower. The first three years flowering should be removed as soon they appear. They seldom bear fruit and their presence would mean suppression of corresponding vegetative growth which is so essential in building up the young trees.

The grafted mango begins to bear fruit from the fourth or fifth year of planting. The time of flowering in different regions is greatly influenced by local weather conditions. In many parts of North India, the mango flowers late in January or in the beginning of February or even as late as March in some submontane districts. In Andhra Pradesh (Rayalasema area) flowing of mango takes place as early as in November-December. Flowering in mango continues in two or three distinct flushes for a period of 6 to 8 weeks on different branches of trees and it takes about 5 months for the fruit to mature and ripen after flowering.

Mango produces blossoms and bears fruit mostly from the terminal buds of its shoots and very rarely from the axillary buds. Dry weather stimulated flowering and cloudy weather or winter rains tend to retard it. Inspite of a favourable dry weather after the month of October, the tree may not flower and it may produce vegetative or leafy shoots only. The chief internal factor that governs and controls the entire phenomenon of flowering in mango is the maturity and age of its seasonal vegetative growth (leafy shoots) which are produced in distinct flushes at certain times of the year.

In Uttar Pradesh, the first flush is produced in March-April and the second in July-August. In Punjab, about five flushes are produced between April and August, but the April-May flushes are the heaviest. The flowers starts in February and continue well beyond the month of March.

In different flushes, the eight to ten month old mature shoots produce flowers. These shoots are produced in spring and early summer and cease growing at least four months prior to blossoming. Other shoots produced in subsequent flushes during late monsoon and after October rarely blossom towards the end of winter or in the beginning of spring which is the flowering time throughout in India. The internal nutritional conditions of the tree favour differentiation of flower buds, if vegetative shoots produced in the spring and summer cease to grow early and accumulate sufficient food reserves in their tissues before October. The spring and summer shoots get sufficient time to grow, rest and mature for the purpose but the later formed growths do not get time to do so.

FLOWER-BUD DIFFERENTIATION

The first indication of the initiation of the flower bud is in the internal structure of the bud. Before this initiation takes place the apical end of the vegetative shoots become dome shaped. As far as the differentiation start, the main axil of the panicles elongates slightly. The axil of the scale also elongate and slightly broaden at the base. The apex broaden slightly gets rounded off and becomes more regular and consists of meristematic cells. The scales grow longer. From the axil of the some of the scale, some conical growth arise which are sign of differentiation of fruit bud in mango.

The time of flower bud differentiation varies from place to place. In Punjab, fruit bud differentiation takes place in August and September. At Saharanpur, the fruit bud differentiation takes place in December. In mild tropical climate of Dharwad, the fruit bud differentiation in Alphonso initiated in early October and reached a peak by November. The application of nitrogen should be given before rainy season to the mango trees before the fruit bud differentiation, so that more flowering, more fruit set and more fruit is retained on the tree and thus increasing the yield of the fruit.

POLLINATION

Cross pollination is very important in mango and give good commercial crop. The cross pollination is done by insects. It has been seen that honey bee is not attracted by mango flowers. It is pollinated by mango fly, especially house fly. Even by cross pollination only 15 per cent or even less hermaphrodite flowers are pollinated, staminate flowers are not pollinated at all.

Monoembryony and Polyembryony : In mango monoembryonic and polyembronic are the two distinct races. When the mango seed contains only one embryo and give rise to only one plant is termed as monoembryonic mango. When the seed contains several embryos which give rise to several plants which can be separated from one another on germination and planted as independent plants is termed as polyemberyonic mango.

In monoembroyonic mango, the embryo is generally a hybrid, being the product of natural crossing of the flowers of two trees of different varieties growing under the same environment. Therefore, such seed gives rise to a plant which shows mixed characteristics of two different kinds and does not look like the parent tree from which the seed is obtained. This type of mango when grown from seed does not usually breed true-to-type.

In polyembryonic mango, out of several embryos in the seed only one embryo may be produced by the crossing of flowers of two different varieties. Even the one plant which is expected to be a product of sexual process is often suppressed and absent. As such, the seed of a polyembryonic mango gives rise to several plants which breed true to the parent.

Almost all the varieties of mango in India are monoembryonic and do not breed true to their parents when grown from seed. So, they have to be propagated by the asexual method. On the other hand, the polyembryonic types of mango are not to be found in any part of India, except in Malbar where few varieties of polyembroyonic nature are found. The famous mango of this type *i.e.* 'Olour grown in Malabar is propagated from seed. The polyembroyonic mangoes are found growing in the moist tropics of South East Asia, such as Malaysia, Philippines and Indonesia.

CLIMATE

Although known to be remarkably tolerant of a wide range of climatic conditions, the mango should always be grown within specific and well-defined ranges of temperature and rainfall for its more profitable cultivation. In general, it does best in comparatively dry regions which receive good rainfall in hot weather from June to September, followed by a more or less dry spell in the subsequent period. A rainfall of about 125 cms falling mostly during the monsoon, is considered very suitable, but much less of it will suffice if irrigation facilities are available. Actually the quantum of rainfall is not so important as its distribution. Rain during the flowering and fruit-setting season (February to April) is particularly harmful as it interferes with pollination which is done by flies, bees, etc. During this period, even thick fog or cloudy weather may ruin the prospects of a bumber crop. Dry and cloudless weather, before blossoming, has been found conductive to profuse flowering. Strong winds and cyclones during the fruiting season can incur immense damage by shedding the fruits.

Temperature is of a basic importance in determining success in mango-growing. Where the temperature ranges are not ideal, both the fruit and the fruit trees may be adversely affected. The favourable temperature for mango is 24–27°C during the growing season along with high humidity. Broadly speaking, temperature rising beyond 115°F and that falling below freezing point is not suitable for this fruit. In the regions where optimum temperature ranges do not prevail, cultivation of mango on a commercial scale is hazardous. Instances are not uncommon when young and even grown up trees were killed or damaged seriously due to abrupt fluctuations in temperature beyond the safe limits, especially due to the fall of temperature below the freezing point. Mango is found growing upto an elevation of 1200 MSL but for better growth and production its cultivation should be limited upto 600 MSL.

The frequency of winds, their intensity and speed has also to be taken into account while selecting sites for mango orchards. Besides causing shedding of flowers and fruits, strong winds also cause mechanical injuries to the trees. The localities reasonably free from the onslaughts of winds should, therefore, be preferred. The damage caused by the winds can, however, be minimised by planting windbreaks of tall and hardy trees around mango groves, especially around those of grafted.

SELECTION OF SITE AND SOILS

Site: Mango is a long-lived tree. If maintained and looked after properly, it continues to yield profitable crops for a longer number of years than many other fruit trees. Its planting, therefore, requires a great deal of pre-planning in the matters of selection of site, provision of suitable drainage, adequate preparatory tillage, systematic lay-out, proper selection of plant material and after care, to achieve good measure of success. The common belief held by growers that mango does not need any special care for its planting and subsequent after care during fruit bearing is highly erroneous and fallacious. The care bestowed on preliminary operations including selection of site may make all the difference between success or failure of a mango orchard.

The site for a commercial mango orchard should be selected as far as possible in a region or locality where this fruit has been growing successfully in the past. Such a selection would ensure the suitability of climate and soils and the adaptability to the agro-climatic complex.

Within the afore-mentioned regional concept, due consideration should also be given to factors like nearness to the market, road and railway station, availability of adequate irrigation facilities, topography of the soil and its physical and chemical composition. It may be borne in mind that while it is possible to improve, in some measure, the physical and chemical properties of the soil and its drainage, it is not possible to alter materially the advantages or disadvantages of its location. Hence one should be over cautious while selecting a site or locality.

Mango orchards should not be planted in the close vicinity of brick-kilns, as fumes emitted by the kilns result in the spoilage of fruit by causing blacktip disease. The safe distance of a brick-kiln from a mango plantation is about two kilometers. There should be no brick-kilns within this range, their chimneys should be raised to atleast 50 feet above ground and they should not be operated, if possible during the entire flowering and fruiting season of the mango.

Soils : Mango is not very fastidious for its soil requirements and can grow and crop well on a wide variety of soils. For its best performance, however, it requires deep and well-drained soils of loamy texture. Soils which lack proper drainage are not suitable for its successful cultivation. Likewise soils with a hard pan or a compact canker layer underneath or with a high water-lable or those liable to be flooded, are also unsuitable. On defective or unsuitable soils, the trees may just linger on with no prospects of profitable production.

Like most other fruit trees, it is not the upper eight to ten inches of soil which is important for mango but the sub-soil down below up to a deapth of six to eight feet matters the most. Before planting an orchard, both soil and sub-soil should be got examined thoroughly by the experts.

Most of the mango-growing soils in India have a low soluble salt content ranging 0.04 to 0.05 per cent and high fertility status. The pH of the most well known mango regions varies from 5.5 to 7.5. Soils with higher or lower values than the above optimum range should be avoided.

CHOICE OF VARIETIES

The pre-historic existence of mango in India, its widespread cultivation all over the country and, above all, its propagation for centuries from seed, has all contributed to the multiplicity of its varieties. The vegetative propagation of mango, which seems to have come into vogue only about four centuries back, has helped in the preservation of outstanding varieties, all of which have originated as chance seedlings. According to reliable estimates, there are, at present, over a thousand recognised varieties of mango grown in India alone. If the countless sucking varieties found growing in various parts of the country are also taken into account, the number of mango varieties would become colossal indeed.

In a commercial orchard, selection of varieties has to be restricted to only a few, which are highly productive, possess superior quality and are well adaptable to the agroclimatic conditions of the tract. Experience has shown that different mango varieties are suited for cultivation in different climatic zones. For example, the Alphanso, a prize mango of the coastal areas of western India, has failed to do well in the interior and north India. Similar is the case with some northern and central Indian varieties, when planted in south India. But this rule does not apply with equal force to all the varieties. There are many instances when certain varieties have done well under diverse climatic conditions. Therefore, it is only through local experimentation and trials that the relative success or failure of a particular variety for a tract can be properly assessed and ascertained.

Bombay Green (Malda) : This is an early variety and has fruit of medium size with lettuce-green colour. The pulp is deep- yellow, firm and fibreless. The taste and flavour are excellent. The **Sehroli** of Delhi is similar to this variety and is beleived to be a chance seedling selection of Bombay Green. Another popular selection from the same stock is Bombay Yellow. It starts ripening by the end of June.

Langra : This is another notable variety which is very popular in northern India. The tree is tall and spreading. The fruit ripens in mid-season (first fortnight of July) and has got a lettuce- green colour. The pulp is lemon-yellow, moderately firm, juicy, creamy and fibreless. It has a very sweet-taste with a fine blend and flavour. Stone is oblong and comparatively small in size. Except for its irregular bearing habit, this variety ranks as one of the best in north India.

Dusehari : This variety is very successful and is becoming increasingly popular with the growers of north India. The size of fruit is small to medium, with an elongated shape. The skin has got an primuline-yellow colour and is medium thick and tough. The pulp is very sweet, firm and fibreless. The fruit has got a good keeping quality and sells at a premium in the market. The tree, though medium in size, has a tendency towards biennial bearing. Besides its superb quality, the fruit is highly suitable for canning. It is a mid-season cultivar, ripens in July.

Samarbahisht Chausa : Out of the late varieties grown in the North India, this is most popular. The tree is very tall and spreading but bears rather erratically. The fruit has a medium to large size and is a good keeper. On ripening, its skin assumes uniform yellowish tinge. The pulp is soft, fibreless, and yellowish creamy in colour, has a sweet taste with delightful flavour. It starts ripening from the end of July.

Fajli : This is another late variety, ripening by the middle of August. The fruit is large in size which remains green from outside even on ripening. It keeps well but its quality is not so good. The variety is medium to heavy copper with biennial bearing habit.

Alphonso : This is one of the finest variety of mango. First medium in size, oval with prominent ventral shoulder. The fruit colour is greenish light yellow with light pinkish blush towards the proximal end. The skin is thin and smooth, flesh cadmium yellow and firm, fibreless, superb taste, captivating flavour and have abundant juice. TSS 17.5 %, acidity 0.35% and stone is small. The fruit maturity takes place in the first week of July. The tree yields 70 kg fruits.

Banganpalli : This is most widely cultivated variety of the south and its fruits are sent in Northern India towards the end of April. The fruits are large, flat and weighing 350 - 400 g. The colour is very attractive golden yellow, pulp is fibreless, firm with sweet taste. It is a fairly regular variety.

Totapuri Red Small : This variety is grown in South India. The beak at the end of the fruit resembles a parrot, hence its name is called Tota (parrot). Fruits are medium to large in size. Flesh is cadmium yelow, fiberless and hard. It is a bit crunchy and tangy. Fruit quality is medium. It has a typical flavour and flat taste. The variety is a regular and heavy bearing type.

Kesar : It is a popular export variety. The variety is grown commercially in Gujarat and Maharashtra. Fruits are medium in size and oblong in shape. Flesh is sweet and fiberless with excellent sugar-acid blend. At ripening, fruit attain attractive apricot yellow colour with red blush. It has good processing quality and being used for mango pulp. However, the variety is moderate in production but has tendency of bennial bearing.

Pairi : It is a prolific bearer variety of western and southern India. The fruits are medium sized, ovate, very attractive with crimson tinted shoulders on a yellowish green background. The ripening time is mid-May and June. It has tendency of biennial bearing.

Swaranrekha : This is an early ripening variety and become ready for harvesting by the end of April. The fruit size is medium, ovate-oblong in shape and have fruits of attractive pinkish red. The flesh is slightly fibrous, good in taste with an acidic blend. It is bienniel in bearing habit.

Amrapali : It is a cross between Dushehari X Neelum. It is very dwarf, regular, late and rich in vitamin A content. The fruits are medium sized, green, apricot yellow in colour. The flesh is fibreless and deep orange red, sweet in taste with high TSS (22–24%). It yields, on an average 16 tonnes/hectare and 1600 plants of this variety are reported to be planted in a hectare.

Mallika : It is a cross between Neelum × Dushehari varieties of mango. It is reported to be good quality variety with regular bearing habit. Fruit size is medium, shape oblong to elliptic and colour cadmium yellow. Fruit quality is good. Keeping quality is good. It is a midseason variety. It is, however, susceptible to bacterial canker in Northern India.

Sucking Mangoes : A good collection of seedling mangoes with good sucking qualities; thin skin, abundant juice of excellent taste and flavour, less fibre, small stones and red blush on cheeks has been established at the Fruit Research Station, Gangian, PAU. The plants of outstanding seven selections under the code names GN_1, GN_2, GN_3, GN_4, GN_5, GN_6, GN_7 and GN_{19} (Gangian Sandhuri) are being propagated for distribution to the growers.

Besides the above varieties, following mango hybrids have been developed in India.

Ratna (Neelum × Alphonso), Sindhu (Neelum × Alphonso), Arka Aruna (Banganpalli × Alphonso), Arka Puneet (Alphonso × Banganpalli), Arka Anmol (Alphonso × Janardan Pasand), Arka Neelkiran (Alphonso × Neelum), Neeleshan Gujarat (Neelum × Baneshan), Neeleshwari (Neelum × Dashehari), Sunder Langra (Sunder Pasand × Langra), Manjira (Rumani × Neelum), Jawahar (Gulabkhas × Mahmood Bahar) and Ruchi (Neelum × Alphonso). Pusa Pratiba and Pusa Shreshtha (Amrapali × Sensation), Pusa Peetamber (Amrapali × Lal Sundari), Pusa Lalima (Dushehari × Sensation).

PLANNING AND PLANTING

Before embarking upon a planting programme, all the preliminaries by way of levelling and demarcation of land, lay- out, digging of pits and their filling up, provision of irrigation channels and planting of windbreaks should be completed. It is also advisable to obtain the requisite number of plants and stock them in the nursery for some time for their proper acclimitization, before their planting to the actual sites. Such a measure has been found to increase success percentage considerably.

Time of planting : There are two planting seasons for mango *i.e.* spring (February - March) and Monsoon (August-September). The latter season gives better results, particularly in the dry and arid tracts where intense summer heat of May-June results in heavy mortalities among the spring plantings.

Lay-out : Proper lay-out not only improves beauty and systematic look to the orchard, but it is as necessary as a sound foundation for a strong building. Mango trees being long-lived, growers should be over-cautious to adopt a well-conceived plan of lay-out both in respect of immediate planting and future extensions. The area of immediate planting should be planned in such a way so as to take different blocks of early, mid-season and late varieties. It is a good idea to place late varieties in the centres and others outside. For mango planting, three systems of lay-out namely, square, hexagonal and quincunx are usually employed. Of these, the square system is most commonly followed in the mango growing regions of the world. This system is easy to execute and permits intercultural operations cross-wise.

Planting distance : The distance of planting in mango depends upon a number of factors, such as locality, varieties to be grown and soil fertility. Seedling mangoes which attain a much bigger size, need more spacing than the grafted trees. Within grafted varieties, certain varieties like Langra and Samarbahist Chausa, being more spreading, require greater space than varieties like Dushehari which has trees of rather small size. A distance of 10.5 metres for seedling mangoes and 9 metres for grafted mangoes is considered adequate.

Some growers have a tendency of giving less distance to their plants. Closely planted orchards become congested within a few years of their planting. Not only cultural operations in such plantations become difficult and costly, but the trees cannot get adequate amount of sunshine and air so vitally necessary for their proper growth and bearing. Given below, are the total numbers of plants that can be accommodated in and hectare with various systems :

Distance between plants (metres)	Number of plants/ha		
	Square System	Hexagonal System	Quincunx System
9	123	137	220
10.5	90	100	162

Planting of grafts : While planting, a hole slightly bigger than the earth ball of the plant, should be dug out in the filled up pit. The packing material around the ball of the graft should then be removed, care being taken that the ball is not injured in the process. Now the plant along with its ball is placed in the hole of the pit and with the help of the planting board, its position is set right. Moist surface soil removed from the hole earlier, should be used in refilling the vacant space and earth around the plant should be firmly pressed. As soon as planting is completed, the filed should be watered.

While planting and setting the plant, it is advisable to keep its collar slightly higher in the pit than it was originally in the nursery, thus keeping a safe margin for setting down of the soil. It is unwise to allow the plants to set either too deep or too high. The graft union should be approximately 23 cm above the level of earth in the pit.

Care of the Young Orchard

Young mango plants, in their early stages of orchard life, *i.e.,* upto first four to six years, need utmost care and attention for their proper irrigation, training, hoeing, weeding and keeping them free of diseases and pests. In regions, where strong winds are rampant, it would be necessary to provide the plants with wooden stakes immediately after planting. It will be advantageous to coat the lower portions of the stakes with coaltar, to save them from white-ants.

Protection against frost : Mango trees are highly susceptible to frost injury. It has been observed that during years of severe frost, young unprotected plants five to six years old or even of more age have been found to have been killed to ground or damaged seriously. In the north India frost usually occurs during the months of December to February. Sometimes late frost may be experienced even in March. Adequate timely measures and precautions against frost are, therefore, necessary. Young plants, especially in the localities which are subject to frost, should always be well-covered up with thatches or kullies of Sarkanda, rice, sugarcane or some other farmwaste straw, keeping the south east side open for aeration and sunshine. When a frost is threatened or imminent, watering the field has a healthy effect as it minimizes the chances of damage. Smudging, *i.e.,* burning heaps of dry matter at several places in the orchard also proves useful in warding off the ill-effects of frost. In short, the grower should keep himself fully equiped and ready to meet the menace of frost to save his valuable trees. Even a little slackness or negligence on this account, may prove disastrous for the young mango plants.

Protection against hot weather : In tracts, where the summer heat is intense and hot winds 'loo' blow, it is advisable to provide some sort of protection to the young mango trees against the vagaries of the hot weather. This can be accomplished by planting quick-growing plants like Jantar and Arhar around the basins or by constructing mud walls. The trunks of the young trees should be white-washed to afford them protection against sunburn injury. The practice of planting bananas around the newly-planted mango plants seems to be helpful in warding off intense heat by increasing humidity but care should be taken that the banana plants are kept reasonably away from the mango plants, because if the banana plants are put too closely, the practice may do more harm than good.

Windbreaks : Mango orchards should always be provided with effective windbreaks to afford protection against the onslaughts of windstorms chilly weather and other scourges. In fact, the planting of windbreak trees should proceed by 2-3 years the actual planting of mangoes so that by the time the plants grow up windbreak is there to provide proper protection. Orchards sheltered by windbreaks are less prone to damage from frost than those which are exposed, without windbreaks. Moreover, in such orchards there is less evaporation of soil moisture as well as less wastage of water through transpiration.

Under conditions obtaining in the North India, growing of tall and hardy trees, namely **Terminalia arjuna,** simbal, Euclyptus and **jaman** is advocated for the purpose of establishing windbreak. Shisham and seedling mangoes are also equally good for this purpose. To make the windbreak more effective it is advisable if tall trees are planted alternating with short statured trees of mulberry, karonda and ber. Usually a distance of 2.5 to 4.5 metres is kept in between the windbreak trees.

Removal of early blossom : Young mango plants often begin to flower in their tender age, which has a detrimental effect on their health and vigour, particularly, if such inflorescences are allowed to set fruit. Such fruiting is always at the expense of the growth of the tree which is so vitally necessary to build up a strong framework and proper size and shape of the tree. Such early inflorescences must always be nipped off immediately till the trees complete atleast four years of age and have attained sufficient size. With a large leaf canopy the tree becomes physiologically fit to bear a good fruit crop.

PROPAGATION AND ROOTSTOCKS

Propagation by seed in mango is the oldest, cheapest and easiest method, but it has several serious defects. Seedlings raised from stones having an influence of mixed parentage seldom come true- to-type. Moreover, they also entail considerably longer period to attain bearing age. This method, therefore, has no place for use in commercial mango-growing where the grower is interested in the perpetuation of the quality of the selected varieties so as to produce fruits of known and superior quality.

As propagation of mango from seed has been practised in different parts of the country from times immemorial, many groves and scattered plantations of mango still have a preponderance of seedlings. The mango industry in the past has suffered tremendously on account of this drawback as the seedlings in most cases yield crops of unsatisfactory and inferior quality. Due to the efforts made by the Agricultural Universities and State Department of Horticulture majority of the growers have now started going in for grafted varieties and new orchards are invariably stocked with grafted plants. This is a happy development and would go a long way to place our mango- growing industry on a sound footing.

Vegetatively, the mango is mostly propagated thorough graftage. Inarching, veneer grafting epicotyl grafting/stone grafting and side grafting are the common methods of propagation, however, side grafting is considered the best method of multiplication of mango plants. Other methods like propagation from cuttings, chip budding, forkert method of budding and air layering, etc. are also employed, though on a limited scale.

Raising of Rootstock

Rootstock used for grafting is grown from stones of seedling trees. For this, the fruits from vigour, disease free and high yielding trees of seedling mangoes are collected during July-August. The stones are sown soon after they are removed from the ripe fruit as they loose their viability very soon. Mango stones gives only 10-15 per cent germination if they are sown after two months of their extraction from the fruit. Before sowing, the stones should be immersed in water and only those stones are sown which sink in water as these are considered to be viable.

The stones are sown in the beds which are prepared throughly after mixing well rotten farmyard manure. In the beds, the seeds are sown in lines which are 45 cm apart and distance of 60 cm is left after every two rows to facilitate the cultural practices and grafting of seedlings. The stones are sown at 15-20 cm distance within the line at the depth of 5 cm. The stones are placed in the soil with the pulmule up as it avoids distortion of seedlings. The stones after sowing are covered with the mixture of sand and farmyard manure. Mulching the beds with sarkanda, rice straw etc. increases seed germination. The beds are irrigated immediately after sowing the stones and subsequent irrigations are given to keep the soil moist but not in too much wet conditions.

The germination of stones starts after about three weeks. The seedlings will be ready for grafting when they have attained the height of about 45 cm and thickness of 0.75 to 1.5 cm. Most of the seedlings become graftable in the next April.

Rootstocks : It has been reported that Muvandan and Bappakai are vigorous rootstocks while Vellaikulamban is a dwarfing rootstock for Alphonso variety of mango. Stones of mango seedling tree are commonly used as a rootstock.

Preparation of scion : Mother trees from where the scion is to be taken should be healthy, vigorous and have sufficient record of good bearing. Before the actual grafting is done, the scion should be prepared carefully. For this, the healthy shoots of the last mature flush having plump terminal buds are selected. These shoots are defoliated 7-10 days before they are detached from the mother tree for grafting. While defoliating the small petioles are left intact. The drop of these petioles and swelling of the terminal buds in week's period is good judgement of preparation of scion wood.

Inarching is done when the sap is flowing and plant is in active growth condition. During rains and dry periods, the process of inarching is avoided as this reduces the graft success. In North India last week of July or the first week of August is the best period for inarching.

Side grafting can be carried out successfully from March to October, but success during the May and October is rather low. The best time for propagation with side grafting in from July to September.

ORCHARD CULTURAL PRACTICES

Irrigation

Amount and frequency of irrigation to be given depends upon the type of soil, climatic condition especially rainfall and its distribution and age of trees. The irrigation requirements of young and non bearing trees are different from those of the bearing trees.

The young non-bearing trees need to be irrigated more frequently in order to grow vigorously and rapidly. The newly planted young mango plants, upto their first four to six months should receive irrigations twice a week in the hot weather. Therefore, the interval of irrigation as well as quantum of water per irrigation may be progressively increased. For the first four to five years, the irrigation must be frequent and regular though of light intensity. During rainy season interval may be adjusted keeping in view the intensity of rainfall and its distribution.

In bearing trees, during the period of two or three months preceding flowering season, profuse irrigation is inadvisable. For the rest of the year, a mango tree should receive irrigation according to its needs which in turn would depend upon several factors such as soil structure, climatic conditions, variety and rootstock and age of the trees. In lighter soils, more frequent irrigation would be necessary than in case of heavy soils. Similarly, irrigation needs during hot, dry and windy weather will be heavier than in rainy and cold weather. The bearing trees with well developed root system usually require irrigation during the fruit development period between April to June at an interval of 10–12 days depending upon the evapotranspiration. One irrigation should be given at the time of addition of fertilizers in the month of February. No irrigation should be given for a period of 2–3 months during October–December.

Generally intercrops are grown during the early years after plantation and hence method of application has to be adjusted accordingly. Upto 5 years after planting, it is better to make basins around the plants and connect them in series so that irrigation could be administered independent of the intercrop. For subsequent age, irrigation can be combined with that of intercrops. However, if intercrops are to be abandoned in fully- bearing orchards then basin system should be followed so as to economise on the water use. Then the basins may be connected in series or to a channel dug in between the rows.

Intercropping

During the first few years of their non-bearing life and until the trees have grown to a big size, the vacant land in between the mango trees can be profitably utilized for the cultivation of harmless types of intercrops like fodders, farm crops, vegetables and pulses preferably of leguminous type. Intercropping should always be judicious and needs of the trees should receive primary consideration, otherwise the practice may prove extremely harmful. Intercropping helps to keep the weeds under check, which otherwise would rob the orchard soil of plant nutrients and moisture. Vegetables like onion, tomato, radish, beans, cauliflower, cabbage, leafy vegetables and leguminous crops like moong, mash, gram and lentil can be grown in pre-bearing orchards. Crops like maize, sugarcane and bajra should not be grown in mango orchard.

While intercropping, the trees should be provided with suitably wide basins and an independent irrigation system. They should also be given regular hoeings and weedings. When the trees grow up to a big size, as it usually happens after their 10-12 years of life, then discontinue the intercropping as at that stage it would impair with their normal growth and fruiting. In order to replanish the organic matter content of the soil, green manuring with leguminous crops like guara, hemp and senji may be carried out, depending upon the need of the soil. Instead of intercropping, temporary quick growing fruit trees can be grown as fillers which are removed when the mango trees assume big size. Papaya, peach, plum, guava and phalsa are grown as fillers. Separate arrangements for manures, fertilizers, irrigation and interculture should be made for the interplants and intercrops.

Interculture

Interculture of the mango orchards is necessary not only to remove the weeds which compete for water and nutrients but also to ensure aeration which is so essential for the proper development of roots and shoots. Hoeing also serves the purpose of mulching and thereby reduces the frequency of irrigation. Interculture may help in reducing the insect-pest population by killing them physically. Frequency and the time of intercultural operations will vary with age of the orchard. If the intercrops are not being raised in the pre-bearing stage due to some reasons, then area in between the basin should also be ploughed atleast three times in a year *i.e.*, pre-monsoon, post- monsoon and in the last week of November.

For the bearing mango orchards, interculture is also equally important. First cultivation should be done before the onset of rains. This help in checking run off losses and facilitate maximum intake of water into the soil. Orchard may be ploughed again after the rainy season is over so as to supress the weed growth and also to break capillaries. Third cultivation may be done in the last week of November or first week of December in order to check the population of mango mealy bug.

Manuring and Fertilization

Although mango grows well even in poor soils because of its deep root system but keeping in view the vegetative growth it has to attain and removal of nutrients through the harvest, it needs some amount of fertilizers. Nutrition requirements may vary with the region depending upon the type of soil and age of the tree. The underfed and under-nourished trees fail to give satisfactory bearing of fruit.

The life cycle of the mango can be divided into five parts, viz. nursery stage, establishment in the field and non-bearing, bearing and a gain periods of trees. Generally, it falls under two main categories viz. non-bearing and bearing stages, while the chief requirements in pre-bearing age are a rapid growth and the development of a strong framework, during the bearing periods good cropping, regular bearing and high quality of fruit are the primary objectives. Nutritional requirements of the trees at different stages, therefore, vary a great deal and are discussed below separately.

Non-bearing Trees : This stage extends from the planting of a tree in the orchard until it begins to yield fruits. The manurial programme during this period has to be designed in such a manner so as to achieve speedy development of the tree together with formation of strong limbs and sound framework. The young trees in this stage need to be given liberal doses of nitrogen, calcium and phosphorus. Potassium would also be needed in reasonable amounts. In soils where calcium content is inherently high and which have a pH ranging from 7.0 to 8.0, the surface application of calcium may not be necessary but in soils where pH is low, ranging between 5.5 to 6.5, it may be necessary to add calcium through delomitic lime. The quantities required to be applied would depend on soil reaction and in certain cases may run as high as 2 quintals per acre.

During the non-bearing period, nitrogen is particularly needed in rather heavy quantities to support healthy and fast growth. It would be advantageous to apply substantial portion of N in the form of organic matter, so that texture of the soil, its moisture holding capacity and ultimately the development of roots therein may be improved. Phosphorus would be needed to cope with high respiration rates and for translocation of carbohydrates. Potash would also be required to meet the need of photosynthesis.

The above different needs can be met roughly if N, P and K applied at the rate of 50-100, 40-80 and 100-200 g of actual nitrogen, phosphorus and potash for each year age of the tree with 40 to 80 per cent derived from organic source.

Bearing Trees : During this stage the manurial programme should aim at two fold objectives, viz. (a) to maintain optimum vegetative growth from year to year, and (b) to ensure regular cropping with superior quality fruit.

In mango, which is a terminal bearer, the fruit-bud differentiation under most situations takes place about four to five months before flowering. There is an antagonism between growth and fruiting in the tree. In the year of heavy flowering and fruiting the vegetative growth remains suppressed which in turn affects adversely next year's crop. If the early flush of vegetative shoots does not come up due to heavy flowering and fruiting, very few mature shoots would be available at the time of fruit-bud differentiation or formation of floral buds and hence there would be little or no flowering next spring. Manuring of the mango is, therefore, quite complex problem and a grower has to keep in view all factors involved in order to get good results.

The following fertilizers schedule is recommended for mango trees :

Tree age (years)	Farm yard manure (kg)	Nutrient (g)		
		Nitrogen	Phosphorus	Potash
1–3	5–20	50–100	40–80	100–200
4–6	25–50	100–200	80–100	200–400
7–9	60–90	200–250	120–160	400–600
10 & above	100	250	160	600

The above doses are for the 'off' year of crop. During the 'on' year apply one additional kg of CAN or half kg urea in June. Apply the whole quantity of farmyard manure and phosphatic fertilizer in December. Apply all nitrogen and potash in February. During 'on' year, split the nitrogen dose into two parts, first part is given at the time of flowering and the remaining half in the month of June.

Ten tonnes of mango fruit produced in one hectare of land use 67 kg N, 16 kg P_2O_5 and 73 kg K_2O.

Doses of manure and fertilizers for bearing trees in different states

States	FYM (kg/tree)	N	P_2O_5	K_2O
			g/tree	
Uttar Pradesh	–	1000	500	1000
Maharashtra	–	1500	500	500
Madhya Pradesh	100	800	440	1440
Tamil Nadu	50	1000	1000	1000
Karnataka	25	730	180	680
Punjab	100	250	160	600

Deficiencies and importance of essential elements

Mineral nutrition of mango plants is an important soil-management practice in an orchard. The life of plant is markedly influenced without these elements. Symptoms of deficiency and excess of essential nutrients have been discussed below :

Nitrogen : The total nitrogen content in mango orchard soils (0- 15 cm depth) in different parts of the Punjab ranges between 0.018 to 0.045 per cent with a mean value of 0.032 per cent. The mango orchard soils around Malihabad (Lucknow) had total nitrogen content of 0.018 to 0.054 per cent.

The most striking symptom of nitrogen deficiency are the severe retardation of growth, yellow and under-sized leaves. Sand culture experiment of 'Langra' mango exhibits retardation of growth under all the degrees of deficiency of nitrogen. The fruit set is greatly reduced and leaves mature without attaining normal size. The leaf stalks form narrow angles with the stem. The mature leaves become yellow. The symptom first appear near the base of the current growth and progress toward the tip. Twigs become stiff and woody, limited in length and diameter. Under acute deficiency, the fruit size greatly reduced, tended to ripe and drop prematurely.

The incidence of physiological disease like softnose is increased with an increase in nitrogen fertilization. This can be reduced by maintaining leaf-calcium at 2.5 per cent either by supplying nitrogen as calcium or by adding limestone or gypsum.

Phosphorus : The deficiency of phosphorus causes stunting of growth in mango. As the deficiency persists, causes premature defoliation following dying back from the tips. The younger leaves become excessively green and slightly smaller than normal. The wood of the main trunk become thin and willowy and cause dying back in some branches.

While growing plants of 'Langra' mango in sand, it was observed that the phosphorus deficiency caused slow plant growth and delayed fruit maturity. An early symptom was the development of raddish purple colour on the underside of the leaf, first starting as spots, later spreading over the entire leaf with veins finally becoming reddish purple. The leaves were thick and stunted. The roots were also stunted. The plants were late in setting fruit.

The high level of phosphorus in shoots of Dusehari mango is found favourable for flower-bud formation. During August, there is not much difference in the level of different fractions of phosphorus in potential flowering and non-flowering shoots. As the time of flower-bud initiation approached nearer i.e. November-December, the level of phosphorus fractions except nucleic acid become quite high in the flowering stems. The leaves from the flowering shoots also has a high level of phosphorus but the differences are not so marked as in the case of stems.

Mango trees appear to be quite sensitive to heavy phosphorus fertilization accumulating as much as 0.84 per cent phosphorus in leaves on dry weight basis against 0.08 - 0.175 per cent in normal leaves. This excessive phosphorus resulted in a spotting of mature leaves in fall, first appearing on the lower surface, but later on also on the upper surface.

Necrotic areas also developed on the margins of some leaves. Leaves become chlorotic and sheds heavily. It also cause some drying of shoots.

Potassium : The mild potassium deficiency is confused with the symptoms of nitrogen deficiency. Pronounced symptoms of potassium deficiency appears as characteristic type of foliage necrosis. The leaves located near the middle or slightly below the middle of the current seasons's growth are the first to be affected. From this portion, the injury spreads towards the distal and basal part of the affected twig. The scorch usually located along the leaf margin and proceeded by dark purplish discolouration. The intensity of the scorch varies with severity of the potassium deficiency.

In Florida, the leaf potassium of 0.3 to 0.8 per cent is suggested as a desirable range for mango. In Philippines, foliar spray of potassium nitrate at 12.5 g per litre induced early, uniform and profuse flowering in 'Carabao' mango. The fruiting was heavy with potassium nitrate application leading to smaller fruits. Potassium nitrate spray has not produced such a response in mango under Indian conditions.

Calcium : The calcium deficiency do not cause any definite leaf patterns but the trees deprived of calcium remain small and slightly lighter green than normal. Increasing the calcium level in the tree with heavy application of limestone or gypsum reduce the incidence of soft-nose.

Magnesium : Magnesium deficiency in mango growing in sand cause stunting of plants which become pale, smaller in height and girth. In the developing leaves, yellowing white areas between the main veins on both sides of the mid-rib run parallel toward the margin. Prominent yellowish specks first visible on both sides of the mid-rib and follows chlorosis.

It was reported that adding more than 98.5 kg of magnesium per tree per year in 'Kent' mangoes is not useful.

Sulphur : The general behaviour of the minus-sulphur trees is somewhat similar to that of phosphorus-deficient trees. In sulphur deficient plant growth is gradually reduced and severe defoliation occurred. The leaves turns very dark green but upon reaching maturity, they develop necrotic areas along the margins and absciss soon-after. The location of the dead leaf areas is the chief distinction between these two deficiencies, being a tip scorch in the case of phosphorus and a side scorch with sulphur.

High concentration of sulphur-dioxide in the atmosphere near the brick-kilns and other industrial units burning coal have resulted in Black tip in mango.

Manganese : Manganese deficiency of mango plants in sand culture cause paling and dropping of plants. Lightening of green between the principal veins develops which gradually turn yellow with a band of green along the mid-rib and the lateral veins in the young leaves. As the deficiency progress characteristic mottling of the leaf appears. Later, prominent yellow colour develop with dark-brown pinhead like spots scattered all over the leaf. This is followed by leaf fall. The size and shape of the leaves is quite normal but the number of the leaves and the twigs are less than the normal.

In an experiment, 800 ppm manganese in the nutrient solution proved highly toxic to mango seedlings. There was marginal necrosis of leaves with deep brown colour between the veins gradually proceeding toward the mid-ribs. This was followed by curling and drying of leaves from the margins inward. Apical buds died, growth remained stunted, ultimately resulting in the death of plants.

Copper : No characteristic uniform symptoms of copper deficiency on plants in sand-culture has been observed. However, severe tip burn in old leaves with grey-brown patches is noticed. The plants are pale green in appearance. The minus copper plants turns slightly lighter green than normal and has S-shape limb growth.

Boron : The deficiency of boron on mango plants in sand culture cause stunted growth and short internodes in some plants. The new terminal leaves in the deficient plants are reduced in size, looking pale green, distorted and brittle. The older leaves are normal green but are smaller than those borne by the control plants. Some leaves curved on one side. The mid-rib turns brown from the ventral side.

Zinc : The zinc deficiency cause stunting of growth within the first six months in sand culture which become more prominent in the second year. The leaves turn pale yellow but less pale than those suffering from nitrogen deficiency, small, thin pointed, narrow and brittle with petioles making acute angle with the stem. Grey brown necrotic patches of irregular shape scattered all over the leaf surface. On some leaves, they spread across the whole leaf surface with distal portion dying. Necrotic areas finally fell off giving a shot-hole appearance. Root growth is also stunted.

Zinc deficiency first appears on terminal flushes with upper part of the tree. The symptoms consists of stunted growth of young leaves with interveinal chlorosis. The affected leaves curl backward giving a cup-shaped appearance. The tips and margins of the curled leaves become chlorotic. The leaves eventually broken down and detach from the lamina. It can be controlled by spraying 1 per cent zinc sulphate or 0.2 per cent zinc oxide, preferably at the beginning of the growing season, thoroughly wetting the foliage. At Ludhiana, a 0.2 per cent zinc sulphate spray gave complete recovery of zinc deficiency symptoms in mangoes growing under field conditions.

Iron : A pot-culture study on mango did not produce any symptoms of chemicals and environmental pollutants may have provided enough iron for normal growth of the plants in the minus-iron cultures. However, in Florida occasional chlorosis observed on young mango trees growing on lime stone area.

Chlorine : Chloride injury in mango manifests as a leaf scorch which starts from the leaf tip, generally 8-10 months after emergence. As the leaf gets older, the scorch becomes brick red and progresses along the leaf margins, slowly covering the major portion of the lamina. Nearly all the affected leaves which emerge in March start abscising in April of the next year. After a few years, the young twigs start drying, giving a sickly look to the tree. The chloride affected mango leaves had 0.02 to 0.09 per cent chlorine as compared with 0.01 per cent chloride in the healthy leaves on dry weight basis.

TRAINING AND PRUNING

The training of the mango plants in the initial stages is very essential to give them proper shape. Specially when the graft has branched too low, the process of training becomes very important. Atleast 75 cm of the main stem should be kept free from branching and the first leader of main branch should be allowed after that. The main branches should be spaced in such a way that they grow in different directions and are atleast 20-25 cm apart otherwise there are every chances of breakage due to smaller crotch angles and heavy top.

Normally mango trees require very less or no pruning. During its first four years of orchard life, the mango plants need not be given any pruning except the removal of dead or diseased branches, if any. The side branches emerging too near the ground may also be removed but it is not a sound practice to cut away the small drooping lateral branches emerging from the head. Such a practice has been found to dwarf the tree and delay its bearing.

A dome-shaped top, neither too near the ground nor too high, avoids exposure to the trunk from the sunburn injury, should be the aim of ideal training and pruning in young mango trees. After the trees are well grown up, the crossed or too close branches which crowd the centre of the trunk and weak branches underneath the main limbs which remain under perpetual shade, should be removed. Always restrict pruning to the barest minimum, as every healthy branch having foliage fully exposed to the sun, is an asset for its future fruiting and bearing. This rule of minimum pruning should apply to mango trees of all categories, young or old, grafted or seedling.

TOP-WORKING OF INFERIOR MANGO TREES

The old unproductive and inferior seedling trees which are found in large numbers everywhere, can be rejuvenated and improved by the process of top-working. Conversion of inferior trees into superior varieties of proven performance, not only improves orchard performance, but increase the income from mango trees in the shortest time.

The selected scaffold limbs of inferior or unproductive trees; desired to be topworked are headed back in February-March with a saw having 2-3 feet long stubs. The cut ends are applied with Bordeaux paint. Many shoots emerge within a short time below the stubs. Out of these, 2-3 vigorous shoots per branch or limb are selected and the remaining are removed. Since the new shoots are very weak at the points of emergence, they are suitably staked to make them grow straight. These shoots make fast growth and become suitable for grafting by August-September of the same year.

REJUVENATION OF OLD MANGO TREES

After a period of about 25 years, when the trees grows very tall should be rejuvenated. The old mango trees have a tendency to develop hollows in their trunks and in main branches starting from crotch or the point of bifurcation. Rain water is deposited here and this causes the bark and wood inside it to rot. This process continues year after year, thus large cavities are formed. Similarly, when a branch is broken by wind or mechanically, the untrimmed stub left behind usually rots and dies. Old trees in neglected condition with unhealthy branches full of diseases and insect-pests need be rejuvenated. The stem-borers should be removed and suitable measures should be taken to check the diseases. Add 100 kg of well-rotten farmyard manure to each plant. Top-working of old mango trees by cleft-grafting, budding or bark grafting is practised. Such trees in weak health can also be invigorated by infusing fresh sap of younger seedlings into them. Many stocks are planted near the old trees and when these have attained the height of one metre or more from ground level they are headed back and the cut ends are then shaped to wedge and inserted into barks of the old tree and tied up.

HARVESTING AND HANDLING OF FRUITS

Mango is highly perishable fruit. It should be harvested when they have attained full maturity but are not ripe. In successful orcharding, harvesting the fruit at its proper stage of maturity, its careful sorting, grading and marketing are the most vital processes. The factors like stage of fruit maturity at harvest, method of harvest, handling during transportation and temperature and method of ripening determine the development of typical aroma and taste. Marketing is dependent on quality of the fruit. Faulty methods of harvesting cause a lot of damage and bruising of the fruits which is the main cause of fruit spoliage. The fruit should be properly handled to fetch better price in the market and to enhance the shelf life.

Harvesting and yield : Harvesting of fruit at its proper stage of maturity is of fundamental importance. The characteristic colour and typical flavour of a variety develop at appropriate stage of maturity. The stage of maturity at harvest effects the fruit quality and its storage life. In Northern Indian conditions, fruit of early varieties become usually ready for harvest by the end of June and the ripening season in case of late varieties may extend upto the end of August. If the fruits are picked when these are not fully mature, they develop white patches and the normal TSS/acid ratio is also not obtained. On the other hand, if the fruits are picked when over-mature or fully ripe, more microbial and physiological spoilage occurs due to the increased susceptibility of the fruits, thus reduced the shelf life considerably. Therefore, the mango fruits should be harvested at the proper and correct stage of maturity. Premature picking should be discouraged because such degreened fruits cannot develop proper taste and flavour.

The fruits are usually harvested when green in colour, fully mature but unripe. Generally, when a few ripe fruits have fallen on their own accord (Tapka) from the tree, the rest of the fruits are considered sufficiently mature, but this criterion is not always reliable and dependable. This stage usually takes 15-16 weeks after fruit set. Development of characteristic colour of spots and appearance of bloom on the skin are also important criteria of fruit maturity. Specific gravity and starch content of the hard fruit have been observed to be associated with maturity. Direct measurement of the percentage of starch in the flesh is found to be a comparatively accurate method for determining the degree of maturity in hard green fruits. Picking fruits at specific gravity give satisfactory results in respect of uniform ripening and keeping quality. Pressure test is also employed to determine the fruit maturity. A practical method of standardization of the stage of maturity for picking would be a combination of various methods for individual varieties in a particular region. Generally, the TSS 12-15 per cent, a pressure 1.75-2 kg. per sq.cm and specific gravity (around 1) will generally give a fair index of maturity. For judging maturity, the physical development of the fruit such as rounding of ventral edge, development of beak, out-growing of shoulders, filling up of the hollow at the stem end and development of the characteristic colour should also be considered together.

The fruit injured or even slightly bruised during the picking operation losses its keeping quality and becomes unfit for despatch to distant markets. The usual practices of knocking down the fruits or shaking the trees violently to get the fruit down need to be discouraged. If the fruit is hanging high, it should be picked up with the help of a step ladder. In no case the picker should climb up the tree as this practice is harmful both for the tree and the picker. The fruits should always be gently cut with special type of clipper and placed in canvas bags or padded baskets and carried to the packing house. A device known as mango-picker, fixed with a long pole, can also be usefully employed for picking of fruits hanging high on the trees. A small fruit stalk (button) should be kept with the fruit which helps in keeping the fruit in better condition in transportation and storage.

The harvested fruits must be placed on a polynet upside down so that the milky ooz flow out and does not stick to the fruit. The fruit is then washed in warm water at 45 – 50°C and dried.

Grafted mango usually start bearing from the fourth to sixth year after their planting. Some trees of the varieties like Dusehari are precocious and start bearing even in the third or the fourth year. A grafted mango tree usually continue to bear till upto 50 years, but its most prolific years of bearing are generally from the tenth to the fourteenth years. During an 'on' years; a well looked after mango tree of 10 to 20 years bears a crop of about 500 to 1000 fruits. During 20 to 40 years its yield may will range between 1000-3000 fruits. Seedling trees usually take about eight years to come into bearing but their productive life is much longer. Many old trees of 100 years of age in mango growing regions are known to be still bearing heavy crops.

Mango orcharding is indeed very paying, especially in the tracts highly suitable for mango culture. It may well bring an income of Rs. one lakh to Rs two lakhs per hectare or even more depending upon the prevailing conditions.

Grading and packing : Sorting and grading are desirable pre- requisites for successful marketing. Through sorting, over-ripe, damaged dull or inferior fruits are removed. The fruits sent to the market after proper grading in different lot, can fetch better price. It is a fact that fruit graded according to size or its stage of maturity brings a higher price than the fruit which is sold without any grading. Some sieves having circular holes of 8.0, 7.5 and 7.0 cm diameter can be used to distinguish fruits. The fruits of mango can be graded according to their weight as follows :

Ist grade : Fruit weight 320 g or more
2nd grade : Fruit weight 270 - 320 g

3rd grade : Fruit weight 200 - 270 g

Grading and packing of Alphonso variety for export

Grade A : 200–350 *g* Grade B : 351–500 *g* Grade C : 551–800 *g*

The fruits should be waxed with paraffix emulsion staFresh and packed in 2.5 to 3.5 kg packing and sent to destination at storage temperature of 13°C.

The common practice is to pack the fruits in bamboo baskets which usually are not of any standard size. Now the wooden boxes are used for packing mangoes. The lining material may be used in the boxes. Individual fruits can be wrapped in tissue paper or ordinary paper which increases the eye appeal. The fruits intended to be shipped should be cleaned before their packing. Thereafter they should be packed in suitable containers in such a way that curing occurs in the pack itself either during transit or at the market site where those are intended to be sold. Such containers used for distant market should be strong and rigid. The fruits packed suitably in boxes or crates reaches its destination in a safe and sound condition and brings more profit in the long run.

Storage : To avoid the gluts in the market, the methods of proper storage of mangoes have proved useful to dispose of the fruit over extended periods. Storage at optimum low temperature has effective in increasing storage life. The treatment of fruits with wax-emulsion not only extends the storage life under cold storage and at room temperature but it also makes the fruits brighter, glossy and attractive. The fruits treated with 4 per cent wax emulsion can be kept at room temperature for 12 days and 35 days in cold storage (37°F ± 1 and 85-90 % relative humidity) after packing in perforated polythene bags. Fully matured but still hard fruits of Dusehari and Langra, mango can be successfully stored for 35 and 45 days respectively at 7°C to 9°C temperature and relative humidity of 85-90 per cent in 2–3 layers in the cardboard boxes of the size of 45 × 25 × 25 cm of five ply. Mangoes meant for cold storage, must always be carefully packed in wooden crates and each individual fruit should be wrapped in tissue paper and packed in sufficient packing material to keep the fruits in position in the crate.

Whereas cold storage of mango does not offer much scope commercially, quick freezing of mango slices in sugar syrup offers bright prospects for the trade. Mango slices thus preserved retain their characteristic fresh flavour for considerable time during frozen storage. Quick freezing of mango pulp and mango slices of green mangoes for preparing mango chutney or other important products can be employed profitably.

The fruits of Alphonso harvested in the last week of June or first week of July can be ripened after 4 days by dipping in 600 ppm ethephon solution for 4 minutes and packing in wooden boxes lined and covered with newspaper.

PLANT PROTECTION MEASURES

The mango is attacked at its various stages of development by a number of insects and diseases. If these are not properly checked or controlled, may occur heavy losses. Some of the most important insect pests and diseases and their control measure are described below :

A. Insect - pests

Most of the mango pests have a seasonal activity and usually make serious attacks during one season or the other. A brief description of biology and control of major insect-pests is given below:

Mango mealy bug (*Drosicha mangiferae*) :

This is a major pests of mango in India and does a lot of damage during the flowering and fruiting stage from January to April. During this time, large number of young nymphs crawl up the trees and congregate on the growing shoots and panicles. Soon after hatching, the nymphs emerge from the soil and crawl up the trees in large numbers from December to April. They suck plant juices thereby causing the tender shoot and panicles to dry up.

Nymphs should be prevented from crawling up the trunk by applying a slippery or sticky band 1 metre above the ground level by mid- December.

Slippery band : To the basal end of the stem, 15-20 cm wide sheet of alkathene is applied and its upper and lower edge is secured with 2-3 nails (2 cm). It is desirable to cover the lower end with compacted soil around the lower edge of the alkathene sheet so that nymphs are prevented from climbing up under the slippery band. In case of severe emergence, apply 50 g of methyl parathion dust (Follidol 2%) on the compacted soil to kill the nymphs.

Sticky band : A 5 cm wide band of Ostico or Esso fruit grease is applied on the trunk. As and when necessary, this can be repeated after scrapping off the crust. The nymphs congregating below the bands should be killed by spraying them with 200 ml of methyl parathion 50 EC in 100 litres of water. In case of the sticky band, a flame can also be used to destroy the mealy bug.

Mango hoppers (*Amritodus atkinsoni sp. and Idioscopus sp.*)

This is the most destructive insect of mango and is very active during February-March at the time of flowering. The nymphs and adults suck the sap from the tender leaves and panicles which become sticky and sooty. Young fruits and dried inflorescence fall to the ground as the summer winds blow.

The insect can be controlled by spraying the trees in the end of February and again in the end of March with either 1 kg Hexavin 50 WP (Carbaryl) or 800 ml of Malathion 50 EC in 500 litres of water.

Mango fruit fly (*Bactrocera dorsalis*)

Maggots of about half a dozen species of fruit-flies occur in various fruits like peach, plum, fig, guava and attacked fruits begin to rot and fall off. The females lay eggs just below the epidermis of fruit or some time little deeper in the pulp. After hatching the maggots starts feeding the pulp of fruit and cause brown rotten path on the fruit surface. On cutting, the wriggling maggots can be seen inside the fruits. The fruits fall and maggots come out of fruit to pupate in the soil. Its attack not only reduces yield but also affects the quality of the fruit adversely.

The maggots are found inside the fruits, the pupae in the soil and adults are active fliers, it is, thus, problematic to control this pest. However, the adults are attacked by a number of natural enemies like wasps and parasites. Affected fruits should be promptly collected and destroyed. Ploughing of the field in January-February to expose the pupae to natural enemies can reduce the population considerably.

Another method to control the incidence is to hang traps containing 100 ml emulsion of methyl eugenol 0.1% and 0.1% Malathion from April-June in the mango orchards. About 10 traps are sufficient for one hectare of orchard.

Spray 1.25 litres of malathion 50 EC + 12.5 kg gur or sugar in 1250 litres of water per ha and repeat sprays at 7–10 days interval if infestation continues.

Mango stem-borer (*Batocera rufomaculata*)

The mango stem borers are well-built large long horn beetles of a dull greyish-yellow colour. The grubs inflict damage by boring galleries in the main trunk and branches, ultimately killing the tree or the branch. Wooden frass come out of the surface holes.

To control this insect remove the frass and inject 4 ml of methyl parathion 50 EC dissolved in a litre of water into the hole and plug it with mud.

Barkeating caterpillar (*Indarbela quadrinotata*)

The larvae of this insect are principal feeders of the bark and spun a loose brownish web of silken strands in which excretal pellets and piece of bark are entrapped. It has single generation in a year. The moths are observed during April-May. Larvae develop from May-

September. Pupation occurs during February-March. The attack is more serious on old trees and neglected orchards.

For its control remove webbing and and inject kerosene oil or chlorpyriphos 20EC (50 : 50) into the holes during September-October and again in January- February.

Mango shoot borer (*Chlumetia transversa*)

Mango shoot borer is a serious pest of mango especially in nurseries. Adults emerge in last week of March. The eggs are laid singly on the upper side of the tender leaves. Larvae on their emergence bore into midrib or leaf stalk. Later on it enters the shoot which later on dries. Full fed larvae came out for pupation. As a result of its attack the fresh growth of the plant particularly in nursery is checked.

For its control remove and burn the dried shoots.

Red ants (*Oecophylla smaragdina*)

Red ants may infest some mango orchards. They are a nuisance and given protection to certain injurious coccids in their nests of leaves formed on the tree. To check this pest remove the nests and burn them.

Mango scale (*Aspidiotus destructor*)

The mango scale sometimes appears as a pest in certain localities. It inflects damage by sucking the sap from leaves. To control mango scale, spray the trees with 500 ml of methyl parathion 50 EC in 500 litres of water during March and September.

Bud-mite (*Eriophyes mangiferae*)

The pest sucks the sap from buds and cause necrosis of tender tissues. It is reported to be associated with mango malformation.

To control the pest, remove all malformed panicles and destroy. Spray Rogor @ 1 litre per litre of water during May-June.

B. Diseases

Mango is subject to a number of diseases at all stages of its development. Almost every part *i.e.,* trunk, branch, leaf, petiole, flower and fruit is attacked by fungi, bacterial and algae. These manifest diseases like rot, die-back, anthracnose, scab, necrosis, blotch, and spots. Some of these diseases have become a limiting factor in mango orcharding in some regions. Some major diseases and their control measures are discussed below :

Powdery mildew (*Microsphaera mangiferae*)

Powdery mildew is one of the worst diseases of mango affecting almost every variety. The disease appears mostly during February- March and sometimes earlier due to congenial temperature and humidity in North India. A whitish powdery growth appears on the inflorescence and the floral axis. The infected floral parts show necrotic streaks and eventually drop. Small fruits may also drop because of the mildew attack on the peduncle. The branchlets and branches of the floral axis show die-back symptoms and eventually drop, leaving the main axis naked. The disease can be kept under control by spraying 0.1 per cent Karathane (500 ml of Karathane in 500 litres of water) or 0.25 per cent wettable sulphur (1.25 kg in 500 litres of water) once before flowering, again during flowering and then after fruit-set. If need be arises one more spray should be given after 10-15 days. The timing of the first spray is very important which must be given as soon as the growers observe the very young inflorescence stalks emerging out from the flowering buds. Quantity of spray suspension will depend upon the age and size of the tree.

Anthracnose or dieback (*Colletotrichum gloeosporioides*)

The disease mostly affects the tender parts of the mango plant. Young shoots, leaves, panicles, flowers and fruits are liable to attack. On leaves dark-brown necrotic areas appear while on the twigs black necrotic patches are observed during the season. On the rachis of the panicle (both on main and secondary rachis) very small and dark spots appears. When young shoots are infected, the attacked parts show symptoms of die-back. Fruits bearing black spots rot during storage. The spread and dissemination of the fungal pathogen is favoured under conditions of high humidity and frequent rains, which also influence the intensity of attack by the pathogen.

The diseased twigs should be pruned and burnt alongwith fallen leaves for reducing the inoculum potential. Immediately after pruning in December or January, some disinfectant solution is applied on cut ends of main branches or twigs followed by the application of Bordeaux paste. To the large cut ends of limbs, Bordeaux paint is applied. Immediately thereafter spray all plants with Bordeaux mixture 2 : 2 : 250. During February, March and April and again during September-October, repeat spraying of all plants with Bordeaux mixture 2:2:250 at monthly intervals.

Leaf blight or twig die-back (*Macrophoma mangiferae*)

Leaf blight disease has become widespread disease. Minute light brown spots appear on large and green twigs. These spots enlarge and cover more than half of the leaf surface. The inner margin of the lesions is dark brown. The severaly affected twigs die-back. Dark brown lesions appear on young and ripening fruits followed by rotting. The measures to check the leaf blight are the same as in anthracnose except applying additional sprays of Bordeaux mixture 2:2:250.

Bacterial canker (*Xanthomonas campestris pv. mangiferae indicae*)

The bacterial blight diseases has become widespread on almost all varieties of mango. It assumes serious form only in humid areas or in seasons when temperature and humidity conditions become favourable for its spread from the leaves on to the fruits in early stage of development. Leaves as well as fruits both are damaged but fruits become severally attacked and disfigured. On leaves, panicles and fruits, tiny spots appear in the initial stages; these spots gradually enlarge in area and later form a raised spot on one side of the fruit. The onset of rain at this cycle of disease, increases widespread dissemination of bacteria which are able to cause severe secondary infection under the prevalent environmental conditions. The disease may assume an epidemic form. The tissue of the fruit which has been attacked begins to show deep cracks, exudating a gummy substance which is full of bacterial cells of the pathogen. The severely affected fruits drop down and become unfit for human consumption. The bacterial ooze is spread by wind splashed rain. A spray of 2 per cent Agromycin 100 (Streptomycin) provide the the best control of the disease.

Stem canker (*Schizophyllum commune*)

The disease causes discoloration and drying of foliage of one or more branches and exudation of gum from the affected bark. Branches may be killed in due course. Small shell-like dirty white fruiting bodies of the fungus, with gills in the lower side, appear in rows on the dead main branches.

The affected trees should be sprayed with Bordeaux mixture (2 : 2 : 250) or 1.5 kg copper oxychloride in 500 litres of water at fortnightly intervals..

DISORDERS IN MANGO

1. Alternate bearing

Alternate bearing is a very serious and an old problem in mango. It is the production of a heavy crop in one year and no crop or very little crop in the next year. Alternation between good and bad bearing year's is not always regular because after a good crop year, two or more poor crop years may follow and conversely after a bad year two or more good crop years may occur. Various causes like varietal differences, growth habit, crop load, cultural practices, sex-ratio, insects-pests and diseases, etc. have been attributed to the occurrence of biennial bearing in mango. Besides, there endogenous level of growth hormones, reserve metabolits and nutrient status had also been considered responsible for the bienniality in mango. Biennial bearing is a characteristic of a variety and some workers emphasised that this is due to the genomic constitution of the particular variety.

Most of the commercial varieties of North India e.g. Dusehari, Langra and Chausa are prone to biennial bearing but varieties of South India like Totapuri Red Small, Neelum and Banglora and regular bearers.

The horticulturists since decades have worked to control this malady but so far no concrete control measures have been put forward. However, application of deblossoming, pruning, better cultural practices and exogeneous plant regulator treatments have shown good results in recent years. Scientists are engaged in hybridising North Indian irregular bearing varieties with comparatively regular bearing varieties from South India. The experiments have started yielding encouraging results and as an outcome, a highly regular variety Amrapali has been evolved by crossing "Dusehari × Neelum" by the Scientists of Indian Agricultural Research Institute, New Delhi.

Recent work to control alternate bearing has shown possibility of using an ethylene releasing compound, ethephon in inducing flowers every year. The concentration of ethephon 200 ppm coupled with 0.1 per cent urea was found effective in inducing regular flowering over the year. Five sprays in all are recommended to be made beginning from middle of September at monthly interval.

Application of paclobutrazol @ 5 g per tree in the tree basin 3-4 months before actual flowering takes place can be helpful in checking alternate bearing.

2. Mango malformation

Malformation is a major malady of mango in India causing heavy losses to the orchardists. This disorder is caused perhaps due to environmental factor, mites, virus or fungus (***Fusarium moniliformae*** var. ***Subglutinans***). Mango malformation is widely distributed in India. Maximum incidence has been reported from Punjab, Haryana and Western Uttar Pradesh, where more than 50% of the plants are affected by malformation. The incidence of malformation is, however, less in Western and Southern India. Almost all the commercial varieties of mango of North India are highly susceptible to malformation.

On seedling over three month old, swelling appear in the axil of leaves. Small clustered leafy-shoots are produced at the apex on the main shoot or lateral. In the case of bering trees the panicles are affected. The peduncles become thickened and fleshy with profuse branching. The floral branches are crowded in the form of a cone. Fertile flowers are rare and fruits are seldom formed. The whole mass turns greyish-brown and then black. A profuse development of numerous small, leafy structures occurs in place of flowers, resulting in a witch's bloom appearance. Each group of the leafy structures represents a malformed floret. A few or all the inflorescence produced by a tree may be malformed. Off season panicles may also be affected.

Malformation has profound influence on the sex expression of mango because malformed panicles mostly produce male flowers and hence no fruit is produced on these panicles. The fungus (***Fusarium moniliformae*** var. ***Subglutinans***) have been isolated from malformed panicles. Recently, floral malformation like symptoms were also induced by a plant growth regulator known as morphactin.

Different methods of checking malformation like pruning of diseased portions; use of fungicides, plant growth regulators and deblossoming have been tried with some success. To control this malady, the affected shoots should be removed every month and destroyed. One spray of 200 ppm Naphthelene acetic acid (NAA) in October (Dissolve 100 g NAA in some alcohol and make volume upto 500 litres) is effective in reducing the incidence of malformation.

3. Fruit drop

Fruit drop is a serious problem in mango and cause great loss to the mango growers. A tree producing several thousand panicles, yields only a few hundred fruits. Most of the flowers falling down after full bloom or at later stage of development. Only 0.1 per cent flower or even less develop into mature fruit. Maximum fruit drop takes place in last week of April or first week of May depends upon favourable condition. The phenomenon of fruit drop in North India has been divided into three distinct phases e.g. pin head drop, post-setting drop and May drop.

The flower drop as well as the fruit-drop is primarily due to the formation of an abscission layer at the point of attachment of the fruit with the twig. Several factors have been considered responsible for the formation of abscission layer. It has been observed that Nitrogen retards and reduces abscission. Low carbohydrates have also been found to lead to leaf, flower, bud and fruit abscission. Fruit drop has been attributed to many other causes e.g. abortion of embryo, degeneration of ovules, poor soil, inadequate irrigation water, attack of insect-pest and diseases, depletion of nutrients, hormonal imbalance, etc.

Fruit drop may be controlled to some extent by the spray of 20 ppm of 2, 4-D (2g in 100 litres of water) in the last week of April or in the first week of May in Langra and Dusehari Cultivars. 2, 4-D should be dissolved in a small quantity of ethanol or methanol and then the required volume of water be added. Do not repeat the spray of 2, 4-D solution.

4. Black tip

The black tip disorder of mango fruits is a very serious problem in mango orchards located in the vicinity of brick kilns. Black tip is characterised by a depressed spot of yellowing tissues at the distal end of the fruit. This spot increases in size with time and also changes colour to brown and finally black. The black-tip affected fruits almost stop further growth and after premature ripening such fruits become soft, thus these fruits never reach maturity and drop down earlier. The fumes that come out of the brick kilns as a result of burning of coal contain sulphur dioxide, ethylene and carbon monoxide. All these gases are toxic to the young developing fruits of mango.

Control of this disorder consists in (*i*) shifting the site of brick kilns two km on east and west and one km on north and south of the orchard, (*ii*) the operation of the existing brick-kilns should be avoided from February to the fourth week of May ; (*iii*) telescopic chimneys, should be 40-50 feet high, if at all, the operations of brick-kiln is necessary during the prohibitive period, and (*iv*) finally the appearance of the disorder can be checked by either (*a*) spraying 0.6 per cent Borax, three times, *i.e.,* before flowering, during flowering and after fruit setting alongwith Bordeaux mixture 2 : 2 : 250 or 1.5 kg of copper oxychloride per 500 litres of water.

5. Spongy tissue

This disorder is commonly found in the ripe fruits of Alphonso variety. The disorder is manifested as a non-edible, sour, yellowish and sponge like patch with or without air pocket develops in the fruit during ripening. The affected fruits have a bad odour and become inferior in quaiity. It is reported that solar radiation which keep soil much heated and that heat emitted by soil by convective flux cause spongy tissue in the mesocarp. Mulching with paddy straw or dry grasses on the soil surface during hot months and early harvesting of fruits reduce the extent of problem. This disorder has adversely affected the export potential of Alphonso. Mango hybrids Ratna and Arka Puneet are free from spongy tissue.

CHAPTER

8

Banana

Banana (***Musa species***) is an important fruit of tropics. This is the only tropical fruit which is exported in large quantities.

ORIGIN AND HISTORY

The edible banana is believed to have originated in the hot, tropical regions of South-East Asia (Assam, Burma-Indo China region). The primary centre of origin of table banana (***M. acuminata***) is the Malaysia region whereas the cooking banana (***M. balbisiana***) originated in southern India. Its cultivation is distributed throughout the warmer countries and is confined to regions between 30°N and 30°S of the equator. Banana is one of the oldest fruits known to mankind. Its antiquity can be traced back to the Garden of Paradise where Eve was said to have used its leaves to cover her modesty. It may be one of the reasons why the banana is called 'Apple of Paradise' and botanically named ***Musa paradisiaca***. Frequent mention is made of the banana in the great Indian epics, Ramayana and Mahabharata.

Introduction of banana to Africa and the West is comparatively recent. It was introduced to East Africa before the time of Christ and spread thence to the West Coast of Africa across the tropical centre of the continent. They reached the mediterranean about 650. A.D. and was taken to the pecific by Polynesian travellers about 1000 A.D. It is believed that the banana has been taken by Arabs from India to Palestinean Egypt. The first introduction to the New World was in 1516 A.D. from the Canary Islands by the Portuguese. The Central American Islands subsequently developed the greatest banana trade in the middle of the 19th Century.

Banana is widely grown in many countries under tropical and sub-tropical conditions like India, Mexico, Philippines, Uganda, Tanzania Thailand, Zaire, Ivory Coast, Kenya, Burundi, Colombia, Brazil, China Venezuela, Ecuador, Egypt, Ghana, Israel, Congo, South Africa, Bangladesh, Fiji, Hawaii, Indonesia, Taiwan, Queensland, SriLanka, Cuba, Panama, Jamaica, Indonesia, Costerica, Malayasia, Guatemala, West Indies and Australia.

AREA AND PRODUCTION

Major banana producing countries in the world are India, Uganda, China, Philippines, Ecuador, Brazil, Indonesia, Cameroon, Tanzania, Guatemala, Mexico and Colombia. The production of banana in the world is 145 million tonnes. India has first position in the world in banana production having 20 per cent share. China, Philippines, Ecuador, Brazil and Indonesia are other leading banana producing countries sharing 7.36, 6.3, 5.5, 5.0 and 4.2 per cent in total production. Banana rank second in area under fruits in India.

Total area under Banana in India is 7.97 lakh hectares and production is 284.6 lakh tonnes. Banana is the largest fruit accounting for 37.2 per cent of the total fruit production from 11.9 per cent of the area. Tamil Nadu leades other states in area under banana cultivation occupying 23.7 per cent of the total area under this crop. The highest productivity of banana is recorded 62.3 mt/ha in Gujarat as compared to average productivity of 35.7 mt/ha in India.Tamil Nadu, Maharasthra, Gujarat, Andhra Pradesh, Karnataka, Bihar, Madhya Pradesh, Uttar Pradesh, West Bengal and Assam are the major banana growing states. There is a regional preference for the cultivar and production system depending upon agro climatic conditions. In the Southern states, banana is also grown exclusively for the leaves used as dining plate or wrapper for edibles. By and large, Dwarf Cavendish is the major cultivar of commercial banana.

Export potential : India is exporting banana to United Arab Emirates, Saudi Arabia. Iran, Kuwait, Bahrain, Nepal, Qatar, Oman, Maldives and Korea Republic. Export of banana from India to different countries during 2011-12 is Rs. 91.54 crores. The export of banana to UAE is 41.4 per cent of the total export from India.

IMPORTANCE AND USES

Banana is a good source of vitamin A and a fair source of vitamin C, and B_2 (Riboflavin). Banana fruits are rich source of minerals like magnesium, sodium, potassium and phosphorus and fair source of calcium and iron. Banana contains water 70%, carbohydrates 27%, crude fiber 0.5%, fat 0.3%, protein 1.2%, potassium 460 mg, magnesium 36 mg, phosphorus 27 mg, calcium 7 mg and ascorbic acid 10 mg/100 *g* of fruit and energy 104 calories per 100 g fruit.

Ripe fruits are delicious and are used for table purpose. In South India, both the plants and the fruits are used extensively in weddings, festivals and for worship. The immature fruits are used for vegetable. The fruits of some cultivars are used as breakfast food after steaming. The end of the inflorescence, technically known as pendant is cooked as a vegetable in Bengal. Many products are made from banana such as banana chips, fig, soft drink, flour and jam. Fruits of cv. Poovan are believed to be good even for diabetics and the dried fruit as an antiscorbutic.

Banana ash is rich in alkaline salts and therefore, can check acidity in stomach, heart burn and colic. Ripe fruits taken with tamarind and salt are said to control dysentery. In Uganada, banana is steamed, roasted or baked and fried. Beer is made out of banana in Africa. Banana flour is prepared from unripe fruits and banana powder from ripe fruits. Starch is manufactured from the Pseudostem. The Pseudostems of banana of all types have been used for manufacturing paper boards. In south India, the leaf of banana is used as a plate for serving meals. The sheathes and leaves are used for making crude ropes. Banana yields a good fibre. The species **Musa textiles** is well known for their strong fibre qualities.

BOTANY

The banana belongs to the family Musaceae in the order scitamineae. There are only two genera types viz. **Ensete** and **Musa** with about 50 species in the family. **Ensete** is an old declining genus which probably originated in Asia and spread to Africa, it has about 6-7 species. In India ***Ensete superba*** is grown extensively in hill ranges of Tamil Nadu and Kerala. ***Ensete ventricosa*** is reported to be grown in Ethiopia as a food crop. Puseglove described genus **Musa** as follow :

Musa (X = 10, 11 : rarely 7 or 9). About 40 species of perennial, stooling or rhizomatous herbs are found in South Eastern Asia and the Pacific. They probably originated in Assam-Burma-Thailand area and are mainly plants of the low land tropics, requiring high temperature, high humidity and high light intensity. Pseudostems composed of tightly clasping leaf sheaths, slightly swollen at base; suckers freely produced ; bracts and flowers inserted independently on peduncle, commonly deciduous by abscission except for functionally female ovaries in basal hands; basal flowers generally female only; male flowers on distal hands ; bracts usually reddish, purple or violet due to anthocyanins; pollen grains with finely granular surface. Seeds 7 mm or less in diameter.

The genus is divided into 5 sections as follows :

(*i*) **Eumusa** (X = 11 ; 2n = 22 in wild sp; 22, 33, 44 in cultivars). The edible cultivated parthenocarpic bananas, except for the Fe' i bananas belong to this section which are derived from ***Musa acuminata*** and interspecific crosses with this species and ***Musa balbisiana***. ***Musa basjoo*** in Japan yields fibre.

(*ii*) **Rhodochlamys** (X = 11 ; 2n = 22) 5-7 species from India to Indonesia. In this parthenocarpy is absent. ***Musa ornata*** and ***Musa velutina*** are sometimes grown as ornamental plants.

(*iii*) **Callimusa** (X = 10 ; 2n = 20) 5-6 species in Indochina, Malaya and Borneo. Plants are small stature and parthenocarpy is absent. **Musa coccinea** is grown as an ornamental plant.

(*iv*) **Australimusa** (X = 10 ; 2n = 20) 5-7 species from Queensland to the Philippines. The Australimusa section is represented by ***Musa textilis*** which yields the Manila hemp or Abaca fibre. It also contains a group of edible bananas.

(*v*) **Incertae sedis** : There are a few species of doubtful affinity. ***Musa ingens*** (X = 7 ; 2n = 14) was discovered in New Guinea whereas ***Musa beccarii*** (X = 9; 2 n = 18) from North Borneo.

CLASSIFICATION

There are several hundreds of cultivars of banana spread throughout the world. In India, the number is estimated to be over 300. According to the recent system of classification recognised the world over, edible bananas or those that originated in the section **Eumusa** have as their progenitors two wild species viz. ***Musa acuminata and Musa balbisiana***. Simmonds and Shepherd have used a scoring technique to indicate the relative contribution of the two wild species to the constitution of any given cultivar. They identified 15 diagnostic characters to distinguish between ***M. acuminata* and *M.balbisiana***. For each character in which the variety agreed with wild ***M.acuminata***, the score of one was given and for each character in which a variety agreed with wild ***balbisiana*** the score 5 was given and intermediate expressions of the characters were assigned scores of 2,3 or 4 according to their intensity. According to the scoring technique, the scores range from 15 (15 × 1) for ***M.acuminata*** to 75 (15 × 5) for ***M. balbisiana.*** A cultivar would have a larger score if it were derived from ***M.balbisiana*** and similar if it were derived from ***M. acuminata.*** An analysis showed that cultivars belonged to six groups of which two were diploid, three triploid and one tetraploid. Given below is genomic classification and nomenclature of Banana.

Ploidy	Score	Constitution	Nomenclature (examples)
2 X	16-23	AA	**Musa** (AA Group) Matti
3 X	15-21	AAA	**Musa** (AAA Group) Gros Michel
			Musa (AAA Group Cavendish sub-group) Robusta
4 X	15-20	AAAA*	**Musa** (AAAA Group) Bodles Altafort
2 X	46-49	AB	**Musa** (AB Group) Ney Poovan
3 X	26-46	AAB	**Musa** (AAB Group) Champa
	59-63	ABB	**Musa** (ABB Group) Kancha Kela
4 X	63-69	ABBB	**Musa** (ABBB Group) Klue Tiparot
2X/3X	70-75	BB/BBB	Musa (BB/BBB Group) Saba

* Not encountered in nature. Bodles Altafort is a synthetic hybrid evolved in the West Indies.

The best known bananas of commerce all over the world belong to the pure **acuminata** AAA Group, but the **balbisiana** genome is associated with greater drought hardiness and resistance to disease. It is not surprising, therefore, that hybrids of AB, AAB and ABB constitution are better adapted to monsoon areas with marked dry seasons, these banana show wide variability and are grown chiefly for local consumption in India and Uganda. The AA and AAA bananas are cultivated mainly in areas where rainfall is equally distributed throughout the year or where water for irrigation is readily available. The greater uniformity of the AAA types makes them particularly suitable for large-scale production for export as in Central America, the Caribbean Islands and northern South America.

The basic chromosome number of **Eumusa** section is 11. Edible bananas belonging to this genus have 22, 33 or 44 chromosomes as they are diploid, triploid or tetraploid respectively. Most of the cultivated types are triploids. Diploids are less and tetraploids are rare. Diploids in general have somewhat stiffer leaves and petioles than triploids and triploids are stiffer than tetraploids. Triploids and tetraploids are bigger and more robust than diploids. Leaf thickness and cell size both increase with increasing ploidy. Most of the triploid clones have steriles pollen whereas diploid pollen varies from sterile to highly fertile.

Several Latin names have been used till recently in the botanical nomenclature of the banana. Three of the earliest employed were ***Musa paradisiaca, Musa cavendishii*** and ***Musa sapientum***. These have been superseded by a genome nomencalture for cultivars in recognition of their derivation from two wild species ***Musa acuminata*** and ***Musa balbisiana***. The cultivated banana is botanically ***Musa paradisiaca***.

BANANA AND PLANTAIN

The word banana is now applied to all table varieties. Formely the word banana was applied to 'Nendran' banana of Kerala which was however called 'Plantain' by Westerners. The English used the word 'Plantain' to represent cooking banana while in parts of South India, even sweet fruited clones were called 'Plantains'. The varient with presistent bracts and male flowers with large fruits held in lax manner and eaten after cooking were grouped under plantains. All other types which had small fruits, held compact in a bunch with softening of the pulp when ripe, dropping of withered bracts and staminate flowers as the banana. Hence, call all the edible varieties as banana.

In other words plantain are starchy, not sweet and cooked as vegetable. They usually resembles green bananas, longer and have thick skin. Bananas are sweet, shorter and have thinner skin. They are eaten as a fruit and have yellow colour when ripe.

CLIMATE

Banana is a tropical plant requiring a warm humid climate. It grows well in regions with a temperature range of 10°C to 40°C and an average of 23°C. In warm dry weather, the fruit stops growth and in the cold weather, it is damaged by frost. In cooler climate, the duration is extended, sucker production is affected and bunches are smaller. Low temperature *i.e.* less than 10°C are unsuitable since they lead to a condition called choke or impeded inflorescence and bunch development. Banana comes up well up to an altitude of 1500 M above sea level in the tropics. The hill bananas of Tamil Nadu are raised between elevation of 500-1500 metres mostly under rainfed conditions.

Banana grows well under high rainfall areas. On an average 100 mm rainfall per month appears to be satisfactory for growth of banana. Hot winds blowing in high speed during the summer months shred and desiccate the leaves. Stagnation of water is injurious and may cause diseases like Panama wilt. Tall varieties are more tolerant to cold temperature above freezing point. The variety 'Monthan' or 'Khasadia' can tolerate low temperature better than any other variety.

Banana cultivation can be made successful under subtropics if planting is so regulated that bunches emerge before winter so that there is minimum frost damage and *choke* condition is avoided. This can be made possible by planting tissue culture raised plants at proper time and of specific size. In Punjab, it is suitable for growing in bet area, river banks and central zone comprising Moga, Ludhiana, Fatehgarh Sahib, SAS Nagar, Sangrur and Barnala districts.

SOIL

Banana are grown in a variety of soils provided soil moisture is available. Deep, well drained, friable loamy soil with adequate organic matter is ideal for its cultivation. The pH range of the soil should be 6.5 – 7.5 but can be grown upto pH 8.7. In coastal areas of Maharashtra soils are sandy. In the plains, banana is grown in well-drained black cotton soils. The medium black and lighter soils of East Khandesh are also suitable. In Tamil Nadu and Andhra Pradesh soils vary from well drained alluvial to the slightly open loamy type of the hill slopes.

Banana is one of the few fruits which has a restricted root zone. Therefore, two soil factors are important for bananas namely depth and drainage. The minimum depth necessary is about a metre.

Saline soils with slinity percentage exceeding 0.05 are unsuitable. Banana can grow well even under slightly alkaline soils. Such soils are found preferable for avoiding the wilt disease which is known to be severe in acid soils. Clones resistant to wilt such as 'Cavendish' group and 'Poovan' can be grown within a reasonable range of pH.

CHOICE OF VARIETIES

The important cultivars of banana are described below :

Poovan: Musa (AAB) Group : Syn. Poovan (Tamil Nadu), Champa (West Bengal), Lal Velchi (Maharashtra), Karpura Chakrakeli (Andhra Pradesh), Palayangodan (Kerala), Kadali (Tamil Nadu), Dora Vazhai (Nilgiris).

It is commercially grown in West Bengal, Andhra Pradesh, Tamil Nadu and Kerala. The plant is tall, hardy and grows vigorously under the ratooning system of cultivation. The fruit is small. Skin is yellow and thin, flesh firm, sweet with a pleasant sourish taste. There is rose pink colouration of the other side of the midrib when leaves are young. It has a good keeping quality. It is resistant to Panama wilt and fairly resistant to bunchy top disease. The average bunch weight is about 15 kg and has 200-225 fruits.

Dwarf Cavendish. Musa (AAA) Group. Syn. Basrai, Loton (Maharashtra), Kabuli (West Bengal), Vaman Keli, Bhusaval (Andhra Pradesh), Pacha Vazhai, Mauritius, Kuzhi Vazhai (Tamil Nadu), Basrai Dwarf (Gujarat).

This variety is grown commercially in Maharashtra, Gujarat, Bihar and West Bengal. The plant of this variety is dwarf with only 1.5 - 2.0 m in height. The fruits are large and curved. The skin is thick and greenish. The flesh is soft and sweet. The variety is susceptible to cold. Fruits ripened at a high temperature often develops black spots on it, hence name Chittidar. It is a high yielding variety but keeping quality is poor. A bunch on an average weighs about 20 kg. The fruits tends to drop off from the bunch when ripe. It does not bear fertile male flowers. The variety is susceptible to bunchy top and leaf spot but resistant to Panama wilt.

Harichhal. Musa (AAA) Group. Syn. Bombay Green (Maharashtra), Peddapachaarti (Andhra Pradesh), Robusta (Tamil Nadu).

It is an important variety commercially grown in Tamil Nadu, Karnataka, Andhra Pradesh and Maharashtra. It is a semi-tall sport of Dwarf Cavendish. It is similar to Basrai except that the fruit is more green and straight, the bunch is more symmetrical and the plant taller. Fruit large, skin thick, greenish to dull yellow, sweet and delicious. The fruits have better keeping quality than that of Dwarf Cavendish. It prefers a moist coastal climate. Average bunch weight is about 20 kg.

Kanchkela. Musa (ABB) Group. Syn. Khasdia (Gujarat), Monthan (Tamil Nadu), Bontha (Andhra Pradesh), Maduranga Bale, Aunda Bale, Mangakai (Karnataka), Khasdi, Bankel (Maharashtra), Bainsa (Bihar), Ponthan (Kerala), Batisa (Orissa), Bluggoe (Trinidad), Pisang Nanka (Malaysia).

This is the most important commercial culinary banana cultivar of India. The plant is tall, robust, light green leaves. The plant is hardy and somewhat drought tolerant. The skin is thick. The fruits having prominent three ridges. It can withstand cold better. Keeping quality is good. Average bunch weight is approximately 15 kg. It has good immunity to Banana Bunchy Top Virus (BBTV) disease and salt tolerance but is highly susceptible to Fusarium wilt disease.

Martaman. Musa (AAB) Group. Syn. Rasthali (Tamil Nadu), Mutheli (Maharashtra), Malbhog (Bihar), Amruthapani (Andhra Pradesh), Rasabale (Karnataka), Sonkel (Kerala), Silkfig (Trinidad).

It is the most liked table variety of Tamil Nadu, Andhra Pradesh, Kerala, Karnataka, Bihar and West Bengal. The plant is tall, yellowish-green stem, the brownish blotches, reddish margins of the petiole and leaf sheath. The average bunch weight is about 12 kg. Fruits are medium-sized and similar to that of Poovan in appearance. It is susceptible to Panama disease and ripe fruit drop off from the bunch. The plant has better root system and can resist wind better than other varieties.

Lalkela. Musa (AAA) Group. Syn. Chenkadali, Sevazhai (Tamil Nadu), Anupan (Bihar), Rathambala (SriLanka), Red banana (Trinidad).

This variety is grown throughout the world. This is the most robust of the bananas grown in India. The height of the plant goes up to 4-5 metres. The colour of the Pseudostem, petiole, midrib and fruit is purplish red. The fruit is of good size and has a characteristic aroma. The skin is thick, pulp is saffron coloured, firm, fairly moist and sweet. The variety has a free suckering habit. It is highly susceptible to bunchy top, fusarium wilt and nematodes

Nendran. Musa (AAB) Group. Syn. Nendran (Kerala), Ethakai (Kerala), Rajeli (Maharashtra), Kochikehal (SriLanka), Plantain (Trinidad).

The cultivar is known in all parts of the world as plantain. It is cultivated on commercial scale in Kerala. It has habit of producing more suckers. The pseudostem has a distinct shade of pink colouration. The fruit is relatively longer and thicker than most other bananas. The bunch is not compact and average weight is 15 Kg. Keeping quality is good. The variety is suitable for the preparation of banana flour, banana chips and drying as fig. It is highly susuptible to Banana Mosaic Virus (BBMV), nematodes and borers.

Gros Michel. Musa (AAA) Group. Syn. Anamalu (SriLanka), Blue Field (Hawaii).

The variety was introduced in South India from Trinidad. It is the best dessert variety and excells other varieties in length of bunch, number of fruits, flavour, attractive skin colour and resistant to bruising. It is susceptible to wilt disease.

Grand Naine. Musa (AAA) Group. It is tall mutant of Dwarf Cavendish. This variety is gaining popularity among the growers of Maharashtra, Karnataka and Punjab. It is more vigorous and robust with well spaced hands, bigger sized fingers and heavy bunches. Bunch weight is 25-30 kg and require propping. It has the potential to bear 40 kg bunch.

Safed Velchi. Musa (AB) Group. Syn. Sonery (Maharashtra), Ney Poovan (Tamil Nadu), Nhali Poovan (Kerala), Kadali (Malabar), Nitka Bale, Deva Bale (Karnataka).

The variety is popular in Kerala and Maharashtra and mostly grown as intercrop in coconut and arecant garden. The plant is tall, stem is slender. Pseudostem is yellowish having reddish petiole margin. The fruits are small, firm fleshed and sweet. Keeping quality is very good. The average bunch weight is about 10-12 kg.

Hill Banana. Musa (AAB) Group. Virupakshi Syn. Mala Vazhai

The banana is a speciality of Tamil Nadu. These are perennial bananas of high quality. Sirumalai and Virupakshi are the two main types. Fruits of sirumalai have better taste. The average bunch weight is about 12 kg. The duration of the variety is about 14 months.

Giant Governer. Musa (AAA) Group. It is popular in West Bengal. The plant is medium dwarf. The fruits are large, greenish to dull yellow in colour. The pulp is firm and taste is sweet. It produces bunch weighing 15-18 kg. The variety is susceptible to (Sigatoka) leaf spot disease but resistant to wilt.

Co.1. Banana : It is a hybrid developed at TNAU, Coimbatore. It is a multi-crosses made among 'Ladan' as female parent and **Musa balbisiana** and 'Kadali' as a male parents. It takes about 14 month duration. The average bunch weight is 10 kg.

Varietal Improvement

The female parents like Angniswar (AAB), Mannan (AAB), Nendran (AAB), Palayankodan (AAB), Harichhal (AAA), Lacatan (AAA) and male parents as Pisan Lilin were used for crossing. The progenies from the cross Agniswar × Pisang Lilin (H–1) showed high bunch weight from 14–16 kg. It is resistant to sigatoka leaf spot, fusarium wilt and burrowing nematode. Vannan × Pisang Lilin (H–2) showed bunch weight from 15–20 kg. It is learnt to sigatoka leaf spot and nematode. BRS-1 and BRS-2 are other promising hybrids developed at BRS, Kannara.

PROPAGATION

Banana is commonly propagated by vegetative means viz. suckers, peepers and rhizomes. When plants are multiplied through suckers, two types of suckers namely sword suckers and water suckers are used. Sword suckers are commonly used as they have a well-developed base with narrow sword-shaped leaf blades at the early stages. The water suckers are having broad leaves and they do not produce a healthy banana clump. Planters throughout the world usually plant sturdy and healthy sword suckers. The sword suckers are vigorous, produce bigger and heavier bunches in 11 months than the water suckers do in more than 15 months. The sword suckers are planted when they attain the height of 80-120 cm. Heading back of tall sucker is beneficial. The suckers should be vigorously growing and must have attained 2 kg weight. The suckers should have narrow, sword- shaped leaves. The base of suckers should be thick and tapering towards the top. Suckers should be free from any pests and diseases.

Peepers (very young suckers) produce late and poor crop.

Rhizomes either whole or pieces (1.5 to 2.0 kg or so in weight) may be planted first in the nursery for sprouting or directly in the main field. For quick multiplication of a variety, rhizome bits may be used, though the plants will require little longer time to fruit. The shape of the rhizome should be conical but not flat. It must have a sound heartbud and side buds.

Plants raised through tissue culture are preferred for planting. Gross Michel, Shrimanti and Grand Naine are commonly produced through tissue culture technique. Disease free plantlets with 3-4 leaves are supplied in pots for raising secondary nursery. At initial stage plants are kept in 50 per cent shade for hardening and shade is reduced gradually. Plants do not require shade after about six months. After two months of this process, banana plants can be planted in the pits.

PLANTING OPERATIONS

The land should be deeply ploughed, harrowed and levelled properly. Pits of 60 cm × 60 cm × 60 cm are dug sufficiently ahead at points fixed for planting. The pits are filled with a mixture of top soil and farmyard manure or compost (50 : 50). The suckers should be detached from the mother plant along with a piece of underground stem with a few roots. The single sucker is planted in the centre of the pit and pressed well around the base. Immediately after planting, light irrigation should be given.

The time of planting of banana depends on climatic conditions and availability of water. Banana can be planted throughout the year except in severe winter and during heavy rains when the soil is very wet. In the areas of heavy and continuous rains, planting of banana should be done after monsoon *i.e.* in September- October. In the areas where rains are not so heavy, planting should be done during June-July. In the areas where assured irrigation is available, planting can be successfully done in February-March. The planting in the hill slopes of South India is done during February-March and on the banks of the Cauveri river in April.

Planting distance : A spacing 2.7 m × 3.0 m (row x plant) for tall cultivar and 1.8 m × 1.8 m (row × plant) for dwarf cultivars were found most suitable. For dwarf varieties, the distance of 1.2 m × 1.2 × m and 1.8 m × 1.8 m can also be kept profitably. On the other hand, for tall and semi-tall varieties, the distance of 2.4 m × 1.8 m, 2.4 m × 2.4 m and 2.5 m × 2.5 m were also found equally suitable. The plant density of 2500/hectare is recommended for Giant Governer.

Spacing in tissue culture plants of 30 cm size should be planted on 15 February to 7 March in the field at 1.8 × 1.8 m distance. Before planting pit of 0.6 × 0.6 m size should be filled with half farmyard manure and half top soil after mixing with 90 g P_2O_5 (180g DAP)

FLOWERING AND FRUITING

The initiation of the inflorescence primordium of the banana bunch takes place in the heart of the pseudostem. It develops to a certain extent before emergence. In cv. Dwarf Canvendish, the emergence of the 11th last leaf indicates approximately the time of transformation of the growing point into inflorescence. The time from initiation of inflorescence to shooting of bunch varies from 3 months in summer to 6 months in winter in the first planted crop. The initiated inflorescence may ascend rapidly from the base of the pseudostem to the top in one month. The flower bud emerges out after all the leaves including the protective leaf has emerged.

Flowers are arranged in two series, numbering about 7-14 pairs. Each of the series is called a hand. The basal nodes of the inflorescence bear female (pistillate) flowers and the upper nodes bear male (staminate) flowers. Sometimes one or two clusters of transitional forms may occur. A bract subtends each cluster. Bracts are large, spatheceous and of various shades of purple, ovate, closely imbricate, spirally arranged and often deciduous. The bracts rise just before flowers become functional. As the ovaries of the female flower develop into fruit, the growing point continues its growth, bracts rising to expose the male flowers.

Flowers are arranged in nodal clusters, each being borne on the obliquely transverse cushion. Female flowers are large, bearing a well-developed ovary with a long style and reduced staminodes. Female flowers develop into the fruit. In the male flowers, the ovary is obortive, the style and stigma selender and anthers well developed. Edible banana rarely contain pollen. Male flowers abscise from the base of the ovary and are shed after exposure for a day. In female flowers, the style and staminodes abscise leaving at the top a scar which persists in the mature banana. The ovary of the female flower is trilocular, each loculus containing an axile placenta. Ovules are 2 or 4 rowed in each loculus.

The common type of inflorescence is the one in which the basal portion bears pistillate flowers, which develops into fruits followed by deciduous staminate flowers *e.g.*, 'Poovan', 'Monthan'. The male bud or heart continues to produce staminate flowers till the fruits ripen but in some groups like 'Nadan' the heart withers and is dried up long before the maturity of the bunch.

In the second group, the whole inflorescence bears pistillate flowers and hence all the flowers develop into fruits *e.g.*, ***'Ayiranka Rasthali'* and *'Moongil'*.**

In the third type, the basal flowers develop into fruits followed by persistant male flowers consisting of green rudimentary ovaries with persistent perianth and bracts *e.g.*, 'Dwarf Cavendish', 'Nendran' etc.

In another type, the basal region bears pistillate flowers which develop into fruits followed by persistent male flowers, which is again followed by deciduous male flowers. The bracts of persistent male flowers are, however, deciduous *e.g.*, ***'Rasthali'* and *'Chakkarakali'*.**

Pollination is mainly by bees and birds which visit the flowers for nectar secreted at the tips of the ovary and collected at the base of the perianth. The ovary of the flowers is trilocular with axile placentation.

The fruit of banana is either seeded or vegetatively parthenocarpic *i.e.*, developed without pollination. The vast majority of edible bananas are not pollinated. Some of the cultivated varieties such as 'Poovan' and 'Kaali' etc. though sterile, set seed when pollinated or when they are grown in the vicinity of a pollen source. Certain cultivars such as 'Dwarf Cavendish' are inherently highly sterile and are not known to set seed. In seeded wild bananas, pollination is essential for fruit development and the mature fruit contains a mass of black seeds. The fruit in the seedless bananas is believed to develop through endogenous auxin stimulation which in seeded bananas is derived from the developing seed. Banana fruit is berry and edible portion is mosocorp and endocarp.

Growth and Development : The growth pattern of the plant suggested a double sigmoid curve, while the dry matter increase followed a normal sigmoid curve. Throughout the period between the third month after planting and harvest, pseudostem contributed maximum to the fresh weight of the whole plant. Seven months after planting, it accounted for more than half of the total fresh weight of the whole plant (51.3%) and was followed by corm and leaf contributing almost equally to the total fresh weight. After shooting, the contribution of the bunch to the total fresh weight become prominent, contributing about 32.2% of the total fresh weight at harvest and was very close to the fresh weight of the pseudostem (36.5%) at the same stage.

Fruit growth pattern : The growth in volume of seeded bananas is sigmoid and that of parthenocarpic fruits is not sigmoid. It was also found that the growth rates are related to certain ovule behaviour and seed content of the fruit and ploidy. In 'Dwarf Cavendish, a concave growth curve was observed. It took 130 days to reach full maturity after the emergence of inflorescence and fruit weight increase was maximum during the final 4 weeks of growth.

The fruit growth in terms of increase in girth, length and volume followed a double sigmoid pattern. Increase in both fresh and dry weight also suggested a double sigmoid curve.

ORCHARD CULTURAL PRACTICES

Irrigation

Banana is a moisture loving plant, therefore, it's water requirement is very high. It requires adequate soils moisture throughout the year. Irrigation is given just after planting. Banana requires irrigation regularly throughout the year except during heavy rains.

In Western Coast of India, it is normally grown as a rainfed perennial crop. In hilly areas also no irrigation is given. In Bihar, irrigation is given after every 10 days from December to June. Banana growing in most inland areas requires 40-50 irrigation from the time of planting to harvest. In North Gujarat and East Khandesh, even more irrigation may be required. In banana, trenches are dug between alternate rows which serve to drain off excess water during the rains and later as irrigation channels. In West Bengal, the plants are irrigated at an interval of 10-15 days during dry periods. Irrigation facility is a must to Cavendish banana, whereas tall cultivars are grown under unirrigated condition or marginally irrigated condition. In Basrai banana, the plants given 45 kg Nitrogen and irrigated at an interval of 6 days, produced mature fruits 83 days earlier than unfertilized plants irrigated at 14 days interval. In Robusta banana, lateral and vertical spread of root mass increased by decreasing the soil moisture.

Water is crucial for its growth. Little moisture stress can lead to decrease in finger size and colour of leaves. Excess water may lead to breakage of pseudostem near root portion, due to rotting. The water requirements of cv. Grand Naine under Punjab condition is as follow :

Months	Irrigation Interval (days)	Months	Irrigation Internal (days)
March - April	7 - 8	July - September	7 - 8 as per need
May - June	4 - 6	October - February	10 - 15

Drip irrigation can reduce quantity of water and increases yield and decreases number of days to harvest and increases leaf production. In banana cv. Robusta, as the availability of water in the soil increases, the stomatal number per unit area and stomatal size increases, resulting in the improved photosynthetic efficiency and ultimately increase the yield. Dry soil conditions adversely affect the banana yield, because there is reduction in stomatal size which interferes with carbon dioxide supply and in turn it reduces the photosynthetic efficiency.

Water use efficiency is more with drip irrigation as compared to basin system of irrigation. The drip irrigation system saves 50 per cent water and also yields higher.

Intercropping

Intercrops can easily be grown in banana plantation at the earlier stage of growth. In some parts of India, mixed cropping is also practised. Planting of banana may be followed by planting of intercrops like brinjal, colocasia, turmeric, chillies, bhindi, radish, cauliflower, cabbage, spinach, maize, etc. depending on climatic conditions. Mixed cropping of banana, arecanut, coconut and cassava is a common practice along the coastal belts of Tamil Nadu. Paddy is also grown as mixed crop. Banana is grown as a shade plant for coffee, cocoa, rubber, young mango trees and orange in different parts of India.

Weed Control

Shallow cultivation at early stage of crop is essential to keep down the weeds and to provide better conditions for plant growth. Weeds can also be checked with the use of herbicides. Diuron @ 4 kg per hectare and Simazine @ 6 kg per hectare control grasses and broad leaved weeds when applied after planting and repeated 30 days after planting. At Bangalore, application of glyphosate @ 1 kg a.i per hectare at the time of planting followed by 0.5 kg *a.i.* per hectare at 30 and 60 days after planting of suckers is recommended.

Manuring and Fertilization

In banana,it is essential to induce quick growth and produce more leaves with longer area. To achieve this, complete dose of manures and fertilizers should be applied by six months after planting. Nitrogen hastens maturity and increases yield. Phosphorus promotes strong root system, healthy rhizome, favours fruit setting and accelerates ripening. Application of potash increases the number of hands/bunch and finger size, improves fruit quality, develops resistance to diseases and reduces water uptake in banana. The third leaf is taken as standard for analysis for establishing critical values. In 'Giant Governer' cultivar, the nutrient values suggested are : leaf N around 2.8, P 0.8 and K 3.8 per cent at the vegetative stage (6 months). Banana needs heavy manure near the soil surface because of their shallow rooting.

The application of nitrogen should be done at 2,4 and 6 months after planting. Phosphorus should be applied at planting time. Potash should be given in two split doses-one at planting and another at the time of initiation of flowers.

In Bangalore, the fertilizers recommended for Robusta banana are 200 g N, 100 g P_2O_5 and 200 g K_2O per plant. Nitrogen and potash are to be applied in four equal splits at 30, 75, 120 and 165 days after planting while phosphorus can be applied at the time of planting. For ratoon crop, the requirement of N and P_2O_5 can be reduced to 100 and 50 g per plant, respectively while K_2O is to be applied at 200 g/plant. Complete fertilizers application before flower initiation which normally occurs within 5-6 months after planting.

For Robusta and Basrai, 180 *g* N, 180 *g* P and 270 K per plant annually has been recommended. In another field trial 150–200 *g*N, 40–60 *g* P and 200–300 *g* K per plant of banana per year is suggested.

In Punjab, the fertilizers for Grand Naine @ 250g nitrogen and 250 g potash per plant is given in 5 equal doses during April, May, June, July and August. At the time of planting in February - March 280 g NPK (12 : 32 : 16) per plant is recommended.

Urea is given 60 g per plant in the Month of May. Again, it is applied 60 g in June, and 80 g per plant each in July, August and September alognwith 40 g MoP in June, 60 g in July and 80 g per plant each in August and September.

The following doses of manures and fertilizers are given to banana crop ber year in different important banana producing states.

States	FYM (kg/plant)	N	P_2O_5 g/plant	K_2O
Andhra Pradesh	10–15	200	50	300
Assam	–	300	50	250–350
Gujarat	10–15	200	50	300
Karnataka	15	400	50	300
Maharashtra	–	300	50	300
Tamil Nadu	10	200–250	40–50	300

DESUCKERING

Desuckering or pruning is the removal of unwanted suckers. These suckers have to be removed periodically as otherwise they compete with the mother plant for nutrients, resulting in lower bunch weight and total yield. It is done either by cutting off the sucker or the heart may be destroyed without detaching the sucker from the parent plant. Sometimes, kerosene is poured into the cavity left after digging the sucker. In South India, crowbar with a chiesel-like end is used for damaging the sucker.

Removal of all suckers upto flowering of mother plant and maintaining only one follower afterwards is the best desuckering practice. However, under high density planting, it is better to leave the follower after harvesting 75-80% of the plant crop so that uniform cultural practices can be followed. It has been observed that sucker removal had no effect on yield in the first harvest, but yield in the second harvest was highest in plants left with one sucker (12253 kg/ ha), followed by plants left with 2 or 3 suckers (8606 and 8879 kg/ha, respectively) and was lowest in plants without removal of suckers (6721 kg/ha).

Removal of style, perianth of male bud

This practice helps in overcoming 'fingertip' disease. Remove the perianth and style while the bunch is still young. The male bud or 'heart' should be removed immediately after the last hand appears and the fruit starts to curve up.

The perianth and style are easily removed by a light brushing movement of the hand a few days after flowering. If not brushed off, they become brown and shrivelled and it is difficult to remove.

The male bud or heart is used as a vegetable in parts of India and as animal or stock feed in some countries. Removal of male bud is said to favour fruit development. It is a practice recommended for improving the appearance of the bunch as well as to ward off 'fingertip' disease.

Spathe Removal

Spathe (pollen inflorescence) should be removed after complete panicle emergence to enhance the filling of fingers.

Trashing

In the banana field, lot of undesirable material is necessary to remove such as dried, diseased and decayed leaves, pseudostem after harvest, male bud, last end of inflorescence, and withered floral parts etc.

Propping

Propping is a method by which support is given to banana bearing plants with the help of the bamboo cruteches, protecting them from bending or falling down due to heavy bunch load and from any damage by wind. Propping is very essential for tall varieties. Wooden props such as bamboo or casuarina or eucalyptus poles are to be given.

Earthing up

Earthing up should be done during the rainy season to provide drainage and to avoid water logging at the base. It is to be done once in 2 or 3 months to prevent soil erosion from the basins and to avoid direct contact of water with pseudostem. Due to earthing up there are fair chances of formation of good root system.

Wrapping of Bunches

It is covering of bunches with polythene or gunny cloth that protects the fruits from intense heat, hot wind, etc. and improves the colour of the fruits.

Mattocking

After the harvest of bunch, the plant stem should be cut in stages at least after 30 to 45 days to facilitate mobilization of the nutrients from the mother to the developing ratoon plant. The pseudostem should be cut leaving a stump of about 0.6 m height.

Frost Protection

Occurrence of frost is very common in North India during December to February. To save the crop from frost damage, irrigate the field and burn the heaps of leaves or farmwaste material to create smoke during expected frost days. In addition, cover the bunches with polythene sheets and stalks with banana leaves to decrease the frost injury and breakage of stalks.

Ratooning

Banana yield three crops which means two ratoon crops after first crop. Under Punjab conditions, one shoot per plant should be retained during September after the emergence of panicle or at the time when about 80 per cent of the panciles emerged in the field.

HARVESTING AND HANDLING OF FRUITS

Banana is categorized as a climacteric fruit. Fruits do not ripe early and uniformly on the plant. Therefore, they are harvested when they are green and fully mature. The fruits are harvested when top leaves start drying. The colour of the fruit changes from deep green to a lighter green. The ridges on the surface of the skin change from angular to round, *i.e.* after the attainment of 3/4th full stage.

Banana comes into flowering in 9 months or so after planting. The dwarf bananas are ready for harvest within 11 to 14 months after planting, while tall cultivars take about 14 to 16 months to harvest. The fruits become ready in 3-4 months after flowering. In India, the main banana season is from September to April. The total period required from planting to first harvesting will also depend on type of variety under cultivation, and climatic conditions. Stage of harvesting of fruits depends on its uses. For vegetable purpose, tender and immature fruits are harvested. For table purpose and for transporting to long distance, the harvesting of mature fruits should be done earlier. The harvesting is performed by cutting the bunch, retaining 15-20 cm stalk, this will help in handling.

Tall cultivars usually yield 15-20 tonnes/ha. Average yield of dwarf varieties is 30-40 tonnes/ha.

Tissue culture raised plants are known to decrease the time of emergence and maturity of bunches and also improve yield over conventional sucker plants.

Banana are not usually allowed to ripen on the tree as it takes long time. Moreover, the fruit-peel splits, fruit ripens unevenly and fails to develop good colour and aroma, hence the marketable quality deteriorates. Therefore, banana needs to be ripened artificially. The bunches of banana are heaped in dry and clean air-tight room and covered with leaves. The fruits are ready within 4 days. Smoke treatment is the common method to induce ripening in Maharashtra and Tamil Nadu. Smoking is done with straw, leaves and cowdung in a closed chamber with bunches arranged in a heap for 18-24 hours in summer and 48 hours in winter. After taking the bunches from the chamber, they are placed in a well ventilated room for development of colour. Besides these methods, chemicals can be used for inducing early ripening. Among them 2, 4-D is the cheapest for inducing artificial ripening. The fruits should be dipped for 10 seconds in 1000 ppm 2,4-D. Ethrel @ 5000 ppm with 5 g of NaOH pellet kept in a beaker in the ripening chamber ripened the banana fruits within 48 hours. Mature banana fruits are generally treated with exogenous ethylene gas at 100 ppm for 24 hours at temp. 16–18°C and RH 90–95%. The fruits attained uniform colour, excellent quality with shelf life of 4 days at 16 – 18°C and 2 days at 30 – 32°C.

The banana fruits harvested at green mature stage can also be successfully ripened in 4 days by dipping in a solution of ethephon 500 ppm (1.25 ml per litre of water) for 2-3 minutes. The fruits should be air dried and kept at 16 – 18°C and 90 – 95 per cent RH. The fruits attained uniform colour, excellent quality with shelf life of 4 days at 16 – 18°C and 2 days at 30 – 32°C.

After harvesting or ripening, the fruits can be stored for some period. The fruits can be stored at a temperature of 13°C and a relative humidity of 85-95% for about three weeks. The bananas should not be placed in refrigerator at low temperature as they become black. The shelf life of banana can be enhanced by keeping the fruit in relatively high concentration of carbon dioxide and low concentration of oxygen. Ripening of banana fruits can easily be retarded for 10-12 days at ambient temperature (30°C) held in sealed polythene bags. Ripening of banana can be retarded significantly with post harvest dip in 150 ppm GA + 500 ppm benomyl or 150 ppm GA + 6% waxol. Giant Governor cv. of banana treated with a trizole derivative (Bas 111W) resulted delayed ripening. Shelf life of banana fruits and their quality can also be extended 3 days more than the control with the use of ethylene absorbent like vermiculite blocks when they are soaked in potassium permanganate at 100 g per litre and inserted into polythene bags each holding one hand with 12 fruits.

INSECT-PESTS

1. Stem borer (*Odoiporus longicollis* Olivier) : It causes much damage to banana plant. The larvae feeds and tunnels inside the corm, leaves turn yellow, wither and ultimately plant die.

Remove all infested plants and destroy them. Spray 0.04% Endosulfan or 0.1% carbaryl. Use celphos (3 tablets per plant) tablets inside the pseudostem and plaster the slit with mud. The pest can be controlled by applying 3g of carbofuran granules per stool

2. Banana aphid (*Pentalonia nigronervosa* Coquerel) : The insect is particularly important as it is the vector of the virus causing bunchy top disease. The nymphs and adults suck sap from young and tender leaves.

Spray 0.3% Rogor 30 EC (dimethoate) or monocrotophos or 0.05 per cent malathion or 0.01 per cent metasystox. Soil application of phorate or Carbofuran @ 4-5 kg/ha near the base of suckers or rhizome at the time of planting is very effective.

3. Rhizome weevil (*Cosmopolites sordidus* Germar) : The pest does harm to the banana crop throughout the year. The grubs bore into the rhizomes. Adults hide in leaf sheathes and suckers.

Remove and destroy infested rhizomes and stumps. Suckers should be dipped in 0.1 per cent quinalphos emulsion or monocrotophos (0.5%) for 30 minutes before planting. Spray 0.05% Fenitrothion or 0.03% phosphamidon around the base of plants.

4. Banana beetle (*Nodostoma subcustatum* Jucoby, *Colaspis hypochlora*) : The pest generally attacks young leaves and fruits. They hide under folded leaves. The spots are seen on fruits. The quality of fruit is deteriorated. Occurrence of pest is maximum during rainy season.

For the control of pest follow clean cultivation practices. Dust with malathion to check the pest.

5. Tobacco caterpillar (*Spodoptera litura*) : It is active during July-September and cause damage on upper and lower surface of leaf blades. Fully grown caterpillars eat up the central whorl of plant thus render the plants stunted in growth.

The pest can be controlled by spraying 1000 ml quinalphos (Ekalux 25 EC) in 500 litres of water when it appear on the plant. Spray can be repeated if need arises.

6. Pseudostem borer (*0diporus longicollis*) : It is active during summer and rainy season. The grubs bore into the stem and feed within it. There is exudation of plant sap and blackened mass that comes out from the hole bore by the grubs. The whole plant dies at later stage.

The affected plants should be uprooted and burnt. Three tablets of celphos per plant should be placed inside the pseudostem and plastered the slit with mud. Treating the plants with carbofuran (3g of granules/stool) is effective treatment. Alternately, Carbaryl 50 WP (0.1%) also check the population of pest.

7. Namatodes (*Rhadopholus similis*) : They are now recognised as an important soil-borne pathogens causing decline in yield in bananas. Affected plants do not response to fertilizer, irrigation or cultural practices. Small dark spots appear on the root. The nematode lays eggs in the root tissue After hatching out, larvae also feed on the root. Plant growth is retarded and yield is affected adversely.

Banana sets may be disinfected either by paring, heat therapy, chemical treatment or by combination of these methods. The pared sets can be disinfected by dipping them in a hot water bath at 55°C for 10 minutes or soil application of carbofuran at 2 kg a.i. per hectare can check the nematodes.

DISEASES

1. Panama disease or Banana wilt : The disease is caused due to the fungus ***Fusarium oxysporum f. cubense.*** The disease was first reported from Panama in early 1900. It is a soil borne fungus and gets entry in the plant body through roots. It is a serious disease in poorly drained soils with planting of banana year after year. The leaves of affected plants turns yellow and later they hang around the pseudostem and wither. Black streaks appear on rhizomes and pseudostems. The disease spreads fast on acid alluvial soils. Warm soil temperature and bad drainage favour the spread of the disease.

The affected plants should be uprooted and destroyed. Always avoid banana planting on infested soil. Disease free rhizomes and suckers should only be used for planting. Apply Bavistin @ 1 g. per litre of water. It is advisable to plant disease resistant varieties like Basrai Dwarf, Poovan, Champa, Raja Vazhai, Vaman Keli, etc. Apply more quantity of farmyard manure for its control.

2. Leaf spot or Sigatoka disease : It is caused due to ***Mycosphaerella musicola***- Sexual stage and *Cercospora musae*-Asexual stage.

Sigatoka is the name of the valley in Fiji where the disease first attracted during 1913. It is a fungal disease. The presence of light yellowish spots on the leaves are the first symptoms. A small number of these enlarge, become oval and changes to dark brown. Infection occurs through the stomata of the young leaves, the lower surface being much more important than the upper. The size of bunch and fruit is reduced due to reduction of leaf area available for photosynthesis. Fruits may ripe prematurely. High humidity occur due to close planting, heavy weeds and failure to remove suckers, favour in spreading the disease.

Proper drainage of field is very important for control of this disease. Avoid too close planting and remove suckers and weeds regularly. Affected leaves should be removed and destroyed. Brodeaux mixture 1 per cent + 2 percent linseed oil spray should be given. Spray with Dithane M-45 at 0.2 per cent.

3. Banana Bunchy Top Virus (BBTV) : The disease is said to be due to virus (Bunchy Top Virus, Banana Virus I or Musa Virus I). The banana aphid (***Pentalonia nigronervosa*** Coq) is the main agent of transmitting the disease. The dwarf banana are very susceptible to this disease. The leaves are bunched together into a rosette at the top and their margins are wavy and slightly rolled upward. The presence of interrupted dark green streaks along the secondary veins of the lamina or the midrib or petiole is a characteristic symptom of bunchy top. The diseased plants remain stunted and do not produce bunch of any commercial value.

It is advisable to always plant virus free suckers obtained from reliable nursery. Remove all affected plants along with complete rhizome. To check aphid, spray 0.3 per cent Rogor or Phosphamidon or Monocrotophos (0.05%). Never allow banana plant/clumps at a place for more than 3 years. Herbicide like 2, 4-D may be applied on the stool after cutting down for effective killing of the plant.

4. Banana Bract Mosaic Virus (BBMV) : Yellow green bands or mottling over an entire leaf appear. Such leaves show abnormal thicking of veins. Development of bunch is adversely affected.

Uproot and destroy the affected plant alongwith rhizome. The cultivation of cucurbits near the banana field should be discouraged.

5. Bacterial wilt or moko disease (*Pseudomonas solanacearum*) : On young plant, one of the youngest three leaves becomes pale green or yellow and collapse near the junction of the lamina with the petiole. The presence of yellow fingers often indicate the presence of this disease. Fruit rot and fruit stalk vascular discolouration, wilted or blackened regrowth of suckers, blackened and dead male flower buds are the characteristic symptoms of bacterial wilt.

Flower visiting insects are main agents for transmitting the disease and this is a good reason for following the practice of removing the bud from the male axis before the bunch mature. Herbicide 2, 4-D can be used to kill infected plants **in situ.** Follow phytosanitation practices in banana plantation.

6. Fruit rot (*Macrophomina musae* and *Gloeosporium musarum*) : Lesions are formed on fruits and stalks followed by rotting. Such fruit ripen prematurely and finally turn brown and rot.

To check the disease, remove affected fingers (fruits) and stalk. Spraying the bunch with Topsin M or Dithane M-45 (0.1%) is effective control of this disease.

7. Pitting disease (*Pyricularia grisea*) : Round, sunken pits appear on the fruit as it approaches maturity or after harvest. Splitting may occur in the centre of the pit. Pits do not extend to the pulp.

All collapsed and drying leaf tissues including transition leaves and bracts should be removed at regular interval, especially during the rainy season. To protect the fruits, spray weekly with Dithane M-45.

8. Anthracnose (*Gloeosporium musae*) : This disease attack the banana plants at all stages of growth. Small, black, circular streaks appears on flowers, skin and distal ends of banana heads. Four sprays of Bavistin (1%) or Prochloroz (0.15%) at fortnightly internal can check the disease effectively.

Papaya

Papaya (***Carica papaya*** L.) is an ideal fruit for growing in kitchen gardens, backyards of homes as well as in orchards, especially those near the cities or big towns. It is also grown extensively as a filler plant in the orchards. Papaya is quick- growing and starts bearing within 8-10 months of transplanting. Papaya cultivation is, indeed, very remunerative, if done on modern lines.

ORIGIN AND HISTORY

The papaya is an important fruit of tropical and subtropical regions of the world. It is a native of tropical America (Mexico). The cultivated papaya originated as a cross between two species of genus ***Carica*** native to Mexico. Dutch traveller Linschoten made first record of papaya is 1576 and observed that plant had been taken from West Indies to Malacca. In India, papaya was introduced by the Portuguese during 1611. It was taken by Spanish to Manila in the mid-16th century. Papaya spread widely in the Pacific Islands by 1800. It was introduced in Hawaian Islands between 1800 and 1823 by Don Moris–a spanish Horticulturist. Today distribution of papaya is extended within 32°N and S latitudes of the equator on the globe. Later on it was brought to India. Presently, papaya is grown extensively in India, Brazil, Indonesia, Nigeria, Mexico, Ethiopia, Democratic Republic of Congo, Thailand and Guatemala.

AREA AND PRODUCTION

India is the leading producer of papaya fruit and has 36.8 per cent share in world production. The area under papaya in world is 4.35 lakh hectares yielding annual production of 12.1 million mt.

Presently in India, papaya is grown in 1.17 lakh hectares with annual production of 44.57 lakh metre tonnes accounting for 1.8 and 5.8 per cent of area and production. Productivity of papaya is the highest (38.1 mt/ha) among the fruit crops, which has attracted the growers for its commercial increase in area and production in last few decades.

Papaya is grown commercially in Andhra Pradesh, Gujarat, Karnataka, West Bengal, Madhya Pradesh and Maharashtra. Andhra Pradesh is producing 26.7 per cent of the total production in the country. It is followed by 23.8 per cent in Gujarat.

Export potential : The Papaya fruits use mainly exported to United, Arab Emirates, Saudi Arabia, Netherlands, Kuwait, Germany, Bahrain, Qatar, Nepal, USA and Ireland. The export value of papaya from India to various countries is Rs. 24.75 crores. UAE is the major country where 37.5 per cent papaya fruits are exported from India.

IMPORTANCE AND USES

Papaya is a very wholesome, refreshing and delicious fruit. It is a rich source of vitamins. Papaya contains about 2500 i.u. of vitamin A and 85 mg of vitamin C per 100 g pulp. It is also fairly rich in calcium and other minerals. The yellow pigment in papaya is due to caricaxanthin. Papaya contains moisture 90.8%, protein 0.6%, and carbohydrates 7.2%. Fruits contain a valuable proteolytic enzyme papain, which helps in the digestion of protein rich foods.

Papain is manufactured from the white latex of unripe papayas. Similar to the animal enzyme pepsin, papain is reputed for its medicinal and industrial uses. It is used for the treatment of ulcers and other ailments. Skin blemishes are said to vanish when treated with papain.

Papaya can be eaten as such as a dessert fruit, when fully ripe or with salt, pepper, sugar or lime juice. Its seeds are also eaten by some people for their slightly flavour and reputed medicinal value. The unripe fruit can be used as vegetable. Papaya fruits can also be made into pickles and preserves of various kinds. The fruits are beneficial in piles, dyspepsia of liver, spleen and digestive disorders. Ripe fruits are used in preparation of jam, jelly, fruity, nectar, soft drinks, ice cream, flavouring crystallized fruits and are canned as syrup. Young leaves are also used as vegetable in Java. Carpaine obtained from papaya is utilized as a diuretic and a heat stimulant.

BOTANY

Papaya belongs to the family caricaceae-a small, somewhat anomalous family with 4 genera and 31 species of which three are in tropical and subtropical America and one in Africa. The genera and the number of included species are, **Carica** : 22, Facaratia : 6, Farilla : 1 and Cylicomorpha : 2. The edible fruits are found only in ***Carica papaya.*** Other species include ***Carica chilensis, Carica goudotiana, Carica monoica*** and ***carica pubescens. Carica candamarcensis*** **(mountain papaya)** grows to a height of about 2.4 m, can withstand low temperature and thrives well at an elevation between 1500-2000 m.

Edible fruits are found only in *Carica papaya*. Other species used in breeding programme are as follow :

Species	Type	Remarks
Carica monoica	Monoecious	Susceptible to virus
C. microcarpa	Dioecious	Susceptible to virus
C. cauliflora	Dioecious	Resistant to virus
C. goudotiana	Dioecious	Susceptible to virus
C. parviflora	Dioecious	Susceptible to virus
C. pennata	Dioecious	Resistant to frost
C. pubescens	Dioecious	Resistant to ring spot
C. stipulata	Dioecious	Resistant to ring spot
C. horivitziana	Dioecious	Susceptible to virus
C. candicans	Dioecious	Resistant to ring spot
C. pentagona	Dioecious	Resistant to frost
C. papaya	Polygamous	Susceptible to virus

Papaya is dioecious but hermaphrodite forms occur. The stem is hollow and softwooded. It is usually unbranched while young but at later stage upright shoots are developed on its terminal growth due to its obstructions. The leaves are palm like with long stalked. Flowers are fragrant axillary panicles. The fruit is fleshy berry. The shape of fruit from pistillate flower is ovoid-oblong to nearly spherical and from hermaphrodite flower it is pyriform cylindrical or grooved. The skin of papaya fruit is smooth, colour is green but turning yellowish or orange when ripe. Flesh is orange or reddish orange, sometimes it is yellowish in colour, central cavity 5 angled. Seeds are many in a fruit depending on climatic conditions and variety. The seeds are spherical in shape, black or greyish, wrinkled enclosed in gelatinous sacrotesta formed from the outer integument. About 20 seeds weigh one gram. Botanically, the fruit type is berry and mesocarp is the edible portion of the fruit

CLIMATE

Papaya is a tropical fruit. It requires warm and humid climate and can be cultivated upto height of 1000 metres above sea level. The temperature below 10°C affects adversely on growth and development of fruits, thus delayed maturity and ripening. At this temperature, the fruits can not develop flavour and also causes poor taste. Dry climate characterised by a meagre rainfall tends to add to the sweetness of fruit whereas wet climate with heavy rainfall tends to reduce the sweetness.

Papaya can be grown successfully all over plains of north India. However, areas free from frost during winter and scorching heat and desiccating winds during summer are highly suitable for its cultivation. Young plants must be well protected against frost. They should be covered with transparent plastic envelops, *Sarkanda*, straw thatches or any other covering material from November to February against frost damage.

Papaya cannot tolerate hot summer or frost. The optimum range of temperature is 22-26°C for papaya. Annual rainfall should range between 1500 to 1800 mm and it should be evenly distributed. It can not stand in water-logged conditions and need protection against winds. For successful cultivation, papaya requires comparatively high temperature coupled with low humidity and adequate soil moisture.

SOIL

Papaya can be grown on a wide range of soils but for better results, a well drained soil, rich in organic matter is desirable. It is a shallow-rooted plant, highly sensitive to wet feet. Water stagnation, even for a short time, may kill the plant. Hence soils with shallow water table or which are subject to stagnation of water should be avoided. Medium black and alluvial soil are also suitable. The pH of the soil should be within 6-7. Generally, calcarious and stony soils with poor organic matter are not suitable.

CHOICE OF VARIETIES

A large number of papaya cultivars is found in cultivation. None of these is a true cultivar since it can not be relied upon to reproduce the parental characters in all the progenies. The following are a few important papaya varieties :

Pusa Delicious : The plants are strong and stout and usually start fruiting at a height of 160 cm or so from ground level. The sex ratio in terms of female and hermaphrodite is 50 : 50. The fruit size is large. The taste of pulp is very sweet. Fruits per plant ranges 30 to 40. The average weight of each fruit is 1–1.2 kg. TSS is 10.0 per cent. It yield 46 kg fruit per plant.

Pusa Dwarf : This is dioecious variety. The plants are dwarf and precocious in bearing. The plants start bearing at 40 cm above ground level within 235 days after planting. The fruits are medium in size weighing 1 to 2 kg. The shape of fruit is oval. The flesh is melting, sweet and red orange in colour having TSS of 8.9 per cent. The variety is suitable for high density planting. Its average yield is 35 kg per plant.

Washington : The plant is fairly dwarf and bears heavily high on the trunk. The proportion of male plant is low, when raised form the seed obtained under controlled self-pollination. The fruit is large, roundish and contains a few seeds. The flesh is yellow, sweet and good flavoured.

Honey Dew : The plant is of medium height and bears fruit quite heavily on the trunk. The proportion of the male plant is low. The fruit is large, enlogated and contains a few seeds. The flesh is extra fine and sweet with pleasant flavour. This variety is also known as Madhu Bindu. The keeping quality of fruit is medium. Fruit bears less number of seeds.

Coorg Honey : This is a selection from Honey Dew. The plant is tall and bears fruits quite heavily, low on the trunk. Most of the plants are hermaphrodite, but a few occasionally produce only pistillate flowers. The fruit is large, of variable shape and contains very few seeds. Its flesh is appreciably thicker, but slightly less sweet than that of Honey Dew. TSS is about 6.0 per cent.

Co-1 : The selection of this variety was made from a variety Ranchi from Bihar. The variety is ideal for table purpose. The plant is of medium height and commences bearing low on the stem. The fruit is roundish and uniform in shape, size and quality. The variety is unisexual with male and female plants occuring separately. TSS is about 7.0 per cent. The keeping quality of fruits is good. It bears 25 to 35 fruits per plant and average yield is 40 kg per plant.

Pusa Nanha : It is a dioecious dwarf mutant variety developed at IARI, Regional Station, Pusa (Bihar). The average plant height and leaf length are 106 cm and 86 cm, respectively. That's why, more plants can be planted per hectare by adopting distance of 1.25 × 1.25 m. Owing to dwarfness, it can escape from strong winds. The variety is precocious in bearing. It is suitable for kitchen gardening. The average yield per hectare is about 60 to 65 tonnes.

Pusa Majesty. It is a gynodioecious variety, tolerant to viral diseases and root knot nematodes. The fruits are medium in size with round shape. Flesh is yellowish in colour and solid in texture. It has good keeping quality. The variety is suitable for papain production.

Punjab Sweet : It is dioecious variety having plant height of 195 cm. Fruit bearing starts from a height of 103 cm from the ground level. Fruits are large, oblong in shape with pointed tip. Flesh colour is deep yellow. TSS ranges from 9.0 to 10.5 per cent. The average yield is 50 kg per plant. It is least susceptible to citrus mite ***(Eutetranychus orientalis)*.**

Pusa Giant : This ia a dioecious variety. Plant starts bearing at one meter height within 260 days after transplanting. The plant can withstand strong winds and storms. The fruit size is 2.5 to 3.5 kg per plant. The fruits are suitable for vegetable making and canning industry.

Surya : Developed at IIHR from the cross between Sunrise Solo and Pink Flesh Sweet. It is a gynodioecious hybrid. Fruits are medium in size with average weight of 600–800 g. The pulp is red, sweet with a TSS of 13.5–15.0 per cent.

Solo. The fruits are small in size with deep pink pulp. Taste is sweet. It is excellent kitchen gardening variety. It is a tuble purpose variety.

CO–2, CO–5, CO–6, Red Lady 786, Pant Papaya-1, Pant Papaya-2 and Pant Papaya-3 are other promising varieties.

CO–3, CO–4, CO–7 and CP–81 are the important hybrids of papaya.

PROPAGATION

Papaya is propagated entirely from seed. The conventional methods of vegetative propagation like cuttings, grafting, buddings etc. have not proved useful for one reason or the other. Seeds used for raising the seedlings should be fresh as their viability is lost in about 45 days. The seedlings can be raised both on raised beds in polythene bags.

Preparation of seed-bed and raising of seedlings : The seedbeds are prepared on well drained soil where the farmyard manure is throughly mixed. Generally 40 sq. meters area is sufficient to raise seedlings for transplanting one acre and for this much area one quintal of well rotten farmyard manure is recommended. The seedbed should be 2 meters long, 1 meter wide and 15 cm high above the ground level.

The seeds are sown in the second week of July to third week of September.. However, the nurserymen should sow the seed in two, three lots of 15 days interval. This will help in regulating the plant sale.

Seeds before sowing are treated with 3 g of Captan per kg of seed. About 150 g seed is enough to raise seedlings for one arce. The seeds are sown 2-3 cm deep and 15 cm apart. The distance from row to row is also kept 15 cm. A light irrigation is given immediately after sowing the seed. Give the subsequent irrigation when the beds are still in 'vatar' condition.

Aftercare and transplanting of seedlings : The seeds germinate in 2 to 3 weeks. When the seedlings have emerged, drench the nursery beds with 0.2 per cent Captan (200 g in 100 litres of water) to prevent the damping off young seedlings. Repeat the drenching of nursery-beds after 4 days, if necessary.

One month after the emergence, the seedlings attain the height of about 15 cm and they are recommended for transplanting in the field.

Top dressing of seedlings in nursery with urea or ammonium sulphate should be avoided as this encourages damping of disease and the development of tall and lanky seedlings which are not suitable for transplanting.

Raising the seedlings in polythene bags

Papaya seedlings raised in polythene bags can stand transplanting better than those raised in seed beds.

Perforated ploythene bags of 25 × 10 cm size with 100 gauge thickness can be used for sowing the seed. About 8 to 10 holes of 1 mm diameter are made on the lower part of the polythene bags for drainage. These bags are filled with a mixture of farmyard manure, soil and sand in equal proportion. Two or three seeds are sown in one bag and after germination only one seedling is retained. These seedlings in the polythene bags should be treated with Captan (0.2%) after their emergence. The transplanting in this case is done alongwith polythene bags. Only care taken in this case is that the bags should be ruptured at the bottom while transplanting.

Vegetative methods

Budding : At Varanasi, patch budding on two month old papaya seedlings when done with a scion cultivar Pusa during mid- September have been proved the best, followed by mid August.

Tissue culture : At IARI, New Delhi, propagation of Pusa Delicious by tissue culture has been done. Such plants when raised in field resulted in uniform growth and produced 1.5 times more fruit yield than plants raised by seeds. The **in vitro** plants showed totipotency with regard to the expression of sex.

PLANTING OPERATION

The best time for papaya planting is either July-September or February-March. After through preparation of land, pits measuring 50 cm × 50 cm × 50 cm should be dug out at spacing of 1.5 m × 1.5 m (4400 plants per hectare) and kept exposed for a few days. These should be refilled with a mixture of top soil and well rotton farmyard manure. To each pit add 10 ml of chlorpyriphos

20 EC mixed in 2 kg soil as protection against white ants. When the seedlings have attained a height of 15-25 cm, transplant three seedlings per pit (10-15 cm apart) and apply irrigation. After flowering, which usually takes place within 5-6 months, only one female or bisexual plant per pit is retained. Rest of the male plants are pulled out. However, well scattered male plants (one for every 10-15 female plants) may be retained for pollination purposes.

The planting distance of 2.5 to 3.0 metre is also recommended. The varieties like Co-1, CO-2 and Solo at 1.8 × 1.8 m, Coorg Honey Dew and Washington at 2.4 × 2.4 m and Pusa Nanha at 1.25 × 1.25 m distance can be planted.

FLOWERING AND FRUITING

The species **Carica papaya** is found to flower throughout the year. The inflorescence is axillary in position. Peak anthesis was found between 5 and 6 AM. The stigma receptivity was found to be maximum on the day of anthesis. The inflorescence of Washington papaya emerged 45-48 days after transplanting. The male flower appears in the axil of the 24th leaf and that of female in 18th to 20th leaf. Female and male flowers developed within 32 and 42 days, respectively, after bud initiation. The flower opened between 8 and 11 A.M. Anther dehiscence was completed within 18 to 36 hours before the flowers opened and the stigma become receptive a day before the flowers opened, remaining receptive for 6 days.

The pattern of fruit growth in papaya followed the double sigmoid type. Depending upon the cultivars, the papaya took 145 to 165 days to attain ripe stage from the date of flowering. The colour break stage was characterised by an increase in vitamin A and proteins.

ORCHARD CULTURAL PRACTICES

Irrigation

Adequate irrigation helps in rapid fruit development and also to obtain regular fruit yield. Papaya cannot tolerate wet feet. Heavy irrigation should, therefore, be avoided as otherwise the papaya trees may suffer from root-rot. In well drained soils, irrigation at shorter intervals during the early crop stages results in good establishment and also encourage better plant development. Generally, papaya crop is irrigated at 4-5 days intervals in summer and 8-10 days in winter depending upon climate and soil conditions. The ring system of irrigation is better because it prevents irrigation water from coming into direct contact with the stem, thus preventing collar rot.

Intercropping

The short duration vegetables like radish, tomatoes, cabbage, cauliflower, onion, chillies can be grown as intercrops during the pre-bearing period. The intercrops should be maintained in such a way that they are competing with the main crop. No intercrop should be grown when the plants are in bearing stage. Papaya itself is a popular intercrop with fruit trees. In mango, litchi and pear during first 6-7 years, one or two rows of papaya between the tree rows can be grown profitably. Papaya does not interfere with the main crop because it produces the fruits only for 2-3 years.

Weed Control

Weeding is necessary and should be done regularly to keep the field weed free. In the field with grown up plants, the interspace remains covered well with the top growth which helps in checking weeds. Two hand diggings one in the beginning of rainy season and other in January-February are necessary for papaya plantation every year. Application of fluchloralin or butachlorine @ 2kg/ha as pre-emergence herbicide two months after transplanting check the weeds for 4 months.

Manuring and Fertilization

Papaya is a heavy feeder and responds well to fertilizers. In Punjab, the plant is manured @1.25 kg of fertilizer mixture *i.e.*, Urea, superphosphate and muriate of potash in the ratio of 1 : 2 : 1/3 twice a year *i.e.*, during February and August. Well rotten farmyard manure is applied @ 20 kg per plant every year in December.

A fertilizer trial conducted at IIHR, Bangalore showed the importance of all the three nutrients for high yields. But the effect of phosphorus on yield was pronounced than that of either nitrogen or potash. 500 g of potash per plant/year was the best fertilizer dose and 250 g of each nitrogen and phosphorus gave an yield of 186 tonnes per hectare in the crop life of 28 months. This dose was applied in six split applications. In the form of fertilizers, each papaya tree should be given approximately the following fertilizers at every two months intervals.

(*i*) Ammonium sulphate 200 g

(*ii*) Single superphosphate 250 g

(*iii*) Muriate of potash 140 g

At Coimbatore, application of 200 g each of N, P and K per plant to Co-1 cultivar in addition to 25 kg of farmyard manure in split doses during the first, third, fifth and seventh month after planting resulted in higher fruit yield. A dose of 250 g N, 250 g P and 200 g K per year in split has been recommended for Solo Cultivar.

The fertilizers should be put in irrigation ring or basin and mixed well by light digging. The male plants which function as pollenizers need not be manured.

Zinc and Boron deficiency : Sometimes plant show deficiency of zinc and boron. Give two sprays of 0.5 per cent zinc sulphate to correct zinc deficiency. One spray of 0.1 per cent borax is sufficient to correct boron deficiency.

POLLINATION

When the plants have started flowering, thin out to one plant per pit, taking care that the final population of plants has only 10 per cent males and these are well scattered throughout the field for adequate pollination.

In hermaphrodite varieties generally single robust female plant is left per pit and others are removed.

SEX EXPRESSION

Sex expression in papaya is very complicated phenomenon. **Storey** identified 8 working categories as staminate, teratological staminate, reduced elongata, elongata, carpelloid elongata, pentandria, carpelloid pentandria and pistillate. He further stated that **Carica papaya** has 3 basic sex forms viz. Staminate, pistillate and andromonoecious. The pistillate plant is stable, while staminate and endromonoecious plants may be either phenotypically stable or phenotypically ambivalent going through seasonal sex reversals during which they produce varying proportions of staminate, perfect and pistillate flowers. Staminate flower is produced by male plant. Teratological flower is produced by sex reversing male plants. Reduced elongata, elongata, carpelloid elongata, pentandria and carpelloid pentandria are produced by hermaphrodite plants. Pistillate flower is produced by female plant.

Changes in the sex expression is accelerated by environmental factors such as low temperature to produce perfect flowers on the male plant. Fertile hermaphrodite types also have some pistillate flowers which may show male tendency in summer and female tendency in winter. A large difference between day and night temperature can produce more female flowers than normal. Long day and high temperature has been reported to promote the formation of female flower in Coorg Honey Dew.

The application of growth regulators has been found to change sex in papaya. GA_3 spray at 50 ppm in Co-1 increased the femaleness. It was reported that SADH treatment proved very effective in Co-1 for the control of height, acceleration of flowering and fruiting at lower node, increase in fruit set and yield. TIBA 100 ppm spray to papaya seedlings increased the femaleness. Application of GA_3 on Coorg Honey Dew increased the production of hermaphrodite and staminate flowers, caused a two fold increase in vitamin C contents but reduced the seed number, fruit size and pectin content. Ethephon @ 240–960 ppm and chlorflurenol @ 20–80 ppm induced intersexual and female flowers as well as male flowers on genetically male plants of Honey Dew cultivar. GA at 25 ppm and ethrel at 100 ppm on 100-125 days old seedlings tended to produce more females. Defoliation has been reported to induce maleness.

SEX IDENTIFICATION

It is difficult to identify the correct sex in dioecious type of papaya varieties until their floral emergence.

The use of peroxidase enzyme system for the identification of sex in papaya was tried at Cuba. Peroxidase zymogram patterns established by polyacrylamide get electrophoresis of extracts of leaf, petiole and root tissues from adult plants of 4 clones differed with sex of the plant and a similar differentiation could be recognized in Juvenile plants. More bands were present in the zymograms of male plants than the female plants. On this basis, hermaphrodite plants may not always be distinguishable from female plants. The results of sex expression in Bangladesh revealed that the level of most amino acids has been similar in both male and female except for proline which is present in female plants only and cysteine which is absent in female plants. The level of tryptophan in female has been twice as high as in male plants.

PROTECTION AGAINST FROST

Papaya is very much susceptible to frost damage during winter. It is, therefore, utmost necessary to provide adequate protection against frost in winter under north Indian conditions. This can be done by covering the plants with rice straw or **Sarkanda** thatche or with white polythene bags of the size of plants in first winter. In home gardens, protection against frost hazard can be provided by planting papaya trees sheltered by walls. Furthermore, papaya plantations need to be protected against strong winds by providing effective windbreaks of **Shisham, popular,** etc.

HARVESTING AND HANDLING OF FRUITS

Papaya trees tend to set too many fruits. Such crowded fruits do not get proper space and light resulting in their poor development and poor quality. Thinning of fruits while they are still of small size, is therefore advisable, so that the remaining fruits develop to proper size and are of good quality.

Papaya trees set fruits within 8-10 months of their planting. In another 4-6 months, depending upon the season, the fruits develop to proper size. In North India, fruits ripen during spring and summer. In hills, it is restricted to three to four months from February to May, because it requires a warm climate during ripening.

High humidity and comparatively high temperature during ripening period may not be conducive to development of attractive colour in fruits which may remain pale green even when ripe. When fruit attains ripening, the colour changes from green to yellowish green. To avoid bird damage, harvest the fruits immediately when mature. The fruit is considered ready for harvesting when the latex of the fruit becomes almost watery. Papaya is a climacteric fruit. The individual fruit is harvested with hands. Fruits are not allowed to fall on the ground or come in contact with the soil while plucking.

The yield of papaya varies considerably due to fertility of the soil, cultural practices and variety. The average yield ranges from 30-50 kg per plant. An average yield of about 40-50 tonnes per hectare in the first year and about 20-25 tonnes per hectare in the second year in obtained.

After harvesting, the fruits to be consumed locally should be stored in a single layer of straw until they become mellow. For distant transport, it should be packed in bamboo baskets with rice straw to avoid bruising. The fruit becomes suscpetible to fungal disease like: ***Colletotrichum gloeosporioides***. It can be checked by immersing the fruits in hot water (50°C) for 20 minutes. Papaya fruit was classified as climacteric. It can be ripened artificially by dipping the fruits in 500 ppm ethephon during the end of December under Punjab conditions. The fruits attained golden yellow colour after 4 days of treatment. The ripening was characterised by an increase in the activities of invertase, cellulase, pectinmethylesterase, catalase, peroxidase, adenosine triphosphatase, acid phosphatase, polyphenol oxidase and mitrochondrial glutamate dehydrogenase and falling levels of amylase, ribonuclease, mitochondrial adenosine triphosphatase, NADH diphorase and malic dehydrogenase and of the RNA, DNA; protein and mitrochondrial protein contents.

Room temperature (28-30°C) was found to be practically unsuitable for storage of fruits. A temperature of 20°C was found optimum both for ripening and satisfactory storage. The fruits get susceptible to fungal attack above 20°C, whereas, the onset of climacteric was delayed at lower temperature. Controlled atmosphere storage in 2% oxygen and 98% nitrogen at 10° C has been found to extend the storage life by a few days. Post harvest decay of papaya fruit can effectively be prevented by dipping the fruits in Aureofungin at 1000 ppm.

INSECT-PESTS

1. Red spider mite (*Tetranychus urticae*) : They suck sap from ventral surface of leaves under silken webs. The yellowish spots appear on the dorsal side of the infested leaves which fall finally when get dried.

Remove the infested leaves and burn them. Spray the plant with 0.06 per cent dimethoate. If needed, repeat the spray once after 15 days.

2. White fly (*Bemisia tabaci*) : Tiny, white scale like objects may be seen clustering between the veins on the ventral surface of leaves and sucking cell sap. The leaves become yellowish, wrinkle and curl downwards. The pest is active during dry season. The curling is due to virus transmitted by white flies.

Spray 0.03% demethoate or 0.04% monocrotophos or 250 ml malathion 50 EC in 250 litres of water.

3. Aphids : (*Aphis gossypii* and *Myzus persicae*) : Nymphs and adults inject their saliva and suck the plant sap. They are known to transmit mosaic virus. The early symptoms of the disease are presence of necrotic spots on the leaves which turn later on to blistered patches of green tissues.

Destroy weeds which are additional hosts. Cut and destroy the virus affected plant immediately. For the control of aphids spray 250 ml Malathion 50 EC in 250 litres of water before virus attack begins.

DISEASES

1. Anthracnose : The disease is caused with fungus ***Colletotrichum gloeosporioides.*** Fruits are severly affected at all stages of growth. The affected spot on the fruit become depressed and bear pinkish masses of spores of the fungus. The infected leaves bearing spots show shredded margins.

Destroy the infected fruits. Spray 0.2% Ziram or Captan or Indofil M 45 (200 g in 100 litres of water) at fortnightly intervals.

2. Collar rot and Stem rot : The disease is caused by a soil-dwelling fungus ***Pythium aphanidermatum*** or by ***Phytophthora palmivora.*** Roots and the trunk of the plant rot. The fungus advances up into the collar and the trunk regions causing the yellowish of the foliage, stunting of the growth and poor fruit development leading to the death of the plant.

For its control improve drainage. Uproot and destroy the affected plants immediately. Spraying of one per cent Bordeaux mixture or Copper oxychloride @ 2 g per litre of water will check further spread of this disease.

3. Damping off : It is caused due to ***Pythium*** sp., ***Phytophthora*** sp. or ***Rhizoctonia solani***. The disease is common in nursery beds and cause mortality of seedlings. The disease is more serious during rainy season.

This could be prevented by sterilizing the soil of the seed bed with 2.5 per cent formaldehyde solution prior to sowing of seeds. Treating of seeds with seed dressing chemical (Ceresan, Agrosan or Thiram) also provides good check.

4. Papaya mosaic : It is caused due to papaya mosaic virus. Leaves become small, curled and wrinkled. The diseased leaves show blister like patches of green tissue of yellow background. The disease is transmitted through sap, graft and several species of aphids.

Spray 250 ml of Malathion 50 EC in 250 litres of water against aphids and white flies before the virus attack begins. Uproot and destroy the affected plants immediately.

5. Papaya leaf curl : It is caused due to Tobacco leaf curl virus. Young leaves at the top of the affected plant become curled, twisted and deformed and deep green. Such plants become stunted and bear no fruit. The vector of this disease is white fly. It is graft transmissible but not by sap.

Uproot and destroy the leaf curl affected plants immediately. Control the vector with Rogor 0.03 per cent or monocrotophos 0.04 per cent or 250 ml malathion in 250 litres of water.

CHAPTER 10

Pineapple

The pineapple (***Ananas comosus*** L. Merr) is one of the most important commercial fruits of the world. It is considered the popular fruit of tropical climate.

ORIGIN AND HISTORY

Pineapple is believed to have originated in Brazil. It has spread to other tropical parts of the world from Brazil. The generic name **Ananas** is derived from the Indian 'nana'. The wild Brazilian pineapple (***Ananas microstachys*** Lindle) is considered to be its ancestor. Pineapple had spread to the other parts of tropical America by the time of Columbus, who took it to Europe. In 1548, it reached India. The important pineapple countries of the world are Thailand. Brazil, Costa Rica, Philippines, China, Indonesia, India, Nigeria, Mexico and Viet-Nam.

AREA AND PRODUCTION

The area under pineapple in the world is 9.3 lakh hectares with total production of 21.7 million metric tonnes. Thailand, Brazil, Costa Rica and Philippines are the leading pineapple producing countries with a share of 12, 10.7, 10.5 and 10.4 per cent, respectively of the total world production.

In India, pineapple is grown on 1.02 lakh hectares with annual production of 15 lakh metric tonnes. There has been phenomenal increase in production and productivity due to adoption of improved production technologies especially in Karnataka, West Bengal and Kerala. At present, the total area under pineapple is only 1.5 per cent of total area under fruits and the production is 2 per cent of total fruit production in India. The productivity of pineapple is low in North Eastern states which is 6-8 tonnes per hectare owing to traditional methods of cultivation against 58 tonnes per hectare in Karnataka.

In India, pineapple is cultivated commercially in West Bengal, Assam, Tripura, Karnataka, Bihar, Manipur, Meghalaya, Nagaland, Kerala and Arunachal Pradesh. The average productivity of pinapple is observed highest in Karnataka (58 mt/ha) and West Bengal (30.7 mt/ha). Normally, area under pineapple cultivation is confined to high rainfall and humid coastal regions in the peninsular India and to the hilly areas of North Eastern region of the country. Of late, it has been shown that pineapple can also be grown commercially in the interior plains with medium rainfall and supplementary protective irrigations.

Export potential : Pineapple fruits are exported Maldives, Nepal, UAE, Qatar, Oman, Bahrain, Georgia, Saudi Arabia, Pakistan and Italy. India his exported 3031 mt pineapple fruits during 2011-12 and earned Rs. 6 crores. Maldives, Nepal, UAE and Qatar are the major countries where pineapple is exported.

IMPORTANCE AND USES

Pineapple is a good source of vitamin A and B and fairly rich in vitamin C and minerals like calcium, phosphorus and iron. It is also a source of bromelain, a protein digesting enzyme. A pineapple fruit contains moisture 85.0 per cent, sugar 13 per cent, protein 0.7 per cent, mineral matter 0.05 per cent, fibre 0.3 per cent, calcium 0.04 per cent, phosphorus 0.011 per cent, iron 0.09 per cent, vitamin A 60 I.U., vitamin B_2 (Riboflavin) 120 mg/100 g and vitamin C 63 mg/100 g of fruit.

The fresh fruit of pineapple is used as dessert fruit in the form of slices. The fruit is used for juice, squash, jam, mixed jam and in canned form. Fruit core is used for preparing candy. Pineapple leaf is a good source of chlorophyll. Leaves yield silky fibre which is used for making a fine fabric popularly known as pina cloth in Philippines and Taiwan. These are also used for Cordage. The other products like oxalic acid, gum and pineapple flavour are also obtained. Pineapple fruit can also be used for making vinegar, citric acid, calcium citrate and alcohol.

BOTANY

Pineapple belongs to the family Bromeliaceae. It is separated from other genera of this family largely on the basis of syncarpous type of fruit which is not found in the rest of the family. Earlier, ***Ananas*** was considered as a monotypic genus including many cultivars but with only one species. Later on two genera ***Ananas*** and ***Pseudananas*** were established. In ***Pseudananas*** syncarp at maturity bears a minute inconspicuous coma of bracts and produces elongated stolens and no slips. In ***Ananas*** syncarp bears conspicuous coma of foliaceous bracts and plants produce slips but never produce stolon. In ***Ananas comosus***, syncarp is well over 15 cm long at maturity, floral bracts are relatively inconspicuous and soon exposing the tops of the ovaries and the flesh is palatable. Fruits are normally seedless and the ovules abort and only traces of them can be found in mature fruits. The genera ***Ananas*** has important species like ***Ananas bracteatus, Ananas ananassoides, Ananas fritzmuelleri, Annas comosus*** and ***Ananas erectifolius***. The genera ***Pseudananas*** has one species ***Pseudananas sagenarius.***

Pineapple cultivars are grouped into five categories.

1. **Spanish Group :** Fruit shape globose with large deep set eyes e.g. Red Spanish, Singapore Spanish.
2. **Queen Group :** Fruit shape conical with deep eyes e.g. Queen, Alexandera, Jhaldup and Bakhat.
3. **Abacaxi Group :** Fruits conical in shape e.g. Perola, Amarella, Abakka.
4. **Cayenne Group :** Fruit shape cylindrical with slight upward taper and flat eyes. e.g. Cayenne, Rothschild, Giant kew, Mauritius.
5. **Maipure Group :** Fruit shape cylinderical - ovoid to cylindrical e.g. Maipure, Randon.

Pineapple fruit type is sorosis. Peduncle, perianth and bracts are the edible portions.

CLIMATE

The pineapple is a plant of humid tropics but is known to adapt well in subtropical areas. The fruit grows well near the sea coasts as well as in the interior, so long as the temperature are not extreme. The optimum temperature range for successful pineapple cultivation is between 22 to 32°C. Leaves and roots grow best at 32°C and 29°C respectively and their growth practically ceases below 20°C and above 36°C. A high temperature at night is deleterious and a difference of at least 4°C between day and night temperatures is desirable.

Pineapple can be grown upto an elevation of 1,100 metres above sea level. It is sensitive to frost. A mildly cool winter improves fruit quality. Pineapple shows a remarkable ability to grow and produce crops under a wide range of rainfall conditions, although the optimum annual rainfall for commercial production ranges from 100 to 150 cm. It grows in Golaghat in Assam with annual rainfall of 75 cm and in Khasi hills with 500 cm. In the areas where the rainfall is less, supplementary protective irrigations are necessary during dry season. The localities facing strong winds should be avoided as ends of leaves get bruised.

SOIL

The pineapple plant comes up well in any type of soil except on very heavy clay soil. Sandy and loamy soils or laterite soils on hill tops are best for pineapple. The soil should be 45-60 cm in depth without hardpan or stones. Low lying areas with high water table should be avoided. The plant prefers the soil pH of 5.0 - 6.0. Alkaline soils are not considered suitable. Light soils produce fruits of good quality whereas yield is comparatively higher in heavy soils. High manganese-ferrous ratio in soil is considered injurious.

CHOICE OF VARIETIES

Kew : The Giant Kew or Kew is the important commercial cultivar of India. This variety belongs to Cayenne group and is considered best for canning in India. The fruits are of big size ranging 1.5 to 2.5 kg in weight, oblong in shape and tapering slightly towards the crown. Eyes are broad and shallow, making the fruits more suitable for canning. The fruit is yellow when fully ripe and the flesh is light yellow ; almost fibreless, very juicy and of agreeable taste. The leaves often have a short sector of small margin of spines just behind the tip and irregularly on the base near its attachment to the stem. The fruit becomes ready for harvesting in August-September.

Queen : This is an earliest ripening variety which ripens in June-July. The plant, fruit and shoots of Queen are smaller that in Kew. This variety is mostly grown in Tripura and partly in Assam and Meghalaya. The fruit is rich yellow in colour and weighs from 0.9 to 1.3 kg. The flesh is deep golden yellow, less juicy than Kew, crisp textured with a pleasant aroma and flavour. Eyes are small and deep, requiring a thicker cut when removing the skin. The leaves are brownish red, shorter and very spiny.

Mauritius : It is a mid-season variety ripening in July-August. The variety is grown in some parts of Kerala. Fruit is medium in size weighing 1.5 to 2.5 kg. Two types with deep yellow and red coloured fruits are found. Yellow variety is oblong, fibrous and medium sweet compared to red type. This variety is exclusively grown for table purpose. Leaves are yellowish green spiny throughout the margin. The red skinned type have round base and sloping abruptly towards the crown. Crown in both types is spiny.

Charlotte Rothschild : This variety is partly under cultivation in Kerala and Goa. The fruit characteristics and taste is similar to that of Kew variety.

Other Varieties : Cayenne, Jhaldup, Singapure Spanish (Ruby), Red Spanish, and Baruipur are other important varieties of pineapple grown in different parts of India.

PROPAGATION

Pineapple is mainly propagated by vegetative methods. It can be propagated by shoot suckers, ground suckers, slips, crown, stem- bits and from splitted crowns. However, suckers, slips and crowns are the three important types of materials used for planting. Suckers arise from the axils of the leaves just below the ground level and the slips are found on the fruit stalk below the fruit. Suckers and slips are usually preferred for planting since they flower comparatively earlier than the crowns. Suckers produce the first crop in 15-18 months after planting while the slips take 20-22 months for the first crop. Crowns take more than 24 months for the first crop. Suckers weighing around 450 g and slips weighing about 350 g are the best planting material for Kew pineapple. Small sized suckers, slips and overgrown suckers may be used only in case of non-availability of the ideal plant material. Fresh suckers and slips should be left to dry and should not be stored for more than 14 days. In shy suckering varieties, sucker production can be increased with high dose of nitrogen, more moisture and application of maleic hydrazide.

When there is shortage of planting material, the leaf cuttings from the crowns can be used for multiplication of planting material. From each crown, ten to fifteen leaf cuttings are made. Cuttings are dipped in 0.3% solution of Dithane Z-78 (3 g in 1 litre of water) for about 5 minutes and then planted. These cuttings will take even more time for flowering than crowns. Thus, they are only recommended where planting material is not available and more area is to be covered under this crop.

The root primordia are present in the basal portion of the planting material which are covered by scaly leaves. After removing scaly leaves, the planting material should be treated with Ekatox (0.05%) and Dithane Z-78 (0.3%) on Difolatan (0.4%) solution to protect against mealy bugs and heart rot, respectively. If the plants are to be stored, these should be arranged up side down under shade instead of heaping them.

PLANTING OPERATION

Double row method of planting is considered best for pineapple. The spacing of 30, 60 and 90 cm between plants, rows and beds respectively in a double row planting system accommodates 43,500 plants per hectare. Little less spacing between plants i.e. 25 cm and 60 and 90 cm spacing between rows and beds accommodates 53,000 plants per hectare. But plant to plant distance of 22.5 cm, row to row 45 cm and trench to trench 90 cm accommodates 63,500 plants per hectare. The plant density of 64,000 with a spacing of 25 cm × 35 cm × 90 cm in double row system is considered most suitable under North Bengal condition. Further increase in plant density to 25 × 35 × 75 cm, accommodates 72, 727 plants per hectare.

The population density ranging from 53,000 to 63,500 plants per hectare could be easily accommodated yielding 85 to 105 tonnes per hectare without adversely affecting the fruit size, quality and canning recovery. In rainfed, high fertile and hilly areas, a lower planting density of 43,500 plants per hectare is recommended. High planting density gives more profits apart from other advantages like less weed infestation, protection from sun burn, increased production of suckers and slips per unit area and non-lodging of plants. Close planting saves the cost of providing shade to the fruits and results in uniformly coloured lustrous fruits. In wider spacing, 20-25 per cent of the fruits get sun- burn. Close planting also helps in moisture conservation of soil, as the transpirational loss is much less when compared to evaporation from soil. It was also been possible to take atleast two crops under high density planting. Hence it is recommended to plant pineapple as close as possible ensuring sufficient space for carrying out the cultural operations.

Usually planting is done during monsoon season to take advantage of soil moisture. The planting in the month of July-August is considered best for establishment and growth of plant. The best months for planting in the North Bengal districts are October and November and in the other districts June-July. Planting should be avoided during heavy rains to prevent heart rot. Where irrigation facilities are available, planting could be taken up all around the year.

FLOWERING AND FRUITING

After attainment of certain vegetative growth and ripeness-to- flower stage, pineapple plants flower 11-12 months after planting and formation of atleast 40 leaves. A pineapple plant produces only one fruit during its life time. It is often observed that even after 15 to 18 months of growth under optimal nutritional and environmental conditions only 40 to 50 per cent plants come to flowering. Irregular flowering behaviour of pineapple is one of the limiting factor in its cultivation. Flowering in pineapple may be induced if the stems are kept in horizontal position, due to geotropism. In this way, accumulation of auxin induces bud initiation.

The fruit growth of pineapple in terms of length, breadth and weight follows a pattern of sigmoid growth. In Kew pineapple, prematuration stage covered 0-120 days, early mature 120-150 days and late mature covered 150-165 days and the fruits ripened after 165 days. Fruit growth increased cantinuously upto 120 days but the rate of increase was less pronounced from 120 – 150 days. The increase in fruit weight was maximum between 30 – 90 days. The juice content increased from 30 – 60 days. Total soluble solids and sugars showed a rise till harvest but rate of increase was more between 60 to 120 days. Starch contents declined during 90-100 days and increased thereafter.

ORCHARD CULTURAL PRACTICES

Irrigation

In India, pineapple is mostly grown under rainfed conditions. Supplementary irrigation can help in production of good sized fruits in areas having optimum rainfall. Irrigation can also be helpful in the establishment of off-season plantings with a view to maintain the year round production of fruits for feeding the canning factories. At Hessaraghatta, it was observed that 20 per cent available moisture, is as good as 80-100 per cent available moisture in the field, without affecting the size, yield and quality. Therefore, 4-6 irrigations in hot months at 20-25 days interval ensure good crop.

Earthing up

Earthing up is most important operation in pineapple culture. The operation gives better anchorage to the plant. This becomes more important in ratoon crops. Earthing up should be done after each fertilizer application and also after the harvest of the crop.

Weed Control

The major factor which contributes to the high cost of production of pineapple is the manual weeding which accounts for nearly 40% of the total cost. Chemicals have proved to be effective in controlling weeds in pineapple plantation and in bringing down the cost of weeding considerably. The weeds can be effectively controlled by spraying a combination of Bromacil and Diuron @ 2 kg a.i./hectare each as pre-emergence herbicides as soon as the pineapple suckers are planted. In established pineapple plantation, the weeds have to be removed before the spray is given as these herbicides do not kill the established weeds very effectively. Simazine and Diuron @ 4 kg/ha as pre-emergene herbicides are very much effective against grasses and sedges. Bromacil alone @ 3 kg a.i./hectare can be as effective against motha (***Cyprus rotundus***). Diuron @ 2 kg a.i and Bromacil @ 3 kg. a.i/ha applied at an intervals of 6 months effectively reduced both dicot and monocot weeds and increase the yield by 18 per cent as compared to control. Bromacil and Diuron work every effectively in sandy and clay loam soils. In areas where the density of weed flora is heavy, the effect of herbicides may break down after one year and a second spray consisting of half the concentration of the first spray may have to be given.

Manuring and Fertilization

Pineapple require nitrogen and potash for better yield and fruit quality. Nutritional removal from pineapple plantation yielding 400 quintals of fruits per hectare is nitrogen 123 kg, phosphorus, 33 kg and potassium 308 kg. At Bangalore, it was concluded that 12 g N per plant is ideal under irrigated conditions. Under rainfed conditions, a dose of 16 g N per plant was found to be necessary for getting higher yield. Potash @ 12 g per plant is recommended for irrigated as well as rainfed crops. No response to phosphorus was observed. For Kew pineapple 600 kg N per hectare is considered optimum for a plant population ranging from 43,500-63,500 plants per hectare.

In West Bengal, it was reported that nitrogen at 12–16 g, phosphorus at 2–4 g and potassium at 10-12 g per plant should be the optimum for a plant density of 51,000 per hectare. However, the highest yield with N, P and K @ 600, 400 and 600 g per hectare, respectively was reported in plant density of 64000 and 72,727 per hectare.

Application of organic manure is done a fortnight before planting. The fertilizers are applied in two split doses, once at the onset of mansoon (May-June) and again at the end of rains (September-October) after the fruits are harvested and slips and suckers are removed.

The ammonium sulphate is considered the best source of nitrogen when applied to soil and was far superior to both calcium ammonium nitrate and urea. It resulted into highest fruit weight, yield and sucker production.

Foliar application of urea at 4 – 5 per cent in dry season and 10 per cent in wet season are useful.

Micronutrient requirements : Usually iron, zinc and copper deficiencies are common in pineapple. Spraying the iron affected plants with a 3 per cent solution of ferrous sulphate is ideal. In very acute iron deficiency, sprayings have to be repeated at monthly intervals. To correct zinc deficiency, foliar application of 1 per cent zinc sulphate solution is given. Application of zinc 2ppm extended the cropping period and improved fruit quality. Copper sulphate cannot be applied as a spray to the leaves since it causes severe scorching. Spraying on the ground near the plants with 1.5 to 2.0 per cent solution, 30 to 50 ml of this solution are distributed at a distance of 3-5 cm from the base of plant.

USE OF GROWTH REGULATORS

Flowering in pineapple can be induced with the use of growth regulators. Among the auxin substances, NAA and planofix have been reported to be very effective in the induction of flowering. NAA at 10 – 15 ppm is very effective in flower induction. Plants raised from suckers and treated with 100 ppm ethrel + 2% urea + 0.04% $CaCO_3$ at 18 months after planting gave 96 per cent flowering. Plants raised from crown similarly treated at 17 months after planting gave 91.8 per cent flowering. Application of ethrel (0.25 ml/litre) in June caused early induction and appearance of inflorescence.

NAA at 200-300 ppm at 2-3 months after fruit set increased the fruit size by 15-20 per cent. Fruit size can also be increased to some extent by partial pinching of crown one month after fruit set. NAA (300 mg/litre) 45 days after emergence of inflorescence showed an increase in weight and size and reduction in total soluble soild and soluble sugar content. Ethrel @ 0.50 ml/1 on NAA treated fruits at 120 days after flower emergence improve the fruit quality.

AFTER CARE OF RATOON CROP

After the harvest of fruit, desuckering should be done immediately leaving only one sucker on the mother plant and all the slips should be removed. Never allow to retain more than two suckers. Plants should be fertilized and earthed up so that they can have good anchorage for the ratoon crop.

HARVESTING AND HANDLING OF FRUITS

Pineapple is non-climacteric fruit and should be harvested ripe. It usually flowers from February to April and ripens in July to September. In Kew variety off-season flowering occurs about 10-15 per cent and such fruits ripens from September to December. The fruits mature in winter are more acidic and not considered for table purpose. In Andhra Pradesh, the fruits are harvested from June to August. The fruits ripens from April to June in West Coast. For local market harvesting should be done at full maturity stage. However, for distant markets, the fruits should be harvested at 75-80 per cent maturity stage. At maturity, the lower most eyelets in the cultivar Kew show orange-yellow colour and eyes get flattened in the centre and bulge on the sides. The bracts become loose and turn brown. The fruits of Kew pineapple harvested between 115 to 130 days after flowering are better suited for canning. Harvesting should be done with a sharp knife severing the fruit stalk with a clean cut and retaining 5-7 cm of the stalk. Crown should be retained otherwise its removal quickens the ripening process and thus reduces the life of the fruit. The fruit should be protected from mechanical injury on the skin to avoid fruit rot. The cut end of the fruit stalk may be dipped in 10 per cent solution of benzoic acid in alcohol to check attack of fungus.

Ethrel treatment was found effective in enhancing uniform ripening in pineapple. Pre-harvest treatment of mature green pineapple cv. Perola with ethrel at 500-2000 ppm resulted in the development of uniform yellow colour in 8 days.

The yield is recorded about 65 tonnes from a population density of 43,500 plants per hectare. The yield goes higher *i.e.* 80 to 100 tonnes when density of plants ranges from 53,000 to 63,500 plants per hectare. In South India, average yield of 125 quintals per hectare has been recorded. Higher yield upto 200 quintals per hec, has been observed in Kew variety. The fruit size and yield decreased considerably with the age of plantation. Thus, plantation should be renewed after every 4-5 years.

The fruits should be handled carefully after harvest. Mechanical injury on the skin can cause fruit rotting during transit or in storage. The fruits are graded on the basis of size, shape and colour. Normally fruits are graded into 5 grades on the basis of weight. The fruits weighing above 1500 g are placed in A grade, 1100 – 1500 g in B grade, 800 – 1100 g in C grade, 550 – 800 g in D grade and less than 550 g in E (baby) grade. The fruits are packed into fibreboard or wood containers for distant transport. A fixed number of fruits are either placed horizontally or vertically in the boxes.

Healthy fruits can be stored well for 15-20 days under ordinary conditions. The mature and ripe fruits can be stored at 11-13°C and 85-90 per cent relative humidity for about 5-6 weeks. Shelf life of fruits can be extended upto six weeks in good condition after treating with 500 ppm NAA or 100 ppm GA.

AVAILABILITY OF FRUITS THROUGHOUT THE YEAR

It is possible to spread the harvesting of fruit throughout the year using following techniques:

(*i*) By using different planting materials.

(*ii*) By planting suckers and slips at regular intervals from July to December.

(*iii*) By applying flower inducing chemicals like ethephon @ 0.25 ml/litre or NAA @ 20 mg/litre.

Studies conducted in West Bengal regarding the harvesting of fruit throughout the year revealed that slips of the pineapple should be planted from July to November.

Ethrel @ 0.25 ml/litre or NAA @ 20 mg/litre be applied between 365 and 415 days after planting. Ethrel solution should be applied at the core of the plant between 7-8 PM in the evening. Application of ethephon at an interval of 7 days from April to November can ensure a steady harvest of fruits almost throughout the year. Fruits from NAA treatment are heavier whereas ethephon induce better quality. NAA causes much delay in fruit maturity. For obtaining a good yield, the plants must have at least 45 to 50 leaves for flowering.

INSECT-PESTS

Mealy bug (*Pseudococcus brevipes*)

The wilting of pineapple is caused either due to toxic secretions of the insects or due to the virus introduced into the plant by the feeding of pest. At first instance, the roots cease to grow, then follow collapse and rotting of the tissue. The wilting of leaves is the prominent symptoms and develope reddish yellow colour.

For its control, collect the plant material from healthy plantation. The basal portion of slips and sucker should be dipped in 0.04% methyl parathion or malathion solution. Application of phorate granules 1.75 kg a.i/ha at 100 days after planting is effectve to control the pest.

Pineapple thrips (*Thrips tabaci*)

Damage is done by adults as well as by nymphs to flowers and leaves. Spray 625 ml of malathion 50 EC in 250 litres of water per ha as soon as the pest appears.

Root-knot nematode (*Meloidogyne spp, Pratylenchus spp, Rotylenchus spp*)

Several nematodes causes large scale damage in pineapple plantations. They attack the roots causing root-knots and lesions or penetrate partially into the roots. The attack is common in light soils. Nematodes can be controlled by fumigation of soil with ethylene dibromide 15 at 250 – 350 litres per hectare or EDB at 100 kg/ha before planting.

DISEASES

1. Heart rot and Stem rot : The disease is caused by fungus *Phytophthora parasitica* and *Phytophthora cinnamomi.*

Poor physical condition of the soil and inadequate drainage are responsible for the spread of this disease. Infected plants loose their turgidity. Leaves start twisting, withering of central leaves and result into their discolouration. The central whorl of leaves when affected will come out with a gentle pull. The fungus can survive in soil.

Select healthy planting material and handle it carefully. Proper drainage of water is essential. Prior to planting, treat the planting material with 4:4:50 Bordeaux mixture. Affected plantation should be sprayed with Captan or difolatan 0.1 per cent.

2. Soft rot, Storage rot and Fruit rot : These are caused by fungus *Ceratostomella paradoxa.* Fruit rot is not seen usually in the field and generally appears in storage and transit. Fruit shows water-soaked lesions which turn yellowish and dark. The affected tissues rot. The stem-end rot and soft rot are also noticed. The fungus invades through wounds or cut-ends and spreads inter and intracellularly.

Collect the affected plants and destroy them. It is advisable to collect the suckers from disease free area for planting. Before planting, dip suckers in 2:2:250 Bordeaux mixture solution. The cut end of the fruit stalk should be dipped in 10 per cent solution of benzoic acid dissolved in alcohol. Expose the fruits for 2 hours to the sun during harvesting. Dipping the fruits for 5 minutes in Thiabendazole 100 ppm minimise rotting.

3. Leaf spot : The disease is also caused due to *Phytophthora* sp. It occurs under moist warm climate. Small water soaked areas develop on the leaves and these gradually enlarge with straw coloured halo and the affected portions gradually dry. The disease can be kept under control by spraying Manozeb/Ziram 200 gm 100 litres of water.

DISORDERS

1. Sunscald

Sunscald is caused due to direct fall of sunrays on exposed area of the fruits and results in damage to fruits. The cells under the skin of exposed surface get damaged. Later shell surface assumes a brownish to black colour and cracks may appear between fruitlets. Affected fruits rot and get easily infested with pests. To control lodging or leaning, special care should be given. The fruits should be covered with dry straw or banana leaves or with own leaves during the month of April-May. Intensity of sunscald is reduced in high density planting.

2. Multiple Crown

Multiple crown may occur due to genetical factors as well as due to soil and environmental reasons which result in impairment in normal growth and development of fruits during ontogeny.Such fruits also taste insipid and are more corky. In fertile virgin soil of warm areas, more abnormal fruits occur as compared to less fertile soil.

CHAPTER 11

Guava

Guava (***Psidium guajava*** Linn) is a tropical fruit but also grows well under sub-tropical conditions. Popularly it is known as 'Apple of Tropics.' It is one of the most common and major fruit of India and considered the fifth most important fruit in area and production after mango, citrus, banana and apple. Guava is hardy, prolific bearer and highly remunerative fruit. It is found favour with the fruit growers due to its wide adaptability and higher return per unit area. Guava is such a fruit which is grown all over the country in the kitchen gardening, near the well and tubewell premises and on a commercial scale.

ORIGIN AND HISTORY

Guava is native to central America and seems to have been growing from Mexico to Peru. It is believed to be introduced in India since early 17th century. Guava is cultivated on commercial scale in Mexico, Peru, Egypt, India, South Africa, USA, Algeria, Brazil, Columbia, West Indies, etc.

AREA AND PRODUCTION

India rank first in guava production in the world followed by Pakistan. The other countries producing guava are Thialand, Indonesia, China, Mexico, Brazil, Philippines, Bangladesh and Nigeria.

In India, guava occupies an area of 2.20 lakh hectares with annual production of 25.10 lakh tonnes and accounting for 3.33 per cent each of area and production. Maharashtra is the largest producer of guava accounting for 12.8 per cent followed by Madhya Pradesh (10.2%), Uttar Pradesh (10.0%) and Bihar (9.76%) although best quality guava are produced in Uttar Pradesh. The district of Allahabad has a reputation of growing the best guava in the country and in the world. In India, guava is widely grown in Maharashtra, Bihar, Madhya Pradesh, Chhattisgarh, Uttar Pradesh, Odisha, West Bengal, Gujarat, Andhra Pradesh, Punjab, Tamil Nadu, Karnataka and Assam.

In Punjab, guava is cultivated on large scale in all the district. It rank second in cultivation after citrus. Total area in the state is 8072 hectares. Whereas the annual production is 177570 tonnes. The districts of Patiala, Ludhiana, Sangrur, SAS Nagar, Ferozepur, Jalandhar, Muktsar, Bathinda, Ropar and Amritsar are known for guava cultivation.

Export potential : India has exported 1382 metric tonnes guavas and earned foreign exchange of Rs. 3.18 crores during the year 2011-12. The guava fruit is exported mainly to

Saudi Arabia, Netherlands, Yemen Republic, UAE, Bahrain, Maldives, Qatar, Switzerland and Japan. The major share of fruits to the tune of 59.6 per cent was exported to Saudi Arabia.

IMPORTANCE AND USES

Guava is the rich source of vitamin C, vitamin A, vitamin B_2 (riboflavin) and minerals like calcium, phosphorus and iron. The vitamin C content of guava fruit is four-five times higher than the citrus fruits. The quality of winter season fruit is considered superior than rainy season fruit. The ripe fruit of Sardar guava (winter season) contains 13.29 per cent total soluble solids, 0.33 per cent acidity, 4.64 per cent reducing sugars, 7.87 per cent total sugars, 1.11 per cent starch, 200-300 mg/100 g ascorbic acid and 1.15 per cent pectin. TSS-acid ratio of Allahabad Safeda is 42:1 and 39:1 in rainy season and winter season crop, respectively. In Lucknow-49, this ratio is 58:1 in rainy season crop and 40:1 in winter season crop.

Guava fruits are used for making juice, jam , jellies and various culinary purposes. The fruit can be canned in sugar syrup. The leaves of guava has been used for curing diarrhoea. Guava fruit contain antioxidant factors and is known to control systolic blood pressure.

BOTANY

Most of the cultivars of guava belong to ***Psidium guajava*** L. Apart from cultivated guava, some other allied species with edible fruits are there. The genus **Psidium** belongs to family Myrtaceae and contains about 150 species. The important species are described below :

1. *Psidium guajava* L. (Common guava)**:** It is a small tree, sometimes growing to 8 or 9 metres. The trunk is slender with greenish brown scaly bark. The young branchlets are quadrangular. The leaves are oblong-elliptic, oval in outline, 7-15 cm long, acute to round at the apex, finely pubescent below, with the venation conspicuously impressed on the upper surface. White solitary flowers or several together upon a slender peduncle are produced on branchlets of recent growth and are 2.5 cm broad. The calyx splits into irregular segments. In the centre of the flower is cluster of long stamens. Ovary is inferior. The fruit a berry is round, ovoid or pyriform, 2.5 to 10 cm in length, commonly yellow in colour with flesh varying from white to deep pink or lemon. Edible portion of fruit is thalamus and pericarp. Numerous small reniform, hard seeds are embeded in the soft flesh towards the centre of the fruit. The flavour is sweet, musky and the ripe fruit is aromatic in a high degree.

2. *Psidium cattleianum* Sabine (Cattley or Chinese or Strawberry guava)**:** It is a native of Brazil. Cattley guava is ornamental in appearance and is a favourite garden shrub in many regions. It is bushy shrub, sometimes becomes a small tree up to 7 metres high. The bark is smooth, grey brown in colour and the young branchlets are cylindrical. The leaves are elliptic to obovate in outline, acute, 5-7 cm long, thick and leathery in texture and deep green in colour. The flowers singly produced upon axillary peduncles are white and nearly about 2.5 cm broad. The calyx is obscurely lobed. The fruit is obovate to round in form 2-3 cm in diameter, purplish red in colour with a thin skin. The flesh is soft, white towards the centre and contains numerous hard seed. The flavour is sweet and aromatic suggesting that of strawberry.

3. *Psidium guineense* Sw. (Brazilian guava)**:** It is a shrub or small tree of slender habit. The young branchlets are compressed-cylindrical and finely hairy. The leaves are ablong-oval, acute or obtuse, 8-12 cm long with lower surface pubescent. The flowers of which one to three are borne upon a single peduncle. The fruit is round or nearly so, 2-3 cm in diameter, greenish yellow and rather hard when ripe. The flesh is whitish containing numerous small seeds. The flavour is sub acid and not so musky as that of common guava.

4. *Psidium friedrichsthalianum* Berg. (Coosta Rican guava)**:** It is a tall tree about 7-10 *m* high having slender and smooth branches, oval or oblong-oval, smooth leaves which are almost glossy above and puberulent below. The fruits of this species are small and globose in shape. The fruits have high acid content. It is a wilt resistant species and used as a wilt resistant rootstock in different parts of the world.

5. *Psidium montanum* Sw. (Mountain guava)**:** It is a shrub about 1-5 m high with flat round branchlets. Leaves elliptic, oblong-elliptic. Fruits are green, subglobose about 2 cm in diameter and very fragrant. It is found on the mountains in Jamaica.

6. *Psidium pyriferum* L. (Pear fruited guava) : It is a small tree, hardy and prefers warm climate for flowering and fruiting. The fruit has white flesh and small seeds with a nice smooth guava flavour. The plant can be easily grown in container for the house or green house.

CLIMATE

Guava cultivation can be extended to varying agro-climatic regions owing to wider adaptability. It is successfully grown under tropical and subtropical climate. Guava does well up to an altitude of 1000 to 1500 metres. It grows best with annual rainfall below 100 cm restricted between June to September. The optimum temperature requirement of guava ranges between 23°C - 28°C. The areas having distinct winter season, is considered best for increasing yield and improving quality. The humid conditions leads to luxurient growth of the trees and yielded poor quality fruits. The young plants are susceptible to drought and cool temperature. It can be grown as rainfed as well as irrigated crop depending upon agro-climatic conditions. At the time of flowering and fruiting, it requires dry climatic conditions. High temperature and high velocity winds at fruit development period lead to heavy fruit drop.

SOIL

Guava is a hardy fruit tree and can be grown to wider adaptability even under marginal soil. It can thrive well on all types of soil. Guava can be grown on poor wasteland soils. It is sensitive to waterlogged conditions. For successful cultivation, the soils for guava are deep, friable, light sandy loam to clay and well-drained soils. Guava is known for its tolerance to salt. It can grow in soil having pH 6.5 to 8.5. Guava is a surface rooted plant, therefore, the surface soil should be rich. Maximum concentration of roots are between 0 – 20 cm soil depth.

CHOICE OF VARIETIES

The following are the important varieties of guava cultivated throughout the country.

Allahabad Safeda: This variety has dwarf tree with a compact, globose, round crown and drooping branches. Tree height is 4.5 - 6 metres, growth upright to spreading, branches heavy with dense foliage, tendency to produce long shoot. Leaves large slightly folded, elliptical to ovate oblong, apex and base obtuse with entire margin. Fruit medium, roundish and slightly depressed at both ends, surface smooth, glossy, skin colour straw yellow. It has thin dots, medium scattered. Calyx medium, closed, cavity shallow. Pulp soft to melting, white, flavour very pleasant, taste very sweet, fruit quality excellent, with 10-12 per cent T.S.S . Seeds about 310 and viable. It bears heavily. In full grown trees, the fruit yield may vary from 120 to 140 kg per tree.

Sardar (Lucknow – 49): It is a selection from Allahabad Safeda made by Dr. G.S. Cheema at Pune. The tree is dwarf, height 6-7 metres, growth upright, spreading, somewhat flattened top, dense foliage, branching heavily. Leaves medium, leathery and folded, ovate oblong, apex obtuse, base round. Fruit medium to large, weight about 182. g, form roundish ovate, rough surface having few ribs on it, skin colour straw yellow, thin dots medium close, base round, apex flat. Calyx large open, cavity shallow. Pulp crispy, soft, cream white, flavour slightly acidic, taste acidic sweet, quality excellent with 10-12 percent TSS. Seed number about 340, viable and bearing heavy. In full grown tree, the fruit yield may vary from 125 kg to 150 kg per tree.

Arka Amulya: It is a hybrid of Seedless × Allahabad Sufeda. The trees are somewhat dwarf with compact, round crown and drooping branches with dense foliage. The fruit is large, round, glossy with white flesh, containing semi-soft seeds. The average yield of rainy and winter seasons crop is 144 kg per tree. The total soluble solids in fruit ranges from 9.3 to 10.1 per cent and acidity from 0.25 to 0.34 per cent.

Punjab Pink : It is a hybrid between Portugal × L - 49 = F1 × Apple Colour developed at Punjab Agricultural University, Ludhiana. The trees of this variety are vigorous with drooping branches. The fruit is medium to large in size with attractive red skin sometimes in summer season and golden yellow in winter season. The flesh is red having pleasant flavour. The total soluble solids ranged from 10.5 to 12.0 per cent. It is a prolific bearer and the average yield is 150 kg per tree.

Shweta : The variety is a selection from Apple Colour and is recently developed by CISH, Lucknow. The trees are semi vigorous with medium height. Fruit medium sized, 195 g in weight and globose in shape. Skin colour creamy white with red spots or blush. Pulp snow-white with excellent quality. The fruits are attractive and have good nutritive value. Seeds semi-hard and 350 in number per fruit. The total soluble solids in fruit ranges from 10.5 to 11.0 per cent. The vitamin C content of fruit is 300 mg per 100 g of pulp. It is a prolific bearer variety yielding 150 kg fruits per tree and has good keeping quality.

Apple Colour: Tree growth spreading, medium foliage, branching medium to poor. Leaves thin, slightly flat, elliptical lanceolate, apex acute and base obtuse. Fruit medium (112g), form round to spherical, surface slightly rough, skin colour red or pinkish, thick dots, base slightly flat, apex round. Calyx large, almost closed, cavity deep. Pulp soft, cream white, flavour pleasant, taste sweet and good in quality. Seeds about 278, viable, bearing is heavy.

Red-Fleshed : Tree height 4.5 to 7.5 metres. Growth upright vigorous, crown uneven, foliage moderately dense, branching medium, barks outer colour grey, inner colour light green. Leaves medium to large, oblong lanceolate, thin apex and base obtuse, margin slightly wavy, upper colour green, lower dull green. Fruit medium to large (170 g), ovate roundish, surface smooth glossy, apex flat, skin thick, pinkish yellow with small dots, base round, stalk medium, thin, cavity shallow, subepidermal layer reddish yellow. Pulp pink, soft, flavour pleasant like apricot, taste sweet with a typical flavour. Seed small, average number 570, light orange. Fruit quality is medium, bearing medium to heavy.

Seedless: Tree height 6.0 - 7.5 metres, growth upright, dense foliage, branching medium to heavy. Leaves large, leathery and folded, ovate to oblong elliptic, apex and base obtuse. Fruit medium, pyriform, ovoid, skin colour dull yellow, thin, dots large, scattered; base flat giving apparent indication of fruits being divided into quarters, apex flat. Clayx large, closed, cavity shallow. Pulp firm to soft, white, flavour mild, taste sweet, pulp thickness completely filled, except a shallow cavity in the centre. Poor keeping quality, fruit is seedless. Bearing is poor.

Pear Shaped: Shape of the fruit is pear like. Fruit medium to large (140 g). Pulp soft to melting, creamy white, pleasant flavour and good quality. Bearing is medium.

Lalit, Arka Mridula and Pant Prabhat are other popular varieties of guava.

Guava Hybrids. Six promising hybrids are developed at Fruit Research Station Anantharajupet, Andhra Pradesh. Out of these hybrid H_1 (Red Fleshed × Saharnpur Seedless) and H_2 (Smooth Green × Nagpur Seedless) are more promising in terms of fruit quality as well as precocity. Two hybrids Safed Jam (Allahabad Safeda × Kohir) and Kohir Safeda (Kohir × Allahabad Safeda) have been released from Fruit Research Station, Sangrareddy. CCS Haryana Agricutural University, Hisar has released two hybrids *i.e.*, Hisar Safeda (Allahabad Safeda × Seedless) and Hisar Surkha (Apple Colour × Banarsi Surkha).

PROPAGATION AND ROOTSTOCKS

It is still common to raise commercial orchards by propagation from seeds. This practice is not advisable because this would lead to lot of variation among the trees not only in the size productivity of the trees but also in fruit size and fruit quality. Hence, it is very important to plant an orchard only with vegetatively propagated plants of known variety. The propagation is commonly done through patch-budding, air-layering and inarching. However, improved patch budding is efficient than simple patch budding and enhances the chances of budding success.

Seeds of Sardar guava are commonly used for raising rootstock which are easily available and possess the qualities of a good rootstock. Portugal rootstock of guava is most suitable for Sardar and Allahabad Safeda varieties, as it improves fruit yield and weight. It also imparts vigour and wilt tolerance to these scion varieties.

Raising of Rootstock

Extraction of Seed: For raising rootstocks, seeds are used to obtain seedlings on which the desired scion variety can be grafted. Seeds may be extracted during winter season from well- sized healthy fruits of recommended cultivars like Sardar (Lucknow-49) and Portugal. Guava seeds retain their vitality for about a year after they are extracted from fruit. After extraction from the ripe guava fruit, seeds should be washed, mixed with ash and then dried and stored in dry container at a cool place.

Sowing of Seeds. Seeds should be sown in March or August on raised seed beds of 2 m × 1 m size. The seeds are closely sown at 2 cm depth in rows, about 8-10 cm apart on raised seed beds which are sufficiently manured during February-March or July-August. The beds should be applied water daily with watering Can. Under favourable conditions, guava seedlings may develop from seed in about 15-20 days from the time of sowing.

Transplanting of Seedlings: The seedlings when attain 10-15 cm height after six months should be transplanted 25-30 cm apart in nursery rows during August-September. The seedlings can also be transplanted in the pots when they are nearly 7 cm in height, if inarching is to be done. The week seedlings should be discarded. Budding is done when these seedlings attain a diameter of 1.0 - 1.2 cm at about 15 cm height. Sometimes, the guava seedlings show sign of wilting due to damping off. To control this, drench the seed beds with 0.3% captan.

Clonal Propagation of Rootstock

Mound layering is used for the propagation of guava rootstocks. In this method of layering, the parent plants are first established in the nursery. The heading back can be done either just before spring or during rainy season. A ring of bark is removed from the stools coming out during spring and rainy season and these are covered with moist soil. These shoots should be planted in the pots or in the nursery for sometime for further development of roots and shoots before budding or grafting with the desired scion variety.

Propagation Techniques

Patch or improved patch budding may be done during May-June when it yields 75-80 percent success. Freshly cut angular bud-wood from current season's growth should be employed for budding. A semi-circular or a rectangular patch of bark (2.5 × 1.0 cm) with two buds is removed from the scion stick taking care that the bark does not split. It is then fixed on the exposed portion of the rootstock and tied immediately with the polythene strip leaving both the buds uncovered. The polythene is removed after a week or so when the bud-take has occurred. When the shoots developing from the buds have attained a length of 15 – 20 cm, retain the vigorously grown shoot and remove the weaker ones. Inarching is another common method of vegetative propagation and about 80-90 percent success can be achieved when it is practised during July-August. Wedge grafting can be performed on rootstock seedlings of 2.5 – 3.0 cm thickness during February. The scion sticks should be defoliated 8 – 10 days prior to grafting. Air-layering is also practised for multiplication of guava plants and the best time for doing this method is February-March and July-August. For better results, the use of indolebutyric acid, indoleacetic acid and naphthalene acetic acid can be made.

FLOWERING AND FRUITING

Guava tree normally produces as many as three crops in a year, a unique phenomenon of the tropical and sub-tropical regions because there is more than one growing season during

SARDAR—A Leading Commercial Variety of Guava

PUNJAB PINK

ARKA AMULYA

Promising Hybrids of Guava

Double - hedge row system of planting with 800 – 900 plants per hectare is beneficial for higher yield in Allahabad Safeda.

ORCHARD CULTURAL PRACTICES

Irrigation

The young guava plants need irrigation at weekly interval during summer month and 2-3 irrigations during winter months. To bearing trees, irrigation should be given for flowering and better fruit-setting at an interval of 2-3 weeks during summer months and at monthly interval during winter months. Irrigation is also essential to check excessive fruit drop during summer months. Irrigation during winter was also found effective in reducing fruit drop and improving fruit size of winter crop. The cropping pattern in guava (for heavy winter crop) can be regulated to some extent by withholding irrigation during hot summer month (May).

Drip irrigation has proved beneficial for guava and increase the fruit size and number of fruits. About 60 per cent water used for irrigation is saved.

Intercropping

The interspace can be economically utilised by suitable intercrops during the pre-bearing period of guava orchards. During initial 3-4 years, the vegetables like brinjal, radish, carrot and okra can be interplanted in the vacant land. The leguminous crops like cowpea, guara, gram, beans etc. should be sown as safe intercrops. Intercropping should be stopped when the trees attain age of being fully grown.

Weed Control

Pre-emergence application of Hexuron 80 WP (diuron) @ 4 kg per hectare can be made during first fortnight of March for rainy season crop and during first fortnight of September for winter season crop when field is free from weeds and stubbles. Glycel 41 SL (glyphosate) @ 4 litres per hectare as post-emergence should be sprayed when the weeds are growing actively; preferably before weeds flower or attain a height of 15–20 cm *i.e.,* during second frotnight of March for rainy season crop and during second fortnight of September for winter season crop. Dissolve the herbicides in 500 litres of water which is enough to give complete coverage on weeds in one hectare. Spray Glycel during the calm day to avoid spray drift to the foliage of the trees.

Manuring and Fertilization

The requirement for manure and fertilizers to guava crop varies with varieties, age of the plants, fertility status of soil, climatic conditions and management practices. The fruit of guava are borne on current season's growth, therefore, manures and fertilizers encourages vegetative growth and fruiting. Fertilization of guava not only increased the yield but also improved the fruit quality. To five year old Sardar cultivar application of 25 kg FYM, 600 *g* N, 300 *g* P_2O_5 and 300 *g* K_2O was recommended for obtaining higher yield. In West Bengal, 260 *g* N, 320 *g* P_2O_5 and 260 *g* K_2O per plant in two equally split doses once in the month of January and another in the month of August was suggested.

The following are general doses of manures and fertilizers given to guava crop for obtaining higher fruit yield and better quality fruits.

Age of tree (years)	Farmyard manure (kg/plant)	Urea (g/plant)	Superphosphate (kg/plant)	Muriate of potash (g/plant)
1 -3	10–20	150–200	0.5–1.5	100–400
4–6	25–40	300–600	1.5–2.0	600–1000
7–10	40–50	750–1000	2.0–2.5	1100–1500
10 and above	50	1000	2.5	1500

Farmyard manure should be applied in May. Half of the inorganic fertilizer should be applied in May-June and the remaining half in September-October.

Zinc Deficiency

Zinc deficiency is a common problem in guava plants. The affected plants produce small leaves with yellowing or chlorosis in between the veins. The plant growth is supressed and the branches die-back. The zinc deficiency can be corrected by spraying the trees with zinc sulphate lime mixture (1 kg of zinc sulphate +1/2 kg of unslaked lime in 100 litres of water). Two or three such sprays should be given at fortnightly interval between June to September.

TRAINING AND PRUNING

Training of guava trees improve fruit yield and quality. Modified leader system of training is generally followed. The main objective of training guava plants is to provide a strong framework and scaffold of branches suitable for bearing a heavy remunerative crop without damaging the branches. The flowers and fruits in guava are borne on current season's growth, hence, a light annual pruning upto 10 cm tip removal may prove useful to encourage new shoots after the harvest (early April). Dead, diseased, intercrossing branches and suckers coming up from the base and sides of the framework should be pruned back annually. Pruned plants, however, certainly reduce yield to certain extent.

CROP REGULATION

Guava bears two crops in a year. The winter season crop is considered superior in quality than rainy season crop, which gets infected with fruit flies. In order to get only winter season crop, the following practices may be adopted.

(*a*) Spray urea 10 per cent or Napthalene acetic acid (NAA) @ 600 ppm during May when maximum flowers have opened. Each tree needs about 10-12 liters of solution.

(*b*) Pruning of terminal portions of the shoots upto 20 or 30 cm between 20 to 30 April avoids completely the rainy reason crop.

(*c*) Irrigation should be stopped during the summer months of April-May.

(*d*) Apply inorganic fertilizers during the month of June to encourage growth in July-August for getting maximum flowering during August-September for winter season crop.

HARVESTING AND FRUIT HANDLING

Guava is climacteric in nature and should be picked when it is mature but firm. Picked at the right stage of maturity, fruits on ripening give excellent taste and flavour, characteristic of a particular cultivar. For successful orcharding, harvesting the fruits at its proper stage of fruit maturity is of utmost importance. The seedling guava comes into bearing very late *i.e.* after 5-6 years of planting. However, the grafted or air-layered plants are precocious in bearing and first crop appears at the age of 2 to 3 years. The fruits change their colour from dark green to greenish yellow at maturity. The fruits should not be allowed to over ripe on the trees as they deteriorate in quality and are more liable to damaged by birds. Individual fruits are picked when they are still hard and firm at regular intervals. Guava fruit must be harvested with great care because of their soft, thin skin. Harvesting is normally carried out by hand to avoid physical injuries. Subsequent handling and transportation of the fruit also need extra precautions to reduce bruising.

The yield of guava varies due to different varieties, age of the plant, fruiting season and orchard management practices. The average yield of seedling trees is obtained approximately one quintal, whereas of grafting trees, the yield can be obtained upto two quintals per tree. It is observed that different varieties produce greater yield in the rainy season compared to winter season.

Guava is highly perishable fruit and should be marketed immediately after harvest. Harvested fruits should be properly cleaned and graded according to the size as follow :

Grade specification and distribution of guava fruits cv. Sardar

Grade	Specification of grade (diameter)	Distribution (%)	Fruit weight (g)	TSS (%)
A	Large-sized (6.6–7.0 cm)	12.0	182	11.0
B	Medium-sized (6.2–6.6 cm)	60.0	143	10.8
C	Small-sized (5.0–6.2 cm)	28.0	104	9.6

The fruits belonging to A and B grades which accounted for 72 per cent has better quality and are acceptable from marketing point of view. Highest distribution of fruits was recorded in grade B *i.e.* 60 per cent. The fruits should preferably be packed in Corrugated Fibre Board Cartons of sizes ranging from 4–10 kg or in bamboo baskets of different sizes.

The fruits of winter guava cv. Sardar harvested at physiological mature stage can be ripened at 20°C in 72 hours and these fruits can be kept for 48-72 hours at ambient temperature in winter.

Proper handling prior to storage is important to preserve fruit quality and to avoid losses due to physical injuries and diseases. Positioning of guava fruits in the natural posture with the pedicel end vertically upward may result in a better keeping quality as compared with fruits kept in reverse or horizontal position. Newspaper should be used as the cushioning material for the fruit. The fruits of Sardar cv. individually wrapped in newspaper impregnated with biphenyl or $KMNO_4$ and kept at room temperature showed less decay and retained a higher level of ascorbic acid than the control. The guava fruits can be stored upto 6 days in perforated polythene bags and wooden boxes. The guava fruits when picked at proper maturity can be kept at room temperature for one week in perforated polythene bags and for three weeks in CFB cartons in commercial cold store at 0–3.3°C temp. and 85–90% relative humidity. Allahabad Safeda variety can be stored for 4 weeks in the cold storage (8.5 -14 °C). Lucknow-49 could be stored well up to one month at 10°C. Dipping of fruits in 6 or 9% wax-emulsion extended shelf life for one month without any spoliage.

INSECT-PESTS

1. Fruit fly (*Bactrocera dorsalis*) : Fruit fly is the most common and a serious pest of guava fruits during monsoon. Being polyphagus, it feeds and breeds profusely on various fruit crops. The fly lays eggs at colour break stage of fruits in the soft epicarp. On hatching, the maggots bore further into fruits and feeds on soft pulp. The infested fruits show depressions with dark green puncture and when cut open the wriggling maggots are seen inside. The infested fruits rot and fall down. Pupation takes place in the soil under trees. Isolated orchards are less infested by the fruit fly.

For its control avoid taking rainy season crop in the orchards with history of severe fruit fly infestations. Harvest the ripening fruits and do not allow the ripe fruits on the tree. Regularly remove the fallen fruits from the ground and burry the infested fruits at least at 60 cm depth. Shallow ploughing with cultivator immediately after harvest is effective in explosing and killing the pupating larvae/pupae which are mostly present at 4–6 cm depth. In infested orchards, spray the trees with 1250 ml (0.05%) Sumicidin 20 EC (fenvalerate) in 500 litres of water at weekly intervals in ripening fruits commencing from July onwards till the rainy season crop is over. Fruits should be harvested on third day after spray. Fix fruit fly traps @ 16 traps per acre in first week of July for the control of fruit fly. Recharge the traps if required.

2. Guava shoot borer (*Microcolona technographa*) : Shoot borer is serious under nursery conditions. It damages the tender shoots of nursery/adult trees of guava. Side sprouting of the vegetative buds just below the larval gallery impairs the quality of the seedlings as the buds below the damaged portion produce lateral shoots and plants give bushy look. The infested shoots dry up which can be located from a distance by the presence of fine black frass on the leaves/shoot parts beneath the site of infestation.

The pest can be controlled by spraying in nursery with 500 ml (0.1%) Durmet 20 EC (chlorpyriphos) or 400 ml (0.1%) Ekalux 25 EC (quinalphos) in 100 litres of water.

3. Mealy bugs (*Ferrisia virgata, Planococcus lilacinus and Nipaecoccus viridis*) : They are causing damage to guava trees. ***Ferrisia virgata*** is active in guava orchards during June to October. It is a major species as compared to other mealy bugs. The other two species are causing damage to the trees during July to October. The nymphs of these mealy bugs suck cells sap from the different parts of the plants like leaves, tender shoots, twigs, branches and fruits. Heavy infestation of these pests encourages the growth of sooty mould due to which the leaves, shoots and fruits become black in colour. All these mealy bugs hibernate on the twigs and branches of trees.

Keep the proper sanitation in guava orchard. Monitor regularly the infestation of trees by observing the underside of leaves, young shoots, branches and fruits. Never allow the branches of trees to touch the group. Prune the infested branches and destroy them. Destroy all the ant nests in the orchard. Drench the trees giving spray of 1875 ml durmet/Dursban/Coroban 20EC (Chlorpyriphos) in 500 litres of water immediately after the appearance of pest. Repeat the spray if need arises.

DISEASES

1. Wilt: The disease is caused due to fungus ***Fusarium*** sp. or ***Cephalosporium*** sp. **or** ***Rhizoctonia*** sp. Symptoms appear on the infested trees many months after their roots are attacked by the fungi. Sparse foliage, denuded branches, the yellowing of leaves and wilting are the important symptoms. In the root, the cambium in between the bark and the wood shows discoloration. Replanted trees bear fruit for a number of years before ultimately succumbing to the disease. The disease can be controlled by adopting the following measures.

1. Plant guava in a well drained field. It is advisable to avoid too heavy soils.
2. Uproot the wilted trees alongwith all the roots and use as fire wood.
3. Rain or irrigation water should not be allowed to stand in the basin around the tree.
4. Drench the soil in the pit with 2 percent formalin solution and cover with sarkanda and old wetted gunny bags. Expose the soil for 14 days and replant healthy guava seedlings.
5. Use Sardar or Portugal cultivars as rootstock for budded plants.

2. Fruit rot/Anthracnose or dieback : The disease is caused by fungus ***Gloeosporium psidii*** and ***Phytophthora parasitica; Rhizopus sp., Aspergilus sp.*** Fully mature fruits are more prone to the attack of the fungus. Circular, slightly sunken, brown spots with definite margins appear on the fruits. The centre of the lesion has a pink sticky spore mass characteristics of the anthracnose disease. Fruits rot completely within 2 to 3 days. The fungus attacks young trees, twigs and branches during the rainy season resulting in the dieback of the shoot from the distal end.

Stagnation of rain or irrigation water should not be allowed in the tree basins. Prune the dead twigs and mumified fruits hanging on the trees. After pruning, spray the trees with 300 g of Blitox or Captan in 100 litres of water. Repeat the spray after fruit-set and continue spraying at 10-15 day intervals till maturity. Burry deep into the soil the rotted and mumified fruits which fall on the ground and are unfit for marketing. Avoid bruising of the fruits.

CHAPTER 12

Sapota

Sapota or sapodilla (***Manilkara zapota*** **(L.) P. Royen) Synonym** (*Achras zapota*.), is commonly known as **chiku** in India. The cultivation of **chiku** is highly profitable as it does not need much spraying and pruning etc. and it is a long-life fruit tree. Moreover, the **chiku** fruit fetches good price as it ripens in July and August, when mango and litchi fruits are scarce.

ORIGIN AND HISTORY

Sapota is native of tropical America and is believed to have originated in South Mexico or Central America. It is believed that from Central America or Southern Mexico, it spread to other countries such as Philippines, Malaysia, Indonesia, Florida in United States, SriLanka, India and Caribean Islands, where it adapted very well. The sapota was taken to Philippines in the early days by the Spanish and from there it spread westwards to Malaysia and other countries. It is not known when sapota was first introduced to India, but the sapota cultivation was taken up for the first time in Maharashtra in 1898 in a village named Gholwad. Thereafter, it spread to other states and now it occupies a significant position among fruit crops.

AREA AND PRODUCTION

India is considered to be the largest producer of sapota in the world, though sapota is considered to be a minor crop in India. The area under sapota is increasing so rapidly owing to a wider range of adaptability, low production costs and high economic returns that in time to come, its marketing may become a problem. In many regions, cultivation of sapota is now preferred over mango. At present, total area and production under sapota is 1.63 lakh hectares and 14.26 lakh tonnes. The productivity is high in Tamil Nadu and Karnataka. Productivity of sapota is much low in Odisha and Maharashtra

In India, sapota is widely cultivated in Karnataka, Gujarat. Maharashtra, Tamil Nadu, Andhra Pradesh, West Bengal and Odisha. The cultivation of sapota on limited scale is also observed in parts of Punjab, Uttar Pradesh, Haryana, Bihar and Brahmputra valley of Assam. In Maharashtra main centres for growing sapota are Thane and Kalaba. It has now spread to many districts of Vidharba, Marathwada and central Maharashtra. In Andhra Pradesh, Vizakhapatnam and Rajamundry have good deal of sapota which has spread to many other districts. In Karnataka sapota cultivation is widely distributed throughout the state. Sapota cultivation in North India is only restricted to sheltered pockets of Punjab, Haryana and Uttar Pradesh as it is susceptible to frost damage. In Punjab, sapota can be introduced on commercial scale in the districts of Patiala, Ropar, Hoshiarpur and Gurdaspur.

Productivity of sapota ranges from 4 tonnes/ha in Maharashtra to 27.8. and 12.3 tonnes/ ha in Tamil Nadu and Karnataka, respectively. Although very high yielding orchards are observed in Bulsar district of Gujarat, the average yields are of the order of 12 tonnes/ha.

Export potential : Sapota fruits are mainly exported to UAE, Bahrain, Canada, UK, Saudi Arabia, Oman, Qatar, USA, Kuwait and Singapore. India has exported 2694 mt sapotas during the year 2011-12 and earned foreign exchange of Rs. 4.28 crores. commodity wise share of export of sapota is 47.2 per cent to UAE followed by 18.5 per cent to Bahrain and 10.4 per cent to Canada.

IMPORTANCE AND USES

Sapota when fully ripe is delicious and is eaten as dessert fruit. The pulp is sweet and melting. It is a good source of digestible sugar which ranges from 12 to 18 per cent and has appreciable amounts of protein, fat, fibre, mineral, calcium, phosphorus and iron. It contains 73.7% moisture, 21.4% carbohydrates, 0.7% protein, 1.1% fat, 28 mg calcium, 27 mg phosphorus, 2 mg iron and 6 mg ascorbic acid per 100 g of fruit. Its carotene content is 97 I.U. The fruit is taken only when fully ripe as it is not edible at immature stage. Although, sapota is primarly cultivated for its edible fruit in India, but in other countries like Mexico, Guatemala and Venezuela, sapota is cultivated mainly for the extraction of chicle gum.

The fully ripe fruits are eaten with skin. Skin is more nutritive than pulp. The pulp of sapota is used for making sharbets and halwas. The fruits are used for making mixed jams and manufacture of industrial glucose, pectin and fruit jellies. Its wood is used for making agricultural implements, building construction, furniture, etc. In the West Indies, seeds are known to be aperient and diuretic and the bark is reputed to be toxic and febrifuge. The bark of sapota is used as a tonic and antipyretic in Guinea.

BOTANY

Sapota (***Manilkara zapota*** **(L.) P. Royen)** belongs to the family sapotaceae. There are several cultivars of sapota in India. They are grouped under four types based on the habit of the tree *i.e.,* nature and branches and colour of foliage.

Trees with Erect Growing Habit : Branches appear in whorls. Foliage is deep green, broad and oval. Fruits are large in size with smooth and yellow skin. Pulp is butter like and sweet.

Trees with Drooping Habit : Branches appear in whorls. Foliage is light green, narrow and eliptical. Fruits are small with rough brownish skin and pulp of inferior quality.

Trees with Spreading Habit–I : Branching irregular. Foliage deep green in colour, broad and oval. Fruits with smooth and yellow skin. Pulp is butter like and sweet.

Trees with Spreading Habit–II : Branching irregular. Foliage light green in colour, narrow, eliptical. Fruits with rough skin. Pulp inferior.

Sapota is slow growing evergreen tree. It attains a height of about 9 metres. The main stem is strong and stout and from it radiating whorls of horizontally disposed branches are produced at more or less regular intervals. The main branches carry an array of short branchlets which bear fruits terminally in the axils of leaves and also give out vegetative shoots from their sides. Leaves are elliptic to obovate, flowers solitary in leaf axils, produced over a long season. Sepals 6, tomentulose, petals 6, staminodes 6, petaloid, stamens 6. The fruit is a drupe, egg shaped and round. The skin of fruit is slightly tough resembling to potato skin in appearance. Each fruit contains 3 to 5 or more black shining seeds.

CLIMATE

Sapota is hardy, tropical fruit crop and can be grown in a wide variety of climate. It prefers a warm and moist weather and grows both in dry and humid areas. Coastal climate is best suited. Areas with an annual rainfall of 125-250 cm are highly suitable. The optimum temperature for sapota should lie between 11 to 34°C. A high temperature of 41°C during summer causes flower drop and fruit scorching. In Karnataka, northern districts such as Raichur, Gulbarga, Bidar and Bellary experience very high temperature in the middle of summer causing scorching of foliage. Sapota has a wide range of adaptability and can be grown successfully upto 1000 m above sea level. Although, in some states like Gujarat, it is grown as irrigated crop, in parts of Karnataka and Tamil Nadu, it has proved to be drought tolerant, suitable for growing even under rainfed conditions.

SOIL

Sapota can be grown on a wide variety of soil but in sandy soils, the plants are uprooted by strong winds. The soils having very high percentage of calcium are not suitable. If the soil is not well-drained or a hard pan is present in sub soil, the sapota tree does not make good growth. It can withstand presence of salt to some extent. Sapota grows well in sandy loam soils of coastal region, red lateritic soils of the heavy rainfall area of Western Ghats and medium black soils. Drainage is most important for sapota growing.

CHOICE OF VARIETIES

Sapota industry in India is based on narrow genetic base and most of varieties are the result of local selections for shape, size and quality of fruits. A dessert sapota of good eating quality should possess a pleasant sweet taste and good flavour. The pulp should be abundant, mellow and melting. Thick skinned, hard fleshed cultivars with sandy texture are considered inferior. The following are the cultivars grown in India :

Kalipatti : It is a leading cultivar of Maharashtra, Gujarat and North Karnataka. It has dark green, broad and thick leaves and spreading branches. Fruits are oval shaped, less seeded with sweet, mellow flesh of excellent quality. Fragrance is mild. Each fruit has 1-4 seeds. Fruits appear singly. The main harvest is in winter. Average fruit yield in 166 kg per tree.

Cricket Ball : It is grown in Tamil Nadu, Karnataka, Maharashtra, West Bengal and Andhra Pradesh. The leaves are light green. This bears the largest-sized fruits which are round in shape. Pulp is gritty and granular and not very sweet. It is a shy bearer and does well in arid climate. This variety produces good quality fruits below an elevation of 300 metres. Average yield is 157 kg per tree.

Chhatri : As the name goes, it bears umbrella like whorls of branches. Its leaves are light green in colour and the fruit is similar to that of Kalipatti in appearance but is slightly less sweet. Though a fairly good cropper, it does not bear as heavily as Kalipatti.

Calcutta Round : It is commercially grown in West Bengal, Karnataka and other states. The foliage is light green in colour. Fruits are large but the flesh is gritty and of moderate quality. It is susceptible to leaf spot disease.

Pala : It is a popular variety of Andhra Pradesh and Tamil Nadu. The fruits are small to medium sized and oval or egg shaped with apex broadly pointed and are very sweet. The bearing is heavy and fruits are borne in clusters. The fruit has thin skin and good flavour.

Efforts have been made to introduce superior hybrids of sapota through planned breeding work. At Coimbatore CO-1 and CO-2 were released. At Dharwar, crosses were made among Kalipatti, Cricket Ball, Calcutta Round and Oval. Two hybrids (DHS-1 and DHS-2) were obtained from the crosses of (Kalipatti × Cricket Ball) and have been released. PKM-1 was released from Periyakulam for its high yield and excellent quality of fruit having better shelf life. Hybrid 2/4 is also promising and has exhibited hybrid vigour. Kirthabharti, Bharamasi and Dhola Diwani are also promising varieties of sapota grown in different regions of the country.

PROPAGATION AND ROOTSTOCKS

Sapota is propagated by both seed and vegetable methods. Propagation by seeds is not advisable because seedling trees are slow growing, take longer time to come into bearing and have lot of variations.

For sexual propagation, seeds are collected from elite trees and sown in pans or beds with light sandy soil as germinating medium and watered at regular intervals. GA_3 promotes the percentage of germination and increases the growth of seedlings.

Propagation by vegetative methods is essential. Sapota is commercially propagated by vencer and inarch-grafting and air-layering. However, veneer/inarching is preferred as compared to air-layering. Propagation by cuttings, budding and stone grafting is also successful.

Veneer grafting. It is a commercial method of propagation for sapota. The rootstock seedlings are raised in pots or bed. Khirni is the best rootstock producing vigorous plants with high productivity. Pencil thickness seedlings of rootstock are suitable for veneer grafting. The best time for doing this propagation method is during raising season *i.e.* July to September. The plants become ready for sale within one year after grafting.

Air-layering : This method is common in Maharashtra, Gujarat, Karnataka, Tamil Nadu and Andhra Pradesh. It is possible to get a sizeable plant in a short time but mortality is high and the root system is shallow. The air-layered plants are likely to be uprooted when heavy winds are experienced in sandy soils. The best time for air-layering is the beginning of rainy season. High humidity prevailing during the monsoon facilitates rooting. The rooting percentage in air layers of sapota increases with a mixture of IBA and NAA at 10,000 ppm. In rooting of air layers, the invigorated shoots produced as a result of beheading a grafted tree, possess a better rooting ability than mature shoots. Invigorated shoots after etiolation treatment, treated with 10,000 ppm IBA gave 91.7 per cent success and 90.9 per cent survival. In another study, etiolated and ringed shoots treated with 2000 ppm IBA gave best rooting percentage of 80.

Inarching : Inarching is a also commercial method of propagation. The different rootstock such as khirni or rayan, sapota seedling and Mahua seedlings are used. The scion remains attached to the parent tree till the union is complete. The rootstocks are raised in pots. One year old seedlings of rayan are suitable for grafting. Inarching is done during spring season. Maximum success was recorded in February (90%) followed by January and March. The graft could be detatched from the mother plant at 5½ months after inarching.

Soft wood grafting : It could be done in one year stock plants during July-August with more than 80 per cent success and in September-October with over 50 per cent success.

Rootstocks : Several rootstocks have been tried in sapota. These include (*i*) sapota seedlings (***Manikara zapota***) (*ii*) Rayan or khirni (***Manilkara hexandra*** or ***Mimusops hexandra***), (*iii*) Adam's apple (***Manilkara kauki*** or ***Mimusops kauki***), (*iv*) Star apple **(*Chrysophyllum cainito*),** (*v*) **Mahua (*Madhuca latifolia*),** (*vi*) **Mee tree (*Bassia longifolia*) and** (*vii*) **Miracular fruit (*Sideroxylon dulicificum*)**. Of all the rootstocks tried (***Mimusops hexandra*** Roxb. Syn. ***Manilkara hexandra*** Dab) popularly known as Rayan-a tropical tree is extensively used as rootstock for grafting sapota as it has a very profuse root yield as compared to air-layered trees and those grafted on self rootstock, respectively.

Raising of Rootstock : *Manilkara hexandra* was found to be most vigorous and productive rootstock. Its fruit are small, oval and sweet. They are washed to get rid of pulp in water and dried under shade and sown. The seeds are soaked in water for a night for easy and quick germination. Seeds are sown in raised seed beds or pots. The seed germinate in about 4 weeks and when they are about 15 cm high they are transferred to small pots.

In Ratnagiri district in Maharashtra and Surat district in Gujarat, self-grown seedlings of rayan from the forest areas are collected for potting. All the side growths are removed up to a height of 30 cm from ground level to get a clean and straight stem. When they attain a thickness of 1 cm they are used for grafting or budding.

PLANTING OPERATION

Sapota being evergreen fruit plant can be planted during February-March and August-September. However, monsoon is the best time for sapota planting. The pits of 60 to 100 cm^3 size are dug in advance during summer. The plants should be planted 9 metres apart in heavy rainfall tracts and 7.5 metres apart in dry zones. In this way, it accommodates 180 to 123 plants per hectare. After planting, the young tree should supported with a stake. Copious irrigation is required soon after planting.

At many places, sapota is planted at 8m × 8m which accommodates 156 plants per hectare. High density planting at 8m × 4m is followed for high productivity, it adjusts 312 plants/ha. High density planting with a spacing of 5m × 5m upto the age of 13 years has been adopted successfully in different regions of the country.

FLOWERING AND FRUITING

The sapota plants raised vegetatively start flowering from second or third year after transplanting. However, economic yield is only obtained from seventh year onwards. Under tropical conditions, sapota flowers throughout the year with two main flowering seasons *i.e.,* July to November and again in February-March and hence two harvesting seasons *i.e.* September-November and January-March. Under Dharwar (Karnataka) conditions, three seasons of flowering were recorded with maximum in June, while in October and March the flowering was less. The peak anthesis was found at 4 A.M. The maximum receptivity of stigma was observed on the day of opening of flowers. Under Ludhiana (Punjab) conditions, flowers opened at 5 A.M. and flowering reached a peak between 5 AM to 7 AM. The anther dehiscence started before anthesis suggesting protandry. The maximum anther dehiscence occured between 8 AM and 11 AM. The cultivar Chhattri had the largest pollen grains (16 μ). The highest pollen viability of 95.8 to 97.6% was noted in Kalipatti cultivar. The pollen germination was observed maximum (45.5 – 57.5%) in 15 per cent sucrose solution after 48 hours. Stigma were receptive from a day before until a day after anthesis. The shape of pollen grains was roundish and their colour being yellowish with an average pollen size of 16.25 μ. The acetocarmine stainability was recorded 96.3 to 97.6 per cent in different cultivars.

Flowers are borne on past season shoot. The flowers are protogynous in nature. Therefore, planting of single sapota tree in home garden is not recommended. The fruit setting is very high but fruit retention is poor. There is a high fruit drop at early stages. In Kalipatti, 22 percent natural fruit set was observed. The maximum fruit drop occurred immediately after fruit setting. Pollination is affected by wind. Sapota is a cross-pollinated crop. The improvement of fruit set at cheaper rate can be obtained by the application of NAA at 300 ppm at flowering stage and repeated at pea stage. Only about 10% of the total fruits setting developed into complete fruits and were retained till maturity. Fruit set as indicated by petal fall took 47 days after anthesis. Maximum fruit drop was observed immediately after fruit-setting.

Fruit growth appeared quite steady throughout the growth period until maturity. From middle of October, increase in fruit length was faster. Fruits reached maximum size and maturity in first week of March. Further retention of fruits rendered them unfit for transport.

Growth of fruit followed a double sigmoid curve. It has been reported that time taken from fruit set to maturity is more than 10 months. Fruits that mature doing March - May are generally better in quality.

ORCHARD CULTURAL PRACTICES

Irrigation

Sapota is grown as rainfed as well as irrigated crop in different regions. It can tolerate drought conditions to some extent, yet it responds well to irrigation. In cv. Kalipatti, scheduling 10 to 11 irrigations each at 80 mm depth to be applied at 30 days interval in winter and 10 – 15 days interval in summer and fertilizing with 1 kg N, 1/2 kg P_2O_5 and 1/2 kg K_2O per tree gave significantly highest fruit yield of sapota and net return. At flowering time frequent irrigation should be applied to maintain humid conditions in the orchard for better fruit set. Normally, young plants are watered regularly during dry season having long breaks in the monsoon and in winter and summer at an interval of 6 to 12 days.

In Maharashtra, young plants are given irrigation once in 8 days from October onwards till monsoon starts. In Karnataka protective irrigation is given during first two seasons for better establishment of plants. Insufficient irrigiation results in dropping of a large number of flowers leading to a loss up to 40 per cent in yield.

Drip irrigation saves 40 per cent water and increase the yield. In drip system during the initial two years, two dripper spaced at 50 cm from the tree should be laid out and subsequently two more dripper can be added. The discharge rate of drippers should be 4 litres per hour depending upon the climate and soil type of the area.

Intercropping

During the first 10 years, when the trees are young, much of the orchard land between rows of trees remains unoccupied. Some vegetables can profitably be taken if, adequate irrigation facilities are available. Peach, plum, phalsa and papaya may be planted as fillers in those orchards which come into bearing rather late. The vegetable crops like bhindi, brinjal, tomato, chillies, onion and leguminous crops like cowpea, moong, urd and cluster bean can be grown as intercrop in sapota.

Weed Control

At Bangalore, Bromacil @ 3 kg/ha proved to be the best herbicide for controlling both broad leaved weeds and grasses and was effective for a period of 6 months. Diuron @ 4 kg/ha also showed almost similar effect like bromacil but nut grass could not be completely suppressed by this chemical.

Manuring and Fertilization

One year old tree should be given 25 kg farmyard manure, 80 g CAN, 63 g superphosphate and 12 g muriate of potash. Thereafter, the above dose should be increased by 5 kg of farmyard manure, 80 g of CAN, 63 g of superphosphate and 12 g of muriate of potash, respectively annually upto the ninth year. From the tenth year onward, 45 kg farmyard manure, 1.5 kg CAN, 560 g superphosphate and 200 g muriate of potash per tree should be applied. The beginning of monsoon is the right time of manuring. From the seventh year onward, the trees bear heavily and therefore, they should be manured twice a year. The second dose of manure can be given in the month of February.

The following doses of manure and fertilizers have been found beneficial for obtaining higher yield of sapota under Andhra Pradesh and Karnataka conditions :

Age of trees (years)	FYM (Kg/tree)	N	P (g/tree)	K
1–3	50	50	20	75
4–7	50	100	40	150
7–10	50	200	80	300
11 and above	50	400	160	450

Manures and fertilizers are applied twice in a year. The first half is applied in beginning of monsoon (June-July) and the remaining half dose at the end of monsoon (September-October).

At Rahauri (Maharashtra) 1.5 kg N, 0.45 kg P_2O_5 and 0.50 kg K_2O recorded the highest yield in Kalipatti sapota. To full grown tree of sapota cv. Kalipati 50 kg FYM, 900 *g* N, 450 *g* P_2O_5 and 450 K_2O per plant per year is recommended in Gujarat.

Under Punjab conditions, sapota at the age of 1 - 3 years is given 25 kg FYM, 220 - 660 g urea, 300 - 900 g SP and 75 - 250 g MoP per tree. At the age group of 4 - 6 years, 50 kg FYM, 880 - 1300 g urea, 1240 - 1860 g SP and 340 - 500 g MoP is applied to each tree. To the next age group of 7 - 9 years, 75 kg FYM, 1550 - 2000 g SP and 600 - 770 g MoP is applied. To full grown tree of 10 years age and above doses are stablised at 100 kg FYM, 2200 g urea 3100 g SP and 850 MoP to per tree. FYM, phosphorus and potash should be applied in the month of December - January. Half of nitrogen should be applied in March and remaining half in July - August.

Micronutrient application also affect productivity and quality of sapota. Deficiency symptoms of Zn and Fe have been observed in field. The deficiencies can be corrected by spraying 0.5 per cent zinc sulphate and ferrous suphate.

TRAINING AND PRUNING

A strong central stem is needed in sapota. In air-layers most of the branches are putforth very near the ground level. In the beginning, the basal branches help in developing a thick central stem and hence care must be taken to maintain proper distribution of branches on all sides. At later stage, the lower most branches weigh down to ground level and become unfruitful. In general, sapota has a well-balanced distribution of branches thus there is no necessity of pruning every year.

The lower most branches of sapota up to a height of 60-90 cm may be removed after 3 to 4 years of planting. The overshaded and crowded branches are also to be removed. The new growth and flowering occur simultaneously and it is a mixed type of bearing habit. Flowers and fruits appear in the axil of leaf on the new growth and hence pruning of branches should not be done.

USE OF GROWTH REGULATORS

Self pollination is seen in stray plar s and pollination becomes difficult. To get higher fruit set and retention of the set fruits, GA, ethrel, CCC and planofix and SADH were tried on Cricket Ball cultivar. SADH at 100 ppm befc e flowering and again at the peak stage resulted in the highest fruit set. Planofix at 300 ppm and GA_3 100 ppm resulted in the highest fruit retention and largest fruits. NAA @ 25-100 ppm at flowering and at 15 days interval resulted in better fruit set at Navsari.

HARVESTING AND FRUIT HANDLING

Sapota is a climacteric fruit, it ripes properly and improves in it's quality after harvesting. It matures in 8 to 10 months after fruit set depending upon cultivar and available heat units. Great difficulty is experienced in determining maturity because of continuous flowering and fruiting. The fruit harvested earlier than physiological maturity takes too long to soften and has poor quality. On the other hand, fruits harvested late soften quickly resulting in spoilage during handling and transport.

Phenols and sugar level increased during development while acidity and ascorbic acid reduced. The fruit nearing physiological maturity sheds off the brown, scaly scurf from the skin. At this stage, fruits become corky brown in colour with intermixed yellowish tinge. Such fruits give a yellow streak when scratched with finger nail, and show practically no green tissue or latex. However, considerable experience is needed to determine the exact stage. Harvesting is done by twisting the individual fruit. Fruit picker is used to pluck fruits at height.

Continuous flowering and fruiting is observed in sapota though there are two distinct periods of harvest viz. September-November and January-March. At some location June-July crop is also obtained in small quantity.

Sapota yields about 250 fruits per tree in the 5th year, in 7th year the yield rises to 800 fruits and between 10th and 15th year it may range from 1500 to 2000 fruits per tree. A 30 year old tree yields about 2500 to 3000 fruits. The yield usually declines after 40th year and it may not be profitable to maintain the orchard thereafter.

The fruits are graded into 3 grades *i.e.,* large, medium and small. They can be packed in CFB boxes, wooden crates, bamboo baskets which are padded with straw, soft grass or dried banana leaves for sending to distant market. The fruits of Cricket Ball and Kalipatti are packed in 3 kg boxes at 15 – 20°C when exported to Middle East. Sapota fruit is highly perishable and cannot be stored for long. Under ordinary conditions, fruits keep well for 5-7 days and spoil within few days from picking due to rapid degradative metabolism. Thereafter, post-harvest losses are enormous. While placing fruits for ripening, care should be taken that they are kept in thin layer otherwise there are chances of rotting and uneven ripening.

Uniform ripening of fruits can be achieved by dip treatment with 1000 ppm ethephon for two minutes. The polyethylene packing was highly effective in checking weight loss and maintaining turgidity and freshness of sapota fruits. GA @ 75 ppm was found optimum and effective in arresting ripening process and weight loss. GA treatment at 75 ppm for 3 minutes dip + 100 gauge polythene with 1.2% vents was the best for prolonging the shelf life of sapota fruits upto 11 days. Treatment of fruit with GA 300 ppm also retarded the ripening by reducing respiration and ethylene production.

Ripe sapota fruits can easily be stored at 2–3°C and 85- 90% RH for 5-6 weeks and firm fruit at 3 to 5°C for 8 weeks.

The storage life at 20°C can be extended for 21 - 25 days by removing ethylene and adding 5 - 10 per co_2 to storage atmosphere. Dipping the fruit in 300 ppm GA_3 and 1000 ppm Bavistin extend the stroage life of fruits. For sending fruits to distant market, Refrigerated vans (12 – 23°C) should be used for transportation.

INSECT PESTS

1. Stem borer (*Indarbela tetraonis*) : The grub bores into the bark of the sapota trunk and feeds on the living tissue inside the bark. The presence of the insect can be detected from the chewed bark thrown out of a hole in the trunk. This insect is commonly found in Tamil Nadu, Karnataka, etc.

Kill the insect by thrusting a stiff wire into the tunnel. Plug the hole with a wad of cotton wool dipped in kerosene and plastered with wet mud. By this, the borer gets suffocated and dies within the tree.

2. Mealy bug : (*Phenacoccus icerjoides*) : It is a sucking insect. Bugs are small, oval with a cottony white waxy covering on their body. Mealy bug stick on the upper surface of the leaves and base of the fruit near the fruit stalks. Leaves have a black coating which gives them a sickly appearance.

Spray dimethoate @ 150 ml in 100 litres of water for its control. Try to keep free sapota plantation from red ants because these help in distributing mealy bugs from one tree to another.

3. Fruit borer (*Virachola isocrates*) : It attack on fruits and sometimes buds which can easily be detected by seeing the latex which comes out on the surface of the infested fruits. The latex crystallizes later on. Sapota bud borer (***Anarsia achrasella***) and sapota moth (***Nephopterix eugraphella***) also infest sapota and do considerable loss.

For their control spray 0.05% percent malathion. Spray Dursban 20 EC (Chlorpyriphos) @ 300 ml in 100 litres of water as soon as attack is noticed.

4. Scale insects (*Pulvinaria psidii.*) : They suck the sap by infesting along the sides or midrib and surface of leaves and twigs. These scales are green or brown in colour and oval shaped.

Spray diamethoate or malathion 150 ml in 100 litres of water.

5. Bark eating caterpillar (*Indarbela sp.*) : This bores into the stem bark and the excreta along with fibrous material hang down outsides the bark.

The pest can be controlled by giving one or two sprays of dimethoate @ 150 ml in 100 litres of water.

6. Leaf miner (*Anarsia gemoniella*) : The tiny caterpillar of a greyish moth mines into the surface of young leaves. Affected leaves curl up, irrigular galleries or mines are seen on the surface of leaves and sometimes caterpillars are found inside the mines. Later on, affected leaves get destroyed, dry up and fall.

Spray once or twice dimethoate or malathion (150 ml in 100 litres of water).

DISEASES

1. Leaf spot : The disease is caused by a fungus ***Phaeophleospora indica.*** It is characterised by numerous, small, pinkish to reddish brown spots with whitish centres. In severe cases, the defoliation of leaves may be noticed and tree becomes partially or fully barren. Leaf spot become severe during rainy season.

For its control, spray Dithane Z-78 @ 0.2 per cent followed by Blitox (0.5%) at an interval of 30 days. Grow resistant varieties CO-1 and Cricket Ball.

2. Sooty mould : The disease is incited by ***Capnodium*** sp. The casual fungal disease develops on the honey dew like excretion by scale insects and mealy bug. The disease adversely affects the photosynthetic function of leaves and disfigures the fruit.

Spray Zineb at 200 g in 100 litres of water to check the disease. Spray starch solution @ 500 g in 100 litres of water. Starch forms thin flakes and drop off.

PHYSIOLOGICAL DISORDER

Flattening of branches or flat limb

The branches become flattened and this disorder has been attributed to a pathogen ***Botryodiplodia theobromae.*** It is observed in Maharashtra, Andhra Pradesh, Karnataka and Tamil Nadu, which reduces production by lowering the fruit set. The affected branches produce small, dry and shrivelled fruits. Affected branches produce leaves of smaller size, the branches have been found to recover to a normal growth during summer months. Phytosanitary measures are beneficial. Prunning and destroying the affected branches is the effective control measure.

CHAPTER 13

Cashewnut

Cashewnut (***Anacardium occidentale*** Linn) is an important tropical tree crops. It ranks second in international trade amongst the major edible nuts. During the past two decades cashewnut gained the status of a horticultural crop. India is one of the world's largest producer of cashewnut.

ORIGIN AND HISTORY

Cashewnut is believed to be a native of Brazil and dispersed from here to many of the tropical areas. It is reported that cashewnut was introduced in the Malabar Coast of India in the 16th century by the Portuguese. The Malabar Coast probably served as a locus of dispersal to other centres in India and South-East Asia. From, India, it was carried eastward to Amboina in Indonesia. The dispersal of the species to South-East Asia appears to have been carried out by birds, bats, monkeys and human agents. The different names of cashew in Indian languages are derived from the portuguese name **Caju** which in turn originated from **Acaju**, the name given to cashew by the Tapi Indians of Brazil.

Major cashewnut producing countries are Viet Nam, Nigeria, India, Cote d' Ivoire, and Brazil.

AREA AND PRODUCTION

Basically, cashewnut is considered as a waste land crop grown for afforestation and soil convervation purposes. The majority of the area, 9.79 lakh ha at present, available in India is covered with non-descript genetically inferior seedling progenies which has resulted in average productivity of around 695 kg per ha as against the national target of one tonne per ha. Viet Nam and Nigeria the world's largest producer of cashew nuts. India rank third in production followed by Cote d'Ivoire and Brazil.

The other cashew nuts producing countries are Indonesia, Philippines, Indonesia, Guinea - Bissau, Tanzania and Benin. The total world production of cashew nuts is estimated 27 lakh metric tonnes with average yield of 0.6 mt per hectare. However, Peru has the highest production yields of 5.3 mt cashew nuts per hectare.

India is producing cashewnuts about 16 per cent of the world production. Maharashtra is the leading cashewnut producing state in India accounting for 32 per cent of total production and 19 per cent of total area with highest productivity in the country. The other major cahsew nut producing states in India are Andhra Pradesh, Odisha, Kerala, Karnataka, Goa, Chhattisgarh, Gujarat, Jharkhand, Meghalaya, Puducherry, Tamil Nadu, Tripura and West Bengal. At present the total area under in India is 9.79 lakh hectares with annual production of 7.25 lakhs mt.. The average productivity of cashewnut in India is 700 kg per hectare. Andhra Pradesh is the second largest producer of cashewnut in India and has an increasing trend in production. This state has 16 per cent of area and contributes 16 per cent of total production.

Kerala which has 7.8 per cent of the area contributes 10.8 per cent of the nut production. Among the states Odisha contributes about 14.0 per cent of the nut production, while the production from other states is less than 10 per cent. This is achieved only because the majority of the area has been planted with recommended varieties namely V-1 and V-4 and plants are raised through vegetative means. In Kerala, the productivity is raised nearly one tonne per ha during the recent years because the crop is grown in the homesteads and receive much better attention. However, in the East-Coast, the productivity levels are much lower mainly due to the poor soils such as degraded soils in Andhra Pradesh and sandy soils of low fertility in Orissa and completely neglected cultivation by the forest plantation in Tamil Nadu.

Export potential : India requires about 12-13 lakh tonnes of raw cashewnuts to feed the large number of cashew processing units engaging over five lakh workers, especially women. Presently, India produces about 7 lakh tonnes of raw cashewnuts annually, the balance of 6 lakh tonnes of raw cashewnuts are imported annually from African and South East Asian countries. India is the second largest exporter of Cashew kernels in the world and exporting 1.1 lakh tonnes of cashew kernals to over 65 countries and earning about Rs. 2900 crores.

There is an ever-increasing demand for cashew kernals in International and domestic markets. Viet Nam and Brazil compete with India in International market.

IMPORTANCE AND USES

The cashew kernels are highly nutritive. They are rich source of carbohydrates, proteins, unsaturated fats, minerals like calcium, phosphorus, iron and vitamins. It contains fat 47%, protein 21%, carbohydrates 22%, carotein 100 I.U. per 100 g, vitamin B_1 630. mg/100 g, Riboflavin 190 mg/100 g and iron 5 mg/100 g. The kernels supply 6000 calories energy per kg. The cashew apple is rich in vitamin C and contains 180 mg ascorbic acid per 100 g juice.

There are many medicinal uses of cashew apple and its juice. It is a good remedy for scurvy, cough and cold and is considered an excellent purgative. The cashewnut shell liquid is an important raw material for a number of polymer based industries like paints and varnishes, resins, industrial and decorative laminates, brake linings and rubber compounding resins.

The wood of cashewnut is used for fire wood and charcoal making. It's wood pulp is used to fabricate corrugated and hard board boxes. Fenny (a type of wine) is commonly prepared from cashew apple which is found very popular in Goa. The remains can be used as cattle feed.

BOTANY

The cashewnut belongs to the family Anacardiaceae. According to Bailey, **Anacardium** is a small genus with few species. As many as 23 species of **Anacardium** are known to exist in Central and South America. The important species of **Anacardium** are as follows :

Anacardium occidentale, A. macrocarpa, A. phemilium, A. orthonianum, A. brasiliense, A. curatellaefolium, A. encardium, A. giganteum, A. humile, A. mediterraneum, A. nanum, A. rhinocarpus, A. spruceanum, A. microsepalum, A. corymbosum, A. excelsum, A. parvifolium, A. amilcarianum, A. kuhlmannianum, A. negrense, A. rondonianum, A. tenuifolium and A. microcarpum.

On the basis of division, **Anacardium nanum** is referred as 'Dwarf' and **Anacardium giganteum** as 'Giant'. Each species is divided into cultivars characterised by colour (yellow or red) and shape (round, pear-shaped or elongated) of apple.

The cashewnut tree is somewhat straggling with shorter leaves, more distinctly viewed and less strikingly coloured. The flowers are borne in terminal panicles and are usually broader and shorter and less compact than those of mango panicles, with staminate and hermaphrodite flowers in the same panicles. The stamens are nearly all normal and produce pollen. The true fruit is the nut.

CLIMATE

Cashewnut is mainly a tropical plant. It does well under hot and humid climate of the west coast. Cashewnut is hardy and drought resistant though it is less resistant to frost and chilly weather. It can not stand dry hot summers. If there is sufficient water supply, it can withstand long period of low relative humidity also. Temperature is a limiting factor in its cultivation and a mild tropical climate is most suitable. The regions where the temperature ranges from 20 to 30°C with annual rainfall of 1000 – 2000 mm are ideal for cashew cultivation. High temperature (39-42°C) during the marble stage of fruit development causes fruit drop. If the temperature falls below the freezing point, the trees are injured. It's distribution is restricted to altitude between 700-900 M where temperature does not fall below 20°C for prolonged period.

Cashewnut seems to thrive on sandy belts along the east coast with about 90 cm of rain per year and with 300-380 cm in the West Coast. It is a sun-loving tree and does not tolerate excessive shade. It is said to be rather highly resistant to strong winds.

SOIL

Cashewnut can be grown in wide variety of soils. It can survive even in the waste land with low fertility levels and those which are prone to soil erosion. It is grown widely on laterite, red and coastal soils in Kerala, Maharashtra, Goa, Karnataka, Tamil Nadu, Andhra Pradesh, Orissa and West Bengal. However, the best soil for cashewnut is deep, well-drained, sandy loam soils without hard pan.

It has been reported that high clay content, high pH more than 8.0, high base saturation, poor drainage or seasonally high water table and the presence of stones or hard pan within 100 cm of soil depth reduced tree size. High sand content and high rainfall are reported favourable.

CHOICE OF VARIETIES

The brief characteristics of some cashewnut cultivars released in India are as follows :

BPP–1 : Nuts are medium-sized (5g) and the shelling percentage is 27.5. The apple is medium sized and yellow in colour with juice content of 68%. The percentage of perfect flower is about 13.2 with the fruit set of 8 fruits per panicle. The average yield is 17 kg at the age of 25 years.

BPP–2 : The nuts are small (4g) and shelling percentage is about 26. The percentage of bisexual flowers is 7 with the fruit set of 8 to 10 fruits per panicles. The average yield is about 19 kg at the age of 25 years.

BPP–3 : This is a selection from Simhachalam in Vishakhapatnam (Andhra Pradesh). The average nut weight is 6 g and shelling percentage is 28. The average yield is 16 kg/ tree at the age of 25 years.

BPP-4 : The nut weight is 6 g and shelling percentage is about 23. This plant has got distinct light pink pigmentation in younger leaves and apple colour is yellow with conical shape. The average yield is 12.5 kg/tree at the age of 17 years.

BPP-5 : This is a collection from Andhra Pradesh. The nut weight is 5.2 g and shelling percentage is only 24. At the time of selection of tree (50 years) the yield was 42 kg/tree/year.

BPP-6 : : This is also a collection from Andhra Pradesh 56. The nut weight is 5.2 and shelling percentage 24. The mean yield in 50th year was 42 kg nuts per tree.

Vengurla-I : This is a selection from Ansur village in Vengurla Tehsil. The nut weight was 6 g with shelling percentage of 31. At the age of 28 years the average yield was 23 kg per plant. The average perfect flowers per panicle were about 8%.

Vengurla-2 : This is a selection from West Bengal. The nuts are small with 4 g weight and shelling percentage 32. The average perfect flowers is 8%. At the 20th year, the average yield was about 24 kg/tree. This selection has very short flowering and fruiting phase (45 days) with pinkish red coloured apples.

Vengurla-3 : Hybrid between Ansur-1 × Vetore-56. The nut weight is 9 g and shelling percentage 27. The percentage of perfect flowers is 25 with the average fruit set of 7% per panicle.

Vengurla-4 : Hybrid between Midnapore Red × Vetore-56. The nut is also bold weighing 8 g and shelling percentage is 31. The percentage of perfect flowers was 35 and fruit set was 6.

Vengurla-5 : Cross between Ansur Early × Mysore Kotekar 1/61. It has medium to small sized nuts with 4-5 g weight and shelling percentage is 30. The average yield at 14th year is 21 kg. This has the highest perfect flowers (50.5%) per panicle. However, the fruit set is only 3.3%.

VR-1 : This is a selection from Vazhisodhanipalayam in South Arcot District of Tamil Nadu. The nuts are medium sized (5g) and give 28% shelling. Bisexual flowers are 14.6% and bear 5-7 fruits per panicle. It has late flowering habit. The mean yield at 17 years is 7.4 kg/tree.

VR-2 : This is a selection from Kathupalli village in Chingalpettu District of Tamil Nadu. The nut size is 5 g, shelling percentage is 28. Bisexual flowers are 10% with 5-8 fruits per bunch. The average yield at 17th year is about 6 kg/tree. It is a late flowering type.

Ullal-1 : This is a selection from Taliparamba in Kerala. The nut is medium to bold sized weighing 7 g and yield 31% shelling. The cultivar has yield potential of 19 kg/tree at the age of 25. Bisexual flowers are 2-3%. The fruiting season is November to mid-March. The duration of harvest is about 110 days.

Ullal-2 : This is a selection from Guntur (A.P.). The nut size is medium (6g) and shelling percentage is 30. It yields 18 kg/tree after 25th year of orcharding. The percentage of bisexual flower is 7. It is a late flowering type (December to February). The duration of harvest is short *i.e.* 85 days.

Anakkayam-1 : The variety is from Cashew Research Station, Anakkayam, Kerala.The nut weight is 6 g and shelling percentage is 28. It yields 35 kg per tree at the age of 20. It produces pinkish yellow apples. This cultivar flowers during October (early flowering) and has a short flowering duration of 25-30 days.

K-22-1 : This is a selection from Karnataka. The nuts are medium in size (6.2 g) and shelling is 22.7%. It gives 13.2 kg nuts from 7th to 15th year of orchard life. It flowers during December- January.

NDR-2-1 : Selection was made from Naduvallur in Kerala. The nuts are bold-sized (7.25 g) and shelling percentage is 26.2. The tree yields 17.1 kg nuts from its 7th to 15th year of orchard life. The flowering is during December-January.

BLA-39-4 : It is a selection from Bapatla. The nuts are medium sized (6.2 g) and gives shelling 26.8 per cent. It records 20 kg yield in its 15th year of orchard life. The flowering season is November-December.

Apart from above selections Goa-1, Goa-2, Madakkathara 1 and 2, BPP-8, Dhana, Kanaka, Amrutha, NRCC Selection 2, Bhoskara, Chitamani-1, Chitamani-2, Bhubaneshwar-1 and Jhargram-1 are promising cultivars grown in different states.

PROPAGATION

Earlier, cashew was usually propagated through seeds planted **in situ** with 3 seeds per hole. Now, vegetative propagation by air- layering, budding and grafting is also possible. For raising rootstock seedlings medium sized nut (120 per kg) are selected from heavy and regular bearing trees of known percentage. These are stored in a cool dry place and sown on carefully prepared seed beds in December. Seeds are also sown in polythene bags with stalk end pointing upward and the suture slightly inclined. Protection against birds, rodents and other animals is needed after sowing of seeds. Generally, the earliest seedlings may appear 15-20 days after planting though many nuts take much longer time. Nuts with high specific gravity germinate more quickly and give more vigorous seedlings, have a higher total viability than the seeds with low specific gravity. Very large nuts having low specific density do not germinate properly.

Budding : The seedlings takes thickness of lead pencil before rainy season. Patch and forkert methods of budding can be employed. In patch budding, the bud-take is about 90 per cent during May-June. The sprouting of bud takes place after about one month. In case of forkert method, the bark is loosened by two vertical incisions, connecting the two with a transverse cut at the bottom. The bud is inserted into the flap by lifting the flap upward and the bud so covered with the flap is wrapped with polythene tape. The wrapper and the flap are removed after about one month of budding. The exposed bud starts developing further.

Grafting : Cashewnut can be successfully grafted by veneer, side, clift and whip grafting. Recently ***epicotyl and softwood grafting*** are becoming popular. Softwood grafting is considered the best method suitable for almost all cashew growing states in the country. The epicotyl grafts give only 25-30 per cent success due to mortality of grafts in the nursery. In case of soft grafting over 60 per cent successful grafts are obtained.

Soft-wood grafting : In this method, rootstock should be 20-25 days old with good growth. Seedling upto two month old were also used as rootstock at Vengurla (Maharashtra). Tall and lanky seedlings should be avoided for grafting. The scions should be 8- 10 cm long of lead pencil thickness with budding tips. The colour of the scion should be turning from green to brown. At the top, 4-5 leaves should be dark green indicating proper maturity. For precuring, leaf blades are clipped off 7-10 days before grafting. When the petiols dry and drop off, the scions can be detached from the tree and used for grafting. While doing grafting, one or two leaves should be left at the bottom and grafting is taken up in the softwood portion above these leaves. Longitudinal cut of 3-4 cm is made and scion wedge is inserted to the rootstock. Tying is done firmly. The grafts are kept in shade for a week and later transferred to open shade. This method gives comparatively higher per cent success.

Air-lyering : This is one of the most common methods of cashew propagation. The best time for air-layering is between February and April. Pencil thickness shoots of last season's growth are selected and a ring of bark about 3 cm long is removed. The ringed portion is applied with IBA @ 500 ppm in lanolin paste. It is then wrapped with polythene sheet. The roots are formed sufficiently within 60-80 days. The layers are separated and planted in pots. The layered plant should be placed under partial shade till transplanting.

Mound-layering : The selected trees are cut down at the ground level and cut ends are treated with fungicides to prevent fungal infection. Within two to three months many buds start sprouting from the ground level and they are covered with sand and soil upto 15 - 20 cm. After 30 - 40 days, shoots which turn green to brown are cinctured and treated with IBA and again covered with sand. Cinctured shoots produce roots in 30 - 40 days. Sand mound around the stump is removed and separated for planting.

PLANTING OPERATION

Before raising new plantation of cashewnut, land should be throughly prepared as soon as pre-monsoon showers are received. The pits of 60 cm × 60 cm × 60 cm should be dug atleast 15 days before actual planting. The planting should be made at the distance of 7-8 m depending upon the soil and climatic conditions. It will accommodate 202-140 plants per hectare according to the square system. The planting is done in the beginning of mansoon *i.e.,* May-June or preferably during July-August.

A closer spacing of 4m × 4m in the beginning (625 plants/ha) and thining out in stages and maintaining a distance of 8m × 8m (156 plants/ha) by the 10th year can be adopted for profitable cultivation. A spacing of 10m × 5m (200 plants/ha) can be adopted in levelled lands planting grafted plants.

FLOWERING AND FRUITING

The cashew tree starts bearing at the age of 3 to 5 years and attains full bearing by the 10th year and continues to yield usually upto 40 years. The inflorescence is an indeterminate of polygamomonoecious type. Each panicle contain 200 - 1600 flowers. Normally, there are three growth flushes in cashew and in South India the flower bud emergence commences by the middle of September and continues till the end of February, the main season being October-November. The fruit ripens from March to May. In West Bengal, panicles appear in December and flowering continues up to May. Late panicles bear little or no fruits.

Flowering in cashew appears in three distinct phases.

(*i*) The first male phase with 19-100 per cent male flowers.

(*ii*) The mixed phase with 0–60 per cent male flowers and 0-20 per cent hermaphrodite flowers.

(*iii*) The second male phase with 0-6.7 per cent male flowers.

The main duration of flowering was recorded as 85 days in which the duration of the first male phase was 2-4 days, mixed phase 69 days and second male phase 13 days. The percentage of hermaphrodite flowers in the mixed phase was 22.2 and the mean fruit set was 4.6.

The maximum number of hermaphrodite flowers are observed in panicles emerging in January which gradually reduced till May. The panicles appearing in the southern side of the tree had the largest number of hermaphrodite flowers. The partially mixed panicles and those appearing on one-month old shoot had longer number of hermaphrodite flowers and were found in the middle portion of the panicles.

The flowers are white to light green at the time of opening, later turning to pink. The flower is typically pentamerous. Number of stamens is 10-11, one or two are large and the remaining small. Yield in cashew is low due to small percentage of hermaphrodite flowers, low fruit set and heavy fruit drop. Average fruit set in cahsew is 3-10 per cent. Ovary is superior and is unilocular and it contains a single anatropous ovule.

Growth patterns of the apple, pericarp and kernel are of different types. Initially, the nut grows much faster than the apple but in later stages, the apple increases in size much more rapidly and soon outgrows the nut. The nut reaches their maximum size in about 30 days. Thereafter, the pericarp hardens and its size decreases. The fruit ripens in about 60 days. Protein contents of kernel increases steadily up to 40 days after fruit set and maintains its level high till harvesting. The sugar also increases upto 40 days, but declines sharply at harvest.

The nut is grey-coloured, kidney shaped and contains a single seed with membraneous adherent testa, semi-lunar cotyledons and short hooked radicle. The fleshy peduncle, the cashew apple is juicy, sweet when ripe and rich in vitamin C and sugar. The nut consists of an epicarp, mesocarp, endocarp, testa and kernel.

ORCHARD CULTURAL PRACTICES

Irrigation

Cashewnut is mostly grown as rainfed crop. But, it responds well to watering during flowering and fruiting. Two or three irrigations during growth and development period of fruits considerably increase the nut yield and reduce fruit drop. Irrigation at the time of flowering should be avoided.

Intercropping

Intercropping is now becoming more common in cashewnut plantation. This would enable higher return from the plantation during the first 4 years till the canopy covers the whole area.

Seasonal crops like horsegram, cowpea, groundnut, sweet potato, ginger, blackgram, can be raised in cashew plantation as intercrop. In Goa, casuarina trees, teak and euclyptus are also grown in the cashew plantation. In Andhra Pradesh and some parts of Odisha, cashew, coconut and casuarina form a popular crop combination. The annuals like pigeon pea and tapioca can also be profitably grown in the interspaces in the initial years of orchard establishment.

Weed Control

Light digging should be done before the end of rainy season to control the growth of weeds. Agrodar-96 (2, 4-D) @2 litres in 500 litres of water and subsequently. Gramoxone @ 2.5 l/500 liter of water can effectively check the weeds. The spray with weedicides can be again repeated after the monsoon.

Manuring and Fertilization

The annual nutrient removal in 30 year old cashewnut tree is 2.8 kg N, 750 g P_2O_5 and 1.26 kg K_2O. The festilizers recommended for a mature cashew free are 500 g N, 125 g P_2O_5 and 125 g K_2O per tree per year in two split doses before (May-June) and after the monsoon (August-September). At Konkan (Maharashtra), cashew tree responded to N at 125 kg, P_2O_5 at 50 kg and K_2O at 100 kg per hectare. Under Utkal region, the trees receiving NPK at 250 kg/ha each resulted in the highest yield. In laterite tract of West Bengal, high nut yield has been recorded in trees receiving N 200 g, P_2O_5 75 g and K_2O 100 g per tree at the age of 3 years. The following fertilizer schedule is commonly followed for cashewnut tree :

Age (years)	N	P (May-June) g/tree	K	N	P (August–Sept.) g/tree	K
1	85	22	22	85	22	22
2	170	42	42	170	42	42
3 & above	250	62	.62	250	62	62

TRAINING AND PRUNING

Normally training and pruning is not practised in cashewnut trees. Only, the young trees are trained by providing support at the time of planting and by removing any water sprouts carrying out on the trunk below the union during the first three years of growth. The branches which are hanging and touching the ground are removed. The plant should be allowed to grow by maintaining a single stem up to 0.75 - 1.0 m from the ground level. All the weak and criss-crossed branches are removed. To avoid lodging of the plant by wind, proper staking of plant is needed. After 4-5 years, the main stem attains a height of 4-5 m. After that, the dead and diseased twigs and dried branches should be removed to reduce losses through disease like 'Die- back' and also to minimise chance of serious losses due to forest fires. The cut ends should be pasted with Bordeaux paste. The training and pruning of plants is done during August - September.

TOP–WORKING

For rejuvenation of old and unthrifty plants in less humid areas, top working can be done with scion from superior genotypes. Under such condition grafting **in situ** was found to give higher success. In top-working, the trees are headed back during November- December at Ullal and during April to June at Puttur. After top- working, two-to-three-fold increase in yield in the second year was observed.

POLLINATION AND FRUIT SETTING

In cashewnut, the flowers start opening by 7 AM and continue upto 3 PM, the peak of opening the perfect flowers is between 9 AM – 2 PM. The stigma becomes receptive for about 24 hours before anthesis and continues to be so for about 48 hours after anthesis. The stigma becomes receptive as soon as the flowers open. Pollination is reported to be carried out by the flies, bees and ants as well as the wind.

Fruit setting is poor because percentage of hermaphrodite flower is less. About 3 to 10 per cent fruit set has been reported depending upon climatic conditions. Fruit set can be increased and fruit drop controlled with the use of growth regulators. Two or three times more nut production can be obtained by spraying 2, 4-D at 10 ppm either at the early or peak stage of flowering. NAA at 10 ppm spraying twice during the flowering period increases fruit set. Two sprays with 50 ppm GA at flowering are the most effective in increasing fruit set and fruit retention.

HARVESTING AND HANDLING OF FRUITS

The cashewnut tree commences economic bearing in third year, attains full bearing by the 10th year and continues to yield for 40 years. The fruit ripens from March to May. It takes two months after pollination for the fruits to be ready. The shell of the nut attains full size in 3-4 weeks after flowering after which the pedicel swells to produce the Cashew apple. The fruits are harvested when fully ripe. They may be allowed to fall on the ground and collected in dry weather, but in wet weather they must be collected daily and dried in the sun.

Harvesting and collection of nuts are done over a period of 10-12 weeks. When apple is not collected, the fruits may be allowed to fall on the ground and nuts collected periodically during the first 4-6 weeks. Later most of the nuts are collected in one or two major harvests.

Yield varies considerably from tree to tree due to climatic conditions, soil type, age of the tree, management practices, etc. On an average, one tree produces 30-35 kg of apples. At present the average yield of nuts in India is only 2.1 kg per tree per year. Maharashtra records the maximum average yield of 11.8 q/ha followed by Kerala 9.6 q/ha. A well raised plantation should yield 2.5 tons of nuts per hectare. On an average 4.6 tons of raw nuts provides one ton of kernels.

Processing : Processing of cashewnuts is the recovery of kernels from raw nuts by manual and mechanical means. Conditioning involves sprinkling of water on dried nuts to bring to an optimum moisture level of 15 - 25 per cent. Roasting makes the shell brittle. Roasting is done with two methods *i.e.* drum roasting and oil bath roasting . Manual shelling gives higher yield of nuts as compared to mechanical processing. After shelling, kernels are dried to reduce the moisture and to loosen the adhering testa. After drying for 6 - 12 hours, peeling is done by hand. The kernels are to be handled carefully to prevent breakage as they are brittle at this stage. The shelling percentage of cashew varies from 20 to 25.

Grading and Packing : Grading is done for export purpose on the basis of count or number of kernels per pound. Sound kernels are named as "Wholes" and broken ones as "Splits". The 'wholes' are packed in several grades viz. Nos. 210, 240, 280, 320, 400, 459 and 500. The popular grade of kernels is 320. The specification for graded kernels are that they should be fully developed, Ivory white in colour and free from insect damage and spots. Packing is done by Vita pack method. It is exhausting the air inside the packing tin, pumping in carbon dioxide and then sealing.

While grading, the 'wholes' are further classified as follow :

(*i*) Whole white kernels (*ii*) Whole scorched kernels (*iii*) Whole dessert kernels. The splits are also further graded into three grades as white pieces, scorched pieces, dessert pieces.

INSECT-PESTS

1. Tea mosquito bug (*Helopeltis antonii*) : They cause severe damage to the tender growing shoots and inflorescence of cashew trees. The adult appears at the time of emergence of new flushes and panicles. The pest population reaches its peak when trees are in full bloom. Both the adults and nymphs of the bud suck sap from the tender shoots, floral branches, tender apples and even immature nuts. The affected panicles and shoots dry up.

The pest can be controlled by spraying carbaryl at 0.15 per cent or dimethoate 0.05 per cent or Quinalphos at 0.05 per cent at the time of emergence of new flushes (October) and panicles (December - January). Spray the plants after 2 or 3 weeks depending upon the severity of infestation.

2. Leaf miner (*Acrocercops syngramma*) : It appears generally in the post harvest and post-mansoon flushes. The caterpillars mine through the tender leaves and severely damage them.

The pest can be effectively controlled by spraying 0.05 per cent fenitrothion at the time of emergence of new flushes. Monocrotophos 36 WSC at 0.05 per cent can also be sprayed.

3. Stem and Root borers (*Plocaederus ferrugineus*) : It has capacity to kill the tree out right. The borers make holes in the collar region of the tree and the gum oozes out from the holes. It leads to yellowing and shedding of leaves. Twigs start drying and ultimately whole tree is dead. Plantations over 15 years old are often infested with this pest.

The pest can be controlled by drenching the basal trunk and the root region with 1.25 litres of lindane 20 EC in 250 litres of water per ha. Inject carbon disulphide into the tunnels and plaster them with mud.

4. Leaf and blossom webber (*Lamida moncusalis* and *Orthaga exvinacea*) : Leaf webber is a major pest in the coastal districts of Andhra Pradesh. The caterpillars web the shoots and inflorescence together, remain inside and feed on them.

Spraying of 0.05 per cent malathion or carbaryl 50 WP 0.1 per cent at the time of emergence of new flushes immediately after the monsoon is recommended for the control of the pest.

DISEASES

1. Pink Disease or die-back : The disease is caused due to fungus ***Corticium salmonicolor*** (***Pellicularia salmonicolor***). The disease is found common during the rainy season. Affected shoots dry up from the tip downwards. During mansoon season, a film of silky thread of mycelium develops in the branches. Later, the fungus develops a pinkish growth which represents the spore form.

Prune the affected branches below the spot of infection and destroy them. Protect the cut surface by application of Bordeaux paste. Spray with Bordeaux mixture 1 per cent in pre-monsoon *i.e.* May-June and post monsoon *i.e.* September-October.

2. Anthracnose : ***Colletotrichum gloeosporioides*** fungus causes the disease. The fungus enters the fruit through the stigma in the flower stage. Rainy season is favourable for the spread of the disease.

Remove the affected parts and spray the plant with 3:3:50 Bordeaux mixture. Plant thick windbreak of tall growing trees like Casuarina, Eucalyptus, Subabul, etc. The windbreak helps in preventing spread of the disease by wind-blown spores.

3. Damping off of seedlings: Different fungi like ***Fusarium*** sp, ***Pythium*** sp., ***Phytophthora palmivora*** and ***Cylindrocladium scoparium*** causes damping off in different areas. The disease occurs under poor drainage conditions in the nursery. The fungi attacks either the root or the collar or both of the seedlings.

Excess water should be drained away from the nursery. Drench nursery beds with Ceresan 0.1 per cent or Bordeaux mixture 1 per cent.

4. Inflorescence blight : The inflorescence blight is caused by fungi ***Gloeosporium mangiferae*** and ***Phomopsis anacardii*** in association with tea mosquito. The disease is characterised by the drying of floral branches particularly when cloudy weather prevails

The mosquitos should be kept under control.

DISORDERS

The appearance of yellow leaf spot, a possible disorder is reported in cashew perhaps due to molybdenum deficiency. The trees sprayed with 0.03% solution of ammonium molybdate once during pre-monsoon and another after cessation of monsoon was found to be effective in reviving the plants.

Little leaf is characterised by small rolled leathery leaves. Foliar spray of 0.3 per cent zinc sulphate is useful to correct the disorder.

CHAPTER 14

Custard Apples

The term custard apple is commonly applied to all the **Annona** species producing edible fruits. These are very delicious fruits. Custard apples are known for their wide adaptability to soil and climatic conditions and freedom from pests and diseases. They are widely grown in tropical and subtropical parts of the world. The commercial plantations of custard apples are not yet established and usually finds a place only in home gardens.

ORIGIN AND HISTORY

All annonaceous fruits are indigenous to tropical America. They spread to different parts of the world after the discovery of the continent. It is thought that few species may be native to Africa. According to Baily ***Annona squamosa*** is a native of West Indies and South America while ***Annona cherimola*** has its origin in the mountains of Ecuador and Peru. The sculptural designs at Ajanta and Ellora and the mention of custard apple in Sanskrit literature, prove that it has been in India since very old times. After being introduced by the Portuguese, the fruits dispersed quickly and got acclimatised throughout South Asia.

Custard apple is now grown in Brazil, China, Australia, Myanmar, Hawaii, Chile, Egypt, Central Africa, Mexico, Israel, Philippines, Spain, South Africa, USA (California), West Indies, India and Sri Lanka.

AREA AND PRODUCTION

In India, the custard apples are very popular in Deccan Plateu and are grown commercially on smaller scale in Andhra Pradesh, Maharashtra, Karnataka, Bihar, Odisha, Assam, Tamil Nadu, Bihar and Uttar Pradesh.The groves are found growing here and there in the gardens or home backyards. Maharashtra and Andhra Pradesh are the leading states in Annona cultivation and annual production. Custard apples in India are cultivated on 19000 hectares with annual production of 1.27 lakh mt/ha. It is accounts for 0.3 per cent of area and 0.2 per cent of the total fruit production in the country. The average production of custard apple is 6.7 mt/ha.

IMPORTANCE AND USES

The custard apples are rich source of carbohydrates, protein, fibre, minerals like calcium, phosphorus and iron and vitamin C. They are considered good energy source with the value of 104 Kcal. *Annona squamosa* fruit contains carbohydrates 23.5 g, moisture 70.5%, protein 1.6 g, mineral 0.9 g, fibre 3.1 g, calcium 17 mg, phosphorus 47 mg, iron 1.5 mg and vitamin C 37 mg. These values are based on 100 g fruit pulp.

Custard apples are mostly consumed as table fruits. They can be preserved as jam, jelly and are also used in ice-creams, and other milk products. Baked fruits are commonly eaten in Andhra Pradesh. The pleasant flavour and mild aroma of custard apples are liked universely. The edible portion of fruit is creamy, granular with an excellent blend of sweetness and acidity. The immature fruits, seeds, leaves and roots are known for their medicinal use in Aurvedic and Yunani system. The seeds contain about 30 per cent oil which can be used in soap and paint industry. The seed cake contains nitrogen, thus can be used as a manure.

BOTANY

The custard apples belongs to family **Annonaceae** and genus *Annona*. In India, the custard apple is ***Annona squamosa,*** in USA ***Annona reticulata*** or ***Annona glabra*** and in Australia ***Annona atemoya***. About 50 species of shrubs and trees belong to this genus bearing aggregate fleshy fruit but only six species produce fruits of commercial importance. A brief description of the **Annona species** is as follows :

1. *Annona squamosa* : Custard apple, sugar apple, sweet sop or **Ate,** Sharifa (Northern India), Sitaphal (Southern part).

It is the most widely cultivated species in India and probably in the tropics of the world. It is a deciduous, tall, woody shrub or small tree. 5-6 m in height with irregular spreading branches. The alternate double-ranked leaves are lanceolate and acuminate. The greenish yellow flowers arise at an extra axillary position, usually in clusters and rarely solitary. Petals is in two whorls. The outer petals are thick, linear and rounded at the apex, while inner petals are minute, ovate or abovate and keeled on the outside. The flower has numerous stamens and carpels. The fruit is composed of cohering carpels forming a tuberculated surface. The black seeds are surrounded by white creamy or custard-like pulp which is very sweet and pleasantly flavoured.

2. *Annona cherimola* : Cherimola or cherimoya

It is considered best fruit among the annonaceous fruit because of its sweet flavour, buttery consistency of pulp and low seed content. It is considered one of the finest sub-tropical fruits in Brazil, Australia, Hawaii, Mexico, California and India. It has been established well in Telangana region of Andhra Pradesh. It is a deciduous, small spreading tree with greyish pubescent shoots. The lower surface of leaf is velvety tomentum. The flowers are usually solitary with narrow outer petals. The inner petals are small and scale like. The fruits are 8 to 15 cm in diameter, green in colour and round to heartshaped. Baily has recognised the following five cultivars on the basis of fruit form are :

Finger-Printed Cherimoya, Smooth Cherimoya, Tuberculate Cherimoya, Mammiliate Cherimoya and Umbonate Cherimoya.

3. *Annona reticulata* : Bullock's-Heart, Bull's-Heart or Ramphal.

It is essentially a tropical fruit require mild climate and thrive well all over South India upto an elevation of 1200 MSL. It is a deciduous tree, 6-8 m in height with lenceloate, long, acuminate and glabrous leaves. The exterior petals are yellowish, fleshy while the interior ones are scale-like. The fruits are smooth, heart-shaped and contain few seeds. Due to low sugar content, the fruit is inferior in quality than custard apple and Cherimoya. It comes into the market late than custard apple because flowering occur from August to October and the fruit ripen in April and May. This species is not cultivated on commercial scale in India.

4. *Annona muricata* : Soursop

It is an evergreen small tree flourishing in tropical climate of central America and Peru. The fruit is also popular in Cuba and Sri Lanka. In Andhra Pradesh and Assam, it is grown on very limited scale. The leaves are short, obovate - oblong to elliptic and shinning above. The exterior petals are fleshy and valvate and interior ones are small and imbricate. The fruits are heart-shaped, extra large with many soft spines pointing towards apex. The white, juicy pulp has acidic mango like flavour which is strained and used in preparing drinks, ice-cream, jelly and other preserves. The acid content is 3-4 times more than custard apple.

It is incompatible with custard apple and cherimoya. The low productivity in soursop has been attributed to the inadequate pollination.

5. *Annona diversifolia* : llama

It is a small tree of subtropical climate and is popular in Mexico and Central America. The leaves are glabrous and papery thin with leaf-like bracts at the base. The outer petals are linear oblong and inner petals are tiny and scale-like. The fruit resembles to the custard apple but is covered by greyish tomentum. It's pulp is cream or rose-coloured.

6. *Annona atemoya* : Atemoyas (Hybrid between Custard apple and Cherimoya).

It is commercially grown in coastal and subtropical regions of Australia. African Pride (Cherimoya × Custard apple) has become an important cultivar of this region. It is a semi-deciduous, sub-tropical fruit tree being tolerant to frost. The quality of atemoyas is similar to cherimoyas but it is near to custard apple in climatic requirements. It differs considerably among themselves in plant and fruit characters due to heterozygous parents. The leaves are very large. The fruit has a thick coating of glaucous bloom. The pulp is juicy with an excellent acidic flavour.

On the basis of isozyme variation pattern at 15 loci influencing 8 enzyme systems, the differences among the cultivars of cherimoya and differences between cherimoya and atemoya can be made.

CLIMATE

Annonas are of tropical origin, prefer warm climate and moderate winter and humidity. The tree remains dormant for a short period during cold season. The prolonged cool weather and frost adversely affect its growth. The temperature above 40°C cause heavy flower drop in northern India. High temperature further affect the fruit growth and yield due to soil moisture strees. Tropical climate might not be conducive for higher fruit production. Hence, warm subtropical conditions show better fruit growth and yields. They can thrive well up to an elevation of 1000 metres above sea level. Annual rainfall of 50-75 cm is considered adequate for its growth and fruiting. Annonas can also tolerate adverse weather conditions at the cost of growth and yield. In northern India during summer season due to high temperature and lack of humidity, no fruit set occurs inspite of profuse flowering. Warm temperature with high humidity and occasional rains are required for good set and development of custard apple fruits. Cherimoya perform better at lower temperature than custard apple and atemoya.

SOIL

Annonas can grow successfully in wide variety of soil ranging from heavy soils to almost sand. The waste lands, marginal, sandy and rocky soils can be considered for growing these fruits. However, for getting better crop, a fertile, well drained sandy loam soil and neutral in reaction is preferred. Waterlogged, heavy soils with poor drainage, sub-soil with hardpan or having high water table needs to be avoided. The custard apple is generally planted in sandy soils with limited nutrients. The growth remains stunted and yield poorly if moisture deficiencies are not compensated by frequent irrigations. These fruits do not thrive well in saline and alkaline soils.

CHOICE OF VARIETIES

Custard Apple : Red Sitaphal, Balangar, Barbados, British Guinia, Brandy, Islander, Washington PI 98797, Washington PI 1070005 and Mammoth are important varieties of custard apple.

1. Balangar : It has better fruit quality than other cultivars. Average number of fruits are 48 per tree. Fruit weight 137 g, pulp 44.9%, TSS 20.7%, acidity 0.20% and total sugars 17.9%. Seed weight 5.7 g.

2. Red Sitaphal : It is distinct cultivar probably originated as chance seedling. The fruits are pinkish dark and pulp erythrite red. Seeds are more. Number of fruits are 22 per tree with 156 g weight per fruit. TSS is 22.3%, acidity 0.24% and total sugars 15.9%. Seed weight 5.2 g, pulp 30.5%.

3. Arka Sahan : It is a hybrid variety of custard apple developed at 11HR, Bangalore. The fruit is large in size and weighing 300 to 500 g. Fruit has good taste. The seeds are fewer and small in size. Skin is tough, the ripening process is slow and has long storage life. Flesh is creamy white, juicy with mild pleasant aroma. TSS is 31 per cent.

4. Washington : The fruit weight is 161 g. Pulp 38 per cent. TSS in fruit is 20.8 per cent.

5. Mammoth : The average fruit weight is 122 g, pulp is 44.5 per cent.

PROPAGATION AND ROOTSTOCKS

Both sexual and asexual methods are employed for propagating the annona plants. However, to maintain the genetic uniformity for obtaining higher yield of better quality fruits, the clonal propagation is a must. The seedlings of local custard apple and Ramphal are good for raising rootstock for improved varieties and hybrids.

Raising of Seedlings

In custard apple seeds very little or no dormancy is observed. The fresh seed germinate in 20-30 days and gives 90 per cent germination. The seed of custard apple do not require any seed treatment like scarification or soaking in hot water. But, soaking of Cherimoya seeds in 500 ppm gibberellic acid improved germination considerably. Seed is sown in beds or polythene bags. The plants raised in polythene bags are perferred because of ease and low mortality during transplanting.

Custard apple as a scion on seedlings of custard apple and Ramphal starts yielding in the 5th year and yields 41 fruits per plant on Ramphal and 29 fruits on custard apple. In another study it has been reported that custard apple on Ramphal shows better tree vigour and fruit quality than on custard apple rootstock. Ramphal as a rootstock also imparted longer life to custard apple as compared to custard apple on custard apple. The atemoya cv. African Pride gave about double the fruit yield on Cherimoya than on custard apple rootstock in the 6th year of planting. The seedling rootstocks, however, exhibit wide variability in growth and yield of the scion.

Vegetative Propagation

Budding and Grafting : These are the commercial methods of vegetative propagation of annonas. Among the budding methods, shield, patch, modified forkert and chip can be employed with 53 to 100 per cent success. Budding is done in early spring when the sap starts flowing or in the autumn. For taking bud wood, dormant last year's shoots should be preferred. The grafting methods like tongue, cleft, veneer, inarching, splice were found successful in annonas.

These methods should be carried out in early spring using one year old mature scion and more than one year old rootstock.

Stooling : The stools of custard apple after treating with 20000 ppm IBA yields 94 per cent success. The rooted stools gave 80 per cent survival on planting. In the month of April, head back 3 years old seedlings at the ground level. After about 3 months, a 3 cm wide ring of bark is taken out from the base of each emerged shoot leaving one to serve as a nurse shoot. Lanolin paste containing IBA is smeared above the ringed portion followed by mounding of all the shoots. The rooted shoots are detached from the mother plant in the month of September. Stooling appears to be very promising method for clonal propagation.

Cuttings : The cultivar African Pride had higher rooting potential from stem cuttings. Etiolation of shoots also improved the rooting. The cuttings of custard apple placed under intermittent mist by etiolating for 15 days and treating with 5000 ppm Naphthalene acetic acid gives 90 per cent success. Higher success from stem cuttings has also been reported in Cherimoya and **Annona** hybrids.

PLANTING OPERATION

It is important that grafted plants should be grown for commercial cultivation. The plants raised in nursery beds from seeds suffer heavy mortality due to damage of roots during lifting and transplanting. It is desirable that the seedlings be raised in polythene bags and after budding or grafting they should be transplanted in the orchard.

The pits of 60 cm × 60 cm × 60 cm should be dug out and filled with a mixture of soil, 20 kg well rotten farmyard manure and 300 g fertilizer mixture of urea, superphosphate and muriate of potash in equal proportion. The distance should be kept 5 m from plant to plant and row to row in square system which thus accommodates 390 plants per hectare. Custard apple can also be planted at the distance of 4m × 4m and 6m × 6m. The planting should be done during the rainy season.

FLOWERING AND FRUITING

Custard apple has a short juvenile phase. The plants begin flowering within 4 years of planting. **Annona** species bear flowers on the current season's growth and very rarely on older wood. The flowering period of custard apples is very long commencing from March-April, continuing up to July-August. The peak flowering is observed in April and May. From initiation, a floral bud develop into flower in 27 to 35 days depending on the species. No fruit set occurs during the entire spring and summer and it commences only in the rainy season, leaving little period for the late set fruits to develop before the onset of winter season. The setting of fruits early in the season is important because immature fruits instead of developing become inedible in winter season and turn into stone fruits.

Annona fruits usually mature in about four months from the time of flowering. The period is reduced when the soil moisture is optimum. Fruits of **Ramphal** mature in about six months.

ORCHARD CULTURAL PRACTICES

Irrigation

The fruit set and development of Annonas occur during the rainy season, thus, they produce a fair crop even without any irrigation. Therefore, Annonas are considered drought-tolerant plants. It has been observed that the custard apple growing in damp and shady situation and receiving irrigation resulted in no fruit drop. The fruit also ripened about two months earlier than usual.

In atemoya, reduced flowering and fruit set has been reported at high temperature due to soil moisture stress. Under such conditions, productivity of cherimoya can be improved by cultural techniques viz, overhead misting, windbreaks and efficient irrigation scheduling.

Two to three irrigations before the onset of monsoon to promote fruit set and one to two irrigations after the monsoon to increase fruit size should be given to custard apples.

Intercropping

During the pre-bearing period, the intercrops can be grown judiciously to compensate the economic loss. Groundnut, linseed and minor millets can be given in the rainy season and pea, oilseeds and gram in the winter season. Intercrops prove beneficial in checking the soil erosion and weed growth.

Manuring and Fertilization

The custard apple is mostly cultivated on poor soils, thus, manures and fertilizers should be applied for better growth and yields. The flowering can be advanced by 10 to 15 days with high doses of nitrogen and phosphorus, but low nitrogen delayed flowering by over two months. High nitrogen rates resulted higher flower production while high N, P and K enhanced the fruit set.

The fertilizer dose for young plant has been recommended as 250 g N, 125 g P_2O_5 and 125 g K_2O per plant. The fertilizers should be applied on the commencement of rainy season. In another trial NPK each @ 240 g per tree resulted higher yield.

TRAINING AND PRUNING

The custard apple is very slow growing plant. It forms a small bush with a large number of branches of various sizes and ages. The fruits are borne on old wood as well as new wood. Light pruning of old wood induces better branching of the plant. Pruning can best be done to avoid overcrowding and to promote well spaced branches. In budded plants, the growth is uniform and there is very little need for any pruning. The custard apple normally goes to dormancy from November to December. The leaves gradually turn yellow at the time of harvest of fruit and drop with the approach of winter. The plants remain in leafless condition for about two months in the winter season and new growth emerges with the onset of spring. Pruning should be carried out when the plant is to put forth new growth in early spring after dormancy.

The completion of leaf fall is essential for the initiation of new growth in annonas. Two sprays of 0.5 per cent potassium iodide at weekly interval resulted in not only early and prolonged harvest but also gave higher yield. In the custard apple cultivar Balangar, manually and chemically defoliated plants and the control produced 17.4, 24.4 and 13.0 kg fruit per plant respectively. In the cultivar Red Sitaphal and Mammoth, manual defoliation was, however, better than chemical treatment.

TOP-WORKING

Large number of **annona** plants from seedlings have uncertain yield and fruit quality. Top working of such uneconomical seedling plants with commercial cultivars is a good proposition. Cleft grafting using two or three scions on large limbs can be employed successfully at the end of dormant season. A large number of one-year old shoots emerged out of the beheaded limbs which may be budded or grafted.

POLLINATION AND FRUIT SETTING

The main constraint in expanding the commercial cultivation of **annona** fruits is due to their low productivity. Enough flowers are borne on a custard apple plant but the poor fruit set causes low yield. Under natural conditions only 1-8 per cent fruit set has been reported. The low fruit set in custard apple is due to poor pollination which has been attributed to both the external and internal factors such as very high and low humidity prevailing at the time of flowering, soil moisture stress, competition between vegetative and floral growth, hypogyny, dichogamy, poor pollen germination and dearth of insect pollinators.

The peak flowering period of custard apple in northern India coincides with the summer season when the temperature goes beyond 40°C, humidity is extremely low, desiccating wind is prevalent and the soil is in dry condition. Neither the pollen is produced nor fruit set occurs in this situation. The pollen grain shrivelles and gets sterile in May and June due to high temperature and low humidity. The fruit set occurs only in rainy season on reversal of environmental conditions.

Poor pollen grain germination has been reported in all the species of Annona. The compound nature of pollen grains, thick exine and absence of germpores are held responsible. In custard apple 85 per cent fruit set was noted by hand pollination in comparison with 30 per cent of the control.

NAA at 10 - 20 pm spray prior to flowering period reduce the flower and fruit drop in custard apples. Dipping of freshly opened flowers of Mammoth cultivar in 50 ppm GA_3 gave 70 per cent fruit set and the developed fruits had more weight but less number of seeds. In custard apple about 18 per cent fruit set is observed by spraying the flowers with 100 ppm GA_3 and NOA.

HARVESTING AND HANDLING OF FRUITS

The custard apple is plucked from the tree while still firm and plumpy. When allowed to remain on the tree, the fruits get damaged due to splitting instead of ripening properly. On the other hand, immature fruits after harvest become soft and rot, though the skin remains intact. It is, therefore, essential to harvest the custard apples at the proper stage of maturity. The custard apple is a climacteric fruit. The fruits of custard apple or sugar apple should be picked when they have attained light green colour. There should be yellowish white colour between the carpels and initiation of cracking of the skin between the carpels. The individual fruit needs to be examined every alternate day to judge the stage of maturity for harvesting. The fruits are hand picked. The fruits in the coastal regions ripen earlier. The harvesting of custard apple starts from August and continues upto December, the peak period being October- November. The cherimoya fruits reach the market after custard apple followed by those of **Ramphal.**

Annonas plants begin bearing at the age of 5 year. The productive life of these trees is approximately 15 years. The 8 year old seedlings yield average number of 149 fruits per plant. The custard apple tree usually produces about 80-100 fruits each weighing 150-300 g. The atemoya cv. African Pride gave 18.7 tonnes yield of marketable fruits per hectare on cherimoya rootstock and 9.2 tonnes on custard apple rootstock in the 6th year of planting.

The custard apples ripen within few days after harvest. In an experiment, when the custard apples fruits were placed in straw, fruit leaves and open baskets; they ripened in 4, 5 and 6 days respectively. The longest shelf-life of four days at room temperature was found in fruits ripened in straw and fruit leaves. The custard apple fruits ripen normally at 15-30°C in storage. Low relative humidity accelerates the process of ripening. The fruits wrapped in perforated polyethylene bags and ripened in wheat straw suffered the least diameter loss compared with wrapping in paper bags and ripening in sawdust or gunny bags.

The ripe fruits being soft and perishable, require careful handling in marketing. The fruits should be wrapped in a piece of strong paper and allowed sufficient ventilation in packing when the fruits are to be sent to the distant markets.

The fruits of custard apple could be kept for about a week after treating with 8 per cent wax emulsion in combination with 400 ppm 2, 4-D and 2, 4, 5-T. Cherimoya fruits can be stored for 12 days at 9°C and 85-90% RH and 2% oxygen plus 10% carbon dioxide in controlled atmosphere storage. The shelf life of custard apple fruits can be extended upto 6 days at ambient temperature and 9 days in zero energy cool chamber after wrapping in tissue paper and placed in cardboard boxes.

INSECT PESTS

Mealy bug (*Planococcus pacificus*) : The pest has been noticed in harbouring on young shoots and in between the fruit segments. The blemished fruits do not fetch premium in the market.

To control the mealy bug, spray the plantation with 0.05 per cent dichlorvos.

DISEASES

1. Leaf spot : It is caused due to ***Alternaria*** sp. The disease appear in November at the fag end of harvesting, thus causes considerable loss in production. The affected leaves drop prematurely. British Guinea and Red Sitaphal are moderately susceptible to this disease.

The disease can be controlled by three fortnightly sprays of benlate or bavistin (0.05%) as soon as the symptoms appear.

2. Anthracnose : It is caused due to ***Glomeralla cingulata.*** The disease is noticed at Udaipur. The control measure is the same as in leaf spot.

DISORDERS

In custard apple some fruits remain very small and become brown. These are known as *'stone fruits'*. They retain on the tree even after harvest. Some physiological factors particularly competition among the developing fruits have been suggested to be cause of stone fruit formation. When the fruiting was spread over a longer period due to defoliation treatment, there was only 7-8 per cent stone fruit formation as compared to 30.7 per cent in the control.

The *'cracking of fruits'* is noticed in custard apple. It is caused due to sudden and high fluctuations in water supply to the plants. Usually, cracking occur from heavy rainfall or irrigation after a prolonged dry spell. Appropriate irrigation scheduling can reduce the problem of fruit cracking.

The abrupt decline of custard apple trees may result due to water logging in sandy or rocky soils. The stagnation of water in the orchards should be avoided.

C. SUB-TROPICAL FRUITS

15. Citrus
16. Grapes
17. Litchi
18. Ber
19. Loquat
20. Date-plam
21. Pomegranate
22. Jamun
23. Phalsa
24. Avocado
25. Aonla

CHAPTER 15

Citrus

Citrus comprising of mandarins, sweet oranges, grapefruit, limes and lemons is most important fruit crop grown in India. Before partition of India, citrus industry has taken a strong foothold in the districts of Layallpur, Montgomery and Sargodha (now in Pakistan). In the present Punjab, then the plantings were restricted to the gardens of Maharajas, Princes, Nawabs and the rich people. To boost up citrus cultivation, the concept of garden colonies was introduced in the Punjab after 1947. Twenty- eight garden colonies were established throughout the State. In the early years of post-independence era, the cultivation of sweet orange to limited extent of local mandarin spread rapidly.

Citrus fruits are grown under varying agroclimatic conditions in all the States of the Indian Union, except in the high hilly temperate regions. The cultivation of citrus in the North-Western States of Indian has steadily increased over the past few years due to its high productivity and adaptability to various agro- climatic regions. The area under citrus is likely to increase further if we try to match the production technology with the protection technology.

ORIGIN AND HISTORY

Most of the **citrus** species are native to tropical and subtropical regions of South East Asia, particularly India and China and in the region between these two countries. The north-eastern region of India is considered as one of the natural home of few citrus species. Most of the taxonomists agree that the mandarin originated in Cochin China. However, Hodgson, a well known American horticulturist, suspected that the mandarin is originated in eastern India. The existence of primitive forms like ***Citrus indica*** and several types of mandarin and mandarin like hybrids, growing wild in the forests of Assam lend support to this thinking.

Chinese literature written during 2200 BC showed evidence of citrus cultivation in China. Citrus was introduced in Greece between 250 and 200 BC. Bonnavia thought that Malaya is the home of lemon while pummelo is thought to be originated in the island east of Malaya archipelago, including Fiji and Friendly islands or in China. Citrus was probably introduced in Europe in 16th century by the Portuguese. It is believed that Colombus took orange and lemon seeds to America.

According to Bonnavia, the mandarin was introduced into Assam by Shan people who migrated westward from Yunan (China) and reached Southern Assam somewhere around the beginning of the Christian Era. The spread of the mandarin from Assam to other parts of India particularly northern India, seems to have taken place during the reign of Babar.

Kinnow, a hybrid between King mandarin and Willow leaf (Mediterranean mandarin), was developed by H.B. Frost in 1915 and released in 1935. A noble introduction of this cultivar made at Fruit Research Station, Layallpur (Now in Pakistan) inspired the growers to extend the cultivation in adjoining areas. In 1958 Dr. J.C. Bakhshi brought the virus-free bud wood of 25 different species of citrus-including Kinnow from California (USA).

The major citrus producing countries of the world are Brazil, USA, China, India, Mexico, Spain, Egypt, Italy, Indonesia, Turkey, Israel, Japan, Iran, Argentina, Morocco, Algeria, South Africa, Greece, Australia, Jamaica, etc.

AREA AND PRODUCTION

In India, citrus fruits (Mandarin, sweet orange and lime and lemons) are grown in 9.15 lakh hactares with total production of 79.22 lakh tonnes annually, accounts for 13.6 and 10.4 per cent of total area and production, respectively. Productivity of citrus varies from 4.4 to 21.9 tonnes per hectare depending agro- climatic regions which is much below the potential. Mandarin and sweet orange are grown mainly in Maharashtra, Andhra Pradesh, Punjab, Madhya Pradesh, Gujarat, Karnataka, Rajasthan, Assam, Odisha, Haryana and Uttarakhand.

Sweet orange (Mosambi) in India occupy an area of 1.62 lakh hectares, producing 12.32 lakh mt fruits accounting for 2.4 per cent and 1.6 per cent, respectively of total area and production under fruits. Major mosambi producing states are Maharashtra, Uttar Pradesh, Odisha, Punjab, Rajasthan, Madhya Pradesh, Kerala, Himachal Pradesh, Nagaland, Arunachal Pradesh, Assam, Meghalaya, Manipur, Tripura, Sikkim, Mizoram, Jammu and Kashmir, Haryana, Karnataka and Chhattisgarh. Blood Red variety of sweet orange is mainly produced in Uttarakhand, Uttar Pradesh, Odisha, Punjab, Rajasthan, Madhya Pradesh, Maharashtra, Tamil Nadu, Chhattisgarh and Jharkhand. Sathgudi variety is mainly cultivated in Andhra Pradesh, Odisha, Tamil Nadu, Rajasthan and West Bengal. The average productivity of mosambi is 7.6 mt/ha. Andhra Pradesh is producing 46.8 per cent mosambi fruits among the states.

The total area under mandarin in India is 3.29 lakh hectares producing 31.29 lakhs mt fruits. The average productivity is 9.5 mt/ha. The area and production under mandarin is accounting for 4.9 per cent and 4.1 per cent, respectively of the total area and production under fruits. The highest production of mandarin *i.e.* 9.15 lakh mt is recorded in Punjab which is 29 per cent of total mandarin production in the country and productivity is 21.4 mt/ha. The other mandarin producing states are Madhya Pradesh, Andhra Pradesh, Maharashtra, Rajasthan, Assam, Karnataka, Manipur and Tripura. Kinnow is the leading cultivated mandarin varety in Punjab, Rajasthan, Haryana and Uttar Pradesh. Nagpur mandarin is mainly growing in Maharashtra, Karnataka, Madhya Pradesh, Uttar Pradesh and Tamil Nadu. Khasi mandarin is grown commercially in Assam, Meghalaya, Manipur, Arunachal Pradesh etc. Coorg variety is cultivated mainly in Karnataka and Tamil Nadu.

Lime and Lemon are generally grown in Andhra Pradesh, Gujarat, Bihar, Karnataka, Maharashtra, Assam and Chhattisgarh. Total area under these is 2.34 lakh hectares and production is 22.7 lakh mt which is accounting for 3.5 per cent of area and 3.0 per cent of production in the country. The average productivity of lime and lemon is 9.7 mt in India. The area in Andhra Pradesh is 47.8 thousand hectares with annual production of 7.18 lakh metric tonnes with highest productivity of 15 mt/ha .

Among the citrus fruits, mandarin is placed at first position with respect to area and production which is followed by sweet oranges and limes. Other citrus fruits viz. grapefruit, pummelo and lemons are mostly grown as backyard plants.

In Punjab, the farmers took the lead and brought back the lost glory in citrus culture. Now kinnow has emerged number one fruit of the state, both from area and production point of view. The total area under citrus in Punjab is 49, 244 hectares out of which kinnow occupies major share of 45, 851 hectares. The annual production of citrus fruits is 10.16 lakh tonnes, Kinnow alone produce 9.89 lakh tonnes. The districts of Fazilka, Ferozepur, Muktsar and Bathinda, occupy, 82% of the area under kinnow in the State. Sweet orange is grown particularly in the arid irrigated region of the Punjab i.e. the districts of Ferozepur, Muktsar, etc.

Kinnow cultivation has also become quite popular in Ganganagar, Bikaner and Jaipur districts of Rajasthan; Sirsa, Jind, Hissar,Ambala and Karnal districts of Haryana; Una, Sirmaur, Bilaspur, Mandi and Kangra districts of Himachal Pradesh and Jammu region of Jammu and Kashmir.

Export potential : The oranges are exported from India to Bangladesh, Nepal, Sri Lanka, Cango P Republic, Oman, Singapore, Canada, Belgium, Saudi Arabi, Russia etc. Annual export of oranges is 34000 mt with value of Rs. 84.93 crores. Alone Bangladesh is importing 86.7 per cent of total export of oranges from India.

Kinnow is exported to Sri Lanka, Saudi Arabia and United Kingdom from Sri Ganganagar. Punjab Agro Industries Corporation exported Kinnow to United Kingdom, Dubai Mauritius and Sri Lanka.

IMPORTANCE AND USES

Citrus fruits are not only delicious and refreshing but also they provide vitamins, minerals and many other substances. Many of the vitamins contained in the citrus fruits are needed by the human body daily. Different species of citrus fruits have different chemical compositions. In sweet oranges, the chief constituents of the edible portions are sugars (glucose and sucrose), and acids (citric acid); the fruits of acid groups contain primarily the acids in the fruit juice. Citrus fruits contains considerable amount of vitamin C. Kinnow contains 60 mg of vitamin C per 100 ml of juice. Lime is also a good source of vitamin C. Lemon has high medicinal value as it is a richer source of antiscorbutic vitamin C than the sour or acid lime. It is also good source of vitamins B, A, and P. Lemon is very useful in the case of the prevention of capillary bleeding and very useful in the case of teeth, hands and face and as a hair rinse. Grapefruit is a rich source of vitamin C and thiamine B_1. The mild bitterness in juice is due to the presence of glucoside called Naringin which is said to have a high medicinal value. Grapefruit is considered very good for prevention against malaria. The total soluble solids in the fruit juice in most of the sweet group of citrus varies from 8-12 per cent, while the titrable acidity usually ranges from 0.5 to 1.5 per cent. T.S.S. acid ratio of 30:1 in Musambi, 14 : 1 in pineapple, Jaffa and Blood Red, 10 : 1 in Valencia Late (Sweet oranges), 12 : 1 to 14 : 1 in Kinnow (Mandarin) and 6 : 1 in Red Blush, Foster and Duncan and 7 : 1 in Marsh Seedless (Grapefruit) is considered to be optimum for marketable fruits.

Most of the citrus fruits such as sweet oranges, grapefruit and mandarins are taken as fresh fruits. The citrus fruits can, however, be utilized in a number of other ways as salads (orange salad, grapefruit-cheese salad, grapefruit-pineapple salad; grapefruit salad), juices, squashes (orange squash, lime and lemon squash), cocktails, syrup, concentrate, marmalades and pickles. The peel of thick-rinded citrus fruits can also be made into delicious candy. Orange, lemon, lime and grapefruit juices are bottled and canned in large scale. Lemon-barely water is prepared from the common lemon. Grapefruit are mainly used as a dessert fruit after adding little sugar due to its slightly bitter taste. It is served in halves, in section or as juice.

The rind of citrus fruits is rich in pectin and certain essential oils. Lime and grapefruit peel is used as cattle feed. Dried lime feed powder and lime sediment obtained when lime juice is clarified are utilized for cleaning metalware. The lemon is used in many culinary purposes. Grapefruit is utilized in the preparation of dry and fortified wines and brandies. It is also used for flavour and in perfumery.

BOTANY

Mandarin and sweet oranges are placed taxonomically in the division Embryophyta; sub-division Angiospermae; class Dicotyledoneae; order Geraniale; suborder Geranianeae; family Rutaceae; sub-family Aurantioedae; tribe Citrae; sub-tube Citrinae, genus **Citrus.**

Swingle recoganised only 16 species under the genus **Citrus** whereas Tanaka described as many as 144 species. Swingle divided the genus **Citrus** into two subgenera viz. Eucitrus having 10 species and Papeda having 6 species. Swingle's treatment was not comprehensive and he considered most species to be of hybrid origin and rejected which were not found to occur in nature in wild form. Tanaka divided the genus **Citrus** into two subgenera viz, Archicitrus having 98 species and Metacitrus with 46 species. His treatment although considered as more comprehensive and detailed, contains excessive number of species, some of them being of doubtful validity.

A good number of citrus species have been exploited commercially some for direct fruit production and some as rootstock. In addition, quite a large number of intergeneric and interspecific hybrids have been developed. Citranges (trifoliate orange × sweet orange), citrumelos (trifoliate orange × grapefruit), citradias (trifoliate orange X sour orange), citrumuats (trifoliate orange × kumquat), Citrangedin (citrange × calamondin), citrandarin (trifoliate orange × mandarin), citremon (trifoliate orange × lemon), limquats (kumquat × west Indian lime) are the intergeneric hybrids, which were developed in hybridization work. In the interspecific hybridization programme, a few other groups like limonimes (lemon × lime), tangors (mandarin × sweet orange), trangelos (mandarin × grapefruit), Lemonnage (lemon × sweet orange), lemandarin (lemon × mandarin) have been developed.

The following are the important citrus species of commercial importance.

A . Acid members group (Citron, Lemon, Lime):

1. *Citrus medica* L. : Citron

A shrub or small tree of irrigular habit of growth, twigs angled, glabrous. Stout, short spines in leaf axils. Leaves glabrous, elliptic-ovate, rounded at the tips, cuneate at the base, margins serrate. Petioles wingless or narrowly margined and faintly joined with the blade. Fruit large, oblong or oval, blunt pointed, rough and lemon yellow. Rind thick.

2. *Citrus limon* (L) Burm : Lemon

A small to medium tree of spreading growth habit and long shoots with small spines and strongly coloured new growth. Leaves medium large, light green, lanceolate and sharp pointed, with sub-serrate margins. Petioles medium, narrowly winged or margined; plainly joined with the blade. Flowers medium sized and purple in the bud. Stamens numerous. Fruit oval pointed commonly at both ends, light yellow. Rind medium, juice abundent and acidic. Core solid. Seeds few, small, embryo white.

3. *Citrus jambhiri* Lush : Rough lemon (Jatti Khatti)

A medium to large tree of spreading growth habit. Spines less than in lemon and colour of new growth much paler. Leaves medium sized, pointed with notched tip and paler in colour. Leaf margin serrate. Flowers smaller, faintly coloured in the bud. Fruit lemon-brown and very deficient in form (round or compressed). Rough and irregular surface and core open at maturity. Flesh colour yellow. Seeds numerous and small, embryo white.

4. *Citrus karna* Raf. : Kharna Khatta

Medium to large tree of upright spreading growth habit. Spines thicker and larger than lemon. New growth faintly coloured. Leaves large and lemon like but broader and darker green. Petioles longer and permanently winged. Flowers large and well coloured. Fruit orange coloured, medium to large, oval with well developed papilla and rough and irregular. Rind surface thick, core open at maturity and flesh colour orange. Moderately seedy and cotyledon white.

5. *Citrus aurantifolia* Swingle (L): Lime

Small to medium tree with numerous small but stiff and sharp spines and faintly coloured new growth. Twigs and shoots slender. Leaves small, elliptic ovate or oblong ovate, obtusely pointed at the tip and rounded at the base, pale green and petioles narrowly winged. Flowers very small, white in the bud. Fruits greenish yellow, small, round to oval. Peel very thin and aromatic, flesh greenish and highly acidic. Seeds small and white inside.

6. *Citrus latifolia* Tanaka : Tahiti or Persian lime

It resembles aurantifolia in most respect. It is a large vigorous tree with many fewer and thicker thorns and new growth more faintly coloured. The flowers are considerably larger and very faintly coloured in the bud. The fruits are much larger. Seeds are very few or lacking. The tree is much harder than aurantifolia and more resistant to pest diseases.

7. *Citrus limettioides* Tanaka : Sweet lime

A medium sized tree with spreading habit of growth. Leaves medium sized, pale green in colour and characteristically somewhat rolled, leaf margin serrate, tip notched, big thorns present generally in the axils of leaves. Flower non coloured. Fruit medium in size, globose to ellipsoid.

B. The orange group

8. *Citrus aurantium* L. : Sour orange

A medium sized tree upto 10 metres height with a rounded top; twigs angled when young, with single, slender spines, often short or stout spines (upto 5-8 cm long) on rapidly growing shoots. Leaves medium sized, ovate, bluntly pointed at the top and broadly rounded at the base. Flowers large, very fragrant. Fruits subglobose, usually slightly depressed at both base and top, peel thick, with a rather rough surface, becoming brilliant orange with a reddish tint at maturity.

9. *Citrus myrtifolia* Raf. : Myrtle-leaf orange

A shrub or dwarf tree with very short internodes often spineless and small myrtle like leaves. The fruits are small, sour or bitter, orange coloured at maturity and contain few or no seeds.

10. *Citrus bergamia* Risso : Bergamot orange

Small to medium sized tree of irregular habit. Thorns variable and not especially numerous. Leaves medium, sharp pointed, with bitter orange aroma, but pale green colour. Petiole long, strongly marginal to moderately winged in upper necked, lemon yellow, often with low flat papilla and persistant style. Seeds few, white inside.

11. *Citrus natsudaidai* Hayata : Japanese summer grapefruit

A medium sized, round topped tree with few thorns. Leaves medium sized, long-pointed with main vein prominent above and dark green in colour. Petiole long and strongly margined from tip to base or winged in upper position as in sour orange. Flowers large and white. Fruit large, subglobose to oblate, yellow at maturity. Flesh yellow. Seed medium large and white within.

12. *Citrus sinensis* (L.) Osbeck : Sweet orange

A medium-sized tree with a rounded top and regular branches; twigs angled when young, usually with slender, somewhat flexible, rather blunt spines in the axils of the leaves. Leaves medium- sized, pointed at the base and petioles narrowly winged. Flowers in small racemes or singly in the axils of the leaves. Fruits subglobose, oval or flattened globose.

C. The pummelo–grapefruit group

13. *Citrus maxima* Osbeck : Chakotra

A large, round-topped tree with angular twigs, often pubescent. Leaves large to very large, oval or elliptic-oval, with a blunt tip and a broadly rounded base and even slightly overlapping the winged petiole, mid-rib and large veins often pubescent; petioles broadly winged and more or less cordate. Flowers very large, borne singly or in axillary clusters or in sub-terminal inflorescence. Fruits large or very large, subglobose, oblate-spheriod. Seeds large, thick, wrinkled.

14. ***Citrus paradisi*** Macf. : Grapefruit

A large spiny, round topped tree with dense foliage; twigs angular when young; glabrous or nearly so. Leaves larger than those of sweet orange, small than those of chakotra; ovate, bluntly tipped and broadly rounded at the base, glabrous or nearly so; petioles rather broadly winged but not so broad as those of the chakotra. Flowers large, borne-singly or in small clusters in the axils of the leaves. Fruits larger than those of the sweet orange but smaller than those of most chakotras. Seeds smaller than those of the chakotra.

D. The mandarin group (loose skin orange)

15. ***Citrus reticulata*** Blanco : Sangtra

A small to medium tree of upright, irregular growth habit and relatively few thorns. Leaves medium in size, lanceolate in form, with prominent midrib and long narrowly winged petioles. Flowers medium small. Fruits depressed globose or subglobose, with thin, loose peel easily separating from the segments. Seeds small, pointed with cotyledons green.

16. ***Citrus unshiu*** Marc. : Satsuma mandarin

A small, spreading, round toppered, virtually thornless tree. Leaves medium large in size, long and sharp pointed with midrib highly prominent above and dark green in colour. Petioles long and narrowly winged from end to end. Flowers medium in size. Fruit medium sized, compressed, orange at maturity and generally seedless.

17. ***Citrus deliciosa*** Tenore : Willow leaf mandarin

A highly symmetrical, broad tappered tree of drooping growth habit, branches fine. Leaves small, long and narrow and sharp pointed, yellowish green leaves. Fruit small to medium with thin rind. Strongly compressed. At maturity yellow to light orange and rind and segments loose. Flavour and aroma mild and distinctive. Seed with cotyledons green.

18. ***Citrus rashni*** Tanaka : Billikichilli or Cleopatra mandarin

The tree is attractive, round-topped, symmetrical, and thornless, with small, dark-green leaves. The fruit is orange red, small, oblate and highly depressed at the apex, with thin, somewhat rough rind. It is used as rootstock.

19. ***Citrus nobilis*** Loureiro : King of Kunembo

The tree and foliage are orange-like in appearance but the fruit is large and mandarin like with a rough, more or less bumpy exterior, a thick, fleshy rind. Flesh colour is deep orange. Seeds few to many having cream-coloured cotyledons.

20. ***Citrus tangerina*** Hort. (Tanaka) : Tangerins

Tree vigorous and large, upright spreading in habit, nearly thornless; foliage moderately dense and of the mandarin type. Fruit medium to large, of high colour, deep orange to red and more acid flavour.

E. Papeda group

21. ***Citrus inchangensis*** Swing : Ichang papeda

A spiny shrub or small tree usually 5-15 ft high; twigs angular when young, with stout, sharp spines, 1.5 - 2.5 cm long. Leaves narrow, 4-6 times longer than wide; petioles very large, broadly winged, obovate or oblong-spatulate, evenly rounded at the tip and narrowed abruptly at the base. Fruits small, glabrous, 3-4 cm diameter in dried specimens, peel rough, seeds large.

22. ***Citrus junos*** Siebold : Yuzu of Japan

The Yuzu is a medium-sized spiny tree; leaves lanceolate- acuminate, with rounded bases but with pointed, usually accuminate tips, slightly crenulate-margined towards the tips, leaf blades 5-7 × 2.5 × 3.5 cm; winged petioles obovate. Fruits depressed - globose, 5-7 cm diameter, greenish in colour when ripe, pulp very acid, seeds plump.

23. ***Citrus latipes*** Swing : Khasi papeda

A thorny tree having leaf blades more variable in size and shape and with the tips subacute or even bluntly rounded, not apiculate or subcandate with blunt points. Fruits are borne singly. Seeds smaller and numerous.

24. ***Citrus macroptera*** Montr. : Melanesian papeda

A tree 15-16 feet high. Petioles broadly winged, distinctly articulated. Leaves elongate - accuminate, only twice as long as the petiole. Twigs subcompressed with one long spine on young twigs and one short spine on old twigs in the axils of the leaves. Fruit with 10-12 segments, pubescent, segments 1-2 seeded with scanty pulp, depressed, almost without juice.

25. ***Citrus histrix*** DC : Mauritius papeda

Low tree or shrub, 2-12 m high; trunk crooked asymmetric or angular, rather thin, branched near the base; crown irregular, densely branched, branchlets thin; spines short, stiff, subulate, green with hard brown or orange coloured tips. Leaves alternate, stalked unifoliate, orbicular-ovate, lanceolate, above dark green, shining, beneath light green or yellowish green, dull, fragrant when bruished. Fruit pendulous, globose, ovoid, ripe fruit yellowish green.

26. ***Citrus macrophylla*** Wester : Alemow

It shows promise as a salt-resistant rootstock for lemons. Leaves large with blade 12-14 cm long and 6-8 cm wide with much smaller, subtriangular, short-winged petioles. Fruits very large 8.5 to 10 cm in diameter, subglobose to oblong, more or less narrowed at the base. Pulp sour, considered inedible.

F. Other species

27. ***Citrus limonia*** Osbeck : Rangpur lime

Tree usually vigorous and productive, medium sized, spreading and drooping, with slender twigs, comparatively few and small thorns; foliage dull-green and mandarin like, and new shoot growth lightly purple tinted. Flowers small and mandarin-like and bud and petals deeply purple-tinged. Hardy to cold.

28. ***Citrus limetta*** Risso : The limette of the mediterranean or Limettas

Small to medium round-topped tree of less vigour and more compact growth habit. There appear to be two form which are identical with the exception of the colour factor. In both, the fruit is small and round shaped or depressed, lemon yellow and acidless at maturity. It's most distinctive feature are the turncate apex, with a strongly depressed ciruclar furrow in the centre of which is a prominent fleshy papilla or nipple.

29. ***Citrus maderaspatana*** Tanaka : Kitchli, Vadlapudi and Guntur Sour orange

An old Indian fruit of unknown origin, the kichli somewhat resembles the bittersweet orange though it is smaller, flatter and rougher in surface texture. Fruit medium sized, depressed globose to broadly obovoid; sometimes slightly necked; colour yellowish orange; seedy; rind rough.

30. ***Citrus madurensis*** Loureiro : Calamondin

Tree of medium vigour, highly productive, upright and columner, nearly thornless; leaves small, broadly oval and mandarin-like. Strongly cold-resistant. Fruit very small, oblate to spherical; red colour orange to orange-red; very thin, smooth; sweet and edible-seeds few.

31. ***Citrus indica*** Tanaka : Indian wild orange

Branches terete, spiny, glabrous. Leaves oblong or lanceolate, thick, sub-entire, attenuate at the apex, acute at the base, veins curved. Fruits small, broadly abovoid or subpyriform, solitary on terminal twigs, pedicels very short; seeds, large, smooth. The leaves resembles with **Citrus sinensis** but small, fig- shaped, fruit containing extremely large seeds is entirely different from any other Citrus.

32. *Citrus pennivesiculata* Tanaka : Gajanimma of India

Tree vigorous having thick shiny leaves, large spines, pitted surface of the fruit. Pulp greenish with juice sacs arranged in a herringbone fashion and the presence of opaque dot. It is used as a rootstock. This species is found in South India.

In citrus (mandarin, sweet orange, grapefruit), type of fruit is hesperidium and edible portion is juice vesicles.

CLIMATE

Citrus plants being subtropical cannot withstand extended cold periods. Temperatures of -2°C to 0°C are injurious to the citrus fruits if such low temperature prevail for long periods. The citrus fruit may freeze at temperatures of – 2.8°C to 2.2°C, or even little higher temperature. Extremely high temperatures are also not conducive to the production of high-quality citrus fruits. Under such conditions, the foliage is killed and much of the fruit drops. Under high temperature conditions, the exposed fruit may become sunburned. In areas which have more total heat available during the growing season, oranges mature early with a high amount of total soluble solids than the oranges produced in places where the temperature is not so high. It is, therefore, clear that the citrus plants thrive best under rather warm conditions.

Sweet oranges require dry and arid conditions with distinct summer and winter seasons with low annual precipitation. It is adapted to arid tropics and sub-tropics. Contrary to the mandarin, it has poor adoption to warm humid conditions. In South India, it is confined to Cuddapah, Kurnool, Chittor districts of Rayalseema and North Circars in Andhra Pradesh. Defined moisture stress period substitutes for winter but the blooming season is not regular and definite, resulting in production of fruits distributed to different seasons. Fruits also remain green to yellowish green at maturity. In Western and Central India, sweet orange cultivar, Mosambi is predominantly grown in irrigated condition in dry climate of Deccan plateau in Ahmednager and adjoinging parts of Hyderabad. In North Western region comprising the Punjab, Northern Rajasthan, Western Uttar Pradesh, Blood Red, Jafa and Valencia are grown in arid-irrigated conditions, favoured by well defined summer and winter for excellent quality and colour of fruits. Kodur Sathgudi which has poor colour under tropics develops excellent deep orange colour when grown under sub-tropics.

Mandarin or losse skinned orange is adapted well to sub- mountainous tracts with elevation ranging from 600 to 1100 m above sea level and rainfall between 200 to 750 mm.

Satpura Hill range in Central India is known for the best mandarin of the continent i.e. Nagpur Santra. This comprises Vindharba region of Maharashtra and adjoining parts of Madhya Pradesh. Predominently budded plants are grown under irrigated conditions and bahar treatment is adopted to regulate the crop. The Vidharba region has a hot climate with the maximum temperature going up to 117°F in May and the minimum touching 43°F in January. The rainfall averages about 113 cm and is received particularly from June to September. The average relative humidity throughout the year is 53%.

In South India, largely comprising of Karnataka, Tamil Nadu and Kerala, mandarin is grown in the warm humid region with tropical climate in Coorg, Wynad, Nilgiri, Palani and Shevearoy Hills. In the North eastern India, hills of Meghalaya (Khasi, Dushai, Garo, Jainta), Mizoram, Manipur, Tripura and Arunachal Pradesh have the predominance of mandarins although many species are found growing. In Brahmaputra valley of Assam, Dibrugarh district is famous for mandarins. It has also been adapted on the hill slopes of Darjeeling district in West Bengal and Sikkim state. Prevalence of sub-tropical climate in these regions favours the excellent colour and quality of fruits.

Kinnow (King × Willow leaf) growing in arid irrigated and mountainous region of North-Western India, especially, Punjab, Haryana, Himachal Pradesh, Rajasthan, etc. is doing very well. It appears to be exacting in its climatic requirement which is evident from its performance in different ecological regions of the country. Obviously, it needs sharply contrasting warm cool temperature with chilling temperature for economical cropping and adequate quality of fruit. This is due to the significant influence of preharvest temperature on acid metabolism and total soluble solids development. The development of carotenoids is also determined by temperature 2-3 months preceding the harvest which is more favourable in sub-tropics than in tropics. Areas with sub-tropical type of climate with temperature range of 10 to 40°C with annual rainfall of 100 to 150 cm and adequate facilities for regular irrigation are most suited for Kinnow.

Commercial growing of lime is common in aridirrigated regions of Gujarat, Andhra Pradesh, Karnataka, Chhattisgarh, Assam and Maharashtra although it is grown throughout the country. Grapefruit, lemon and sweet lime are mostly grown in homesteads and have much local significance.

The amount and distribution of annual rainfall and seasonal humidity regions are very important aspects of the environmental complex which influence the adaptability of citrus culture to various climates. In subtropical regions annual use of water by evapo-transpirational losses in a well-watered mature citrus orchard ranges some where between 762 mm in cool climate to 1245 mm in the hot semi-arid climate. On an average 1000 mm to 2000 mm of rainfall would be required to maintain ideal soil moisture throughout the year.

The frequency and velocity of wind also determine the suitability of a region to citrus cultivation. The major influence of these factors are of two types. The first is the form of effect of cold or hot wind on the vegetative growth and fruiting. Secondly it may mechanically damage the trees and fruits.

SOIL

The soil requirements of citrus like those of other fruit plants are more exacting than those of annual crops. The soils which support the excellent growth of crops such as wheat, maize or cotton may be totally or partially unsatisfactory for citrus cultivation. All the citrus fruit trees are very sensitive to high salt concentration in the soil. Under such conditions, the plants cannot absorb adequate water from the soil and consequently remain stunted. In addition, the toxicity due to high salt concentration in soil shows up in the form of typical leaf burn symptoms. This condition may further result in the reduction of plant growth and yield. Presence of excessive free lime leads to deficiency of phosphorus, manganese, zinc and lime induce chlorosis. Therefore, the soil with high salt concentration and having an electrical conductivity of the saturation extract of more than 2 mmhos per cm should be avoided when planting citrus.

The citrus plants thrive best in soils having slightly acidic reaction with a pH range of 5.5 to 7.0. Under such conditions, most of the nutrients are readily available to the plants. The soils having pH more than 8.7 pose many production problems and should never be used for planting citrus. The soils which are water-logged or have a very high and fluctuating water-table should not be put under citrus. Soils with inadequate surface drainage should be avoided. Citrus orchards should not be planted in areas where water stagnates for many days during the monsoon season and those fields which get flooded after every fall of rain.

For best citrus cultivation, well drained medium to light loamy soil, which should be free from injurious salts and which have a slightly acidic reaction should be selected for planting citrus orchards.

The sweet orange can be grown on wide range of soils but medium to light loamy soils rich in organic matter, well drained having the pH range from 6 to 8 are most suitable. The soil for sweet oranges should be at least one metre deep. In shallow soils, the tree remains stunted and die early for want of proper moisture and nutrient.

For mandarin, well drained light loam to loam soils which are easy to work should be preferred. Too light or sandy soils, even though deep and well drained, may pose problems as they would tend to dry out quickly at the surface and the feeder roots lying within the first

30 cm of the soil may be transiently starved for moisture. Frequent and light irrigations in such soils would be needed and mandarin cultivation should be attempted in them only if adequate means of cheap irrigation are available. The soils at and around Nagpur are coarse, free working, well drained, black and loamy, about 6 feet deep and overlying coarse sand, mixed with lime nodules. Mandarin can grow successfully on a wide variety of soils, which are not excessively saline or alkaline, have no hard pan or kankar layer within 2 metres from the surface and the water- table remains well below 3 metres. The PH range from 5.0 to 8.0 is suitable for mandarins.

Calcarious soils, in general, are not satisfactory for citrus cultivation, because the presence of lime depresses the uptake of several micronutrients. Hence soils having no free lime or lime cancretions, but having sufficient calcium on the exchange complex and with values of pH and conductivity close to the optimum may be desirable.

In general for citrus fruits, pH should be less than 8.5, conductivity based on 1 : 2 soil water suspension within 0.5 mmhos/cm, free lime less than 5% and lime concentration less than 10%. These limits may well apply to sweet orange mandarin as well.

CHOICE OF VARIETIES

There are a large number of citrus varieties grown in different citrus growing regions of India. Only those which have show promise are being discussed and described in this chapter.

1. **Sweet orange (*Citrus sinensis*)**
   - A. Common group or Mediterranean oranges :
     (*i*) Pineapple (*ii*) Hamlin (*iii*) Jaffa
     (*iv*) Valencia (*v*) Sathgudi (*vi*) Shamouti
   - B. Acidless group :
     (*i*) Mosambi (*ii*) Succari
   - C. Pigmented group :
     (*i*) Blood Red (*ii*) Ruby (*iii*) Moro
     (*iv*) Tarocco (*v*) Blood oval or Doblefina
   - D. Naval group :
     (*i*) Washington Naval (*ii*) Roberston (*iii*) Bahianiana
2. **Mandarin (*Citrus reticulata*)** - Loose skinned orange
   - A. Reticulata group :
     (*i*) Nagpur santra or Ponkan (Chhina)' (*ii*) Coorg
     (*iii*) Khasi mandarin (*iv*) Local
   - B. Mediterranean group or Deliciosa group :
     (*i*) Kinnow (King × Willow leaf)
     (*ii*) Wilking (Sister hybrid of Kinnow)
     (*iii*) Willow leaf (*iv*) Emprior
   - C. Satsuma group :
     (*i*) Ovari (*ii*) Wase (*iii*) Kara
   - D. Tangerine group :
     (*i*) Dancy (*ii*) Beauty (*iii*) Naartja
   - E. Nobilis group :
     (*i*) King (*ii*) Kunembo
   - F. Mitis group :
     (*i*) Calamondin (*ii*) Billikichilli (*iii*) Cleopatra
3. **Mandarin–like Tangers** (Hybrid between Tangerine × Sweet orange)
   (*i*) Temple (Natural hybrid) (*ii*) Clementine
4. **Mandarin–like Tangelos** (Hybrid between Grapefruit × Tangerine)
   (*i*) Orlando (*ii*) Minneola

5. Grapefruit (*Citrus paradisi*)

A. Seeded Group :

(*i*) Duncan (*ii*) Triumph (*iii*) Pink marsh
(*iv*) Ruby (*v*) Foster (*vi*) Star Ruby

B. Seedless group :

(*i*) Marsh seedless (*ii*) Cecily (*iii*) Red blush

6. Pummelo (*Citrus maxima*)

(*i*) Kao pan (*ii*) Red fleshed
(*iii*) Chakaiya (*iv*) Aijal
(*v*) Jorhat (Pink flesh)

7. Lime (*Citrus aurantifolia*)

A. Acid or Sour lime :

(*i*) Kagzi (*ii*) Mexican (*iii*) Palmetto

B. Large fruited or Tahiti lime :

(*i*) Tahiti (*ii*) Pond (*iii*) Bearss

C. Mandarin lime :

(*i*) Rangpur lime

D. Sweet or Acidless lime (***Citrus limettioides***)

(*i*) Palestine (*ii*) Sweet (*iii*) Local

8. Lemon (*Citrus limon*)

A. Eureka group :

(*i*) Eureka (*ii*) Villafranca (*iii*) Nepali oblong
(*iv*) Galgal (*v*) Italian round
(*vi*) Punjab Baramasi Lemon (*vi*) PAU Baramasi Lemon-1

B. Lisbon group :

(*i*) Bonnie (*ii*) Kennedy (*iii*) Lisbon

C. Anamalous group :

(*i*) Meyer (*ii*) Cuban (*iii*) Ponderosa

D. Sweet or Acidless lemon group :

(*i*) Mill sweet

The brief description of important cultivars is given below :

A. Mandarin

1. Nagpur Santra : This is the premier mandarin of India and is one of the finest mandarin variety grown in the world. It does well under Nagpur conditions where it is usually raised by budding on the rough lemon rootstock. The fruits are medium in size, sub-globose in shape. The fruit colour is often greenish orange to light orange. The surface is smooth and glossy. The stalk end (base) is slightly drawn out and warty with glandular furrows. The rind is thin and slightly adherent. The segments are 10–11. Juice content is abundant, yellow in colour with excellent flavour, sweet in taste. The number of seeds per fruit is 6-7. The maturity period is generally January-February.

2. Kinnow : It is a hybrid between King × Willow leaf. It was brought to Fruit Research Station Abohar from California in 1958-59 and to Jalandhar a litter earlier. Fruit medium to globose to oblate. Skin golden yellow when fully ripe. Acidity moderate with fine sugar/acid blend, flavour very rich. Seeds 12-25. Ripen in January-February. Less prone to fruit drop. The average yield is 150-200 kg fruits per plant.

3. Local : Fruit small to medium, oblate to subglobose. Skin cadmium coloured. Base short necked and furrowed. Flavour fair, Juice abundant, slightly acidic. Seeds 3-7 Ripens in December- January.

4. Khasi : It is commercially grown in Assam. It is a prolific bearer. Fruits are depressed, globose to oblate in shape. Colour of mature fruit is orange yellow to bright orange. The surface of the fruit is smooth, glossy. The stalk end is even or obtuse, occasionally necked, slightly ribbed. The rind is thin and is separated very easily, number of segments 8-10, rag little to medium. The pulp vesicles uniformly orange coloured, coarse, very melting, juice abundant, orange coloured. Sweetness and acidity well blended. Seeds 9-25.

5. Coorg : It is the important commercial variety of South. The fruits are oblate to globose, bright orange yellow in colour. The base necked or depressed with grandular ribs extending through the collar. The rind is thin and soft, slightly adherence, easily separated. The number of segments 9-11. Rag is little; juice abundant, deep chrome in colour. Seeds 14-30.

6. Daisy : It is a cross between Fortune and Fremont mandarin. Fruit medium to large, mid-season fruit with an attractive dark orange rind. Fruit weight is 210 *g*. It peels and sections moderately well. The tree produces a heavy crop with the fruit held in large culusters. Moderately seedy with 1-3 seeds per section, seed number 9. TSS is 11.5 per cent, acidity 0.54 per cent and juice content 41.8 per cent. Ripens early in 5-20 November. It is suitable for the area having soil pH less than 8 and raised on carrizo rootstock.

7. W. Murcott : Tree moderate in size and vigour. Fruit is usually flattened with a thin, smooth orange rind, easy to peel. Fruit weight is 200 *g*, seed number 10. Low seeded in the absence of cross-pollination but seedy when cross- pollinated. The flesh is orange coloured and juicy, with a rich and sweet flavour. TSS is 9.6 per cent, acidity 0.68 per cent and juice content 39 per cent. Ripens in 1-20 January being a mid-season variety. It is suitable for the area having soil pH less than 8 and raised on carrizo rootstock.

B. Sweet orange

1. Mosambi : Fruits small to medium, subglobose. The fruit surface smooth with longitudinal furrows. Apex marked with a circular ring. The colour of the flesh is pale yellow or whitish. Juice has low acidity. Seeds 20-25 per fruit. Ripens in November.

2. Jaffa : Fruit medium to large, round to oblate in shape. Skin orange yellow to orange red. Acidity and sweetness well blended. Flavour rich. Seeds 8-10. Ripens in December. The average yield per plant is 54 kg.

3. Blood Red : Fruit medium to large, roundish to slightly ablong in shape. Rind thin, deep orange, tight and glossy. Flesh fully red when ripe, rich flavour with sweetness and acidity well blended. It is an excellent variety. Seeds 8-10. Ripens in December. The tree can yield 42 kg fruit per plant.

4. Pineapple : Fruit medium to large, round to slightly oblate and deep orange. Juice abundant, acidity and sweetness well blended, flavour excellent. Seeds 12-25 Ripens in December.

5. Valencia : Fruit medium slightly oval. Skin deep golden yellow. Juice abundant, subacid in taste. Flavour rich. Seeds 2-6. Ripens during February-March.

6. Sathgudi : Fruit is medium, subglobose, areole absent. Rind is medium thick smooth and finely pitted. The pulp is straw coloured, juicy with good flavour. Seeds 12-20. This is a famous variety of Andhra Pradesh and Tamil Nadu. Ripens from October to February.

7. Shamouti : The fruit is ellipsoidal in shape, medium to large sized. Rind thick, firm, surface finely pitted, but relatively smooth. Pulp colour is light orange, juice medium, sweet in taste with rich in flavour. It is practically seedless (0–1 seed/fruit)

C. Lemon

1. Eureka : Fruit medium, oblong, apex nippled. Skin lemon yellow, smooth. Juice abundant, clear, strongly acidic with excellent flavour. Seeds rarely present. Ripens in August-September.

2. Punjab Baramasi Lemon : The tree of baramasi are vigorous, spreading and thornless. New growth and flowers are purple. The trees flower and fruit throughout the year. The fruit is medium to large, lemon yellow, round, tapering towards the base, apex is rounded. The skin is smooth and thin. Fruit is very juicy with low seed content. This variety is more suitable for growing in the irrigated arid region of Punjab. It mature in first week of July. Average yield is 84 kg fruit/plant.

3. Galgal : Its trees are vigorous. Fruit is medium in size, oval in shape, peel is smooth, glossy, medium thick and yellow at maturity. Its juice has 5.2 per cent acidity and 5–8 seeds per fruit. It matures in last week of November in North India and gives 80–100 kg fruit per tree.

4. Pant Lemon-1 : Fruits medium in size, round in shape, smooth, juicy with thin rind. This lemon is a selection from kagzi kalan at Pantnagar (Uttranchal).

5. PAU Baramasi Lemon-1 : The fruit is lemon yellow, round, tapering towards the base and apex is round. Skin is smooth and thin. Fruit is very juicy and seedless and contains about 7 per cent acidity.

D. Lime

1. Kaghzi : Fruit small, round and thin-skinned. Pulp greenish white. Juice strongly acidic.

E. Grapefruit

1. Marsh Seedless : Fruit medium to large, oblate-roundish in shape. Skin lightly yellow, smooth. Acidity and sweetness medium. Seeds 0-6. Ripens in December-January. Average yield is 93 kg fruit/plant.

2. Duncan : Fruit large, oblate in shape. Skin pale light yellow, flesh pink. Acidity and sweetness well blended, bitterness well- marked. Seeds 40-50. Ripens late in January. Average yield is 84 kg fruit/plant.

3. Foster : Fruit medium to long, oblate in shape. Skin pale yellow, flesh pink. Acidity and sweetness well blended, bitterness well marked. Seeds 40-50. Ripens in November-December. It yields 51 kg fruit per plant.

4. Red Blush : Fruit small to medium, oblate, peel smooth, glossy and deep yellow having crimson colour in patches at maturity. Deep bright crimson blush in juice vesicles. Mildy acidic and high in TSS. Seeds 0–8, mostly aborted. Ripens during last week of November. Average yield is 77 kg fruit/plant.

5. Star Ruby : The trees are medium in size. Fruits small to medium having oblate-roundish shape. Peel smooth, glossy, yellow with distinct bright red blush. Flesh colour is deep red. Fruits juicy, have high TSS, well bended with acidity and rich in vitamin C. Fruits are seedless (1-2 seeds/fruit). It is an early variety which ripens during last week of November. The average yield is 53kg fruit/tree.

F. Sweet lime

1. Local : Fruit medium globose to ellipsoid. Rind smooth with distinctive aroma, juice abundant, lacking in acidity and insipid. Seeds 5-6. Ripens in the beginning of September.

PROPAGATION AND ROOTSTOCKS

The sexual as well as asexual methods of propagation are used to raise plants of different species of citrus. The seedlings of acid lime and mandarins are still planted in some regions of Karnataka, Tamil Nadu, Kerala and North-East region. The rootstocks are also grown from seeds and then scion cultivars are budded/grafted upon these seedlings in sweet oranges, mandarins and grapefruits. Vegetatively propagated plants raised from cuttings/layers are used in limes and lemons. Seeds of most citrus species are polyembryonic and thus nucellar seedlings are used both for raising uniform rootstocks as well as for direct planting especially in acid lime and mandarins. This also helps to raise healthy plants as citrus viruses are not transmitted through seed.

All the commercial citrus fruits grown in India are generally propagated through 'T-budding'. Jatti Khatti (***C. jambhiri***) is the common rootstock used for the propagation of these fruits. This rootstock is tolerant to viral diseases like tristeza, exocortis etc., and the plants raised on it are vigorous and produce fruits of good quality.

The propagation of quality plants need utmost attention because of susceptibility of citrus to viruses and mutation. The quality of nursery plants has a major contribution in the productivity of citrus orchard and decline problem.

RAISING OF ROOTSTOCK

Preparation of Seedbeds and Sowing of Seed : For raising the rootstock, seeds freshly extracted from mature fruits of Jatti Khatti collected from healthy and vigorous tress are sown on raised beds. The land used for preparing the seedbeds should be well drained and fertile. The beds should be 2-3 meters long, 60 cm wide and 15 to 20 cm high from the ground level. There should be sub-channels on both sides of the beds for irrigation. The seeds of Jatti Khatti may preferably be sown in September. The sowing of seed on the raised beds is done in the first week of September. If the sowing is delayed, the germination reduces due to onset of winter and also the growth is slowed down.

The seed is sown in rows 10 cm apart and in these furrows the seeds are placed 2 cm apart and 1 cm deep. After the seeds are sown, they are covered with layer of sand and farmyard manure mixture about 1/2 cm thick. The seedbeds are irrigated immediately after sowing. The first irrigation is usually applied by sprinkling with hand hose and the next few irrigations are applied in a way that the beds are moistened through seepage.

The seeds should be sown immediately after extracting from the fruit as its viability decreases during storage. For facilitating sowing, the seeds should be washed and dried in shade.

Care of Young Seedlings and Its Transplanting : The germination of seed starts about 3 weeks after sowing. These young seedlings are likely to be damaged by frost during winter. It is advisable to cover them with Sarkanda to avoid any damage from cold. It will also improve the growth of seedlings. The seedbeds should be kept free from weeds by doing hand weeding or with small khurpa from time to time.

Light dressing of nitrogenous fertilizers makes the seedlings to attain the height of about 15 cm by the next March, which is the optimum size of transplanting. By sowing the seed in September and transplanting the seedling in March, one can save a year in the propagation of plants. If the seedlings do not attain the transplanting size by March, their transplanting should be done in August-September.

From most of citrus species used as rootstocks, many seedlings arise from one seed. One of these seedlings is sexual seedling and others are nucellars. So, while transplanting only the uniform seedlings are selected and too vigorous and too week seedlings are rejected. This helps in maintaining the uniformity of rootstocks used for nursery production. Generally 20% seedlings are rejected at the time of transplanting.

The field in which the seedlings are to be transplanted, should be well prepared and levelled thoroughly. The seedlings of 10-12 cm height should be transplanted at the distance of 15 cm in rows which are 30 cm apart and a distance of 60 cm after every two rows should be kept for facilitating the budding and hoeing operations. After transplanting a light irrigation is applied to the field. Thereafter the irrigation are given at 8-10 days interval.

Budding the Seedlings : The transplanted seedlings become buddable 6 to 12 months after transplanting depending upon the time of transplanting. The seedlings which are to be budded should be of pencil thickness at about 20 cm from the ground level. All the seedlings may not attain the buddable size at the same time. Inspite of the fact that the uniformity was maintained at the time of transplanting, some of them may become more vigorous and some may remain week. Most of them, however, grown uniformly. It is necessary to do second culling at this stage. About 10 per cent seedlings are discarded at the time of budding. The remaining uniform seedlings are budded. Spray of 1.5 per cent urea on Rough lemon seedlings at monthly interval from March to December increases number of buddable plants, improves budding success and produces healthy kinnow plants. Citrus plants can be budded either during February-March or August-September when the sap flows in the seedlings. 'T' budding or shield budding is the common method of propagation in citrus.

Selection of Scion Wood, Preparation of Rootstock and Budding Operation : For the propagation of quality plants, the scion should be true to variety, excellent in vigour and productivity. Select virus free bud wood. If not available, it may be taken from perfectly trees showing no symptoms of decline and ill-health. Trees from which bud-sticks are taken should have a good record of producing satisfactory crops of high quality fruits over a number of years.

In citrus, budwood selected for taking the buds should be round especially in Kinnow variety of mandarins where the availability of round budwood is a problem. It should be taken from trees which are vigorous, heavy bearer and free from diseases.

Before budding, the stock should be prepared by removing the leaves and thorns from the place where the bud is to be inserted. The bud removed from the bud stick is used without any piece of wood. A 'T' cut is given on the stock at a height of about 20 cm from ground level. The flaps are lifted with the help of the back side of the knife and the bud is inserted into it. To hold the bud in a position tightly, it is wrapped with alkathene tape both at the upper and lower ends, leaving actual bud uncovered.

Containerized nursery production of Kinnow. Mix two parts of soil, one part of FYM and one part cocopeat for preparation and sterilization of potting mixture and stack on concrete floor. Solarize the mixture with 100 micron UV stabilized polythene sheet during last week of April and May for 4-6 weeks and fumigate with Basamid Granular (Dozomet 98%) @ 50 g/m^2 during May-June. For raising rootstock, sow rough lemon seed (2 seeds/bag) in black plastic polythene bags of 250 gauge (12" × 7") filled with sterilized potting mixture during second week of August under screen/shade house. About 75 per cent seedlings attain buddable size in first fortnight of May and become saleable during September-October.

After Care of Budded Plants

When the uptake of bud is assured, remove half of the top of the rootstock above the bud union. This will help in quick growth of the sprouted buds. When the sprouted buds have made about 15 cm growth, remove the remaining portion of the rootstock leaving 2-3 cm from the bud union. The nursery plants after budding should be kept well supplied with nutrients and moisture. A light irrigation after budding helps to improve the bud uptake. The subsequent irrigations should be given at weeks' interval during summer and 15-20 days during winter.

One or two light dressings of nitrogenous fertilizers help in the rapid growth of sprouted buds. The nursery area should be kept free from weeds. But care should be taken that the buds inserted on the stock are not disturbed.

All other shoots emerging below or above the bud union should be removed from time to time. Otherwise these sprouts will compete with the growth of inserted bud and the plants will not attain the appropriate size in a given period. The young budlings should be staked to train them properly.

Propagation of Limes and Lemons

For propagation of sweet lime and lemons, stem cuttings 15-20 cm long are made from mature terminal growth in the month of February-March and August-September. These cuttings are planted in the field at a distance of 20 cm in the row and the distance between two rows is kept 30 cm. After every two rows the distance of 60 cm is kept to facilitate weeding and hoeing operations. However, no weeding is done till the cuttings have rooted completely, otherwise hoeing will disturb the cuttings and rooting will be affected adversely. The cuttings can be planted in polythene bags of about 5 × 7 cm size during February or September. These cuttings are watered regularly so that they may not dry up. If these cuttings are treated with some growth substance like IBA (50 to 100 ppm) the root formation is increased considerably.

Kagzi lime is usually propagated by air-layering or ground layering in the end of February or in March or in August-September. When the sap starts flowing the terminal branches 45 cm in length and of pencil thickness are selected. A ring of bark is removed from these branches and burried in the soil. The apex of the branch is kept above the ground level. The soil is kept moist continuously. After 2 to 3 months the rooted layers are separated from the parent tree and planted in the nursery. The branches which are near the ground level are most suitable for this purpose.

Propagation of High-Grade Plant Material

The propagation of superior quality plants deserves the utmost attention. In citrus this aspect has acquired added importance in view of the widespread decline problem. For raising healthy and high-grade plants of citrus, consider the following points while selecting the rootstock:

(*i*) Always obtain Jatti Khatti (***Citrus jambhiri***) seeds from healthy fruits from vigorous trees. Immerse the seed in hot water at 52°C for about 10 minutes to check Phytophthora infection

(*ii*) Use only nucellar seedlings

(*iii*) For selecting nucellar rootstocks, rogue out the slow growing seedlings in the nursery when attain 10-12 cm height. Discard approximately 25 per cent of them which are either too tall or too short.

(*iv*) For Blood Red, Cleopatra should be used as a rootstock. The seeds of Cleopatra ripen in January and should be sown in the first week of February for raising the seedlings.

(*v*) For Mosambi, Pectinifera should be used as a rootstock. Its seed should be sown during August-September to raise the seedlings.

Choice of Rootstock

The most commonly and widely used citrus rootstocks in the world include sour, sweet and trifoliate oranges and rough lemons. Sour orange has been employed in the propagation of sweet orange, mandarin orange, grapefruit and lemon. It is more hardy than other rootstocks except trifoliate orange and rough lemon. Rough lemon is the second most important rootstock. It is vigorous and somewhat resistant to gummosis. Trifoliate orange is hardy and tolerant to severe frost, highly tolerant to phytophthora root rot and succeeds in soils too moist for other rootstocks.

In India, rough lemon is one of the leading rootstocks for most scion varieties. Next in importance is kharna khatta, which is more popular in Uttar Pradesh.

From the trials conducted in the Punjab, Jatti Khatti for Blood Red, Valencia, Jaffa and Pineapple; Kharna Khatta for Malta local, Santra and grapefruit were reported to be the best rootstocks. Cleopatra for Blood Red orange and pectinifera for Mosambi are recommended in Punjab. In Uttar Pradesh, Italian 76 and Sweet lime performed exceedingly well for Mosambi and Kharna Khatta was found to be best for Naval and Sevella sweet oranges.

Rough lemon has been found to be the best rootstock for acid lime in Tamil Nadu. In a long range rootstock trial; performance of Sathgudi on Sathgudi, Billikichilli and Gajanimma showed promise, however, rough lemon became the commercial rootstock. Superiority of Rangpur lime has been proved as it is considered to be highly tolerant to drought added with high productivity and comparable quality of fruits.

In Karnataka, Kitchilli, Rangpur lime, rough lemon, Kodakithuli, Cleopatra and Trifoliate orange appeared to be promising for Coorg mandarin. Kata Jamir (**Citrus jambhiri**) was found promising for Khasi mandarin in Assam followed by Kharna Khatta. However, in the recent trials, Rangpur lime has been found to be promising.

Performance of Nagpur Santra on rough lemon and Rangpur lime has been highly satisfactory under Maharashtra conditions. Rangpur lime is considered to have long life and heavy yields added with comparable quality of fruits. Marmalade orange, a strain of Rangpur lime was found to be the best for Kinnow mandarin. Under Bihar conditions Rangpur lime gave the highest yield and longevity to scion of Nagpur santra. Rangpur lime appeared to be the best rootstock for Mosambi and Sathgudi under Bangalore conditions.

Troyer and carrizo citrange are hybrid between sweet orange × trifoliate orange. Trees on these rootstocks are vigorous and adaptable to all types of soils except to high level of available calcium. They are somewhat susceptible to citrus nematode and to **Phytophthora** root rot and are resistant to **Phytophthora** gummosis and tristeza.

Overall situation of rootstock in the country is for shift towards the use of Rangpur lime from rough lemon owing to the best performance of this rootstock in different agro-climatic regions.

FLOWERING AND FRUITING

The flowering in citrus takes place mostly in spring and in growing season when soil moisture and temperature both remain favourable. In Lime and lemons, flowering takes place almost throughout the year. In northern Indian conditions, major bloom of almost all the species occurs during early spring (February- March) when the atmospheric temperature starts rising after the cold winter and soil moisture condition also improves. In South India, where there is no well defined winter with very low atmospheric temperature, the flowering season is longer and not very distinct. It is very common to get two crops, occasionally three also in many citrus types grown in South India. However, the flowering can be regulated by withholding soil moisture or through fruit thinning by chemicals and adjustment of fruit harvesting.

In Kinnow, flowering takes place during end February to early March in North India. It starts bearing flower and fruits 4-5 years after planting. It is precocious in bearing and give very high yield during early years of its life. Due to heavy bearing the trees get exhausted leading to collapse or gradual decline.

The sweet lime trees bear two types of flowers viz. Staminate and hermaphrodite on the same tree, but the formation of staminate flowers is more. The fruits mature about six months of their blossoming. Sour lime starts bearing flowers and fruits from the fourth year onwards after planting. Under normal conditions, the trees flower all the year round each flush bringing forth new blossom. The fruits mature in six months after flowering. In North India, the main harvesting season is in the months of August-September. Grapefruit tree produce flowers and fruits once in a year under North India in spring and yields mature fruits 8 to 9 months later in the following November to December.

In citrus, pollen development is a normal phenomenon except in Washington Naval, Satsuma mandarin and Bearss etc. where no viable pollen is produced. The cultivars where pollen is produced in abundance, self pollination is a general rule. The stigma remains receptive for 6-8 days. Honey bees are common pollinating agent. Cross pollination is reported to increase seediness in certain citrus cultivars like Shamouti orange, Clementine mandarin and Minneola tangelo. Both male and female sterility, partial self-incompatibility and normal male and female fertility conditions prevailing in genus Citrus which have resulted to different degree to seediness in the fruits i.e. Seedless (with no seed), commercially seedless (0-10% seed) and seedy (numerous seeds). Self-incompatibility has been reported in Nepali Oblong and

Lucknow Seedless lemon, pummelo, Clementine mandarin and Sweet lime. Nagpur Santra was found to be self- compatible and cross compatible except with grapefruit.

Poor fruit set and high fruit drop resulted into poor yield, especially under unfavourable enviornmental conditions such as late frosts, drought or excessive rain etc. in most of the citrus species. Due to considerable loss of soil moisture during summer months leads to severe fruit drop.

The growth of the fruit as represented by a change in the diameter is rapid upto the middle of October in Hamlin and up to the end of November in Valencia Late. Therefore, the first seven and eight months after blooming are the periods of most rapid fruit growth in sweet orange varieties grown under North Indian conditions. Increase in fruit weight and volume followed corresponding increases in fruit diameter. Rind thickness in both the varieties decreased during the early stages of maturity and thereafter remained practically unchanged. Juice percentage increased with the development of the fruit and the maximum was attained when the rate of growth had slowed down.

PLANTING OPERATIONS

Citrus is planted twice in a year. The spring planting season, suitable for citrus plantings, starts after the 15th of February. The monsoon season starts from middle of July and continues upto the end of September. Citrus is however, commonly planted when rains have set in and the weather has cooled down sufficiently.

Kinnow and Baramasi lemon plants can be successfully transplanted bare-rooted during December-February. After digging the plants from nursery, remove the one fourth foliage and cover the rest with moist wrapping material.

Preparation of land : The land on which young citrus trees are to be planted should be prepared well in advance. Soil should be thoroughly ploughed up and levelled. Preferably, soil should be planted with a green-manure crop such as guara or senji. These crops should be burried when they have attained the maximum vegetative growth and field should be irrigated immediately. The land should be heavily manured with farmyard manure a few months before the actual planting.

Planting distance: It depends upon the variety, the rootstock, the type of soil and the climate. The spacing commonly given to citrus plants in north India is **6 m × 6 m** in square system and accommodate 275 plants per hectare. The tree should not be planted closely, because they grow tall and slender and make spraying, pruning and picking difficult. The trees planted too closely bear poor crops of inferior quality and are susceptible to the attack of many insects-pests and diseases. Cultivation in closely spaced orchard is also very difficult.

Kinnow is precocious bearer and starts bearing in the 3rd to 4th year of its age. Different planting distances are being followed by the kinnow growers. Kinnow is being planted at 20′ × 22′ and 10′ × 11′, 15′ × 15′, 17′ × 17′, 20′ × 15′ and 20′ × 10′ and also as a filler tree in mango, pear and litchi. However, the uniform spacing of 20′ × 20′ should be generally followed.

Where the soil is loamy and well drained, the pits may be dug deep enough only to accommodate the ball of the plant. If the soil is of heavy texture, pits 1 × 1 × 1 metre may be dug to facilitate better root penetration.

Care of Young Plants : The young trees must be protected against high or low temperature and strong winds. The trunk of the young trees should be white washed to protect them against the hot sun. A row of Jantar (***Sesbania egyptica***) planted on the south-western side is very effective in reducing sunburn and wind damage to young trees. The young citrus plants are susceptible to frost and must be protected during the first two winters. This can be done by providing a cover over the young plants with farmwaste material. The southern side of the plants should be kept open to receive sunshine. The young plants must be watered regularly in the arid regions. Apply water 2-3 times a week for the first few weeks after planting. After this, during the first year, the plants should be irrigated after a week. The sprouts which develop on the trunks of the trees below the scaffold branches should be removed. The top should be left unpruned and only the dry and dead-wood should be removed.

ORCHARD CULTURAL PRACTICES

Irrigation

Water is one of the critical inputs for successful production of citrus fruits. There is a differential response of citrus trees to water requirement during vegetative and reproductive phases. Soil moisture stress is detrimental to plant growth which is linearly related with water use.

The success of citrus cultivation on light and medium textured soils of the Punjab, Haryana and Rajasthan depends largely on irrigation. Generally, kinnow requires more water as compared to sweet orange. The irrigation requirements of lemon, however, are the highest. Grapefruits require more water than oranges but less than lemons. The water requirement of young trees is lower than that of the bearing trees. The closely spaced trees and those with intercrops require more water because of a greater competition for soil moisture. The use of fertilizers and the spray materials are also known to increase the water requirement of plants. Kinnow trees cannot grow and fruit well in the absence of proper soil moisture. The twig die-back and leaf drop could occur due to water stress. The lower fruit set, excessive fruit drop and reduction in fruit size are associated with unfavourable soil moisture which consequently account for poorer yield.

The weather in north-western India turns increasingly hot and generally dry from March through June. The active growth of plants and fruits of kinnow and other citrus also taken place during this period. As such, it is a peak period of water use for citrus orchards.

It is suggested that young citrus trees upto 8 years may be profitably irrigated by basin system. The application of irrigation at right time and in right quantity is more important. Under North India weekly irrigation during March to June and fortnightly irrigation during November to February are followed. In Punjab, it is reported that the young plants up to the age of 3-4 years, should be irrigated after 7 days intervals, whereas older trees after 15-20 days interval depending upon climate, rainfall and type of soil. Utmost care needs to be given to irrigation before sprouting in February, after fruit set in April and in the hot weather, otherwise the growth of the trees may be adversely affected resulting in the excessive shedding of flower/fruits.

In the states of Maharashtra, North Western Region, parts of Tamil Nadu and Andhra Pradesh, plants experience water deficit due to negative balance between precipitation and evaporation. The situation is aggravated by low humidity and high temperature which accentuates evaporative demand. In heavy rainfall areas of North Eastern states, no irrigation is practised.

Mandarin growing in Malnad, Wynad, Palani, Shevaroy and Nilgiri Hills are mostly under rainfed conditions. Moisture stress caused during November to March induces dormancy and is a substitute for low temperature. But the failure of blossom shower and subsequent failure of precipitation demands for irrigation otherwise no flowering or fruit set occurs.

Water requirement of acid lime under tropical conditions of South India was found to be 875 mm per year. Application of 40 litres water per tree was found to be optimum in Dehradun valley. Minimum water need of seedling to save it from permanent wilting was found to be 2.25 litres per plant which could maintain turgidity. It is a practice to supply 60-90 litres water per tree at 7-10 days interval depending upon season in well grown orchards of mandarin and sweet orange under Maharashtra conditions. Maximum water use efficiency in Kinnow, when irrigated was provided at 100-135 cumulative pan evaporation (CPE). Vegetative growth and the second stage of fruit growth are most sensitive to soil moisture conditions. The average weight and juice content has positive correlation with water while sugar and acidity has negative correlation.

Citrus trees are highly sensitive to excess moixture and waterlogging conditions. The trees require good soil aeration. The excessive irrigation may result in poor soil aeration leading to reduced growth and yield, predisposing the trees to root rot and other diseases. Excessive irrigation also results in the leaching of essential nutrients from soil as well as in accumulation of certain undesirable salts if the irrigation water is not of good quality. Citrus trees are sensitive to salinity and the total soluble salts in the irrigation water should not exceed 1000 ppm. Over-irrigation of citrus causes decline of orchards in most cases. Waterlogging, particularly near the tree trunk can be avoided by providing mounds of earth around the tree trunk well below the bud union.

Drip Irrigation in Kinnow : The drip irrigation system in kinnow enables efficient and judicious use of water alongwith improvement in yield. The requirement of water per day and per plant during different months according to age of the trees is given below :

Amount of water to be applied to Kinnow through drip irrigation (litres/day/plant)*

Month	Age of kinnow plants (Years)				
	0 – 2	3 – 4	5 – 6	7 – 8	9 and more
January	3	6	9	12	15
February	6	12	18	24	30
March	9	18	27	36	45
April	13	25	39	52	60
May	16	32	48	64	80
June	17	34	51	68	80
July	13	26	39	52	65
August	12	24	36	48	60
September	11	22	33	44	55
October	8	16	24	32	40
November	5	10	15	20	25
December	3	6	9	12	15

Intercropping

In order to utilize the vacant land to generate income till the plants become productive, intercropping is recommended. However, indiscriminate use of exhaustive intercrops may lead to decline of orchards.

Intercropping should not be done in the bearing orchard. But in young and non-bearing orchards, intercropping upto 4 years with a leguminous crop such as guara, moong, mash, cowpea, gram and pea may be done. Guara-wheat rotation with guara as a green manure can be taken in sweet oranges for 5-6 years. Sufficient space should, however, be left unsown to permit young trees to make unrestricted growth. More of fertilizers should be added to meet

*1. Amount of irrigation water may vary by 10 - 15 per cent depending upon the prevailing weather conditions.

*2. For lifting water from canal storage tank, a booster pump with solar/electric motor of 2HP will be sufficient for 10 acres kinnow plantation. However, for 15 and 25 acres orchard, a booster pump with Electric motor of 3 and 5 HP respectively will be required for lifting water.

*3. In the beginning, 1-2 dippers/plant are required and may be increased to 4-5 drippers depending on the soil type, age of the tree etc. Sub-lateral loops of the drippers should be used around each plant for efficient use of water.

the requirements of the intercop. The fruit tree and intercrops should be provided with independent irrigation system. Tall and exhaustive crops like cotton, **chari, bajra,** maize, **berseem, bhindi** and creeper types vegetables should not be grown in the orchards.

During summer season, vegetables like round melon, pumpkin, onions and bittergaurd and leguminous crops like moong, mash, moth and cowpeas may be grown. Guara may be grown as fodder or as green manure crop. Chillies should not be grown in a citrus orchard as they have proved to be harmful to the citrus plants. During winter season, turnip cauliflower, carrot and radish can be grown. Peas and gram make excellent intercrops as they enrich the orchard soil. Senji may be grown as fodder or as a green manure crop.

In Darjeeling, cabbage and peas were found beneficial in mandarin orchards from the cost-benefit analysis. Under Coorg conditions, mixed cropping with Robusta coffee was more remunerative than monoculture, though plant vigour of Coorg mandarin was comparatively suppressed. The best arrangement was Coorg mandarin altered with six rows of Robusta coffee.

Berseem proves to be harmful to citrus trees because it requires frequent irrigation while the citrus trees do not require the same amount of water during winter. Therefore, **Barseem** is incompatible in irrigation requirements with citrus.

Weed Management

The citrus orchards are infested with monocot and dicot weeds which compete with the main crop for winter, nutrients and space. Besides harbouring the insect pests, the weed roots also secrete toxins which adversely affect growth and fruit bearing.

Cultivation has been the major method of weed control in citrus orchards but it has many drawbacks as it damages feeder roots. Frequent tillage destroys the structure of the surface soil, thus lowering the water holding capacity and permeability of the soil. The weeds like *Cynodon dactylon* and *Cyprus rotundus* are difficult to eradicate by light digging or other cultural practices. Moreover, hand weeding is expensive and laborious. Weed management has become an expensive aspect in the cultivation of citrus crops. The cost of cultivation can be considerably reduced by adopting chemical weed control in place of conventional hand weeding.

Chemical weed control : Best results in citrus were achieved with diuron at 5 or 6.25 kg/ha and tafazine at 7.5 - 10 kg/ha when applied at pre-emergence stage at Abohar. Diuron at 4 kg/ha was the most effective to control monocot weeds in sweet orange orchard at Ludhiana.

Paraquat at 5 kg/ha applied twice annually gave better weed control than dalapon at 8-12 kg/ha. Oxidizon at 5 kg/ha was the most effective treatment for controlling weeds in Kinnow orchard for 90 days when applied at post-emergence stage of weeds. Similarly in Kinnow orchard, Diuron, atrazine and simazine @ 5 kg/ha as pre-emergence and paraquat and glyphosate 5 kg/ha as post-emergence treatments were adjudged best in checking weeds.

In a long term adaptive trial conducted at different locations of Punjab, it was concluded that glycel 41 SL (glyphosate) @ 41/ha as post- emergence (second fortnight of March) followed by glyphosate/Gramaxone 24 WSC (paraquat) @ 3 1/ha (second fortnight of July) in 500 litres of water effectively control broad spectrum of weeds in kinnow orchards.

Manuring and Fertilization

One of the major causes of citrus decline in India is improper and inadequate nutrition. In Punjab, the deterioration and unthriftly growth of citrus trees is reported to be due to lack of adequate nutrition. Citrus trees require a judicious supply of plant nutrients for proper growth and regular harvest of high quality fruits. The ill-fertilized trees may have hidden hunger and in acute cases may show a variety of deficiency symptoms. Fertilizer recommendations have been made based both on experience and experimental results to achieve optimum orchard performance.

For proper growth and development of citrus, about 17 elements have been known to have important role to play. Apart from major nutrients like N, P, K, Ca, Mg, and S, citrus requires micronutrients like Zn, Cu, Mn, Fe, B, Mo, etc. Inadequate nutrition of citrus plants causes serious disorders and may eventually lead to decline of the orchards. Chapman reported that about 18 tonnes of citrus fruits remove about 21 kg nitrogen, 5 kg phosphorus, 41 kg potassium, 19 kg calcium, 3.6 kg magnesium, 2.3 kg sulphur, 40 g boron, 9 g copper, 50 g iron, 13 g manganese and 13 g zinc.

A brief description of the deficiency symptoms of some of the essential elements is given below :

Nitrogen : The deficiency symptoms of this element are easily recognized. The deficient trees show a general lightening of green part of the leaves. The leaves become distinctly yellowish green and some may even lose the green entirely when the deficiency persists for a longer time. The trees which remain severely deficient in nitrogen for long time, become stunted, have sparse foliage and produce dead-wood. Such trees bear very little fruit.

Phosphorus : The deficiency of phosphorous is rare in North India and is not easy to recognize in the field. The tree deficient in phosphorus have reduced growth and have more lack-lustre, smaller and narrower leaves than the normal trees. The fruit borne by such trees is rough in texture, having thick and coarse rind. The fruit has a hallow core and tends to drop prematuerly.

Potassium : The symptom of potassium appears as reduced growth and smaller leaves. The new growth is very weak and the twigs break very easily. The fruits remain small and have a very thin, smooth and well-coloured rind.

Magnesium : The deficiency symptoms usually occur in old citrus leaves when the fruit is mature. The symptoms first appear as chlorotic spots at the tips and between the veins. The leaves become abnormally thin. The yellow spots enlarge until an inverted V-shaped area remains green near the base of the leaf. In acute deficiency, the entire leaves become yellow and later drop prematurely. In North India, soils have adequate magnesium content.

Zinc : The symptoms of zinc deficiency appears on fully mature new leaves as irregular interveinal chlorosis commonly known as "mottled leaf". The terminal leaves become small and narrow referred to as "little leaf". Fruit bud formation is severely reduced, twigs die back. The deficiency symptoms of zinc in citrus are widespread in north India.

Manganese: In the young citrus leaves, it is hard to distinguish it from zinc deficiency, but when the leaves are full grown, the deficiency can be easily recognised. The deficiency manifests itself by green veins on a light green background. In the mature leaves, bands of green develop along the mature leaves, with light-green tissue. In severe cases of deficiency, the dark-green leaf areas become dull green and the light-green areas turn grey or whitish. The leaves become thin and the die-back of the twigs starts.

Iron : With the iron deficiency, there is a general chlorotic condition of the areas between the veins and when the deficiency persists, the areas between the veins become yellow. In such cases, therefore, the entire leaves become like old ivory. There is premature defoliation and in severe cases, twigs start dying back.

Copper : The copper status of the North Indian soil is usually low, however, its deficiency in citrus has not been noticed. Grapefruit seems to be more sensitive to copper deficiency than sweet orange. The fruits develops symptoms of deficiency before the branches are affected. The fruits become misshapen, have dark- brown-gum-soaked eruptions, varying in size. There are gum pockets in the albedo. The leaves of deficient trees are deep green, over-sized and coarse. The shoots are long, vigorous and of S-shaped giving the appearance of excessive nitrogen fertilization.

Manuring and Fertilizer schedule : The citrus soils in Punjab are sandy to sandy loams, low in N, P and medium in K, low in Zn, high in pH and with $CaCO_3$ concretion in sub- soil.

In full grown Kinnow annual application of farmyard manure @ 100 kg per tree, N @ 400 g/tree, P_2O_5 @ 440 g/tree are recommended as a general practice and three foliar applications of 0.3% $ZnSO_4$ in April, June and September are also recommended.

Generally, Nitrogen is found to be in deficient in all the citrus growing areas of Punjab. The following fertilizer schedule is recommended for citrus orchards.

Age of the tree (years)	Farmyard manure (kg/tree)	Nitrogen (g/tree)
1–3	5–20	50–150
4–6	25–50	200–250
7–9	60–90	300–400
10 and above	100	400–800

The whole quantity of farmyard manure should be applied in December. Nitrogen dose is given in two split doses, the first part is given in First half of February and the second in April-May after the fruit-set. Apply phosphorus alongwith the first dose of nitrogen.

In majority of trials response to P and K has not been observed while significant response to N application is reported. Optimum dose of N is found to vary from 600 to 680 g per plant for mandarin. For Khasi mandarin in Assam, 300 *g* N, 250 *g* P_2O_5 and 300 *g* K_2O is given to full grown trees. In Andhra Pradesh for Sathgudi orange and in Karnataka for Coorg mandarin, application of 400 *g* N, 200 *g* each P_2O_5 and K_2O per tree is recommended. Nitrogen 400 g, P_2O_5 200 g and K_2O 400 g annually in addition to 30–40 kg FYM was found to increase the yield of Darjeeling mandarin by 32 to 58 per cent. Under Maharashtra conditions, for Musambi 800 g N, 100 g P_2O_5 and 400 g K_2O and for Nagpur mandarin 600 gN, 200 P amd 400 g K was found optimum. Application of 600 g N, 200 g P_2O_5 and 300 g K_2O was also found optimum for acid lime in Tamil Nadu.

Correction of Zinc deficiency : Nutrient status of soil and leaves of citrus orchards in the Punjab, Haryana and Himachal Pradesh was conducted and it was concluded that Zn deficiency is widespread. The trend suggests that zinc is most critical among the micronutrients although nutrient like Mn and Fe are found deficient and need attention. The symptoms of zinc deficiency appear on fully mature new leaves as irregulur interveinal chlorosis commonly known as 'mottled leaf'. The terminal leaves become small and narrow referred as "little leaf". Fruit bud formation is severely reduced and twigs die-back.

To control zinc deficiency, spray the affected trees with 0.3% zinc sulphate solution without addition of the lime to spring flush in April-May, to summer flush in June and to late summer flush in August-September. Under acute deficiency conditions, 0.45% zinc sulphate solution without lime can provide better and early recovery. Foliar application should be applied to fully develop flushes. Since zinc deficiency becomes acute after first fruit bearing in the fourth year, one maintenance spray of 0.3% zinc sulphate solution should be given in April right from the start of the third year. A gap of one week should be kept between the foliar application of Bordeaux mixture and zinc sulphate solution.

TRAINING AND PRUNING

To the young citrus plants, staking should be given to help them grow, upright and straight. Sweet orange trees does not require pruning except removal of unwanted, intercrossing and diseases branches. In sour lime, the branches which are profusely growing on the ground and the water sprouts should be removed. Pruning operation provides good framework to the trees which should be attended to yearly. Luxurient growth of branches in sweet lime causes overlapping and more height. It is, therefore, essential to prune the tree for maintaining even growth. In Haryana, moderate pruning of 20 kg per tree in late November to early December results in higher fruit yield of sweet lime.

In lemon, the plants should be trained in such a way to develop open centre. This can be achieved only by removal of twigs yearly. It is essential to prune lemons very light annually to stimulate new growth and maintain production. Grapefruit trees requires less pruning than orange trees. Under humid conditions, the drooping branches should be pruned to avoid infection by gummosis and foot rot fungi. Due to more dense foliage and heavier cropping, it give out more dead wood than orange trees. Therefore, all such dead wood should be suitably pruned.

Off shoots or water sprouts are common phenomenon in Kinnow. These are characterised by long thorny growth with sparse foliage. They bear profusely but the quality of fruit is rather poor. Trees under stress are more prone to produce sprouts. The water sprouts unnecessarily rob the food material from the plant. Judicious modification of these off shoots should be done from time to time by pruning and balancing them with rest of the tree. The pruning is carried out early in the spring after the danger of frost has passed and before the tree starts a new growth cycle. For getting better yield of high quality fruit, pruning of crowded branches is necessary to open up the tree for proper ventilation and provide more chances for innerwood to bear fruit. Removal of dead and dried wood is necessary to check the further spread of disease.

THINNING OF FRUITS

The Kinnow mandarin are capable of producing heavy crop even when they are 3 to 4 years old. This is more common on light soils. Under such conditions thinning of fruits be restored to. At this stage, the crop needs to be regulated through judicious thinning especially during first few years of bearing. If heavy crops are taken from the trees during initial years, not only the tree health gets impaired but also the fruit size is reduced.

Thinning of the fruit and floral buds should be done to keep a balance of the tree foliage and number of fruits per tree. Crops should be so regulated that proper flushing continues throughout the year. Hand thinning can be done during early years of fruiting. Chemical thinning or even water or normal pesticidal sprays if applied at floral bud opening can reduce crop to a great extent.

Sometimes in third year Kinnow may bear 400-500 fruits on young plants. If such a heavy load is allowed to remain on the young plants, their health may suffer badly and some of the plants may even die. In order to maintain good health of the trees and to ensure regular cropping, the fruits of young Kinnow trees must be thinned out judiciously soon after setting in the month of May.

Quality Improvement

To improve fruit size and increase yield in kinnow mandarin, three foliar sprays of potassium nitrate @ 1 per cent at the end of May, June and July should be applied.

PHYSIOLOGICAL AND PATHOLOGICAL FRUIT DROP

Fruit-drop is a serious problem in citrus. Generally the trees bear large numbers of flowers and fruits, all of which they are unable to carry to maturity. It is a common observation that not more than 7-8 per cent of the flowers develop into mature fruits. First, the unfertilized flowers drop from the trees and, later, some of the fruits also drop in two or three definite waves. A considerable number of fruits drop in April soon after the fruit- set. Another drop comes when the fruit is about 3-5 cm in diameter. Usually, these two drops are not of such intensity as to materially affect the total yield. The last fruit-drop, known as pre-harvest drop, occurs just before the fruit is matured. It, however, reduces the yield considerably. There are two main causes of fruit drop, *i.e.*, physiological and pathological.

1. Physiological causes of fruit-drop

Causes : The following are the possible physiological causes of fruit drop :

(*i*) Climatic factors
(*ii*) Disturbed water relations
(*iii*) Lack of nutrition
(*iv*) Relation of seed to fruit drop

Symptoms : The flower-drop, as well as the fruit-drop is primarily due to the formation of an abscission layer at the point of attachment of the fruit with the twig. The growth-regulator balance within the tree is responsible for setting in motion the processes leading to the abscission layer.

Control : For checking excessive pre-harvest fruit drop, spray the trees with 10 ppm of 2, 4-D (Sodium salt of horticultural grade) in September about 2 months before harvesting. For spraying one acre of sweet orange trees add 5 g of 2, 4-D in 500 litres of water. Do not spray 2, 4D when dicot crop is intercropped in citrus orchard. Do not spray 2, 4-D when the adjacent fields are cultivated with cotton or other dicot crops. Spray 200 ppm GA_3 instead of 2, 4-D when cotton or other broad leaf crop are cultivated in or around the orchard.

2. Pathological causes of fruit-drop

A good proportion of fruit-drop in citrus has also been reported because of incidence of pests and diseases.

Causes :

(*i*) Stylar-end rot
(*ii*) Stalk-end-rot

Symptoms : The casual organism of the stem-end fruit rot is ***Colletotrichum gloeosporioides*** and ***Alternaria citri.*** Dark circular depressions with yellowish margins appears on leaves, branches, and fruits. Later the spots become raised, rough and light brown and the yellow margins disappear. Sand paper texture on the surface of leaves and fruit.

Control : The stem-end-fruit rot can be effectively checked by spraying the trees with Ziram 27SC (1250 ml) or Propiconazole 25 EC (500 ml) or Bavistin 50 WP (500 g in 500 litres of water) in mid April, August and September and two additional sprays of Ziram 27SC (1250 ml) or propiconazole 25 EC (500 ml)or Bavistin 50 WP (500 g) in end July and September in 500 litres of water per acre.

CITRUS DECLINE

Citrus decline may be due to several causes such as unhealthy planting material carrying viruses and similar diseases, improper rootstock, mis- management of the orchard, defective soil, poor drainage, malnutrition, insects, nematodes and diseases.

Rejuvenation : For the rejuvenation of declining citrus orchard, the following schedule is recommended :

1. Remove dead wood during January-February before the new growth starts. Spray 2:2:250 Bordeaux mixture immediately and apply Bordeaux paste to the cut surface and the trunk of the trees. Apply Bordeaux paint to the trunk after a week.
2. Add farmyard manure and nitrogen to the plants as per recommendations.
3. Follow strictly spray schedule for the control of insects pests and diseases.
4. Spray the solution containing 1.5 kg of zinc sulphate in 500 litres of water and Bordeaux mixture, separately in April, June and September on new growth flushes when the leaves have attained two-third of their size. There should be a minimum gap of one weak between the two sprays.

GRANULATION

Granulation is a complex pre-harvest disorder of citrus fruits characterised by apparent drying up of juice vesicles which become hard, assume a greyish colour and are enlarged with an increase in pectin, lignin and other polysaccharides, resulting in considerable decrease in total soluble solids, acidity and juice percentage and sugars. A good proportion of fruits is affected by this malady causing huge economic loss to the orchardists, particularly in the arid-irrigated areas of Punjab *i.e.* Ferozepur, Fazilka Bathinda and Faridkot districts as well as in the adjoining states of Rajasthan and Haryana. The problem of granulation has been reported from other places of India, though it constitutes a major problem in aforementioned areas. The sweet orange cultivars such as Mosambi, Hamlin, Blood Red are much more prone to this disorder than mandarins. However, this disorder has also been reported in other citrus fruits like grapefruits, pummelos and tangelos. Dancy tangerine is highly prone to this disorder, whereas most of the mandarins, notably Kinnow are almost free from it.

Factors affecting granulation

Climate : This disorder has been reported to be influenced, to varying degrees by weather conditions. Citrus trees growing in humid climates are reported to have a higher incidence of granulation than trees growing in dry regions. In Punjab, incidence of granulation was the highest at Ludhiana followed by at Abohar, Attari, Hoshiarpur and Pathankot.

Species and cultivars : Sweet oranges are more prone to granulation than mandarins, grapefruits and tangelos. Under Delhi conditions, Valencia Late and Kinnow were found to be almost free from granulation. Granulation is reported to be serious in Hamlin, Blood Red, Mosambi, Jaffa, Valencia Late and Pineapple sweet oranges; Dancy, Kinnow, Wilking and Kara mandarins; Duncan and Marsh grapefruits; and Pearl tangelos. Kinnow was found less susceptible than Nagpur mandarin.

Rootstocks : The vigours rootstocks like rough lemon induced higher incidence of granulation. Highest incidence of granulation was also noted in Blood Red on Jalandhari Khatti, a strain of rough lemon. It was followed by the trees budded, on Kharna khatta, sweet orange and grapefruit. Blood Red budded on galgal (***Citrus limon***) and sour orange (***Citrus aurantium***) rootstocks had the lowest percentage of granulated fruits. Fruits of Blood Red, Mosambi, Valencia and Pineapple exhibited the highest incidence of granulation on rough lemon while those of Jaffa did so on Kharna khatta. Blood Red on Cleopatra and Pineapple on Troyer exhibited the least granulation.

Mineral nutrition : The granulation is considered to be due to nutritional disorder. The trees having boron and zinc deficiency were found to have a greater tendency to produce granulated fruits, whereas manganese and iron were of little consequence in this regard. Trees with high nitrogen content in the leaves showed the highest granulation in the adjacent fruits. With the development of granulation in the fruits of Mosambi and Blood Red, the leaf N, P, K, Mg, Zn and Cu were found to increase, whereas Ca, B and Fe decreased but Mn content remain unaffected.

Enzymes and Plant growth regulators : An enhanced formation of lignin, probably due to Zn shortage, induced low auxin content and an increase in pectin and a decrease in pectin esterase activity were associated with granulation. The activity of diastase was found to be 15-25% lower in the granulated fruits of Kaula, Dancy and Butwal mandarins as compared to normal fruits. It was observed that a higher diastase activity in Kinnow was associated with little granulation. Higher level of auxins, cytokinins and abscisic acid and low gibberellins were noted in the granulated fruits than in the normal fruits.

Crop load : Higher incidence of granulation were recorded in trees carrying a heavy load.

Tree location : Incidence of granulation was noted more on northern side and in interior of the tree.

Control measures

Although, no successful method to control granulation has yet been found but certain measures for reducing its incidence and intensity have been reported. Early picking of larger fruits before the granulation become serious has been recommended. Restricted amount and frequency of irrigation has been reported to reduce granulation. Sprays of lime, zinc sulphate and Bordeaux mixture singly or in combination reduced granulation. A combined spray of $ZnSO_4$ and $CuSo_4$ each at 0.5% was more effective than their individual application. Three sprays of 25 ppm boric acid, 1% potassium nitrate and 2% calcium hydroxide at monthly intervals starting from 10 September reduced granulation. Granulation was reported 5% less with 2, 4-D and 23 to 42% less by 10 or 20 ppm GA. Three sprays of 300 ppm planofix and 15 ppm GA each in August, September and October decreased granulation by 50% in Kaula mandarin. Lead arsenate at 250 to 500 ppm was found effective in checking granulation in sweet orange and mandarin. In Dancy tangerine, three applications of GA, 2,4-D and 2, 4, 5-T (20 ppm each) and NAA (200 ppm) in August, September and October significantly reduced the incidence of granulation.

HARVESTING AND HANDLING OF FRUITS

Most of the orchardists sell citrus fruit to the professional fruit contractors who harvest the fruits before they are fully ripe and market them for getting more profit. It is a common sight to see green and unripe orange and mandarin do not properly ripen before November-December, yet one finds lot of green and under ripe maltas and oranges in the market as early as in September-October. Extraction and sale of juice from such oranges has become a big business with fruit vendors.

The sale of under-ripe citrus fruits is, indeed, a very deplorable practice. The consumption of under-ripe fruits is harmful for human health. The practice of selling unripe fruits should be curbed by the fruit growers and others concerned, in the interest of overall well-being of the fruit industry and to save our nationals from the ill-effects of immature fruits on their health. Wherever feasible, the growers should carry out harvesting and disposal of their fruits themselves or directly under their supervision.

Harvesting : The citrus fruits should be harvested when they are fully ripe as they are non-climacteric in nature. Citrus fruits develop their characteristic flavour and aroma at fully ripe stage. The fruits do not at all improve in quality after they have been harvested from the trees. Total soluble solids: acid ratio is a scientific and reliable index for adjusting maturity of citrus fruits. The studies on fruit quality at maturity and ripening of Kinnow mandarin on different rootstocks were conducted at the Regional Fruit Research Station, Abohar. The growth of fruit in terms of length, diameter and weight increased rapidly up to 30th January on Jatti Khatti and Kharna Khatta and upto 20th January on Troyer and Carrizo rootstocks. Thereafter, a slight decrease in fruit growth was observed. The best harvesting time of Kinnow mandarin on Jatti Khatti and Kharna Khatta fell between 20th January to 9th February and on Troyer and Carrizo between 20th January to 30th January. The optimum harvesting time of fruits and varieties of citrus growing in north India is given below:

	Kind/variety	Harvesting time	Solids/acid ratio
1.	**Sweet orange**		
	Mosambi	November	30 : 1
	Pineapple and Jaffa	December	14 : 1
	Blood Red	December-January	14 : 1
	Valencia	February-March	10 : 1

2.	**Mandarins**		
	Daisy	November	21 : 1
	Local	December-January	
	Kinnow	Mid-January-mid-February	12 : 1 to 14 : 1
	W. Murcott	January	14 : 1
3.	**Grapefruit**		
	Red Blush	November	6 : 1
	Foster	November-December	6 : 1
	Marsh Seedless	December-January	7 : 1
	Duncan	January	6 : 1
	Star Ruby	November	6 : 1
4.	**Lemons**	August-November	

Faulty harvesting and rough handling at the farm directly affect market quality. Bruises and injuries later show up as brown and black patches making the fruits unattractive. Kinnow fruits are susceptible to damage from handling when harvested wet. The rind may be turgid when wet and is liable to easy bruising and sunscald. Harvesting in the early hours of the day especially on the day when there is a heavy dew on the fruits or immediately after rains should be avoided. Fruit spoilage can be reduced by dipping kinnow fruits in 125 ppm benlate for one minute, drying them in air followed by wrapping in 100 gauge perforated polythene bags.

Harvesting should be done by clipping from the tree. A sharp clipper or shear is used. A short, slightly curved blunt shear is best suited for this purpose. The 'Secateur' is commonly used as clipper to harvest Kinnow fruits. The stems are cut as short as possible without actually cutting into the bottom or the fruit itself. Stem left on the fruit is source of mechanical injury during packing and transport. Kinnow fruits are likely to torn off easily if pulled with hand, hence this method should not be used. Fruits borne on high branches present a problem. Commonly a long pole with a curved blade is used. The best means of reaching high fruits is with a ladder. Fruits should be collected in a picking bags carried over the pickers shoulders. The sack is then lowered into appropriate containers and unhooked to open an outlet at the bottom. The fruits are pooled in the shade for grading. After harvesting, kinnow fruits should be washed in clean water followed by dip in 0.01 per cent chlorinated water (sodium hypochlorite 4% @2.5 ml/litre water). The fruits should be partially dried under shade and Citrashine wax should be applied with foam. Waxed fruits should be again dried under shade before packing. This will helps in improving the appearance and maintains the fruit quality during transit, storage and marketing for two weeks. The fruits can be packed in paper moulded trays followed by wraping with shrink film (15 micron).

The full grown sweet orange tree yield 500-1000 fruits. However, yield varies with climatic conditions, soil type, varieties grown, age of plantation, and orchard cultural practices. Well grown up Kinnow tree of about 10-12 years age bears about 1000- 2000 fruits depending the prevailing conditions.

Grading and sizing of fruits : Grading is necessary to get suitable returns commensurate with quality. During grading split, puncture, deformed fruits and incipient rots must be removed. Off grade fruits should be removed from the packing house line as early as possible so that dump-rate can be proportionately increased to replace defective fruit with sound fruit that will return to profit. After grading, the fruit is sized for uniformity. The fruits of mandarin and sweet oranges can be graded into 4 categories as follows :

(*i*) Extra special : With minimum diameter of 8.1 cm
(*ii*) Special : With minimum diameter of 7.5 cm
(*iii*) Good : With minimum diameter 6.8 cm
(*iv*) A : With minimum diameter of 6.2 cm.

The fruits can be packed in boxes in 3 or 4 layers in such a way that they do not get pressed while in transit.

Export Specification : Nagpur mandarin exported to Middle East with specification having light orange colour, fruit weight 150-175 g and grade 40-45 mm and 60-70 mm. The fruits with grade 60 mm are packed in 7 kg and of 40 mm in 2.5 kg packing with storage at 5-7°C.

Shelf life : Fruit harvested at optimum maturity, dipped in 125 ppm Benlate and wrapped in perforated polythylene bags (100 gauge) and packed in wooden crates can be stored upto 85 days at O°C–3.3°C temperature with relative humidity 80-90%.

The healthy unbruised Kinnow harvest during first week of February can be stored for 8 weeks at prevailing room temperature by individually seal packaged with electric sealer or rubber band in 10 micron thick high density polyethylene bags. The kinnow fruits harvested at optimum maturity, packed in ventilated CFB boxes should be stored at 5 – 6°C and 90 – 95 per cent RH. The fruits remain in acceptable condition for 45 days.

Large sized March Seedless grapefruits store better than the small sized fruits at room temperature. These can be stored for 60 days at 15°C–20°C. Gibberellic acid at 30 ppm in polythene (100 gauge) wrapping give better results.

The non alcoholic naturally carbonated lemon beverage can be shelf stabilized with optimized concentration of clarifying agents and optimized heat treatment with a shelf life of 4 months.

INSECTS PESTS

1. Citrus psylla : ***Diphorina citri*** (Kuwayana) : It is more active in March-April, June-July and September- October. The population density of pests is more in arid-zone. The adult psyllid is grey coloured and actively flying. It rests on the leaves with closed wings and hind end raised upwards. Orange yellow nymphs and grey adults of citrus psylla suck the plant sap from the growing shoot which ultimately dries up. It also acts as a vector of greening disease.

Spray 1250 ml of Rogor 30 EC (dimethoate) or 200 ml Imidacloprid 200 SL or 160 g Actara 25 WG (thiamethoxam) or 200 ml Confidor/Crocodile 17.8SL in 500 litres of water per acre in the second week of March and again in the first week of September. Adjust time of application with the appearance of the pest.

2. Citrus leaf-miner : ***Phyllocnistis citrella*** (Stainton) : It is serious pest and cause substantial economic damage to mandarin, acid lime and sweet orange. It attacks tender leaves in which larvae feed making shinning silvery serpentine mines. It also mines young tender shoots. The leaves become distorted and crumples. Severe infestation causes difoliation. The pest is more serious problem in the nursery and young plantation during flushing seasons. The pest is active from end March to November with its maximum infestation during April-May and September-October. The attack of this pest encourages the development of citrus canker.

The pest can be controlled by spraying on nursery plants 250 ml of Sumicidin 20 EC (fenvalerate) or 1000 ml of Ripcord 10 EC (cypermethrin) or 1250 ml Hostathion 40 EC (triazophos) or 1875 ml Durmet 20 EC (Chlorpyriphos) or 200 ml Imidacloprid 200 SL or 160 g Actara 25 WG (thiamethoxam) or 200 ml Confidor/Crocodile 17.8SL in 500 litres of water during April-May and August-September

3. White or Black fly : ***Dialeurodes citri*** (Ashmead) **and** ***Aleurocanthus woglumi*** (Ashby): White fly became devastating in Vidharba region of Maharashtra. Both nymphs and adults suck the sap from the foliage and reduce the plant vigour. Severely infested foliage turns yellowish green, becomes curled and finally shed. Sooty mould developed on honey dew excreted by the whitefly, give black appearance to the foliage. Affected trees have less chlorophyll, nitrogen and crude protein and produce few flowers which may shed. The fruits are insipid. Nymphs of whitefly are small pale yellow insects with red eyes. Citrus black fly lays eggs in spiral rings on the lower side of new leaves and nymphs are black in colour. Freshly emerged adults are redish but later on gets covered with a heavy pulverulence of salty bluish look. Both

Bunches of
PUNJAB-MACS PURPLE Grapes

THOMPSON SEEDLESS Grapes

UMRAN—A Commercial Variety of Ber

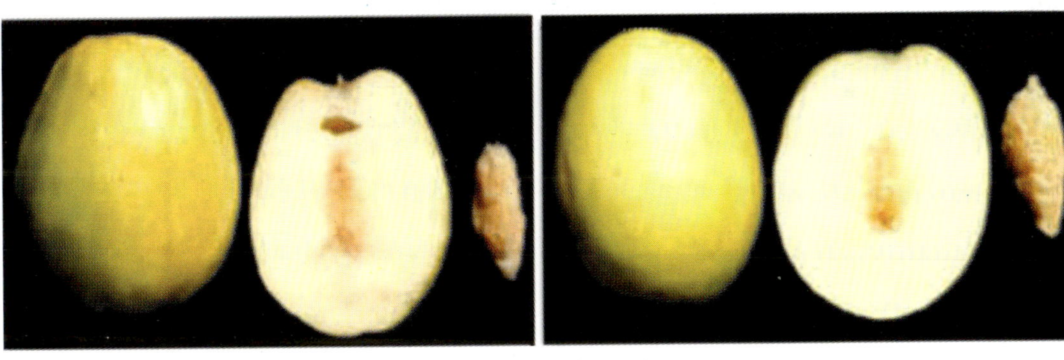

UMRAN

SANAUR-2

WALLAITI

DANDAN

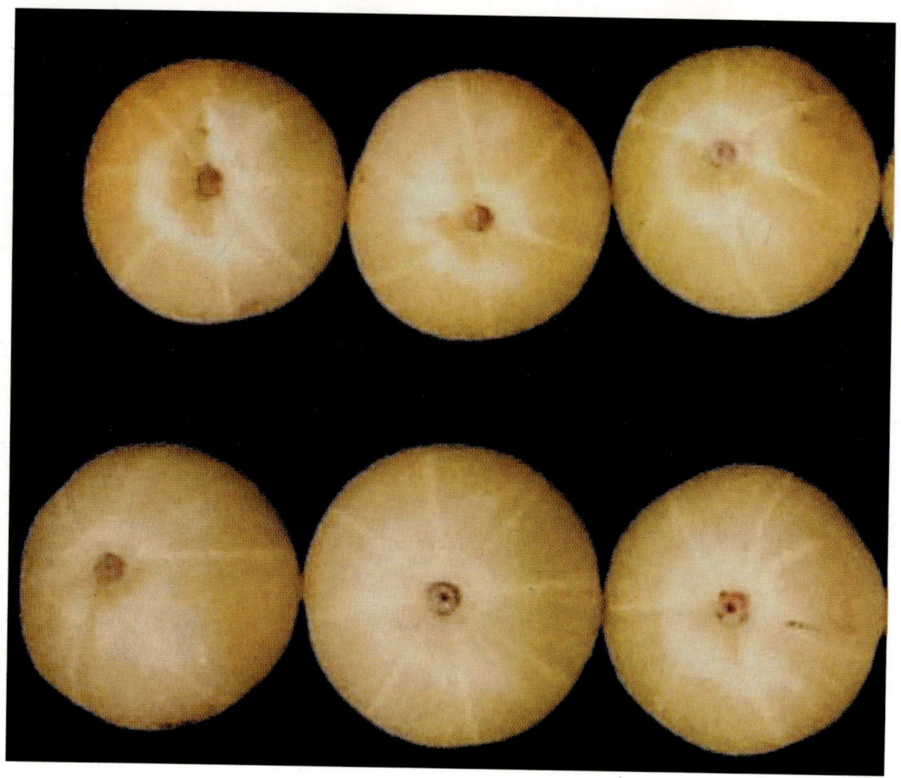

FRANCIS – An Aonla Variety

BHAGWA - A Pomegranate Variety

infested branches and destroy them. All the ant nests in the orchards should be destroyed. Drench the plants with 1875 ml Durmet/Dursban/Coroban/Massban 20 EC (chlorpyriphos) in 500 litres of water on appearance of bugs. Repeat the spray if need arises.

DISEASES

1. Canker : The bacterial Canker is caused by ***Xanthomonas axonopodis*** pv. ***citri*** (Hasse). The disease is highly infectious, spreads from tree to tree through the water splash. Disease appears on leaves, twigs and fruits. On leaves canker appears as yellowish spot, which gradually enlarge, turn rough and brownish and become raised on both the sides of the leaf. These spots are surrounded by a yellow halo. Fruit lesions become rough and croky and are confined only to the rind. Kagzilime and grapefruit are highly susceptible. It is one of the most serious disease of acid lime prevalent all over the country.

The disease can be controlled by three spraying of 100 ppm streptocyclin, the first in October, the second in December and the third in February. Prepare solution by mixing 50 g Streptocyclin in 500 litres of water. Also add 25 g copper sulphate to increase the potency of the antibiotic in the mixture. Bordeaux mixture (2 : 2 : 250) or 50 per cent copper oxychloride (0.3%) can also be sprayed.

2. Scab : The diseased is caused due to the fungus ***Elsinoe fawcetti*** (Bittan Court and Jenkins). Small, dark brown, rough, irrigular raised lesions appears mostly on under side of the leaves. Twigs and fruits are also infected.

Clipping of infected leaves should be done in July. Apply three sprays of ziram 27 SC (0.25%) or Dithane M–45 (0.25%) or Bordeaux mixture (2 : 2 : 250) or 50% copper oxychloride (0.3%) during last week of June to August at 20 days interval.

3. Gummosis (*foot rot*) : It is caused with fungus ***Phytophthora parasitica***. Phytophthora diseases produce symptoms of decline through rotting of the rootlets, girdling of trunks and dropping of blighted leaves. Important symptoms above ground include dead areas of bark, exudation of small or large amounts of gum, a yellow gummosis zone at the cambium beyond the invaded, killed area and later drying and longitudinal cracking of bark. Symptoms known as foot rot below ground include dead area with less noticeable gum, being soluble in soil water. Symptoms on leaves appear as dark, watery patches either on the edges or on the tops. The blighted leaves drop and complete defoliation may take place near ground. The gummy lesions may also appear on branches/limbs.

Treat foot rot, gummosis and cankers by decortication. The methods of treating gummosis is the removal of the diseased bark alongwith 5-10 cm strip of healthy bark beyond the diseased portion, disinfecting the wound with mercuric chloride (0.1%) or sodium hypochloride (0.1%) solutions. Cover the wound with Bordeaux paste. After the paste dries up in about a week, apply Bordeaux paint. Afterwards, give a spraying of copper oxychloride (1.5 kg) in 500 litres of water or preferably Bordeaux mixture 2 : 2 : 250 or give two application of Ridomil Gold 68 WP/Curzate M8 or Matco 8-64 as paint (2g per 100 ml of Linseed oil) to the infected trunk and drench (25 g per 10 litres of water per tree) the soil at the base of the tree in February-March and again in July-August.

Give two sprays of Aliette 80 WP 0.25 percent (2.5 g/litre of water) in April and September in addition to soil drenching with Ridomil Gold 68 WP/Curzate M8/or Matco 8-64 (25 g in 10 litres of water/acre) in February – March and July – August.

4. Anthracnose or die back or withertip : The diseases is caused due to the fungus *Colletotrichum gloeosporioides* (Penz.) or physiological causes. The disease manifests itself as light green spots which soon turn brown. If the spot has sufficient moisture, pinkish masses of spores ooze out of the surface. Sometimes fruiting bodies appear like black dots on pustules. The spots may be at the margins or tips of the leaf blades and sometimes near the midrib. The lesions are usually surrounded by concentric rings. In advanced stages, lesions are found on the twigs which start dying back. Unfavourable conditions such as extreme temperature and moisture make the plant more vulnerable to the disease. Kinnow being early and prolific bearer is prone to this disease.

Regulation of the crop in early years, pruning of the diseased twigs and sprays with Bordeaux mixture (2:2:250) or 50% copper oxychloride (0.3%) during March, July and September help in reducing the disease.

5. Citrus greening : It is caused by a bacterium. The disease manifests as stiff, upright multiple twigs and buds. Leaves of infected trees show chlorotic pattern similar to zinc deficiency. The leaves may be completely yellow or yellow with green veins. Mature leaves show yellowing of midribs. Leaves become small, thick and upright. Pre-mature defoliation occurs. Die-back of branches and greening of fruits takes place. The disease is spread through the vector ***Diaphorina citri*** which is most effective in transmitting the disease.

For its control use disease free budwood and spray against the vector citrus psylla.

6. Virus and Virus - like Diseases :

(i) **Tristeza :** It is caused due to virus **(*Citrus tristeza virus*)**. The appearance of a tree infected with tristeza is that of a tree which roots have been injured. This is due to the sieve tube necrosis at the bud union which check carbohydrate transportation from top to roots resulting in root starvation and heavy bearing which exhaust the tree. The first noticeable symptoms are chlorosis and bronzing of leaves, lack of new growth, off season flowering, heavy bearing, gradual defoliation and finally decline of the tree. Under filed conditions, the only fairly specific symptom of tristeza is honey combing-a fine pitting of the inner face of the bark in the sour orange portion of the trunk below the bud union. Stem pitting in many citrus varieties is also caused by this disease. Although the disease is graft transmissible, spread is caused by vector (aphid). Its incidence has been found to be very high in Southern India.

For its control use disease free bud wood and tolerant rootstocks such as rough lemon and Trifoliate orange. The vector (aphid) should be checked by giving timely spray.

(iii) **Exocortis :** Exocortis is caused due to viroid **(*Citrus exocortis viroid*)** : It is not common on kinnow and sweet orange budded on *Jatti Khatti* rootstock. Cracking and scaling of bark of trifoliate, citranges and Rangpur lime rootstocks is noted. Epinasty and curling of leaves, yellow blotches and cracks appears on shoots of some citrus species. Trees shows stunted growth.

The disease spreads through contaminated budding knives and also through infected bud wood. No insect vectors is known. Use only resistant rootstock like Jatti Khatti. Sterilize the budding or cutting tools after each contact with infected plants to avoid spreading to healthy trees.

(iv) **Ring spot (*Citrus ring spot virus*) :** The disease appears as yellow rings on mature leaves. The ring number varies from one to several per leaf with variable diameter. These rings may coalesce to form bigger patches by covering the entire leaf. The severely infected plant shows die-back and decline symptoms with low fruit yield. The virus is transmitted through the infected bud wood. Use virus free plants for raising the citrus orchard.

7. Melanose or stem and fruit-rot : Disease is caused due to ***Phomopsis citri.*** Dark circular depressions with yellowish margins appears on leaves, branches and fruits. Later, the spot become raised, rough and light brown and yellow margins disappear. Sand paper texture appears on the surface of leaves and fruits.

To check this disease, spray of Bordeaux mixture (2:2:250) or 50% Copper oxychloride (0.3%) during July-August and September is recommended.

8. Citrus sooty mould : The disease is caused by fungus ***Capnodium citri***. It producer black velvety superficial coating on leaves, twigs, stem and fruits.

Spray Ziram 27 SC @ 1250 ml in combination with Ethion 50 EC (Phosmite 50 EC) @ 1000 ml in 500 litres of water per acre during August, September and October for the control of citrus sooty mould syndrome.

CHAPTER 16

Grapes

The grape (***Vitis vinifera*** L.) is an important and an economic proposition for the farmers among the horticultural crops grown in India. It is one of the commercially important fruit crops of Maharashtra, Karnataka, Tamil Nadu and Andhra Pradesh in South India. Grape is also cultivated profitably in the northern States of Punjab, Haryana and Uttar Pradesh. Grape growing has been regarded as one of the most remunerative enterprises, but a major impediment in the expansion of area under this crop is the heavy initial establishment cost and recurring expenditure. Besides being grown on commercial scale, it can also be planted in Kitchen garden.

ORIGIN AND HISTORY

The grape (***Vitis vinifera***) is the most important species grown in India and is considered to be a native of Armenia - a district near Capsian Sea in Russia. Recently, scientists have reported grapes amongst the oldest flora of the earth, on the basis of discoveries in Western Kazakhastan. Clear imprints of vines and their leaves in createaceous chalk deposits dating back to 90-95 million years have been discovered, a time at which dinosaurs flourished.

Grapes were known in India since 11th century B.C., but much of its antiquity was not known until the Muslim invasion. Muslim invaders introduced grape from Iran and Afghanistan by the end of 12th century. Later grapes were taken to South by Mohamed Bin Tuglak when he shifted his capital to Daultabad in 1338. The cultivation of grapes in India, has known to be prevalent at the time of Susruta and Charakha (1356 B.C.). The ancient Aryans knew about grape culture as well as preparation of beverages from it. Recent historic facts can be traced back to 16th Century when Akbar encouraged grape cultivation in India. Later Mughal rulers introduced many more varieties during 1758.

In India, as far as Tamil Nadu is concerned, the grapes seems to have been introduced in the year 1832 by a French priest at Melapatti in Darmapuri district. Introduction of variety Anab-e-Shahi by Abdul Banquer Khan from the middle east about the year 1890 revolutionised the grape cultivation. Sardar Bahadur Lal Singh in 1928 at Layallpur introduced as many as 116 grape varieties from different grape growing countries. Extensive collection of grape varieties made at IARI in 1950. The Late Chief Minister, S. Partap Singh Kairon imported the Anab-e-Shahi variety and also obtained one lac cuttings of Perlette cultivar from California (U.S.A.) in 1962.

The important grape growing countries in the world as China, Italy, USA, France, Spain, Turkey, Chile, Argentina, Iran, Australia and India.

AREA AND PRODUCTION

The total area under grapes in India is about 1,16 lakh hectares with an annual production of 22.21 lakh tonnes, though the area under grapes is 1.7 per cent of the total area under fruits, its production accounts for 2.9 per cent of the total production of the fruits in the country. Grapes are grown largely in Maharashtra, Karnataka, Tamil Nadu, Andhra Pradesh as tropical grape and in Punjab, Haryana and parts of Uttar Pradesh as sub-tropical grapes. It is also grown in Kinnaur district of Himachal Pradesh as temperate crop. Productivity varies from region to region and the best orchards of Maharashtra and Karnataka yield 17-20 tonnes per hectare. Of the total grape production, about 95 per cent is contributed by Maharashtra and Karnataka.

The grape cultivation in Punjab is of recent origin. The grape cultivation has been spread in the districts of Bathinda, Ferozepur, Ludhiana and Mansa districts covering an area of about 438 hectares. The total production of grapes in Punjab is 12,523 tonnes. The major grape growing areas in Maharashtra State are situated in the districts of Sangli, Nasik, Solapur, Pune, Ahmed Nagar, Latur, Satara, Osmanabad and Buldhana as table grapes and Nasik, Sangli, Osmanabad and Buldhana as wine grapes. The area under grapes in this State is 92000 hectares. In Andhra Pradesh, grapes are grown in Hyderabad, Rangareddy and Anantapur. The Hyderabad-Secundrabad twin city regions forms a nucleus for the largest concentration of vineyards around any urban area in India. In Karnataka, the grape culture is mainly concentrated in the district of Bijapur, Bengaluru, Kolar, Belgaum, Gulbarga, Koppal and Bidar and grapes are being cultivated in an area of about 16800 hectares. In Tamil Nadu, grapes are cultivated in Coimbatore, Dindigul and Theni having total area 2900 hectares.

Export potential. India is exporting grapes to Netherlands, Bangladesh, UAE, UK, Russia, Saudi Arabia, Thailand, Sweeden, Sri Lanka and Nepal. The export of grapes during 2012-13 was 1.73 lakh mt worth of Rs. 1258.6 crores. The major share was exported to Netherlands (21%) and Bangladesh (20%).

IMPORTANCE AND USES

The grape is one of the most delicious, refreshing and nourishing fruit. Ripe grapes are easily digestible. It is fairly good source of minerals like calcium, phosphours, and iron and vitamins like B_1 and B_2. Grapes are good source of sugars like glucose, fructose and sucrose. The total soluble solids in different varieties ranges from 12 to 18 per cent. Brix°-acid ratio in Perlette is 23-30, in Thompson Seedless 28-35 and in Anab-e-Shahi 22-28.

Among the grape products, unfermented grape juice is universally popular. Grape juice is very delicious and energy giving beverage. For bottling fresh grape juice, it is necessary that the fruit should be juicy and aromatic. The juice is mild textured and acts as laxative and stimulant to kidneys. Ripe fruits are supposed to be the best table fruit. Wine making from grapes is a flourishing industry in many countries. Grapes also make good jelly and syrups. Fruits are used for making raisin. Grape vinegar from Perlette is a popular product.

BOTANY

The grape belongs to the family **Vitaceae** which is made up to 12 genera and about 600 species. The only genus **Vitis** is containing food plants. This genus is subdivided into 2 subgenera, **Muscadinia** and **Euvitis**. The member of **Muscadinia** have 40 somatic chromosomes, while that of **Euvitis**, 38. **Muscadinia** can easily be identified by tight bark that does not shed, simple tendrils, nodes without a diaphragm and small clusters with berries that detach as they mature. **Vinifera** has forked tendrils, bark that sheds, a diaphragm at the nodes, and elongated clusters with berries that adhere to the pedicels at maturity. It also has intermittent tendrils, thin, smooth shinny leaves with 3, 5 or 7 lobes. Berries are round or oval with edible skins that adhere to the flesh. Grape is berry and edible portion is epicarp and mesocarp.

The genus **Vitis** consist of about 60 species and only 3 species in **Muscadinia. Vitis vinifera** produces over 90 per cent of the world's grapes which are either pure **Vinifera** or **Vinifera** hybrids. The most important species of **Vitis** are as follow

1. ***Vitis vinifera*** Cultivated grapes
2. ***Vitis labrusca*** Fox grape
3. ***Vitis aestivalis*** Summer grape
4. ***Vitis rupestris*** Sand grape
5. ***Vitis cadicans*** Mustang grape
6. ***Vitis riparia*** Forst grape
7. ***Vitis berlendieri*** Spanish grape
8. ***Vitis cordifolia*** Winter grape
9. ***Vitis monticola*** Sweet mountain grape
10. ***Vitis longii*** Bush grape.

CLIMATE

Grapes are grown commercially in climate ranging from temperate to tropical around the world. The most successful area for grape cultivation is warm temperate zone between 34° North and 45° South latitude. Grapes are grown outside this zone also but in scattered areas. In tropical climate vine is evergreen.

Grape do best under a long, hot, dry and rainless summer with adequate sunshine, followed by a winter cold enough to induce dormancy in the vines. Temperature is considered as a major factor influencing composition and quality of grapes. The total amount of heat received can be expressed in terms of temperature time value called 'degree days' or heat units. Certain specific heat units are required for ripening of a particular cultivar. The early ripening varieties require 1600 heat units whereas the requirement of heat unit for late ripening varieties is 3500. The sugar content of berry generally decreases slightly with increasing altitude. For the production of good quality grapes, dry weather is essential at the time of flowering and when the fruit is developing and maturing.

The vines can tolerate low temperature or frost with little damage in the dormant period. Low temperature in winter helps in leaf fall and the vines enter dormant period. Occurrence of late frost during spring causes damage to sprouting buds.

Heavy and early rains are not good for cultivation of late ripening superior varieties of grapes, as they result into cracking of the berries and spoilage of the crops. Under such conditions, the berries do not develop sweetness and remain insipid. Moist weather also favours the spread of fungus diseases. Regions receiving heavy rainfall area, therefore, are not suited for grape cultivation. Hails during fruiting season may cause considerable damage to the vine.

Labrusca grapes or hybrids having labrusca blood will withstand humid summers and cold winters better than pure **Vinifera** varieties.

SOIL

Grapes are adopted to a wide range of soil type and grown on wide variety of soils in different regions both within India and other parts of the world. Grapes have a strong root system, therefore, most of the soil type are considered ideal for its cultivation. The best soil for grape, however, should be sandy loam, well drained and fairly fertile with good amount of organic matter. One should avoid the heavy clays, very shallow soils, poorly drained soils and those that contain high concentration of salts. The grape vines are relatively tolerant to salinity and alkalinity as compared to many other fruit crops. But, excessive lime is harmful for grape growing. The upper salt tolerance limit of grapes has been found to be 0.3 per cent.

The soils that retain water for long do not allow the vines to go into dormancy. Therefore, such soils should not be selected for grape cultivation. Well drained, clay loam, black clay loams and even shallow soils produce successful grape crops. Salt affected, nematode infested and water-logged soils should be avoided. Soils having EC upto 1.5 mmhos/cm, calcium carbonate up to 10 per cent, lime concretion upto 20 per cent and pH upto 8.7 are suitable for successful grape cultivation.

Some grape cultivars can be grown up to 7 mmhos per cm Electrical conductivity. However, salt injury can be expected when conductivity of soil is more than 2.5 mmhos/ cm and chloride is more than 10 ppm. This injurious effect of salt is reported more toxic on heavy soils compared with light soils. The exchangeable sodium percentage (ESP) of 45 and above is also injurious to grapes. Anab-e-Shahi is more susceptible to higher ESP than Cheema Sahibi and Bangalore Purple. The cultivar Perlette is more susceptible to salinity, whereas Himrod is moderately tolerant and Thompson Seedless and Beauty Seedless are tolerant.

CHOICE OF VARIETIES

There are about 8000 grape varieties which have been named and described but not more than 20 per cent of them may be growing somewhere in vineyards, gardens and varietal collections. In India also more than one thousand varieties have been collected and maintained in varietal collections. However, the varieties which have shown promise and established in a particular state of the Indian union are few. Anab-e-Shahi which was one of the major variety in the southern States in the mid seventies has not been replaced by Thompson Seedless. There is also some area under new clones of Thompson Seedless viz. Tas-A-Ganesh, Chaman Manak, Sunaka and a selection namely Dil Khush from Anab-e-Shahi. Other varieties which are being grown in South India are Bangalore Blue, Cheema Sahebi, Bhokri and Karachi Gulabi. Under the favourable conditions for grape growing in North West India comprising Punjab, Haryana, Rajasthan, the area is fast increasing and consistant efforts are being made to make it a success.

The first effort was made during the pre-partition days by the then fruit section to introduce grape cultivation in Punjab. They introduced 116 varieties from places like USA, France, South Africa and Australia. Distinguishing characters of these introductions were described and Thompson Seedless, Khalili, Kandhari, Black Prince, Foster's Seedling, Black Hamburg, Pandhari Sahebi and Dakh were recommended for semi commercial scale. Despite all this work, grape growing failed to make an impact as a commercial venture among the growers, perhaps because of disturbed political conditions leading to the partition of the country. A breakthrough was, however, achieved in 1962 when the Punjab Government started making sincere efforts. One of the major steps was the introduction of Anab-e-Shahi grape variety from Hyderabad on a large scale and import of one lac grape cuttings of an early ripening cultivar 'Perlette' from California, U.S.A. Varietal collections were also established at the Regional Fruit Research Station, Abohar and at the main campus of the Punjab Agricultural University, Ludhiana by getting varieties from within India and abroad. It is worth mentioning here that only those varieties came to be established in this region which have short internodes, have more branching habit, bear on the basal buds, are not easily spoiled by rains, ripen before onset of monsoons, possess character of abundant flower bud differentiation and whose flower primorida are not damaged by rainy season. Even varieties which are traditionally cane pruned e.g. Thompson Seedless, give good success only when pruned as long spurs. As a result of observations recorded at these centres Panjab Agricultural University, Ludhiana recommended cvs. Perlette, Thompson Seedless, Beauty Seedless, Flame Seedless and Punjab Purple for commercial cultivation in the Punjab State. Similarly, CCS Haryana Agricultural University, Hisar has categorised their recommended varieties in two groups viz. Seedless Varieties: Beauty Seedless, Delight, Perlette and Thompson Seedless, Seeded Varieties : Banqui Abyad, Champion, Early Muscat, Gold and Cordinal. Apart from the above mentioned varieties, a new clone of Thompson Seedless namely Tas-A-Ganesh and an introduction from California, U.S.A. namely Flame Seedless are finding favour.

A brief description of some of the above mentioned varieties is as follows :

Perlette : This variety was evolved at the University of California, Davis by Dr. H.P. Olmo. It is a hybrid of Scolokertek Hiralynoje 26 × Sultanina Marble and resulted from a cross made in 1936. This variety has a definite place in grape variety situation because of its being earliest maturing seedless variety in existence. It was introduced and released for commercial cultivation in the Punjab State in 1964 and has now spread in whole of the North-West India. The bunches of this variety are medium to large in size, conical, heavily shouldered, compact and attractive. Berry is whitish green, medium in size, spherical, ripens from the beginning of 2nd week to end of 3rd week of June. However, for fear of spoilage by the early monsoon showers, the growers start picking it by the end of the May when the quality is not good. It has a T.S.S. of 16 to 18 per cent, acidity of 0.5 to 0.7 per cent and juice about 70.0 per cent. The yield averages 30 tonnes per hectare from well managed vineyards. The major drawback in this cv. is compactness of bunches having large number of shot-berries. Although, it is a table variety but can also be used for wine with good success.

Thompson Seedless : This variety originated in Asia Minor. It is believed to be grown in every viticultural country of the world. The bunches are medium large, long, conical to cylindrical, shouldered, well filled to compact. The berries are yellowish green to golden yellow when fully ripe, small and seedless. It ripens during the second to third week of June before the onset of rains and has an excellent keeping quality. The T.S.S. ranges from 18 to 22 per cent, acid content 0.5 to 0.6 per cent and juice 70-75 per cent. It is a multipurpose grape variety being used for table, wine and raisins. The yields are almost half of that of Perlette in North-West Indian plains. This variety is getting renewed attention and importance due to its quality.

Anab-e-Shahi : It was introduced in Hyderabad by A.B. Khan from the middle east around 1890. The bunches are very attractive, medium large to large (400 to 600g), medium long, cylindrical to long conical, neither shouldered nor winged and well filled. Berries greenish yellow when raw and amber when fully ripe, bold and seeded. Ripening is uniform, mid season to late i.e. last week of June to mid July in North India. The quality is average in North and good in South and West India. Total soluble solid varies from 14 to 16 per cent, acidity 0.5 to 0.6 per cent, juice 65-75 per cent, very light cropper on kniffin but very prolific bearer on bower system. The average yield is 35 tonnes per hectare but yields up to 80 tonnes per hectare have been reported from Maharashtra and Andhra Pradesh. This variety is over vigorous and as such the canopy management is bit difficult. Lot of area has been uprooted under this variety in Punjab due to barrenness of the vines which was due to complete shadowing of canes. The important defect in this variety is of low sugars, flat taste and erratic bearing habits.

Flame Seedless : It is an introduction from California (USA). This variety is a descendant of three cross breed, the Cardinal and Red Seedless, Red Malaga and Tifahfi, and the Muscat of Alexandria and the Thompson Seedless. The clusters are medium in size with small, bright red, crisp seedless berries. It ripens a week later than Perlette (2nd to 3rd week of June) and yields upto27 kg per vine. Its juice is light yellow in colour having 18.0 percent T.S.S. and 0.7 cent acidity. This is excellent table grape variety and holds promise for North-West Indian plains.

Cardinal : This is also a introduction from U.S.A., where it was evolved as a cross between Flame Tokay and Ribier. The clusters are small to medium in size and mostly loose. The berries are very large and somewhat round in shape, dark red to reddish black in colour and seeded. It ripens in the first and second week of June. This is a heavy yielder and yields about 3/4 of Perlette can be expected from a bower trained vines. The T.S.S. ranges from 16 to 18 per cent, acidity 0.4 to 0.6 per cent and juice about 70.0 per cent. Because the berry is thin skinned and the stem attachment is week, the clusters must be handled carefully to avoid injury to the fruit. This is an excellent table grape variety and holds promise for commercial exploitation under conditions of North-West Indian plains.

Tas-A-Ganesh : This is a selection from Thompson Seedless in Maharashtra State. This is different from Thompson Seedless in the shape of berries which are comparatively bigger and more elongate. The bunches are medium to large in size and comparatively loose. The T.S.S. ranged from 18 to 20 per cent, acidity 0.8 to 1.0 per cent and juice 60 per cent. It ripens in the second week of June in Punjab and earlier than Thompson Seedless. There is lot of curiosity among growers for this variety.

Banqui Abyad : A variety of Russian origin, Banqui Abyad is an excellent table grape. The bunches are large, shouldered and compact. The berries are very bold, green in colour, roundish, skin very thin, seeds 2-4 per berry. It ripens a little after or alongwith Perlette i.e., last week of May to first week of June. It contains 80 per cent juice, 18 to 20 per cent T.S.S. and 0.7 per cent acidity. This is a medium cropper and yields about 18 kg per vine. This variety has been used most extensively in breeding programmes for evolving early ripening hybrids. This also holds promise for commercial cultivation in North-West Indian plains.

Delight : It is a sister seedling of Perlette evolved by Dr. H.P. Olmo at Davis, California, USA. It is less vigorous than either Perlette or Thompson Seedless. Ripening is uniform and early, from last week of May to middle of June. Its bunches are medium to long and berries are green and small. It has a T.S.S. of 18-21 per cent, acidity 0.5 to 0.6 per cent and juice 70.0 per cent. At prime maturity, it is as good as Thompson Seedless. It has good keeping quality and can ship well to distant markets. It is a good cropper, but yields are less than Perlette.

Beauty Seedless : It is an introduction from California, U.S.A. It is an early ripening, coloured, seedless, sweet and prolific bearing grape variety. Its bunches are medium to large in size, berries are bluish black, spherical, small, size moderately variable, bloom thick, flesh tender watery. It ripens along with Perlette in the end of May to first week of June. The T.S.S. content varies from 16-18 per cent, acidity 0.6 to 1.0 per cent and juice 70-75 per cent. The average yield is 25 kg per vine. On account of high juice percentage, sweetness and high yield potential, it is likely to prove useful in the processing industry for juice and raisin making. Because of low keeping quality, its scope of cultivation is limited to only near big cities and towns.

Lamanto : Lamanto is considered to be a complex hybrid between ***V. champini* × *V. labrusca* × *V. vinifera* × *V. aestivalis*.** The vines of this cv. under subtropical conditions are moderate to vigour and carry medium sized bunches weighing on an average 80 g. The yield per vine varies from 5 to 6 kg. The berries are bluish black, spherical, small to medium having thick bloom. The skin is thick and of slip skin type. The juice is purple coloured and acidic. The seeds per berry may range from 1 to 5. Ripening is uniform and mid season (2nd week of June) in North India. It contains 14.0 per cent T.S.S., 1.0 per cent acidity and 80.0 per cent juice. Having non-vinifera blood, it has been observed to be highly resistant to anthrancose and cercospora leaf spot and other fungal diseases. Moreover, the fruit is neither attacked by birds nor the berries spoil easily by rains. This is its advantage over other coloured varieties, because mostly their skin, not juice, is coloured. To make coloured wine, the juice has to be kept in contact with the skin for long times creating processing problem. This is a rare character in vinefera varieties commercially grown in the region. It can be used for juice and wine making purpose. The deep purple coloured juice is also used for Blending.

Kishmish Charni : This is an introduction from USSR, where it is a highly valued seedless variety of Uzbekistan. This is mainly used for raisin and table purpose in its home country. The bunches are large and compact. Berries are brick red, spherical medium large, size highly variable. Pulp juicy, pinkish yellow, very sweet and aromatic. Ripening is uniform, mid season, *i.e.*, 3rd week of June in North India. The T.S.S. ranges from 20-22 per cent, acidity 0.5 to 0.8 per cent, juice 70-75 per cent. In Russia the T.S.S. goes upto 28 per cent. The average yield is about 21 tonnes per hectare.

Punjab-MACS Purple : The fruit is rich in anthocyanins - a source of antioxidants and is suitable for processing into juice, nectar and RTS. It contain 60-65 per cent juice with total soluble solids 17-18 per cent and acidity 0.50 per cent. It has medium and loose bunches. The berry is medium in size, seeded and purple colour at maturity. The ripening time of this variety is first week of June.

Pusa Seedless, Manak Chaman, Bangalore Blue, Gulabi, Cheema Sahebi, Sharad Seedless are another popular varieties of grape. Some good hybrids have been derived by hybridization at IARI, New Delhi and IIHR, Bangalore. The important hybrids are Pusa Navrang (Angenine × Rubi Red), Pusa Urvasi (Hur × Beauty Seedless), Arkavati (Black Champa × Thompson Seedless), Arka Hans (Anab-e-Shahi × Bangalore Blue), Arka Shyam (Bangalore Blue × Black Champa), Arka Sweta (Ana-e-Shahi × Thompson Seedless), Arka Majestic (Angur Kalan × Black Champa), Arka Chitra (Angur Kalan × Anab-e-Shahi), Arka Soma (Anab-e-Shahi × Queen of vineyards) and Arka Trishna (Bangalore Blue × Convent Large Black).

PROPAGATION AND ROOTSTOCKS

All the commercial grape cultivars are grown over rootstocks in Europe, U.S.A., Australia and Russia due to soil borne problems. In India, all the commercial cultivars are grown on their own roots as self rooted cuttings.

The grape is best propagated by hard-wood cuttings. The cuttings are made from one year old shoots (canes). The cuttings should be taken from healthy and vigorous vines with well-matured canes. The best cuttings are those which are made from mature vines free from fungal and viral diseases and have a good bearing record. The vines which are poorly nourished and have suffered from drought and frost are not good for the preparation of cuttings. The medium sized canes with internodes of moderate length are preferred for making cuttings. The outer bark of the canes should be of clear colour *i.e.,* light brown or purple brown, depending upon the variety. There should not be dark blotches, dead streaks or immature areas on the canes. The inner bark of the canes on cut should appear green. Usually the flat or angular canes are not used for making the cuttings. It is observed that cuttings made from the middle part of the cane give higher percentage of rooting.

The cuttings are prepared at the time of pruning in January when the vines are dormant. The cuttings should be prepared promptly after the pruning is done. The length of the cuttings varies from 20 to 25 cm and each cutting should have at least three buds. The general thickness of the cuttings should be 0.75 to 1.25 cm. In making a cutting, the lower cut should be given immediately below the bud, while the upper cut should be 3-4 cm above the bud in a slanting manner to avoid injury to the top and to hold and orientate the cutting in handling and planting. The finished cuttings should be tied in bundles of 100-200 and should be buried in moist sand or saw dust for about a month for callusing. The callused cuttings start well in the nursery and give a higher percentage of rooting.

Planting of Cutting and After Care : The cuttings are planted on well-prepared soil in the nursery during February with a spacing 15 cm in rows that are 30 cm apart. After every two rows, a space of about 60 cm is left to facilitate for cultural operations. The cuttings should be planted vertically, keeping only one-third portion above the ground and the remaining two-third portion is burried in the soil. The cuttings are allowed to remain in the nursery beds for a year after which the rooted cuttings become fit for transplanting in the field. After care of the nursery beds should be regular through frequent watering, hoeing and weeding. The attack of white ants and anthracnose should be checked properly as they cause serious damage. The best time for transplanting the rooted cutting is January-February when the vines are dormant.

Rootstocks : All the grape varieties in India are multiplied through hard-wood cuttings. With the result, yields have been declining in Anab-e-Shahi and Thompson Seedless due to nematodes in peninsular Indian States. In the arid irrigated regions of Punjab, 80 per cent vineyards are found to be infected with nematodes. The reason being, more than 50 per cent of the plant material was supplied from single source which showed high infestation of nematodes. Soil salinity is also posing a threat to the grape industry in the north Indian States.

Rootstocks have been found to impart resistance to soil borne fungi, drought tolerance and vigour to the scions. Phylloxera is another problem of vinifera grape growing area of the world which have necessitated the use of rootstocks with selective resistance/tolerance to a particular disorder to make the grape industry a success. Given below are the characteristics of some important rootstocks.

St. George : It is also known as Rupestris St. George. This rootstock is a pure seedling selection chosen from the wild type species ***Vitis rupestris***. It has been planted more extensively than any other rootstock in most of the grape growing countries. It is vigorous, roots-well from cuttings, grafts well and is highly resistant to phylloxera and drought. This rootstock produces only staminate flowers.

Dog Ridge : It is seedling selection from ***Vitis champini***, which is recommended for use with heavy producing wine and raisin varieties on light sandy soils. It is highly resistant to nematode infestations and produce most vigorous grafted vines. Cuttings of this rootstock root with great difficulty and once rooted they bud and graft readily.

Teleki 5-A : It is a hybrid between ***Vitis berlandieri*** and ***Vitis riparia*** showing moderate degree of resistance of nematodes and highly resistant to phylloxera.

16 16 (Syn. Couderc 16 16, Solonis Riparia 16 16) : It is hybrid between ***Vitis solonis* × *Vitis riparia***, having moderate resistance to phylloxera and highly resistant to nematode. In sandy loam soils, it produces scions of moderate vigour that yield good crops. Cuttings of .this variety root with ease and graft readily.

1613 (Syn. Couderc 1613, Solonis × Othello 1613, Solonis-othello) : This rootstock is a hybrid arising between the species ***Vitis solonis*** and the fruiting variety Othello. It produces moderately vigorous scions, is resistant to namatodes and moderately resistant to phylloxera. Cuttings root readily and it buds and grafts easily with all fruiting varieties.

Salt Creek (*Vitis champini*) : It imparts great vigour to its scions, resistant to nematodes. This rootstock roots its cuttings with difficulty but buds and graft readily

FLOWERING AND FRUITING

The flowers in grape are borne in clusters. They are perfect, pistillate or staminate. Berry set from pollination, fertilization and seed development. In seedless varieties berry develop by parthenocarpy. Pollination provides stimulus for berry set. This type of parthenocarpy has been reported in Black Corinth cultivars. In other seedless varieties like Perlette, Beauty Seedless, Pusa Seedless, Thompson Seedless and Delight in which fertilization occurs but after sometime embryo aborts (known as stenospermocarpy). Most of the grape varieties are self pollinated but varieties like Banqui Abyad and Hur having pistillate flowers require cross pollination.

Flowers in grape mostly develop in spring. The parts of flower differentiate in the following order: 5 sepals, 5 petals, and 5 stamens. First the petals are free but later on join along their edges to form the cap or calyptra which covers the flowers bud. There are three main types of flowers. In hermaphrodite or perfect flowers, the stamens are erect with anthers producing functional pollen and pistil is functional. In pistillate flowers found on female vines of dioecious species of cultivars, the pistil is well developed and functional but stamens are more or less reflexed and pollen is generally sterile. Staminate flowers found on male vines have erect with viable pollen and more or less aborted pistils. Anthesis occurs most frequently between 6 to 9 A.M. and may also occur between 2 to 4 P.M. Anthered dehiscence coincides with the anthesis of flowers. In certain cultivars like Bhokri and Angur Kalan, it is observed to be completed well before anthesis. In Gulabi cultivar dehiscence started only after anthesis. Pollen tubes have been observed in styles within 3 hours after pollination at 16-27°C. The consequences of fertilization appears 2-3 days after pollination. The berries do not fall from the cluster and are said to have set.

Grape berry grows in three stages. The first and the third stages are the fast and the second one is very slow which is termed as lag phase. The lag phase has been reported due to the presence of higher levels of endogenous growth regulators.

PLANTING OPERATIONS

Before planting grapevine, it is essential to prepare land thoroughly by deep ploughing and follow up by tillage so that noxius weeds are killed by it. The land should be levelled thoroughly.

Spacing of vines varies greatly in different grape growing areas. A number of factors influence spacing such as temperature, soil fertility, moisture supply, variety etc. Wide spacing of vines, particularly between the rows make it easy and more economical. The initial cost of vines, planting stakes and training are directly proportional to the number of vines. Wide spacing between rows overcome crowding between the rows and improve leaf exposure to the light.

In Northern India, grapes are planted according to square system. Vines are generally trained on head system and wire trellis system. In head system, the distance is kept 2.0 × 1.5 metres, which thus accommodates 3300 vines per hectare. In case of kniffin and Y- trellis system, the vines are planted at the distance of 3 × 3 m which accommodates 1100 vines per hectare. When the vines are trained on Bower system, the planting distance is maintained at 3.0 × 3.0 m which adjusts 1100 vines per hectare. Spacing of vines on Y-trellis should be kept 1.5 × 4m, it will accommodates 1650 vines per hectare. To facilitate proper inter cultivation and management, it is always advisable to keep spacings at the end of rows.

The direction of rows will matter only in the case of Kniffin and Telephone system and not in head or Bower systems. In deciding the direction of rows, it should be taken into consideration the usual direction of the wind. Planting the grapevine rows right angle to the wind need to be avoided, as that, when blowing across is likely to damage the young shoots and the fruit bearing canes, especially in the localities which are effected by wind storms of strong velocity. In plains of north India, where there is intense heat at the time of ripening of grapes, the rows should preferably run from East to West, so that the ripening bunches are saved from the direct rays of the sun. In localities where the climate is comparatively cool, it would be advisable to set the rows from north to south so that the sunshine is well distributed on both the sides of the vine to facilitate proper maturation and colouring of the fruit.

The planting of vines under north Indian conditions is done in January to first fortnight of February when they are still dormant. The size of the pit should be 1 × 1 × 1 metre dimension. If the soil is light, the size of the pits can be reduced. The refilled pits should be watered a few days before planting the vines. In each pit, add 5 ml of chlorpyriphos 20EC mixed in about 2 kg soil against white ants. Plants with buds which have sprouted require special care in setting as compared to those that are still dormant. At the time of planting, it would be necessary to train the plants properly. It is usual practice to prune the top three to four buds, keeping only one cane. The staggling roots are also trimmed, broken and damaged roots should also be removed. Vigorous and healthy, one year old rooted cuttings are considered best for planting.

ORCHARD CULTURAL PRACTICES

Irrigation

The growth and fruit production of grape vine is directly associated with the presence of water throughout its life. The yield from a vineyard is an end product of a series of biochemical and physiological processes that take place in living cells of grapevine. These processes proceed at maximum only when turgor pressure of cells is optimum. The excessive depletion of soil would bring about corresponding increase in diffusion pressure deficit within the tissue fluid of the vine. Consequently, the growth is affected adversely. The root elongation ceases when the turgor pressure approaches zero.

The dormant mature vines exhibit a high degree of tolerance to waterlogged soils. But these are prone to damage if subjected to waterlogged conditions for a long period during active growth season. The roots of grapevine in saturated soil may die from lack of aeration. The remaining fewer healthy roots are not able to absorb sufficient water to meet the needs of the vine even from the very wet soil. The saturated soil conditions also cause reduction in microbial activity and leaching of nutrients. The grapevine under excessive soil moisture conditions may tend to produce excessive vegetative growth at the expense of fruiting. Also, the vines will continue to grow or initiate new vigorous growth after harvest if readily available water is in ample supply. Such a late growth utilizes carbohydrates and does not allow their storing. The late growing new shoots fail to mature properly and are subject to injury by frosts. Such vines are likely to show bud failure and less crop in the following year than the vines that ceased growth early and matured their wood well. This situation is more pertinent to the cane pruned varieties.

Under the Punjab conditions, one irrigation is suggested after pruning in the first fortnight of February. The second irrigation is applied in first week of March. After fruit set in April till first week of May, the irrigation is recommended at 10 day intervals. Vineyards are to be irrigated weekly during rest of May. The interval is decreased to 3-4 days during June. During July to October, the irrigation is given if there is prolonged dry spell or insufficient rainfall. Only one irrigation is recommended from November through January, if the soils get extremely dry.

The grapevine need regular irrigation in southern India except at the time of pruning and monsoon. Irrigation is given at 6-8 days interval during fruiting period. In Madurai, the vines are irrigated four times a week during summer and two times a week during winter.

The irrigation timings should also be based on the requirement of the vines at the critical stages of bud burst, flowering and harvest. Other irrigations should be arranged to provide a reasonable moisture supply between these times. The water needs of vineyard are influenced by the following factors :

(*a*) The time to irrigate, the number of irrigations and the amount of water at each irrigation are determined by the age and condition of the vines and soil type. The climatic factors such as temperature, humidity and wind influence greatly the water needs of vineyards.

(*b*) Young vines need more frequent irrigation than grown up vines. The vines trained on bower system need more water than those on kniffin or telephone or head system.

(*c*) The irrigation is seldom applied during winter when the vines remain dormant. Hence, the soil moisture depletes to a very low level. As such, vines would not resume normal growth in spring unless irrigation is applied to replenish the soil moisture. Irrigation soon after pruning hence is necessary.

(*d*) The period between fruit set and maturity is the most critical. Adequate water should be available to vines during the period.

(*e*) During the hot period from mid May to mid June, there is great need of water. The sugar accumulation in berries occurs during this period.

(*f*) Irrigation should be withhold a little ahead of fruit maturity. This improves the fruit quality.

(*g*) Irrigation should never be ignored after harvesting of the grapes.

According to estimates made in Uzbekistan, 1.5 per cent of the water is used from beginning of growth to flowering, 10 per cent between beginning of flowering and fruit set, 43 per cent during fruit growth and 45 per cent during ripening. It is, therefore, essential that the amount of irrigation water is regulated according to the stage through which the plant is passing.

Intercropping

Actually no intercrop should be sown in vineyards as it comes into bearing one year after planting and commercial crops start after 2-3 years of planting. Apart from this, the distance between vines is 3 × 3 metres and as such much space is not left between the plants for growing of intercrops. Another factor is that almost entire plantations are trained on bower system of training. This structure with the spread of grapevines on it causes partial to complete shading in the 3rd year. Also, the grapevine is a shallow rooted crop, therefore, root injury is quite possible in case of deep ploughing.

Keeping in view the above facts, intercrops should not be grown in the vineyards. But it has been observed that grape growers have started planting of intercrops like radish, cucurbits, bhindi, brinjal, cabbage and potato for the first two to three years after planting the vineyards. Short duration crops like cucurbits are planted during summer months when irrigation can be applied to these intercrops alongwith grapevine without any loss.

However, to augment organic matter in the soil, it is better to grow cover crops of leguminous types like guara, senji and cowpeas and burry them into the soil, while they have attained maximum vegetative growth. The purpose is to keep the soil loose and friable. Exhaustive and tall crops should never be sown. The winter season vegetables like cabbage, cauliflower and peas should not be grown during dormant period because they disturb the vineyards. By giving irrigation to these vegetables during winter, the vines would continue to put some growth which affects very badly in the next cropping. Only, the short term intercrops like moong and mash can be sown during the first two-three years.

Weed Management

The vineyards are infested with weeds which compete with the grapevine for water and food. Also they harbour the harmful insects viz. defoliating beetles, stem girdler and the jassids. These insects hide in underneath and subsequently emerge to attack the vines when the conditions are favourable for them to do so. The weeds root secrete toxin's which adversely affect the vine growth and fruit bearing. Cultivation is effective if done frequently but it may reduce yields from root pruning and cause affect on soil moisture. Moreover, hand weeding is labour intensive and costly, owing to the steady increase in labour wages and their non-availability. Weed management had become an expensive input in the cultivation of grapes. Recently, the control of weeds through the use of chemicals has come to light which is not only economical but also convenient and efficient as it consists of one or two applications.

Hexuron 80 WP (diuron) @ 3.0 kg/ha (first fortnight of March) after thorough cultivation to remove the established growing weeds/plant debris can effectively control the weeds when applied at pre-emergence stage or glycel 41 SL (glyphosate) or gramoxone 24 WSC (paraquat) @ 4 1/ha as post-emergence should be sprayed when the weeds are growing actively and attain the height of 15-20 cm. Dissolve the herbicides in 500 litres of water per hectare so as to give a thorough coverage to the weeds in the field. Spray glycel/gramoxone during the calm day to avoid spray drift to the foliage of the grapevines. Total uptake of nitrogen, phosphorus and potassium by weeds per unit area in vineyards was significantly more in control than other treatments which show that there was a positive correlation between weed population and nutrient uptake by weeds. The fruit yield was recorded higher under glycel treatments. The quality of fruits in terms of total soluble solids was improved with hexuron and glycel treatments.

Manuring and Fertilization

It is basically essential to know the role of different nutrients on growth, fruit yield and quality in order to include them in various proportion in vineyard manuring at different stages of growth and fruit development.

Nitrogen : Nitrogen was found to have a role in the flowering of grapes. Absence of Nitrogen in the fertilizer was found to delay the floral initiation in Anab-e-Shahi. It was also found to have influence on the number of bunches per vines and the mean bunch weight ultimately increasing the yield per vine. The need of this element is greatest and the response is most rapid on sandy gravelly soils. On heavier soils, nitrogen availability and response will occur more slowly. Crop yield may be reduced before the deficiency symptoms of this element appear.

Phosphorus : Phosphorus appears to have a clear cut role in the floral bud initiation. Application of phosphorus was found to promote fruitfulness in Anab-e-Shahi vines. Increasing levels of applied phosphorus were associated with increased fruit yield in Anab-e-Shahi and Thompson Seedless.

Potassium : Potassium was found to be favourable for the inflorescence formation. Its application made those buds fertile which under normal conditions remained sterile through increased carbohydrates accumulation. Increased yields were obtained with increasing levels of K in Anab-e-Shahi and Thompson Seedless grapes. Potassium was reported to have an important role in the quality of grapes. Higher level of applied K was associated with higher total soluble solids content of grape juice.

The deficiency of this element has been associated with vineyard areas with very sandy soils. Potassium fertilizer must be placed near the active root zone. Measurable response to K fertilizer has only been obtained where visual deficiency symptoms have appeared.

Magnesium : Magnesium requirement of vines is more during berry ripening. Mg deficiency is very common in the vineyards of peninsular India, particularly in Anab-e-Shahi. The deficiency is mostly induced due to over manuring with potato and is more prevalent in light sandy soils. Thus, Mg requirement is more during fruit development stage and in low Mg soil, it moves from leaf chlorophyl to the developing fruit causing chlorosis.

Calcium : Deficiency of calcium makes the berry skin susceptible to necrosis and rotting. Higher levels of petiole calcium were associated with reduced yields in Anab-e-Shahi and Thompson Seedless. The exact role of Ca in vine production is, however, not clear.

Micronutrients : Among the micronutrients, boron, zinc, iron, manganese and copper are important in viticulture. Boron is essential for the regulation of carbohydrate metabolism. It is also important for the pollen germination, growth of pollen tube and normal fruit set. Its deficiency is commonly known as hen and chicken disorder of the clusters. Boron is considered to be delicate among the micronutrients because of the narrow range between its status of deficiency or excess. Shoot growth, bunch and berry size and sugar content of the juice was found to increase with boron application in Perlette grape. Boron spray, increased the protein and RNA contents of grape leaves. Thus, it seems to improve productivity and quality in grapes. Boron deficiency can be corrected by either soil application or foliar sprays of boron containing materials like boric acid or borax.

Zinc deficiency symptoms start appearing in the mid summer when secondary or auxiliary growth begins. The secondary growth and the primary shoot tips are affected first. The main foliage symptoms of zinc deficiency are the chlorotic pattern, the location and the small size of affected leaves and particularly the widened angle formed between the two basal lobes of the leaf blade when the petiole is attached there, the primary veins tend to draw together, resulting in a fan like appearance. Foliar application of zinc improves vine growth, fruitfulness, fruit set, fruit yield and quality of berries.

Iron is needed for the activation of several enzyme systems. Its deficiency impairs chlorophyll production resulting in the characteristic chlorosis of the young leaves. Deficiency of Fe is common in calcarious soils and in vines with weak root systems. Beneficial effects of iron on vetgetative growth, fruit yield and quality of berries were reported. The concentration used ranged between 0.05 to 0.2 per cent iron sulphate.

Magnesium serves as an activator for enzymes in growth processes and helps in chlorophyll formation. Therefore, its deficiency manifests in leaf chlorosis which is common in acidic sandy soils. The deficiency can be corrected by spraying 0.2 per cent neutralised manganese sulphate as soon as the deficiency symptoms appear on the vines.

Nutrient requirements

Under the Bangalore conditions for Anab-e-Shahi vines of less than 5 years age, a combination of 500 kg N, 125 kg P_2O_5 and 750 kg K_2O per hectare per year was found to be optimum. While the optimal combination for the vines of more than 5 years of age was found to be 500 kg N, 500 kg P_2O_5 and 1000 kg K_2O per hectare per year. Individually, N at 1000 kg, P_2O_5 at 500 kg and K_2O at 800 kg per hectare were found to be optimum under western Maharashtra conditions. Under Southern Karnataka 666 kg N, 888 kg P_2O_5 and 666 kg K_2O per hectare were found optimum doses.

In Punjab, to one year old grapevine 20 kg farmyard manure, 400 g urea, 1.5 kg superphosphate (16% P_2O_5) and 250 g muriate of potash are recommended. To full grown vine of 5 years and above, 80 kg farmyard manure, 1 kg urea, 4.5 kg single superphosphate and 800 g muriate of potash is added. To newly planted vine apply 60 g urea and 125 g muriate of potash in April and repeat the same dose in June.

Time of application : Under Maharashtra conditions where vines are pruned twice, application of 60 per cent of annual dose of N, 50 per cent of P_2O_5 at April pruning and rest of N and P_2O_5 and the entire K_2O at October pruning is recommended. Application of P after 30-40 days after pruning was found to promote fruitfulness in Anab-e-Shahi vines. Irrespective of the time of application, K was found to promote bud fertility. Application of K on 20th day after pruning improved the fertility status of promixal buds, while application on 50th day in the distal region. Early application of N *i.e.,* 20th day after pruning and later application of P and K 35-50th day after pruning, was found to favour fruit bud differentiation.

In Punjab, the whole quantity of farmyard manure, superphosphate and half nitrogen and half potassium is applied after pruning. The remaining nitrogen and potassium is applied in April. The use of high dose of fertilizers results in excessive vegetative growth and barrenness. In the case of bower system, complete shade under the bower is an indication of excessive growth. In that case, the nutrient content of the soil should be re-checked with a soil test and the fertilizer dose be adjusted. Give two sprays of urea @ 1% first at full bloom and second at fruit set to get higher yield and better fruit quality in Perlette grape.

Foliar Application : Application of nutrients through foliage is yet another method to increase the efficiency of applied nutrients. It overcomes the soil and translocation factors in the absorption of nutrients and envisages at greatest economy of the nutrients. Foliar application of N as urea, P as calcium phosphate and K as potassium chloride resulted in the increased contents of N, P and K for improving the yield and quality of the fruit.

TRAINING AND PRUNING

Training is a distinct process in grapevine and a number of different systems have been developed to create favourable microclimate to manipulate the physiology of the vine for increased productivity and fruit quality, and to give it a desired shape that maintains its vigour for a long period and facilitates requisite leaf exposure and different cultural operations including harvesting and plant protection. Grapevine bears on new growth that emerges from the last season's mixed buds. Pruning is necessary to regulate yield, size of bunches and quality of fruit. Proper pruning also regulates the number of buds and adequate number of bearing shoots each year, prevents the accumulation of old and unproductive wood and keeps the vine within manageable shape.

(a) Training of grapevine

In nature, grapevine is a slender climber clinging with the help of tendrils and bearing scanty fruits at the tops. To domesticate it, channeling its energy from vegetative growth to enhanced bearing, an artificial support is a must. In fact, improper training may lead to complete barrenness of the vine.

Methods of Support

Grapevine cannot be grown satisfactorily without some form of support, temporary or permanent, to obtain a well formed vine with strong straight trunk quickly and economically. Varied forms of support, viz., arbours (bowers), stakes and trellis have been devised and used, the first one being the most common in India. The short time supports or stakes especially in hard-pruned vines, provide support until the vines are large and rigid enough to stand on their own. The permanent supports, bowers and trellis are required for vines that are either cane-pruned or cordon trained. It is advisable to construct a durable bower or trellis before planting of vines to avoid frequent repairs or replacements.

Bower or Arbour or Pergola : In spite of being the most expensive systems of support, this is commonly adopted for Thompson Seedless, Perlette and Anab-e-Shahi varieties. It is best suited in warmer climate where the vine grows vigorously. It provides good protection against hot desiccating winds. The bunches hang from the vines under the extensive vine spread and are saved from damage by birds and sun scorch. It is also capable of giving high yield of quality fruit. The wood growth is suppressed due to shading effect as vines cover the overhead net completely. But the establishment of this system is rather tedious besides being expensive. The cost of establishment may range between Rs. 2.5 to 3.0 lakh per hectare at current price.

A bower consists of a criss-cross network of wires usually 2.1 to 2.5 metres above ground and 30 to 45 cm apart, supported by pillars made of concrete, stone or iron, angle iron or even bamboo. For roof, strong angle iron of about 6.4 × 6. 4 × 0.64 cm section or steel ropes of 10 mm diameter are used to run on peripheral poles making a rectangle. Steel ropes perform better than angle iron. The wire used for making nets should be of 8 to 10 gauge according to the pressure to be sustained by the arbour.

Sometimes, holes are drilled in the angle iron arms at 60 cm distance to create a criss-cross network of wires but it is not considered a good practice. Instead, the net wires should be fastened as such to the angle iron or steel rope at the periphery. If the wire sags, it can be restretched by twisting. Each pillar is supported with a deadman fixed 100-150 cm deep in the ground which should be 15 × 30 × 60 cm in size in loamy soils and one and half times larger in sandy soils and should be made of reinforced cement brick concrete having a single steel bar of 12 mm diameter or of cut stone. The peripheral poles are kept inclined at 75° angle. The end poles are stretched with ropes made of 3 wires of 8 mm diameter, while each corner pole needs three such ropes.

Trellis : Although not used in tropical and subtropical regions, it may be of some worth in high hills. The most common types are two-wire vertical trellis and overhead trellis.

Three-wire vertical trellis once prevalent in north India were erroneously known as six-arm kniffin. Steel posts of about 6. 4 × 6.4 × 0.64 cm sections and 2 to 2.5 m above ground are firmly fixed in earth with a cement concrete foundation. The end of posts are firmly anchored or braced. The spacing of the poles depends largely on the planting distance. Two or usually three wires are stretched horizontally at the height of 1.2, 0.9 and 0.6 metre supported by single iron pole at 5 metres distance. The establishment cost of vertical trellis is about Rs. 1.5 to 2.0 lakh per hectare.

The telephone system or three-wire horizontal trellis or overhead trellis was used is north India for moderately vigorous varieties with more apical dominance. The poles are about 2 m high. All the wires run only in one direction and thus movement in the vineyard is unrestricted. The air circulation between rows was better and it was considered better than bower.

Y-Trellis is recently introduced in North India for higher yield and excellent fruit quality. Y-shaped structure is build up by maintaining 110° angle between the Y. The horizontal wires are stretched maintaining a distance of 9″ to 1′. This is an open canopy system allowing more sunlight and more aeration which leads to less build up of humidity.

Stakes : These are commonly used in kitchen gardens where head system of training in practised. A good support may be a strong bamboo or a 5 cm diameter wooden pole of about 2 m height. The stakes should be charred over fire or treated at the bottom with solighum or coaltar to protect from white ants. The stakes are either fixed soon after or at the time of planting the vines keeping their 30 to 40 cm length in the ground to provide support till vine trunks gain strength to stand on their own.

The initial cost for providing stakes is high as the planting distance is reduced in head system to 2.0 × 1.5 m accommodating nearly three to four times more plants than in bower system. Not only the digging of more number of pits involves higher cost, the watch and ward of stakes and fruit is also expensive.

Training Systems

The training systems were developed to suit the various needs, conditions and personal preferences. In Andhra Pradesh, Anab-e-Shahi vines were commonly trained on bower system. Bangalore Blue of Mysore was mostly trained to the **mandap** system. In Puna, Baramati, Phalton and Nagar areas of Maharashtra, two-wire trellis and bower systems were favoured but in Nasik and Marathwada regions, head system of training to a live stake of Pangara (*Erythrina indica*) was commonly followed. In Punjab and Haryana, Anab-e-per *** predominant variety is mostly trained on bower and Y-trills and, to a limited extent, on horizontal and vertical trellis. Thompson Seedless and Black Prince varieties of grapevines were once trained on arbour with wires fixed on live poles of Kiluval (*Commiphora candata*) in Dindigul, Krishnagiri and Madurai. In Periyakulam, maximum yield from grapevine was obtained when trained on **pandal** system.

The choice of training system depends on factors, such as apical dominance, vigour of the vine, bearing zone on the shoots, soil type, cultural practices, economics of the system and prevailing climatic conditions.

Bower : The training of vines, both under tropical and subtropical regions of India, is done by forming two major limbs on which several cordons are developed one on either side of each limb running along each wire. This is the most successful and popular system.

In the plains of north-west India, the grapevine undergoes sufficient chilling in winter while in summer the temperature may go as high as 43°C with very low relative humidity which prevent normal metabolism in the vine since most cultivars show little carbon dioxide assimilation beyond 35°C. In South India, high sunshine and low relative humidity occur during berry development and ripening. Bower system creates the required microclimate under the dense canopy of vines with a temperature difference of over 10°C compared to that in the open. More than 100 per cent increase in relative humidity has also been recorded under the canopy.

The two primary limbs (cordons) are developed bidirectionally and the secondary cordons are developed on the main arms so that the vine covers the overhead area of about 9 square metres when planted at 3 × 3 m. Short or long fruiting spurs are allowed to develop on the secondary cordons only. Being an extensive systems, the fruiting area of the vine spreads over the entire nine square metres space which enables it to retain more fruiting wood than in other systems of training.

The formation of two primary limbs is sometimes encouraged by pinching off the apical shoot close to the wire. Two vigorous shoots growing in opposite directions are selected at the wire level for training as primary arms. These are allowed to grow upto to the length provided for the purpose. One secondary limb (cordon) is allowed to develop along each wire from these two primary arms. Generally, the entire length of primary arms is attained in two years but will be better if it is achieved in three or even four years. Quick attainment of the length of primary limbs results in weak secondary cordon on the proximal parts of the main cordons and too much growth at distal parts. In three metres, there are usually eight wires and, therefore, eight secondary cordons should be developed on either side i.e., approximately four on either side of primary cordon. Once the primary and secondary cordons have been developed, the rest of the pruning it is similar to that on any other cordon. It is customary to retain 100 to 200 fruiting spurs in Parlette and about 100 short canes in Thompson Seedless vine planted at 3 × 3 m distance.

On the basis of yield, bower system proved superior to kniffin system. Among several training systems in Beauty Seedless bower system was found to give the highest yield. Perlette, Muscat Hamburg, Himrod and Thompson Seedless bear much more heavily on bower system to more than compensate its high cost. Best growth, yield and fruit quality was obtained in Beauty Seedless grapevines trained on bower system. Yields in Karachi Gulabi were the highest with bower system. In Beauty Seedless bower system gave 1.5, 1.9 and 3.1 times higher yields than telephone, kniffin and head systems, respectively. In Himrod, bower gave 1.6, 1.9 and 2.7 times higher yield than telephone, kniffin and head systems, respectively.

Bower system of training is most successful as it provides a unique microclimate, cuts excessive sunshine, increases the humidity and lowers the temperature under it, ensures maximum spread of foliage and best interception of light resulting in maximum yield and quality of fruit. Harvesting is very easy and bird damage is much less. The system is difficult to adopt and requires lot of skill and labour, the cordons become barren if the vines are not trained and pruned properly, spraying and fruit haulage are difficult and the cost of establishment is much higher than in the other systems.

Vertical Trellis : If the main trunk extends horizontal on one side of the wire, it is termed as unilaterally horizontal cordon. When one cordon is trained to extend on either side of trellis making a T-type structure, it is termed as bilateral horizontal conrdon. The long trunk of the cordon enables good crop distribution. The fruit quality is excellent because clusters do not touch each other and shoots do not rub against or grow through the clusters. Cordon system tends to make lower buds on canes more fruitful. Thus, varieties which bear on long spurs on head system will bear normal crop even on short spurs on cordon system. This system is simple and involves relatively lower cost.

In cordon trained vines, the height of wires from ground level varies depending upon agroclimatic conditions. Where it is intended to make use of ground heat and the cultivar is not vigorous, it may be as low as a few centimetres from ground. After planting, one erect growing shoot is selected and the others are removed. This shoot is directed to grow along the horizontal wire and loosely tied with it. Side shoots arising on the upper side of the cordon are allowed to grow.

In Perlette, maximum intensity of anthracnose infection was observed on vertical trellis followed by horizontal trellis, bower and stakes in descending order. Anab-e-Shahi was noted most susceptible and Himrod least susceptible to anthracnose when trained on vertical trellis.

The initial training in these systems is expensive, laborious and requires more skill. The varieties which bear on long canes and have unfruitful basal buds cannot be trained on this system. The renewal of cordon is also difficult.

Kniffin (Storey) : This system, first developed by William Kniffin in 1850, is being used, to some extent in India, in highly modified form named as Indian storey system. It is also called espalier system in some countries. In India, it was once believed to be good for varieties such as Thompson Seedless, Pusa Seedless, Black Prince and Muscat of Alexandria.

The training in this system is basically similar to that in cordon system. The permanent branches (arms) are arranged horizontally and tied loosely on the wires so that annual growth arises at the same level. The vines are trained to usually three and sometimes to two pairs of horizontal arms. On two wires, four-arm and on three wires, six-arm storeys are developed. Thus, there are no cordons and only four or six arms, one on each side of the main trunk running along each wire.

The maximum number of infected buds were found in Perlette (77 per cent) followed by Anab-e-Shahi (37 per cent), Himrod (34 per cent) and Thompson Seedless (17 per cent) when trained on Kniffin system. Perlette on Kniffin system was first to be infected by anthracnose and was rated moderately resistant whereas Anab-e-Shahi, although got diseased quite late, was more severely damaged. Thompson Seedless trained on this system had 28 per cent dead canes due to anthracnose infestation.

The fruit yield on this system was only about half of that in bower system. The overall development of the vine and leaf area were much less because of under utilization of space and the bird damage was more..

Overhead Trellis (*Telephone*) : In this system, as the name suggests, the trellis looks like telephone wires. One or two tier trellis may suit semi-vigorous varieties. The young vines are supported by wooden sticks. After reaching the height of about 2 metres, the tip is pinched off to encourage side shoots close to the wires. Two vigorous shoots across wires are selected as primary arms from which six laterals, one on each side along the wires, are allowed to develop as secondary arms.

Vines trained on this system produce considerably higher yield than on vertical trellis but not as much as on bower. Similarly, higher yield in Himrod vines was recorded when trained on telephone system than on espalier (kniffin) and head systems. Its effect on bunch characters, maturity and quality of fruit in Beauty Seedless has been reported. Thompson Seedless vines trained on overhead trellis had lesser number of dead canes due to anthracnose than on bower. Similar results were obtained in other cultivars also. Drooping of vine from the first and third wire forming a tunnel is conducive for the spread of diseases and bird damage. This method needs a lot of skill and expenses and is not suitable for varieties having low to moderate vigour. The system is best suited to the varieties which have comparatively lower vigour and bear fruit on basal buds of the canes, *e.g.* Beauty Seedless, Perlette and Delight.

Y-Trellis : Vines are trained to H system of training. Vines are headed back at the height of 5 feet from the ground. Two secondary arms are developed on which fruiting canes are maintained. This training system is found highly suitable for Perlette and Flame Seedless. The system offers plenty of sunshine to the bunches and improve the quality of bunches. Grapevines on Y-trellis are spaced at 1.5 × 4 m which gives high yield, improves fruit quality and enhance maturity.

Head : The vines are supported by stakes during the first 4-5 years or till their trunks become strong enough. After planting, the growing shoot is cut at a height of about one metre. Four to five well placed branches arranged in the form of a goblet are selected. All the other side branches are pinched off. At the first pruning, the laterals are pruned to spur with one or two buds. These spurs will produce a number of shoots to provide arms for the framework. At the subsequent prunings, a sufficient number of spurs are retained at the end of each arm in different directions for bearing as well as to provide canes for the next year's spurs. Normally, 15-20 fruitng spurs of 3-4 buds and an equal number of renewals of one to two buds are retained on a vine. But, as in other systems, the renewal spurs put forth only a weak growth or die and are of no use.

The head system is considered the most economical. But, the cost per unit production of grapes was highest with this system. Berry size is usually bigger. The maximum bud and flower drop was noted in Beauty Seedless on head System. Disease intensity on both leaves and canes was the lowest in this system. Thompson Seedless vine trained on this system had the least number of dead canes due to anthracnose infection. The yield on head system is very low. On an average, the vines at full bearing yield only 4-5 kg fruit. This system is not suitable for vigorous varieties pruned to long canes which do not bear on basal buds. In windy location, the vines trained on head system are likely to lodge. Installation of stakes costs a lot and require watch and ward.

Apart from these, other systems of less significance are also followed in certain areas *e.g.*, factory system employed in South Africa. Guyot system of training is followed under conditions where the temperature is very low during the fruit development and maturity. Chautauqua system is followed for long bearing varieties as Sultanina and Corinth. Fan system is suggested for extreme cold conditions and is suitable for cultivars bearing on long canes *e.g.* Thompson Seedless. Umbrella system is suitable for Thompson Seedless, and Black Corinth. Tatura trellis is followed for training grapevines in Australia.

(*b*) Pruning of Grapevine

Pruning comprises the removal of living canes, shoot, leaves and other vegetative parts of the vine. In nature, grapevine shows acropetal growth and if left as such its branches continue to elongate climbing with the help of tendrils. Acropetal growth is more pronounced under warmer condition. When pruned keeping 8-10 buds, only the terminal 2 or 3 nodes usually put forth growth and those at proximal positions either do not sprout or produce only weak shoots bearing small bunches that do not ripen. Vine pruning regulates or encourages good yield and improves size and quality of fruit. The aim of pruning is to properly distribute the bearing wood over the vine and to regulate the crop maintaining its vitality for consistent productivity. Generally, pruning has a depressing effect on vine growth and reduces bearing. However, over-bearing also has similar effect and delays the ripening.

Pruning Methods

(*i*) Spur Pruning : The retention of 1-4 basal buds after pruning as fruiting canes is called spur pruning. For the most economical production of all varieties of grapes that produce medium sized clusters on shoots arising from buds at the base of the canes, spur pruning should be used. Perlette variety is spur pruned.

(*ii*) Cane pruning : It is practised by leaving more than four buds on a cane. It should be used with varieties of which the lower buds on the canes are usually sterile such as Thompson Seedless.

(*iii*) Mechanical pruning : Cane pruning with less number of canes per vine of same length is being used for more varieties. It permits positioning of the fruit for machine harvesting better than the other system.

Type of Pruning

1. Dormant pruning : The principal pruning is done while the vine is dormant, between leaf fall in autumn and the starting of the buds in spring.

Time of pruning : In north west plains, the pruning is generally practised from middle of January to first week of February when the vines are in dormant condition.

In tropical areas of Maharashtra, Andhra Pradesh, Karnataka, and Tamil Nadu, the vine continues growth all the year round and does not undergo dormancy. Pruning is, therefore, done twice a year, once in summer and again in winter. Summer pruning is done during March-April, except Tamil Nadu, where it is done in June when the canes are cut back to 1-2 buds to induce vegetative growth and is called back pruning or growth pruning. During winter, pruning is done between the last week of September and first week of October in northern districts of Karnataka and in December in Tamil Nadu when it is done to induce fruiting depending upon the variety.

Amount of pruning : Amount of pruning depends on the bearing behaviour of different cultivars. Number of canes per vine and number of buds per cane varies from variety to variety. Following intensity of pruning is recommended for different varieties on bower system at 3×3m spacing in Punjab:

Variety	Number of canes to be left/vine	Number of buds to be left/cane
Perlette, Beauty Seedless and Punjab-MACS Purple	60–80	4
Thompson Seedless	40–50	8–10
Anab-e-Shahi	80–100	5 or 6

Unit of pruning : When a vine has reached the stage of full bearing, pruning consists of removing all the growth except (*i*) **Bearing units :** for the production of fruit and new wood or fruit only, (*ii*) **Renewal spurs :** for renewal or the production of wood for the next year and (*iii*) **Replacement spurs :** In the older vines, for the replacing or shortening of arms.

(2) **Summer pruning :** Summer pruning, of which there are many forms, consists in removing buds, shoots, or leaves, while they are green herbaceous. Thus, it is done while the vine is growing or active. Summer pruning has various uses, principally as follows:

(*a*) **Correction of shape :** To direct the growth into the parts that will form the permanent frame work of the vine such as the trunk, branches and arms and to keep these parts active and healthy. This is accomplished by such operations as disbudding, pinching and suckering.

(*b*) **Shading the fruits :** To increase the shade on the fruit by topping, which promotes the upright position of shoots and growth of laterals.

(*c*) **Opening the vine to light :** To open the vines and thus expose the fruit more favourably to light and air.

In Punjab, summer pruning was substituted by three summer pinchings, one in May and two in August - September to increase fruit yield and quality since the former is a cumbersome process.

Rejuvenation and Top-working

The old Perlette vines trained on bower system can be successfully rejuvenated by heading back the primary arms leaving behind 1' stubs in the month of December – January. Bordeaux paste should be applied after heading back of primary arms.

Flame Seedless variety can be successfully top-worked on Perlette vines. For this purpose, tongue grafting should be done in the last week of February on one year old shoots (canes). This technique advances maturity by 4 – 5 days of Flame Seedless. The fruit quality is also improved.

CONCEPT OF DOUBLE CROPPING IN NORTH INDIA

In the Southern and Western parts of the country, where vine remains evergreen, the grape growers are in a great benefit and have to prune the vines twice a year to get two crops annually. In Western India, severe pruning is done in March after harvesting to encourage fresh vegetative growth. The crop from this growth ripens at the end of October but the fruit is poor, thus, the crop is not common. A second light pruning is done in October and the crop is harvested in March.

In the northern India, vines go into dormancy during winter because of distinct summer and winter seasons. The scientists were of the opinion that summer pruning will not be able to produce second crop. Grapes are being grown since long in countries like Afganistan, Iraq, the Mediterranean Coast, California and parts of Southern Australia where the vines remain dormant during winter and put forth growth only once in spring. At present also, only one crop is taken. Same is the case of northern India. Now, a new thinking has emerged, that is to obtain two crops (winter and summer) with the technique of double pruning. The idea behind this is to retain fruit on the vine for a longer period with no risk of rain damage as it is a major limitation to the summer crop. Trials have been undertaken at different places in Punjab and Haryana with different dates of pruning *i.e.,* 1st, 10th, 20th and 30th July on Perlette and Tas-e-Ganesh varieties. It was found that 10th July was the best date of pruning. However, the yield is very low in comparison to the summer crop. The trial may prove helpful for improving yields and having fruit during winter also with better quality and without risk of rain damage.

Beauty Seedless grapes in the arid-irrigated region of Punjab can give two crops in a year. Pruning for the summer crop has to be carried out during the first week of February and for the autumn crop from 20th-30th June. The autumn crop is harvested from mid-September to mid-October. Alternate sprays of Bavistin (0.1%) and Bordeaux mixture (2:2:250) are applied at weekly intervals during July and August to protect this crop from anthracnose.

THINNING OF FRUITS

The removal of flower clusters before flowering or parts of such clusters after fruit set is called thinning. Like pruning thinning consists removal of living parts and it concentrates the activities of the vine into the left parts. In other aspects, however, thinning has the opposite effect of pruning it strengthens the vine by limiting the crop without reducing the leaf area. Thus thinning offers for greater possibilities for improvement of fruit quality than does pruning. In winter, when pruning is done the next years crops can be estimated by experience or on the basis of fruitfulness of the buds. After the clusters appear, however, the potential crop can be seen hence pruning accompanied by thinning permits a better balance of capacity and crop than does pruning alone. Thinning makes it possible to grow as much crop as the vines can bear without sacrificing quality with thinning, it may actually be possible to increase bearing capacity, since vines that are to be thinned can be pruned longer to produce a greater, leaf surface, which is not possible when crop load is to be determined by pruning alone.

Fruits of thinned vine is less prone to decay. Properly thinned fruit is less costly to pick because clusters are more uniformly coloured and less time is required in selecting the ripe cluster. Different grape varieties do not set the fruit equally well with normal thinning. Some tend to set straggly clusters, others nearly perfect clusters while some like Perlette over compact clusters. To obtain maximum improvement in fruit quality in these variations in set different methods of thinning have been recommended.

(*i*) Flower cluster thinning : It is done between leafing out and blooming. Flower cluster thinning is practised in cultivars which tend to set straggly clusters. It reduces the number of clusters without reducing the number of leaves. With an increase in leaf cluster ratio, the flowers on the retained clusters are better supplied with food materials. The flower parts develop more perfectly, fruit set will be more and there will be a large percentage of normal berries. This method is generally applied to grape cultivars like Cardinal, Muscat of Alexandria. Flower cluster thinning can also be practised to rejuvenate weekened vines.

(*ii*) Flower thinning : Flowers thinning by the use of mechanical means like plastic brushes or removal of some of the laterals by hand before the fruit set needs to be practised in grape cultivars like Perlette which tend to set heavily. In this variety, the cluster become over compact and are susceptible to berry rot at the time of ripening and also a high percentage of berries remains under sized. In Perlette, Gibberellin (30-50 ppm), Sevin (1000-2000 ppm), ethephon (5-10 ppm) and use of plastic brush at the time of full bloom have found to be very effective in flower thinning.

***(iii)* Cluster thinning :** It consists of removal of entire clusters after the fruit set. This method has no effect on fruit set or cluster length. It is essentially a grading and sorting of clusters at an early stage. Misshapen, small sized and over sized clusters are removed. This provide more favourable conditions of growth for the remaining clusters, giving larger berries. It is employed in cultivars like Empror on heavy soils. Cluster thinning is easiest and best means of reducing crop on overload vines of highly productive wine grape or raisin grape vineyards. Cluster thinning, however, is a time consuming and costly affair. In case of Perlette, thinning of bunches is necessary so that the remaining bunches develops properly. It is recommended that not more than 100 bunches be left on each vine (trained on bower), planted at a distance of 3 m × 3 m. The thinning should be done soon after the berry set and all small and under developed clusters should be removed.

***(iv)* Berry thinning :** Berry thinning consists of removing parts of clusters or individual berries after fruit set. The rachis of the cluster can be cut back to retain the derived number of berries. In addition to its removal of some of the laterals it provides more space for berry development and prevents compactness of the clusters. Berry thinning should be done soon after fruit set especially in seeded cultivars. The removal of individual berries is very time consuming and uneconomic. Berry thinning is not as effective in increasing the berry size in seedless cultivars. It is, however, very important in preventing overcompactness of the clusters when berry size is either increased by girdling or use of growth regulators.

BUD DIFFERENTIATION

Normally, the grapevine forms compound buds at each node all along the length of its shoots. The compound bud consists of 3 to 5 buds, in some cases upto 6 buds as seen in Anab-e-Shahi cultivar. The buds are enclosed by the common protective scales and appear as one large bud called 'eye'. When the vines leaf out in the season, one of the buds (usually the middle one or primary bud) bursts open. In the case of death of the primary, the accessory buds bursts open as laterals. The buds of the grapevine are classified as leaf bud and fruit bud depending upon the nature of the structure they contain. The leaf bud is a rudimentary sterile shoot which upon leafing out gives a vegetative shoot. The fruit bud contains a shoot having both rudimentary leaves and flower clusters or inflorescence primordia which could be easily distinguished under the stereo microscope or magnifying lens prior to pruning for the subsequent crop.

The rudiments of the flower clusters are formed during the season preceding the year in which the fruiting takes place. The differentiation that results in the formation of fruit buds begins in the end of April under Punjab conditions in Perlette. The differentiation of the buds starts in lower part of the shoot, that are farthest along in their development. The process of bud differentiation proceeds rapidly once this process starts and by the end of June more than 80 per cent of the buds from the nodes 1-10 get differentiated. The time of fruit bud differentiation depends upon the geographical location of the place and the cultivar involved. In California, the differentiation of the buds in Thompson seedless starts in early June at Davis.

The calyx, corolla, stamens and pistil are differentiated in the order named. The calyx is discernible on the side of the merismetic tissue of the primordia of the flower one week after leafing out. The development of the parts of the flower is very rapid under tropical conditions. At Hyderabad, the differentiation of floral parts in Anab-e-Shahi grape was regular in the order of calyx, corolla, stamens and pistils after bud burst. The calyx initiated on the 5th day after bud burst and developed fully by 7th day. Corolla was initiated on 7th day and was fully developed by 9th day. Stamens initiated on 7th day developed as a pad like structure by 9th day and differentiation into anthers and filaments by the 11th day. Initiation of the carpel was initiated on 11th day and attained full development by the 13th day with two ovules appearing clearly inside the ovary.

GIRDLING

Girdling was introduced into Greece accidentally as a means of improving the set of Block Corinth in 1833. Girdling as practical in commercial vineyards, consists in removing a narrow ring of bark entirely around some member of the vine like arm or cane. The common width is 4-5 mm. Girdling of the trunk affects the whole vine while girdling a cane affects only the shoot supported by it. It is essential that the ring be completely removed and even if a small portion of the bark is left, there is no effect. The immediate affect of a complete girdle is to interrupt the supply of carbohydrate and hormones so that their level increases in the parts above the girdle. The width of the girdle should be such that the wound heals in a short time. It is specially true when the trunk is girdled otherwise restricted food supply to the roots results in death of the vine. Similarly removal of wood below the bark injures the vine. Vines are girdled to accomplish one or more of the three objectives viz. to improve fruit set, to increase berry size and to advance maturation.

Fruit set in variety like Perlette can be improved by girdling the vine before blooming. Sizing of the Seedless cultivar like Thompson Seedless and Perlette can be hastened and their ultimate size can be appreciably increased by girdling timed to be effective during the period of rapid berry enlargement. If girdling is done to improve berry colour or enhance ripening, the girdle must be open and effective during the early part of the ripening period.

QUALITY IMPROVEMENT IN GRAPES

To get optimum yield and quality of grapes the following package of treatments should be adopted.

(*i*) Thin flower buds one week before flowering by leaving 100–120 flower buds per panicle.

(*ii*) When berry size is 4 mm, girdle the vine by removing a 4 mm wide ring of bark from the main stem and dip the clusters in 40 ppm GA_3. While girdling, there should be no injury to the wood and no piece of bark should remain attached with the wood.

(*iii*) One week after the first GA_3 + treatment, give a second dipping in 40 ppm GA_3.

(*iv*) The field should have sufficient moisture during girdling and atleast 3 weeks after that.

(*v*) Harvest the crop when attained the requisite TSS content.

Two foliar sprays of potassium sulphate @ 1.5 per cent, first one week after fruit set and second at colour break stage, improve the quality and colour of Perlette grapes.

USE OF GROWTH REGULATORS

Plant growth regulators are well established as important cultural tools in grape production. They can control specific plant processes that cannot be conveniently or economically controlled by any other means. The growth regulators now can be applied either for promotion or reduction of growth, root initiation, bud or seed dormancy, fruit set, berry size, fruitfulness and total yields of seedless grapes, loosening of clusters, induction of seedless berries in seeded grapes and post harvest keeping quality of the berries.

The most commonly used auxins for rooting of grapevine cuttings are IBA and IAA. Soaking of the basal ends of the cuttings in IBA 2500 ppm solution for 15 seconds ensures better rooting of the cuttings.

B-9 at 1000 ppm hastened termination of bud rest in grapes. Early bud break in Thompson Seedless grapevines can be achieved by dipping the canes in plastic cylindrical jar containing 1500 ppm paclobutrazol solution. NAA at 750 to 1000 ppm were widely practised in France to delay bud break by 16 to 27 days.

When the flower bud clusters of the male vine were dipped in an aqueous solution of the cytokinin at 1000 ppm three weeks before anthesis, they produced typical hermaphrodite flowers with normal fruit set.

Spraying of SADH at 2000 ppm on Himrod just before anthesis resulted in cent per cent increase in fruit set. GA at 75 ppm 2-3 days after full bloom on Pusa Seedless variety increased bunch length, berry size and weight.

The excessive vegetative growth of vines can be curtailed by spraying the growth retardants like B-9 and phosphon - D at 0.12 and 0.05 per cent, respectively at 10 leaf stage.

Maturity of grapes can be hastened by 6 days by dipping the clusters in ethephon at 500 ppm at the onset of ripening. Ethrel application at 250 ppm two months after set reduced the percentage of green berries to as low as 6.3 and 3.3 in Bangalore Blue and in Muscat respectively as against 30.9 and 25.9 in control. Ethephon at 600 ppm in Perlette at colour break stage advanced ripening.

A pre-bloom spray of GA_3 at 15 ppm results in thinning of flowers and cluster elongation in Thompson Seedless and Tas-A-Ganesh cultivars. CCC at 2000 ppm and IBA at 100 ppm were found to be most effective in checking flower and flower bud drop.

Application of GA_3 at 50 ppm to Anab-e-Shahi variety 8 days before bloom decreased the bunch weight and the number of berries while one-third of the treated flowers developed seedless berries.

Post harvest berry drop in Anab-e-Shahi grape is nearly 10 per cent during transit and storage and NAA at 100 ppm was found to be optimum for checking such type of losses. Shattering of berries during storage can be minimised with pre- harvest sprays of cycocel and kinetin at 4000 and 100 ppm concentrations, respectively.

2,4-D at 1.5 kg/ha is recommended to control weeds in vineyard with precaution not to drift the chemical on to the grapevines.

Maleic hydrazide at 500 ppm sprayed at 5 leaf stage was most effective in increasing the overall fruitfulness of the canes from 22.4 to 59.4 per cent.

CCC treatments significantly increased the number of bunches per vine in Thompson Seedless. Maximum fruit set was recorded with CCC 600 ppm.

To increase the berry size, first application of GA 20 ppm at bloom time for flower thinning and the second application of GA 40 ppm on the same vine at fruit set stage (usually after 10-14 days) proved beneficial. GA 30-50 ppm and Sevin 1000-2000 ppm and ethephon 5-10 ppm at the time of full bloom were found very effective in flower thinning of Perlette grapevine.

Canopy interashading effects cannot only be manipulated by pruning alone yet the use of growth retardents have come to rescue. Paclobutrazol PP 333 (4-chlorophenyl-4, 4-dimethyl-2- (1, 2, 3-trizol-l-Yl) penton-3-01) inhibits synthesis of plant sterols and specifically GA. PP 333 has been used as pre-bloom sprays and soil application. Pre bloom sprays of paclobutrazol @ 1000, 1500, 2000 ppm in cultivars Roumi Red reduced shoot growth, internodal length but bud fertility was increased. The soil application @ 4 ml per vine was also equally effective. A single application of PP 333 was effective in reducing vegetative growth for a period of two years if the rate of application was greater than 1.1 kg/ ha.

For uniform colour development of Flame Seedless grape, retain 80-90 bunches per vine (75% crop load) immediately after bunch emergence and spray 400 ppm ethephon at colour break stage.

BARRENNESS

It is a major problem in grapevines found by the growers in north west Indian plains. The problem is sometimes so acute that vines are left with too few canes after pruning. The apparently healthy canes and arms when given cuts are observed to be dry or partially so. The vines do not bear flower bunches and if a few bunches are found, their size is small. The lack of flower bunch formation can be either due to lack of flower bud formation or their subsequent death. The causes of death of the floral primordia was reported to be shading. The excessive foliage creates such ecological conditions due to which some saprophytic fungi turn into parasitic leading to the death of tissues. The excessive foliage is due to over-fertilization especially with nitrogen. Barrenness is a common phenomenon in Anab-e-Shahi cultivar of grapes.

In this cultivar, loss of floral primordia was found to be a factor contributing to barrenness. The fruitfulness of a bud varied both with the diameter of the cane and its nodal position. The fruitfulness of canes declined when the cane diameter increased or decreased from 1.2 to 1.4 cm. In most fruitful canes, buds at 9th and 10th nodal position had invariably floral primodia. Fruitfulness was more uniformally distributed over various nodal positions in canes of medium vigour but for low vigour canes, it was mostly confined to middle nodes. With increase in diameter of canes, a decrease in the percentage of floral buds was accompanied by an enhancement in dead buds, but no change in vegetative bud counts. This shows that floral buds were susceptible to death with increase in cane diameter beyond 1.2 cm. The loss of floral primordia occured between February-March.

Varietal differences have also been reported in loss of floral primordia. The maximum number of infected buds were found in Perlette (77%) followed by Anab-e-Shahi (37%), Himrod (34%) and Thompson Seedless (17%). In Perlette and Himrod, low bearing may be due to flower bud mortality alone but in Anab-e-Shahi and Thompson Seedless the flower bud differentiation is a part of the problem.

There are reports which indicate that syndrome of barrenness is associated with drying of canes. The mortality of the canes extended to the secondary arms of the vine and in some cases even to the primary arms. The removal of all the dead tissue evidently necessitated extensive pruning. There is a close and highly significant relationship between the vigour of a vine and the mortality of its canes. The intensity of mortality is very acute in Anab-e-Shahi trained on bower which gives about 12 kg of dead wood per vine.

The death of flower buds can be checked by using some agronomic measures such as by discouraging excessive vegetative growth and by decreasing azotic fertilization. The excessive growth of the vines can also be controlled by the application of 2000 ppm CCC coupled with removal of dead wood. CCC should be sprayed in mid-October. A simple removal of dead wood at monthly intervals from mid October to mid January was observed to be helpful in reducing the mortality of canes.

HARVESTING AND FRUIT HANDLING

Grape is harvested when it is fully ripe as it is a non-climacteric fruit. It is said to be in ripe stage when it attains characteristic colour, flavour and aroma which constitute the quality of grapes. After harvesting the grape, its quality remains same without subsequent change in colour. Also, over-ripening of grapes on the vine, do not fetch premium in the market and pose serious problems in its transit and storage. Therefore, harvesting of grapes at the optimum stage is of prime importance.

Sugar-acid ratio might be a more reliable indicator for grape harvesting. However, the harvest of varieties with lower acid content (0.40 - 0.75%) could be based on TSS content alone, while for the varieties with high acid (more than 0.95%), the criterion should be acidity alone. The varieties with medium acid content (0.75 - 0.95%) should be harvested based on the TSS/ acid ratio. The ratio must be higher for low acid varieties than for high acid varieties to maintain a given Ievel of acceptability.

Berries at the apical end of the bunch ripe faster while those at the distal end ripe slow. Only 38-50% berries in a bunch can match the quality standards of the berries in the middle of the bunch.

pH of the juice is another criterion used for predicting maturity. pH measurement is an expression of the free or active acidity at any stage in the development and represents the state of balance of the chemical constituents at that time. During growth, the pH of grapes constantly undergoes change, starting with low in the immature grape and reaching a high value in the overripe stage. It would appear reasonable, therefore, to draw the conclusion that pH can serve as an indicator of maturity. In Thompson Seedless, a pH of 3.7 may be suitable for table grapes if drying and rotting have not set in. General recommended pH for Thompson Seedless is 3.45 - 3.50 for harvest.

Harvesting : Grape should not be harvested until they are fully ripe. There are many indicators to the proper stage of ripeness of grapes for picking but the taste is the most valuable indication of the ripeness of the bunch. For this purpose, the greenest barries, which are always near the tips, should be tasted. If they are good to eat, the entire bunch is ripe for picking. Fully ripe bunches should be picked for local consumption while for distant markets, bunches should be picked when still hardripe so that they do not spoil during transit. Ripe grape bunches should be clipped with scissors without injuring the berries. During handling, the natural bloom on berries must not be rubbed off. Harvesting should be done during the coolest period of the day. Bunches should not be exposed directly to the sun. Trimming, grading and packaging should be done in shade.

Undesirable berries viz. unripe, over-ripe, small, mis-shapen, sun-burnt, decayed, soft and bruised should be trimmed. Bunches should be graded according to the fruit quality, maturity and size and different grades should be packed in different containers. For nearby markets, mulberry or bamboo baskets can be used, whereas for distant market, wooden boxes of 2-4 kg capacity or Corrugated Fibre Board (CFB) cartons should be used.

Being a perishable fruit, it cannot withstand high temperature and low humidity prevailing at the time of harvesting which causes 25-30 per cent losses through spoilage and cut down the already meagre storage life of grapes under ambient conditions. Thus after harvesting it has limited possibility for transport to the distant markets in a good condition which further restricts its marketability. It is, therefore, desirable to store the sufficient quantity of grapes at harvesting time to spread its marketing over a longer period.

In Perlette grapes, ethephon at 400 ppm if applied at colour break stage-advances fruit maturity, increases total soluble solids and reduces fruit acidity.

Export specifications : Thompson Seedless and Sharad Seedless varieties are exported to Middle East, Holland/Germany and United Kingdom. Berry size for export varies from 16 mm to 18 mm having amber, white and white/amber colour. Grapes sent to Middle East are packed in 1 kg capacity. The packing size for Holland/Germany and UK is kept 4.5 kg and 9 kg. The storage temperature is maintained 0 to 1°C. Flame Seedless variety is exported to Holland/ Germany and UK with berry size 16 - 18 mm in 4.5/9 kg packing maintaining storage temperature 0 to 1°C.

Yield : Well managed vineyard can be expected to start yielding after 3 years under North Indian conditions and even less than 2 years under tropical conditions of pennisular India.

Vineyard can satisfactorily be maintained at least for more than two decades. The productivity per hectare in India is much higher than in many countries. The yield of 60 tonnes/ha in Anab-e-Shahi is the highest in the world. The cultivars like Perlette and Thompson Seedless may yield around 25-30 and 15-20 tonnes/ha, respectively.

Use of polyliner : Wrapping of grapes in polyethylene bags is useful because it exchanges gases and allows permeability to water vapours with reduced moisture loss. It checks stem or berry shrivelling and provides good visibility of the packed produce. Sufficient perforations should be made in the polyethylene bags before packing.

Grape Guard (Sulphur dioxide generators) : In package SO_2 generators, both slow release and quick release type, have been introduced for commercial use. Popularly known as Grape Guard, the quick release type is a craft paper coated with a thin layer of mixture of sodium bisulphite and a plastic polymer. The slow release (dual release) one is based on two poly plastic coated papers, pasted together leaving 12 to 16 unpasted rectangular pockets in rows of 3 or 4 is spread at equidistance on the entire surface. These empty pockets carry sodium bisulphite powder.

Grape Guard paper is kept in perforated polyethylene bags having grapes with its coated surface out ward while brown uncoated paper side of Grape Guards must face the grapes and then the bag is placed in the corrugated fibre board (CFB) cartons. At the bottom, some paper clippings or shavings or wood cushion is spread over which the perforated polyethylene bag is placed. Finally the polyliner is folded and attached with stapler. The quick release paper is claimed to give protection to grapes against decay for about 4-7 days during transit while the slow release paper ensures a protection for 40 days in the cold storage. The humidity activates the Grape Guards creating a controlled release of sulphur dioxide in the box. Potassium metabisulphite, in touch with moistures from Potassium bisulphite which after giving out sulphur dioxide molecules forms potassium sulphite. On reaction with atmospheric oxygen potassium sulphite forms potassium sulphate, a stable compound.

By using grape guards in each box, table grapes can be kept in commercial cold storage for upto 40 days. The spread of **Botrytis** decay, which is capable of growth at low storage temperature, is retarded throughout the storage period, therefore, high quality grapes can be marketed at premium.

Pre-cooling : Climatic conditions, prevailing at the time of grapes in north India favours rapid transpiration and development of decay causing fungi. The loss of water is very damaging to the grape quality. A reduction in temperature of grapes 9.5°C halves the rate of respiration and doubles the keeping period. A fruit temperature below 4.4°C greatly retards growth and development of all fungi. The prompt removal of the field heat of grapes after packing is the best means of maintaining the initial quality of the fruit. Pre-cooling checks stem desiccation, browning, berry softening and shatter. Forced air cooling in which cold air is forced a cross wise through the packed boxes is the most beneficial and technically sound method of pre-cooling. The pre-cooling temperature of air is 1-2°C less than the storage temperature.

Storage : Factors in storage environment that effect grape quality are temperature, atmospheric humidity, air movement and fumigation with sulphur dioxide. Recommended temperature for cold storage of grapes is 0°C to 2°C and relative humidity between 85-90 per cent. These grapes can be kept upto 40 days. Shelf life of grapes can further be improved in storage by removing field heat by forcing the air through the boxes at 2°C less than cold storage temperature. Good refrigeration is needed in storage, because **Botrytis** decay growth at 2°C is double than that at 0°C. In controlled atmospheric storage, grapes can be stored for 2–3 months at 1°C and 95% relative humidity with oxygen and carbon dioxide concentrations at 10 and 3 per cent, respectively.

Flame Seedless grapes harvested at optimum maturity with firm berries having light purple colour and packed in ventilated CFB boxes of 4 kg capacity lined with polythene film containing one sheet of grape guard can be stored at 0 – 2°C and 90 – 95 per cent RH with acceptable quality for 45 days. Grapes packed in LDPE bags with single sheet of SO_2 generating pad and kept in CFB boxes can be stored for 30 days at 0-2°C temp. and 90-95 per cent RH with acceptable quality.

Processing : Processing technology of grape vinegar from Perlette at 5 L scale has been standardized at PAU, Ludhiana. This will provide an alternate use of grapes cv. Perlette. It is a fruit based natural vinegar with properties of grapes and vinegar blended together. Grape vinegar has shelf life of two years.

Disorder of grapes in storage : During storage, grapes are subjected to a variety of disorders some of which result from conditions existing during storage and others due to conditions which already exist in storage. Grey mould is the most common cause of fungal spoilage. **Cladosporium** rot, **Alternaria** rot, Blue mould and **Rhizopus** rot are also important diseases of grapes. Grapes harvested after rains are much more subject to decay losses than those harvested after a dry period. In Pusa Seedless grape, decrease of arginine and rise in proline is related to senescence. In Thompson Seedless, internal browning of the berries after 2-3 months of storage is reported. It begins in the vasicular area and extend into the flesh. Desiccation in storage is evidenced by dry stems, shrivelling of the berries near the capstem and loss of weight. To reduce this, fruit should be harvested in early hours of morning and late in evening.

INSECT PESTS

1. Grapevine thrip (*Rhipiphorothrips cruentatus.* Hood) : This is most destructive pest of grapevine in India. The nymphs and adult rasp the ventral surface of tender leaves and flower stalks and suck the oozing cell sap. As a result of their intensive feeding, the leaves develop silvery white scorchy patches with curly tips, gradually get deformed and ultimately fall down. Attack on flower stalks results in shedding of flowers. Sometimes the fruits are also attacked resulting in scab formation or russetting on the berries. The peak infestation is during February-March and September-October. The pest breed throughout the year, excepts in winter, when it is found as a pupae in the soil at a depth of 8-18 cm under the host plants.

For its control spray 500 ml of Malathion 50 EC in 500 litres of water before flowering and after fruit set. In case of Perlette, carbaryl @ 0.15% should be preferred over Malathion as apart from killing the pest population, it also takes care of thinning when sprayed at pea-nut stage.

2. Leaf-roller (*Sylepta lunalis* Guenee) : It is a serious pest of grapevine during August-September. A female lays 100 to 150 eggs, usually on ventral surface of leaves. On hatching, the young caterpillars feed on the epidermis of leaves and skeletonise the same. Later, these caterpillars roll the leaves and feed within. Pupation takes place within rolled leaves. Generally each leaf-roll contains only one caterpillar. The activity of the pest is accelerated with the onset of monsoon and continues till October.

In the initial stage of attack, remove the rolled up leaves and destroy the same with larvae pupae within. In case of severe infestation spray 500 ml Malathion 50 EC in 500 liters of water as soon as the attack begins.

3. Hepper (*Arboridia viniferata* Sohi & Sandhu) : Nymphs and adults of hoppers usually suck the cell sap from the ventral surface of leaves. The feeding spots on the leaves become pale. In case of severe infestation, the affected leaves turn yellow, gradually start curling, become brown and ultimately fall down. It is serious after rainy season. It is also responsible for an indirect loss by producing honey dew which serves as a substrate for the growth of sooty mould fungus on foliage and fruits. It affects the production of fruit and also depreciate the quality of grapes.

For its control spray 1.5 kg of Sevin/Hexavin 50 WP (carbaryl) in 500 litres of water.

4. Yellow and Red wasps (*Polistes hebraeus* (Fb.) and *Vespa orientalis* (Linn) : They cause much damage by feeding on ripe berries having thin skin and high sugar content.

Burn or smoke the wasp nest in hedges, on trees etc. at sunset. On a small scale, the damage by wasp, can be avoided by covering the bunches with muslin bags.

5. Defoliating beetles (*Adoretus* spp) : Adult beetles are nocturnal, they come out of the soil after dusk and feed on leaves making innumerable holes in leaf lamina. In case of severe infestation, the entire leaf lamina may be eaten away and also attack the fruit near the apical end. Eggs are laid in the soil, grubs feed on roots and other organic matter and sometimes the grubs feeding on roots cause the death of tree. The adult beetles appear soon after the first heavy shower in June and are active for about one month.

Spray in evening one kg Carbaryl 50 WP in 500 litres of water as soon as the damage starts. Repeat the spraying after 5 or 6 days, if the damage continues or the insecticidal deposit is washed away by rain.

6. Mealy bugs (*Nipaecoccus viridis and Maconellicoccus hirsutus*) : Mealy bugs are active during July to October in vineyards. First Species is the major one causes damage to twigs, branches, leaves and fruits. Second species is active on tender shoots.

Spray 1875 ml Durmet/Dursban 20EC (chlorpyriphos) or 750 ml Curacron 50 EC (propenophos) or 500 g Asataf 75 SP (acephate) in 500 litres of water after the harvest of grapes in July to avoid the residue of insecticides.

DISEASES

1. Anthracnose or die back : The disease is caused by the fungus ***Elsinoe ampelina*** Shear. Small light brown spots appear on young leaves which later enlarge, turn dark brown and give shot-hole appearance. In severe attack, early defoliation occur. Dark brown sunken spots with raised margins develop on new shoots/canes leading to their death from tip backwards. Similar spots appear on laterals of clusters. Under favourable conditions dark brown depressed spots appear on berries also. On the berries, the disease is referred to as 'bird's eye spot' because of the grey centre surrounded by a reddish-brown zone.

Control :

(*i*) Prune the shoots and canes during January-February and give one dormant spray of Bordeaux mixture (2:2:250) after pruning using 125 litres of water per acre.

(*ii*) Spray with Bordeaux mixture (2:2:250) in the last week of March using 250 litres of water per acre.

(*iii*) Spray Bavistin 50 WP @ 500 g per acre in last week of April using 500 litres of water.

(*iv*) Spray Bordeaux mixture (2:2:250) in the last week of May in 500 litres of water per acre.

(*v*) Spray Score 25 EC @ 500 ml in mid-July and Bavistin 50 WP @ 500g per acre in end July using 500 litres of water.

(*vi*) Spray Score 25 EC @ 500 ml in mid-August and Bordeaux mixture (2:2:250) in end August in 500 litres of water per acre.

(*vii*) Spray Score 25 EC @ 500 ml in mid-September and Bordeaux mixture in end September using 500 litres of water.

2. Cercospora leaf spot : The disease is caused by ***Cercospora* spp.** The disease appears in March-April but becomes serious from August onwards with maximum attack during September-October. Necrotic small area on leaves with straw coloured centre and reddish brown margins appear. Severe attack results into drying of leaves and early defoliation.

Control :

(*i*) Proper fertilization of the vines results into reduced attack of leaf spot,

(*ii*) Spray the fungicides as recommended for anthracnose.

3. Downy mildew : Downy mildew is caused by fungus ***Plasmopara viticola*** (Berk and Curt). Light yellow oily spots appear on upper surface of leaves which on the lower surface are covered with white downy growth of the pathogens. Later, the spots become brown and brittle. Leaves with many active spots drop pre-maturely. The diseases start appearing in nursery and on grown up vines in March-April. After rainy season *i.e.,* August-September, it assume serious proportions and continue to appear in humid weather. It affects tendrils and fresh growth of the shoots also.

Control :

(*i*) All the pruned canes should be destroyed as the buds may contain dormant mycelium.

(*ii*) Old fallen leaves should be collected from the orchard soil and destroyed.

(*iii*) Other control measures are the same as for anthracnose. Give one additional spray of Bordeaux mixture (2:2:250) in mid-September using 500 litres of water per acre.

4. Powdery mildew : The disease is caused by an Ascomycite ***Uncinula necator*** (Schw). The fungus spreads over the new shoots, leaves and canes in the spring and later infects the berries. It is one of the most important and widely distributed disease of grapes. The disease may be found on new growth and is more conspicuous on the upper surface of the leaves. The entire leaf surface may be covered by indistinct white patches which later have a powdery appearance. Usually, they enlarge so that the entire upper surface of the leaf has a dusty coating. The severly attacked leaves curl upwards during warm dry weather. They, however, usually retain their normal green colour but may show some discolouration towards the end of the season Spots on the canes are of the same general appearance as on the leaves. The young berries may have spotting as on the leaves and show powdery growth of the fungus on its entire surface. Damage to the fruit may result in rusty spotting and misshapen berries. Sometimes the fruit splits as a result of the retarded growth of the infected area.

Control :

(*i*) Spray the vines with 0.25% wettable sulphur (1.25 kg in 500 litre of water).

(*ii*) Spray Bayleton @ 200g or Topas 10 EC @ 200 ml in 500 litres of water in mid March, last week of April and first week of May.

5. Foot rot or collar rot : This disease is especially present in grape cuttings and young vines and is caused by ***Rhizoctonia*** sp. In the case of young vines the roots and the collar region turn brownish with the shredding of bark and internal brown discoloration. Ultimately the vines wilt and die. Leaves turn yellow and ultimately the vines wilt and die.

Control :

(*i*) The cuttings for planting should be dipped into 0.2% Ziram suspension (2 g per litre of water).

(*ii*) The soil in the pit should be drenched with 0.4 percent Captan (400 g in 100 litres of water) thoroughly before planting the cuttings.

6. Rotting of berries : Various kinds of air-borne fungi like ***Penicillium, Aspergillus, Rhizopus, Botrytis*** etc. attack the maturing or matured fruit and cause blue mould rot, black mould rot, Rhizopus rot and Botrytis rot, respectively. Grapes berries, are attacked when still on the vine. The wasps aid in injuring the berries and releasing the juice which serves as substrate for the growth of fungi. In Perlette, which has compact bunches, the growth pressure ruptures some berries and released juice flows into other berries where fungi grow and causes various types of rotting.

Control :

(*i*) In case of compact bunched varieties such as Perlette, practice the thinning of bunches as recommended under thinning.

(*ii*) Use insecticides or repellents to guard against wasps and other insects causing injuries to berries.

(*iii*) During June, spray grapevine with 0.2% Ziram (1 kg per 500 litres of water) at 7 day interval. Stop spraying a week before harvesting the bunches.

SPECIAL PROBLEM

Water berry : This disorder is caused due to water stress or excessive nitrogenous fertilizer or over-bearing. The drying of berries is at the tips or is scattered all over the bunches during May and June. Berries look like small cellophane bags, half filled with sap and remain hanging on the bunches.

Control :

(*i*) Apply frequent irrigation during the summer (May and June).

(*ii*) Practise a proper thinning of the over bearing vines.

CHAPTER 17

Litchi

The litchi (***Litchi chinensis*** Sonn.) is a delicious fruit and generally consumed as a table fruit. It is one of the most popular fruits of India which is commonly taken as fresh or in dried forms. The fruit of litchi comes to the market in May or early June when very few other fruits are available, thus, they fetch remunerative prize in the market.

ORIGIN, HISTORY AND DISTRIBUTION

It is indigenous to Southern China, particularly the provinces of Kwangtung and Fukien. The litchi has been grown in China for over 3000 of years. In 1059, T-Sai Hsiang wrote a monograph on litchi cultivation which is considered to be the oldest publication on this fruit.

The spread of litchi from China to other parts of the world was slow probably due to the exacting soil and climatic requirements of this fruit as well as very short life span of its seeds. The litchi had reached the West Indies by 1775, South Africa in 1869, the Hawaii Islands by 1873 and in Florida in 1833. It spread into other countries like Vietnam, Indonesia, Southern Japan, Formosa, Australia, New Zealand, Mauritius, Brazil, etc.

In India, litchi reached through Burma. It was first introduced into Bengal about the end of the 17th Century and spread further into other parts of India.

The litchi was introduced into Punjab around 1920 by Mahajan family from Dehradun to Pathankot. Justice D.K.Mahajan went to Bihar in 1934 and brought with him one hundred litchi plants. In this way, a beginning was made for the commercial cultivation of litchi in Punjab.

The major litchi producing countries are China, India, Taiwan, Thailand, VietNam, Israel, Australia, Africa, Mexico and Central and South America.

AREA AND PRODUCTION

China is the biggest producer of litchi in the world. India ranked second in the world in respect of area and production. India and China account for 91 per cent of the world litchi production. In India, it occupies an area of 80400 hectares with annual production of about 6.7 lakh tonnes. The states growing litchi are Bihar, West Bengal, Jharkhand, Assam, Punjab, Chhattisgarh, Odisha, Uttarakhand and Tripura. Bihar in the leading state in litchi production with a share of 43.9 per cent. The average productivity of litchi in India is 6.7 mt/ha.

Litchi is ideally suited to be sub-montane areas of Gurdaspur, Hoshiarpur, SAS Nagar and Ropar districts of Punjab. The total area under this fruit is about 1752 hectares and it constitutes only about 2.4 per cent of the total area under fruits. Annual production of litchi in Punjab is 15137 metric tonnes.

Export potential : The litchi fruits are exported to Bangladesh, Nepal, Maldives, Ireland, UAE, Germany and Singapore. During the year 2011 – 12, 320 mt litchi fruits are exported to different countries and Rs. 39 lakhs was earned as foreign exchange. Bangladesh has 61.6 per cent share of total export of litchi fruits from India. It was followed by Nepal where 34.8 per cent litchi fruits were exported.

IMPORTANCE AND USES

The litchi fruit is very popular and mostly eaten fresh in our country. Litchi squash is a popular product which has a pleasant flavour and is very refreshing. The pickles, preserves and wine are also made from litchi in China. Dried litchi commonly known as 'litchi nut' is very popular among the Chinese living all over the world. The fruit is dried either in the sun or in an oven. Sun dried litchi is considered better than artifically oven dried fruit. Litchi fruits can also be frozen with minimum handling. The natural covering of the fruit is a good packing material by itself. The whole frozen fruit makes an attractive product. The litchi fruit makes an excellent canned product and liked very much.

Litchi is a rich source of minerals like calcium and phosphorus and vitamins. It contains minerals 0.7 per cent, riboflavin (vitamin B_2) 122 mg per 100 g pulp, protein 0.9 per cent and vitamin C 64 mg per 100 g pulp. It is a rich sources of sugar and different varieties ranging from 6.7 to 13.8 per cent.

BOTANY

The litchi is an evergreen tree belonging to the family Sapindaceae (Soap berry family) and sub-family Nepheleae. Rambutan (***Nephelium lappaceum***), Longan (***Dimocerpus longan***) and Pulasan (***Nephelium mutabile***) are other members of the sub-family. Rambutan bears fruits of good quality which are considered even superior to those of litchi. This plant does well on the lower slopes of the Nilgiris. Longan (anshpal), sometimes called 'Little brother of litchi' bears edible fruits in which the aril does not separate readily from the seed. It is grown in Southern India, Assam and Bengal. Both can be used as a rootstock for litchi.

The genus **Litchi** has two species, ***Litchi philippinenis*** and ***Litchi chinensis.*** The former is a wild plant grown extensively in the Philippines. This species is not of commercial importance except being used as a rootstock.

The litchi (***Litchi chinensis*** Sonn.) trees are medium to large, much branched, round-topped, handsome evergreen tree, reaching up 15 metres or more in height. The plants have alternate, pinnate and leathery leaves, having 5-7 opposite or alternate leaflets. The leaves are glossy green above and greyish green on the under surface. The bark is greyish brown and rough. The litchi plants bear three types of petalless flowers. The first flowers to open are males. The inflorescence is a compound raceme developing both from terminal and axillary buds. The first type flowers are the staminate flowers in which the pistil is aborted almost completely. After two to four days, the pistillate hermaphrodite flower appear. These flowers bear fruit. There is a transitional period of two to three days and then the staminate hermaphrodite flowers with united stigmas appear. These flowers continue for 10 to 14 days. The flowers of different sexes on the panicles do not open simultaneously. The panicles on the same branch flower during the same period but flowers on panicles borne by different branches appear on different days. So, for effective pollination and fruit set of litchi mixed planting, *i.e.*, growing of several varieties together in an orchard is recommended. Pollination is done by insects, which include the honey bee and flies. The seedless varieties seem to be self or cross sterile, while those with normal seeds are probably self and cross fertile.

FLOWERING AND FRUITING

In North India, the flowering takes place in February. Opening of flowers starts in second or third week of March. Flowering period ranged from 26 to 35 days in different varieties. In Eastern India, the emergence of flower panicles starts during the second week of March and continues upto second week of April in different cultivars. The total duration of flowering in different varieties ranges from 25 to 40 days. The cultivar Shahi is early to flower followed by Rose Scented, Purbi and Bedana. In litchi fruit, seeds develop initially at a high rate, followed by membranous mesocarp and aril which grow very fast towards the later stage of fruit development. In litchi, from fertilization upto the second week of May is the period of active seed growth and marked by a complete lack of flesh growth. The increase in fruit diameter during this period is mainly due to the increase in seed diameters. The flesh growth commences from May 14 and increased rapidly upto the harvesting date. The period between the second week of May and first week of June is critical for fruit cracking.

The fruit of litchi is a one-seeded nuts, usually develop in bunches. The fruits tend to be 3-5 cm in diameter and usually oval in shape. The fruits have a thin leathery shell (pericarp) which turns pinkish red when the fruit is ripe. The aril or edible portion which separates easily, lies under the pericarp and completely surrounds the seed. The pulp is translucent, pearly white and soft in texture.

CLIMATE

Litchi, being a subtropical fruit, thrives best under moist subtropical climate. In China, where the litchi originated, the summer months are hot and humid and the winter months are cool and dry. The litchi usually likes low elevation but can be grown up to an altitude of 800 metres with varying degree of success. The site selected for litchi should be free from frost, have high humidity and abundant soil moisture. Frost in winter and dry heat in summer are limiting factors for its successful cultivation. Under these conditions tree makes poor growth and fruit cracking is a very serious problem. The young trees require protection against frost and hot desiccating winds for several years till they are firmly established. The temperature during summer should be less than 41°C and during winter between 1.1°C to 4.4°C for successful litchi cultivation.

In Punjab and Haryana, litchi does well in submontane tract of Gurdaspur, Hoshiarpur, SAS Nagar, Ropar and Ambala. The litchi can also be grown in the districts of Amritsar, Jalandhar, Ludhiana and Patiala under protected conditions. In these areas summers are quite hot to encourage vegetative growth of plants and winters are cool enough to provide 200–300 hours of chilling temperatures to facilitate bud differentiation in litchi. Quite frequently, summer temperature rises above 40°C during the period of fruit growth and development. This is favourable for sun burning and cracking of fruits to varying intensities in all the cultivars.

In South India, litchi grows only on hill slopes upto an elevation of 1067 metres which are cooler than the plains. In Western Uttar Pradesh, where annual rainfall is not more than 89 cm, litchi grows successfully with artificial irrigation. Prolonged rain is not desirable, especially at the time of flowering, when it interferes with pollination.

SOIL

Litchi grow best in a deep, fertile, well-drained loamy soil rich in organic matter. It is must that the soils do not have a hard pan within 2.5 metres of the surface. Litchi seems to do well under slightly acidic conditions. In acidic soils the roots are covered with tubercles containing mycorrhizal fungi which grow on the roots of the litchi to the mutual benifit of the fungus and the plant. Preferably, the soil pH should be 7.5 to 8.0. In high pH and saline soils, litchi is difficult to establish and flourish. The litchi roots can stand immersion for a considerable length of time provided that the water is flowing. In no way it can stand in stagnant water as it causes root decay. The soils with adequate sub-surface drainage are suitable even if they remain wet for long periods.

PROMISING VARIETIES

While selecting litchi varieties for planting in an orchard, a few points should be kept in mind. The fruits of the variety should be bright red and the average fruit diameter should not be less than 4 cm. The fruits should not be prone to splitting. The customers prefer fruits which have smaller seeds and pleasant taste. In Bihar, which has the largest area under litchi in India, the important varieties are Shahi, China, Deshi, Dehra Rose, Purbi, Bedana, Mclean, Swarna Roopa and Muzzafarpur. The varieties grown in Uttarakhand and Uttar Pradesh are Seedless Early, Seedless Late, Early Large Red, Late Large Red, Calcutta, Dehradun, Rose Scented, Khatti and Gulabi. The varieties recommended for growing in the Punjab and Haryana are Saharanpur, Dehradun, Calcutta, Muzzafarpur, Seedless Late and Rose Scented. In West Bengal, the varieties grown are Muzzafarpur, China, Deshi, Purbi, Elachi Early, Elachi Late, Bombai and Kasba.

The characteristics of the important litchi varieties are as follows :

Dehradun : This variety is mainly grown in Uttarakhand, Punjab and Haryana. It is an early, regular and heavy bearing cultivar, with fruits ripening in the second week of June. Its fruits have an attractive colour. The fruit is susceptible to sunburn and cracking. The pulp is sweet, moderately juicy, medium soft in texture, TSS 17 per cent and acidity 0.48 per cent. The pulp/seed ratio is 3.75:1.

Calcuttia : This variety has proved very successful for growing in comparatively hot and dry areas. It is a heavy bearing cultivar with excellent fruit quality and yield 80-100 kg fruit per tree. Its fruits are large, attractive and mature in the third week of June. The fruit is less susceptible to sunburn and cracking. The pulp is sweet, soft in texture, moderately juicy with good flavour, TSS 18 per cent and acidity 0.49 per cent. The pulp/stone ratio is 4.78 : 1.

Seedless Late : This is a descriptive name signifying a rather shrivelled seed and a much greater proportion of flesh in the fruit. Its fruit mature in the third week of June and are more prone to splitting than Calcutta. It is prone to irregular bearing. Fruits are deep, carmine red, pulp is soft, sweet and very juicy with an agreeable flavour. The juice has 18.7 per cent TSS and 0.53 per cent acidity. The pulp/stone ratio is 28:1. This variety comes into bearing rather late.

Rose Scented : The fruits of this variety have distinct rose aroma and hence called rose scented . The fruits have attractive pink skin. This is a medium yielding variety producing 80-90 kg fruits per tree. Fruits are mostly heart shaped, pulp greyish white, soft and very sweet. The juice has 12.79 percent TSS and 0.33 per cent acidity. The pulp/stone ratio is 6.40 : 1. Fruits are moderately susceptible to sunburn and cracking.

Saharanpur : This is an early variety ripening in the first week of June and yield heavily. The fruits are large, heart-shaped and deep orange to pink in colour. This variety resemble with Early Large Red and Pinjore Common and is considered to be a synonym of these varieties.

Muzzafarpur : This is one of the important litchi varieties mainly grown in Bihar. This variety bears profusely and yields around 80-100 kg fruit per tree. The fruits are deep orange to pink in colour and are less prone to splitting. The fruits of this variety generally mature in the first week of May in Eastern India and in the middle of June in Northern India. The juice has 18 per cent TSS and 0.48 per cent acidity. The pulp/stone ratio is 4.78 : 1.

Some litchi cultivars were developed through selection and hybridization in India. Swarna Roopa is a selection made at Central Horticultural Experiment Station, Ranchi. It has attractive deep pink colour, small seed and high TSS/acid ratio. Its fruits are resistant to cracking. Saharanpur Selection is a chance seedling selection. Its fruits ripen late in the third week of June. It has a very low percentage of fruit cracking. Two hybrids namely Madhu and H–73 have been released. Madhu (Purbi × Bedana) has higher number of fruits about 24 per panicles. H–73 is also a product of cross between Purbi × Bedana and has better fruit quality than Purbi.

PLANTING AND AFTER CARE

Planting : Plantation of litchi in spring season has not proved to be a desirable practice because of the high rate of mortality during the hot dry spell of May-June. Litchi should be planted towards the end of the rainy season. During the rainy-season, the temperature in Northern plains becomes moderate and the atmosphere has high humidity. Considering this, litchi should be planted in September-October.

Litchi trees are usually planted 7.5 - 9.0 metres apart both ways i.e. in rows and between plants in a row, thus accommodating 180 - 123 plants per ha . The distance may be reduced to 8 metres when the climate is comparatively dry and the soil is not so fertile.

The success of an orchard depends upon the selection of a plant from the nursery. One should always go in for a healthy and true-to-type plant of a recommended variety. Two year old plants should be planted in the field. By doing so, the field mortality is considerably reduced. Preferably, the young litchi plants, should be planted in the nursery and transplanted when they have attained good size.

Before planting, pits of one metre in diameter and one metre deep should be dug a few weeks before the actual planting. The pits are then allowed to remain open for a few days and then filled with top soil mixed with manures and fertilizer at the rate of 20-25 kg farmyard manure, 2 kg of bone meal and 300 g of muriate of potash. If available, a basket of soil from litchi orchard which contains mycorrhizal fungi should be added to this mixture. The pits are then watered so that the soil settles down. At the planting time a small hole is made at the centre of the refilled pit and the desired plant is planted with the help of planting board. Water should be applied immediately after planting.

Planting of windbreak : Hot and desiccating winds in summer and cold winds in winter adversely affect the growth of litchi. The young litchi plants should be protected against these adverse conditions which can cause the uprooting of trees and drop of flowers and fruits. So, two to three years before the litchi trees are planted in the orchard, a windbreak should be planted at the orchard boundary. The windbreak should be at a right angle to the direction of the prevailing winds. A row of tall-growing trees such as jamun, seedling mango, eucalyptus, arjun and simbal alternating with low-headed trees, such as mulberry, ber and neem should be planted.

Protection of young plants : The irrigated sub-montane areas of the Punjab and Haryana are ideally suitable for litchi cultivation. In spite of its being well suited to these areas, there is no headway in area under litchi. This is mainly because of its being a delicate plant which is subjected to high rate of mortality in the initial years due to frost and hot summer winds. After planting, the young litchi plants need protection against winter frost and summer hot winds (loo) up to four-five years. This can be done by covering the plants with farmwaste materials like **sarkanda,** rice straw (parali), maize stalks, sugarcane trash, etc. Growing of Jantar (dhaincha) around the young litchi plants also provides good protection in summer and winter. The Jantar seed should be sown around the plant in the basin in the middle of February. It grows sufficiently by the middle of April to provide shade to the plants. The tops of the Jantar can be tied in winter to act as protection against frost. The open spaces in Jantar can be plugged with locally available straw. Root pruning of Jantar plants is necessary to avoid competition with litchi roots. It should be done three to four times in a year.

Besides, a few weeks after planting 50 g of CAN (calcium ammonium nitrate) per plant should be added to the basins, leaving a width of about 15 cm around the stem. A light irrigation is given after mixing the fertilizer with the soil. This dose of the fertilizer should be repeated every two months. This would help the young plants to make quick and vigorous growth. The diseased, dried or dead portions of a branch, if any, should be removed. The branches which tends to grow into the centre of the tree and crowds or crosses the framework branches may also be removed.

PROPAGATION TECHNIQUES

Litchi can be propagated from seed or through vegetative means.

Seed propagation : The trees raised from seeds are very slow to come into bearing and may take ten years or even much longer time to come to bearing. The seedling trees do not produce true-to-type and often yield fruits of inferior quality. The litchi seed also loses its viability within 4-5 days of its extraction from the fruit. However, seed proagation may be followed for raising rootstock. In such case, the seeds should not be allowed to become dry but should be sown fresh just after extraction. The seeds may be kept viable for about two months by leaving them in the fruits or keeping them in moist packing material. So, considering these problems, litchi is usualy propagated vegetatively.

Vegetative propagation

Litchi can be propagated through cutting, layering, budding and grafting. Layering is the common method of propagating litchi in most parts of the world. Air (gootee) layering is used commercially for raising litchi plants. This method being less tedious than inarching and due to high percentage of success, is adopted by the nurserymen throughout of India for litchi propagation. The plant prepared by this method are ready for sale within a year and quarter, the date of layering. A terminal branch, 45–60 cm long and 1.0–1.25 cm thick is selected. A 4 cm wide ring of bark is removed with a sharp knife. Place wet moss or roots of water hyancinth on the exposed portion and wrap it with polythene sheet. The ends of wrapped polythene sheet should be tied tightly. The rooting starts after about 4 weeks. However, the **gootee** should be severed from the mother tree, remove the polythene sheet and immediately plant the **gootee** in a nursery bed.

Although, layering in litchi can be done in February-March and July to October, yet the period from middle of August to September is the best for this operation.

Preparation of nursery beds : The nursery beds should be prepared under partial shade: For this, raising the janter in between the nursery beds is quite useful. But care should be taken that jantar rows do not compete with the growth of nearby plants. So, root pruning of jantar plants which are near the litchi row is very necessary. To the soil where the nursery beds are to be prepared should be added large quantity of organic matter. It is generally recommended that upper 22.5 cm soil should be added with 50 per cent of farmyard manure.

Planting of layers : After two or three months of layering, when adequate root system has developed, the layers are separated from the parent plants. Care should be taken that there is proper balance of the top with the root system. If need be, excess branches and leaves should be removed. The roots of litchi in the beginning are very tender and break away very easily. The rooted layers should, therefore, be very carefully planted in the nursery. These layers in the nursery beds are planted in the rows which are 45-60 cm apart. The plant to plant distance in the rows is kept 20 to 25 cm. After planting, the layers should be irrigated immediately. The subsequent irrigation should be given at week's interval. The interval during irrigations can be decreased or increased according to the need of the plants. Only thing which is kept in mind is that the soil remains in wet condition. The dry condition decreases the growth of the nursery plants considerably. Frost injury is very common in young litchi plants. So, these plants are protected by making thatches of **sarkanda** on the beds.

The layers after separating from the parent plants can be planted in the polythene bags. The bags should be 22.5 cm wide and about 20-25 cm in length. These are filled with soil and farmyard manure mixed in fifty, fifty ratio. This planting of layers in polythene bags helps in better transportation and thus enhances the success of litchi plants in the fields. Nursery plants of litchi also need some fertilization for its better growth. For this, the light dressing of nitrogenous fertilizers like calcium ammonium nitrate or ammonium sulphate or urea after 2-3 weeks interval should be given.

Cutting, budding and grafting

Soft wood cuttings may also be made to root with bottom heat and carefully controlled condition. However, soft-wood cuttings do not root well even with the use of growth regulators.

Budding and grafting have also been tried in many countries but the percentage of success with these methods has been very low, ranging between 10-20 per cent only. A method of splice grafting was developed in South Africa with considerable success. Propagation of litchi by inarching has also been tried by the Chinese. It is very tedious and time consuming method and takes several months before an inarched plant is severed from the mother plant. Longan as a rootstock gives quick growth but the bearing is uncertain.

ORCHARD CULTURAL PRACTICES

Irrigation

Adequate soil moisture is considered essential for successful litchi cultivation. In areas, where annual rainfall is more than 125 cm and is well distributed through -out the year, litchi can be grown without irrigation. The young plants neither establish well nor do they make optimum growth if there is shortage of water. Copious and frequent watering is essential for the bearing litchi trees.

Litchi should be carefully irrigated at all stages of development. Their irrigational needs are especially more in summer. The young plants need irrigations twice a week during April-June. In winter, weekly irrigation would be sufficient.

Adequate frequent watering is essential for the bearing litchi trees. The development of litchi fruits takes place during March to May when the temperature starts rising in the plains of India and the atmospheric humidity remains very low. Evapo- transpiration consequently rises considerably. If the litchi orchard is not frequently irrigated during the spring and summer months, there is chance of severe fruit drop. The fruit which remain, do not develop fully, often split and become unfit for consumption.

At fruit set, irrigation is given at three weeks' interval which is reduced as the atmospheric temperature increases. During fruit development period i.e. from the second week of May to the end of June, irrigation should be given twice a week. Irrigating litchi tree twice a week during this period reduces cracking of fruits to a great extent and helps in proper size development. After the withdrawl of monsoon bearing orchards should be irrigated at the end of November or first week of December to protect them from frost injury. Later on irrigation during winter should be applied depending upon rain and soil moisture conditions. Irrigation of young trees should be done by the basin system. As the trees grow, the basin should be gradually enlarged.

When the trees are fully grown and have occupied the entire soil with their root-system, then the flooding system of irrigation should be introduced.

Intercropping

The litchi is a slow growing tree and takes at least six years to come into bearing. During the early years, the vacant space in between the trees may be utilized profitably by growing intercrops. The choice of intercrops depends upon the climate and soil and also on the marketing facilities. The vegetables may be grown near the cities, while leguminous crops like pulses, guara and senji may be grown at places away from the market. During karif season, vegetables like pumpkin, ridgegourd, bitter gourd, cucumber and leguminous crops such as moong, mash, moth and cowpeas may be grown. Guara may also be grown as a green manure crop which will protect the young litchi plants against hot desiccating winds in addition to enriching the soil. In winter season, radish, carrot, turnip, cauliflower, peas and gram may be grown as intercrops. Senji is also grown as fodder or as a green manure crop.

Beside vegetables and pulses, some quick-growing fruit plants can be grown in the early years. Phalsa and papaya are the execellent intercrops during the initial years. The phalsa bushes can be kept low by severe annual pruning and do not crowd around the litchi plants. Papaya because of there upright growth, do well as an intercrop. The most productive period of the papaya plants would be over by the time the litchi trees comes into bearing and it can then be removed from the orchard.Peach, plum and kinnow are also good intercrops. The intercrops should be manured separately and protected from the attack of insect pests and diseases.

Weed Conrol

In the litchi orchard, cultivation should be kept to the minimum. The main objectives of tilling the orchard should be weed control or the mixing of manures and fertilizers with the soil. The litchi is a shallow-rooted plant and deep ploughing of the orchard soil should be avoided as it damage the root-system. Most of the presistent weeds in litchi orchards could be controlled by the application of post-emergence herbicides like glyphosate and paraquat. Diuron @ 5 kg/ha as pre-emergence herbicide can effectively check the weed flora in litchi plantation. Post-emergence herbicide glyphosate @ 1 – 2 a.i *l*/ha or paraquat @ 0.6 – 1.2 a.i *l*/ha are very useful for weed control in litchi orchard. Mulching the orchard with black polythene is very useful practice which preserve the soil moisture and controls the weed population.

Mulching

The moisture of the soil can be preserved by providing mulch over it. The use of mulch enhance the rate of penetration of rain- water or irrigation into the soil. Apart from this, it also check the growth of weeds, thus eliminating the competition between the weeds and the fruit trees. The use of mulch in young litchi plants encourage the development of a better root system than in the case of the plants growing in a bare soil. The farmyard manure, compost or straw can be used as mulch. The farmyard manure and compost are the excellent mulch material, because they enrich the soil in addition to conserve soil moisture. When straw is spread over the soil as mulch material, an additional dose of 2.5 - 3.5 kg of calcium ammonium nitrate per quintal of dry straw is given to hasten the rotting of straw. The litchi plants will suffer from nitrogen starvation if additional dose of nitrogen is not given along with the straw mulch. Besides, cutting down of tall weeds growing in the orchard and leaving them spread over the orchard soil also provide a good mulch. Polyethylene preferably black polythene can be used as best mulch material to maintain high moisture level and to control the growth of weeds.

Manuring and Fertilization

The special attention should be given to maintain the optimum levels of NPK in the orchard soil. When nitrogen is present in the soil in sufficient quantities, the plants make luxuriant growth, have dark-green leaves and produce high yield. The trees growing under nitrogen deficient conditions remain stunted. The leaflets are rough in texture with curling margins. The yellowing first appears in the old leaves and when the deficiency continues, the young leaves may also become yellow. When phosphorus is deficient the leaflets become abnormally large and dark green. The texture of the leaves is little rough and dark brown scorched areas appears in the old leaves. The deficiency of potassium causes considerable stunting of the plants. The leaves are small and soft in texture. The scorching of leaf margin starts from the tip and progress gradually towards the base of a leaflet.

Fertilizer schedule for Litchi orchards : The recommended doses of manures and inorganic fertilizers for full litchi trees grown commercially in following states are given below :

State	FYM (Kg/tree)	N	P_2O_5 (g/tree)	K_2O
Bihar	50	200	320	500
West Bengal	80	600	200	600
Uttarakhand	–	1000	500	1000
Punjab	60	800	360	360

In Punjab, to young litchi plants of 1 – 3 years age, FYM 10 – 20 kg, Urea 150 – 500 g, SP 200 – 600 and MoP 60 – 150 g per plant is applied. In the age group of 4 – 6 years, FYM 25 – 40 kg, Urea 500 – 1000 g, SP 750 – 1250 g and MoP 200 – 300 g is given to per plant. When the plants are between 7 – 10 years age, the doses are increased further as FYM 40 – 50 kg, urea 1 – 1.5 kg, SP 1.5 – 2.5 kg and MoP 300 – 500 g per plant is applied. To full grown plant of 10 years and above, the doses of manures and fertilizers are stabilized at FYM 60 kg, Urea 1.6 kg, SP 2.250 kg and MoP 600 g per plant.

In North India, Farmyard manure, superphosphate and muriate of potash should be applied in December. Half of urea should be applied in the middle of February and the other half in middle of April after the fruit set.

Zinc deficiency : In litchi, the deficiency of zinc appears as bronzing of leaves. The leaflets also become small and pointed and internodes remain short.The zinc deficiency can be corrected by spraying 4 kg of zinc sulphate in 500 litres of water. The trees should be sprayed in spring as soon as they put new leaves.

TRAINING AND PRUNING

Training of litchi plants is done according to modified leader system. Training of plants should be completed upto fourth year of planting.

To give proper shape to the litchi plant, little pruning is often necessary after planting. Once the desired shape is achieved, no pruning is usually necessary, except the removal of dead, diseased and criss-crossed branches. Litchi flower are borne mostly on current year's growth and old shoot rarely produces flowers. So, to promote new growth, snipping of old branches is desirable. However, this is done indirectly when a part of the shoot bearing the cluster, the fruit is removed during harvesting. If litchi tree makes too much vegetative growth, both root and shoot pruning may be done. But, heavy pruning causes profuse vegetative growth which takes place at the expense of flowering and fruiting. When the trees become too old and produce fruits of small size, heavy pruning may be done.

FRUIT DROP

Maximum fruit drop occurred during second and third week after fruit set. Seedless Late and Calcutta cultivars are less prone to fruit drop than Dehradun and Muzzafarpur. Apart from the competition among fruits for water and nutrients and other physiological causes, strong wind significantly affects drop. Irrigation to bearing litchi trees twice a week from April onwards and good windbreak minimize fruit drop to a great extent.

Foliar spray with zinc sulphate at 0.5, 1 and 1.5 per cent considerably increased the zinc content of the leaves and affectively reduced fruit drop in Dehradun cultivar. Higher level of zinc in the leaves might increase the endogenous production of auxins and thereby reduce the fruit drop. Similarly, NAA and 2,4-D at 15 ppm in combination with 1 per cent zinc sulphate resulted in more fruit retention till harvest. Foliar spray of NAA @ 40-50 ppm at pea stage and again 3 weeks later promote fruit set and reduce fruit drop.

HARVESTING AND HANDLING OF FRUITS

Harvesting : Layered litchi begin bearing fruit when they are about six years of age. The yield goes on increasing every year till the trees are 20 to 30 years old. Early varieties of litchi like Dehradun start ripening in early June, where as the mid season and late varieties ripen in the second fortnight of June. The fruit colour changes from greenish to attractive red or pink. Litchi is a non-climacteric fruit usually do not improve in quality after harvest. So the fruits should be allowed to ripen properly on the tree. For the local market the fruits should be picked at complete ripening stage. However, when the fruits are to be shipped to a distant market, they should be harvested when they are still hard-ripe or have just turned pinkish and the sharply pointed tubercles on the skin have become flattened. The maturity of the fruit for harvesting is judged from the tubercles on it. When the fruit is mature, the tubercles become somewhat flattened and the epicarp becomes smooth.

The litchi fruit is picked in whole clusters with a portion of the leafy stalk attached to each of them. In this way, the fruit does not wilt soon after harvest. The fruit cluster are spot picked several times as they do not ripen on the tree at the same time. The harvested fruits should be kept in shade because atmospheric temperature is very high at harvesting time. If allowed to remain exposed to the sun, the fruits lose their freshness, become dull in colour and deteriorate in quality.

Grading and packing : Litchi fruits should be graded and then packed in mulbery baskets of suitable size. Soft dry grass or banana leaves should be placed in the baskets before litchi clusters are piled up. The clusters should not be packed too deep or too high as the bottom fruit get crushed. The fruit clusters are covered with some more grass or banana leaves and a piece of moist gunny bags should be wrapped around the basket and tied securely.

Marketing : A full grown litchi tree of different varieties bears about 80 to 150 kg of fruit. The average yield per adult tree is 4000 to 5000 fruits. After the litchi trees come into bearing, the yield goes on increasing till the trees are 30 years old. With proper care and management and under suitable environmental conditions, a litchi tree may continue bearing economic crop for over 100 years of age. Litchi is a highly perishable fruit, its marketing should be done as early as possible. During transit, care should be taken to avoid crushing of fruit and damage of the skin.

Storage : The bulk of the fruit is consumed in the fresh form. The fruit does not keep for more than a few days at room temperature. It looses its bright red colour and turns brown within 2-3 days after harvest. The availability of litchi can be prolonged by keeping the fruits in the cold storage. The most important post- harvest need of litchi is the retention of fruit colour and quality for longer period so that the marketing is phased out to avoid the glut and ensure better premium to the growers. The shelf life of litchi fruits can be enhanced up to 35 days in cv. Seedless late by storing them in perforated polythene bags of 100 gauge thickness in the commerical cold storage (0-3.3°C and RH 85-90 per cent) after treating with 6 per cent wax-emulsion. The fruits of litchi cv. Bombai packed in perforated polyethylene bags can stored for 18 days at 4°C. A storage temperature of 5–7°C further minimise the losses of litchi fruits. It is reported that litchi fruits of cv. Rose Scented treated with hot water at 55°C and10 per cent oxalic acid for 15 min. stored well upto 18 days under cold storage condition (temp. 5°C and 85 ± 5% RH).

PLANT PROTECTION MEASURES

Litchi was considered to be free from serious insect-pests and diseases. But observations have shown that litchi also suffers from many insect-pests which include nut borer, leaf roller, grey weevil, mites, mealy bug and snails.

INSECT-PESTS

Litchi nut borer (*Blastobasis sp*) : It damages the fruit by entering through a small pin-head size hole near the attachment of peduncle and feeds inside it. Infested fruits become unfit for consumption. For the management of the pest, clean cultivation is necessary *i.e.,* removing of fallen fruits (mummies) from the orchard and ploughing destroys the carry over of pests to the next crop. Alternate sprays of 750 ml Sumicidin 20 EC (fenvalerate) or 1000 ml Ekalux 25 EC (quinalphos) in 500 litres of water at fruit setting stage followed by another spray 20 days later should be given with the appearance of pest and at colour break stage.

Leaf roller (*Tortix epicyrta*) : This pest is active from March to November. It is the most destructive pest and eat fresh growth coming out during September-October. A very active green caterpillar rolls the leaf and feeds the green matter within the roll. No Hibiscus plants should be grown near the litchi orchard. The rolled leaves should be collected and destroyed at the initial stages. Spray 800 ml of Malathion 50 EC in 500 litres of water per acre during September-October or as soon as the attack begins. Repeat after 15 days if necessary. The orchard should be ploughed and irrigated during December-January to kill the hibernating caterpillers.

Mites (*Eriophyes sp.*) : Both adults and nymphs infest the leaves. They live at the base of hairs on the under surface of the leaves and cause a brown velvity growth of the leaves with pit formation. The leaves become thick, curl up and eventually dry. The attack of mites starts in March and the maximum activity is in July. The mites can be controlled by spraying the trees with 0.05 per cent Dimethoate.

Back eating caterpillar (*Indarbela tetraonis*) : It is pest of neglected litchi plantation. Larvae after hatching make holes in scaffold crotches and feed on surface of bark. The excreta of wood hangs down at the holes. The girdling caused by the feeding of bark can be harmful to tree.

Clear the holes with a wire and inject kerosene oil and chlorpyriphos solution 50 : 50 and plug the holes with mud.

Mealy bug (*Planococcus citri*) : Mealy bug does a lot of damage during flowering and fruiting stages i.e. January to April, when a large number of nymphs crawl up the tree and congregate on the growing shoots and panicles and suck the sap. The nymphs should be prevented from crawling up the trunk by applying a slippery or sticky band one metre above the ground level from end of December to beginning of January. Apply a 15-20 cm wide sheet of alkathene to the basal end of the stem and secure both its upper and lower edges with twine. It is desirable to apply mud to the cracks on the bark under the lower edge of the alkathene sheet so that the nymphs are prevented from climbing up the slippery band. Or apply 5 cm wide band of Ostico or Esso fruit tree grease. Repeat as and when necessary after scraping off the crust. In case of severe emergence apply 50% of methyl parathion dust (Follidol 2%) on the compacted soil to kill the nymphs.

The nymphs congregating below the bands should be killed by spraying them with 200 ml of methyl parathion 50 EC in 100 litres of water. In case of sticky band, a flame can also be used to destroy the mealy bug. Drench the plants with 1875 ml Durmet/Dursban 20 EC (chlorpyriphos) in 500 litres of water on apperance of bugs. Repeat the spray if needed.

Snails : It is a minor pest of litchi and is active during July- August. The pest can be controlled mechanically or by applying 5 per cent Malathion dust during July-August.

Bats and birds : They also cause considerable loss to fruits. They can be scared effectively by beating drums or by firing crackers.

DISEASES

Anthracnose (*Botryodiplodia theobromae* and *Colletotrichum gloeosporioides*) : The spots start from the tip or the margin of the lamina which are chocolate in colour. Anthracnose (*Colletotrichum gloeosporioides*) attackes leaves and branches, flowers and fruits. Lesions on the leaves may appear as small round light grey areas or irregular brown marks at the tips. It is also obvious on the flowers and fruits. The organism gets associated with fruits in the orchards and cause infection during transit or storage.

Prune the affected plants and burn such shoots. Spray 50% copper oxychloride (0.3%) or Bordeaux mixture 2 : 2 : 50 in February, April and September – October. It was found that fruit kept at 10°C remain free from infection.

Fruit rot : It is serious problem in litchi. Fruit rot at the time of harvest in certain orchards. Such rotted fruits also cause rotting in healthy fruits and adversely affect the marketing of fruits.

The disease can be checked by spraying Bavistin @ 500 g in 500 litres of water one week before harvesting of fruits. Fruit stored at 5°C result slow rot development in fruits. Hot benomyl dip to fruits at 48 – 52°C slow rot development.

PHYSIOLOGICAL DISORDERS

Splitting or cracking of fruits

It is quite common in almost all the litchi growing areas of India, particularly under dry conditions. In severe cases, the crop losses due to this malady may be as high as 20 per cent or even more.

Causes : Splitting of fruits has been generally attributed to abrupt changes in atmospheric temperature, relative humidity and soil moisture conditions, following rain or heavy irrigations. This disorder may occur shortly before maturity when rains follow a prolonged period of drought during which the fruit gets checked in growth. Excessive soil moisture aided by fluctuations in temperature and humidity may aggravate fruit splitting.

Early maturing varieties (Dehradun and Saharnpur) are more susceptible to cracking significantly possess higher number of stomata per unit leaf surface area than mid-late season ripening and less susceptible varieties (Calcuttia and Rose Scented).

Control measures : The following measures are generally considered appropriate for adoption to minimise fruit splitting.

1. Regular irrigation in the orchards helps in maintaining growth and expression in the fruit.
2. In the absence of rains during summer months, water spray may prove useful in keeping the ambient atmosphere of the fruit humid, as moisture has a good local effect on the fruit against splitting.
3. Some filler trees can be planted in quincunx system of layout in which the trouble is minimised.

4. The litchi plants should be trained to keep low headed. Such trained plants with dense foliage, can withstand more hot and desiccating winds as compared to tall trees and thus fruit splitting is the least in their case.
5. One or two rows of tall trees e.g. Eucalyptus alternating with small sized trees having dense foliage (mulberry, Jamun, desi ber, etc.) may be planted around the orchard as windbreak. This wall of trees help to create humid conditions in the orchard, which prove favourable for the developing fruits and thus splitting is avoided to a great extent.
6. The varieties which are less prone to splitting should be planted. Early varieties like Dehradun and Saharanpur split more than the mid-season or late varieties.
7. The litchi orchard should be planted by a hillock or near the large bodies of water or in between tall and dense trees like mangoes.
8. The plants can be guarded immensely against high temperature by sowing Jantar or Arhar along the tree rows or in the periphery of the plant basin. These helps to minimise splitting of fruits, beside protecting the fruit trees from the vagaries of hot weather.
9. NAA and 2,4,5-T at 35-100 ppm has been found effective in checking fruit splitting and increasing fruit size.

CHAPTER 18

Ber

The ber or Indian jujube (***Ziziphus mauritiana*** Lamk.) is one of the ancient and common fruit of India and China. It has wide adaptability because of which it is cultivated practically all over India especially the drier parts of Indian sub-continent for its fresh fruits. It can be successfully cultivated even in the most marginal ecosystems of subtropics and tropics. It is often called the poor man's fruit. However, grafted varieties of ber are no longer the poor man's fruit as they fetch even higher prices than several other fruits. Of late, the cultivation of ber, has received a great impetus as a commercial crop in the North India especially in the States of Punjab, Haryana and Rajasthan because of its potential for high yields and excellent economic returns to the growers. It is an ideal fruit for cultivation in the arid and semi-arid zones of Northern India because it has the least irrigation requirements in the summer months of May and June when it sheds its leaves and enter a period of dormancy.

ORIGIN, HISTORY AND DISTRIBUTION

The ber is said to be indigenous to the area stretching from India to South-Western China and Malaysia. The ber has a long historic background, and is mentioned in the earliest Sanskrit literature and with many other names in different Indian languages. Ber fruits are used in religious rites by Sanatanist Brahmanas in north India (Kashmir). In Valmiki's Ramayana use of ber is mentioned in **pind dan** – a ritual after death. It is intimately connected with the folk-lore of the people in Northern India particularly in the Punjab. Its abundant presence in the wild state proves its ancient domestication. Its commercial cultivation is said to have started when a Muslim cultivator won prize by presenting delicious fruits of ber from a budded plant to Raja Raghoji Bhonsle II.

It is believed that the ber tree from Garhwal (U.P.) has been introduced more generally into other parts of India. From India it spread gradually to south, South East Asia, Zanzibar and the East-African coast and then further into the African continent, The process of spreading would have started only a few hundred years ago. It is found in many tropical countries of both hemispheres often in naturalized state.

Ber is distributed between 30°S and 30°N latitude mainly in India, Pakistan, Bangladesh, Central and Southern Africa and North part of Australia. Ber plantation on large or small scale exist in China, Afghanistan, Russia, Iran, Iraq, Israil, Syria, Italy, Spain, Burma and U.S.A.

The ber plant is considered the most sacred one in Sikh and Hindu religion. The Sikh Gurus preferred to plant ber trees in Gurdwara. The Golden Temple, Amritsar is the highest Religious Abode of Sikhs. The oldest ber tree about 440 years old named as *Ber Baba Budha Sahib* is located near to holy *Sarowar* in the periphery *i.e. Parkama* of Golden Temple. This ber tree is associated with highly respected religious Saint Baba Budha Ji, hence it is a called *Ber Baba Budha Sahib*. *Dukh Bhanjani* ber and *Lachhi* ber are another old plants located in the premises of Golden Temple.

AREA AND PRODUCTION

China is the biggest producer of ber in the world. India with an area of about one lakh hectares, ranks second among ber growing countries of the world. The important provinces for ber cultivation in India are Maharashtra, Gujarat. Uttar Pradesh, Tamil Nadu, Jammu and Kashmir, West Bengal, Chhattisgarh, Haryana, Rajasthan, Madhya Pradesh, Punjab, Karnataka, Bihar and Andhra Pradesh. The annual production of ber in India is estimated 10 lakh tonnes. It accounts for 1.49 and 1.31 per cent of total area and production of fruits, respectively. Productivity of ber in India is 10 metric tonnes per hectare.

The improved budded varieties of ber have been planted on a large scale in Punjab, Haryana, Rajasthan and Gujarat because of high economic returns. In the Punjab and Haryana, there is perhaps no other fruit tree that grows wild so extensively as the ber. In the Punjab, the districts of Sangrur, Bathinda, Ferozepur, Ludhiana, Patiala, Muktsar are the most famous for grafted ber varieties. The total area under ber in Punjab is about 1828 hectares with annual production of 30160 tonnes. In Haryana, the districts of Hisar, Rohtak, Jind, Panipat, Mohindergarh and Gurgaon are famous for commercial cultivation of ber. In Rajasthan, its orchards are spread in Bharatpur, Jaipur and Jodhpur. In Gujarat, ber orchards are found in Banaskantha, Sabarmati, Bhav-nagar, Surendranagar, Patan, Ahmedabad, Bharuch, Vadodra, Sabarkantha and Mehsana. In south India ber is found around Tirunelveli, Ramanathapuram, Dharmapuri and Salem district in Tamil Nadu and Bijapur, Bellary, Gulbarga, Belgaum, Raichur and Bidar in Karnataka. In West Bengal, this fruit is quite popular in Murshidabad, Malda, Bankura and Birbhum.

IMPORTANCE AND USES

The ber is one of the most nutritious fruits. The pulp of different varieties contains 13.0 to 19.0 per cent total soluble solids and 0.20 to 0.60 per cent acidity at fully ripe stage. It is one of the richest sources of vitamin C, next only to aonla and guava but better than citrus fruits and apple. Ripe fruits of Umran ber contains 120 mg ascorbic acid per 100 g of pulp. Ber fruit contains β-carotene (vitamin A) at 81 μg per 100 g of fruit.When fully ripe, ber contains 5.6 per cent sucrose, 1.5 per cent glucose, 2.1 per cent fructose, 1 per cent starch and 13.6 per cent total carbohydrates.

Ber is also a good source of minerals and proteins. Ripe fruit contains 0.031 per cent calcium, 0.036 per cent phosphorus and 1.14 per cent iron. Protein forms 0.94 per cent of its content. A comparison of nutritive value of ber with apple reveals that it (ber) excels in calcium, phosphorus, protein, mineral matter, vitamin C and vitamin A. Ripe fruit of Umran ber contains amino acids like aspergine, aspartic acid, arginine, glutamic acid, glycine, serine, threonine, α-alanine, valine, methionine, leucine and isoleucine. The ber tree is utilized chiefly for its edible fruits.

It is also one of the principle host plants for rearing lac insects. Secondary uses of the tree are for carpentry and building wood, fodder, hedges, fences, fuel and medicinal purposes.

The roots are used as decoction in fewer and as powder applied to ulcers and old wounds. The fruit has been used in traditional medicines as an emollient, expectorant, coolant, anodyne and tonic. The fruit is given to receive abdominal pains during pregnancy. The fruit also helps to lower cholesterol levels and blood pressure. Some of the triterpenic acids isolated from the fruit are also believed to be useful in fighting cancer and HIV. The fruit is co-prescribed to the patients of open heart surgery for quick healing and speedy recovery.

The ber fruit is eaten mostly fresh but it can be utilized profitably for the preparation of several delicious products. The fruit of the choice grafted varieties is very tasty, the pulp being juicy, sweet and rich in flavour, the fruit is easily digestible and can act as a mild laxative. Drying it in the sun is a common practice in the dry region of Northern India where it is often the only fruit locally available. The dried fruit is kept for use during the off season. Umran is highly suitable for sun-drying and dehydration and excellent Chhuhar's can be prepared. Fully mature unripe fruits of ber can be used for the preparation of murabba, candy, pickle and chutney. The juicy varieties can be converted into pulp to serve as base material for squash, nectar and ready to-serve beverage. The fully mature fruits of ber can be canned in sugar syrup. Ber candy is an excellent product and the fruits of Umran variety gives an excellent product when candied. A nice jelly, prepared from the ripe fruit, retain a good amount of vitamin C. As ber is now being cultivated as a commercial crop, there is scope for canning these products.

BOTANY

The ber belongs to the genus **Ziziphus** of the family Rhamnaceae and order Rhamnales which has about 50 genera and more than 600 species. The genus **Ziziphus** includes about 170 species throughout the world. Some species of this family are cultivated either for edible fruits or as ornamentals. The India jujube ***Ziziphus mauritiana*** Lamk. is very common in India and is widely distributed in warm countries. This species is summer deciduous, sheds its leaves in summer after the harvest of the fruit. It is thorny shrub or small tree upto 12 metres in height. Leaves are alternate, simple, 3-nerved, minutely denticulate, obtuse, broadly oval to rounded-elliptical, slightly equal to the base, up to 8 cm long and 5 cm broad, densely tomentose underside and has stipular thorns. Inflorescence is axillary cyme and sub-capitate in the leaf-axils. Flowers are small, greenish-cream, bi-sexual, actinomorph, pentamerous, upto 0.8 cm in size and acrid-scented. Petals 5, arising between and smaller than the calyx-lobes. Calyx 5-lobed, shortly tubular and lobes valvate. Stamens 5, opposite to the petals and arising outside the margin of usually conspicuous disk. Style is thrum as it is shorter than stamens. Anthers 2-locular and opening lengthwise. Stigma is bi-lobed. Ovary superior to half inferior, 2-locular, ovules in each locule on basal placentas and anatropous. Fruit drupaceous, persistent lower part of calyx often evident, ellipsoid to subglobose, greenish yellow to golden yellow, 2.2 - 5 cm long and 2 - 3.5 cm broad. Edible portion is epicarp and mesocarp.

The Chinese jujube **(*Ziziphus jujuba* Mill.)** grows in China, Southern Europe, South and East Asia. It is a winter deciduous and has leaves that are glabrous at the underside. The tree is up to 9-10 metres in height and spiny. The branchlets are often slender and frequently give appearance of pinnate leaves. The leaves are serrate, 2.5 - 5 cm long, oblong-ovate to lanceolate. The fruit is dark-red or brown.

The **mallah** ber **(*Ziziphus nummularia*** (Burm. F.) Wright & Arn.**)** grows as a small shrub in wastelands of Rajasthan, north-western India and Andhra Pradesh. The fruit from the bushes of mallah being poor in quality is not of much commercial importance. It has a peculiar acrid taste and very little pulp. The seedlings of mallah ber are commonly used as a rootstock for cultivated varieties of ber.

The Jujubie de Palestine **(*Ziziphus spina – christi*** (L.) Desf.) : It grows is Iran and Iraq as a commercial crop.

The other important wild ***Ziziphus*** spp are as follows :

Ziziphus xylopyrus (Retz.) Willd
Ziziphus oenoplia (L.) Mill.
Ziziphus joazeiro Mart.
Ziziphus mistol Griseb.
Ziziphus rugosa Lamk.
Ziziphus funiculosa Buch.-Ham.
Ziziphus glabrata Heyne ex Roth
Ziziphus oxyphylla Edgew.
Ziziphus lotus (L.) Lamk.
Ziziphus sativa Gaertn.
Ziziphus vulgaris Lamk.

FLOWERING AND FRUITING

The flowering period in north India lasts for about two and a half months from September to November. In Rajasthan, flowering has been observed to began in July reaching its peak in September. In the tropical climate of Southern India, flowering continue through out the extended summer *i.e.,* May to September. Flower buds appear both on current season growth and one year old mature shoots. The inflorescence is axillary cyme on the main as well as the lateral shoots. The number of flowers per cluster varies from 16 to 28. The whole period of bud development is divided into eight stages. It takes 21 days to 22 days for passing through various stages of bud development. The peak of flower anthesis is at 6 A.M. in Sanaur-2, Sanaur-5 and Chhuhara cultivars and 2 P.M. in Thornless, Khaithli and Umran cultivars. The dehiscence of anthers starts just after anthesis and completes within 4 hours. Pollen grains are highly viable-the viability ranging between 87 to 91 per cent in different cultivars. Pollen grain germinability is also quite high to 36- 48 per cent. The peak receptivity in stigma is found on the day of anthesis. It does not set any fruit by self-pollination, thereby shows self-incompatibility.

Fruit-setting starts in second week of October and continues upto first fortnight of November. The ber fruit reaches to ripe stage in about 180 days after fruit-setting. The fruit growth in terms of length and diameter shows three distinct phases and follows a pattern of 'Double Sigmoid' curve.

The **Indian jujube** has a somatic chromosome number of 2n=48. This might indicate polyploidy and may be tetraploid. The chinese jujube has chromosome number of 2n=24. This has polyploid variants with 2n=48 and 2n=96.

CLIMATE

The ber is a hardy fruit tree and can grow successfully even under unfavourable climatic conditions, where most other fruit trees fail to grow. It can be grown up to a height of 1,000 metres above sea-level, beyond this it does not bear well. Ber relishes hot and dry climate for its successful cultivation, but the trees need adequate watering during the fruiting season. Excessive atmospheric humidity is considered a limiting factor for satisfactory fruiting. Temperature below freezing is injurous to the young twigs and developing fruits and result in substantial crop loss. It can very well withstand hot and dry weather during summer months of May-June, its tree enters into dormancy by shedding its leaves. New growth starts in July with the advent of rains and the growth period continues till the middle of November when it is inhibited with the onset of cold weather.

SOIL

Ber provides a good scope for cultivation on soils which have so far been considered marginal or even unsuitable for growing other fruits. Its tree develops a deep tap-root system within a short period of growth and as such adopts itself to a wide variety of soils. Ber is well known for its ability to thrive under adverse conditions of salinity, drought and water-logging. The ber can flourish even in soils with pH as high as 9.2. Ber cultivation can succeed even under constraints of irrigation and fertilization, however, for good tree growth and yield, deep sandy-loam soils with neutral or slightly alkaline reaction and good drainage are more desirable.

PROMISING VARIETIES

The choice of suitable varieties is of paramount importance for successful cultivation,. More than one hundered cultivars of ber are grown in India which have been developed by selection in different regions. Given below, are the salient features of some varieties which have proved promising for commercial cultivation.

Umran : This variety is cultivated in a large scale in Maharashtra, Gujarat, Rajasthan Punjab and Haryana. The fruit is large, oval in shape with a roundish apex and has an attractive golden yellow colour which turns into chocolate brown at full maturity. The fruit is sweet, with 14-19 per cent TSS and has pleasant flavour and excellent dessert quality. It is a prolific cropping variety, yielding 150-200 kg of fruit per tree. The fruits ripen late from second fortnight of March to mid-April in north India and have a good keeping quality. It is susceptible to powdery mildew.

Sanaur-2 : This is a selection from Sanaur - a small town near Patiala, which is known for ber cultivation. The fruit is large and oblong with a roundish apex. On ripening, fruits atain a light yellow colour and TSS of 18–19 per cent. Like Umran, it is also a prolific bearer-yielding about 150 kg fruit per tree. It is a mid-season variety, ripening during second fortnight of March under north Indian conditions and has been found fairly resistant to powdery mildew disease.

Wallaiti : Trees semi-erect. The fruit is medium in size, oval in shape, skin smooth and light golden yellow to golden yellow at maturity. Pulp soft, sweet with 13.8 to 15.0 per cent TSS. It is an early variety and ripens during first fortnight of March. Average yield is 114 kg per tree. It is moderately susceptible to powdery mildew disease.

Kaithli : This variety is a selection from Kaithal in Haryana. The fruit is medium in size, oval in shape and has a tapering apex. Fruit pulp is soft and sweet with TSS of 14-16 per cent. Fruits ripen in the second fortnight of March to first week of April. The average yield is 120 kg fruit per tree. This is an excellent variety but appears to be more susceptible to powdery mildew disease.

Z.G.-2 : The fruit is medium in size and roundish in shape with smooth skin. The fruit pulp is soft with an excellent sugar-acid blend. When ripe the fruits attain light-yellow colour and TSS of 13.0 per cent. The average yield amounts to 150 kg fruit per tree and the ripening time extends from second fortnight of March to first week of April. This variety is recommended for growing for local markets only. It is less susceptible to powdery mildew.

Gola : This is an early variety and popularly grown in Haryana and Rajasthan. The fruits are round in shape, medium in size and attain golden yellow colour at maturity. The pulp is soft, taste sweet with TSS 16–20 per cent. The quality of fruit is excellent but cannot stand long transportation. The average yield is 80 kg fruit per tree.

Banarsi Karaka : Trees tall and vigorous. This is a very popular mid season variety of Banaras and Uttar Pradesh. Fruits globose, oblong to long in shape with tapering to pointed styler end. The average weight of fruit is 40–50 *g* and develops greenish yellow to yellow colour at maturity.

Dandan : The variety is grown commonly in Patiala district of Punjab and in Hansi and Jind areas of Haryana. The fruit has a pointed apex (beak) like tooth. The fruit is medium in size, oval in shape with round base, smooth surface and has an attractive golden yellow colour at maturity. The fruit has 92 per cent pulp, 11.2 per cent TSS, 0.24 per cent acidity 8.8 per cent total sugars and 109 mg/100 g vitamin C. The average yield is 94 kg fruit per tree. It is a mid-season variety, ripens during second fortnight of March. It is moderately susceptible to powdery mildew disease. The variety is suitable for diabetic patients.

Varietial Improvement

Selection of Darakhi – 1 and Darakhi–2 resistant to powdery mildew disease was made at Rahuri. Kakrola Gola and CAZRI Gola selections were made from cultivar Gola. Goma Kirti, a clone developed from cultivar Umran mature earlier than Umran. Thar Bhubharaj and Thar Sevika (Seb × Katha) are recently released varieties. Ber hybrid (Chinese × Sanaur-2) is free from attack of powdery mildew and the fruit colour is quite appealing due to light red tinge at the tip.

PLANTING AND AFTER CARE

Planting : The budded plants can be planted in February-March and again in August-September, but the latter season of planting gives a better success. The ber plants can also be transplanted bare-rooted (without earch ball) during December-January with equal success.

Before the plants are put in the field, the orchard site should be properly laid out according to the square system. One metre deep pits of one metre diameter should be dug and left exposed for one month before actual planting. Pits should be refilled with a mixture of top-soil, about 20 kg well-rotten farmyard manure and 1 kg superphosphate per pit. To avoid the attack of white ants 15 ml of chlorpyriphos 20 EC mixed in about 2 kg soil is added to each pit. The refilled pits should be about 2-3 cm higher than the ground level and irrigated thoroughly, so that the loose soil settles down firmly. A plant may be set in the centre of a pit with the help of planting board, maintaining the same level of soil at which it stood in the nursery. The budding point should remain about 15-20 cm high from the ground level. The plants should be immediately watered after plantation. They should be irrigated after every 4- 6 days atleast during the first two months and subsequently after every 7-10 days for another 3-4 months or until the plants get fully established.

The grafted ber is spreading in habit and grows into a big tree. The tree requires proper spacing for its healthy growth and fruiting. For obtaining good income, ber plants should be planted 7.5 metres apart in square system (from row to row and plant to plant) thus accommodating 180 trees per ha. However under rainfed and arid conditions ber plantation can be made at 6 × 6 m distance. Similarly, a closer spacing of 6m × 6m can be kept on semi-vigorous rootstock ***Z. mauritiana*** (Coimbatore) Umran trees grafted on this rootstock show a spread of 6 metre as compared to the recommended rootstock viz. ***Ziziphus mauritiana*** (Elongated Dehradun) on whom the tree spread to an area of 7.5 metre. Thus about 50% more plants/ha can be accommodated with over 20% increase in yield of equally good quality fruit.

In semi-arid regions of India, ber plants are spaced at 7 – 8 m × 7 – 8 m, 7.2 – 9.6 × 7.2 – 9.6 m and 11 – 12 m × 11 – 12 m.

Lifting plants from the nursery : The budded ber plants should be transplanted during February-March or August-September. The plants are dug out from the nursery with good-sized earth-balls so that their root-system is not much disturbed. The plants should be packed carefully to keep the earth-ball intact. The earth-ball should be kept moist throughout the period of transportation and upto plantation so that the roots of tree do not dry up in the intervening period.

While lifting bare-rooted plants, the leaves and shoots of the budded ber plants are removed before uprooting them from the nursery. These plants are also headed back at a height of 60-75 cm from ground level. Then, these plants are dug from the soil wih the help of spade and Khurpa to keep maximum feeding roots with them. These plants are tied loosly in bundles and are wrapped in moist rice straw. Such plants can easily be trained according to modified central leader system. The bare-rooted plant should be lifted from nursery from mid-December to early-February.

After-Care of young plants : The plants do not make much progress without proper care in the initial stages. The newly set plants should be given frequent but light irrigations. It is essential that all the shoots emerging from below the budding point of a plant should be regularly removed, so as to encourage scion growth. The plants should be properly staked to help them grow upright. The plants can be protected from the strong winds by making a mound of earth around the trees to give them support against the uprooting. They should be protected against the hot sun and excess water should be drained away. Insect-pests and diseases should be kept under check by suitable plant protection measures.

Planting as Windbreak : Besides regular ber plantations, the tree can also be successfully planted as a windbreak around the commercial orchards to provide an effective wind screen.The tall- growing trees like Eucalyptus, arjun and simbal should be interplanted with ber, being a low-headed tree.

ROOTSTOCKS AND PROPAGATION

Seeds of **Katha ber (*Ziziphus mauritiana*** Lamk.**)** are generally used for raising rootstock, which are easily available from the wild growing trees and possess the qualities of a good rootstock. The ber plants should be budded on ***Ziziphus mauritiana*** (Elongated Dehradun) for higher fruit yield. Ber plants raised on semi-vigorous rootstock ***Ziziphus mauritiana*** (Coimbatore) can profitably be planted at a closer spacing of 6 x 6 m.

Seeds of **Mallah ber (*Ziziphus nummularia*)** can also be used as rootstock. The seedlings of Mallah ber are slow growing and become buddable after longer period than the seedlings of **Katha ber.**

In Rajasthan, ber trees on Barodi **(*Z. mauritiana* var. *rotundifolia*)** produce vigorous growth and result in higher fruit yield. Budding on ***Z. nummularia*** results in an inverted bottleneck graft union as the rootstock remains thinner than the scion. ***Z. mauritiana*** Ecotype-291 and ***Z. mauritiana*** (Ecotype – Assam Gauhati with Banarsi Karaka, Ponda and Gola cvs. were compitible with perfect union. At IARI, the Jhar ber rootstock showed incompatibility with inverted bottleneck symptoms budded with 'Gola' cultivar.

At PAU, Umran on ***Z. joazeiro*** and ***Z. xylopyrus*** rootstocks produce greater diameter and resulted in inverted bottleneck union. The ber plants on ***Z. jujuba*** develop typical proliferation of cambium tissues at bud union.

Raising of Rootstock : The germination of ber seed is quite a difficult process on account of the stony nature of the shell (endocarp) which contains the seed. A large percentage of seed stones are non-viable and require elimination at the time of sowing. Seed stones collected from dropped fruits contain 50-70 percent non-viable seeds. Seeds should be dipped into a salt solution of 17-18 per cent concentration for 24 hours before sowing. The floating seeds should not be sown as these are generally non-viable. The ber seeds can also be sown by cracking the hard shell (endocarp). They germinate rapidly in about 8–10 days. However, for commercial purpose, stones should be sown as such to avoid injury to embryos. To get best rootstock material, it is important that seeds should be collected only from healthy and vigorous growing Katha ber trees.

The ber seedlings raised from **Katha** ber stones, which are sown during March-April, after fresh extraction, in well-prepared nursery field at a distance of 15 cm in rows 30 cm apart. Germination starts in about 3-4 weeks and seedlings make a rapid growth. The seedlings should be trained to the single stem. Nearly one-fourth of the seedlings attain buddable size of a lead pencil by August, while the rest are ready for budding by April next.

In sandy or sandy-loam soil, seed can be sown in the polythene bags in April and the seedlings can be transplanted in the field during July-August without disturbing the root-system. Budding **in situ** can be done on these seedlings during September or when they become buddable. The ber seeds can also be sown in the field (Sandy **TIBA** land) at desirable distances and budding is done **in situ,** but success is less as they need a lot of labour and irrigation during the dry and hot months. In another method of raising seedlings, the ber stones may be germinated in small containers and removed to one a pot at the four leaf stage after which they may be planted in the field in the beginning of rainy season.

Raising of seedlings in polythene bags and tubes : The ber seeds can also be sown in the polythene bags of 30 × 10 cm size in the month of April. Transplanting of very young seedlings at the two leaf stage gave field survival up to 82 per cent and subsequent bud take up to 72 per cent. The budded plants of ber can be raised in the polythene tubes (25 × 10 cm) of 300 gauge thickness. The seeds are sown in the polythene tubes filled with well prepared compost in the first fortnight of April. These tubes should be protected from direct exposure of sun. Three months old seedlings are budded in July and plants become ready for transplanting in August - September or next spring season.

Budding : The propagation of ber by budding is the most successful method. Both Shield or T-budding and ring-budding methods are employed but the former is preferable, because it is easier to perform. Budding operation should be done when there is proper flow of sap in the stock to be budded. The bud take efficiency in the 'Umran' was achieved highest (84.9%) in June. Shield-budding is done during March-April or August-September, but it has been found that August-September budding gives a far better success. The buddlings make growth at a very fast speed. Plants budded in April usually become saleable in August-September, where as those budded in rainy season are ready for planting by February-March next. The ring-budding is preferable during June-July when the new growth starts. Shield-budding done during August-September has given success of 75 to 81 per cent, whereas budding in April has given a little success.

Selection of Stock and Scion : The stock seedlings should be healthy and vigorous and it is allowed to grow as a single stem only. The budding is done when the stock stem has attained the thickness of a lead pencil.

It is essential that bud sticks are taken only from selected trees which are known for bearing a heavy fruit crop of good quality. The mother plant from which the scion bud-sticks are obtained for budding should be healthy, vigorous, free from diseases and insect-pests and should be true-to-type. Two to three months old shoots with plump buds should be selected. Bud-sticks, about 30 cm long, are cut from the selected mother plants. For sending to distant places, about 20 cm long bud- sticks should be taken. The leaves of the bud-sticks should be cut away, keeping the leaf stalks attached to the buds. These should be tied in small bundles and wrapped in moist piece of cloth. The bud-sticks should be kept moist till they are used for budding. The bud sticks can be kept for 2-3 days in good condition.

ORCHARD CULTURAL PRACTICES

Irrigation

To young ber plants (first 2 years) for initial establishment and better production, application of 8–11 irrigations per year on the basis of climatological approach irrigated at 100 and 75 mm cumulative pan evaporation (CPE) are recommended.

Irrigation is essential during the development of fruit, i.e. from October to February at intervals of 3 or 4 weeks depending upon the weather. Trees will continue to bear even if no irrigation is applied during this period but the yield is substantially reduced because of heavy fruit drops and smaller size of the remaining fruit. The quality of fruit is also very poor. It has been observed that the fruit become large and their quality is improved and the fruit shedding is very much minimised if irrigation is applied during fruit development period. Irrigation should be stopped in March as fruits on the branches lying on the ground get damaged and their ripening is delayed. The harvesting of fruit is over in April and they become dormant in May-June and shed their leaves. They need little or no irrigation during this period. If irrigation is applied during the dormant period, the trees would continue to put forth growth haphazardly which is not desirable. Under north Indian conditions there are sufficient rains during July to September when the tree produce the maximum fresh growth. During the second half of September and in October the trees come into flowering. At this time, light irrigation should be given. Heavy irrigation during this period should be avoided which leads to heavy flower drop.

Intercropping

The ber tree begins to bear after one year of its planting in the field. To develop the tree properly, it is advisable that no fruit should be taken at least for the first two-three years. Intercropping can be successfully practised on the vacant land in the young orchard during the first 3-4 years. Only leguminous crops of short stature like gram, moong and mash can be grown to get some income from the land in these initial years. These crops also enrich the soil by fixing nitrogen. The other exhaustive and tall-growing crops should not be grown in the ber orchard as they deplete the soil of its nutrients to a greater extent and compete for light with the trees.

Manures and fertilizers, irrigation and plant protection measures should be given separately to the fruit trees and intercrops according to their needs.

Cultivation

Generally, no cultivation is practised in the ber orchard. However, cultivation of orchard land can help to kill the weeds like **baru, kahi, motha,** etc. which propagate vegetatively through rhizomes/bulbs are indeed very difficult to eradicate. Cultivation with tractor or ploughing rather helps their further spread. The land infested with such obnoxious weeds should be dug up and all rhizomes/bulbs collected and burnt. Cultivation of orchard land, apart from checking weeds, is helpful in promoting aeration of the soil, in conserving soil moisture, in burying the green manures, in exposing grubs/pupae of various insects as well as in imparting a neat look to the orchard. However, only shallow cultivation should be carried out in the orchard land. It has been seen that deep cultivation especially near the root zones of the fruit trees may do serious harm by destroying fibrous roots, which are mostly in the upper soil.

One summer ploughing immediately after pruning exposes the harmful insect-pest and fungal organisms to the bright sun which checks their further growth. Another ploughing at the time of manuring and in September-October proves useful in checking the growth of weeds.

Weed Control

Among the various problems with which ber cultivation is confronted, one serious problem is of excessive weed growth. The sub-tropical climate of Punjab is very conducive for the rapid multiplication of weeds in the ber orchard. The traditional method of controlling weeds *i.e.* manual weeding is very expensive and time consuming. So the use of herbicides seems to be the efficient, convenient and more economical method of controlling weeds in berorchard.

Pre-emergence application of Hexuron 80 WP (diuron) at 3 kg/ha can be made during the first fortnight of August when field is free from growing weeds and stubbles. Glycel 41 SL (glyphosate) at 3 litres/ha or gramoxone 24 WSC (paraquat) at 3 litres/ha as post-emergence should be sprayed when the weeds are growing actively preferably before weeds flower and attain a height of 15-20 cm. Dissolve the herbicide in 500 litres of water per ha to give complete coverage of weeds/field. Spray Glycel and Gramoxone during the calm day to avoid spray drift to the foilage of the fruit trees.

Manuring and Fertilization

Studies on the removal of NPK in ber cv Umran reveals that a total of 142 to 191 *g* nitrogen, 57 to 87 *g* phosphorus and 467 to 684 *g* potassium was removed by a full grown tree during one growing season.

Proper nutrition of ber tree is necessary to get good crop over the years. The fruit becomes large and attractive and get decent price in the market. 20 kg farmyard manure and 100 g nitrogen (200 g urea) is recommended for one year old ber tree. Similar amount of farmyard manure and nitrogen should be increased every year up to the age of five years. The quantity of farmyard manure and nitrogen should be stabilized at 100 kg and 500 g (1 kg urea), respectively, after the age of five years. Farmyard manure should be supplied in May-June. Half of the urea may be applied during rainy season (July-August) and the other half at the time of fruit-set (October-November). The fertilizer should be evenly spread in the basins of trees upto the periphery. After adding the fertilizer, light hoeing with spade or khurpa should be given to the basins to mix it thoroughly with the soil.

The higher yield have been obtained in Umran by application of 400 *g* N, 100 *g* P and 200 *g* K per tree under Punjab conditions. Application of 1 kg N, 1 kg P and 150 *g* K per tree to full grown trees of Gola variety was suggested. For established orchard of Umran, Urea and superphosphate each @ 1250 per plant has been recommended under Haryana conditions. Half the quantity of urea is applied in July and second half during November. Superphosphate is applied in June – July to enhance the yield.

Leaf Sampling : In order to diagnose or confirm nutrient deficiency in ber and to determine nutrient status in ber leaves, leaf sample should be taken. Five to seven months old 70 leaves from middle of shoot during November to January should be collected. Collect 4 – 8 leaves per tree from each direction at working height (1 – 2 m), removing one leaf per shoot. Cover 10 to 12 per cent trees from the block for properly diagonising the nutrient status. Collect leaf samples in polythene bags, keep the bags in ice-box and immidiately send to leaf Analysis Laboratory.

TRAINING AND PRUNING

Training : The ber plant start bearing within 2-3 year of their planting in the orchard. In the fourth year, the trees bear commercial crop. Hence, the ber plants should be properly trained during the first 2-3 years, to build up a strong framework. The young budlings should be given support with a bamboo stake to avoid the breakage of the bud-union and to support the main stem. The commercial varieties are spreading in nature, therefore, staking is absolutely essential during the first two years to train the tree properly. The plant will make vigorous growth during the first year. Many secondary branches will emerge from the main stem. The ber trees are trained according to modified leader system. All the branches upto 75 cm from the ground level should be removed. Four or five laterals which are most favourably located around the main stem should be selected to make the proper framework. At the end of the year, the main stem should be headed back to some outgrowing laterals.

Pruning : The pruning of ber trees is highly desirable to maintain their vigour and productivity as well as to improve fruit size and quality. Pruning also saves the fruit from being affected by the powdery mildew disease and strong winds. The ber tree remains young upto 30 years, if proper pruning is done regularly. Ber fruit is borne in the axils of leaves on the young growing shoots of the current year. Hence, a regular annual pruning is essential to induce a good and healthy growth which will provide a maximum fruit bearing area on the tree as well as to improve fruit size and quality. In unpruned ber tree, the canopies of the trees get un-necessarily enlarged, the growth and branchlets become weak and both fruit size and quality gets impaired. Ultimately, such trees become economically unproductive besides occupying large orchard space. Some thinning out of the branches of ber trees is also necessary to avoid too much crowding so as to admit adequate sunlight and facilitate proper aeration. Ber pruning experiments have shown that light pruning, i.e. heading back of 25 per cent of the previous year's growth (branchlets, shoots, etc) is desirable to obtain heavy yield, good fruit size and better quality. The lower branches should be pruned suitably to prevent them from spreading on the ground. The diseased, broken and intercrossing branches should also be thinned out. Severe pruning after every four-five years, is recommended.

The ber trees shed their leaves and enter into dormancy during summer months. The best time for taking up pruning would, therefore, be be the second fortnight of May.

Pruning of Sanaur-2 cultivar should be done during the third week of April when the trees are dormant. Pruning by heading back at 8 buds length of previous year's growth gives higher yield of better quality fruits. The cv. 'Umran' pruned on 9 May by retaining 6 buds yielded superior quality fruits. It has been observed that the selective pruning of late flowering branches (21 October to 5 November) has slightly improved fruit size, weight and palatability rating in Umran cultivar of ber.

Top working : Inferior ber trees growing on neglected lands and along the borders of the fields yield crops of small and inferior fruits, and do not fetch any income. Such uneconomic and inferior trees can be made to yield good income, if top-worked by budding with improved varieties The method of top-working wild ber trees is quite simple and can be practised by the growers themselves. The wild ber trees are headed back during April-May (to a height of about 1 metre) when they are in the dormant stage. After heading back, Bordeaux paste should be applied to the cut end of thick branches. The headed-back trees produce a number of healthy shoots from below the cut-ends during June- July. Of these, two strongest shoots should be retained and the other removed. The selected shoots of 2-3 cm diameter should be T-budded in July-August with the buds from the desired variety. The portion of the shoots above the point of insertion of a bud is cut off entirely soon after the buds begins to sprout. The successfully top-worked trees develop sufficient head growth within a year to bear a small crop of fruit. In the subsequent years, they start bearing normal drops.

REJUVENATION OF OLD TREES

The ber trees if not pruned properly every year, start giving diminished yields and small fruits after bearing normal crops for a few years. In unpruned trees, the old wood goes on accumulating every year. Such trees become unproductive with weak growth and may get easily infected with diseases like powdery mildew and insect-pests like fruit-fly, lac insects and termites. The fruit size is reduced and the fruits become mis-chapen, curved, corky and fall prematurely. Such old trees can be revived and rejuvenated by severe pruning in May. The operation will consist of drastic heading back of branches, to the extent of 50-75 per cent as well as removal of diseased, broken, intercrossing and lac-infested branches entirely. The trees should be sprayed with Captan (0.2%) after pruning. With the onset of rains in July, a heavy dose of nitrogenous fertilizer (about 1 kg of actual nitrogen) should be applied to a 12-15 year old tree. The trees should also be sprayed twice with 0.05 per cent Karathane or Bayleton 25 WP before flowering in August-September. The fruit yeild would be produced by 30-50 per cent during the first year depending upon the severity of pruning, but the trees would again start giving full yields and normal fruits of superior quality during the later years.

Ber trees need to be rejuvenated after the age of about 25 years. Head back the main limbs to about 30 cm during second fortnight of May. The average height of main stem should be about one metre from ground level and each tree have 4 or 5 main limbs. During the rainy season, number of shoots emerged from the stub. Thin out 12–18 shoots per tree in the fourth week of August. The second thinning of shoots should be done during second fortnight of September (before flowering) to retain 8–12 branches per tree. Trees bore 2–20 kg fruit per tree during first year and about one quintal fruits during second year. Tree starts giving commercial crop with higher yield of excellent fruit quality during the third fruiting season.

PROBLEM OF FRUIT DROP

The problem of heavy fruit drop in ber is of great concern to the ber growers. Premature fruit drop of about 50 per cent produce is the major problem in 'Umran' cultivar which adversely affect the yield and profit of the growers. It is estimated that only 20 – 30 percent fruits attained marketable size of 25 – 30 g per fruit. The ber crop produced only 8 – 9 per cent fruits which could reach full maturity. The different types of fruit drop occurred in ber are as follow :

1. Physiological fruit drop. It might be attributed to two main reasons. Firstly, it may occur due to abortion of embryo. During the early stage, the drop in mainly due to shriveling of fruits which occurred up to December. Out of the total dropped fruits 30 per cent has aborted embryo. Secondly, a pre-mature fruit drop may occur due to premature formation of an abscission layer in the stalk of ripe or nearly ripe fruit. This abscission has been reported to occur as a reault of natural exhaustion of growth regulators present in the fruit or when they cease to flow from their production centre because of some disorders in the tree or climatic conditions. The maximum fruit drop was recorded from first week of November to end January which account for 60 per cent of the total fruit set. During this period, the mean temperature decline from 19°C to 10.6°C in January and RH increased from 65 per cent in November to 81 per cent in February. From first week of February to mid-March, the per cent drop decreased and only 17.7 per cent fruits dropped.

The ber fruit 'Umran' require 24-26 weeks (180 days) from the time of setting to reach the stage of maturity. The growth is most active during the first six and last twelve weeks but is slow during the middle six weeks. The synthesis of auxin and gibberellin decreased during the slow growth period due to formation of inhibitors. The deficiency of promotors leads to the formation of abscission layer and cause heavy drop during slow period of fruit growth. Auxins inhibits abscission of fruits by preventing physiological break down of calcium pectate of middle lamella. Spray application of 20 – 30 ppm NAA once in the second fort night of October and again in the second fortnight of November check 10 per cent fruit drop in Umran ber.

2. Drop due to climatic factors. Some times severe cold occurs in the month of December which persists for longtime and continues even up to end January. This condition further deepens when cold waves blow. This leads to heavy leaf fall and fruit drop. Heavy reduction in leaves and leading to sparse foliage results into poor photosynthetic activity in plants. The leaves fails to provide the required amount of food substance, thus, fruits stops in growth, shrivelled and falls.

To avoid such condtions, apply light irrigation to the ber orchards as and when there is chances of occurrence of frost/cold. Heaps of dried leaves should be allowed to burn slowly to provide a thick smoke screen over the field, which helps in raising the atmospheric temperature. This can save to some extent the heavy drop that occurs during December – January.

3. Drop due to white ant attack. White ant is a major problem in ber orchards. It attack the root system, on the main trunk and main limbs. This block the smooth flow of sap in xylem and phloem. Ultimately there is reduction in supply of available carbohydrates to the fruits and results into fruit drop. Apply chlorpyriphos to tree basin @ 1 ml in litre of water once in April again after rainy season in September. Prepare thick solution of chlorpyriphos (100 ml in 1 litre of water and apply this solution with the help of brush in the form of paint to the trunk and main limbs after scrapping the affected portion.

4. Pathological fruit drop. Due to attack of fungus (powdery mildew) white powdery mass deposits on fruits and underside of the leaves. The fruits become cankered, corked, disfigured and de-shapened. Such fruits drop heavily before reaching maturity. Spray the affected plants with 0.05% Karathane or Bayleton at flowering, mid-October, mid-November and mid-December to check the disease and subsequently fruit drop.

HARVESTING AND FRUIT HANDLING

Harvesting : The ber tree grows quickly and the first crop can be harvested within 2-3 years of planting. The fruit itself requires about 22-26 weeks to mature after fruit-setting. The peak season for harvesting in north India is in mid-March to mid-April but some early varieties may ripen by end-February. This period being a slack season for other kinds of fruits, ber sells readily at remunerative prices. In South India, the fruits are ready for harvest in October to November. The harvesting season of ber in Gujarat is December to March and in Rajasthan it is January to March.

Ber is a late peak type climacteric fruit. The fruit should always be picked at the right stage of maturity, i.e. when it is neither under-ripe nor over-ripe. It should be picked when it has acquired normal size and characteristic colour of the variety, e.g. golden yellow colour in Umran. The specific gravity of Umran fruits at maturity should be less than one. Normally four to five pickings have to be made as all the fruits on the tree do not ripen at the same time. In no case, the fruits should be allowed to become over-ripe on the trees, as they deteriorate in taste and quality and thus fetch lower price in the market.

Ripening : Umran a commercial cultivar of ber in north India ripens late. The optimum harvesting time of this cultivar is around first week of April in south-western districts of Punjab. The technique to induce early and uniform ripening permit staggering the harvest which avoid the bothersome operation of picking in 4-5 lots. Ethephon at 400 ppm at colour break stage (250 ml in 300 litres of water in first week of March) advance ripening by two weeks in Umran and produce attractive, uniform, better quality and deep golden yellow with chocolate tinge coloured fruit.

Ber fruits harvested at early maturity on 15 March ripen unevely. Ethephon (2000–3000 ppm) and hot water dip regardless the stage of maturity enhance ripening percentage and develops the best colour of fruits after ripening. Delaying the picking of fruits to later maturity stages results in higher TSS, vitamin C, total sugars and PME activity and low acidity and total phenolics. Ber fruits should be picked upto 29 March for distant markets and between April 5–12 for local markets.

Marketing : Ber trees are regular and heavy bearers and the mature trees of different grafted varieties can bear 100 to 200 kg of fruit per tree. It is relatively easy and inexpensive to grow a ber orchard. Yet the returns from it can exceed the profits from the cultivation of several other fruits. The grower can get an income of about Rs. one lakh to Rs. two lakh per hectare or even more by growing selected varieties and using latest techniques.

Grading and Packaging : The grading should be regularly practised before the fruit is marketed so that they sell at a premium. The ber fruits should be graded into four grades namely, A grade – large sized; B grade – medium sized; C grade – small sized and D grade – under ripe, over ripe, deformed, misshapened and cankered fruits. Highest distribution of fruits is found in B grade (33%), which is closely followed by grade A (27%). The extent of C and D grade fruits is 21% and 19%, respectively. The fruits of Umran belonging to A and B grades which accounted for 60% of the total crop have deep golden yellow colour are more acceptable to the consumers and considered the best for marketing.

The ber fruits should be packed properly in CFB cartons, wooden crates, baskets, polynets and gunny bags of convenient size on the basis of grades. The fruits should be sent immediately to market after packing those properly.

Packing of ber fruits in hard board corrugated cartons of 8 kg (40 × 25 × 20 cm size) with 6 holes of one cm diameter on two sides and paper shavings as cushion retained good quality for 9 – 12 days. Packing in bambo baskets using dry grass as a cushioning material could be useful for local or a short distance transport. Gunny bags could be useful for packaging of poor quality produce. Packing of ber in polynets of one kg capacity and perforated polyethylene bags of varying sizes could be used for local sale of fruits (consumer packs). CFB cartons of 4 and 8 kg capacity are preferred for packing of ber fruits. Gunny bags of 16 to 40 kg sizes are used for long distance transportation of ber fruits.

Shelf life : The ripe fruits of Umran ber could be stored for about three weeks in the home refrigerator (0–4°C) in perforated polythene bags. The storage life of fruits can be extended upto 10 days in Umran and 12 days in Sanaur-2 by storing them in perforated polythene bags at room temperature after treating with 6 per cent wax-emulsion. The shelf life of fruits can be enhanced up to 30 days in Umran and 40 days in Sanaur-2 by storing them in perforated polythene bags of 100 gauge thickness in the commercial cold storage (0–3.3°C and RH 85-90%) after treating with 6 per cent wax-emulsion.

The colour deveopment of ber fruits proceeds slowly when packed in HDPE bags and CFB cartons and retain its original colour up to 20 days in cold storage (0–3.3°C temp. and 85–90% RH). The fruits in paper bags develops browning after 30 days of cold storage. The palatability rating of fruits in CFB cartons and HDPE bags remain excellent upto 20 days of cold storage with better consumer's acceptance. The shelf life of ber fruits cv. Umran can be extended upto 20 days after treating with GA_3 25 ppm, packing in CFB cartons and storing in commercial cold store (temp 0-3.3°C and RH 85-90%).

The ber fruits remain in good condition in preforated polythene bags for one week at ambient temperature. The fruits of Umran harvested at colour break stage can be stored at 7.5 ± 1°C and 90 – 95% RH for two weeks with acceptable colour and quality.

Pre-harvest spray of TIBA 25 – 50 ppm and SADH 2000 ppm showed higher and morphactin 10 – 25 pm and ethephon 300 – 400 ppm registered lower pectin methylesterase (PME) activity in paper bags after 40 days of cold storage.

PLANT PROTECTION MEASURES

The leaves and fruits of ber are attacked by several kinds of insect-pests and diseases. The affected fruits become small, disfigured, fall prematurely and become inedible. The suitable plant protection measures should be adopted to get yields of healthy and normal fruits of superior quality.

INSECT-PESTS

Fruit-fly (*Carpomyia vesuviana* Costa) : It causes great damage to ber fruits. Fruitfly deposits eggs in the epicarp of developing fruits. After hatching, the larvae enter into pulp and start freeding. The infested fruits become deformed, turn brown, rot and drop off. Fully grown maggots emerge out of the fruit by making a hole and pupate in the soil. To control the pest, pick and destroy the infested fruits. To escape egg laying on fruits, harvest at green and firm stage and do not allow the fruit to ripe on the tree. Rack the soil around the tree during summer to expose the pupae to heat and natural enemies. Spray 500 ml of Rogor 30 EC (Dimethoate) in 300 litres of water during February-March, care being taken that sprayings are stopped atleast 15 days before fruit harvest.

Leaf-eating caterpillar (*Euproctis spp.*)and **ber beetle (*Adoretus pallens* Arrow) :** The plantation should be watched carefully during rainy season regarding the attack of these insect-pests. The young caterpillars initially remain gregarious and scrap leaves and tender fruits. Later, instars disperse and devour leaves, fruits and tender shoots. The affected fruits become unmarketable. To control these, spray with 750 g Hexavin 50 WP (Carbaryl) in 250 litres of water as soon as the damage is noticed. At early and smaller scale, pluck the leaves with egg masses and young caterpillars and destroy.

Lac insect (*Kerria lacca*) : This insect also causes serious damage by sucking the sap from the twigs which usually dry up. Their presence on ber trees is considered as harmful because they devitalize the trees and affect adversely the yield of fruits. To control this insect, remove and destroy the infested dry twigs. Spray the trees with 250 ml of Rogor 30 EC (Dimethoate) in 250 litres of water in April and again in September.

DISEASES

Powdery mildew: The disease is caused by ***Oidium erysiphoides*** f.sp. ***Ziziphi*** and appears from September to December. It has become a big menace to ber orchards in north India. If not checked in time, the disease can wipe out the entire crop. Young developing leaves and fruits are covered with whitish powdery mass of the causal fungus. The disease causes premature defoliation and heavy fruit-drop. Affected fruits remain small and become cankered and disfigured. Sometimes the attack is so severe that the entire crop is lost either through drop or rendered unmarketable, thus causing heavy economic losses to the growers. The disease can be controlled by 3-4 sprays of 0.05 per cent Karathane 40 EC (50 ml in 100 litres of water) or 0.25 per cent wettable sulphur (250 g in 100 litres of water) or 0.05% Bayleton 25 WP (50 *g* in 100 litres of water). First spray must be given at flowering (September). second spray after fruit-set in mid October, third in mid November and fourth to mid December. Another spray in January can be given if need arises.

Leaf spots : Two leaf spots of ber are very common in ber growing regions i.e. 'Phoma Leaf Spot' caused by ***Phoma macrostoma*** Mont. and 'Black Mould of Leaf' caused by ***Isariopsis indica.*** Both diseases are caused by different fungi, while the Phoma leaf spot appears on the upper surface, the black mould make its appearance only on the lower surface of leaves. In case of Phoma leaf spot symptoms appear when the leaves have fully expanded, in the Black mould case the symptoms can appear even on young leaves. Phoma leaf spot appears with grey centre, yellow margin and dark fungal growth on the mid-rib, main vein, petioles and the leaves. Black mould spot appears as small circular, small finger-like projections like softy tufts. Both the leaf spots of ber can be controlled by spraying the following fungicides as given below:

First spray : Bordeaux mixture 2 : 2 : 250 or with 0.3% copper oxychloride 50% (300 g in 100 litres of water) should be sprayed both on upper and lower surface of leaves with the appearance of disease in August or when the leaves have expanded.

Second spray : This spray should be given after 14 days of the first spray with 0.2 per cent Dithane M-45 WP 75% (200 g per 100 litres of water) both on upper and lower surface of leaves.

First and second spray should be repeated alternatively at 14 days interval till the fruits are fit for marketing. Thereafter sprayings are stopped a week before harvesting.

Black fruit spot : The disease is caused by ***Alternaria alternata***. Disease produces small, irregular, sunken, black spots on fruits. Sometimes, ***Phoma macrostoma*** is also associated with the disease at later stages. The infected fruits become disfigured and may drop off before harvest. The disease starts its appearance during January and is very severe during February – March.

The disease can be controlled by spraying 0.25% Mancozeb 75 WP (250 g in 100 litres of water) in end of January and mid-February.

PHYSIOLOGICAL DISORDER

Fruit Cracking

Fruit cracking in ber can be caused due to high temperature rise in March, irregular irrigation interval, imbalance in endogenous level of growth regulators and varietal characters. Higher level of gibberellic acid and abscisic acid in the skin and stone leads to fruit cracking. The cultivar Umran has less cracking problem due to hard skin and texture of fruit. ZG-2, Sanaur-2, Gola and Kaithli are prone to splitting due to soft skin and high TSS at maturity.

It has been reported that uptake of water and solutes is mostly governed by presence of certain chemicals. The enhanced water uptake causes accumulation of solutes within the fruit with consequent rupturing of fruit skin. Irrigation at proper interval will help in regulating water uptake and solutes. Spray of NAA @ 20-30 ppm at pit hardening stage once in second fortnight of October and again during second fortnight of November increase the promotor level and thus reduce the cracking of fruit skin.

CHAPTER 19

Loquat

The loquat (***Eriobotrya japonica*** Lindl.) can be grown successfully in sub-tropical regions. Nevertheless, this fruit merits more attention as it ripens in April- May in north–India at a time when there is hardly any other fruit available in the market thus commands price in the market.

ORIGIN AND HISTORY

Loquat originated in middle western China. It has long been cultivated in Japan. Several important loquat varieties have originated in these two countries. Meyer mentioned that the loquat is in all probability indigenous to the hills of the mild wintered, moist regions of central-Eastern China. Specimens were observed growing wild among the scrub in the region near Tangsi, Chekiang province.

The loquat has been cultivated in Japan for more than a thousand year and grows in almost every district except the extreme north- eastern part. Large loquat groves flourish and fruit abundantly in South and South Eastern Japan. The loquat was brought to Europe by the French in 1784 and planted in the National Garden at Paris. It was first imported to England from Canton and placed in the Royal Botanical Garden at Kew under the auspices of Sir Joseph Banks in 1887. The loquat fruit is also commercially grown in Australia. The tree is common in Italy and Sicily and good varieties have been developed there. The loquat has for many years been a familiar fruit in the orchards and gardens of Hawaii. In Chile, the loquat has been grown since the clonial days. The loquat was introduced into St. Michael Island in about 1823. The exact date of its introduction into the USA is not known. It was probably grown in Florida earlier than in California. The loquat came to California directly from Japan. The loquat tree finds a congenial home in Gulf States and large trees are found in Louisiana, Mississippi, Georgia, Alabama, Florida and North Carolina.

AREA AND PRODUCTION

Loquat is mainly cultivated in China, Japan, Pakistan, India, Madagascar, Mauritius Island, Turkey, Spain, Italy, Greece, Israel, UAE, Venezuela, Brazil and Australia. China with more than 80 per cent of the world production is the main producing country. It is followed by Spain, Turkey, Japan and Pakistan.

The commercial cultivation in India is mostly confined to Uttarakhand, Uttar Pradesh, Delhi, Punjab and Himachal Pradesh. It is also cultivated to small extent in Assam, Maharashtra and Nandi hills of Tamil Nadu and Mysore. Dehradun, Saharanpur, Muzzafarpur, Meerut and Farrukabad are known for loquat growing.

In Punjab, one come across a few old and new loquat orchards here and there, mainly in Gurdaspur, Hoshiarpur, Ropar, Amritsar, Patiala and Jalandhar Districts. The area under this fruit has, however, remained more or less static, mainly on account of the reason that not much research work has been done on various aspects of its cultivation and there is no regular selection and standardization of varieties.

IMPORTANCE AND USES

The loquat is very delicious and refreshing in taste. The fruit consists of 60-70 per cent pulp and 15-20 per cent seed. The edible part of fruit contains 88.2 per cent moisture, 0.6 per cent protein, 0.3 per cent fat, 9.6 per cent carbohydrates, 0.03 per cent calcium and phosphorus, 1.3 mg iron/100 g fruit, 0.5 per cent mineral, 0.9 per cent fibre and 559 I.U. vitamin A, respectively.

The fruit is generally used for dessert purposes as well as for jelly, jam and preserves, juice, squash, canning and chutney. A large proportion of the loquat crop is sold for fresh consumption. The loquat fruit has a tough plum like skin and a firm flesh, nearly melting in some varieties; ranging in colour from almost white to deep orange. The fruit has a mild, acid–sweet flavour, enriched in some varieties by a apple – like ester.

The fruit is considered to be a sedative and is used in allaying vomiting and thirst. The flowers are used as expectorant. An infusion of the leaves is given in diarrhoea. The tender branches are used as a fodder. The wood is hard and close-grained and may be a substitute for pear wood for ruler and drawing materials.

BOTANY

The loquat ***Eriobotrya japonica*** Lindl.) belongs to the family Rosaceae and subfamily Pomoideae. It is a true pome fruit. The word **Eriobotrya** is derived from the two Greek words **erion** (wool) and **botrys** (a cluster) is implied to wooly inflorescence.

The tree is symmetrical, evergreen, attains a height of about 7 m and has a hairy dense crown. The trunk is short, usually branching 60-90 cm from the ground to form a crown, round or oval in form and is normally compact and dense. The leaves are somewhat crowded towards the end of the stout wooly branchlets. They are large, alternate, subsessile, stiff, coriacious, elliptic, lanceolate to obovate, lanceolate in outline, 21-32 cm in length with remotely toothed to sharply dentate margins, dark glossy green on the upper surface and rusty tomentose beneath. The base is obtuse or narrowed into a very short, stout, wooly, stipulate petiole. Nerves varying from 12 to 15 and very prominent beneath the surface. The small branches are also covered with a rusty tomentum.

The fragrant white flowers are 1-2 cm broad and are borne in terminal wooly panicles, 10-20 cm long. The calyx is composed of 5 small imbricate, acute teeth, the carolla has 5 oblong-ovate clawed petals, white in colour and delicate in texture, the stamens are 20. There are 5 pistils joined towards the base. The fruits, borne in clusters are commonly round, oval or pyriform, 2.5-8.0 cm in length, pale, yellow to orange in colour and somewhat downy on the surface. Fruits small sized, 4 cm lengthwise. Fruit skin thick but slightly tougher. The flesh is firm and meaty in some varieties, melting in others. Flesh colour ranging from almost white to deep orange, juicy and with sub acid flavour. The seeds are as many as 10, since there are 5 cells in the ovary and 2 ovules in each cell. Several ovules are aborted and not more than 3 to 5 seeds develop. The seeds are large, smooth and brown, ovat, flat on the sides when more than one seed is in the same fruit. Seed 2 cm long. Sometimes only one seed is found in the fruit. Loquat is a pome fruit and its edible portion is fleshy thalamus.

CLIMATE

The loquat has long been naturalized in India. It is grown nearly throughout the country upto an elevation of 1525 m above sea level. It can be grown throughout the tropics wherever there are elevations of a few thousand feet. The loquat succeeds well under subtropical climate. It can grow successfully to regions in which the temperature does not fall below the freezing point. In general, a mild climate with an average annual rainfall of 60-100 mm, well distributed throughout the year, is ideal for loquat cultivation. Since the tree bloom between November and late January at certain places, the crop may be destroyed by moderate winter frosts. The plants especially foliage are heavily injured when the temperature falls to 0°C and remains so for any length of time. The fruit of loquat is most susceptible to frost injury when it just starts colouration. Heavy damage is noticed in early ripening varieties.

In the areas where scorching hot winds begin to blow before the fruit ripens, the fruit either remain too small or do not properly ripen. Under such conditions, the pulp does not produce abundant required quantity of juice. Further, the fruit become sunburnt and remained unfit for marketing. Under cool and foggy weather at the time of ripening, the fruits lack in sweetness and flavour.

The loquat trees are, however, resistant to heat and drought. The thick, leathery leaves are well adapted to withstand seasons of neglect without serious injury.

Although an evergreen fruit, loquat is unique in tolerating cold weather conditions. However, warm and dry climate is essential at the time of fruit ripening. In arid and dry zones, the fruits are prone to sun burn injury. Consequently, loquat should be cultivated only in the submontane or other areas with mid climate or places free from severe hot weather condition.

SOIL

The loquat can thrive in a wide variety of soils. In some places seems to do best on a light sandy loam; whereas at other places it has faired well on heavier soils. Good drainage is, however, essential and the subsoil should be free from hard pan. Stagnation of water in the land, even for a short time may damage or kill even grown up trees and such soils should be discarded. According to the opinion of an expert from Israel, heavy soil of medium type should be preferred than a very light soil.

CHOICE OF VARIETIES

No systematic attempt has so far been made for the selection or improvement work of varieties. However, there are generally two types of varieties having small or large size fruits. Depending upon colour of rind, the varieties may be called 'Surkha' or 'Sufeda'. The small-fruited varieties are usually sweeter than the large fruited ones but the latter get premium price due to their larger size and attractive appearance. The shape of the fruits also varies from round to oval and various shape in between or some may be egg-shaped.

Most of the loquat plantation in India are of seedling type. The following are the important varieties of loquat.

Golden Yellow : It has medium sized, egg-shaped fruits with attractive golden yellow colour. Flesh is yellowish which tastes sour-sweet. Each fruit contain 4-5 dark brown, medium sized seeds. Ripens during third week of March.

Pale Yellow : It has large fruits, which are slightly conical to roundish in shape and pale yellow in colour. Flesh is white and tastes sour-sweet. Each fruit contains 2 or 3 medium-sized seeds. Ripens during second week of April. Loquit is a pune fruit and its edible portion is fleshy thalamus.

California Advance : Fruit medium-sized, conical to round in shape, external colour yellow. Flesh creamy white, sour-sweet in taste. Fruit contains 2 or 3 medium-sized seeds. Ripens during fourth week of April.

Tanaka : Fruit medium, 4-5 cm long, 3-7 cm broad, ovate in shape, smooth and moderately pubescent. Rind medium, firm. Pulp medium completely filled, sayal brown, coarse, firm, juiceness abundant, taste pleasant, subacid. Seeds 2 to 4 per fruit, medium in size.

Loquat Selection : Trees tall. Fruit medium in size, oval in shape, weighing 37g and attain orange colour at maturity. Pulp percentage 53, pulp seed ratio 1.95. Each fruit contain 4 – 5 seeds. The average yield is 20 kg fruit per tree. Ripens during fourth week of March.

Pathankot : Trees medium in height. Fruits medium to large in size, ovate in shape, weighing 40 g and attain orange colour at maturity. Pulp 61 per cent, pulp seed ratio is 2.9. Each fruit contain 3 seed. The average yield is 25 kg fruit per tree. Ripens during third week of March.

Improved Golden Yellow : Fruits are golden yellow in colour, pyriform in shape. The fruit flesh is orange coloured, crisp and sub-acid. Each fruit contain 3 – 5 seeds. Ripens in end of March.

PROPAGATION AND ROOTSTOCKS

The loquat is rather difficult to propagate. The seeds grow readily but seedlings trees often bear fruits of variable and inferior quality. Thus, vegetative propagation is very important to raise the good quality true-to-type plants for commercial orcharding. Air-layering is possible but the success is low. The usual technique followed by nurserymen is to raise the plants through inarching which is time-consuming and cumbersome. Thus, there is need to standardize better and quick methods for loquat propagation. Improvement in this fruit is needed by a) carrying out extensive survey of loquat orchards for spotting out and selecting some meritorious trees and b) by importing promising loquat cultivars from foreign countries, particularly from China and Japan, from where this fruit actually originated.

Raising of Rootstock : The loquat seeds germinate readily when it is sown immediately after extraction from the fruit. The seed should not be allowed to dry after extraction as exposure to heat and light tends to results in poor germination and stunted seedling growth. Fresh seed are sown during April-May in moist sand for germination. When the seedlings are 4-5 cm tall, they are transplanted in the nursery under the mother trees for inarching. If the mother plants are high headed, the seedlings are transplanted in the pots and brought in contact with the mother plants by raising platforms when they attain incharchable size. The seedlings grow rapidly and are fit for grafting in the following rainy season.

Promising loquat varieties are generally grafted upon domestic loquat seedlings of the commercial varieties. Several other rootstocks such as pear, apple, quince ***(Cydonia oblonga)*** and **Mespilus** have also been used in certain occasions.

Propagation Techniques: The usual technique followed is to raise the plants through inarching. The best time for inarching is July-August. Air-layering can also be tried but success is much less.In air-layering 3 months old shoots are used. The use of 3 per cent indole butyric acid enhances the success in air- layering.

PLANTING OPERATION

There are two planting seasons for loquat plants viz. February- March and August-September. The plants should preferably be planted during August-September when the weather has cooled down sufficiently. In general, loquat is planted at a distance of 6.5 m × 6.5 m in square system, thus accomodates 225 plants per hectare.

The pit should be made 1 × 1 × 1 m. While mixing add 3-4 baskets of farmyard manure and 200 g of single superphosphate per pit. Add 15 ml of chlorpyriphos 20 EC mixed in about 2 kg soil to ward the attack of white ants.

FLOWERING AND FRUITING

In India, the flowering period of loquat is very long, lasting from mid July to January or sometimes even up to May. Three reproductive flushes under tropical conditions are noted, out of which the intermediate ones give the higher yield of better-sized fruits. At Saharanpur only one flush continued flower from september to February. The number of inflorescence was higher in beginning but only a few of them bore fruits. The number of inflorescence continued to decrease with the advancement of season, but the percentage of fruit-bearing panicles gradually decreased. The fruit size seemed to be inversely proportional to the number of fruits per panicle. Earlier panicles gave best-sized fruit and size reduced afterward.

In northern India only one continuous reproductive flush appears. No peak hour of anthesis was observed. The opening of flowers continued throughout the day. The dehiscence of anthers took place in longitudinal fashion. It took more than a day to complete dehiscence in all the varieties except Improved 'Golden Yellow' and Pale Yellow' in which case it was completed only in one day. The time of dehiscence was found to have hastened with the increase in temperature.

In Punjab, the flowering period in loquat is very lengthy. The flowering starts sometimes in the first week of October and continues upto third week of December. The number of flowers per cluster may very from 50 to 100 but in general, not more than 15- 20 fruits per cluster are set. Some of the varieties are good pollinizers for others.

Loquat trees grow singly or in small groves, though produce perfect flowers, yield negligible or no crop. This is reported to be due to self-incompatibility in commercial loquat varieties.

After fertilization, the loquat fruit develops very rapidly. The first indiction of fruit enlargement is a thickening of the toral rim immediately above the carpel level. The whole toral region undergoes cell division and enlargement is more of less uniform throughout. The sepals grow towards the centre and cover over in 'hood' fashion, the distal portions of the carpels. The sepal bases thicken and persist as permanent structures, whereas the petals, stamens and styles dry up. The hood or cap enclosing the distal portions of the carpels may be excised from immature fruits and the 5 carpels are exposed to view. The functional ovule develops into a fertile seed (occupy central region) and the confines of the individual carpal walls, surrounding non-functional ovules are wholly disrupted. By the time, the fruit is mature, the carpal wall are more or less parchment-like. The seed is extremely hard. The skin of the mature fruit is comparatively tough and leathery.

The edible portion in loquat is entirely toral in nature, consisting of pith and cortical areas. The development of edible portion consists of rather uniform growth of receptacle tissue throughout the fruit . The toral cells of mature fruit are large, thin walled and very juicy.

ORCHARD CULTURAL PRACTICES

Irrigation

The loquat is more tolerant to drought. However, the best results are obtained when the orchard is irrigated judiciously. There must be sufficient moisture in the soil in order to enable the shoots to develop and the mature terminal buds to fill out properly. As the trees blossom early, the orchard must be irrigated just before the swelling of blossom buds. During fruit growth to maturity (November to March) three to four irrigations are generally advisable.

During winter and rainy season, no irrigation is applied to loquat trees. After the withdrawl of monsoon, young orchards should be irrigated at weekly interval/fortnightly intervals from September onwards. To the bearing orchards, irrigation should be applied at the end of November or first week of December to protect from frost injury.

Interculture

Thorough cultivation of loquat field should be given to check the weed growth. It prefer clean cultivation management practice. Mulching with brown, black, or transparent polythene film from November to June in loquat orchard was found effective.

The cultivation of leguminous cover crops is, however, considered beneficial. Winter cover crops may be planted before September, the purpose is that their sufficient growth to be turned under before the harvesting starts. The leguminous crops like gram, peas, mash etc. should be preferred as intercrops.

Manuring and Fertilization

It is generally recognized that loquat tends to exhaust the soil and that for good regular cropping it needs adequate nutrition. Given below is a broad nutritional schedule recommended for loquat.

Age of tree (years)	Farmyard manure (kg/tree)	Urea (46% N)	Superphosphate (16% P_2O_5) (kg per tree)	Muriate of potash (60% K_2O)
1-3	10-20	0.15-0.5	0.2-0.5	0.15-0.4
4-6	25-40	0.6-0.75	0.6-1.2	0.6-1.0
7-10	40-50	0.8-1.0	1.5-2.0	1.1-1.5
10 & above	60	1.0	2.0	1.5

The farmyard manure should be applied in September alongwith entire quantities of phosphorus and potash. However, one-half dose of nitrogenous fertilizer should be applied in October before flowering and remaining half in February-March *i.e.* after the fruit-set.

TRAINING AND PRUNING

Loquat is generally trained according to modified leader system or open centre system. During initial stages, stem up to height of 50 cm should be kept clean. Later on, pruning is confined to removal of dead and diseased branches in the full grown tree. Harvesting of mature bunch is a kind of pruning and it encourages new growth. The best time for pruning is during summer after the crop has been harvested.

Top-working

A large percentage of the loquat seedlings trees are unprofitable. Such healthy trees should be top-worked with some improved commercial varieties. The vegetative method of propagation such as inarching, T-budding and bark grafting could be employed. Grafting plants will start bearing superior quality of fruit after third years. Top-working of inferior loquat tree should be done during May. Good number of healthy shoots will emerge from the headed back plant during the rainy season. Only one or two healthy branches should be retained for grafting purpose.

THINNING OF FRUITS

The loquat is a prolific bearer fruit plant. The tree has tendency to over bear. Thinning of fruit in the clusters or removing of some of the cluster may, therefore, be practised, for improving the size and quality of the remaining fruits. The thinning should be done when the fruits are less than 1.2 cm in diameter.

POLLINATION

The recommended cultivars of loquat are either self-incompatible or partially self compatible. It is, therefore, advisable, not to plant solid blocks of one cultivar alone, California

Advance is known to be a good pollinizer for Golden Yellow, Pale Yellow and Tanaka and should be planted along with these varieties. But when Tanka pollinated with Pale Yellow gave lower set than the self one, indicating thereby a partial cross-incompatibility. Under Saharanpur conditions Golden Yellow was found totally self-incompatible, whereas California Advance, Pale Yellow and Tanaka were partially self-incompatible.

Self-incompatibility in the loquat is a gametophytic nature. The pollen tube penetrate the stylar canal upto one-fourth to one-third of its length and fail to go beyond even after 72 hours of pollination. This suggests that self-incompatibility in the loquat is of gametophytic nature because in sprophytic type of self-incompatibility, only germination of pollen grain is inhibited.

HARVESTING AND HANDLING OF FRUITS

Harvesting : The loquat tree starts bearing fruit after third year of planting. The yield goes on increasing as the trees grow older and maximum yield is obtained after fifteen years of age. The harvesting of immature and green fruits should be avoided. All fruits in a cluster usually mature uniformly, then entire cluster may be cut at once. But, in some cases where the fruit at the base ripens before that at the tip of the cluster, the pickers will have to clip the ripe fruits by hand. The fruits should never be pulled from the tree by hand, as the stem would separate from the flesh and cause decay to set in at once. The fruit should preferably be harvested with clipper.

The average yield of loquat tree is about 16 kg. Well maintained and healthy tree can yield fruit upto 40 kg.

Grading : The fruits should be suitably graded before packing into two grades. The large sized fruits free from blemishes should be placed in one box while all the remaining marketable fruits should be packed separately. The undersized and mis-shapen fruits should be collected in a separate lot which can be sold for the preparation of jam, jelly or other products. All superfluous stems should be clipped off and badly bruised, shrivelled or scarred fruit should be discarded.

Packing : The fruit requires careful packing. Paper is placed at the bottom of each box. The larged sized choice fruit should receive better handling and packing. The paper cuttings can be used for providing cushion. The wooden boxes of 14 kg size should be used for sending fruit to nearby markets. However, for distant markets, smaller packages are used to give considerable protection to the fruit.

INSECT-PESTS

1. Bark eating caterpillar (*Indarbela quadrinotata* Walker) : Incidence of bark eating caterpillar is noticed during October - November : It causes damage by boring holes into the stem and branches and feeding on the bark under the cover of its excreta.

Remove webbing and apply Kerosene into the holes during October - November and again in January - February. Treat all the alternate host plants in the vicinity.

2. Fruit fly (*Bactrocera dorsalis*) : The fruits are attacked by fruit fly during April - May. The maggots are found inside the fruits. The fruits fall and maggots come out of the fruit to pupate in the soil.

Affected fruits should be collected and destroyed. Ploughing the field in January - February to expose the pupae to natural enemies can reduce the population considerably. Hang traps containing 100 ml emulsion of methyl eugenol 0.1% and 0.1% malathion in April in the loquat orchards. Spray 1.25 litres of malathion 50 EC + 12.5 kg sugar in 1250 litres of water per ha and repeat sprays at 7–10 days interval if infestation continues.

DISEASES

1. Shoot/fruit blight and Bark canker : The disease is caused due to fungus ***Phoma glumerata.*** The cankers appear on the bud scars, wounds, twig stubs or in crotches. Small circular brown spots appear around a leaf scar. As the canker enlarges the centers become sunken with the edges raised above the surrounding healthy bark. The fungus prepetuates itself on the trees in bark cankers.

The canker should be removed and the dead bark decorticated alongwith 2 cm of healthy bark. The dead-wood and prunings should be destroyed. The wounds should be covered with a disinfectant solution and painted with Bordeaux paste and later with Bordeaux paint. The trees should be sprayed with 2:2:250 Bordeaux mixture immediately afterward and also in March and June.

2. Crown rot : It is caused due to fungus ***Phytophthora*** sp. The water loving fungus attacks the bark producing canker extending from the ground level up to the main points where the main limbs emerge. The rot girdles the trunk during the next 2-3 seasons. Flowering is very profuse on the affected trees, but fruiting is sparse and of low grade. Yellowish green foliage is characteristic of the crown rot disease. Often the half side of the tree affected by crown-rot may show symptoms. Some branches may be killed every year and ultimately the whole tree may succumb to the disease and dry up completely. The pathogen is soil borne and perpetuates itself in the dead cankers.

Remove the severely infested trees and use them as fire wood. Remove the diseased bark during the dry season by extending the cut an inch beyond the diseased zone on all sides. First treat the cut with a disinfectant solution and then apply Bordeaux paint after a week. Immediately after this, spary the tree with 2.2.250 Bordeaux mixture. Repeat the spray just before the monsoon, during the monsoon and thereafter, too, till October.

3. Root-rot–White rot : The disease is caused due to ***Polyporus palustris.*** The bark and the wood of the root including the root collar is affected. The decayed wood is pinkish to dull violet in colour whereas in the advanced stages, small, white, elongated pockets appears and they form a mass of spongy white fibres. The affected tree begins to show symptoms of wilt, early leaf fall and increase in the fruit-set. The fruiting bodies conks **(gidder peehree)** which may grow up to 30 cm or more in diameter usually appear when the rot is fairly well advanced. They are either hidden by the litter or lie exposed on the surface of the soil.

Locate the affected trees in early stages by examining the roots and the root-collar region of the tree showing weakening signs. Dig out decayed roots and cut them completely right from the collar region. Treat the cut end of the roots immediately with disinfectant solution. When dry, apply Bordeaux paste on these cut ends. Drench the soil from where the dead roots have been dug out with 2 : 2 : 250 Bordeaux mixture. Do not allow irrigation water to come into contact with the stem. Avoid deep hoeing and interculture to obviate injuries to the roots, through which fungus attacks.

CHAPTER 20

Date-Palm

The date palm (***Phoenix dactylifera*** L.) is considered to be the oldest among the cultivated tree fruits. It is a prominent tree of desert Oasis. Date palm is considered a symbol of life in desert because it tolerate high temperature, drought, and salinity more than many other fruit plants.

ORIGIN AND HISTORY

Date palm is believed to be indigenous to countries around the Persian gulf of the Middle East where it has been cultivated for atleast 6000 years. The dates were already commercially grown and appreciated by people in Mesopotamia (Southern Iraq) as far back as 3000 B.C. It has been under cultivation in Egypt since the prehistoric days. On the basis of Mahenjodaro excavations, the date palm was cultivated in Indo-Pakistan as early as 2000 B.C. In the Old World, the date growing areas stretched from Indus valley in the East to Tunisia. The date land in Southwards fall up to Sudan, then follow the coasts of the Red sea and Gulf of Aden, northern part of Somalia and Southern Coast of Arabia. In Western hemisphere, the date palm was introduced in the late 18th or early 19th century by the Spanish missionaries.

The principal date growing countries in the world are Egypt, Saudi Arabia, Iran, UAE and Pakistan. The other major date growing countries are Algeria, Iraq, Sudan, Oman, Libya and Tunisia.

AREA AND PRODUCTION

Date palm is grown in more than 40 countries. The annual world production of dates is around 7.52 million tonnes out of 1.15 million hectares area. Arab countries produces 5.4 million tonnes annually and possess 70 percent of the world date palm production. Pakistan is the fifth largest dates producing country having production of 6.2 lakh tonnes which is 9 percent of the total world production of dates.

In India, date palm is cultivated commercially in Gujarat and Rajasthan. Efforts are made to grow date palm in Haryana and Punjab. It is estimated that total population of date palm trees in India is approx 105 million trees covering an area of 80000 hectares.

At present India is importing Chhuharas (dry dates) and **Khajoor** (Soft dates). To meet the need of this fruit, the Indian Council of Agricultural Research sanctioned a Coordinated

Scheme for the Improvement of Date palm in 1955 at Abohar. This place was considered to provide congenial conditions for date cultivation due to scanty rainfall (23-30 cm) with sufficient canal irrigation facilities. During 1958, a good number of suckers of twenty cultivated varieties from the USA were brought at Abohar station. In addition, 30 other varieties were procured from Muscat, Egypt, Aden, West Pakistan and from within the country up to 1961-62. Since then, research on different aspects of date growing has been continuing at Abohar and good progress has been made on propagation and curing of fruits. To further step up the work on date, ICAR has sanctioned another scheme during 1976 for Abohar (Punjab), Jodhpur and Chandanwal (Rajasthan) and Kheebi (Gujarat). Later on, a research scheme on date palm was also introduced at Bikaner (Rajasthan).

Presently date palm is cultivated in coastal Saureshtra, *i.e.* Jamnagar, Bhavnagar, north Gujarat ; Jaisalmer 'Barmer, Bikaner' Nagaur, Jodhpur, Churu and Sri Ganganagar districts of Rajasthan, Hisar in Haryana and Abohar in Punjab. In Kutch, approx. 14 lakhs heterogenous date palm trees are spread over about 12500 hectares yielding about 85500 tonnes of fresh fruit annually.

IMPORTANCE AND USES

The date palm is highly nutritious delicious and is known to contain mostly sugars. The flesh of fully ripe date (tamar) consists of 75-80 per cent sugars (Glucose and fructose). The fresh dates (Khalal) with a 20% moisture contain 60-65% sugars, 2.5% fibre, 2.0% protein, 2.0% fat and 2.0% minerals like iron, calcium, potassium and moderate quantity of chlorine, copper, magnesium and sulphur. In this way it furnish 3000 calories of energy per kg. It also contains small amount of vitamin A, B_1 and B_2. The fruit is also a good source of nicotinic acid.

Date palm provide food, shelter and timber products. All parts of the palm can be used for various purposes. Different products are prepared from dates in Iraq. A liquor known as **arak**, alcohol, vinegar, liquid sugars, **dibbis** (date juice) and a concentrate protein for poultry birds from date stones are generally prepared. In California, the products for use in breakfast and for bakery purpose are prepared with special reference to date paste and sugar. For the manufacturing of paper, the leaves of date palm have special significance.

BOTANY

The cultivated date palm is botanically known as ***Phoenix dactylifera*** **L. and** belongs to the family Palmae. The genus ***Phoenix*** is distinguished from other genera of pinnate leaved palms by the upward and lengthwise folding of the pinnae and the peculiarly furrowed seeds. About 12 species of genus ***Phoenix*** are identified which are native to tropical or subtropical parts of Africa and Southern Asia. In India, another species ***Phoenix sylvestris*** (L.) Roxb is cultivated as a rich source of sugar. ***Phoenix dactylifera*** is distinguished from this species by the production of-off shoots or suckers. All species are dioecious, male (staminate) and female (pistillate) flowers are produced in clusters on separate palms in the axils of leaves of the previous years growth.The inflorescence or flower cluster is a branched spadix and is enclosed before maturity in a protecting sheath or spathe. Leaves of date palm are 3 to 6 metres long and have a normal life of 3-7 years. Old and dead leaves are not shed but they are removed under cultivation. ***Phoenix dactylifera*** has 36 chromosomes (n=18, 2n=36)

In addition to ***P. dactylifera***, the other five species bear edible fruits but grown as ornamentals are as follow :

P reclinata Jacq. Dwarf palm ;
P acaulis Roxb. Dwarf palm
P farinifera Roxb. Pigmy palm
P humilis Royle
P atlantica A. chev.

The other species viz. *P. carariensis P. rupicola, P. paludosa, P. robelinic* and *P. hanceana* are grown as ornamental or other purposes.

Date palm fruits are drupes, thick skinned with thick and sweet flesh and large seed in the centre. Endocorp is thin and membranous. The fruit is a single seeded berry.

CLIMATE

The date palm as a tree flourishes well under varied sets of climate. However, for proper maturity of fruit, the date requires prolonged summer heat without rain or high humidity during the ripening period. A light shower with prolonged periods of cloudy weather and high humidity may cause more damage than a heavy rain followed by clear weather and drying winds. The mean temperature between the period of flowering and ripening of the fruit should be above 21°C rising to 27°C or higher for at least one month. For successful fruit maturation, nearly 3000 heat units are required. The heat units available in most of the north-western districts of India, counted from the time of flowering, *i.e.* end February to July, indicate that these are suitable for date palm cultivation. It is a general quotation about date palm that their heads in fire and feet in water are essentialities for successful cultivation. Taking into this consideration, parts of Rajasthan extending from Sri Ganganagar to Anupgarh, Jaisalmer and Barmer and Kutch district of Gujarat will be suitable for date cultivation. The climate of Abohar (Punjab) should be considered marginal because of rainfall (30 cm) and high humidity at the time of ripening (July-August) being the limiting factor.

In Mediterranean region no rain occurs during February to September and thus its fruit matures up to **pind** or **tamar** stage in about 180 days. In India, no such location is available which could meet this requirement although fairly dry conditions are available in north-western India. In different parts of India, fruit development period is cut short to 122-170 days and the fruit yet not full mature is harvested early before rains to avoid heavy fruit spoilage.

SOIL

The date palm can be grown in soils containing more alkali or salts. It can tolerate such condition better than many other fruit plants. In view of the large investment required to bring a date garden into bearing and maintain it on profitable production, sandy loam soil, 2 or 3 metres deep with good water holding capacity and drainage is most desirable. Date palm can tolerate high soil salinity. In the soil having 4 per cent salt concentration, dates can survive well provided the root system does not come in contact with a stratum of soil where the sodictiy is more than 1 per cent.

CHOICE OF VARIETIES

Date palm varieties are generally divided into 3 groups on the basis of flesh consistency *i.e.* soft, semi dry and dry. Soft dates are those which pass through **doka** (Rutab) stage and remain soft when they reach **pind** (Tamar) stage. These dates are mostly of the reducing sugar type. Semi-dry dates are those varieties which pass through a **rutab** stage but make a dryish tamar. The sugar is generally of reducing type. Most dates are this type. Dry dates are those varieties which do not pass through a rutab stage. They are mostly of sucrose type.

During 1956 to 1962 at Abohar (Punjab) about 50 varieties were collected indigenously and from the USA, Egypt, Pakistan, Muscat and Aden. As a result of assessment of the performance of these varieties done so far, Hillawi, Barhee and Hayani are considered good as raw-eating dates. Medjool, Hillawi, Zaidi, Khadrawi and Shamran are suitable for making **Chhuhara.** Khadrawi, Hillawi and Shamran also yield good quality soft dates. The brief description of these varieties is given below.

Hillawi : It is soft date from Iraq. This variety is relished both in **doka** and **dang** stages. Total soluble solids range between 28 to 42% and astringency in the fruit at **doka** stage is low or almost absent. It is an early variety yielding good crops and is somewhat more tolerant to rains. Dry dates (Chhuhara) of good quality and cured soft dates (Khajoor) can be prepared. Its fruit at **dang** stage (fresh form) is very delicious. Average yield ranges from 50 to 80 kg per palm.

Khadrawi : It also originated from Iraq. This veriety proved successful under Abohar conditions. The trees of this variety are comparatively less tall and yield good crops. It can be used both for dry dates and soft dates. The yield ranges from 40 to 70 kg per palm.

Shamran : It is a mid-season cultivar tolerant to high humidity. The variety yielding prolific crops. The fruits can be cured into good quality **Chhuhara** and also softened with salt treatment. Fruit is medium to large, oblong to oblong-oval and yellow at **doka** stage. Its yield per palm is 40 to 70 kg.

Medjool : The variety originated in Morocco and has large size fruits. It is late in ripening and has proved particularly good in preparing dry dates of attractive bold size and good quality. Its yield is 35 to 50 kg per palm.

Barhee : It is soft date from Iraq. The variety has proved extremely good for table use in the fresh form **(doka** stage). The **doka** fruit contains about 32% TSS, has golden yellow colour and has a very pleasant taste because of low astringency and high pulp content. The trees of this variety are prolific in yields and the fruit is ready for eating late in the season *i.e* first fortnight of August at Abohar. Its yield ranges from 60 to 110 per palm.

Hayani : It is soft date originated from the UAR. The berries have attractive deep colour. The fruits could be consumed as fresh in the **doka** stage as ripening does not proceed further under Abohar conditions. The yield per palm ranges from 30-40 kg.

Zaidi : It is a mid-season variety, slightly tolerant to rain or high humidity. The fruit is small to medium, obovate and yellow at **doka** stage.

Khalas. It is a mid-season variety. The fruit is small to medium in size, oblong oval, yellow and sweet at *doka* stage. The variety is suitable for processing as soft dates and for table purpose.

PROPAGATION TECHNIQUES

Dates can be grown either from seeds or from suckers (offshoots). When grown from seeds, approximately half of the palm will be male and produce only pollen. Its sex will be known only when it comes into flowering after four or five years. In this case, most of the female plants are inferior (not true-to-type) to the mother palm. For breeding purpose, propagation through seed provides an ideal material, or sometimes seedling palm appears outstanding and then this can be further propagated from offshoots.

The date palm are always propagated through suckers (offshoots) for commercial plantation. The suckers usually arise near the ground around the trunk. The offshoots arising at a higher level from the ground on tree trunk and with no roots give very poor survival. These are separated from the mother palms during March or August-September. The leaves are trimmed off 4-5 days before their detachment. The inner leaves should be cut back by one-half and the outer ones by two-thirds'. The tender young unopened leaves near the central bud and parts of the bare stalks of the old leaves necessary to protect it, should be kept on the offshoot. The outer whirl of leaves may be fastened to afford protection from heat and cold to the central bud also facilitate detachment and transport.

The suckers weighing approximately 25 to 30 kg and are well rooted should be removed. Expose the point of detachment and set a chisel (12 cm wide and 19 cm long) sharpened at the face and welded to a 150 cm long handle of 4 cm diameter. Drive in the chisel by hammering at the other end. It is very important that no injury is caused to the mother palm. Cut surface should be coated with tarcol or some suitable material immediately and earthed up.

Date palm is usually propagated through its offshoots which is a slow and laborious task due to limited number of offshoots produced during its life cycle. Mass production of date palm plants with tissue culture is possible to produce uniform date plants with proliferation but no callus formation or through somatic embryogenesis from a proliferating callus. Tissue culture raised plants yields the highest quality of dates. This technique provide best quality planting material *i.e.* true to type, healthy and disease free plants.

PLANTING OPERATION

The offshoots are planted 6 to 7 metres apart in the already prepared pits of 1 × 1 × 1 m size immediately after detachment. In this way 202 to 275 plants/hectare will be accommodated. If transported from long distance, the offshoot may be kept in the nursery for one season. The maximum diameter should be in level with the soil and top straight. The soil around the offshoots should be pressed firmly. The field is irrigated immediately after planting. Thereafter, frequent light irrigations are given to keep the soil always moist. At Abohar, the offshoots removed in March survived better in direct field planting than those removed in August-September. However, the separation could be done both in February-March and August-September.

The date palm plantation can be made at 8m × 8m accommodate 156 plants per hectare. In certain areas date palm is also planted at 6m × 6m having 275 plants per hectare.

ORCHARD CULTURAL PRACTICES

Irrigation

There is a proverb for date irrigation, that it should have its head in fire and feet in water. Date palm is known as drought resistant fruit tree and is able to survive for long periods without irrigation. However, continuous drought condition retards the growth of the plant. If water is available, date palm used it lavishly. Date palm is highly tolerant to excessive irrigation and floods. Continuous stagnation of water or waterlogged conditions are injurious for its growth. To maintain maximum growth, the root zone up to 2-3 m should be kept moist and not allowed to dry. Light but frequent irrigation should be given after planting.

The full grown trees on the lighter soils are usually irrigated 7 to 10 days during mid-summer and every 15 to 30 days during winter. Such soils require 2.75 to 3.75 acre-meters of water per year and 30 to 45 acre-centimeters per month is needed during summer. On heavy soils, half the amount may be enough. Each irrigation of 10-15 acre-centimeters is usually sufficient. Irrigation is withheld when ripening starts to facilitate harvesting, hasten fruit ripening and to reduce fruit drop caused by high humidity.

Intercropping

Intercropping in date palm with suitable crops bring good income and also improves the fertility of the soil. During the first few years, intercropping can be practised with no shortage of irrigation. Intercrops such as gram, peas, mash, moong, moth, senji and lentil can be sown during summer. Intercropping of some vegetables in plantation located near the cities, can be practised if sufficient irrigation and manuring facilities are available. The filler trees like grapes can be tried with good success.

Manuring and Fertilization

Generally the farmers do not apply manure to the date palm. The trees certainly respond to manuring as indicated by increased vigour and growth. The results of studies conducted at Abohar shows that 25 to 50 kg of farmyard manure and 1 to 2 kg ammonium sulphate per palm should be added. The quantities may be reduced if some leguminous crop has been grown in the date palm. Farmyard manure is applied during December-January. The nitrogen dose should be given a fortnight before flowering *i.e.* in the first week of February.

To get better yield a full grown date palm tree should be given 20–40 kg FYM, 500–1000 *g* N, 250 – 500 g P_2O_5 and K_2O each annually. Farmyard manure should be applied after monsoon in September to December. The whole quantity of phosphorus and potassium and 60 per cent nitrogen should be given three weeks before flowering. The remaining 40 per cent nitrogen should be applied during fruit development period in March - April.

POLLINATION

In date palm, male and female flowers are borne on separate trees being a dioecious plant. Therefore, hand pollination is necessary for production of commercial crop. A female palm usually carries 6 to 12 clusters but the actual number may vary according to the variety and season. A cluster may carry 50-100 strands with 16-30 set fruits on each. The female flowers are pollinated as and when they emerge out of the spathe. This is accomplished by smearing the flower buds with cotton plug dusted with pollen grains and then placing 1 to 3 strands of freshly opened male inflorescence in an inverted position into the female inflorescence. A twine or a thread pulled from the leaflet is tied with a slipknot around the pollinated cluster about 10 cm from the outer end to hold the male flowers in place. As the cluster develops, the knot slips to leave the cluster open. To avoid re-visits, female spathe about to rupture is cracked open and pollinated. It has been observed that one male palm is enough for about 20 females. If pollen is in short supply, it may be mixed with talc. If the time of opening of male and female spathes does not synchronise, the pollen can be stored dry at room temperature till the completion of pollination.

FRUIT THINNING

Excess load of fruit may cause shrivelling of berries, breaking of spathe stalks, more damage due to rain and humidity, delay in ripening and alternate bearing. It also reduced size and produce poor quality fruit. It is , therefore, necessary to keep only optimum quantity of fruit and thin out the rest. This is usually accomplished either by reducing the number of fruits on each bunch and or by removing some of the bunches. The number of fruit that a palm can safely carry depends on the cultivar, age, size and vigour of the palm and number of green leaves on it. Under normal conditions, 1-2 bunches in the 4th year and-3–4 bunches in the 5th year may be left. Normally 8-10 bunches per palm are retained in India. Small, defective and broken bunches should be removed.

In short-stranded varieties like Khadrawi, the strands are generally cut back to even, up the bunch from the top. Most of the fruit thinning is done by the removal of half to two-third of strands from the centre. In the long stranded varieties like Deglet Noor, one-third to half strands are cut in similar way as in Khadrawi, in addition strands are also cut back to remove about one-third of the flowers.

The desirable number of fruits to be left is between 1300 and 1600 per palm depending on the variety. The per cent thinning is generally done 40-50 in Khadrawi, 50-55 in Hillawi, 50-60 in Zaidi and Barhee. Ethephon 100-400 ppm after 10 to 30 days from fruit set was found effective in fruit thinning of cv. Hayani. The biennial bearing habit of the treated palms were found to reduce by ethephon treatment. It also advances the ripening of fruit.

STAGES OF FRUIT RIPENING

The datepalm fruit can be divided into four stages on the basis of fruit development and ripening. The Arabic names for these four stages are **Kimri, Khalal, Rutab** and **Tamar**. In

Punjab these stages are termed as **gandora, doka, dang** and **pind**, respectively. **Kimri** or **gandor**a is a stage when the fruit has grown a little and attains a clear apple green colour. The second stage **Khalal** or **dok**a is marked by the turning of the colour of the fruit skin from green to yellow to chrome or to yellow, finally spotted with having characteristic of its variety. In this stage, the fruit has attained the full size.

The third stage known as **Rutab** or **dang** characterized by the date becoming more or less translucent and softening starts from distal end by darkening of the skin from yellow, chrome or scarlet to brown or to nearly black. The final stage in the ripening of date is called **Tamar** or **pind,** when the fruits get fully mature and has lost much of its water, enough to make the sugar to water proportion sufficient high to prevent fermentation. This stage is equivalent to that of raisin in the grape.

HARVESTING AND PROCESSING

Harvesting of dates generally depends upon the weather conditions. The rain and high humidity in the atmosphere at the ripening time is a limiting factor in its cultivation. When the climate is favourable, it is preferable to leave the fruit of most varieties on the palm until it reaches the stage of maturity at which it is to be consumed or stored. The changes associated with ripening and the period during which the fruit may be consumed extend from the peak of the **khalal** stage, when the fruit has its most intense red or yellow colour and maximum weight, to the final **tamar** stage, when it has lost the greater part of its moisture content and will keep without special attention to storage. Most of the people like to eat the fruit in **khalal** stage. At least two varieties of dates-Hillawi and Barhee, are liked most for eating in **khalal** stage. Dates are hand-picked at the stage of maturity. All the dates in the same bunch do not ripen at the same time, it has been the practice to make several pickings to harvest the fruit during a season. Sometimes, when the season is favourable and more than 70 per cent fruit is ripe, the entire bunch is harvested.

The research conducted on curing of dates at Abohar have revealed that the rain and high humidity in the atmosphere at the time of ripening (July and August) do not allow the ripening process on the tree to proceed satisfactorily beyond **doka** stage. If the fruit is retained on the tree, there is checking, splitting and rotting. High humidity and rainfall also cause the fruit to drop. Therefore, the crop has to be harvested at **doka** stage. Though in comparatively drier seasons partial crop on some trees may become **dang** (mellow and soft) but the quantity of such fruit is limited. The berries are removed and graded manually on the basis of size and colour.

At Abohar (Punjab) a technique has developed to transform satisfactorily the date fruit at **doka** stage into dry dates **(Chhuhara)** of good quality. At least four varieties Hillawi, Khadrawi, Shamran and Medjool have yielded very good product. **Chhuhara** obtained from Medjool, which is a large-sized variety, compare very well with the high quality **Chhuhara** imported from Middle East counties. The technique developed involves immersion of fruit at **doka** stage in boiling water for 6 to 8 minutes and then drying either in temperature-controlled oven (air-circulation type) for 80 to 120 hours at 48 to 50°C or in the sun for 10-15 days if weather is dry. Thus, an average of 45 per cent fruit product is obtained. Fruits at advanced **doka** stage or when they attain one-fourth, one-half or full **dang** (the berries become mellow and soft starting from the distal end) can be converted into soft dates **(khazoor)** of good quality by drying either in the oven at 40°C or in the sun. Thus, for soft dates, only drying the berries at partial or full dang stage is required with no other treatment and this way a final product of soft **Khazoor** ranging from 50-60 per cent is obtained.

Hillawi and Barhee yielded 50-100 kg fruit per palm at doka stage. The average yield from Khadrawi and Shamran is obtained 40-70 kg fruit per palm. The yield from Medjool palm is upto 50 kg but its fruits are very large in size.

Artificial ripening of fruit at **doka** stage to transform it into **dang** stage was also attempted at Abohar. For these studies, berries were treated with 0.5 per cent to 2.0 per cent common salt (sodium chloride) and similar concentrations of acetic acid in combination with 1.0 per cent salt. The fruits to be treated with salt were spread on polythene sheet and requisite quantity of salt was applied by rubbing and smearing uniformly on the berries. The fruits which were given acetic acid plus salt treatments, were first dipped in solutions of desired acetic acid concentrations for 2 minutes followed by salt application by the method described above. Each treated lot was packed into wooden boxes lined with old newspapers and packed in laboratory at room temperature. The boxes were opened after 24 hours. From these studies, it was found that with 2 per cent salt, 60 to 70 per cent of the **doka** fruit were transformed into **dang.** However, the **dang** obtained by this treatment was not as good in taste as that of naturally ripened on the tree, but still it was edible and generally acceptable on account of its having lost the astringency. But such product cannot be stored more than 24 hours and, as such, should be consumed to as early as possible.

Low energy X-ray irradiation can be used as a potential commercial treatment for retaining the quality and ensuring the safety of dates.

Storage : The shelf life of fresh dates can be enhanced for two weeks in cold storage (5–7°C temp. and 85–90% RH). Fresh dates at *Khalal* stage can be stored up to two months at 0–1°C. Dried dates (Chhuharas) can be stored for one year at ambient conditions after packing in gunny bags.

INSECT-PESTS

The most important pests of dates are follows :

(*i*) **Date Stone weevil (*Coccotrypes dactyliperda* F.) :** It attacks unripe fruits and the adult penetrates the fruit and reaches the stone by constructing a direct circular hole through the pulp and both adults and grubs feed inside on the pulp and results in the drop of unripe fruit. Hillawi and Khadrawi, which ripen early, are more susceptible to this pest. Spraying the plants with 0.075 per cent Malathion has proved effective for its control.

(*ii*) **Nitiduled beetle (*Haptoncus luteolus* Eri) :** The larvae penetrate the fruit and eat the inner portion of the pulp. Their attack is followed by fungal decay. The adult is brownish yellow, oval, slightly oblong, 2.3 ± 0.13 mm long and 1.16 ± 0.21 mm broad. Initially, the dropped fruits are attacked. Then the pest spread to fruit bunches on the tree and cause the fruit to drop. The pest over winters as pupae in the soil. Spraying with Malathion (0.075 per cent) gave satisfactory results. Regular removal of dropped fruits and their destruction also helps in minimising the effect.

(*iii*) **Date palm scale (*Parlatoria blanchardi* Targ).** The scale affected leaves first show a yellow discoloration around areas of sucking activity followed by brown necroses. In severe incidence, fruits are also affected. The pest can be controlled by spraying 500 ml of malathion 50 EC or 375 ml dimethoate in 250 litres of water per ha.

(*iv*) **Rhinoceros beetle (*Oryctes rhinoceros* L).** The beetles throw out a fibrous mass while feeding in the burrows made in young fronds. The injury is seen as a series of holes on the fronds when they open out. Due to its attack top leaves wither and drop. Treat the breeding places with 2 kg of carbaryl 50 WP in 250 litres of water per ha.

(*v*) **Red palm weevil (*Rhynchophorus ferrugineus* Olivier).** The larvae feed on the soft tissue of trees and often cause very severe damage especially when a large number of them bore into the soft growing parts. The weevil is attracted to the trees by the smell of palm juice, which flows as a result of the wounds by man or other agents. Inject emulsion of dimethoate 30 EC

@ 400 ml or carbaryl 50 WP @ 250 *g* in 25 litres of water into the live holes and plaster them with mud after application of chemicals.

(*vi*) **Termites (*Odontotermes obesus* Rambur) :** They feed on the roots of the newly transplanted suckers which may ultimately cause them to wither and die. As a preventive measure, chlorpyrphos 20 EC mixed in each pit @ 10 ml in 2 kg soil before planting is recommended.

DISEASES

(*i*) **Graphiola leaf spot (*Graphiola phoenicis*) :** It is also called as false smut or palm leaf pustule. It is a serious disease. This disease is more acute in the areas where humidity is more. Numerous hard black smut like pustules are seen scattered developing epidermally on the upper and lower surfaces of leaflets and also on rachis. The pustules at maturity consist of round, hard, black cups about 0.50 × 0.25 mm. These cups contain yellow spores. Older leaves are more affected, they loose their chlorophyll and dry up. For its control, remove and burn the affected leaves to check further contamination and spray the trees with 2: 2: 250 Bordeaux mixture (2 kg copper sulphate + 2 kg unslaked lime mixed in 250 litres of water).

(*ii*) **Fruit rot :** It often causes considerable loss when humid weather occurs during the ripening season. Under such conditions, various fungus may develop in the fruit and cause spotting, dropping and rotting. The damage may be reduced by better ventilation of the branches and protecting the fruit from rain. In addition, spray the bunches with a mixture of 5 per cent fahana (ferlic dimethyl dithiocarbamate) in sulphur.

CHAPTER 21

Pomegranate

The pomegranate (***Punica granatum*** L.) is a common table fruit and is very much liked for its refreshing juice, which has a high medicinal value. The hardy nature, low maintenance cost, high yields, better keeping quality and survival without irrigation make pomegranate cultivation a paying proposition.

ORIGIN AND HISTORY

Pomegranate belonging to the family Lythraceae is a favourite table fruits of tropical and subtropical regions. The fruit is native of Iran, where it was first cultivated in about 2000 B.C. ago. It spread to Mediterranean countries like Spain, Morocco, Iran, Egypt, Afghanistan and Baluchistan at a vary eraly date. The pomegranate is known to have been cultivated in the middle east more than 5000 years ago. It is now extensively cultivated in Baluchistan, Pakistan, India, Morocco, Iraq, China, Egypt, Iran, Spain, Afghanistan, Japan and Russia. The fruits grown in Kabul and Baluchistan considered extremely superior in quality. The north-western region of Pakistan is known for production of high class pomegranates.

AREA AND PRODUCTION

India ranks first with respect to pomegranate area and production in the world. The other pomegranate producing countries are Iran, Turkey, Span, Tunisia, Morocco, Afghanistan, China, Greece, Japan, etc. India contribute 70 per cent to the world pomegranate market. The good quality pomegranate is produced in Turkey, Iran, Afghanistan, Syria, Moroco and Spain.

In India, pomegranate is cultivated on 1.12 lakh hectares area accounting for 1.7 per cent of the area under fruits. Pomegranate growing states in India are Maharashtra, Karnataka, Gujarat, Andhra Pradesh, Madhya Pradesh, Tamil Nadu and Rajashthan. Maharashtra has maximum area of 82000 hectares under this fruit crop with annual production of 4.78 lakh mt.

Maharashtra contribute about 73 percent of the total area followed by Karnataka and Andhra Pradesh. The productivity of fruit is the highest (26.4 mt/ha) in Tamil Nadu. Major pomegranate producing areas in Maharashtra are Nasik, Sangli, Solapur, Satara, Ahmednagar, Buldhana, Beed, Aurangabad, and Washim. In Karnataka, it is growing mainly in Bijapur, Bellary, Koppal, Bagalkot, Belgaum etc.

Export potential : India is exporting pomegranate to UAE, Netherlands, UK, Saudi Arabia, Russia, Bangladesh, Egypt, Baharain, Kuwait, Thialand, Nepal and Oman. About 40 per cent of pomegranate crop is exported from India to other countries. India exported 30158 mt fruit valued at Rs. 1473 million in 2011-12.

IMPORTANCE AND USES

Pomegranate is considered highly nutritious fruit. The edible portion in this fruit is 68 per cent. It contains moisture 78%, protein 1.6%, carbohydrates 14.5%, calcium 10 mg/100 g, phosphorus 70 mg/100 g, iron 0.3 mg/100 g, riboflavin 0.10 mg/100 g and vitamin C 16 mg/100 g fruit.

The fruits are mainly used for dessert purposes. The fresh fruit is of exquisite quality while its processed products like bottled juice, syrups and jelly are highly appreciated. The juice is considered useful for patients suffering from leprosy.

The fruit juice easily ferments and may be used for the production of wine. The juice of wild pomegranates is used in the manufacture of citric acid and sodium citrate for medicinal purpose. The bark of the stem and root contain a number of alkaloid belonging to pyridine group. It is also employed in the therapeutics in dysentery and diarrhoea. The pomegranate is known best for curing the chronic stomach ailment. The pomegranate seed contains oil which has a potential for industrial use.

BOTANY

The genus **Punica** has two species viz. **granatum** and **protopunica.** ***Punica protopunica*** is found wild in Socotra Island and ***Punica granatum*** is cultivated in tropical and subtropical parts. ***Punica granatum*** has been classified into 2 subspecies *i.e.* **cholorocarpa** and **porphyrocarpa. Chorocarpa** is found in Transcaucasus region and **porphyrocarpa** in Central Asia.

1. *Punica granatum* : It is a deciduous shrub or tree upto 6.5 m in height and relatively long lived (upto 50-70 years). Leaves petioled, oblong or oval-lanceolate, 2.5-5 cm or long lenghwise, obtuse, glabrous and shinning. The handsome brilliant orange red flowers are axillary, solitary or in small clusters and borne towards the ends of the branchlets. The calyx is tubular, persistent, five to ten-lobed, the petals five to seven in numbers, are lanceolate, inserted between the calyx lobes. The ovary is embedded in the calyx-tube and contains several locules in two series one above the other. The fruit is berry and edible portion is fleshy testa of seeds.

2. *Punica nana* L : It is also called as Dwarf pomegranate. It seldom grows higher than a man and usually treated as a pot plant in the North. It is the best kind for green house use. The double flowered habit is more common. It is as hardy as granatum species and is suitable for outdoor work where the climate is not too severe. On the pacific coast it is grown as a hedge plant.

CLIMATE

Pomegranate is sub-tropical fruit. It can adopt itself to a wide range of climatic conditions and can grow up to 1800 m above sea level. The fruit tree grows best in semi-arid climate where cool winter and hot and dry summer prevail. The tree requires hot and dry climate during the period of fruit development and ripening. The optimum temperature for fruit development is 38°C. The tree can not produce sweet fruits unless the temperature is high for a sufficient long period. Under tropical and sub-tropical climate, it behaves as an evergreen or partially deciduous. Under humid conditions, the sweetness of fruit is adversely affected. Therefore, it is considered that pomegranate is a hardy fruit and can thrive well under drought conditions, though yield is low. The plant bear well only under irrigation.

In areas of low temperature, the tree behaves as deciduous in nature and sheds its leaves during winter months. It is also rated as winter hardy fruit tree. Two years old shoots of hardy cultivars are not damaged even at 2°C. When temperature falls below–14°C, visible damage due to frost occurs. Aridity and frequent anomalies of the climate cause leaf shedding and fruit cracking

SOILS

It can be grown on diverse types of soil. The pomegranate is not very particular about its soil requirement. The deep loamy or alluvial soils are ideal for its cultivation. It can tolerate soils which are loamy and slightly alkaline. It can thrive well on comparatively poor soils where other fruits fail to grow. Pomegranate can also be grown in medium and black soils. It is rated as salt-hardy fruit plant.

CHOICE OF VARIETIES

Different cultivars have been recommended for the commercial cultivation in different states in India on the basis of physico-chemical characteristics. In north India, there are no well recognized commercial varieties. Brief characters of important cultivars are given below.

1. Ganesh : It is an improved variety known as GBG No. 1. Ganesh is a seedling selection by Dr. G.S. Cheema at Pune. It is a selection from Alandi and considered to be the best variety. The fruit is medium in size. It has soft seeds. Ganesh is a high yielding variety and is a good cropper. The flesh is pinkish and has juice with agreeable taste. Its main crop (ambe bahar) in North India matures in mid August. TSS of Juice is 13 per cent with low acidity (0.5%). The average yield is 15-18 tonnes per hectare.

2. Alandi : Fruit medium in size, fleshy testa, blood red or deep pink with sweet slightly acidic juice. Seeds very hard. The variety is named after the name of the village where it was grown extensively.

3. Dholka : Fruit large in size, rind greenish white, fleshy testa, pinkish white or whitish with sweet juice. Seeds soft. Juice is acidic. It is medium cropper. It is an important variety of Gujarat.

4 Kandhari : It produces large fruit. The rind is deep red. The flesh is dark red or deep pink. The juice is slightly acidic. The seeds are hard. The variety is successfully grown in Himachal Pradesh. The juice is sweet with 12 per cent TSS and well blended with acidity (0.61%). It is regular bearer variety and yield 10 – 13 tonnes fruit per hectare.

5. Muskat : This variety is also largely grown. Fruits small to medium in size. Rind is somewhat thick. Fleshy testa, with moderately sweet juice. The seeds are rosy in colour. Fruits are tasty.

6. Nabha : Tree is medium in growth, fruit skin yellowish and smooth. Cracking medium. Juice is 65 per cent. The arils are light pink in colour. Seeds are medium soft. Taste is good.

7. Jalore Seedless. It is soft seeded variety of Rajasthan. The fruits are large in size with average weight 200 *g*. Fruits are attractive in appearance with pink to deep red skin. The arils are pink to red having soft seeds.

8. Mridula. It is a soft seeded hybrid with excellent fruit quality. The arils are blood red in colour with TSS 17.8 per cent and acidity 0.47 per cent.

9. Bassein Seedless. It is soft seeded red coloured variety grown in Karnataka. The average weight of fruit is 327 *g*. The arils are light pink in colour with TSS 15.6 per cent and acidity 0.49 per cent.

10. Jyothi. It is variety with soft seeds and pink aril has been released from University of Agricultural Sciences, Bangalore. This is a selection from the seedlings of Bassein Seedless and Dholka varieties. The average fruit weight is 219 *g*. Its TSS is 15.0 per cent and acidity 0.58 per cent.

11. PAU Selection. It originated as a chance seedling from Ganesh. Plants are vigorous and evergreen. Fruits medium to large, weight 450 g. Aril's are white transparent with little pink tinge but seeds are little hard. The juice percentage is 71, TSS 13 per cent and acidity 0.7 per cent. The average yield is 8 tonnes per hectare.

12. Bhagwa. The tree is medium in size, bushy, partially deciduous. The fruits are medium to large in size, rind smooth, glossy, red in colour with soft seeds having red coloured aril. The fruit weight is 215 g, juice 45 per cent, TSS 14.2 per cent and acidity 0.48 per cent. The average yield is 14.6 kg per plant. The main crop mature between mid-August to mid-September.

PROPAGATION TECHNIQUES

Pomegranate plants raised from seed vary widely and are undersirable. Thus, they must be raised vegetatively. Among the vegetative methods of propagation, cuttings are universally used for raising pomegranate plants on commercial basis.

Mature wood is used for making the cuttings and these are 8 to 10 cm long. The cuttings are planted in the nursery fields in such a way that not more than one-third of the cutting is exposed. The best time of making the cuttings is December-January when the plants shed leaves. The cuttings made during September-October can also root satisfactorily. The cuttings in the nursery fields are planted directly after making them from the plants. For getting high percentage of rooting dip cuttings in 100 ppm IBA for 24 hours before planting in nursery beds.

Pomegranate may also be propagated by air-layering or gootee. Treatment with 10000 ppm Indole Butyric acid in lanolin as carrier was found to improve rooting. Ground layering is another method used for multiplying the pomegranate plants.

PLANTING OPERATION

Land is prepared thoroughly and levelled prior to pit digging. The layout is done following square or hexagonal system. The size of the pit should be 60 × 60 × 60 cm. Pits should be filled with 22-25 kg of farmyard manure or compost, 1 kg of superphosphate and good soil mixture.

The plants are planted at the distance of 6m × 6m apart in square system and it will accommodate 275 plants per hectare. In higher but deeper soil, the planting distance can be reduced to 5 × 5 m.

Planting density is the most important yield contributing factor which can be manipulated to attain the maximum production per unit area. The optimum spacing is important for the maximum utilization of land and good income over a long period. At MPAU, Rauhari, it was observed that as the plant density was increased, yield per hectare also increased without affecting fruit quality. A density of 1000 plants per hectare gave 2-3 times higher yield and 2.44 times more profit as compared with normal plant population of 400 per hectare. It was also recommended that for higher yields for the first four to five years after planting, a distance of 5 × 2 m may be adopted and alternate plants may be removed after wards maintaining a planting distance of 5 × 4 m. The cultivar Ganesh can be planted at the distance of 3 × 3 m and Kandhari at 4 × 4 m apart.

The best time of planting pomegranate in northern India is dormant period *i.e.*January to mid February and in South India during monsoon season.

FLOWERING AND FRUITING

In evergreen pomegranate cultivars, the flower buds of the spring flush are borne on mature wood of one-year old shoot, whereas the flowers which appear during July-August are borne on the current year's growth. In deciduous cultivars, the flowers are borne on the current year's growth between July and August. The flowers are found mostly in clusters, either terminally or in axils of the leaves. The inflorescence is cyme and due to heavy drops of secondary and tertiary buds they appear to be solitary in clusters.

In Western India, three flowering seasons *i.e.,* Ambe Bahar (January - February), Mrig Bahar (June - July) and Hasth Bahar (September - October) have been reported. Ambe Bahar is most commonly favoured by the growers because of high yield consequent to profuse flowering. In Punjab, only one flowering season is observed from April to June. In Bihar, flowering occurs twice, once during February - March and again during July - August. In Karnataka, flowering was observed in July - August, March and September. The flowering period extended for 80 to 87 days in first flowering and 22 to 30 days in second and third flowering. The flowering period of different cultivars is also quite variable. Under Delhi conditions, Dholka, Kandhari, Muskat and Patiala flowered only once in a year while Ganesh and Japanese Dwarf flowered twice. Heterostyly is common in pomegranate flowers.

The time of dehiscence of anther varied in different cultivars and no general sequence was found in the time of anthesis. Anthesis in Punjab started at 8 AM and was complete by 4 PM with a peak at 2 PM. The stigma was receptive one day before anthesia and remained receptive for upto 5 days. The percentage of pollen grains that germinated was over 90 in most of the 21 cultivars studied. After open pollination, fruit set was highest in cultivar Dholka (63.8%), Bedana, (63.0%) and Kali Shirin (62.7%). After self pollination, fruit set was appreciably lower. Fruit development was determined at fortnightly intervals between 18 April and 8 August. On 8th August, the cultivars Kazki, Shirin Anar and Achikdana had the largest fruits, 6.50, 6.32 and 6.26 cms in diameter, respectively. Fruit cracking was lowest in the cultivars Kazki, Guleshah and Bedana.

ORCHARD CULTURAL PRACTICES

Irrigation

The newly set plants require regular irrigation so that the roots become well established and the plants can start growth. The plants may be individually watered daily or about a week after planting. In northern India where planting is done during the spring, regular watering may be given every 7 to 10 days till the start of the monsoon. In areas where planting is done during the monsoon, irrigation may be given whenever there is no rain for a prolonged period of time. After the plants are well established, in about 6 months, they can stand considerable amount of drought and irrigation may be given at intervals of 2 to 4 weeks depending upon the soil, climate, weather conditions and intercrops grown. However, during summer irrigate the plants at an interval of 10-15 day.

Regular irrigation is essential from flowering to ripening of fruits, as irregular moisture condition results in dropping of flowers and small fruits. It may also cause development of cracks on mature fruits which reduces market value and consumer acceptance.

Intercropping

Intercropping in pomegranate orchard is highly desirable because it takes about 6-7 years to come to commercial bearing. Vegetables viz. cabbage, cauliflower, tomato, radish, cucurbits, moong, peas, beans or green manure crops can easily be followed in pomegranate orchard. The growing of intercrops should be carried out for the first four years of the life of the plantation. It is usually advisable to allow the intercrops to grow throughout the year. Intercrops can be continued for another 3 to 4 years after the plants had started bearing. It is best to grow a green manure crop during the monsoon and burry in it, when it has completed its vegetative phase and started flowering.

Manuring and Fertilization

In northern India, farmyard manure is applied during December. Nitrogen should be given in two split doses, first half should be added in February and other half in April. In other areas, manuring may be done just before the start of monsoon in case of young plants. The one year old tree should be manured with about 5-6 kg of farmyard manure and 20 g nitrogen. This amount is increased by the same amount every year so that a five year old tree gets 25-30 kg of farmyard manure and 100 g of nitrogen. Experiment carried out at the MPAU indicate the following schedule :

Age of plant (years)	Nitrogen	Phosphorus g/plant	Potassium
1½ – 2	250	125	125
2½ – 3	500	125	125
3½ – 4	500	125	250
4 and above	625	250	250

At Mahatma Phule Krishi Vidyapeeth, Rahuri, an application of 500 g N, 125 g P_2O_5 and 125 g K_2O is recommended for 'Ganesh' variety. Under Udaipur conditions of Rajasthan, application of 240 g N, 160 g P_2O_5 and 60 g K_2O per plant is suggested for variety 'Jodhpur Red'. In Gujarat state pomegranate is applied with 50 kg farmyard manure, 500 g N, 250 g P_2O_5 and 500 g K_2O per plant per year. Application of fertilizers is done in December-January for **Ambe bahar,** in May-June of **Mrig bahar** and in October-November for **Hasth bahar.**

In Andhra Pradesh, adult bearing trees are applied with 800 g N, 400 g P_2O_5 and 400 g K_2O per tree alongwith 100 kg FYM per tree. In Karnataka a dose of 200 kg N, 300 kg P_2O_5 and 100 kg K_2O alongwith 12.5 tonnes per hectare farmyard manure is applied.

In Orissa, 45 kg N, 115 kg P_2O_5 per hectare along with 10 kg FYM + 100 g sterameal per tree are applied. In Tamil Nadu, 600 g N, 500 g P_2O_5 and 1200 g K_2O alongwith 30 kg FYM is incorporated per tree per year.

TRAINING AND PRUNING

Training

Pomegranate may be trained as multi-stemmed tree or single stemmed tree.

(*i*) **Multi-stemmed tree :** In this method 3-4 stems are left at hill and remaining shoots are removed, this will give a bush from look to the resultant tree. In Maharashtra, the growers prefer multistem training by retaining all stems. But yield has not been found to be affected by number of stems per plant.

(*ii*) **Single-stemmed tree :** The single stem up to 30 cm is left by removing all the side shoots at the time of planting. The main stem is headed back at a height of about one metre results in the formation of branches. Four or five well distributed branches on all sides above 60-70 cm from the ground level are allowed to grow. In the third year of planting one can maintain desired shape of the pomegranate. Single stemmed tree has tendency to produce less number of shoots.

Pruning

Pomegranate does not usually require pruning except for removal of suckers, dead and diseased branches and developing a sound framework of the tree. It is essential to remove the suckers as soon as they arise. The fruits are borne terminally on short spurs produced all along the slow growing mature wood. These bear fruits for 3 to 4 years. Therefore, only a limited pruning of bearing tree is required. Annual pruning in winter during dormant period should be confined to shortening of the previous season's growth to encourage fruiting.

For getting a good crop, a set of new shoots should be allowed to develop every year on all sides of the tree and gradual growth of new shoots should be encouraged by restricted cutting back of the bearing shoot.

CROP REGULATION

The pomegranate starts fruiting in about 4 years after planting and continues for about 25 to 30 years. Economic yield is generally obtained after 10 years of planting.

To regulate flowering, water is withheld for about two months in advance of the normal flowering season. After two months, manures and fertilizers are applied and light irrigation is given. Three to four days later, heavier irrigations at normal interval are followed. The tree readily responds to this treatment by producing new growth and blooms and bears a good crop.

A full grown pomegranate has tendency to bear flowers and fruits throughout the year. To obtain higher fruit yield during a particular period, plants are given a resting period by which the natural tendency of the tree is altered with artificial means. It is done by withholding of water for about 2 months in advance of normal flowering, root exposure and also use of chemicals. By adopting such methods flowering can be induced in June-July **(Mrig bahar)** coinciding with the break of monsoon, February-March **(Ambe bahar)** and September-October **(Hasth bahar)**. These practices are knows as bahar treatment.

Mrig bahar is taken in Deccan areas where water is so scarce during the hot weather. The flowering, therefore, is so forced that the maximum requirement of water falls during the rainy season. For this treatment, watering is withheld from December to April-May results in sufficient suppression of growth. In the month of March-April leaves are shed as plants go to dormant stage. The manures and fertilizers are applied and the light irrigation is given which is followed by two heavy irrigations at 7 days interval before rain set in. Within 15 days, trees will put on profuse growth along with the formation of flowers and fruits. The fruits ripen in October and continues upto December.

Ambe bahar is taken in the areas where enough water is available during hot weather. The fruits are available during June and July and no irrigation is given after the start of the rainy season. The trees shed their leaves by October-November, when a shallow hand digging or ploughing is done. During December-January, manures are applied. The first irrigation is given in January and the flowers appear within a month of this irrigation. In dry regions of western Maharashtra **Ambe bahar** has been found to be better treatment than **Mrig bahar.**

Hasth bahar is seldom taken. The trees have to be made dormant during August-September. This is rather uncertain because of the rains that occur during this period.

Pollination

Both self and cross pollination are recorded in pomegranate. Greater percentage of fruit set was observed by hand pollination and pollination under natural conditions *i.e.* open pollination.

HARVESTING AND FRUIT HANDLING

Pomegranate is a non-climacteric fruit. Its fruits become ready for harvesting in 5-7 months after the appearance of blossoms. Mature fruits become slightly yellowish and further pink to red. On tapping, the fruits give metallic sound and when pressed they give a 'Crunch' sound. The fruits are harvested with the help of secateurs.

The period of fruit harvest is November to March in *Mrig bahar*, June to August in *Ambe bahar* and February to May in *Hasth bahar*. The corresponding flowering period is June to August in *Mrig bahar*, January to February in *Ambe bahar* and October to November in *Hasth bahar*.

The trees begin to bear fruit in the fourth year when a small crop of 20-25 fruits (4-5 kg) per tree may be harvested. In the 10th year, it rises to 100-150 fruits (20-25 kg). The average yield in well managed plantation may be as much as 200-250 fruits per tree.

After harvesting, sorting of fruits should be exercised to remove undesirable fruits. The fruits should be properly graded before packing to fetch higher premium in the market. The fruits are graded in to 5 grades viz. A, B, C, D, E grades. A grade fruit should have minimum 400 g weight and 90 mm in diameter. The fruit weight and diameter should be 350 g – 80 mm in B grade, 300 g – 70 mm in C grade, 250 g – 60 mm in C grade and 200 g – 50 mm in C grade. The fruits should preferably be packed in CFB cartoon of 4 – 5 kg. capacity.

Export specification are variable for different countries. Ganesh and Bhagwa varieties are exported to Middle East having 300 – 350 g weight of red coloured fruits and to Netherlands/ Germany and UK having 250 – 300 g weight of red coloured fruits. Arakala and Mridula varieties are exported to Middle East, Netherlands/Germany and UK having 200 – 250 g weight and deep red fruits. The fruits are packed in 3 – 5 kg capacity boxes and sent at 5°C temperature.

The healthy fruits are packed mostly in bamboo baskets and wooden crates containing 10-12 kg with a padding of paddy straw or dry grasses. The fruits can be transported to distant market without any loss.

The fruits can be stored for about 5-6 months at 4.5°C and 80- 85% relative humidity. The shelf life of wax treated and intact film wrapped fruits of cv. Ganesh could be extended upto 6 weeks at 4 – 5°C and upto 4 weeks at ambient temperature (26 – 27°C). The storage life of pomegranate fruits in sealed polythene bags (0.02 mm) at 10°C is extended upto 12 weeks.

INSECT-PESTS

1. Fruit borer or pomegranate butterfly (*Deudorix isocrates*) : This is a serious pest found all over India. Infestation starts from flowering to button stage. The caterpillar bore inside the developing fruits. Such infested fruits are also invaded by bacteria and fungi and causing fruit to rot. Such affected fruits fall down.

Collect and destroy the affected fruits. Spray young fruits with 625 ml of monocrotophos 40 EC in 500 litres of water per ha. Also, bag young fruits with coarse cloth or muslin cloth or polythene of 300 gauge thickness.

2. Bark eating caterpillar (*Indarbela tetraonis*) : This pest bore into the bark of pomegranate tree and feeding inside. Trees become weak and do not bear fruits.

Avoid over crowding of trees by removing unwanted twigs. Clean the affected portions by removing all web. Inject kerosene oil or petrol and plug the hole with cotton wool soaked in carbon bisulphide.

3. Stem borer (*Coeleosterna spinator*) : The caterpillar of this pest makes a hole and bores through the main trunk or main branches. It comes out at night and feeds on bark.

Clean the hole by removing insect excreta with the help of a hooked wire. Plug the hole with cotton plug dipped in petrol, chloroform, carbon bisulphide or kerosene oil followed by sealing it with mud or painting with coaltar.

4. Sap sucking insects : These are mealy bugs, scale insects, thrips, aphids, mites cause shedding of buds, flowers and fruits at very young stage.

(*i*) Spray Durmet/Durban 20 EC (chlorpyriphos) @ 3.75 ml in one litre of water on the appearace of mealy bugs and scale insects.

(*ii*) Spray 500 ml Rogor 30 EC (dimethoate) in 500 litres of water for the control of white flies, aphids and thrips.

(*iii*) Spray water soluble sulphur 1.25 g/litre for the control of red mites.

DISEASES

1. Leaf spot : *Xanthomonas punicae, Colletotrichum gloeosporioides* : The former pathogen is bacterium and the latter is fungal. The bacterium pathogen causes irregular water-soaked spots on leaves. They are light brown to dark brown in appearance. The leaf spot caused by fungus, produce minute, violet black or black spots on leaf.

For their control, collect the fallen leaves and fruits and destroy them. Spray 0.2 % Captan or Dithane M-45 at fortnightly interval.

2. Fruit rot : *Phomopsis* sp. : The flowers are affected and fail to set fruit. The young fruits may drop pre-maturely. Yellow or black spots appear all over the fruit. The disease spreads through the seeds of affected fruits. The incidence is wide spread during rainy season.

Remove all affected twigs, fruits and burn them. Spray Dithane Z-78 at 0.2 per cent at fortnightly interval.

3. Black rot (*Xanthomonas axonopodis pv. Punicae*) : The disease is caused by a bacterium. Black spots develop on the mature fruits as soon as the rain starts. The intensity increases with the increase in humidity.

The disease can be controlled by spraying Bordeaux mixture (2 : 2 : 250) during May and again in June and July.

DISORDER

Cracking or Splitting of Fruits

This disorder is reported to be due to boron and calcium deficiency. There is further attack of insects or fungal attack on the cracked fruits. So fruits become unfit for marketing. The **Mrig bahar** crop is more susceptible to cracking than the crop of other bahars.

Main cause of this malady is the wide variation in moisture content of the soil as well as in the humidity of air due to monsoon. If there is a sudden break in the rains during August, the growth of fruit is arrested. So as a result of the dry atmosphere that follows, the elasticity of the skin is lost ; then there is rain again and growth restarts, results in cracking of fruit skin.

Thus cracking of fruits is mostly due to irregular water supply to the trees. **Ambe-bahar** crop is regularly irrigated, so it does not crack badly. The best treatment is to give regular irrigations to the **Ambe-bahar** crop taking care that at no stage there is a scarcity of water. In case of **Mrig-bahar** crop, the splitting of fruits cannot be controlled altogether as the variation in humidity cannot controlled cracking and can, however, be minimised if the plants are regularly irrigated whenever there is a break in rain. Cracking is correlated with rind thickness. Cultivars like Karkai, Gule-Shah, Bedana, Khog and Jalore Seedless are comparatively tolerant to fruit cracking.

For checking fruit splitting in pomegranate, supply soil moisture regularly through light irrigations. Plant windbreak around the pomegranate plantation. Spray borax @ of 0.1 per cent. In the month of June, give a spray application of GA_3 at 250 ppm. It is better to plant only those varieties which are less prone to fruit cracking.

CHAPTER 22

Jamun

The jamun (***Syzygium* cumini** Skeels) is an important indigenous minor fruit of India. It is known by different names like black plum, Indian black cherry, **Ra jamun** etc. in various parts of India. The jamun is tall, handsome evergreen tree

ORIGIN AND HISTORY

The jamun is native to India or the East Indies. It is also found in Thailand, philippines, Madagascar and some other countries.

The jamun has been successfully introduced into many other tropical countries like West Indies and East and West Africa, and also some other subtriopical regions including Florida, California, Algeria, and Israel. It is widely distributed in India, Sri Lanka, Malaysia, Australia and USA.

AREA AND PRODUCTION

India is the second largest producer of Jamun fruit in the world after China. It is also found growing in Bangladesh, Nepal and Pakistan.

Maharashtra is the largest Jamun producer in India followed by Uttar Pradesh, Tamil Nadu, Gujarat, Assam etc.

In India, the maximum number of jamun trees are found scattered throughout the tropical and subtropical region. It grows in the Indo-Gangetic plains, lower ranges of Himalaya and Tamil Nadu. Jamun is seldom planted in the from of an orchard and generally scattered trees are found in fruit plantations. Organised orcharding of Jamun is still lacking in India. They are also seen growing in parks, on road sides, avenues and as windbreak.

IMPORTANCE AND USES

Jamun is highly nutritive fruit. It is a good source of iron, minerals, protein and sugars. The fruit contains 0.07% protein, 0.04% mineral matter, 0.015% calcium, 0.015% phosphorus, 1.2% iron, 0.9% fibre, 14.0% carbohydrates. 48 I.U. carotene and 18 mg/100 g vitamin C.

The fruit of jamun is tasty and has pleasant flavour. Mostly, the fruit is used for dessert purposes and it is very much liked by the people. The fruit is usually shaken with salt before eating. The fruit has sub-acid spicy flavour. It can be used for making Jam, jellies, squash, beverages, vinegar, pickles and wine. Jamun squash is very refreshing drink during the summer months. Its fruit syrup is very much useful for curing diarrhoea. Fruits are effective medicine against heart and liver trouble. The seed powder of Jamun reduces the quantity of sugar in urine very quickly. Jamun juice mixed with mango juice is very good for quenching thirst for diabetic patient. The vinegar prepared from slightly unripe fruit is stomachic, carminative and diuretic. Small jamun fruits contain high amount of acidity, tannins and anthocyanins are found very suitable for use in the beverage industry.

Jamun seed can be used as a concentrate for animals because it is rich in protein, carbohydrates and calcium. Its wood is used for railway sleepers. It is not attacked by wood decaying insects or fungi.

BOTANY

The genus ***Eugenia*** comprises about 1000 species of evergreen trees and shrubs, most of which are tropical in origin. Some of the old World ***Eugenia*** sp. are now placed in the genus ***Syzygium***. It belongs to the family Myrtaceae. Many of the species yield edible fruits and some of these are of ornamental and medicinal value.

The large evergreen tree has small dark purple fruit with prominent elongated seed. The fruit is astringent even when ripe. A popular fruit, is the rose-apple or *gulab* jaman (***Syzygium jambos***). It is found in South India and West Bengal, the tree is very ornamental. The fruit is yellow in colour, generally insipid in taste and has high pectin content. The species (***Syzygium zeylanica***) grows as a small tree with edible fruits, is found on the Western Ghats of India. A few trees of species ***Syzygium malaccense*** (Malay rose-apple) are found in South Africa. The species ***Syzygium densiflorum*** is used as rootstock in jamun and it is resistant against the attack of termites.

The tree of ***Syzygium cumini*** is 16-25 m high, branchlets white. Leaves broadly oblong or oval, bluntish acuminate. The tree can live more than 100 years.

In jamun, new vegetative shoots emerge as terminal growth on the previous season's branchlets. The new shoots in jamun emerge in two distinct flushes, *i.e.* from February to May and August to October. The growth of these shoots is completed in two phases *i.e.* from first week of March to second week of April and from second week of August to last week of October or second week of November. The flush which appears in the month of February produces maximum growth and flowering. Flower bud differentiation has been observed on 5 to 10 month old branches and it started from last week of January and continued for 43 days. Thee floral parts arose in acropetal succession.

CLIMATE

Jamun is successfully grown under tropical and subtropical climate. It also occurs in the lower range of the Himalayas up to an elevation of 1300 metres and in the Kumaon hills upto 1600 metres above sea level. It is widely grown in the larger parts of India from the Indo-Gangetic plains in the North to Tamil Nadu in the South. It is one of the most hardy fruit crop and can be easily grown in neglected and marshy areas where other fruit plants can not be grown successfully. Jamun is somewhat more susceptible to cold and drought than the seedling mango trees. It requires dry weather at the time of flowering and fruiting. For ripening of fruit and proper development of its size, colour and taste, early rains are considered very beneficial. The fruits show remarkable improvement in these respects after the very first shower of rain.

SOIL

Jamun tree is exact in its soil requirements. The tree requires deep, loam and well-drained soil for its optimum growth and good fruiting. Its cultivation should be avoided in very heavy or light sandy soils.

CHOICE OF VARIETIES

No named or standard varieties of this fruit are cultivated on commercial scale. The common variety grown under North Indian condition is as follows.

Ra Jamun : It produced big sized fruit with average length of 2.5-3.5 cm and of diameter 1.5-2.0 cm. Fruits are oblong in shape, deep purple or bluish black in colour at fully ripe stage. The pulp colour of ripe fruit is purple pink and the fruit is juicy and sweet. The stone is small in size. It ripens in the month of June-July. The variety is very common among the people.

Small sized Jamun : It is a late maturing variety. The average length of fruit is 1.5-2.0 cm and diameter is 1-1.5 cm. The fruit is slightly round in shape, deep purple or blackish in colour at full ripe stage. The colour of the pulp is purple, less in juice, weight and sweetness of pulp in comparison to that of 'Ra Jamun'. The stone is very large. Fruits ripen in the month of August.

CISH-37 : This is a variety from CISH, Lucknow. The fruits are large in size and oblong in shape. TSS is 16 per cent. The average yield in 2.0 q fruits per tree. Ripens in second week of June.

CISH-42 : This is seedless type variety from CISH, Lucknow. The fruits and small in size and round in shape. TSS in 14.7 per cent. The averate yield is 1.5 to 2.0 q fruits per tree. Ripens in second week of June.

Konkon Bahadoli : The variety is from Regional Fruit Research Station. Vengurla, Maharashtra. Fruit weight 15 g. TSS is 16 per cent.

Badama : The fruits are large in size. It is very juicy variety.

Bhado : The fruits ripens in the month of August.

Narendra Jamun - 6 : The variety is recommended by NDUAT, Faizabad.

Goma Priyanka : The variety is recommendation from Central Horticultural Experiment Station, Godhra, Gujarat

Ashada, Jathi and Kaatha varieties are also cultivated in different Jamun growing regions of the country.

PROPAGATION TECHNIQUES

Though lot of jamun plantation is seen on road side or scattered plantation at farmer's field, yet no single well established orchard is reported in North India. Also no systematic work has been done on its propagation.

The most common method of jamun propagation is by seed. Seedling plant bears fruit of variable size and quality. For improved and selected true-to-true, vegetative methods of propagation like inarching, air-layering, grafting and budding have been advocated.

Sexual propagation : Seed are sown fresh in flat nursery beds during July when this fruit ripens. Seeds of Jamun remain viable upto three months after extraction from the fruit. The seeds should be sown at a distance of 15 cm in rows which are 25-30 cm apart. The seedlings can also be raised in ploythene bags of 22.5 - 30 cm size. The bags should be filled with a mixture of soil and farmyard manure in equal proportion. To drain out the excess water the polythene bags should be pricked from all sides before filling the mixture. It has been seen that more than one seedlings come out from a single seed. These seedlings are separated in different bags when they are about two weeks old. The seedling become ready for transplanting after one year.

Plants grown from seed become transplantable during next spring season. But it is advisable to keep them in the nursery upto next rainy season which is the best time of its plantation.

Vegetative Propagation

T-budding and patch budding : According to the recent research conducted at Punjab Agricultural university has revealed that jamun can be best propagated through T-budding and as well as through patch budding. The seedling of jamun is used as a rootstock. The per cent success is higher in T-budding (70%) than patch budding (60%). The best time for budding in both the cases is either during February-March or during August-September. However, the success during August-September is higher.

Inarching : The rootstock used for propagating jamun is the jamun seedlings. For raising the rootstock, seeds are collected from healthy, vigorously growing and high yielding jamun trees. Seedlings are raised either in bed or in pots singly. In the month of June-July one or two year old rootstocks are inarched with the matching thickness of scion. Rootstock are watered if necessary till the grafts are separated from the parent tree. The union will complete in a period of about six weeks.

Veneer grafting : Veneer grafting gives 31 per cent success when one year old seedlings are used as rootstock. The shoots are taken from spring flush and the method is employed in the month of July.

PLANTING OPERATION

Jamun can be transplanted during spring (February-March) or during monsoon (August-September). However, the later season of planting is considered better because the plants easily get established during the rainy season. The plants are transplanted with earth ball and are given irrigation till they get established. The size of the pit should be 1 × 1 × 1 m and these should be filled with a mixture of surface soil, silt and well rotten farmyard manure.

The jamun is planted at the distance of 10-12 metres in square system, thus accommodates 105-75 plants per hectare. The grafted and budded plants can be spaced at 8m × 8m and seedling trees at 10m × 10m.

FLOWERING AND FRUITING

The flowering in jamun starts in the first week of March and continues up to the middle of April. The trees are in full bloom in the second week of April. The inflorescence in jamun is generally borne in the axils of leaves on branchlet. The flowers ae hermaphrodite, light yellow in colour. The maximum anthesis and dehiscence were recorded between 10 A.M. and 12 Noon. The pollen fertility was higher in the beginning of the season. The maximum receptivity of stigma was observed one day after anthesis.

Jamun is a cross-pollinated fruit. The pollination is done by honeybees, house flies and wind. The maximum fruit set *i.e.* 32.6 - 36.0% was obtained when pollination was done one day after anthesis. Thereafter, a sharp decline was observed in fruit set.

Three distinct phases of fruit growth in jamun are recorded. During the first phase (15-52 days after fruit set), the rate of growth was slow. In the second phase (52-58 days after fruit set), the rate of development was quite rapid and the third and last phase (58-60 days after fruit set) comprised comparatively slow growth with little addition of the fruit weight. The length and diameter of fruit showed a continuous increase with advancement of maturity. The colour of jamun fruit changed from dark green at fruit set to light reddish colour at partial ripening and dark or bright purple at full ripe stage. The fruit took 63 days for compete ripening from fruit set. The ripe jamun had 76 per cent edible portion and 3. 1 : 1 pulp to seed ratio. TSS and sugars followed an increasing trend, while tannin content followed a decreasing trend during growth and development.

ORCHARD CULTURAL PRACTICES

Irrigation

During the initial year, the jamun plants required 8-10 irrigation in a year while bearing trees (full grown) required 4-6 irrigation during the summer months of May and June when fruits ripen. In the remaining period of the year, irrigation may be given when there are no rains or dry spell persists. During winter month, irrigation proves useful as it protects the plants from frost injury.

Jamun trees can thrive well under rainfed condition as it develop deep tap root system and able to extract water from the deeper layers of soil.

Intercropping

To supplement the income from pre-bearing period of jamun, intercropping should be practised judiciously. Intercropping also improved fertility of the soil. Fruit crops like, peach, plum, guava, kinnow, kagzi lime, phalsa, and papaya can be grown as filler trees. Such filler trees can be uprooted when the jamun trees starts bearing commercial crop. The leguminous crops like gram, peas, moong and mash can be grown successfully. In addition, intercrops of vegetables near established market may be taken with cauliflower, cabbage, knol khol, radish, brinjal, turnip, carrot etc.

Manuring and Fertilization

During the per-bearing period of jamun, a dose of 20 kg well rotten farmyard manure should be applied. To the bearing tree 80 kg FYM per tree should be supplied annually for proper growth and fruiting. Sometimes in a highly fertile soils, the plants produce profuse vegetative growth and fruiting is delayed. Under such conditions, the manures should not be given and irrigation should also be given sparingly and withheld in September-October and again in February-March. This procedure will prove beneficial in fruit bud formation, flowering and fruit setting. Ringing and root pruning are also helpful.

The Jamun trees should be manured and fertilized judiciously for obtaining commercial crop. One year old plant can be given 5 kg FYM, 125 g nitrogen and 50 g each phosphorus and potash. Every year same quantity of fertilizers should be increased and stabilize the dose at the age of ten years when the tree is considered full grown. At this age and after that add 50 kg FYM, 1250 g nitrogen and 500 g phosphorus and potash to each plant for economic bearing.

TRAINING AND PRUNING

Jamun plants should be trained according to the modified leader system. Regular pruning is not required in jamun plants. However, in later years, the dry twigs and crossed branches are removed. While training the plant, the framework of branches is allowed to develop above 60-100 cm from the ground level. The branches of the Jamun tree are brittle, thus wider crotch angles in scaffold branches should be developed for better frame work. Annual corrective pruning is done after harvesting the fruits.

Top working : The jamun plants, on account of their tap root system, do not stand transplanting well unless the operation is performed at a fairly young stage. The raising of budded plants in the nursery takes at least 2 to 3 years from the time of sowing the seed to the time of transplanting the plants in their permanent places. During this period, the root system goes rather deep and is badly injured while removing the plants from the nursery. This generally results in a fairly high percentage of mortality of the plants after transplanting. In order to avoid this, the seeds may be sown *in situ* or very young seedlings transplanted in their permanent places and when they get established in 2 to 3 years and give out 3 to 4 branches, the branches as well as the leader are budded *in situ*. The operation should be done in stages completing it in two years as otherwise if the branches and the leader are headed back in one stroke, the tree will receive shock and a set back in growth. Keeping of one or two ungrafted shoots or nurse shoots as they are called for a year or so, keeps the root system well fed and they also give protection to the scaffold limbs and the trunk from sun-burn and frost injury. The trunk and the exposed portion of scaffold limbs should be protected against sun burn by white-washing them with unhydrated lime and wrapping the exposed parts with old gunny bags or dry straw.

FLOWER AND FRUIT DROP

In jamun, the flower and fruit drop start just after opening of flowers and continue up to maturity. About 65 per cent flower and fruit drop in the first five weeks and since then a maximum of 19-21 per cent flowers and fruits drop off up to maturity. Only 12-15 per cent flowers reach maturity. The flower and fruit drop are found at 3 stages. The first drop takes place during bloom or shortly there after. This proves to be the heaviest drop as about 52% of the flowers drop off after 4 weeks from flowering. The second drop starts about 35-40 days of full bloom and apparently there is no difference between the developing and aborting fruits. The third drop takes place after 42-50 days of full bloom and continues till 15th July.

Control : The extent of flower and fruit drop in jamun may be reduced by two sprays of 60 ppm GA_3, one at full bloom and the other 15 days after initial setting of fruit.

HARVESTING AND FRUIT HANDLING

The grafted jamun starts bearing after 6-7 years while the seedling one after 8-10 years of planting. The fruit ripen in the month of June-July and takes about 90 – 120 days to ripen after fruit setting. The main characteristic of ripen fruit at full size is deep purple or black colour. The jamun fruit is non-climacteric in nature. The fruit should be picked immediately when it is ripe, because it can not be retained on the tree in ripe stage. The ripe fruits are picked singly by hand and in all cases care should be taken to avoid all possible damage to fruits. For harvesting, the picker climbs the tree with bags of cotton slung on the shoulder. The fruits of jamun is generally harvested daily and sent to market on the same day. The fruit is highly perishable and can be kept in good condition for about 2-3 days under ordinary conditions.

The average yield of fruit from a full grown seedling jamun tree is about 80-100 kg and from a grafted one 60-70 kg per year.

The storage life of jamun fruit is 6 days at room temperature and 3 weeks at low temperature (9°C and RH 85-90%) when pre-cooled fruits are kept in perforated polythene bags.

INSECTS-PESTS

1. White-fly (*Dialeurodes eugeniae*) : It damages the tree in all parts of India. Sometimes the fruits of jamun get wormy due to attack of fruit fly.

Pests can be controlled by maintaining sanitary situation in the orchard. Pick up the affected fruits and burry them deep in soil. The area under the tree should be dug so that the maggots in the affected fruits and the pupae hibernating in the soil may be destroyed.

2. Leaf eating caterpillar (*Carea subtilis*) : It is reported to damage the plant in South India at Coimbatore. The insect infest the leaves and may defoliate the trees.

The pest can be controlled by spraying 625 ml Rogor in 500 litres of water.

3. Bark eating caterpillar (*Indarbela quadrinotata*) : It is a polyphagous pest of major importance on **Jamun** especially in north-western India. As a result of larvae feeding inside the branches and the trunk, the translocation of cell-sap is disrupted and growth as well as fruiting capacity of the tree is reduced. Remove the webbing and inject kerosene oil into the holes during September - October and again in January - February.

4. Squirrels, Parrots, Crows and Birds : The jamun fruits are also damaged by these squirrels, parrots, crows and birds. For keeping them away, beating of drum or flinging small dry earthern balls through a sling is useful.

DISEASES

Leaf spot and fruit rot : The disease caused due to ***Glomerella cingulata***. Affected leaf shows scattered spots, light brown or reddish brown in colour. The affected fruits rot and shrivel.

The disease can be controlled with fungicide like Dithane Z–78 at 0.02% or Bordeaux mixture (2 : 2 : 250).

CHAPTER 23

Phalsa

The **phalsa** (*Grewia asiatica L.*) being a hardy fruit, can be grown successfully even on inferior and marginal lands. Though grown on a small scale, this fruit has bright prospectus for extending its cultivation, especially in lands near cities and towns. **Phalsa** groves grown on modern lines, with proper care to cultural practices like manuring, irrigation, pruning, control of diseases and pests etc. can be made to yield good crops and handsome returns to growers.

ORIGIN, HISTORY AND DISTRIBUTION

The presence of its name in Sanskrit and also in many other Indian languages such as Punjabi, Bengali, Tamil and Telgu show that **phalsa** is native to India. It has also been mentioned in early **Vedic** writings. The **phalsa** belong to the family Tiliaceae which includes 18 genera and about 350 species. Some of the genera and species are of Indian origin. The members of this family occur all over the world, especially in the tropics of both the Northern and Southern Hemisphere. The plants of this family, however, are not met with in very cold regions, such as arctic and antarctic.

Phalsa has been distributed to north and central Thialand and the Philippines. It is widely cultivated in Bangladesh, India and Pakistan.

AREA AND PRODUCTION

Phalsa is grown on about 400 hectares in India. It is commercially cultivated in Uttar Pradesh, Rajasthan, Madhya Pradesh, Maharashtra, Gujarat, Pujnab and Haryana. Besides these States it is also cultivated on limited scale in Andhra Pradesh, Bihar, West Bengal, the Western Ghats, the Malabar Coast in South India and Himachal Pradesh.

In Punjab, its cultivation is becoming popular in Fazilka and Abohar area. It is also grown in Amritsar and Ferozepur districts.

IMPORTANCE AND USES

Ripe **phalsa** fruits are sub-acidic and good source of vitamin A and C. They are fair source of phosphorus and iron. The edible portion of the fruit is 69 per cent and moisture content is 80.8 per cent. **Phalsa** is very rich in nutrition and contain 1.3 g protein, 0.9 g fat, 14.7 g carbohydrates per 100 g fruit. It is a rich source of mineral matter and contain 129 mg calcium, 39 mg phosphorus, 3.1 mg iron. Its carotene content is 419 I.U. and contain 39 mg vitamin C per 100 g of fruit.

Phalsa fruit contains various bioactive compounds like anthocyanins, tanins, phenolics and flavonoids.

Phalsa is mostly consumed as fresh fruit and have cooling effect on human system. Its fruits, roots and leaves form an important ingredient of many recipes used to cure a variety of ailments, according to the Indian and **Unani** systems of medicine. The fruits are excellent for making juice, syrup and squash.

The **phalsa** fruit is astringent, cooling in its effect and has beneficial gastric properties. The water extract obtained from the **phalsa** bark is very soothing and relieves irritation. The roots of the **phalsa** plants are used for curing rheumatism. Its leaves are ground and applied to boil and other swollen body parts. Phalsa fruits possess anticancer and antioxidant properties.

The yellowish-white phalsa wood is close-grained, strong and elastic. It is used for preparing shoulder poles, bows, spear handles, baskets and shingles. The phalsa bark is treated to yield fibre which can be put to many uses. The shoots of the plants after pruning can be utilized either for making baskets or supporting vegetable crops. Pruning of one full grown phalsa plant is sufficient for making one or two baskets.

BOTANY

The genus **Grewia** has about 150 species, out of which about 40 occur in India. One of most important plant of this genus, which yield edible fruit is phalsa ***(Grewia asiatica)***. It belong to family Malvaceae and sub-family Grewioideae. Earlier *Grewia asiatica* L. was called *Grewia subinaequalis* DC. In Pakistan 10 species belonging to genus *Grewia* have been identified. *Grewia asiatica* is a cultivated species. It is also cultivated in South Asian countries.

The **phalsa** is a deciduous bush and when unpruned can grow into a tree upto 10 metres or more with a trunk nearly 30 cm in diameter. In the cultivated form, however, it is kept as a bush by heavy annual pruning. Its stem is hard and woody, circular and non-hairy. It has rough grey bark which yields a mucilaginous juice used for clarifying sugar. Leaves are 7.5-15 cm long, dull green on the upper surface and light green on the lower surface. Leaves are petiolate, stipulate, orbicular or broadly ovate. The leaf margins are coarsely and irrgularly toothed. They are rounded or more or less cordate at the base, rounded acute or accuminate at the apex. The leaf venation is reticulate, multicostate and divergent. The leaf base is 5-nerved, the smaller nerves are not arched, they are prominent beneath, transverse one being more or less parallel. The leaves are softly tomentose on both upper and lower surfaces, becoming less hairy and rough when mature. Petioles 1.5 to 2 cm long. There are 2-7 peduncles and a peduncle has 3-6 pedicellate yellow flowers in auxillary clusters. Generally, the flowers are hermaphrodite. A normal flower has 4-5 sepals, 4-5 petals, 70-80 free stamens and fully developed gynoecium. The phalsa fruit is drupe, globose in shape and pea sized. It is red or purple in colour, is indistinctly lobed and has 1-2 seeds in it.

CLIMATE

Phalsa relish distinct winter and summer for best growth, yield and quality. In regions having no winter, the plant does not shed leaves and produce flower more than once, thus yielded poor quality fruits. Full grown plants can tolerate freezing temperature for a short period. The plants can tolerate temperature as high as 44°C. High temperature during fruit development favours ripening of fruits. At flowering time, clear weather is needed, whereas rains at that time affect fruit-setting adversely.

The **phalsa** is one of the hardiest fruit plants and can be grown successfully throughout the Punjab and Haryana. Being deciduous in habit, it can withstand frost quite well. However, care should be taken to select sites which are not subject to very low temperatures during winter. It can also grow successfully in hot and dry climatic conditions, such as those prevailing in the districts of Ferozepur, Bathinda and Sangrur of Punjab. It can withstand occassional drought and water shortages better than fruit plants. However, for raising profitable crop of **phalsa,** satisfactory arrangements for irrigation need to be made.

SOIL

The **phalsa** is not at all fastidious in its soil requirements and can grow quite successfully in almost every kind of soil. Around Amritsar (Punjab), where the soils are comparatively heavy, its plants grow well and bear bumper crops. At many other places such as Ludhiana, it yields well under lighter soil conditions. Though the ideal soil for growing **phalsa** is the rich loamy type. Under water logged conditions plants become chlorotic and make poor growth.

Proper soil drainage is another factor which should be kept in mind. However, soils where water stagntes for many days during the reainy season or those which have a poor sub-surface drainage and are water-logged should not be selected for commercial cultivation of **phalsa.**

CHOICE OF VARIETIES

In **phalsa,** no distinct cultivar is identified. Some growers have, however, given names as Local and Sharbati. Two distinct types i.e. Tall and Dwarf were recognised at Hisar. Dwarf type was found to be more productive.

1. Tall type : Plant height is 4.5 m, leaf size 20 × 18 cm. Leaves are light green in colour. Average fruit size is 2.07 cm and weighing 0.48 g. Average yield per bush is 5.2 kg. Pulp is 81.5 per cent, juice 5.4 per cent. TSS 14 per cent and Acidity 4.64 per cent.

2. Dwarf type : Plant height is 3.4 m, leaf size 18 × 15 cm. Leaves greenish white in colour. Fruit size 2.26 cm, weight 0.54 g. Average yield is 3.5 kg per bush. Pulp 60.3 per cent, juice recovery is 34.6 per cent. TSS 12.1 per cent with acidity 3.63 per cent.

PROPAGATION TECHNIQUES

The **phalsa** is usually propagated from seeds, which is the easiest and most commonly used method of propagation. The propagation of phalsa from cuttings is also possible and the success can be improved with the use of growth regulators.

Raising of seedlings : For raising the **phalsa** seedlings, large sized, purple black coloured fruits are collected when the crop is ready in the end of May or beginning of June. After extracting from the fruits, the seeds should be washed and dried under shade. These seeds are sown in raised beds when there is sufficient humidity in the atmosphere. Rainy season (July-August) is the best time for sowing of seed. The seeds on raised beds are sown in lines which are 10-15 cm apart from each other. In the rows, the seed should be sown 4-5 cm apart and 1.5 to 2 cm deep. The seeds should be covered with sand or light soil mixed with well rotten and dry farmyard manure. The beds should be watered regularly with water Can but too much watering should be avoided as the excessive moisture conditions cause poor development of the plants. The beds should be kept free from weeds. Initially, one hand weeding is recommended, otherwise the roots of small plants get damaged if weeding is done with khurpa etc.

When the seedlings come out and have made 5-7 cm growth, light dressing of calcium ammonium nitrate or Ammonium sulphate at the rate of 50 g/sq metre of nursery area is applied. This encourage rapid growth of the seedlings. Seedlings are ready for transplanting in the following winter i.e. during January-February.

Propagation through cuttings : The **phalsa** plants can also be multiplied through hard-wood cuttings. The cuttings should be prepared during December-January and kept for callusing. The use of root promoting harmones such as Indole butyric acid @ 100 ppm enhances the success of rooted cuttings.

PLANTING OPERATION

Land is prepared well before the plants are set in the field. When there is enough time, a cover crop such as **guara, jantar or senji** may be sown in the soil. After these crops produce enough vegetative growth, they should be burried into the soil. Before planting, the orchard site should be properly laid out according to the square or the hexagonal system. Half metre deep pits of half metre diameter should be dug and refilled with a mixture of top-soil and well rotten farmyard manure in the ratio of 1 : 1. To save the plants from possible attack of white ants add 10 ml of chlorpyriphos 20 EC in 2 kg soil to each pit. After this, the field is thoroughly irrigated and transplanting is done when the soil is in friable condition.

The **phalsa** plants are spaced at various distances in different regions of India. Eight to twelve months old seedlings are better for planting in the field. The plants are spaced at 1.5 metres apart by which 4400 plants are accommodated in one hectare by the square system of planting.

The **phalsa** plants should preferably be transplanted in the field during January-February before they start new growth. The plants being dormant at that time, they can be lifted from nursery with bare roots. However, for transplanting during August-September, the seedlings have to be lifted from the nursery alongwith earth balls. Transplanting in the rainy season, is, therefore, a little more cumbersome and riskier than that done in the spring, when the plants are dormant.

FLOWERING AND FRUITING

Flowering in **phalsa** starts from February-March and continues till May. The first flower to open is at the base. Flowers are borne in the axil of leaves. The flowers are mostly cross pollinated and honey-bee seems to play major role in pollination.

The flower buds become plumpy before anthesis. The first sign of anthesis is the appearance of a slit in sepals at the base of the bud. The slit widens and at first only one sepal falls apart. The other sepals fall one by one and the whole process of flower opening is complete within half an hour. The dehiscence of anthesis in phalsa takes place before the flowers are completely open.

ORCHARD CULTURAL PRACTICES

Irrigation

As **phalsa** is regarded a drought resistant fruit plant. However, it has been observed that in Punjab, Haryana and other neighbouring northern Indian regions, irrigation is essential for securing high yield of better quality fruits. Its plants not needed any irrigations till January. Adequate supply of irrigation water at regular intervals specially during flowering and fruiting periods is very essential for ensuring better health of plants and more profitable yields. A light irrigation should be given after pruning and fertilization of the plants. During the early part of the spring, when the new growth starts and the temperature is usually low, the irrigation interval may be kept at about 2-3 weeks. The demand for water increases after the middle of April and consequently the irrigation interval may be reduced to 7-10 days. At this time, the plants should not be allowed to suffer from water shortage; as it would adversely affect the yield and quality of fruit. Regular irrigation should be applied to the plants till the fruit is harvested and the monsoon sets in.

As the roots of the plants are active even during winter, adequate soil moisture should be maintained in the root zone. During winter, one or two light irrigations may suffice if there are no rains.

Interplanting

Many fruit plants grown in the plains of North India such as mango, litchi and pear comes into bearing on commercial scale very late. These fruit plants have a slow rate of growth and the space between the tree rows remains unoccupied for several years. The growers can, therefore, utilize the empty space between the permanent fruit trees for raising some quick-growing fruit plants like phalsa. **Phalsa** has another advantage over other quick-growing fruits suitable for interplanting that it is kept low-headed by severe pruning every year and does not cause overcrowding in the orchard. **Phalsa** being a deciduous plant, does not require much water during the dormant period (winter months). **Phalsa** should be interplanted only in the middle of the permanent tree rows. As soon as the permanent trees come into bearing, the **phalsa** plants should be uprooted, so that the main fruit crop does not suffer.

Manuring and Fertilization

Generally, **phalsa** is planted on comparatively poor soils. Some cover crop such as **guara, jantar** or **senji** should be grown in the field where **phalsa** is to be planted. This practice add sufficient quantity of organic matter to the soil and enriches it.

In order to get profitable crops of good quality, full grown **phalsa** plants should be given 10-15 kg of well rotten farmyard manure, soon after planting. Nitrogenous fertilizers (170 g urea per bush) should also be applied, preferably in two split dose-one at the time of flowering and second after fruit-setting. Higher yield of **phalsa** can be obtained by application of 100 kg N, 40 kg P and 25 kg K per hectare, respectively. Trials at Rajasthan Agricultural University, Udaipur revealed that application of NPK @ 100, 40, 25 kg per hectare gave higher yield.

Zinc and iron were found to influence berry size and juiciness in phalsa. $ZnSO_4$ @ 0.4 per cent at prebloom stage and after berry set improved the juice content. Ferrous sulphate at 0.4 per cent alone or in combination with zinc improved the berry size.

TRAINING AND PRUNING

Phalsa is usually trained as a bush. The plant can also be trained as head system with a single stem. The height of the single stem should be kept at one metre. The plant produce shoots above one metre just as in bush system.

The **phalsa** fruit is borne in clusters in the axils of leaves on the new growing shoots produced during the current season. Annual pruning is, therefore, very essential to have new vigorous shoots to ensure regular and heavy fruiting.

The general practice of cutting back the **phalsa** plants to the ground level every year during the dormant period is not in order. Investigations carried out on this aspect have shown that the phalsa plants pruned to a height of one metre during January- February produce a greater number of new shoots than those which are pruned to the ground level. The growers are, therefore, advised to prune their **phalsa** plants at a height of one metre from the ground level.

The **phalsa** plants are rather slow in shedding their leaves in winter. The best time for their pruning is when the plants have shed their leaves and in all cases the operation should finished well before the start of new growth.

USE OF GROWTH REGULATORS

Growth regulators have proved effective in increasing the fruit set and yield in phalsa. GA_3 at 10 ppm increased the setting of fruit and yield appreciably. CCC at 250 ppm sprayed twice at an interval of 7 days after 50 per cent fruit set increased the fruit size. Ethephon at 1000 ppm resulted in maximum ripening in 5 days after application. SADH 1000 ppm at early stage of plant growth reduced the plant height and brought improvement in yield and fruit quality. Spraying of GA_3 at 60 ppm once at the beginning of flowering, another after 15 days and ethrel at 1000 ppm when ripening of berries had just started, increased the fruit retention percentage and yield. They also reduced the harvesting span and increased the TSS of the fruit.

HARVESTING OF FRUIT

The **phalsa** plants begin to bear fruits in the second year. A good commercial crop is usually obtained during third year. In the Punjab and Haryana, the harvesting season of phalsa fruit starts by the end of May and lasts till the end of June. The fruits should be picked when the colour has changed to a deep reddish brown and the pulp tastes sweet. Several pickings are necessary as all the fruits do not ripen at one time. The fruit-picking is usually done on alternate days. The fruit is packed in small baskets or 2 kg packs.

Under optimum conditions, a **phalsa** bush yields on an average about 4-5 kg of fruit.

INSECT-PESTS

1. Plum hairy caterpillar (*Euproctis fraterna*) : The caterpillars feed gregariously on leaf lamina skeletonizing it completely. Subsequently, the caterpillars segregate and gnaw the leaves. In case of severe infestation, the entire plant may be denuded.

Collect and destroy the egg masses and the gregariously feeding young caterpillars. Spray Dursban 20 EC (chlorpyriphos) @ 200 ml in 100 liter of water when caterpillars are noticed.

2. Bark eating caterpillar (*Indarbela tetraonis*) : Larvae feed inside the branches and trunk, thus translocation of cell-sap is disrupted. Growth and fruiting capacity of the tree is reduced. Remove the webbing and inject kerosene oil into the holes in December-January after pruning.

3. Psylla *(Diphorina grewia)* : The pest suck cell sap from young leaves. The growth of the plant is reducing and fruting is affected.

It can be controlled by spraying Rogor 30 EC (dimethoate) 1000 ml in 500 litres of water in first week of March.

DISEASES

1. Brown spot : The disease is caused by fungus ***Cercospora grewiae.*** The brown spot of phalsa is quite wide spread in the Punjab and is very severe from June to August. It results in premature leaf-fall when the attack is severe. The disease first appears as tiny lesions on the upper and lower surface of the leaf. In the beginning, these lesions are covered with a white mass of fungus. Gradually, the lesions enlarge and become reddish brown to dark brown. Many times, several lesions coalesce to form big spots which are very conspicuous and may cover a large part of the leaf.

To control this disease, the leaves and prunings should be collected soon after removal and destroyed to check the fresh infection of the new leaves coming out in spring. As soon as the first symptoms appear on the leaves, the plants should be sprayed with Bordeaux mixture 2 : 2 : 250 or 0.3 per cent Dithane Z-78.

2. Pinspot of phalsa : The disease is caused by ***Phyllosticta grewiae.*** The disease can appear any time during the growing season of phalsa and may cause considerable damage to the foliage. Small brown to dark brown, circular to irregular pinspot like lesions appear on the leaves.

This disease can be controlled by sprays given above for the brown spot of phalsa.

3. Powdery mildew *(Oidium Sp.)* : Leaves are affected. White powder appear on shoots and under side of leaves. The disease appears after rainy season. It cause defoliation of the plant.

The disease can be checked by spraying the plants with Wettable sulphur @ one litre in 500 litres of water as soon as the white powdery mass appears on leaves and shoots.

CHAPTER 24

Avocado

The avocado (***Persea americana*** Mill) is the highly nutritive fruit. It is an evergreen sub-tropical fruit. It is also called as Butter fruit. Avocado fruit is a single seeded berry.

ORIGIN AND HISTORY

The avocado is native to Mexico in Central America. The early Spanish explorers recorded its cultivation from Mexico to Peru. It was introduced to Southern Spain in 1601 and into Jamaica in about 1650. In Florida it was first recorded in 1833 and in California in 1856. It has also been found to grow wild all over South America and West Indies and has lately spread to many other tropical countries like Hawaii, Philippine Islands, Cuba, Sri Lanka and India. It is not exactly known when avocado was first introduced into India but it seems it may have been introduced in the south and west coasts of India about 75 to 100 years ago from Sri Lanka. In Western India, avocado was for the first time imported from Sri Lanka in the year 1941 and planted at the Ganeshkhind Fruit Experiment Station, Poona.

AREA AND PRODUCTION

Avocado is cultivated commercially in Mexico, Chile, Dominican Republic, Indonesia, USA, Calombia, Peru, Kenya, Brazil, Rawanda and China. The annual production of Avocado's in the world is 45 lakh metric tonnes growing on 6 lakh hectares area. Avocado is most important fruit of Mexico producing 28 percent of the total world production.

In India, avocado is grown in Karnataka, Kerala, Tamil Nadu, Andhra Pradesh, Maharashtra and Sikkim. Production of this fruit is estimated 500 – 1000 mt annually for domestic market. Presently area under avocado growing in India is limited. But, there is great scope for its cultivation in the country on account of providing nutritional security to the people. Sizeable acreage can be brought under this fruit crop in the near future.

IMPORTANCE AND USES

Avocado has twice as much energy value as in bananas. It is a rich source of fat, potassium, phosphorus, magnesium, calcium, chloride and ascorbic acid. It contains 245 calories, 26.4% fat, 368 mg potassium, 10 mg calcium, 38 mg phosphorus, 35 mg magnesium, 11 mg chlorine and 16 mg ascorbic acid per 100 g of edible portion. The protein content forms 1-4 per cent. Avocado also has fair amount of vitamin A and B.

The pulp of avocado has a buttery consistency and blend in taste with a nutty flavour. It has a pleasant aroma of the interior shell of a tender coconut. A person normally gets used to the taste and starts relishing it after tasting once or twice. Its pulp is used as a sandwich filling or spread, in icecream and milk shake. The fruit is considered better for diabetic patient due to low sugar content. It's fat is harmless. The oil from avocado is widely used for the preparation of cosmetics. The purple variety contains as much as 17 per cent of oil. The avocado for all purposes is a salad fruit and should be eaten fresh.

BOTANY

The avocado belongs to the family Lauraceae. The three ecological races have been recognised *i.e.* Mexican race, Guatemalan race and West Indian race. The Mexican race is included in the group ***Persea drymifolia*** and the Guatemalan and the West Indian races are included in the group of ***Persea americana.***

1. Mexican Race: The leaves of this race are smaller than those of Guatemalan and West Indian races and sharper at the apex. It is characterised by small fruits weighing less than 250 g. The fruit tends to ripen within six to eight months after flowering. Fruits have thin, smooth skin with a large seed fitting loosely in the central cavity. The flowers are heairly pubescent. This is a high land race. Amongst the three races, this is the most resistant to cold temperature. It does not thrive in tropical region.

2. Guatemalan Race: This race is native to the highlands of Central America. It tends to bear larger fruit weighing 600 g which requires a longer time to develop and ripen. The fruits ripen 9 to 12 months after flowering. The fruits have thicker, harder and rougher skin as compared to Mexican race. It's seed, held tightly in the cavity of the fruit are small. The oil content ranges between 8-15 per cent. The trees are less resistant to cold than those of the Mexican race.

3. West Indian Race: This group is native to the low lands of Central America. The fruits are medium sized, skin is smooth but leathery and glossy. Fruits are borne on long stalks and require upto 9 months for ripening from flowering. Seeds are large, fitting loosely in the cavity. The oil content is low *i.e.,* 3- 10 per cent. The race is the least resistant to cold. This is the race which is likely to be successful in most parts of tropical India.

CLIMATE

The avocado prefers mild winters of the tropics and sub-tropics. The trees are tender to frost and do not stand hot dry winds. The range of mean maximum and minimum temperatures in the Nilgiri hills in Tamil Nadu, where avocado is grown are 27.2°C to 33.9°C and 14.9°C to 22.2°C, respectively. Avocado is successful in South India especially in areas with rainfall of 75 to 190 cm. It grows fairly well on the slopes of Nilgiris between altitude of 610 and 1524 metres. The West Indian varieties will probably grow well in the equable climate of moist regions of south, west and east India from sea-level to elevations ranging from 305 to 914 metres, but Guatemalan varieties may require much higher altitude. In region, where minimum winter temperatures of -0.5 to 3.5°C occur, only the Mexican race survives. Mexican and Guetemalan cultivars withstand low temperature of 10 – 15°C.

SOIL

Avocado can be grown on a wide range of soil types. It thrives best on a loam of medium texture overlying a porous sub-soil. The plants are extremely sensitive to poor drainage and cannot stand waterlogging. Heavy clay soils should be avoided as avocado succumbs quickly to wet area. Some of the loams and sandy loams of alluvial origin are excellent.

The optimum pH for avocado is 5-7 and are intolerant to saline conditions. Shallower soils less than 60 cm in depth and with rocky or gravelly substrata close to the surface should be strictly avoided. The root system does not fully develop in such soils. The trees remain dwarf and die a premature death at a very early age and are also liable to be seriously damaged or totally uprooted in exposed windy situations.

CHOICE OF VARIETIES

The following are the important cultivars of avocado :

Purple: It was introduced into India from Sri Lanka. This cultivar belongs to West Indian race. The fruit is pearshaped. Its size is 12 – 15 cm × 6 – 9 cm with a long neck and about 250 g in weight. The skin is smooth, shinning, deep crimson or maroon in colour and leathery in texture. It can easily be removed from pulp. The seed is set loose in the cavity. Flesh is thick, firm, smooth and fine in texture, deep yellow and with a rich nutty flavour.

Green: It was also introduced into India from Sri Lanka. It belongs to the Guatemalan race. The fruit is large and oval in shape. The surface is slightly rough and yellowish green in colour. Skin is thin. Seed is large, roundish and sits tight in the cavity. The neck is solid. The flesh is thick, greenish yellow, changing to green and has a mild nutty flavour.

Fuerte : This is the most popular cultivar of avocado. It belongs to group B and is a hybrid between Mexican and Guatemalan races grown in California. Fruits are pyriform in shape. Average weight of fruit ranges between 225-450 g with 18-26 per cent oil content. Fairly resistant to cold. The cultivar is better suited to subtropical climate.

Hass: It is also grown in California and mature much earlier than Fuerte. It belongs to Group A cultivar. Fruits are medium sized, roundish and turn purple on ripening. The cultivar is suitable to subtropical climate.

Yulia: The cultivar was selected from California. It has excellent flavour. The average weight is 200 g. The yield is good but tree bears alternately.

Lula, Pollock, Ardith, Ace, Pino, Green Gold and Pinkerton are other important varieties of Avocado.

PROPAGATION TECHNIQUES

The avocado is commonly propagated by seed in most of the tropical countries. Seedlings usually vary somewhat in their characteristics from their parents and do not generally breed true to type. To ensure parent quality in the progeny, it is necessary to propagate the avocado by vegetative methods such as cuttings, layering, budding or grafting.

Vegetative propagation: The rooting capability of avocado cuttings varies greatly depending on the races and cultivars. The Mexican race is relatively easy-to-root whereas the West Indian race is quite difficult. The Guatemalan race is intermediate in rooting ability on cuttings.

Avocado should preferably be propagated vegetatively by budding or grafting. The shield-budding, Forkert-budding or side grafting can be successfully followed. In Tamil Nadu, layering as well as appraoch grafting gave up to 75 per cent success. In West Bengal, chip budding was found more successful. The grafted plants become ready in six months and may be planted in the field after another six months.

Purple avocado serves as a good rootstock for avocado. The Guatemalan rootstocks are more sensitive to cold and has also proved more susceptible to high pH, chlorosis and to **verticillium** wilt. Mexican race rootstocks are used generally in Israel and in South Africa. West Indian rootstocks are preferred in warmer regions or where salinity is a problem.

PLANTING OPERATION

The planting distance will have to be determined according to the vegetative vigour developed by the tree of a particular variety in a given set of environments.

The tree is planted in pits (1 × 1 × 1 m) filled with top soil mixed with well rotton farmyard manure, compost or leaf mould. The distance between plants must not be less than 10 metres. In this way 105 plants will be accommodated in one hectare. Under Poona conditions, a spacing of 8-9 metres may be adopted for both the Purple and the Green varieties. The commonly followed spacing in different areas is 7 × 7m but it may vary from 6 – 12 m in the square system. On the sea coast and on alluvial soils where the vegetative growth of the trees would be more luxuriant, wider spacing may be necessary. The plants are planted with a ball of earth around the roots. The grafting joint should be well above the ground while planting and supported by stakes against possible damage from strong winds. If there is any danger of water-logging, they should be planted on mounds, as avocado cannot withstand waterlogged conditions.

The plants should be watered regularly during the seasons other than the monsoon and particularly during the summer, as otherwise the branches are likely to be scorched and the tree vitally damaged. The avocado tree is particularly subject to wind injury. For this reason, windy localities and sites should be strictly avoided.

FLOWERING AND FRUITING

Vegetatively raised plants usually bear earlier whereas seedling trees start bearing at 5-6 years age. The plants have a marked tendency to biennial bearing and girdling increases the yield of such plants.

The inflorescence in avocado is a compound panicle of raceme with a unique flower behaviour, thus, termed as protogynous, diurnally synchronous dichogamy. The female and male parts mature at different times, it synchronises in such a way that all the open flowers on a tree are female at one time and male at a different time. The synchronisation is diurnal for each tree, flower is functionally male at one part of the day and functionally female during another part of the same day. The dichogamy is also protogynous, the pistil maturing earlier than the stamen. While the flower is structurally bisexual, it is functionally unisexual. Each flower opens twice and is closed in between, the first time it functions as a female, the second time as a male.

Based on this unique flower behaviour, avocado cultivars can be divided into two groups *i.e.* A and B. In group A, first opening takes place in the morning, second opening during the afternoon. In group B, the first opening is in the afternoon and the second opening in next morning. Therefore, every morning A- pistils can be fertilized by B-pollen, while during afternoon B- pistils are ready to receive A-pollen. It is reported that not all cultivars or seedling trees follow this pattern and rhythum is upset by cold or cloudy weather. The single tree is often unfruitful and mixed planting of cultivars is desirable. Pollination is done chiefly by honey-bees.

In the climate of Poona the avocado produces flowers from November to January in three main flushes. The three flushes of flower clusters do not raise from different branches but arise in succession from the extension of the same leafy shoots. The flowers produced from November to December fail to set fruit, while those produced in January set a successful crop. Similarly in the lower foot hills of Nilgiris, it has been observed that November-December flowering are occasional and not very dependable for successful setting of crop but the March and April flowering do set successful crop.

ORCHARD CULTURAL PRACTICES

Irrigation

The first watering should be given soon after the application of manures and the second watering on the third day, so as to ensure the wetting of the full root zone. The subsequent irrigations from February to June may be given after 6-10 days depending upon the availability of moisture in the soil and the intensity of heat in the weather. Irrigation during the rain from July to September is not required except during prolonged dry spell. After rainy season is over, the avocado trees may again be irrigated after 15 days till the end of November. During December, water may be withheld for about a month and the orchard soil cultivated and manured prior to the flowering of trees in January.

Intercropping

Intercropping can be practiced to compensate the economic loss of initial years. Legumes or shallow-rooted crops as intercrops may be done in young orchards. The modern practice in California is to plant 400 trees per hectare (5 × 5 m) and gradually thin to a ultimate 140 trees per hectare (10 × 7 m).

Manuring and Fertilization

The avocado need fertilization for yielding good crop over the years. Application of Nitrogen was found to be most essential for cultivation of avocado. The most productive range for yield was associated with leaf nitrogen levels between 1.6 and 2.0 per cent. Application of K had little effect on yield increment. The young avocado trees should get N, P, K in the proportion of 1 : 1/2 : 1 and the older trees in the proportion of 2 : 1/2 : 2.

To avocado plants of 1 – 3 years age, apply FYM 25 kg and NPK @ 40, 20, 35 g/plant respectively. To full grown trees of 10 years and above apply FYM 50 kg and NPK @ 200, 45, 165 g/plant, respectively. Application of nitrogen influence fruit size and yield markedly.

At Poona, good results have been obtained by applying 45 kg of farmyard, 5 kg of castor cake and one kg of superphosphate to 7 years old trees in the month of January.

PRUNING

No pruning is needed for atleast a period of 7-10 years after planting, except for removal of stock growth below the graft union. The trees are pruned sparingly, mainly by heading back the central shoot in upright growing cultivars like 'Pollock' to develop a spreading habit. In spreading cultivars like 'Fuerte', branches are thinned and shortened. To facilitate harvesting operation and other orchard operations, old tall trees may be headed back. After harvesting of fruits, only old devitalized branches should be suitably pruned. Heavy pruning results in excessive vegetative growth and ultimately leads to poor yield.

HARVESTING AND HANDLING OF FRUITS

Seeded avocado fruits are 8-10 times larger than seedless ones. The avocado tree start bearing fruit after 4 – 5 years of planting. The fruits are harvested in August – September in South India. The fruit is clipped as soon as it changes colour from purple to deep maroon and green to greenish yellow so that it may be marketed before becoming soft with ease. The fruit (berry) is something like a pear in shape with a single large seed surrounded by buttery pulp and a hard skin. The harvested fruit should take 4-5 days to soften after which it does not keep long. The purple avocado should be picked as soon as it shows a blush, a purple colour on its skin. In Green avocado, the brightness of the green colour of the skin usually diminishes and a slight yellowish tint develops. In storage, the purple avocado develops a deep maroon colour all over the skin within a day or two of harvesting and the Green avocado similarly becomes greenish yellow.

The purple avocado tree of 10-15 years in age may bear about 200 to 300 fruits. It has been reported that 20 – 25 years old avocado tree can yield 1000 – 1500 fruits. However, good orchard in California have been found to give a yield of 6000-12000 fruits per acre per year.

Avocado is a climacteric fruit. Mature avocado fruits ripen in 4 – 5 days after harvesting. Ripening of fruits at 15 – 21°C takes place satisfactorily.

Treatment of avocado fruits with ABA methyl ester at 220 mg/g of fresh weight immediately after picking, enhanced the soluble polyphenol oxidase activity in the mesocarp, indicating an association between ABA level and fruit browning potential.

The avocado fruit is best packed in single layers in small, flat, well-ventilated wooden boxes. The fruit is padded with sufficient wood-wool to keep in position in the boxes.

The West Indian cultivars are more sensitive to low temperature than the Guatemalan and Mexican cultivars. Cold tolerant cultivars store best at 4.4°C whereas cold intolerant ones store at 10-13°C. Fruits wrapped in polythene bags and stored at gradually decreasing temperatures (2 days at 17°, 2 days at 14°, 4 days at 12° and then 8°C) do not soften for 23 days in Fuerte and 46 days in Nabal. For most varieties, the ideal storage temperature seems to be about 5.6°C to 8.9°C.

INSECT-PESTS

Mealy bug (*Planococcus pacificus*) : The pest causes damage to the avocado during flower and fruiting.

It can be controlled by spraying the plants with 0.05 per cent dichlorvos.

DISEASES

1. Fruit spot : It is caused by fungus ***Colletotrichum gloeosporioides.*** It results in shedding of young fruits. The remaining fruits on the tree do not attain normal size and become deformed. In some fruits, the infection may be latent.

The controlled atmospheric storage of fruits in 2 per cent oxygen and 10 per cent carbon dioxide at 7.2°C for 3-4 weeks prevent development of this fungus.

2. Root rot : The disease is caused by ***Phytophthora cinnamomi***. It is a serious disease of avocado and may kill the tree. Root rot is accentuated by poorly drained soils.

Ridomil mixed with the soil before planting @ 1 g a.i. per 10 kg soil or applied as a drench to the soil surface around established plants (1 g a.i. per 10 litres) controls root rot at least 4 months after treatment.

3. Cercospora spot (*Cercospora purpurea*) and scab (*sphaceloma perseae*) : They causes lesions on leaves as well as the fruits. Scab is a wide spread fungal disease cause severe losses from fruit drop and reduces fruit quality by marking fruit.

The disease free plants should be planted. Regularly watch the presence of pests and unusual symptom. Spray copper fungicide to central this disease.

Corcospora spot infects the leaves and fruits during the period of rainy season. It can be controlled by spraying systematic fungicide (captan or manozeb 0.2%) during the growing season.

CHAPTER 25

Aonla

Aonla or the Indian gooseberry (*Emblica officinalis* Gaertn.) is an important minor crop grown in sub-tropics and tropics. The cultivation of aonla is highly remunerative due to its high productivity even on marginal lands. The plant is quite hardy, heavy bearer and giving better income to the farmers. The crop is also doing well on wasteland across the country resulted in efficient utilization of resources.

ORIGIN, HISTORY AND DISTRIBUTION

Aonla is native to tropical southeast Asia specially in Central and Southern India, Sri Lanka, Bangladesh, Malaya and China. It grows wild in foot hills of northwest Himalayas to eastern Himalayas in Assam, Meghalaya, Manipur, Mizoram and Tripura and at elevation from 1250 to 1800 MSL in South India.

Aonla is grown and known in India for last 3500 years. Sushruta mentioned its use in Ayurveda during 1500 BC – 1300 BC. It finds a prominent place in ancient India literature especially in Vedas, Ramayana, Padmapuran, Kadambari, Charak Shanghita, Sushrut Shanghita, Askandhpuran etc. Aonla is regarded sacred by 'Hindus' and has great mythological significance. **Pind Dan** is done near the base of the tree to get **Mukti** (Salvation) of the elders.

Aonla is grown as a commercial fruit crop in many parts of the world. Now it is cultivated in different countries like India, Sri Lanka, Malaya, China, Hawaii, Cuba, Singapore, Pakistan, West Indies, Florida (USA) and Thialand. In India, its cultivation was first started in Varanasi (Banaras). The crop is growing with great success in Faizabad district of Uttar Pradesh.

AREA AND PRODUCTION

India ranks first in the world in area and production. It is found growing in different countries of the world like Bhutan, Nepal, Pakistan, China, Sri Lanka, Cuba, Puerto Rico, Iran, Iraq, Malaysia, Thialand, Vietnam, USA (Hawaii and Florida), Phillipines, Trinidad, Panama and Japan. The cultivation of this crop is very common in India. Uttar Pradesh is the leading state and commercial aonla orchards spead in Azamgarh, Pratapgarh, Varanasi, Bareilly, Faizabad, Sultanpur, Jaunpur, Kanpur, Agra, Banda and Mathura districts. The commercial cultivation of aonla has come up in some parts of Gujarat, Tamil Nadu, Andhra Pradesh, Karnataka, Maharashtra, Rajasthan, Punjab, Haryana, Madhya Pradesh and Himachal Pradesh.

The wild aonla is found growing in Himalayas, Chota Nagpur, Bihar, Odisha, West Bengal, Karnataka, Madhya Pradesh and Western Ghats.

The total area under aonla cultivation in India is 95000 hectares with annual production of 9.6 lakhs mt. The average productivity is estimated 9.6 tonnes/ha. The Gujarat state has 17000 hectares area under aonla with annual production of 1.5 lakh mt. The Kandi belt of Punjab and Himachal Pradesh is highly suitable for aonla growing and producing excellent quality fruits. In Punjab, the area under aonla is 271 hectares producing 3680 mt fruits with average productivity of 13.6 tonnes/hec.

IMPORTANCE AND USES

Aonla fruit is highly nutritive and popularly known as a 'Amrit Phal'. It is the richest source of vitamin C among the fruits and contains 600-700 mg of ascorbic acid per 100 g of pulp. Aonla is also rich in protein, minerals and iron. The fruit contain corbohydrates 14 per cent, protein 0.5 per cent, iron 1.2 per cent, vitamin B_1 30 mg/100 g fruit, mineral matter 0.7 per cent and fibre 3.4 per cent.

It is useful in harmorrhages, diarrhoea, dysentary, diabetes, jaundice, dyspepsia, anaemia and cough. It is main ingredients of Chyawanprash ayurvedic medicine system. Aonla is one of the ingredient in Triphala and used in the treatment of headache, biliousness, constipation and enlarged liver.

The fruits are used as preserve (murabba), pickle, jam, jelly and candy. It can be dried and powdered for off season use. It is commonly used in the preparation of ink, hair oil (amla oil) and hair dyes. Aonla is known to restore health and vitality.

BOTANY

Aonla belongs to genus ***Emblica*** and family Euphorbiaceae.

Emblica officinalis : The tree is evergreen in the tropical climate but is deciduous under sub-tropical conditions. The tree is speading in nature and attain height of 10-20 metres in different types of soil.

Emblica myrobalan : It is a small sized deciduous tree. The fruits are 1.5 – 4.0 cm in size and are used for preparation of various products.

Emblica fischeri : It is a small tree with large leaves. Its fruit is used for making pickle and chutney.

Earlier, aonla was categorised under genus *Phyllanthus* which comprises of about 500 species. ***Emblica officinalis*** is a monoecious plant having male and female flowers separately on the same panicle. Male flowers appear in clusters and bear in very high proportion. Female flowers have tiny green parianth and number of segments varies from 5 to 6 or even upto 7. These flowers bear on upper end of few branches. Fruit is capsular berry (drupaceous) with fleshy exocarp. Edible portion of the fruit is epicarp and mesocarp. The endocarp forms the hard stone which encages the seed. Seeds are 6-8 tightly embedded in the centre. The seed coat is dark chestnut brown and hard.

CLIMATE

Aonla is a sub-tropical fruit but can be grown successfully in tropical climate. It is a hardy tree and can be grown in variable agro-climatic conditions. The mature plant can tolerate temperature as high as 46°C. However, it relishes distinct winter and summer for high productivity. In India, it is being grown near sea coast to upto 1800 MSL. It can't withstand much hot and frost but can tolerate mild frost under north Indian conditions. The tree can be damaged with the occurrence of severe frost. Grafted plants are more prone to frost injury as compared to seedling plants. The young plants upto 3-4 years should be protected from hot desiccating wind in summar and heavy frost during winter. Low temperature from 7°C to 10°C is conducive for floral bud initiation.

After fruit-set in spring, the fruit remain dormant through summer without any growth, thus it makes the crop highly suitable for arid region. Aonla tree can tolerate drought for longer period. The Cultivar Chakaiya tolerate drought conditions better than the commercial cultivar Banarsi. The growth of the fruits takes place during July-August and at that time sufficient humidity is very useful to attain proper size.

SOIL

Aonla trees can be grown on wide variety of soil ranging from sandy loam to clay loam. But, well drained, fertile loamy soil is best for aonla cultivation. It is a potential crop for degraded lands and the marginal soils having soil pH of 6.0 to 9.0. It has good tolerance to saline, sodicity and moderately alkaline soils.

Aonla is considered ideal plant for various kinds of wastelands and road side plantation. The areas having high water table should not be considered for aonla growing. Stagnation of water during rains is harmful for its growth and root system. It is high salt tolerant crop and has great possibility for commercial cultivation in salt affected soils. The cultivars Francis and Kanchan have better tolerance to sodicity and salinity than cultivar Banarsi.

The kandi area of Punjab is considered ideal for aonla cultivation and producing excellent quality good-sized fruits.

CHOICE OF VARIETIES

The varieties like Banarsi, Chakaiya, Kanchan, Francis, Krishna, NA-7 and NA-10 are growing popularly in north India. Varieties are screened and evaluated at various Agricultural Universities and recommended for different regions. On the basis of their performance, the important characteristics of selected varieties are described below :

Banarsi : It is a seedling selection from Varanasi (Uttar Pradesh). The trees are semi-tall with spreading growth habit. Fruits are large in size, slightly conical at apex and light yellow at full maturity. The average fruit weight is 30g with light stone. Fruits are preferred for making preserve. Shelf life of fruit is poor. It is shy bearing and prone to heavy fruit drop.

Chakaiya : It is a seedling selection. The trees are tall with upright growth habit. Chakaiya is a prolific and regular bearing variety. Fruit is small to medium in size, flattened at base and have round apex. The average fruit weight is 28 g. Fruit skin is smooth, at maturity appears rusetted, light green in colour. Keeping quality is very good and suitable for pickle and other products. It is a heavy bearer most popular variety but has tendency to bear in alternate year.

Kanchan (NA-4) : It is a chance seedling from Chakaiya. The trees are tall with upright growth habit. Fruit is medium in size having high fibre content. The average weight is 30 g. Fruit skin is smooth, light green. It is preferred by industries for pulp extraction and preparation of various products. The variety is growing well in semi-arid regions of Gujarat. It mature late in mid-December. The average yield is 111 kg fruits per tree.

Francis : It is also known as Hathi Jhool which originated from Uttar Pradesh. The variety is a seedling selection. The tree is erect and tall with drooping branches. Fruit is large in size weighing about 60 g. The fruits are oval roundish, light green and slightly fibrous. Fruit skin is smooth, thick at upper side and thin at base. It is prolific bearer variety but has serious incidence of fruit necrosis.

NA-7 : It is a seedling selection from Francis. The average fruit weight is 40 g, skin is smooth, semi-translucent and yellowish green. Flesh is almost fibreless and soft. Stone medium is size and oval round in shape. It is precocious, prolific and regular bearer promising variety. Fruit is free from necrosis and is suitable for preservation and processing purposes. It is a mid-season variety, matures in end November. The average yield is 121 kg fruits per tree. It is recommended with the name of 'Neelum' in Punjab.

NA-10 : It is a chance seedling developed from cultivar Banarsi. The trees are semi-tall with semi-spreading growth habit and dense foliage. Fruits are moderate in size and flattened round in shape. Fruit skin is rough, yellowish green with pink tinge. Flesh is slightly fibrous, whitish green, soft, juicy and highly astringent. Stone is moderate in size and nearly rectangular in shape. It mature in mid-November. The average yield is 121 kg fruits per tree. It is recommended with the name 'Balwant' in Punjab.

Krishna (NA-5) : It is a chance seedling of cultivar Banarsi from Pratapgarh. The trees are semi-tall with spreading growth habit. The average fruit weight is 40-50 g, skin is smooth, attractive, compressed at distal end with red spots. Its pulp is fibreless. The variety is suitable for preservation. It is early maturing variety and have shy bearing habit.

PROPAGATION TECHNIQUES

Aonla is raised both through sexual and asexual methods of propagation. Seed propagation is though a commonly used in various parts of the country but does not ensure true-to-type plants due to cross pollination. Aonla is now commercially propagated through patch budding during June-September.

The fruits of seedling aonla (desi) are collected during January-February and seeds are extracted and used for raising of rootstock. The seed should be sown in first fortnight of March in north India. The seeds can be sown on seed beds or in polythene bags. The seeds can be soaked in GA_3 @500 ppm for 24 hours to improve the germination percentage. The seeds germinate in 5-7 days and within 4-6 months plants become ready for budding. Patch budding is done when the seedling become 1.0 to 1.2 cm in diameter at 15 cm above the ground level from June to September. When the bud take has occurred, the rootstock should be cut above the bud union. When the shoots from the bud attain a length of 15 – 20 cm, retain the vigorously growing shoot and remove the weaker one. The suckers below the bud union needs to be removed regularly to attain a good sized healthy plant.

The vegetative propagation can be done with forkert method of budding which give high success from July to September. The plants can be propagated through T-budding method during rainy season from July to September. This method also gives high success up to 80 per cent. Inarching or approach grafting can also be practised. Use of poly and net house, containers and rooting media proved useful in multiplication of aonla plants.

PLANTING OPERATION

Aonla plants can be planted twice in a year *i.e.* during August-September in rainy season and mid-January to February-March in spring. Bare-rooted plants can be planted during January with good success.

The planting distance is kept 7.5 × 7.5 m in square system which accommodate 180 plants per hectare. It is cross-pollinated crop, therefore, plants of two or more varieties should be planted together to get proper yield. The cultivar NA-7 (Neelum) may be planted as filler to serve as pollinizer. Hedge-row planting at a distance of 8 × 4 m and triangular planting system is also becoming popular for effective utilization of space and solar radiation. In certain areas, wider spacing of 8 to 10 m is followed in heavy soils. The young plants should be protected from frost by making thatches during winter.

FLOWERING AND FRUITING

Flowering in aonla takes place on new determinate shoots begin to appear at the nodes in spring season. The flowering takes place from March to May in north India. Aonla tree is senstitive to day length. Flower bud differentiation takes place in first week of March. In South and West India, flowering occur in June-July.

Male flowers appear in clusters in the axil of leaf all over the branchlet. Female flowers appear only on the upper end of a few branchlets. Early flower initiation was found in cv. Chakaiya and late initiation in cv. Kanchan. Initial fruit set in aonla varies from 12 to 18 per cent. Fertilization takes place within 36 hours after pollination. Immediately after fertilization, zygote rests for 120-130 days and endosperm nucleus may rest for 70-80 days after fertilization in cv. Banarsi. Thereafter, fruits do not show any growth during summer months. Dormancy breaks as a result of division in endosperm nucleus in end July to early August. Fruit starts growing continusouly and maximum growth occurs in the month of September.

The fruit growth follows a pattern of double sigmoid. The growth of fruit after dormancy is slow in first fifteen days. It show rapid growth from mid-August to early October. The growth of fruits slow down again between second week of October to early November and registered slight increase after that. It cease to grow after November. The seed length and weight increases rapidly during first rapid growth period of fruits when their size varies from 1 to 3.5 cm. Fruit is drupaceous with a freshly exocarp. Endocarp is thick and massive.

The fruits attain maturity in end November to early December and continue ripening upto February. At maturity and ripening, fruits become dull and greenish yellow.

Pollination : Aonla is a cross-pollinated plant. Honeybees are the main pollinating agent. Wind also play an important role in pollination process. Pollen viability and pollen grain germination varies from 82-96 and 16.7 to 37 per cent, respectively. Most of the aonla cultivars are self-incompatible and need pollinizer in order to improve fruit set and retention. Krishna (NA-5) and NA-6 are found to be best pollinizer for NA-7 cultivar.

ORCHARD CULTURAL PRACTICES

Irrigation

Aonla is generally cultivated as ranifed crop and little or no irrigation is provided. But for better establishment of orchard in early years few irrigation are essentially required.

After planting, young plantation should be irrigated at 3-4 days intervals and at 10-15 days intervals during summer. In bearing orchard, regular watering is needed for the development of embryo. Irrigate the plants at 10-15 days interval from March to mid-July in light textured soils. During rainy season, no irrigation is given to the aonla orchards. During fruit development period in September and October monthly irrigation should be scheduled. The fruit maturity takes place from November to January, only one or two light irrigation can be given if need arises.

During peak winter period, if there are chances of occurrence of frost, light irrigation should be given to afford protection against frost. Avoid giving irrigation to aonla plants during flowering period.

Intercropping

During the initial 4 – 5 years of pre-bearing stage sufficient space is available for raising intercrops. In winter months from November to February, when tree has sparse or no foliage, vegetables like pea, cauliflower, spinach, tomato, brinjal etc. can be grown. Leguminous crops can be intercropped during pre-bearing orchard which enrich the orchard soil. The fillers like karonda, phalsa and ber can be intercropped in each square or between the tree rows to supplement the income during prebearing period.

Mulching and Weed Control

Mulching in aonla plantation is very helpful in minimissing water requirement and checking the weed growth. The surface area or tree basin are covered with organic or inorganic mulches during active growth period. Mulching with black polythene and paddy straw is found effective in induction of early and uniform flowering which regulate fruit maturity and produce better coloured furits. The practice of covering the soil with black polythene is very effective in conserving moisture, checking weeds and reducing the fruit drop.

Organic mulch like straw, paddy straw, sugarcane trash, hay, banana leaves are also used in aonla orchards. The thickness of organic mulch should be 20-30 cm and not be in close contact of the tree trunk. Paddy straw mulch is commonly used in north India due to its easy availability. Mulching in aonla should be done during December-January after addition of manures and fertilizers.

The weeds can be removed by doing regular hoeing for better root growth and moisture conservation. Pre-emergence herbicide diuron @ 3 kg/ha in first fortnight of March or glyphosate @ 3*l*/ha in second week of March in 500 litres of water can be sprayed to check weed flora in aonla orchards. An additional spray of gramoxone @ 3 *l*/ha after rainy reason can be very helpful in controlling the weeds round the year.

Manuring and Fertilization

Aonla bear heavily and continue to bear upto about 50 years under proper conditions. The doses of manures and fertilizers are fixed on the basis of soil fertility, age of plant and productivity.

Under Punjab conditions, 15-20 kg farmyard manure is applied to young plants and 30-40 kg to mature plants during July-August. In addition, 30 g nitrogen per plant as applied for each year of age of the plant upto 10 years and afterwards 500 g of nitrogen to full grown plants.

In another fertilizer schedule followed by the growers, one year old plant is given 10 kg FYM, 100 g urea, 150 g single superphosphate (16% P_2O_5) and 40 g MoP (60% K_2O). The doses are increased almost in similar way and stabilized at 10 years of age, when plant is given 60 kg FYM, 1 kg urea, 1.5 kg superphosphate and 1/2 kg muriate of potash. The whole quantity of FYM, superphosphate and muriate of potash and half quantity of urea is given in January - February before flowering. The remaining half quantity of urea is given during August.

In Rajasthan, five years old aonla plant is given 50-60 kg FYM, 600 g nitrogen, 300 g phosphorus and 375 g potash. FYM, phosphorus and half potash and nitrogen is given in February before flowering. Remaining nitrogen and potash is applied during August.

Boron deficiency occur in aonla plants which cause problem of necrosis. Spray application of borax @ 0.6 per cent in September - October at fortnightly interval has been suggested. If zinc and iron deficiency is noticed, a spray of 0.5 per cent zinc sulphate and iron sulphate can be given for their correction. Soil application of zinc sulphate @ 250-500 g per plant is beneficial to overcome the zinc deficiency.

TRAINING AND PRUNING

The trees should be trained to single stem up to the height of 75 cm. Select 4 to 6 well spaced main branches on all directions around the trunk. Aonla bear heavily and due to fruit weight tender and lengthy branches tend to break. The trees should be trained to modified leader system for proper framework. There will be little or no limb breakage if tree is well trained.

The tree does not require regular annual pruning. However, to give proper shape to the tree and to allow primary branches at regular space all around the trunk, corrective pruning should be done. After harvesting the crop, remove dead, diseased, intercrossed and infested twigs for further normal growth of the tree.

FRUIT DROP

Fruit drop in aonla is a great concern to the growers as it is reducing fruit yield to considerable extent. Flower and fruit drop in aonla occur at different stages. Initially, about 70 per cent flowers drop off within three weeks of flowering due to unfertilized ovaries and degenerated ovules. Second time, the young fruitlets drop off at the time of dormancy from June to August which may be due to lack of pollination and fertilization. Finally, fruit drop spread over a period of rapid growth from August to October may be due to embryological and physiological factors such as lack of auxins, improper nutrition and moisture stresses.

Heavy fruit drop in aonla cultivars has been reported 12 to 38 per cent in August and 35 to 54 per cent in September. The minor elements play pivotal role in aonla nutrition with regard to fruit size, yield and quality. Zinc @ 0.6 per cent as foliar application proved helpful in checking fruit drop in Banarsi cultivar. The minimum fruit drop upto 50 to 56 per cent was recorded with zinc application.

HARVESTING AND HANDLING OF FRUITS

Budded aonla plants start bearing after 4-5 years of plantation and the trees starts giving regular yield at the age of 10 years. Seedling trees give commercial bearing after 10-12 years. Productive life of aonla tree is 50-60 years. The fruits are ready for harvest in November-December in North and West India and continue bearing upto the month of February. The availability of fresh aonla in South India is from March to December and in East India from October to January. Aonla fruits should be harvested at full maturity. Maturity can be judged by the change of seed colour from creamy white to black or by development of translucent exocarp. Fruits are harvested individually or fully loaded branches can be cut. Shaking of tree is not a good practice and fruits should not be allowed to fall on the ground. The injured fruits cause spoilage to good fruits during packaging, transporation and storage. Banarsi, Krishna and NA-10 are early maturing cultivars. Francis and NA-7 are mid-season cultivars whereas Chakaiya and Kanchan are late maturing cultivars.

Ladder can be used for ease in harvesting. Use of plastic trays is good for collection and transportation of fruits. All the fruits on the tree do not ripen uniformely. Therefore, two to three pickings should be done for harvesting of all the fruits on the tree. Peduncle should be properly clipped to check the spoilage during transportation. The bearing trees of different varieties can yield 100 to 150 kg fruits per tree.

The fruits should be graded into three grades viz A, B and C grades on the basis of size. In general, the fruit diameter should be 4 cm and above in A grade and less than 4 cm in B grade. All the defective fruits should be placed in C grade. Both A and B grade healthy fruits are used for preserve and candy making. It is common practice in industry that small-sized fruits are used for making Chyawanprash. The fruits are commonly packed in gunny bags and baskets. However, the fruits should preferably be packed in CFB boxes for profitable marketing.

Aonla fruits are highly perishable in nature. The fruits should be handled quickly as period between harvesting and consumption is very limited. Shelf life of aonla fruits at ambient temperature is about one week but can be extended upto 120 days by storing in perforated polythene bags. The spoilage starts after a week at room temperature which is caused due to blue mould.

The fruits can be kept at low temperature (10°C) for two weeks. Shelf life of fruits may be extended upto 75 days in 15 per cent brine solution. Pre-harvest spray of calcium nitrate 1 per cent proved beneficial in extending storability of fruits at ambient temperature.

PLANT PROTECTION MEASURES

A. Insect-pests

Bark-eating caterpillar (*Indarbela tetraonis* Moore) : The pest is very common in aonla plantation. It causes damage by eating the bark and boring holes into the stem. Due to bark eating, shoots and main trunk get girdled and dries up. Under severe attack full grown tree dries up. The infestation of this pest starts in April with the emergence of moths.

Remove the webs and inject water emulsion of 0.05 per cent chlorpyriphos and plug the holes.

Shoot gall caterpillar (*Betonsa stylophora* Swinhoe) : The insect causes gall formation on stem and shoot from June to August. However, the pest remain active from June to December. The infestation leads to stunted growth of the trees. In the beginning, terminal shoots swell and increases in size later on. The galls are quite visible in October-November.

The pest can be controlled by cutting the galled shoots. Spray 0.05 per cent monocrotophos or chlorpyriphos in beginning of the season. If need arises, repeat spray at fortnightly intervals.

Mealy bug (*Nipaecoccus vestator* Newstead) : Both nymphs and adults feed on tree from April to November and results in drying and dropping of leaves and flowers.

Prune the affected parts of the tree and destroy them. Spray 0.05 per cent monocrotophos or 0.05 per cent quinalphos.

Leaf rolling caterpillar (*Garcillaria acidula and Tonica* (*Psorosticha*) *ziziphi* Stainton) : The pest rolls the leaf and feeds inside, reducing the photosynthetic capacity of leaves and causes leaf shedding.

Collect the rolled leaves and destroy them alongwith the larvae. Spray 0.04 per cent monocrotophos or 0.05 per cent quinalphos.

Aonla aphids *[**Cerciaphis emblica*** (Patel and Kulkarny), ***Schoutedonia emblica*** (Patel and Kulkarny) and ***Setaphis bougainvillea*** (Thunberg)] : Leaves turn yellow and dry up. Shoots appear bended and twisted at the growing points. The nymphs and adult females suck the sap. Tree growth and vigour is affected.

Prune the infested leaf and shoots. The plants should be sprayed with 0.06 percent dimethoate.

B. Diseases

Ring rust (*Revenelia emblicae* Styd.) : It appears as circular, reddish solitary or gregarious spots on leaves in the beginning of August. Initially few black pustules appear on fruits which later develop a ring. These postules join together and cover large area on the fruit.

The disease can be controlled by giving three sprays of 0.4 per cent wattable sulphur in July. Repeat the spray at monthly interval. Dithane Z-78 @ 0.2 per cent from July to September after 2 - 3 weeks interval is also effective for checking the disease. Banarsi and Chakaiya cultivars are comparatively free from this disease.

Blue mould (*Penicillium citrinum*) : It causes brown patches and water-soaked areas on the fruit surface. As the rot progresses, three distinct colour zones viz. bright yellow, purple brown and bluish green are seen. There is exudation of drops of yellowish liquid on the fruit. The fruit finally gives a bluish-green, pustuled appearance and emit a bad odour.

Affected fruits should be discarded for marketing. Bruising and injury at the time of harvesting should be avoided. The fruits may be treated with 0.6 per cent borax or 0.1 percent carbendazim after harvesting.

Soft rot (*Phomospsis phyllanthi* Punith) : The fungus cause infection mostly on mature fruits in November - December. Brown to black round lesions develop within 2-3 days of infestation. Later on, lesions show olive brown discolouration with water soaked areas and cover the whole fruit within a week.

Bruising and injury should be avoided to the fruits. After harvesting of fruits, treat them with 0.1 per cent bavistin in November for further spread of the rot.

Anthracnose (*Colletotrichum gloeosporioides* state of *Glomerella cingulata* (Stoenm.) Spauld and Schrenk) : Minute, circular, brown to grey spots appears with yellowish margin on leaves. Depressed lesions are formed on fruits and later on turn dark. Affected fruits become shrivelled and rot. The disease appear during August-September. It is favoured by hot and humid weather.

Spray the trees with Bordeaux mixture (2 : 2 : 250) or 50% copper oxychloride (0.3%) or carbendazim (0.1%) when the infestation is noticed.

PHYSIOLOGICAL DISORDER

Internal fruit necrosis

The symptoms starts with the browning of innermost part of the mesocarpic tissues at the time of endocarp hardening in the second and third week of September. Browning of mesocarp extends towards the epicarp resulting into brownish black areas on the fruit in the second and third week of October. In severe incidence, mesocarp of fruit turns black and becomes corky and gummy pockets develop. The deficiency of boron has been reported for the cause of this disorder.

Francis and Banarsi cultivars are highly susceptible to this disorder. Chakaiya and NA-6 and NA-7 are almost free from this problem. To control the disorder, three sprays of borax @ 0.6 per cent in Septermber and October at fortnightly interval should be given. Zinc sulphate (0.4%) + Copper sulphate (0.4%) and borax (0.4%) in September-October has also been found effective in controlling the internal necrosis.

D. TEMPERATE FRUITS

26. Apple
27. Pear
28. Peach
29. Plum
30. Almond
31. Apricot
32. Walnut
33. Cherry
34. Strawberry

CHAPTER 26

Apple

Apple (***Malus domestica*** Borkh) is the premier table fruit of the world. It is the typical temperate tree fruit, about 48 per cent of the world's supply being produced in China. The States like Jammu and Kashmir, Himachal Pradesh and Uttarakhand has achieved distinction in the cultivation of apples.

ORIGIN AND HISTORY

The cultivated apple (***Malus domestica***) is reported to have originated in south-western Asia, in the Caucasus region near Gilan in Turkestan. It has existed in Europe, both in wild and cultivated forms since prehistoric times and have been well developed there at the beginning of Christian era. Records of apple cultivars are available as early as 100 BC. Apple cultivation by Greeks and Romans seems to have been started from a few centuries BC in the Middle-East and South-Eastern Europe as a result of their travels and invasions. It was introduced in America after it has been cultivated for more than 2000 years in Europe. It is not known when the apple was introduced in the cooler parts of India but evidence showed its presence in Agra in 1632. Baring variety Ambri which is indigenous to Kashmir, all other varieties were introduced first by the European Settlers, missionaries and later on by elite growers, nurserymen and Research Introduction Centres. Emperor Jahangir praised Kashmir apples in his book Turk-e-Jahangir which gives proof of their cultivation during 16 century.

The first apple orchard in Himachal Pradesh was established at Bandrole in Kullu Valley by Captain A.A. Lee, an Englishman around 1870. Besides, many apple varieties were introduced by Alexander Coutt's in his orchard called 'Hillock Head' at Mashobra during 1887. The famous Delicious varieties were introduced by Samuel Nicholar Stokes, a resident of Philadelphia, USA, in 1918 at Kotgarh in Shimla Hills. In Kumaon and Garhwal apple was introduced by Britishers in the later half of 19th century. Mr. Allen and Mr. Smith introduced apple in Kumaon hills at Chaubattia around 1872. The first apple orchard was established in Ramgarh area of Nainital district. Apple was also introduced in Bangalore and Nilgiris, but it was destroyed by wooly aphids in 1897.

Apple cultivation is a new introduction to a few isolated hilly tracts of Bihar, Darjeeling, Sikkim, Arunachal Pradesh, Meghalaya, Manipur, Nagaland and Assam hills. Scattered orchards are also found in Ooty – Nilgiri hills which were planted during 1850.

The major apple producing countries in the world are China, USA, India, Polland, Italy, France, Iran, Brazil and Russian Federation.

AREA AND PRODUCTION

The total production of apple in the world is 74.95 million metric tonnes. China is the largest producer of apple in the world producing 48 per cent of the total world production. Total area under apple cultivation in the world is 4.8 million hectares. The average productivity of apple fruit in 15.6 mt/hectare.

Apple is the fourth most important fruit crop in India. This fruit grown in 3.22 lakh hectares having annual production of 22.03 lakh tonnes accounting for 4.8 per cent of total area under fruits and 2.9 per cent of total fruit production in the country, respectively. It is largely grown in Jammu and Kashmir, Himachal Pradesh, Uttarakhand and Arunchal Pradesh accounting for 53.0, 32.19, 10.47, 4.13 per cent of area, respectively. Area under apple in Nilgiri hills of Tamil Nadu, Nagaland and Sikkim is negligible. The average productivity of apple in India is 6.8 tonnes per hectare in comparison to 35.2 and 31.9 mt/per hectare in Brazil and USA, respectively.

The production of apple is the highest in Jammu and Kashmir which is 80.6 per cent of total production in India. The average production in the state is 10.4 mt/ha against the average productivity of 6.8 mt/ha in India. In India apple occupies 4.8 per cent of the total area under fruits constituting 2.9 per cent of fruit production. Jammu and Kashmir, Himachal Pradesh and Uttarakhand occupy major share of apple production (98.61%).

The low average yields are on account of poor setting of the largely grown delicious varieties due to low pollinizer ratio and the prevailing low temperature at the time of flowering and fruit setting coupled with irregular bearing tendency and low yield potential.

Export potential. The future prospects of apple cultivation in India are bright on account of introduction of advance technologies and export potential. India has exported 30060 mt apples to Bangladesh, Nepal, Congo, Maldives, Pakistan, UAE, Singapore and Liberia during 2011-12 and earned value Rs. 91.45 crores. The share of export of apple from India was 84.15 per cent to Bangladesh alone.

IMPORTANCE AND USES

Apple is a rich source of carbohydrates, proteins, minerals like calcium, phosphorus, iron, sugars, potassium, thiamine and vitamin B_6. Carbohydrates found in apple consist of sugars, dextrins, starch, hemicellulose, cellulose and pectic substances. The apple fruits have been found to contain appreciable amount of sorbital and various sugars (sucrose, glucose, fructose). In cv. McIntosh, the sorbital, sucrose, glucose and fructose contents were recorded 8.4, 6.5, 18.4 and 48.9 mg per g fresh weight, respectively. The major acids in apple are recorded maleic and citric. Apple contains 86% moisture, 14.5% carbohydrates, 0.3% protein, 110 mg potassium, 10 mg phosphorus, 6 mg calcium, 90–120 I.U. vitamin A, 5–40 mg vitamin C, 10 *g* thiamine and 0.3 mg iron per 100 *g* fruit.

Apple is believed to reduce the incidence of dental caries, helps to control obesity and supply extra energy for heavy exercise. Apple is chiefly used as table fruit. The various products like jam, jelly, preserve, slices, saucer, apple butter, apple chips, apple rings, wine, juice, concentrated juice, cider and powder are prepared from apple.

BOTANY

The genus **Malus** belongs to the subfamily Pomoideae and the family Rosaceae with a basic chromosome number of 17. The genus **Malus** has 25 species and several subspecies of so called Crab apples. The cultivated apple has been designated as ***Malus domestica.*** The description of some principal **Malus** species are as follows :

Malus domestica Borkh (Cultivated apple) : The tree is a round headed, grows up to 10 m or more. It is a deciduous rarely evergreen and rarely with spiny branches. The buds are ovoid with several imbricate scales. The leaves are serrate or lobed, folded or convolute in buds, stipulate. The flowers are white to pink or carmine in cymes, petals usually sub or bicular or obovate. Stamens 15-30 with usually yellow anthers. The ovary is inferior, 3-5 cells, styles 2-5, connate at base. The fruit is pome, usually without grit-cells, persistent or deciduous calyx, with depression at either end. The edible portion of fruit is fleshy thalamus.

Malus baccata (L.) Borkh. (Siberian Crab) : It grows wild from Siberia to Manchuria and the Himalayan region. It is a spreading tree, flowers are white and showy. Fruits yellow or red, firm and translucent.

Malus sylvestris Miller (Wild Crab-apple) : It is considered to be native of Western Asia and south eastern Europe. Trees are large. There are several cultivars differing in form, size, colour and taste.

Malus floribunda Siebold (Flowering Crab) : It is a native of Japan. Trees are small and thorny. Flowers are highly ornamental, rose-red colour. Fruits are small in size and red in colour.

Malus angustifolia (Aiton) Michaux (Narrow-leaved Crab-apple) : It is distributed from Pennsylvania to Tennessee and Florida. Leaves are small, narrow and lanceolate. Flowers are pink in colour, fruits small.

Malus coronaria (L.) Miller (America Crab-apple) : Trees are small, bushy and thorny. Flowers are large with persistent calyx. Fruits are greenish yellow, fragrant and waxy.

Malus soulardii L.H. Bailey (Britton) (Soulard Crab apple) : It is a natural hybrid of *M. pumila* × *M. oensis*. Trees are small. Fruits are large with good aroma.

Malus ioensis (Alph Wood) Britton (Prairie Crab apple) : Trees are small, flowers large , fruits are green with light coloured spots.

CLIMATE

Apple has diverse temperature climatic adaptation. It is the most widely planted fruit of the temperate zone. Most of the apple varieties require 1000-1500 chilling hours below 7°C to break the rest period. These conditions are available at an altitude ranging from 1500-2700 m above mean sea level. The average temperature should be around 21-24°C during the active growing season. Low temperature rains and cloudy weather hamper bees activity during pollination.

Abundant sunshine is important in growing apples since it is largely responsible for good colour development. In general, sites located in north eastern aspect at lower altitudes and south western aspect at higher altitudes are suitable for apple growing. The localities should be free from hail storms and spring frosts. For optimum growth and fruitfulness, apple trees require 100-125 mm of rainfall equally distributed over the growing season. Apple trees are particularly sensitive to low soil moisture supply. Water stress during growing season reduces number and size of fruits and increases June drop. Excessive rains and fog at the time of fruit maturity deteriorate the fruit quality and increase the incidence of sooty blotch, fly speck and other diseases. High winds are not desirable for apple cultivation. Abundant sunshine is important for the growth development of apples and is repsonsible for high colour in fruits.

SOIL

Apple can be grown on all types of soils. Proper drainage and fertility of soil are important. Most suitable soil for apple is deep and well drained loams. Loamy soils, rich in organic matter with pH ranging from 5.5 to 6.5 and having proper drainage and good aeration are most suitable for apple cultivation. The soil should be free from hard substrata and water logging conditions. Water logged soils favour soil borne diseases particularly collar rot and root rot. When apples are grown on calcareous soils, they suffer from iron and manganese deficiencies. Apple suffers from potassium and magnesium deficiencies if grown on light soils. Soils with heavy clay or compact sub soil should be avoided for planting apples as in clay soil, most roots slope downwards and grow in sub-soil.

CHOICE OF VARIETIES

The following are the important varieties of apple grown in different regions :

Commercial Varieties : Red Delicious, Starking Delicious (Royal Delicious), Richared, Mollie's Delicious, Vance Delicious, Topred, Granny Smith.

Colour Strains : Top Red, Vance Delicious, Hardeman, Red Gold, Skyline Supreme.

Spur Types : Red Spur, Red Chief, Starkrimson, Oregon Spur II, Gold spur, Silver Spur, Well Spur, Scarlet Spur-2

Low Chilling Varieties : Tamar, Vered, Tropical Beauty, Maayan, Michal, Schlomit.

Scab Resistant Varieties : Sir Price, Priscilla, Prima, Liberty, Redfree, Coop12, Freedom, Macfree

Maturity Basis Varieties : The varieties are categorised on the basis of their maturity *i.e.* early, mid and late season.

(*i*) **Early season varieties :** Mollie's Delicious, Michal, Maayan, Schlomit, Anna, Chaubattia Anupam.

(*ii*) **Mid season varieties :** Red Delicious, Vance Delicious, Richared, Royal Delicious, Starkrimson, Red Cheif, Well Spur, Oregon Spur, Red Spur, Gala Selection, Hardeman, Skyline Supreme Delicious, Bright-N-Early, Cooper-4, Golden Spur, Silver Spur.

(*iii*) **Late season varieties :** Lal Ambri, Firdous, Topred, Sunhari, Golden Delicious, Ambri, Fuji, Red Gold, Yellow Newton.

New Varieties :

Fuji	:	cross between Red Delicious × Rall's Janet
Gala	:	cross between Kidd's Orange × Golden Delicious
Ambred	:	cross between Red Delicious × Ambri
Ambstarking	:	cross between Starking Delicious × Ambri
Ambrich	:	cross between Richared × Ambri (Semi Dwarf, Semi spur type)
Ambroyal	:	cross between Starking Delicious × Ambri (Semi Dwarf)
Lal Ambri	:	cross between Red Delicious × Ambri
Jonagold	:	cross between Golden Delicious × Jonathan
Empire	:	cross between McIntosh × Delicious
Chaubattia Princess	:	cross between Early Shanburry × Red Delicious
Chaubattia Anupam	:	cross between Early Shanburry × Red Delicious
Sunehari	:	cross between Ambri × Golden Delicious

Brief description of some commercially important apple cultivars are presented below :

Red Delicious : The cultivar was evolved as a chance seedling in Iowa, USA. The fruits are large, oblong conical with five knobs like protrusions at the calyx. Skin smooth, covered with red streaks on a pale background. Flesh creamy white, tender,crisp, fine grained, sweet, highly aromatic. It requires 133-139 days from full bloom to maturity. Ripens during end of August.

RED DELICIOUS Apple

PATHARNAKH–Hard Pear Variety

PUNJAB BEAUTY–Semi-So Pear Variety

SHAN-I-PUNJAB
Popular Variety of Peach

PARTAP - Early Variety of Peach

SATLUJ PURPLE - A Hybrid of Japanese Plum

Golden Delicious : Tree moderately vigorous. Fruit medium to large, oblong, skin golden yellow with russetted prominent small dots scattered all over. Flesh creamy white, fine, crisp, sweet with a blend of acidity. It is a good pollinizer for all the Delicious group. It requires 148-154 days from full bloom to maturity. Ripening time is second week of September.

McIntosh : Tree vigorous. Fruit medium, oblate round, skin smooth, shinning carmine colour on a pale green background. Flesh white, develops red shade after storage, tender, crisp, sweet with a good acid blend, juicy and mild flavoured. It is susceptible to scab.

Jonathan : Tree medium sized. Fruit round to conical, medium to small and reddish in colour with good quality. Fruits are susceptible to black Jonathan spots.

Starking Delicious : Fruits oblong conic with red stripes, juicy and sweet in taste. Require 115-120 days from full bloom to maturity. It ripens during the first fortnight of August.

Starkrimson : Fruits conical, red wash, hard but sweet and juicy. It ripens with in 100 days after full bloom i.e. third week of July. It gets dark when harvesting is delayed.

Yellow Newton : Fruits oblate in shape with green colour, sub-acidic and juicy. It is a late variety, ripens during first week of October and require 172-178 days from full bloom to maturity. It has good shelf life. The variety is susceptible to stem end russet, bitter pit and internal browning on storage.

Granny Smith : Fruits round in shape having green colour, light yellowish on ripening. Flesh very firm, crisp, greenish yellow to whitish and sub-acidic in taste. It ripens late during second week of October and require 176-182 days from full bloom to maturity. The variety has good shelf life.

Ambri : It is indigeneous variety grown in India. The fruit is medium to large in size and oblong in shape. It has red streaks over a greenish yellow background. It is a late ripening variety and ripens in September-October.

Richared : It is a budsport of Red Delicious. The fruits are large sized and oblong conical in shape. The yellowish ground colour is overlaid with a bright red wash. Lenticells are conspicuous. It ripens in third week of August.

Red Gold : It is a regular bearer variety. Fruits round to slightly oblong. Skin highly red blushed, waxy, glossy. Flesh white with pinkish tinge near the surface, firm. Ripens in third week of August.

Red Chief : Tree spur type. Highly productive. Fruit red striped and large. Flesh creamy, crisp. Ripens is second week of August.

Red Spur : Tree spur type. Fruit conical, solid red skinned. Tree with small internodes resulting in a tree about two third of size of standard one. Ripens in second week of August.

Mollie's Delicious : A seedling from the cross [Golden Delicious × Edgewood] × [Gravenstein × Close]. Fruit large conical with 50 – 75% red colour. Quality moderate. Ripens in third week of July. Susceptible to powdery mildew.

Vance Delicious : It is bud mutant of Delicious. Fruits conical, Skin solid red with deep red stripes. colouring two weeks earlier to Red Delicious. Ripens in second week of August. It is a high yielding variety.

Gala Selection : Fruits medium in size, conical, red in colour with yellow background. Flesh yellow white, crisp and juicy. Texture smooth and spicy sweet flavour.

Red Free : Fruit with red broken inconspicous stripes. Slightly oblate. Flesh light yellow to cream coloured, firm, crisp, juicy, sweet with sub acid taste and pleasant flavour. Good dessert quality. Resistant to scab, cedar apple rust. Moderatly resistant to powdery mildew. It is highly productive variety.

McIntosh : A chance seedling. Popular variety. Fruit medium to large, flat round in shape. Ground colour pale greenish yellow, flushed with deep purplish red. Flesh white, soft, fine textured, juicy and sweet. Fruit mature before the appearance of colour. It is a hardy and very productive variety.

Anna : A variety for low hills upto 5000 ft. Fruits large, oblong conical, skin yellowish overlaid by red blush on cheeks about 30-40 percent. Flesh creamish white, juicy, subacid to sweet, mild flavoured. Ripens in end June to early July. It is regular bearer variety.

Top Red : Fruits large, conical, skin striped. Fruit colour up earlier than Starking Delicious. Flesh yellowish, firm, tender, juicy, aromatic, sub acid. Repens in second week of August. It is a high yielding variety.

PROPAGATION AND ROOTSTOCKS

Apple is mainly propagated by grafting and budding. The rootstocks are raised from the seeds of selected hardy varieties suitable for this purpose. For raising seedling plants, the seeds are stratified in sand at a temperature of 4-7°C for 60-90 days. Stratification can also be done by direct sowing of the seeds in the nursery in early December. Seed after stratification are sown in February-March at a distance of 5 cm in rows 10 cm apart. The seedbeds are covered with mulch in order to protect the germinating seedlings from heavy rains. The seedlings can also be raised in polythene bags or in earthenware pots. The seed can also be stratified for 2-3 months at 2-5°C.

Clonal Propagation

The clonal rootstocks are propagated by mound layering. The clones are planted at distance of 30 cm in rows 60 cm apart during winter which give rise to numerous shoots in the spring. All these branches except the central one are ringed before treating with Seradex during the rainy season to encourage the root development. The ringed shoots are then covered with soil and the rooted clones are separated at the onset of dormancy and planted in nursery beds for further grafting. The following are the important rootstocks used for clonal propagation.

(*i*) Very dwarfing : M 27

(*ii*) Dwarfing : M 9

(*iii*) Semi Dwarfing : M 26, M 7, MM 106

(*iv*) Vigorous : MM 104, MM 109, MM 111

(*v*) Very Vigorous : M 12, M 16, M 25

Rootstock M 27, M 9 and M 26 has weak anchorage. MM 106 is susceptible to collar rot. MM 111 is resistant to drought. M 25 is precious. The cross are as M 26 [M 16 × M9], MM 106 [M2 × Northern Spy], MM 104 [M2 × Northern Spy], MM 111 [Northern Spy × Merton 793], and M25 [Northern Spy × M2]. Six hardy clonal stocks are produced by Ottawa Research Station, Canada. Ottawa 3 is a dwarfing rootstock.

The performance of apple trees in Himachal Pradesh is less satisfactory on clonal rootstocks on account of low fertility status of the soil, sloppy lands and inadequate irrigation facilities. The Crab apple seedlings (***Malus baccata***) is widely used as rootstock. Seedling rootstock can also be raised from seeds of scion cultivars. Seeds of Ben Davis, Delicious, Yellow Newton, Rome Beauty, McIntosh give good germination.

Gafting and budding : The rootstocks are grafted with desired scion variety during February-March. Usually tongue grafting gives a good successs and is performed about 20-30 cm above ground level. Seedlings which fail to show success with tongue grafting, shield budding should be done in the month of June and chip budding during mid-March. Old trees can also be top-worked. Rootstocks have influences on scion with respect to tree size, vigour, cropping and precocity. The intensity of fruit colour, and flavour are also influenced favourably.

The effect of certain scions have also been recorded on rootstocks with respect to volume of roots, their direction and colour. The uniformity and vigour of resultant apple trees are obtained on rootstocks of the varieties viz. Delicious, Rome Beauty and 'Wine Sap'. Malling 9 rootstock has dwarfing effect which is used in home gardens where dwarfing is desirable. However, none of the known varieties is completely resistant to wooly apple aphid. Apple rootstocks are easily propagated by hardwood cutting with the aid of growth regulator like IBA at 2500 ppm.

PLANTING OPERATION

While planting an orchard, proper decisions about the selection of varieties, rootstocks, tree size and spacing, pollination and planting procedures must be made with understanding. The commercial bearing life of a standard apple orchard has been estimated about 50 years.

The pits are dug on well cultivated land during summer in the month of April-May in advance of planting. Generally the dimension of pit should be kept 1 × 1 × 1 m but on rich and deep soil, it may be kept 60-75 cm^3.

On steep slopes, the tree rows are planted along the contour to avoid excess erosion and improve safety in operation of equipment. Apple planting is done with its one year old plants during the dormant period preferably in the early spring avoiding low temperature injury. Planting is done in square or hexagonal systems. Planting is done from December to March. However, early planting in December – January is desirable.

The planting distance varies according to variety, the vigour of rootstock, the fertility level of the soil and general climatic conditions of the area. The planting distance is kept 3.0-7.5 m under different conditions. Too close planting should always be avoided, otherwise it will cause many problems like shading, root crowding, less availability of nutrients and moisture, hindrances in cultural operations, difficulty in pest and disease control. The grafts should be planted in such a way that the point of their union remains 25 cm above ground level to prevent from incidence of collar rot.

The commonly followed planting distance and number of plants accommodated per hectare are given below :

Tree vigour	Rootstock	Planting distance (m)	No. of plants (per ha)
A. **Spur Type Varieties**			
Dwarf	M 7, MM 106	3.0	1100
Semi Dwarf	MM 109, MM 111	3.6	772
Semi Vigorous	Seedling	4.8	434
B. **Non-Spur Type Varieties**			
Dwarf	M 9	3.0	1100
Semi Dwarf	M 7, MM 106	4.5	494
Semi Vigorous	MM 109, MM 111	6.0	275
Vigorous	Seedling	7.5	180

FLOWERING AND FRUITING

The time of flower bud initiation in apple is closely related to the growth cessation of shoots on which they are set. The period ranging from growth cessation upto the appearance of floral primordia is the period of physiological differentiation of flower buds. During this period, differentiation processes proceed within the buds, increasing in number of nodes and inducing some physiological changes. When the bud reached a certain stage, it may become a flower bud or may terminate its differentiation becoming a leaf bud. The fruit buds are usually developed on spurs, laterally on two/three year old wood. However, buds may also develop on tips of one-years old shoots, which are found mostly when dwarfing rootstocks are used.

A good correlation was found to exist between the leaf area and flower bud formation. In cvs like Granny Smith and Delicious, no flower bud formation was found at leaf/fruit ratio below 10 which was found to increase progressively by increasing the ratio from 20 to 50.

The average maximum and minimum temperature around 20° and 10°C, respectively during flowering in April in Himachal Pradesh resulted in good fruit set. High relative humidity (more than 50%) in March delayed flowering without affecting fruit set, but high rainfall and relative humidity during flowering in April adversely affected fruit set, while low rainfall and relative humidity in April improved fruit set and yield. Very low temperature i.e. less than 4.5°C reduced fruit set by interfering pollen germination and bee activity. Sprays of aminoethoxyvinylglycine inhibit ethylene production and increase fruit set in treated apple flowers, suggesting that endogenous ethylene level limits fruit set.

A continued enlargement of the receptacle takes place during the development of the fruit. The throat of the receptacle becomes narrow through which the style protrudes. The connection between the receptacle and carpel tissues becomes so close one that the receptacle makes up the greater portion of the flesh of the apple. A rapid phase of cell division occurs in the first few weeks after pollination which ceases abruptly 30-40 days after full bloom in Cox's Orange Pippin, and after 4 weeks in Granny Smith. The subsequent fruit growth occurs mainly due to cell expansion. The fruit growth pattern follows a smooth sigmoid curve. In apple, fruit growth is dependent on the presence of growing seeds up to the end of the June drop. After this stage, removal of the seeds no longer results in cessation of fruit growth.

The water content in apple fruits varies from 75-90 per cnt. The water content increases with the increase in fruit size with a slight decrease towards the end of maturity. The bulk of the carbohydrate in fruit is sugar which is mainly synthesized in leaves and transported to the fruits although, a very little sugar is also synthesized by the fruit. Fructose, glucose and sucrose are the three main sugars found in the fresh apple. The reducing sugars (fructose and glucose) and sucrose content of the fruit increases with the increase in fresh weight. Light and temperature during the first four months after fruit set have a marked effect on sugar content of fruit. Starch accumulated at very early stage of fruit development. The accumulated starch is hydrolyzed into sugars with the advancement of maturity. The disappearance of starch is higher at the later stages of fruit development. The titratable acidity of the fruit steadily decreases as the fruit matures but the actual or absolute amount of acid present in the fruit increases until just before harvest when it decreases slightly.

ORCHARD CULTURAL PRACTICES

Irrigation

Water requirement of an apple tree varies according to climatic conditions, types, age of the trees and its different stages of growth and development and management practices. The very first irrigation is done just after planting. The further irrigations are done to provide adequate soil moisture so that young plants do not suffer for want of adequate moisture. Due to lack of moisture plants show stunting effects of their growth.

During the period from June/July to September, it is necessary to irrigate the apple plant for proper fruit development. Irrigation before June is also necessary, particularly for newly planted trees, especially those on shallow, light or gravelly soils.

The water requirement of Starking Delicious apple grafted on M 7 rootstock was worked out and irrigation was applied at different levels of field capacity (75, 50, 25%). It was observed that 8 irrigations were needed in total to the trees irrigated at 75% field capacity. However, only 3 irrigations were applied to the trees irrigated at 50% of the field capacity, 2 irrigations at 25%

of the field capacity and 1 irrigation to the control. The quantity of water applied was 212, 429, 646 and 212 litres per tree at 75%, 50%, 25% field capacity and in control, respectively. The consumption of water by an apple was estimated to be 127, 113, 108 and 94 cm/acre when irrigated at 75, 50 and 25% of the field capacity and control. The consumption of water was low in early growth stages (March - April) of tree and fruits. It increased from May onwards the period corresponding to greater foliage and rise in atmospheric temperature. The peak water consumption reached in July just before harvesting of fruits. During the period from July to September, irrigation is important for fruit development. For newly planted trees, irrigation before June is also necessary particularly on shallow, light or gravelly soils.

The modern systems of irrigation, like, drip, sprinkle or trickle have been proved very effective with respect to plant growth and fruit yield in apple. Through drip irrigation, nitrogen fertilizer can easily and economically be given. This system also suits the trees on hill slopes. Water consumption and soil losses through erosion are considerably less than with furrow irrigation. Drip irrigation at 100, 80 and 60 per cent ET_C to Scarlet Gala and Red Fuji was found to enhance vegetative growth compared to basin irrigation. The growth increased with volume of water applied through drip. The yield was improved with 100 per cent ET_C.

Intercropping

Intercrop for apple orchard should be well planned, beneficial and profitable. Crops should be selected for intercropping in apple which do not interfere with normal irrigation and other management practices. Intercrops should not encourage incidence of insects and diseases. The crops such as melons, beans, strawberries, etc. are preferred as intecrops. Forage crops can also be raised between the rows of young plants. Sometimes, filler trees between apple trees are also planted. Thus, income is obtained earlier and the trees are rather easily removed when crowding seems apparent.

Orchard Management Practices

The tree growth, yield and fruit quality is greatly influenced by orchard soil management practices. The most suitable system of soil management for a particular area, however, depends largely on type of soil, amount of precipitation, topography and planting system.

Clean cultivation : The whole area between the trees is cultivated during the first initial years of planting. During the summer months cover crops are grown and ploughed into the soil afterwards. Clean cultivation is found suitable where the slope of the land is less than 10 per cent. This system, however, reduces the uptake of phosphorus and potassium following damage to tree roots in the surface soil.

Sod culture : The various grasses and legumes are grown as a permanent cover. The grasses are cut when 7-10 cm high and left in the orchard for decomposition. This system is followed where the slope of the land is more than 10 per cent. This system is popular in Kotgarh orchards. The fruit colour is improved through Sod culture system. Soil erosion is prevented and penetration and percolation of moisutre into and through the soil is facilitated. Scab control is difficult since infected leaves from the previous season do not easily decompose.

Mulching : Mulching improves soil moisture conditions and tree growth with respect to trunk diameter and shoot length. In Himachal Pradesh, where most of the orchards are rainfed, use of mulches particularly, in areas affected by summer drought, can greatly reduce the water losses from the soil and further improve the availability of nutrients. Straw, hay, sawdust, composted conifers, farmyard manure, and black polythene are mostly used as type of mulches. Mulching encourages development of roots near the surface and increases the availability of K, N, P, Ca, Mg and B in the soil. The system's demerit is that frost damage to the blossoms is slightly increased due to insulating effect of straw mulch.

Clean basin management : It is the most common method of orchard floor management and is highly suitable for young trees to develop deeper root system and to avoid any compitition for nutrition or water by weeds to young trees. However, it is not advocated for bearing trees due to its effect on feeding root system and soil moisture levels. Most of the apple orchards in HP are located on steep slope vulnerable to run off and soil erosion. The present system of sod culture with clean basins helps to prevent run off and soil erosion. Herbicides should be applied in April when the weeds are not more than 10 cm in height followed by mulching. The mulches may be removed before rains in high rainfal areas, otherwise aeration of the soil is seriously reduced which may induce rotting of the roots. Cultivation of basins after harvest, facilitates the application of fertilizers in winter.

Weed Control

The use of herbicides to eliminate weeds and grasses enables tree roots to exploit the surface soil more effectively than in grassed or cultivated orchards. Apple orchard sprayed with glyphosate at 1.7 kg/ha or mechanical weed control showed considerably higher yield than trees on unweeded plots. Hexuron 80 WP (diuron) @ 4kg + glycel 41 SL (glyphosate) @ 0.8 *l*/ha control the broad spectrum of weeds effectively in apple orchards.

Application of 10 – 15 cm thick grass mulch + glyphosate @ 800 ml/800 litres water per hectare provides acceptable level of weed control in apple orchards. In higher hills, black polythene has also been found effective for checking weed growth.

Manuring and Fertilization

The doses of manures and fertilizers depend upon soil fertility, type of soil, kind and age of the tree, cultural practice and climate. The following fertilizer schedule is followed in Himachal Pradesh, Jammu & Kashmir and Uttarakhand.

Age of trees (years) Himachal Pradesh	FYM (Kg/tree)	N	P (*g* per tree)	K
1–3	10–30	70–210	35–105	70–210
4–6	40–60	280–420	140–210	280–420
7–9	70–90	490–630	245–315	490–630
10 & above	100	700	350	700
Kashmir				
15 & above	–	600	130	750
Uttaranchal	50	500	100	400

In fertile and rich soils, doses can be reduced by one-third to one half. In Arunachal Pradesh 50 kg FYM, 350 g N, 180 g P_2O_5 and 180g K_2O is recommended. To full grown apple tree, the doses of fertilizers in Tamil Nadu are scheduled as 25 kg FYM, 250 g N, 1 kg P_2O_5 and 1 kg K_2O.

Farmyard manure alongwith phosphorus and potash should be given during December-January to the bearing trees. Nitrogen is applied 2-3 weeks before bud break. When irrigation facilities exist, nitrogen can be applied in two split doses and the second half can be given one month after flowering. Complete NPK fertilizers should be applied as a single dose during February. In Himachal Pradesh, the retention of phosphorus in soil is good, therefore, its excess application should be avoided. The phosphours should be applied after three years under such conditions. The fertilizer should be broadcasted on the soil surface under the spread of the trees and slightly mixed with the soil. Fertilizers should be applied at least 30 cm away from the trunk in old trees and should not be applied in too wet or too dry soils. In high rainfall areas with steep slopes, band application of nitrogenous fertilizers should be preferred.

Nutrient Deficiencies

The deficiency symptoms of different elements are given below :

Nitrogen : The deficiency of nitrogen may cause restricted growth, narrowing of top-root ratio, less elongation of branches and reduction in size and colour of fruits. The bark of the tree may be reddish or yellowish green in early stages, but later developing tints of yellow.

Phosphorus : Shoots short, thin and upright. Leaves small with dull purple and bronze tints, early defoliation of older leaves. Opening of buds in the spring is delayed. Lateral buds may remain dormant, therefore, few lateral shoots appear.

Potassium : Deficiency of potassium is seen on spurs of old branches which progressed towards the younger leaves as the season advances. The first evidence of scorch might be loss of normal green colour at the widest part of the leaf margin, accompanied by a water-soaked or stained appearance, which was followed by necrosis. Severely affected trees were mostly stunted in growth with small-sized leaves. The fruits in affected trees do not develop properly, remain small in size with poor colour development.

Calcium : The young foliage of calcium-deficient plants showed an upward cupping of the margins. In older leaves, the margin turns necrotic and they may fall. Death of growing points followed by die-back. In better pit, slight indents appear on the skin usually towards the clayx end of the fruit. The areas turn brown and the flesh below these areas also turn brown and corky. Symptoms become more pronounced in the storage conditions. In cork spot, hard brown spots appear on the surface skin. Flesh and these spots become hard due to abnormal tissue proliferation. Measles on the bark result from a complex involving low calcium, high manganese and sometimes low boron. The deficiency can be corrected by giving one spray of 0.5 per cent calcium chloride.

Magnesium : In severe cases, the symptoms shows marginal scorching of leaves. Severe defoliation of terminal shoots progresses from base to tip. Green colour starts fading on the terminals of older leaves progressing interveinally towards the base and midrib, giving the very typical 'Herringbone' appearance to the leaves. In severe cases, the fruit may fail to mature and drop early.

Zinc : Buds along shoots fail to develop. Leaves remain small and narrow (little leaf) tending to form rosettes at tips. Foliage is sparse throughout the tree. Older leaves may fall in severe cases leaving tufts or rosettes at the terminals. Fruits become small, pointed and mis-shapen. The deficiency can be corrected by spraying 0.5% ZN SO_4 in two sprays at 15 days interval during May to July.

Boron : Symptoms normally appear on the fruits before vegetative parts are affected. Fruits do not develop normally and become mis-shapen caused by depression usually underlaid by hard corky tissues which rapidly turn brown when exposed. Surface colour is dark green. Leaves become dark green, thick and brittle, starting at shoot tip. Boron deficiency is also known as corky pit, corky core, spot necrosis and drought spot. For the correction of Boron deficiency give one or two sprays of 0.1 per cent Boric acid at 15 days interval in the month of July.

Iron: The deficiency symptoms first appear on young leaves at tip of the shoot. It is characterised by interveinal chlorosis of young leaves. In severe cases, the new leaves may unfold, but completely devoid of green colour. The veins, however, may turn green later.

Manganese : The characteristic chlorosis first appears at the leaf margins and progresses interveinally toward the midrib. Early defoliation occurs particularly on the top of the tree. Fruits remain poorly coloured. Give one or two sprays of 0.4 per cent manganese sulphate at 15 days interval in June.

Copper : Whither tip, leaf margins burned and ragged with some cuping. Tree defoliation progresses from tip to the base of the shoots.

TRAINING AND PRUNING

Pruning is done with a view to giving desired shape to a tree during early growing years and is termed as training. Even after proper training, the yearly pruning of bearing trees is quite important so that it could support a full crop of large and coloured fruits during the subsequent bearing period.

A. Training of Standard Trees

These are trained according to modified leader system. A leader develops on the young tree until it reaches the height of 2-3 m when the growth is restricted. The plant is pruned 60-90 cm above ground immediately after planting.

First year summer pinching: The scaffold are selected at equal distance with the lowest branch 30-60 cm above the ground and the others are spaced vertically at 10-15 cm apart. The growth of retained scaffold may be encouraged by depressing the growth of other shoots by pinching the top 3-5 cm of other shoots. Summer pinching is done from mid April to mid May or when the shoots are 10 to 20 cm long.

First year dormant pruning : This is done in winter following the first summer growth. Three scaffold at equal distance should be selected preferably with a vertical spacing of 10-20 cm. The primaries are headed back to achieve a balance in growth among them. Two good limbs available may be headed back to 45 cm from the trunk to supress their development until a third scaffold can be selected at the end of second growing season. Cut the laterals back to one bud and defer scaffold selection until the next year. Such trees will generally grow vigorously and will benefit by summer pinching during the second growing season.

Second year dormant pruning : In second dormant season 5-7 secondary branches per tree usually two on each primary scaffold are selected. These secondaries are directed partially outward. New growth from such branches will fill in laterally giving the tree a well shaped framework. Secondary limbs should be left full length until it is necessary to maintain balance with the primaries or other secondaries. If the primary scaffold branches is over-vigorous, it can be retarded by heading back to balance with the rest of the tree. Most trees will produce short laterals and spurs during the second year and these should not be immediately removed as these provide shade and some early fruit.

Third year dormant pruning : This consists of thinning and removal of unwanted branches and cutting others to desirable side limbs. During the third growing season, secondary branches often form fruit spurs, but on young trees fruit bud may be found at the tip of unpruned shoots.

Fourth Year dormant pruning : By this time, training has been largely completed. The tree should be thinned out and the remaining branches cut to side limbs. A moderate number of small shoots should be left in the centre of the tree for fruit bearing wood. Adequate thinning out of branches and fruiting wood will maintain a well distributed bearing area throughout the tree and reduce excessive spread and breaking of branches. By fifth summer after planting, most apple varieties produce enough crop to be considered a bearing orchard.

B. Training of Dwarf Trees

Spindle bush, Dwarf Pyramids, Palmets, Head and Spread and Cordon methods are followed for training dwarf trees. Head and spread system for central leader tree is also adopted for moderate and ultra high density plantings. Spindle bush is found most suitable method. In this case one year old apple plants are cut back to a bud about 60 cm above the ground.

First summer pruning : This time 2-3 laterals 30 cm from the base may be used to form the main scaffold branches. Such laterals should have a wide angle with the main stem and should spaced at equidistance around it. The vigorous growing laterals are tied down in August. The ties can be removed after leaf fall or left till the following summer. They should be tied so that they are straight, not arched, otherwise strong vertical shoots will arise from the top of the arch.

First winter pruning : Two or three well spaced laterals should be retained and unwanted branches arising on the main stem should be removed. The scaffold branches may be cut back by one third to half of their length to a outward growing bud if the growth is weak. Otherwise the main branches should not be pruned. The vigorous upright growing shoots arising directly below the shoot forming leader and competing with it should be cut.

Second summer growth : During the third summer, spindle bushes may carry a fruit. During August of the second year suitable laterals are tied down to form branches.

Second winter pruning : To check excessive vigour of the central leader it may again be cut back to the next suitably placed rather weaker growing lateral which is tied and trained to take the place of the central leader. Delaying pruning until late winter or early spring will also help in checking vigour.

Subsequent growth and pruning : Branches are allowed to grow from the central leader at regular intervals, choosing wide angled shoots. To allow sufficient light to reach the lower parts of the tree, the higher placed branches must be kept shorter than the lower ones.

The main branches should be so trained and spaced that there is plenty of room for fruiting laterals, for the same reason they should not be allowed to fork. The branches should be spread to about 45° angle to the trunk for the development of strong scaffold limbs. When the growth of the leader in comparison with the lower branches is too vigorous, it is best to prune the central stem back to a weaker lateral and train it as a replacement.

Spindle bush system on M_7 or MM 106 rootstocks may be followed under mid hills for high density planting.

Pruning

When the pruning of *bearing tree* is done the main purpose is to maintain a proper balance between vegetative growth and fruit production. An ideal mature tree should produce at least 25 cm of new terminal growth each year. Thus, the tree increases and maintains its fruiting area while producing satisfactory annual crops. The trees receiving regular pruning require light thinning and cutting back of the terminal branches to laterals. This prevents the tree from getting too high for economical spraying and picking operations.

The centre of the tree should be kept fairly open to impart better colour to the fruits. If this is not practiced for several years, it is best to thin out surplus branches over a period of two or more seasons. Heavy pruning will encourage vegetative growth and expose scaffold branches to sunburn damage. Old bearing trees producing small fruits will benefit from heavy pruning which stimulates new shoots and fruiting spurs. The larger pruning wounds should be protected by covering with Bordeaux paste and Bordeaux paint.

In *standard trees* start pruning from the top of the tree and work downwards. The upward growing limbs should be cut back to strong laterals. Remove the crowding branches and thin the remaining limbs, leaving the vigorous fruiting wood well spaced along the length of the limbs. Remove diseased, dried and broken branches. Remove large limbs if growing parallel and crowding other limbs. While making large cuts direct sun light should not sunscald remaining exposed branches. Remove all water sprouts except needed one. While removing a thick side branch, the first cut should be made on the under side of the limb where the weakest wood occurs. Thin out the interfering branches growing upward from the top of the limbs. Divert branches to open areas by pruning back to desirable laterals.

In *dwarf trees*, once the central leader has reached its alloted height of 2.5 m, the extension growth should be cut back each year to a weaker side branch. The strong growing shoots and branches towards the top of the tree should be removed competely. Renewal pruning of the fruiting branches lower down should be carried out each year for maintaining the vegetative growth and fruit quality in the lower parts of the tree. Lower branches should not be heavily shaded by branches higher up and some of them must be completely removed. A stub should be left while cutting back branches to the main stem so that regrowth of the moderately vigorous fruitful bud is encouraged. Avoid removing too many branches. When the main branches lose vigour these can be stimulated by pruning.

FRUIT THINNING

Generally, an apple tree sets heavily. Thinning is important for better development of fruits. Thinning of fruits can be done either by hands or chemicals. Usually one or two fruits per cluster are allowed to develop their large size, colour and taste, reduces the leaf: fruit weight ratio and reduces the incidence of better pit in storage. Approximately 100 sq. inch leaf area (20-40 leaves) per fruit is recommended for proper fruit development. An application of 10-15 ppm Naphthalene acetic acid or 0.075 per cent carbaryl (Sevin) 7-10 days after petal fall is quite effective in thinning the fruits. For delicious group and Golden Delicious, NAA has been found effective, whereas for Red Gold, Sevin is considered better. Ethephon at 100-200 ppm at petal fall stage in also recommended for fruit thinning.

PRE-HARVEST FRUIT DROP

The total number of fruits retained for final harvest decides the total yield per tree or per unit area. Therefore, it is essential that there must be minimum fruit drop after setting and during the period of fruit development. There are three distinct fruit drop in apple.

(*i*) Early drop–which is due to unpollinated and unfertilized flowers.

(*ii*) June drop–which occurs during the summer months and is mainly caused by fruit competition and moisture stress.

(*iii*) Pre-harvest fruit drop—which is severe in early ripening cultivars, ranging from 40-60 per cent of crop load. In mid season cultivars like Delicious group and Golden Delicious, the range of pre-harvest drop varies from 15-20 per cent.

The pre-harvest fruit drop can be checked conveniently with the application of 10 ppm NAA a week before the expected fruit drop or 20-25 days before harvest. Application of 2, 4-DP (Dichloroprop) at 0.5% (5 ml per litre of water) has been found to reduce harvest fruit drop more effectively. When applied to apple trees 25 days before harvest, 2,4-DP (Dichloroprop) at 20 ppm and fenoprop at 20 ppm have been found equal effects in reducing pre-harvest drop. Application of Alar at 2000 ppm 40 days after fruit set has been reported to increase fruit yield.

POLLINATION AND FRUIT-SETTING

Apple cultivars are diploid and triploid. The diploid cultivars are self-fruitful because they have plenty of good pollen. The triploid cultivars are self-unfruitful and are having high female sterility. The flower structure in these cultivars does not facilitate pollination by bees. Partially or fully self fruitful cultivars like Red Gold, McIntosh, Granny Smith, Golden Delicious, Tydeman's Worcester are suitable pollinizers for Delicious group of apple cultivars. Crab apples have been found to be very effective pollinators for apple cultivars. They have the advantages viz. abundant flower production, prolonged flowering period, production of large open flowers, attractive to bees, annual formation of flower buds, high pollen production, high pollen viability and fertilizing ability and small tree size allowing high plant density.

A good pollinizer must produce plenty of viable pollen and compatible with the commercial cultivars. The flowering period of pollinizer should overlap with the commercial cultivars. It must produce fruits of good quality, attractive colour and appealing appearance.

For effective pollination, insect activities are important. It is also desirable to place atleast 6-8 beehives per hectare of apple orchard. Cross pollination by honey bees significantly increases the fruit in apple. Incliment weather, particularly temperature below 4.4°C at bloom inhibits bee activity and hinders pollen germination. Optimum conditions for pollen germination and growth are between 21.1 to 26.7°C. High winds, high humidity and continuous rains also adversely affect the fruit set. Placement of beehives about 4-8 bee colonies per hectare help to give a good fruit set.

HARVESTING AND HANDLING OF FRUITS

The apple fruits should be harvested at proper picking maturity. It is a climacteric fruit. For distant markets, picking is done in advance to full maturity whereas for home markets properly ripe fruits are harvested. Picking of immature fruits results in poor quality with poor flavour and taste. Such fruits shrivel during storage and are subjected to physiological disorders such as scald, bitter pit and soft core. The over mature fruits in some cases may develop soft scald and internal breakdown with poor shelf-life. The time taken from full bloom to maturity is rather constant over a wide range of climatic and cultural conditions and is considered as one of the most reliable indexes of maturity. Red Delicious should be picked after 133-139 days after full bloom. The cultivar Golden Delicious should be picked after 148-154 days, Royal Delicious after 115-120 days, Granny Smith after 176-182 days and Tydeman's Worcester after 88-94 days. Change of the colour of fruits from green to yellowish green indicates that fruits are ready for harvesting. However, fruits of green variety are judged by taste. The flesh firmness can be determined by removing a thin slice of the skin and flesh with a knife and recording the pressure. Most of the commercial varieties require the flesh firmness of 16-18 lb/sq. inch to give maximum picking maturity. Delicious group should be picked before it attain pressure of 15-16 lb/sq inch. By and large flesh firmness, change in good colour and total soluble solids should help to judge the picking maturity.

Method of picking : All the apple fruits do not ripen at a time on the tree and more than one pickings are required. The apple fruits are harvested with great care. Careless handling by pickers, especially for fresh market can cause waste. Picking should start with the lower branches advancing to the top. Apple should be grasped in the palm of the hand and removed from the spur with a quick, upward twist of the wrist. A straight pull will usually result in pulling the stem out of the fruit or the spur from the tree. Fruit stalk should remain with the harvested fruits. Harvested fruits are carefully placed in the container. Fruits are kept under the shade until they are picked up and prepared for their planned outlet. The yield of apple fruits varies greatly due to climatic conditions of locality, soil types, cultivars, management practices. A well grown apple tree yields 30-50 kg fruit per tree.

Sorting and grading : After harvesting, unwanted fruits are sorted out. The healthy fruits are cleaned by washing to remove dust and spray residue. Washing can be done with tap water or a dilute solution of 1 per cent hydrochloric acid to remove lead carbonate residues. Apple fruits are graded according to size and shape, colour and permissible skin blemishes. They are graded into super, fancy, selected and commercial grades depending on market demands. For local market fruits are also graded into extra large, large, medium, small, extra small and pittoo.

Generally, following proportion (%) of fruit size of different grades is found on a tree :

(*i*) Large, super and extra large : 20–24%

(*ii*) Medium : 35–40%

(*iii*) Small : 15–20%

(*iv*) Extra small, pittoo and culls : 20–25%

Large, medium, small and extra small grade fruits are packed in four layers. The fruits of extra large grade are packed in three layers. Pittoo grade fruits are packed with wrappers. The mechanical graders can be employed for quick and efficient grading of apple fruits.

Table 1. Arrangement of different grades of apples in wooden box

Grade	Fruit dimeter (cm)	Box size, inner dimension (cm) L × B × H	No. of Layers	No. of fruits (per box)
Super large	85	45.7 × 30.5 × 27.9	3	54–57
Extra large	80	45.7 × 30.5 × 25.4	3	60–63
Large	75	45.7 × 30.5 × 30.5	4	96
Medium	70	45.7 × 30.5 × 27.9	4	112
Small	65	45.7 × 30.5 × 25.4	4	128–132
Extra small	60	45.7 × 30.5 × 25.4	5	160
Pittoo	55	45.7 × 30.5 × 25.4	Loose	Variable

Table 2. Arrangmenet of different grades of apple in CFB carton

Grade	Number of fruit layers	Number of fruits/layer	Number of fruits/box
Super large	4	18	72
Extra large	4	20	80
Large	5	20	100
Medium	5	25	125
Small	5	30	150]
Extra Small	5	35	175
Pitto	Loose	–	Loose

Packing of fruits : The fruits should be properly packed to get premium in the market. Generally, the fruits are marketed after packing in gunny bags, wooden boxes, Tray packed wooden boxes (Table 1), Pine needle board boxes, Bamboo mat boards boxes, CFB cartons (Table 2) and plastic crates. While wrapping fruits in papers, the paper is kept flat in one hand and the fruit is put at its centre with the calyx end downwards. The paper is then wrapped round the fruit in such a way that all the ends come over the stem. While placing fruits in the box, the stem end is put downwards and the calyx end upwards. The size of the boxes is so adjusted for the different grades that in all cases the packed fruits will weigh 16-17 kg. The weight of box and other packing material is about 5 kg giving a gross weight of approximately 21-22 kg per box. While packing the fruits, the boxes are lined with newsprint to cover the bottom, sides and the top of the packed fruits. The bottom and top of the box are also given extra padding with grass and pine needles to avoid spoliage during handling. Paper liners are given in the box and in between every two layers. Paper liners are also given between two rows lengthwise.

Storage of fruits : In order to get higher price and to make available apple fruits in off season their storage at low temperature is essential. The deterioration of apples starts after the climacteric stage. Quick removal of heat from the fruits is a pre-requisite for an effective storage. Pre-cooling is essential for Delicious apples, which otherwise show poor shelf life during August and September. Cold storage and controlled atmospheric storage help to extend the market life of fruits. Apple fruits are stored in racks or in the wooden boxes (30 × 30 × 45 cm). The recommended storage temperature for most varieties is –0 to 1°C with 90–95% relative humidity and shelf life of fruits can be extended for 4-6 months.

In controlled atmospheric storage, carbon dioxide, oxygen, temperature and humidity are controlled in gas tight rooms. Generally, the level of carbon dioxide is increased to 2.5-3.0 per cent with a temperature of 30-32°F in controlled atmospheric storage. CA storage at 0-1°C in 2-5 per cent CO_2 and –3 per cent oxygen prolongs the storage life of Golden Delicious, McIntosh, Rome Beauty and Stayman Early Worcester cultivars for 8-9 months.

Pre-harvest spray of silver nitrate 100 ppm, sodium benzoate 500 ppm, benzothiodiazole 200 ppm proved effective in enhancing the overall quality of Starking Delicious apples both at harvest and after storage for 150 days at 0°C and 85–90% RH.

There are certain growth retardants that can help in increasing storage life of fruits while maintaining acceptable quality. The storage life of Red Delicious fruits prolongs with 1000 ppm CCC by a week. Post harvest dipping of apple fruits with calcium chloride maintains higher quality and very less storage disorders. Waxol at 8% in combination with Alar at 400 ppm for 40-60 seconds by dip method improve quality of Red Delicious fruits. This treatment inhibits respiration and pectin hydrolysis and reduces weight loss and organic acid content.

Colour Improvement and Enhancement of Ripening

In general, buyers prefer red or yellow apples to green ones. Nearly all red colours in apples are due to soluble anthocyanin pigments. The red colour development in Delicious varieties is generally very poor in warmer and low lying apple growing areas below 1800 m above sea level. Application of ethephon at 500 ppm about 10 days before harvest improves the red colouration. Since ethephon accelerates the fruit abscission, naphthalene acetic acid at 10 ppm should be added to ethephon solution to check the abscission.

The maturity of fruits is over delayed at higher ranges i.e. above 2100 m and simultaneously the red pigment becomes too intense giving deep red to blackish appearance to fruits which become unacceptable to the consumers and give low returns. Under such conditions an application of ethephon at 1000 ppm in combination with 10 ppm NAA about 3 weeks before harvest enhances the ripening by 7-10 days and improve the colour of fruits in mid hills. The growth regulators should be sprayed separately and not to be mixed with nutrients, fungicides or insecticides.

INSECT-PESTS

1. Wooly apple aphid (*Eriosoma lanigerum* Hausmann) : The aphid lives in colonies and suck plant sap from the young shoots, cut-ends, cracks of main limbs and trunks and roots of apple plant resulting in the formation of galls and the plants become weak and prone to the attack of cankers. They remain active from March to December. In the winter season, they migrate from the aerial parts to the roots and in the reverse direction in the summer.

Spray with 0.03 per cent dimethoate during March-April and again in June (summer). Apply dimethoate at 15 g (a.i.) per metre at 8-10 cm deep in trenches during spring and summer to control aphids on the roots. Raise the plants on aphid resistant rootstocks such as Morton 778, 779, 789, 793.

2. San Jose Scale (*Quadraspidiotus perniciosus* Comstock) : The pest is active from March to December. These scales are very small in size and greyish in colour. The poplars and willows are the host plants of this pest. Heavily infested trees appears as if they are covered with wood ash. If not checked timely, the plants may die within 2-3 years. The pests are also spread by crow, maina and bulbul birds. The pest may carry from plant to plant at the time of fruit picking and nymphs may crawl along the ground and infest new plants.

Remove all the infested wild plants from the apple orchard. Fumigate nursery stock before planting. In winter spray the dormant trees with 3 per cent miscible oil impregnated with methyl parathion 0.05%. Spray 0.03% dimethoate 10-15 days after petal fall or in the second week of May. Combination of tree spray oil (2%) with chlorpyriphos @ 0.04 % at tight cluster stage has been found effective in checking the population build up of scale and mite during the reason.

3. Apple root borer (*Dorysthenes hugelii* Redt) : The grubs feeds on the roots and confines to one root about 10–20 cm deep. Leaves show reduction in size and typical yellowing and withering symptoms. Adults become active at night

Plantation in sandy soils should be discouraged. Drench basin area of the plants with chlorpyriphos or triazophos 0.04% during July and October. Once the infestation has occurred, treat tree basin with phorate granules @ 100 g a.i per tree.

4. Codling moth (*Cydia pomonella* L.) : Caterpillar feeds on the pulp in a small cavity and makes transverse tunnels into the core region and feeds as immature seed.

For its control, give two sprays of 2 kg sevin in 500 l of water in the second half of June and another 2-3 weeks later.

5. Blossom thrips (*Taeniothrips* sp., *Thrips carthami* and *Thrips flavus*) : Thrips suck the sap from leaves, flowers and young fruits and reduce the production. The maximum population of thrips is noted during spring (February-April). The population declines from May onward and make steady revival in October-December.

Follow clean cultivation practice. Spray fenitrothion at 0.05 per cent.

6. Indian gypsy moth Hairy caterpillar (*Lymantria obfuscata* Wlk) : Caterpillar feed on the leaves and all tender twigs. It lay eggs in clusters on the lower surface of the leaves.

Collect egg clusters and destroy them between August-March. Spray Rogor at 0.03 per cent for the control of this pest.

7. Tent caterpillar (*Malacosoma indica* Walker) : It is a pest of apple in North Western India and more serious in Shimla hills. It is active from March to May. Pupation takes place in stem, between leaves and among dry debrish in ground. The entire plant may be defoliated in severe infestation.

Prune the twigs containing egg mass in December – January and burnt them. Use pole tied with rag and dip in kerosene to destroy the pest. Spray 0.05 per cent nimbecidine to control the pest.

8. European red mite (*Panonychus ulmi* Koch) : Mite feeds on leaves and injury produces browning and loss of colour in the leaves.

A dormant spray with oil emulsion should be given for killing eggs. Spray the plant with fungicide 0.02% clofentezine or fenazaquin for control of mite population at motile and egg stages.

9. Apple stem borer (*Apriona cinerra* Cheverlot) : The grubs and adult cause damage by making a tunnel and reaches close to trunk of tree. The vitality and productivity of plant is greatly impaired. Adult feed on bark and cause damage.

Prune and burn the affected shoots and branches during winter. Insert a cotton wick soaked in carbon disulphite and seal the tunnels with mud. Place paradichlorbenzene 0.5 g inside the holes and plug them.

10. Leaf-rollers (*Archips termias* Meyrick) : It feeds on young leaves from April to September. The insect also scraps the skin of the fruit from July onwards. Attack on fruits is pronounced in storage.

Spray endosulfan 0.05 per cent in the last week of May and Malathion 0.05 per cent in early July or at least three weeks before harvest.

DISEASES

1. Scab : The causal fungus is ***Venturia inaequalis***. Typical scab symptoms appear on the leaves and fruits. Light brown or olive green spots which soon turn black appear either on or both sides of the young leaves in spring. The affected leaves may dry up or fall prematurely, resulting in loss of vigour and reduced yields. Affected fruits show scabby, knotty, mis-shapen appearance. Mild temperature and rainy weather are most favourable for the severity and spread of the disease.

To control scab disease follow clean cultivation practices. Collect all affected plant parts, fallen fruits and destroy them. Spray Bordeaux mixture (4 : 4 : 50) when the buds are showing pink colour, when petals have fallen and about three weeks later. Spray at least three times Dithane M-45 (Mancozeb) at 0.5 per cent or Bavistin at 0.05 per cent.

2. Pink disease : It is caused due to ***Corticium salmonicolor***. Light brown lesions appear on twigs and stem. Affected bark gets broken after sometimes into small protuberances of white or buff coloured fungal structures. It spread from June to September. The disease is favoured by over-crowding of branches, poor drainage, warm and humid conditions.

Remove the affected plant part. To large cut ends apply Bordeaux paste. Application of Triademefon 2% on scarified cankers followed by Triademefon @ 0.05% spray soon after harvest in rainy season is very effective.

3. Powdery mildew : The disease is caused by fungus ***Podosphaera leucotricha*** Salm. The disease mainly affects the new shoots and the affected leaves and produces white powdery patches. The affected terminals remained stunted and die, while the leaves curl and crinkle. The fruits of Jonathan cultivar show russeting. The leaves fall and the plant is robbed of its carbohydrates production. The blossoms are deformed and fruit setting is reduced drastically. Dry weather with mild temperature conditions favour disease development.

Prune the affected twigs in winter to reduce the disease. Spray with wettable sulphur (300 g/100 litres of water) or carbendazim fungicide (50 g/100 litres of water) i.c. (*i*) during the late dormancy (*ii*) At bud swell (*iii*) At petal fall and (iv) two weeks later.

4. Silver leaf canker : The disease is caused by fungus ***Chondrostereum purpureum.*** Silvering of foliage appears soon after petal fall. The wood of dead tissue turns black. Toxic substances produced by the fungus on translocation to leaves, induce silver leaf symptoms.

Prune the affected plant parts and wounds should be covered with Bordeaux paint. Young trees show recovery when their vigour increase by fertilization and other cultural practices. Post-harvest spray of carbendazim (0.05%) or Blitox (0.3%) on trees can check the infection. Also spray these chemicals on ground to reduce the inoculum in the orchard.

5. Sooty blotch and fly speck : Sooty bloch is caused by ***Gloeodes pomigena*** and fly speck by **Microthyriella rubi.** Sooty blotch is characterised by dull black to grey spots with indefinite outline. Fly specks appears as definite circular specks black in colour. Both spots make fruit skin smoky and reduces its market return.

To control three diseases, give two sprays of Captafol/Mancozeb/Zineb/Captan at fortnighly interval 15-20 days prior to harvest.

6. Brown rot : The disease is caused by ***Monilinia fructigena.*** The fungus over winters in mumified fruits. It hibernates in the fruiting spurs and branches and producing canker on the base of the spur.

During summer remove all affected spurs and branches. Discard all affected fruits and destroy them properly.

7. Root rot : The disease is caused by ***Dematophora necatrix.*** Affected trees show sparse foliage, slow growth and bronzing and yellowing of leaves. Ultimately such plant die. The roots turn brown and remain covered with white cottony mycelial mat of the fungus in rainy season. Heavy, water-logged soils favour the development of the fungus and the disease.

Improve drainage of the orchard for the control of disease. Cut the affected roots during November-December. Apply Brassicol paint (10 kg/litre linseed oil) on the cut ends and the healthy portions of the roots. Uproot and burn the dead plant and treat the soil with 1 per cent Brassicol solution. Give atleast 3 drenching of carbendazim (10 g/10 litres water) at 15-20 days interval during monsoon.

8. Collar rot : It is caused due to ***Phytophthora cactorum***. The disease spread maximum in poorly drained soils. It manifests itself in the form of brown, soft, spongy, cankered area around the collar of the tree at or below soil level. The girdled trees succumbs to attack.

Remove the soil around the collar region during November-December and expose the affected portion to sun. Remove the cankered area to the healthy portion and apply copper oxychloride paint (Blitox in linseed oil). Drench 30 cm radius around tree trunk with Mancozeb (300-400 g/100 litres water) or copper oxychloride (500-1000 g/100 litres water) or Brassicol (1 kg/100 litres water). Always keep graft point 20-25 cm above the soil level at the time of plantation.

DISORDERS

1. Bitter Pit : The symptoms appear as small, dry, brown pockets usually spherical in shape below the skin and also in cortex. The cultivars like Northern Spy and Delicious are more prone to this disorder. Large fruits and immature are more susceptible than others. Heavy doses of nitrogenous fertilizers, excessive shedding and heavy pruning are reported to favour bitterpit. Storage at 32-34°F under high humidity (85-95%) controls pitting.

2. Scald : It first appears as light mottling on the greener surface of fruit. Darkening becomes more severe with the elapsed time and ultimately extend to red surface also. Scald usually affects the skin only but in severe cases it may extend to fruit flesh. The immature fruits are most susceptible to scald which is aggravated by warmer temperature. Light scald fruit in storage may be severely affected during marketing.

3. Internal Browning : It is characterised by brownish streaks radiating into flesh from the core. It can be controlled by storage at 36°F. Controlled atmospheric storage with higher temperature can also be helpful in the control of this disorder. It is mainly associated with Yellow Newton apples.

ALTERNATE BEARING

The apple cultivars Royal Delicious, Red Delicious and Golden Delicious have the tendency to bear heavy crop in a year followed by poor cropping season, setting a rhythm of irregular bearing. Once this pattern of irregular bearing sets in, the fluctuating rhythm of yield continues year after year. The alternate bearing can be checked to certain extent by adopting following practices :

- (*i*) Thinning of fruit in one year often increases the return bloom in the following year. In a heavy cropping year, thinning is particularly essential for return bloom as the trees become exhausted due to heavy crop.
- (*ii*) Nitrogen application early in the 'off' year has a slight tendency to promote annual bearing in trees having low-nitrogen level.
- (*iii*) Judicious pruning of spurs in winters preceding 'on year' to reduce crop load.
- (*iv*) Application of growth retardant like SADH 2000 ppm or paclobutrazol 1500 ppm in June-July before the flower bud differentiation should be given in an 'on year'.

CHAPTER

27

Pear

Pear is one of the superior temperate fruits having good taste and flavour.. In India, pear is largely grown for consumption as a fresh fruit. The cultivation of Japanese pear ***Pyrus pyrifolia*** (Burm F. Nakai). has received a boost as a commercial crop in Northern India and acreage under this fruit crop has been steadily increasing because of its high yield potential and good economic returns. The pear needs relatively less care due to its hardy nature which enables it to flourish well even on water-logged soils, where most other fruit trees fail to grow. It is also well known for its keeping quality and stands transportation well. Besides local consumption the Patharnakh fruit is transported to distant consuming centres like Mumbai, Kolkata and Chennai.

In the wake of serious problems like 'Citrus decline' in citrus fruits, 'malformation' and 'alternate bearing in mango', pear is the only fruit which offers good prospects, as it is relatively free of any such serious problems. This is one of the main reasons that fruit growers of Punjab, Haryana and Himachal Pradesh are switching on to pear cultivation on a large scale.

ORIGIN, HISTORY AND DISTRIBUTION

Most of the **Pyrus** species are native to the Northern Hemisphere of the Old World. No species of pears is indigenous to either North or South America or to the continent of Australia. European and West Asian species (Occidental Group) are native to Eastern Europe and South Western Asia, including South Afghanisthan, Caucasus and Asia Minor. East and Northern Asian species (The Oriental Group) are native to Eastern Asia, including China, Japan and Manchuria. Vavilov proposed three centre of origin for cultivated pears *i.e.,* chinese centre, central asiatic centre and near eastern centre. Zeven and Zhukovsky proposed fourth centre for pear *i.e.,* Siberian centre. Chinese centre comprising the region of north and central China, Japan and Korea. ***P. pyrifolia, P. ussuriensis, P. betulifolia*** and ***P. calleryana*** originated in this tract. Central asiatic centre includes Western Tian–Shan, Pamir Alai, Uzbekistan, Tadjikistan, Afghanistan and north west India. ***P. communis, P. salicifolia, P. regeli*** and ***P. pashia*** are indigenous sps of this centre. Near eastern centre comprising Asia minor and Cancasus mountains. ***P. syriaca*** and ***P. caucasus*** species found in this centre. Siberian centre species are ***P. communis, P. cordata, P. nivalis*** and ***P. salvifolia.***

Pyrus pyrifolia (Burm F) Nakai, is the most widely distributed of the Oriental pears, extending over the entire Central and Southern region of China, as well as in Formosa and

Japan. The pear (***Pyrus pyrifolia*** (Burm F.) Nakai originated in China, where its culture dates back to 2500-3000 years. It may have been introduced into India from China during the time of Lord Kanishka (120-170-A.D.), who settled some Chinese hostages around village Harsa Chhina (Amritsar distict) by them. Its cultivation appears to have spread to other parts of Northern India from this place, but this is only a possibility.

AREA AND PRODUCTION

The main pear producing countries in the world are China, Italy, USA, Argentina, Spain, Turkey, South Africa, Netherlands, India and Japan. The total production of pear in the world is 22.5 million metric tonnes. China is producing 16 million metric tonnes of pear annually accounting for 71 per cent of the total production in the world.

In India, pear occupies the second place among temperate fruits both in area and production. Because of the wide range of its adaptability, the cultivation of this fruit has spread to the temperate and sub-tropical regions of Jammu & Kashmir, Himachal Pradesh, Tarai region of Uttar Pradesh. Punjab, Uttarakhand, Haryana, Arunchal Pradesh, Assam and South India. The area under pear in India is 48,000 hectares with its annual production of 2.94 lakh tonnes.

The area under pear fruit has been steadily increasing in Punjab State. It ranks next only to citrus, guava and mango. It occupies about 2787 ha with annual production of 6,3040 mt. This fruit is doing very well in the districts of Taran Taran, Amritsar, Jalandhar, Ludhiana and Patiala. The pear orchards of sand pear (Patharnakh) are coming up in very hot and arid tracts of South-West Punjab.

IMPORTANCE AND USES

Pear is very delicious and juicy fruit. It is a rich source of protein and mineral like phosphorus. Ripe fruit of different pear cultivars contains 10.0 to 13.0 per cent total soluble solids and 0.20 to 0.32 per cent acidity. Pear fruit contains protein 0.6%, calcium 8 mg, phosphorus 15 mg and vitamin A 60 I.U. per 100 *g* of fruit. Sugars, starch and cellulose are the main carbohydrates found in pear fruit. Brix°-acid ratio in Patharnakh is 36 :1 in LeConte is 47 : 1 and in Baggugosha is 60 : 1.

Pear fruits can be used in the preparation of several delicious products such as pear preserve, pear jam, pear chuteny, pear juice and canned pear. Pear preserve has attractive amber colour with characteristic flavour. Patharnakh and Kieffer varieties are considered good for canning.

The fruits of Punjab Nectar, Punjab Soft and Punjab Gold are suitable for the preparation of RTS, Nectar and Shelf Stable Squash products.

BOTANY

The pear belongs to the genus ***Pyrus***, of the family Rosaceae. Twenty two primary known species of genus ***Pyrus*** have been described. The important species which are either grown for commercial cultivation or for raising rootstocks are given below :

1. *Pyrus communis* L. : European pear : Trees grows in upright manner. Bark light brown to grey in colour. Lenticells are present on the twigs. Young shoots are light brown in colour. Leaves small, ovate, 5-10 cm long, margin serrated, base obtuse, apex acuminate. Leaves are dark green above and light green under surface. It has persistent calyx, fleshy pedicels and pyriform shape in different form.

2. *Pyrus pyrifolia* (Burm F.) Nakai, var. Culta: **Japanese or Chinese or Sand pear** : Tree 9-10 metres in height, having spreading habit of growth. Bark light brown in colour with the presence of lenticells. Bark surface rough and splitted. Branches are in drooping habit.

Pubescence present on young shoots. Leaves mostly ovate, 10-15 cm long, margin crenate, base round, apex narrowly acuminate. Leaves are dark green above and light green below, mibrib pale green. It has deciduous calyx, non-fleshy pedicel and fruit shape like that of apple.

3. *Pyrus serotina* Rehd **: Shiara :** Shiara is a wild relative of pear and is widely used as rootstock. Tree 8-9 metres in height, spreading in nature. Leaves ovate, 8-10 cm long, pointed at the tip, medium in size. Spines long, stout and pointed. Leaf margin finely serrated. It has deciduous calyx and fruit shape like that of apple.

4. *Pyrus pashia* Hamilton : **Kainth :** This species is commonly used for raising of rootstock. Trees having upright habit of growth, 9 metres in height. Branches are thicker than pear. Leaves elliptical, margin serrated, base and apex acute, 5-7 cm long. Spines present, long and pointed. Fruits about 1 inch long, sub-globose and brown. It is found wild in the Himalayas to Northern China.

5. *Pyrus communis X Pyrus pyrifolia* : Hybrid pear : Trees medium in vigour and spreading. Leaves medium in size, 8-10 cm long, heart shaped, broader at the base and narrow towards the apex, upper surface glabrous, undersurface light green. Fruits small to medium is size and pyriform in shape with attractive greenish yellow-colour.

Pear is a pome fruit and its edible portion is fleshly thalamus.

FLOWERING AND FRUITING

The flowers are epigynous and the ovary is inferior. The type of inflorescence in pear is *Corymb.* In common pear, the flowers are 4-12 in umbel-like clusters on slender pedicels, white, appearing with the leaves, calyx persistent or rarely deciduous, stemens 15-20. Flowers of Patharnakh pear are white,3 cm or more across, 4-12 together on slender pedicels, appearing with the first foliage. The flowering starts in the last week of February and continues upto third week of March. The fruit is borne on spurs. It is pollinated through insects. The pollen is highly viable.

The pear cultivars grown in the plains of Northern India are self-fruitful or partially self-fruitful. Patharnakh which occupies about 90 per cent of the area under pear in the Punjab, usually give commercial crop when planted in solid blocks. The cultivars like 'LeConte', 'Baggugosha', 'Smith' and 'Kieffer' will give commercial crops, only when atleast two of these are planted together. Honey-bees usually prefer flowers of other plants to those of pears. This is due to the fact that pear flowers provide a relatively small quantity of nectar which is low in sugar content. In orchards where heavier fruit-set is desired, two or three colonies of bees per acre should be provided.

Fruit-setting in pear starts by end of March. The fruit is borne on spurs. The fruit (Patharnakh) reaches harvest maturity after 155 days of fruit-set. The fruit growth in terms of length and diameter shows three distinct phases and follows a pattern of "Sigmoid Curve".

CLIMATE

In India pear cultivation is mainly confined to the temperatre Himalayn mountains at 1700 – 2400 MSL. This condition is ideal to grow a large number of European and Japanese/ oriental pears.

Pear can be grown successfully in mid-hills at an elevation of 1,200 to 1,800 metres above sea level, where mean maximum temperature of 15°C-25°C in winter and 20°-32°C in summer and minimum temperature of 2-10°C in winter and 10-18°C during summer prevail. Large number of pear cultivars require 900–1200 hours below 7°C during winter to complete their chilling requirement in order to flower and fruit satisfactorily. Bartlett pear has a chilling requirement of about 1500 hours. An annual rainfall of 100-125 cm is considered adequate. The best flavour and keeping quality in Bartlett pear develops in locations where summers are fairly hot and dry. Cool nights (10°C) during a month before harvest cause softening and premature ripening of this cultivar, thus impairing fruit size and quality.

Patharnakh pear is a very hardy tree and can be successfully grown in the sub-tropical climate prevailing in the Punjab and Haryana States. The submontane tract as well as the central part of the Punjab State have been found to be quite suitable for its cultivation. It can also be successfully grown in the Bet area. This cultivar require 200 to 300 chilling hours and can withstand high temperature and hot winds during the summer. Being deciduous in habit, it escapes damage from frost. However, care must be taken to plant pear orchards in frost free locations. The absence of rains during flowering period is one of the pre-requisites for the successful cultivation of pear. Rain at flowering not only washes away the pollen but also interferes with the activity of pollinating insects, thus adversely affecting fruit-set. Areas exposed to excessively hot winds during summer also have an adverse affect both on fruit and foliage.

SITE AND SOIL

Site has a decisive influence on regular cropping. In plains the pear orchards should be at a distance from Eucalyptus plantations so as to save the fruit from bird damage. The site should be such from where excess of rain water should not stagnate for long, which may cause heavy mortalities. Pear should be grown on a land which is at a slightly higher level than the surrounding area to reduce the chances of damage by frost.

It can grow well on a wide variety of soils provided these are well drained. The pear tree is hardy and can flourish even on rather inferior lands with relatively less care. It can tolerate water logged conditions to some extent, however, the areas frequented by floods and where the water stagnates for many days during the rainy season should never be selected for pear growing. The most desirable soil for pear is one which is of medium texture, deep, well drained and has a water table below 200 cm around the year. Pear trees are short lived on sandy and loam soils. A neutral pH range of 6.0–7.5 is desirable because iron deficiency is encountered on highly alkaline soils. It can grow on soils having pH upto 8.7, if the electrical conductivity of the soil is below 0.5 mmhos/cm. Highly fertile soils very rich in nitrogen are not suitable for pear growing as they increase the incidence of psylla and fire blight.

CHOICE OF VARIETIES

Pear varieties grown in India are grouped into three categories *i.e.* European pear, Asian or Japanese pear and Hybrid pear. The following varieties are grown in pear growing states.

1. Kashmir Valley : Kings Pear, Vicar of Winkfield, Red Bartlett, China Pear, Fertility, Williams, Starking Delicious, Bertlett, Conference, Comice, Hardy, Clapp's favourite, Winter Nelis, Flemish Beauty, Chinese Sandy Pear (Nakh Kashmiri).

2. Himachal Pradesh :

(A) High Hills :

Early Varieties : Early China, Laxton's Superb

Mid Season Varieties : Bartlett, Red Bartlett, Max-Red Bartlett, Flemish Beauty, Starkrimson

Late Varieties : Conference, Kashmiri Pear, Doyenne-du-Comice.

(B) Mid, low Hills and Valley areas : Patharnakh, Kieffer, China Pear, Punjab Beauty

3. Uttarakhand and Uttar Pradesh :

(A) High Hills : Max-Red Bartlett, William Bartlett, Winter Nelis, Hardy, Clapp's Favourite, Conference, Flemish Beauty, Comice

(B) Lower Hills and plains : Patharnakh, LeConte, Gola, Punjab Beauty

4. Punjab :

(A) Hard Pear : Punjab Nakh, Patharnakh

(B) Semi Soft Pear : Punjab Gold, Punjab Nectar, Punjab Beauty, Baggugosha

(C) Soft Pear : Nijisseiki, Punjab Soft

More important and promising ones are as follows:

Bartlett : It is the popular commercial cultivar. The tree is prolific and regular bearer. The fruit is medium to large, ovate pyriform in shape and turn yellow in colour on ripening with thin skin. The pulp is soft, juicy, sweet and scented but keeping quality is poor. It is mid season variety and starts ripening from the first week of August. The fruit is suitable for dessert purpose, drying and canning.

Conference : It is a regular and heavy bearer variety. The fruit is medium in size, pyriform in shape and pale yellow in colour at maturity. The pulp is salmon coloured, sweet and juicy. It is a mid season variety and ripened from last week of July to first week of August.

Clapp's Favourite : It is a good and regular cropper. The trees are large, spreading, round topped and very productive. The fruits resemble Bartlett in size, shape, colour and flavour. Skin is pale lemon yellow with brown dots. The texture is fine, melting, buttery, juicy and flavoured.

Flemish Beauty : The trees are medium in size, vigorous and spreading with drooping branches. Fruit is large, obovate or roundish, colour clear yellow, overspread on the exposed check with a dotted and marbled red blush. The flesh is tender, granular, juicy, sweet and aromatic with a slight musky flavour. It ripens in September.

Starkrimson. Trees are moderately vigorous. It grow well in mid hills upto 4000 feet. The fruits are medium in size, obtuse pyriform in shape with attractive dark red colour. It attain crimson colour in storage. The flesh is white with fine melting texture, sweet and have pleasant flavour. It ripens in second week of July.

Patharnakh : It is a hard pear variety of ***Pyrus pyrifolia***. This is the most popular variety because of heavy bearing and good keeping quality. The fruit is tough and firm and can stand transportation very well for long distances without any spoilage. The fruit is medium round and green in colour with prominent dots. The flesh is gritty, crisp and juicy. It ripens in the last week of July. It is a heavy yielding variety with an average yield of 150 kg fruit per tree.

Baggugosha : It is a variety of ***Pyrus communis***. Trees are upright and vigorous and has irregular bearing habit. It has small, greenish, yellow fruits with tapering stem-end. The flesh is sweet and somewhat gritty. It ripens in August and has an average yield of 60 kg per tree.

Punjab Beauty : It is a Interspecific hybrid between ***P. communis*** × ***P. pyrifolia*** and called as semi-soft variety. The trees are upright, medium in vigour and regular in bearing. The fruit is medium, yellow with red blush. The flesh is white and more juicy and sweet than LeConte and Baggugosha. Fruits mature in third week of July. The average yield is 80 kg per plant.

Punjab Nector : It is a Interspecific hybrid between ***P. communis*** × ***P. pyrifolia*** and called as semi-soft variety. The trees are upright, medium in vigour and precocious. The fruit size is medium to large, ground colour is yellow green. The flesh is whitish, very juicy, TSS 13.6% and acidity 0.21%. The mature fruits are less gritty and become mellow when ripe. It mature in fourth week of July and yields 80 kg fruits per tree. Suitable for processing like ready to serve (RTS), nectar and squash.

Punjab Gold : It is a Interspecific hybrid between ***P. communis*** × ***P. pyrifolia*** and called as semi-soft variety. It is a sister line of Punjab Nectar. The trees are upright, medium in vigour and precocious. The fruit size is large, ground colour is golden yellow. The flesh is whitish, TSS 13.3% and acidity 0.22%. It mature in fourth week of July and yields 72 kg fruits per tree. Suitable for processing like RTS, nectar and squash.

LeConte : It is a hybrid between ***Pyrus communis* X *Pyrus pyrifolia***. LeConte is a variety having low chilling requirement. Tree medium in growth, upright and become spreading in fully mature trees. Trees bear good crop, but are blight susceptible. Its fruits are small to medium in size and pyriform in shape with greenish yellow in colour. It repens by the end of July and yields about 60-80 kg fruit per tree.

Kieffer : Kieffer is a hybrid between ***Pyrus communis X Pyrus pyrifolia***. It is a variety requiring longer chilling hours than LeConte and Patharnakh. Tree is very productive, widely adaptable, hardy and disease resistant. The fruit is medium to large, pointed at the ends, brownish red in colour and grity, hard, well suited for canning. It ripens in August-September. Average yield 100 kg per tree.

Punjab Nakh : It is hard pear selection from Patharnakh and belongs to *P. pyrifolia*. Trees are spreading and vigorous. The fruit is medium, weight 155g, ovate and light yellowish green with prominent dots. The flesh is gritty, crisp and juicy. Its keeping quality is good. It repens in fourth week of July. The average yield is 190 kg per plant.

Nijisseiki : It is soft pear variety and belongs to **P. Pyrifolia.** Trees are spreading and medium in vigour. The fruits are medium in size, ground colour golden brown. The flesh is whitish, mature fruits are very soft, fruit firmness is 11.2 lbf. TSS 12.9 per cent, acidity 0.21 per cent and very juicy (74.6% juice) variety. It mature in end June to first week of July. Its fruit ripen on the tree. The average yield is 80.2 kg/tree. It is suitable for processing like RTS, nectar and squash.

Punjab Soft : It is soft pear variety and belongs to *P. pyrifolia.* Trees are upright, spreading and medium in vigour. The fruits are medium in size, ground colour yellow green, flesh is white. Mature fruits are very soft and juicy. TSS 11.3 per cent with acidity 0.135 per cent. It ripens in first week July. The average yield is 85 kg per plant. The variety is suitable for processing.

PROPAGATION AND ROOTSTOCKS

The pear plants are raised on **Kainth (*Pyrus pashia*),** or rootsuckers (Batank) of ***Pyrus pyrifolia*** or Shiara **(*Pyrus serotina*)** or Quince A **(*Pyrus ussuriensis*)**

Common Rootstocks

1. ***Pyrus Communis* :** Clonal rootstocks (Old Home × Farmingdale) resistant to blight with high yield potential are as follows :

Dwarf	:	OH × F51
Semi dwarf	:	OH × F69, OH × F230, OH × F333
Semi vigorous	:	OH × F217, OH × F267, OH × F361
Vigorous	:	OH × F18, OH × F112, OH × F198

2. ***Pyrus pashia*** (Kainth)	:	Commonly used in Punjab a Himachal Pradesh
3. ***Pyrus pyrifolia*** (Rootsuckers)	:	Used in Punjab
4. ***Pyrus ussuriensis***	:	Quince A standard rootstock Quince C semi-vigorous rootstock
5. ***Pyrus serotina*** (Shiara)	:	Commonly used in Himachal Pradesh
6. ***Pyrus betulifolia***	:	Oregon 260, 261, 264
7. ***Pyrus calleryana***	:	Oregon 211, D-6.

The Patharnakh pear plants are raised both by budding and grafting on pear suckers and Kainth seedlings. Of the various methods of grafting tongue and cleft graftings are the most common ones for pear propagation. When the scion and stock are of equal thickness, tongue grafting can be successfully employed, whereas when the stock is thicker than the scion, cleft grafting may be practised. Tongue and cleft grafting are performed during December-January, when the plants are still dormant. T- budding is also practised from May to July. Pear plants can also be propagated through hard-wood cuttings.

Raising of rootstocks from Kainth (*Pyrus pashia*) seed : Fully mature fruits of Kainth are collected in September or first week of October. These fruits are dumped for softening and easy extraction of seed. The seeds need stratification before they are sown in the field or on raised nursery bed. The seeds of Kainth have a period of rest which should be broken by low temperature. The seeds are placed in moist sand in wooden boxes in layers one above the other during October or November. The sand is kept moist. The seeds are kept in the stratifying medium till the upper most layer of seeds pushes the sand upward and protrudes the radicle. The stratification is completed in about a month. The seeds germinate in 10 - 12 days. The sprouted seeds should be sown in the nursery beds in January at a distance of 15 cm in rows 30 cm apart, immediately. The seeds start germinating within 10 days. One month old seedlings are planted in nursery at a distance of 10 × 60 cm. These seedlings become buddable in May-June or can be graftable in January next year.

Sowing seeds on raised beds : The Kainth seed is also sown on raised beds during November-December. The stratification of seed on these beds is completed by natural process and the seedlings come out in about two months. These seedlings are allowed to grow on raised beds for about a year and transplanted in the nursery in the following January. The distance from seedling to seedling and row-to-row is kept 15cm and 30cm, respectively. These seedling become buddable during August-September and graftable in December-January.

Raising of Kainth roostock without stratification : The seeds extracted from mature fruits in last week of September or first week of October can be sown directly. Freshily extracted seeds should be placed in moist sand in wooden boxes for germination. The seeds germinate in 10–12 days. These seedlings are planted in the field in lines at 10 cm apart leaving 60 cm space after every four lines at 2 to 4 leaves stage. These seedlings become buddable in May-June or can be grafted in December-January.

Clonal propagation of Kainth : The rootstock raised from Kainth seed is not uniform in growth and vigour and takes two years for the seedlings to become buddable or graftable. Therefore, clonal propagation of Kainth becomes essential to get uniform and ture- to-type rootstocks. For raising clonal roottstock, hard-wood cuttings has been found to be suitable method of propagation. The rootstock raised from cuttings become graftable after one year, thus, one year is saved as compared to raising of Kainth seedlings.

Raising of rootstock from pear suckers (*Pyrus pyrifolia*) : This rootstock is widely used in Punjab for propagating pear. The rootsuckers (Batankan) are collected from the underneath of old pear trees during November-December. These are headed back leaving two to three buds from the ground level and planted 10 cm in rows 30 cm apart leaving 60 cm space after every two rows. Out of the newly emerged shoots, single healthy shoot is retained which become buddable during August-September. Those suckers which do not become buddable during August-September are grafted in the following December-January with the scion cultivars. The pear suckers which have well developed root system can be bench-grafted and directly planted in the nursery field at the above mentioned distances.

Raising of plants through cuttings : The pear plants can also be raised through hard-wood cuttings. The cuttings are prepared from juvenile shoots during December. The cuttings are kept for callusing for about a month and are planted in the nursery field at a distance of 10 cm apart in rows 30 cm apart. Treating the cuttings with 100 ppm IBA for 24 hours prior to callusing gives better rooting success. The nursery fields are constantly kept moist with frequent and light irrigations. Flooding of the nursery should be avoided. The cuttings of *Kainth* are also prepared and treated with IBA100 ppm for 24 hours to raise clonal rootstock. These are later budded or grafted.

Clonal rootstock of Quince A : Quince A is most commonly used clonal rootstock producing trees 50 - 60 percent of the standard size. However, this rootstock has poor compatibility with most of the commercial cultivars. Incompatibility can be covercome by double grafting with Old home or hardy varieties. Mound layering is generally done to propagate this rootstock clonally.

PLANTING AND AFTER CARE

The best time for planting pear trees is from mid-January to first fortnight of February before they start new growth. One year old, healthy and vigorous plants should be used for planting. Older plants of 2-3 years age can also be planted with good success. Before the plants are put in the field, the orchard site should be properly laid out. The trees may be planted at a distance of about 7.5 metres apart by which 180 plants are accommodated in one hectare by the square system of planting. The pear may also be planted by the hexoganal system by which 207 plants are accommodated in one hectare.

Peer can also be planted at 5 × 5 m distance. Using quince rootstock, high density planting in pear have been attempted. Planting distance of 3 – 3.5 × 1.2 m on Quince MA has been recommended for cv William's.

The pear cv. Patharnakh can be planted at 8 × 4 m distance and the trees are trained by bending of main scaffolds and two secondaries. This also helps in reducing juvenility by two year. Soft pear can be planted at 6m × 6m by which 275 plants are accommodated in one hectare.

Basins should be pepared immediately after planting. The level of soil near the trunk should be kept slightly higher than the level of basins so that water may not come in direct contact of the trunk. Irrigation should be given immediately after planting so that soil may settle down properly around the roots. After two or three days, second irrigation should be given. Subsequent irrigations should be given as and when required. The irrigation interval upto March may be 15-20 days, but later on as the season warms up the interval may be reduced to 10-12 days upto June. Irrigation during rainy season is not required. The trunk of young plants should be white washed once in March, again in May and then in the rainy season to avoid injury from sun-burn and to prevent cracking of bark. Farmyard manure should be mixed in the basins at the rate of 20 kg per tree in January-February. Irrigation should be applied immedately after it is thoroughly mixed in the basins. To check the attack of white ants, the trees should be given chlorpyriphos 2 ml per litre of water once in April and then after rains. The surplus shoots not required for building the framework of the trees should be removed. The shoots appearing on the rootstock should also be removed, otherwise they will have an adverse effect on the growth of plants. Trees should be protected from insect and pests by following the proper spraying schedule.

ORCHARD CULTURAL PRACTICES

Irrigation

Water is needed during summer months, which is the active growing period and when young fruits are developing. Shortage of water during the month of April, May and June restricts the tree growth and leads to the formation of hard and small fruits of poor quality. During summer months pear should be irrigated at an interval of 5-7 days depending upon the soil conditions. Plants should be irrigated after 15 days interval in August and September. No irrigation should be given in January. Bearing trees should be irrigated through flood method during summer months at an interval of 5 to 7 days so that fruit size may be increased. Irrigation is not required during rainy season. As regards the colour composition, dessert and keeping quality of fruits, neither too little nor too much water is needed. If the plants suffer from extreme water deficiency, the fruits may lack colour, become tough and somewhat meaty without the crispness of fruits, having a higher water content. When water is excessive, the colour may again become less attractive and the keeping quality deteriorates. Under relatively dry conditions fruits develop higher acidity and better flavour. After harvesting of fruits in August, the trees should be irrigated at an interval of 20 days or so upto the end of October. After this no irrigation may be given till January.

Intercropping

Judicious intercropping not only gives good income from the land, but also maintain its productivity at a high level and keep down the weeds. Intercrops like moong, mash and toria can be grown during **Kharif** season, while wheat, peas, grams and senji may be grown during **rabi** season in young and rejuvenated peas orchards to get some income during the non-bearing period. Even in bearing orchards crops like peas, grams, senji can be grown during **rabi** while moong, mash and sunflower during **kharif.** Additional dose of fertilizers should be given for intercrops.

Some fruit plants such as peach, plum, papaya, and phalsa may also be interplanted as fillers. However, the fillers must be removed when the pear trees come into bearing. Additional doses of the fertilizers should be added to filler trees according to their requirements, so that they do not compete for nutrients with the permanent trees. It should be kept in mind that once the peaches are planted as fillers, no intercropping with crops like berseem, patato, tomato, etc. should be done during the rabi or kharif seasons. Otherwise the peaches as fillers or the main pear plants may suffer from the on slaught of root rot or any other devastating disease, because of the excessive watering to the intercrops, which is not required at any cost by the deciduous trees due to dormant condition in winter months.

Soil Management

Cover crops : It refers to planting an intercrop in an pear orchard for providing cover to soil surface. These crops are usually cut and mulched or mixed into the soil. These are useful as provide cover to the soil during winter and prevent erosion during heavy rains. Soil cover keeps the soil warm in winter and cool in summer. Peas, beans, soybean, cowpeas, lentil and sumhemp are the suitable cover crops.

Mulching : Under rainfed conditions, where water scarcity restrict severely the growth and yield of the trees, mulching is often used to conserve moisture which helps in checking weeds, erosion and temperature fluctuation in pear orchards. Black polythene as a mulch increase the yield of pear by 14 per cent over the clean cultivation.

Weed Control

Weeds can be effectively controlled by spraying the herbicides namely hexuron or glycel or gramoxone. Spray hexuron 80 WP (diuron) at 4.0 kg/hectare as pre-emergence (first fortnight of March) after thorough cultivation so as to remove the established growing weeds/plant debris. Gylcel 41 SL (glyphosate) at 3 litres/hectare or gramoxone 24 WSC (paraquat at 3 litres/hectare should be sprayed as post- emergence when the weeds are growing actively and to a height of 15-20 cm. Dissolve the herbicides in 500 litres of water per hectare so as to give a thorough coverage to the field/weeds. In case there is emergence of weeds during/after rainy season, another spray of glycel/gramoxone at the same rate may be done. Spray glycel/gramoxone during calm day so as to avoid spray drift to the foliage of the fruit tree.

Quality improvement : Foliar application of KNO_3 @ 1.5 per cent after full bloom improve fruit yield and quality of Patharnakh pear.

Manuring and Fertilization

Pear trees should be adequately manured and fertilized so that thay may make good vegetative growth and bear better crops of high quality fruit. Based on experimental evidence the following schedule of manuring and fertilization is recommended :

Doses for full grown trees

State	FYM (Kg/tree)	N	P_2O_5 (g per tree)	K_2O
Himachal Pradesh	100	700	350	700
Jammu and Kashmir	–	600	130	750
Punjab	50	500	320	900
Uttarakhand	–	500	–	400
Arunachal Pradesh	500	350	210	210
Tamil Nadu	40	600	150	300

Under sub-tropical conditions of Punjab, the entire dose of farmyard manure, superphosphate and muriate of potash is added in December. Half of nitrogen is added in early February before flowering and the other half in April after the fruit-set.

To full grown plants of Punjab Beauty, a supplemental dose of urea @ 500 g is given in September in addition to recommended fertilizer doses to get better fruit size and higher yield. In hills, 60 – 100 kg FYM, 700 N and K_2O each and 350 g P_2O_5 is given to ten years old plants.

Micro-nutrient deficiency : Pear is susceptible to zinc and iron deficiency. On calcarious soils or where irrigation source is drainage water of cities, pear develop chlorosis due to lack of avilable iron, manganese or zinc. Iron deficiency appears on apical leaves which develop characteristic symptoms of dark green veins on a pale green background. Boron deficiency may cause blossom blight to pears in which the blossoms wilt and die but leaves remain normal. In severe cases, leaves also die and the limbs may or may not put on new buds for a few weeks. In copper deficiency, terminal leaves on current year's shoots are first to be affected. The leaf tips first become, yellow and this is followed by necrosis. Later in the season, most of the new shoots develop die back. Due to zinc deficiency, the plants remain dwarf, slow growing and show little leaf symptoms. Shoot terminals exhibit rosette like appearance.

To correct zinc deficiency, zinc sulphate 3 kg + 1.5 kg unslaked lime per 500 litres of water is suitable for spraying non-bearing trees in April-May and bearing trees after fruit harvest. Iron chlorosis in young trees can be controlled by spraying chlorotic young trees with a solution of 0.3 per cent ferrous sulphate. Boron deficiency can be corrected by broad-casting borex in the tree basins at the rate of 100 g per tree in early fall. Such a treatment usually prevents boron deficiency for three years. Copper deficiency can be controlled by spraying copper sulphate at the rate of 0.5 per cent after fruit harvest.

TRAINING AND PRUNING

Proper training and pruning of pear trees is essential for the development of proper framework and to control the size of the tree for the convenience of horticultural operations, to maintain the vigour and growth of the tree, to spread the fruiting area uniformly on the tree, to secure fruit of good size and quality and to encourage regular bearing. Pear trees can be trained according to modified leader system, free standing, pyramid, spindle bush, palmette and tatura trellis. For high density planting, tatura trellis system of training is followed. Pear trees are usually trained according to the 'Modified Leader System'.

Training in the first year : In low-headed trees, the lowest branch is allowed to develop upto a height of 60 cm and accordingly top the plant is cut at about 90 cm. If high-headed trees are required, then the plant should be headed back at a height of 1.2 to 1.5 metres.

Training in second year : The top most shoot in the centre is left as the leader but is cut back where immature portion starts. Three is five laterals (main scaffold branches), spaced at a distance of 15 to 22 cm from each other are kept in different directions. It is advantageous if these laterals are bent downward by tying with rope or thick thread to the ground. The tying of these laterals will encourage the development of secondaries.

Training in Third year old trees : The laterals left at the end of second season's growth will branch off to form new laterals, one or two of which should be selected to form the secondary scaffolds framework. The laterals should be headed back to encourage sprouting of buds to develop tertiary branches.

Training in fourth-fifth year old trees : The unwanted secondary/tertiary branches should be removed. The leader should now be cut back to a well-placed, outward going lateral.

Pruning of young bearing trees : The pear trees bear fruit on shoots of limited growth which are called spurs. These spurs make only a few millimetres growth every year and bear fruit for 8-10 years. Therefore, the pruning of young trees is only of corrective type for the first 10 years. Diseased, dried and embracing branches should only be removed. Severe pruning should not be done during this period which would lead to the loss of fruiting spurs. Care should also be taken to avoid the injury to the spurs during harvesting of fruit.

Pruning of older trees : The older trees need renewing and invigorating the bearing wood of the trees. This is accomplished by thinning out the bigger branches entirely. This helps opening up the trees for more light for better colour. The process of renewal is completed in stages in 3 or 4 years. The trees again develop new fruiting spurs which bear fruit for another period of 10 years. The pruning of pear should be done in January to early February.

The Patharnakh pear trees should be pruned at the height of 2.5 m for better quality and fruit production. For this closer spacing of 4m × 4m should be done. Bordeaux paste should be applied after pruning of plants.

Rejuvenation of old pear orchards. Pear trees tend to become less productive at an age of about 20 years. Production on such trees can be restored by rejuvenating them. It can be achieved by heading back the 3–4 main scaffolds to about 15 cm during December-January. The rest scaffolds should be completely removed. Paint the cut ends with Bordeaux paint. Mainy sprouts shall emerge on these stubs in March. In May, retain only one to two out going shoots on each stub with a total of 6 to 8 shoots per tree. Rejuvenated trees start fruiting in third year and bear commercial crop in the fifth year.

CROP REGULATION

Normally pear trees come into bearing at the age of six to seven years. Pear trees tend to overbear, resulting in smaller fruits. The number of fruits a tree will carry and develop to good marketable size varies with its vigour and growth conditions. One fruit per cluster may be retained after thinning. This operation should be performed soon after the occurrence of the natural fruit drop in the middle of April. In each of the commercial varieties nearly 30 to 40 leaves per fruit are essential for building materials that go to make fruit.

Many of the fruiting spurs are lost as a result of fruit harvesting with the help of hooks or downward pull of the fruit with hand. Hence a little or no fruit is set for the subsequent crop. To compensate this loss, the fruit set can be increased by spraying 20 ppm of Gibberellic acid at full-bloom stage. To check spur breakage harvesting should be done with hand. The use of hooks should be avoided. The fruit should be pushed with a little force towards the base of the spur by using the right hand and holding the spur with the left hand. Saving the spurs from breakage during fruit harvesting helps regular fruiting throughout the life of the pear tree.

Quality improvement : Foliar application of KNO_3 @ 1.5 per cent after full bloom improve fruit yield and quality of Patharnakh pear.

HARVESTING AND HANDLING OF FRUITS

Harvesting : Pear is climacteric fruit which ripens on the tree as well as after harvesting. Harvesting of the pear fruit at proper stage of maturity is very important. The criteria for maturity of pear fruits are change in external fruit colour, decrease in firmness of the fruit flesh and increase in the total soluble solids (TSS) content. Lenticels of the fruit turn brown on maturity.

The fruit of Baggugosha, Punjab Beauty Punjab Nectar and Punjab Gold reaches harvest maturity after 140 days and of Patharnakh after 150 days of fruit-set. The size and weight of the fruit continued to increase till harvest in August. The colour of the fruit changes to light yellow at the final stage of harvest.The optimum harvesting time of pear cultivars is from July to August.

Preharvest spray of ethephon at 100–300 ppm hasten maturity of fruits by two weeks. Most pear cultivars ripens and develop best dessert quality at 15.6–21°C and RH 80–85%.

The fruit should be picked carefully without any bruises and injuries. Care should be exercised during picking so that the fruit bearing spurs do not get damaged. Once the spurs are broken or damaged, that will take long time to become fruit-bearing spurs again and will ultimately affect the fruit yield in the coming bearing seasons. For distant markets the fruit should be picked when it is still in a hard ripe stage and without injury and bruises. A small stalk (button) should be kept with the fruit to avoid fruits rot, due to fungus, in storage.

After harvesting, pear fruits are cooled to a temperature – 0.6 to – 1.6°C to remove field heat and arrest ripening. Pre-cooling enhance the shelf-life of fruits. Hydro-cooling reduces the incidence or shriveling and brown core without affecting weight loss or incidence of rot.

The average yield of hard pear varieties like Patharnakh and Punjab Nakh ranges from 150 – 190 kg per tree. A well managed pear orchard under subtropical condition normally yields around 20 – 30 tonnes/ha. The different semi-soft and soft varieties yields 80 – 90 kg fruits per plant.

Ripening : For improving ripening and eating quality of Punjab Beauty fruits should be chilled at 0°C and ripened at 20°C for 3 days. The frutis of Patharnakh should be chilled at 0°C for 3 days and ripen at 20°C for 4 days. For proper ripening and improving quality of pear, fruits should be treated with 100° ppm ethephon for 3 – 4 minutes or exposed to 100 ppm ethylene gas for 24 hours and stored at 20°C. The fruits of Patharnakh would be ready in 8 days and of Punjab Beauty in 4 days.

Grading and packing : The fruits should be carefully sorted and graded before sending to markets. In this way, the consumers gets the quality of his choices, while the fruit grower earns a premium for his product. Sand pear fruits can be categorised into four grades and specified as A, B, C and D grades. Highest distribution is found in B grade (46%) followed by C grade (30%) and A grade (14%). The fruits belong to grade A and B which accounted for 60 per cent are more acceptable to the consumers.

The pear fruits can also be graded according to AGMARK grades as follows :

Agmark grades of Pear

Grade	Diameter (cm)
Extra large	7.5
Large	6.5
Medium	5.5
Small	5.0

When the fruit is to be despatched to distant places, it is generally packed in wooden boxes. For sending the fruit to short distances, baskets and CPB cartons are largely employed. The base of the wooden box is given thick layer of dried grass. A sheet of paper is then spread to cover the grass as well as the sides of the box. The fruit is arranged in the box in layers. The upper most layer is covered with paper. It is then followed by layer of dried grass. Then, the lid is closed with the help of nails.

Marketing : The fruit growers normally do not conduct direct sale but generally auction the crop to the contractors when the fruit is on the tree. The contractors pick the fruit according to their convenience and sell it in the market. Only few orchardists market their crop directly in the main markets. In order to ensure due remuneration to orchardists, sales cooperatives need to be organised and such organisation should be helped in grading, packing and transportation of the fruit. The facility of storage chambers can also play an important part in improving the marketing of pear fruit.

Shelf life : Patharnakh and other standard varieties keep well in cold storage if properly handled. The fruits of Patharnakh and Baggugogha pear can be stored for 90 days and 45–50 days, respectively at 0- 3.3°C temperature with 85-90 per cent relative humidity after packing them in polythene bags. The fruits of Patharnakh, Punjab Beauty and Punjab Nakh can be stored at 0 to 1°C with RH 90 – 95 per cent for 60 days. The fruits of Patharnakh have post storage life of 2 days at room temperature and 4 – 6 days in refrigerator, whereas post storage life of Punjab Beauty is 1 – 2 days at room temperature and 4 days in refrigerator. The fruits of Punjab Soft and Nijisseiki can be stored at same conditions for 4 weeks. Pear fruits has excellent storage potential in CA storage at temp 0-5°C (2-3% oxygen and 0-1% CO_2). Brown heart and soft scald arc the disorders occur during CA storage.

The pear fruits particularly those of Patharnakh variety have a long post-harvest life and unique shipping quality and can be transported to distant markets like Bombay, Calcutta, etc. This quality alone has encouraged several growers to take up pear cultivation, especially in the far-flung areas.

PLANT PROTECTION MEASURES

A. Insect pests

Hairy-caterpillar (*Euproctis sp*) : The gregarious caterpillars first feed on the epidermis of the leaves. The epidermis of the leaves is shelled out with the result that rest of the leaf surface dry up and turn brown. In case of severe infestation, the entire tree may be defoliated. The outer coat of the young fruits is also beaten up as a result of which the attacked portion of the fruit becomes black and hard. As soon as their attack is noticed, collect and destroy the gregariously feeding young caterpillars.

Bark-eating caterpillar (*Indarbela quadrinotata* Wlk) : Bark-eating caterpillars cause damage by boring hole into the stem and branches and feeding on the bark under the cover of its webbing containing its excreta. The pest is active in neglected orchards.

For the control of this insect, remove webbing and apply kerosene into the holes during September-October and again in January-February. Treat all the alternate host plants in the vicinity.

Aphids (*Schiazaphis* sp. and *Toxoptera* sp.) : Sometimes cause serious damage to the plants by sucking the cell-sap from the leaves and tender fruits. Aphid attacks the pear as soon as the sprouting starts (February-April). The attack is more severe on semi-soft pear than on hard pear.

They can be controlled by spraying 200 ml Imidacloprid 200 SL or 160 g Thiamethoxam 25 WG in 500 litres of water first at initiation of foliage (2nd fortnight of February), second at full bloom (first fortnight of March) and third at fruit set (2nd fortnight of March) on semi-soft pear. On Patharnakh single spray of any of these insecticides at full bloom (2nd-3rd week of February) is effective.

Spider mites (*Eutetranychus orientalis* and *Tetranychus uriticae*. They attack in April-June. Initially yellowish white specks appear on the leaves followed by leaf scorching and premature leaf fall. Infested leaves gather dust.

Apply frequent irrigations during April-June. Remove castor and *bhang* which are the alternate sources of mites. Spray 1000 ml of Dicofol or Fosmite 30 EC (ethion) or 750 ml of Fenazaquin 10 EC in 500 litres of water/acre as soon as mite population appears on underside of leaves. If need arises, spray can be repeated.

Fruit fly (*Bactrocera dorsalis*). It is a serious pest of pear. Fruits nearing maturity are punctured by the fruitfly for egg laying and the maggots after hatching bore into the fruits thus render the fruits unfit for consumption. Isolated orchards are less infested by fruitfly.

Harvest the ripening fruits and do not allow the ripe fruits on the tree. Regularly collect the fallen fruits from the ground and bury the infested fruits atleast at 60 cm depth. Shallow ploughing immediately after harvest is effective in exposing and killing the pupating larvae/pupae which are mostly present at 4–6 cm depth. Spray 1250 ml (0.05%) Sumicidin 20 EC (fenvalerate) in 500 litres of water in the end of June. Repeat the spray at weekly interval if required. Fruits should be harvested on third day after spray. Fix fruit fly traps @ 16 traps acre in the first with of June for the control of fruit flies Recharge the traps if required.

B. Diseases

Pear scab : *Venturia pirina* : Infection appears on young pear shoots. Olive-dark mouldy sports appear, especially on the under-side of the leaf. Later the spot turn grey and necrotic. Similar olive spots develop on the pedicel, calyx and petals. The affected blossoms and petals usually drop. Dark-brown spots are produced on the fruits. The spots join together, become corky and crack.

To check this disease, apply bulky organic manures of the trees. Spray 0.2 per cent Captan at pre-bloom stage when the trees are dormant and continue till petal fall at 10 days interval. Seven or eight sprays may have to be given if the disease persists. Collect and burn or carefully plough under the fallen leaves to minimize ascospore discharge and consequent infection with the disease. Prune the trees to promote good aeration.

Shoot-fruit blight and bark canker : *Botryodiplodia theobromae* and ***Phoma glomerata*** : Cankers appear on bud scars, wounds, twig stubs or in crotches. Cankers are elliptical, small circular, brown spots appear around a leaf-scar or superficial wound. As the canker enlarges, the centres become sunken with the edges raised above the surrounding healthy bark. The fungus perpetuates itself on the trees in bark cankers.

To control this disease, cankers on the trunk and in the crotches should be removed and the dead bark decorticated along with 2 cm of the healthy bark. All the dead wood and pruning should be destroyed. Cover the wounds with a disinfectant solution and after this apply Bordeaux paste to them. After a week cover the dried paste with Bordeaux paint. The whole operation should be immediately followed by spraying the pruned and canker treated tree with 2 : 2 : 250 Bordeaux mixture. Spray may be repeated in March, June and January.

Root-rot and Sap-wood-rot: *Polyporus palustris, Ganoderma lacidum, Schizophyllum commune* : Gummosis of main trunk, limbs and secondary branches occur. The bark and wood of the roots rot and turn brown with white mycelial mat in the crevices. The affected trees begin to show symptoms of wilt, early leaf-fall and increase in fruit-set before collapsing. Rotting of roots leads to toppling over the trees, especially those with bulky tops.

To each full grown tree (4-6 years) apply 10 g Bavistin 50 per cent WP +5 g Vitavax 75 per cent WP mixed in 10 litres of water along the trunk and around the drip area twice-once before the monsoon (April-May) and second after the monsoon (September-October). Immediately after the treatments, apply light irrigation to the trees. In younger trees, the dose of fungicides should be reduced to half.

Spray Bordeaux mixture or 0.3 per cent copper oxychloride 50% in March and again in June. After the leaf fall again spray with same as in March. Locate the trees showing distress signs.

Avoid deep hoeing to obviate injuries to the roots, through which the fungus attacks. Also avoids growing intercrops which require excessive irrigation during winter. Avoid pilling up of the soil around the trunk of the tree.

Pear leaf spot (*Phyllosticta piricola and Alternaria Sp.*). Severe defoliation occur due to the disease. Leaf spotting is followed by yellowing and dropping of leaves. Spots of different size and shape, brown to dark brown appears on the leaves in June-July. Leaves fall off pre-maturely.

Spray Manozeb 600 g, carbendazim 100 g and Zineb 600 g from the appearance of disease in May-June at three weeks interval one after the other.

CHAPTER 28

Peach

Peach (***Prunus persica*** Batsch) has a good position amongst stone fruits and is rated as third most important temperate fruit in India. In the plains of north India, cultivation of peach has attained a significant position during the last few years and still there is scope for putting more area under this fruit. With the introduction of low chilling varieties, the crop is becoming popular in sub-tropical plains of north India.

ORIGIN, HISTORY AND DISTRIBUTION

Early writers were of the opinion that the peach is native of Persia. However, the cultivated form of the peach came from China. DeCandolle claims to have found references to the peach in the Chinese literature of 2000 B.C. F.N. Meyers reported finding many wild peaches in China. Theophrastus, 332 B.C. gives the first account of the peach in Greece, and it is highly possible that this fruit was introduced there as a result of Alexander's expedition to the East. Virgil 71-19 B.C. gives the first account of the peach in Rome. The references of peach in the English literature were found in the twelveth century but when it was brought to England is not known.

The Spanish introduced the peach into America and 50 years after Cortez it was a common fruit in Mexico. Indian tribes of the South soon took up the culture of the peach and were instrumental in its dissemination. Father Hennepin claims to have found many peach trees on his voyage to Louisiana. From the early domestication of the peach in Mexico and Southern U.S., a distinctive type or race of peaches has developed, which recognized as the "Indian Race" of peaches. During colonial times the peach was commonly grown in Virginia and adjacent colonies.

The peach is grown as a commercial and home fruit in most of the temperate countries of the globe. Extensive plantings of peaches occur in Turkistan and Persia. Of late years peach has assumed importance in several parts of Africa. It is the most common fruit of Argentina and grown for drying purpose in Chili. Considerable plantings of the peach are found in Australia and New Zealand. France has long been famed for its peach orchards. In Japan, peach is among the leading fruits. China also grows many peaches and here a large number of forms and types are found. In USA, the peach ranks second only to the apple in commercial importance.

AREA AND PRODUCTION

The major peach producing countries are China, Italy, Spain, USA, Greece, Turkey, Iran, Chile, France and Argentina. China is the leading producer of peaches accounting for 50 per cent of world production. The world production is estimated 21.5 million metric tonnes with average productivity of 13.7 mt/ha. The other peach producing countries are Brazil, Mexico, Egypt, India, South Africa, Australia, Tunisia and Algeria.

In India, varieties which need more cold for breaking the dormancy are commonly cultivated in Jammu and Kashmir, Himachal Pradesh, Uttarakhand and the hilly tracts of the Punjab. The varieties which need a subtropical climate are grown in Punjab, Uttarakhand, Haryana, Delhi, etc. Peach is also grown on a limited scale in the hills of South India and the northeastern region of India.

In India, high chilling peaches are grown in Jammu and Kashmir to Khasi hills. Low chilling peaches are grown in Punjab, Haryana, Western Uttar Pradesh, Uttarakhand, and Himachal Pradesh. Total area under peaches in India in 36400 hectares with annual production of 2.86 lakh mt annualy. The total area under peach cultivation in Himachal Pradesh is about 5101 hectares. In Punjab, the area under peaches is 1649 hectares which produce 29134 tonnes of fruits per year.

IMPORTANCE AND USES

The peach is delicious, juicy and highly palatable fruit. It is a rich source of vitamin A, iron and protein. Total soluble solids in different varieties ranges from 10.0 to 12.0 per cent and acidity 0.4 to 0.6 per cent. Fruits contain about 8% sugar, 0.8% minerals and 1.5% proteins.

The fruit is generally consumed fresh but delicious squash is commonly prepared. It can also be processed as canned and dried products, frozen preserves, jam, nectar, juice, beverage and marmalade etc. Peaches are also good source of low calorific diet.

BOTANY

The peach belongs to the genus **Prunus** of the family Rosaceae. The important species of peaches and nectarines are as follows :

1. *Prunus persica* (L.) Stokes [Syn. of *Prunus Persica* Batsch]

It is a low headed tree with glabrous twigs. Much like the almond in botanical characters. Leaves broadly lanceolate or oblong lanceolate, 10-22.5 cm long, acuminate, finely sharp-serrete when young, otherwise, coarsely crenate-serrate, shinning above and somewhat lighter beneath. The petiole usually gland bearing, flowers solitary, pink, appearing before the leaves, the sepals more or less pubescent on outside, fruit soft, pubescent at maturity, the stone deep pitted and very hard.

There are two well marked horticultural forms, the clingstones (***Persica vulgaris,*** Risso) and the freestones (***Persica domestica,*** Risso).

Ornamental forms of peach :

A. ***Prunus persica*** **var.** ***nucipersica,*** Schneid: The Nectarine

A smooth-skinned form of peach. Fruit smooth, usually smaller, leaves usually more strongly serrate but not always so.

B. ***Prunus persica*** var. ***platycarpa,*** Bailey : Saucer Peach

Fruit much flattened endwise and scarcely thicker in that direction than the length of the stone, with a calyx-like eye or broken cavity at apex. Stone small, clingstone, flat, compressed, rough and irregular. Fruit greenish with a red cheek, medium in size, flesh light yellow and of good flavour but with a slight bitter-almond taste.

2. *Prunus davidiana*, Franch. Father David's Peach.

It is a slender willow-like tree. Leaves narrower and smaller than those of the common peach, tapering from near the base into very long acuminate points, very sharp-serrate, light green, willow-like. Flowers appearing very early, one inch or more in diameter, light pink, solitary, the sepals glabrous. Fruit nearly globular. The suture prominent, pubescent, greyish or yellowish, stone small nearly spherical, ruminated, free from the whitish dry flesh.

3. *Prunus mira*, Wilson

The tree is small, bushy, with rather slender branches. Leaves narrow, long, pointed. Fruit roundish or oval, pubescent, flesh white and freestone. Stone unusually small and smooth. The tree has late blooming habit.

THE NECTARINE

The nectarine is a hairless or fuzzless peach, smooth skinned, somewhat like a plum. Its tree differs in no essential respect from that of the peach. Genetically speaking, the absence of fuzz on the nectarine is fundamentally the only difference between it and the peach. Its fruits, aside from the absence of the pubescence, is likely the peach. It may be a little smaller in size, firmer fleshed and may possess stronger flavour and aroma. Even the varieties of the two fruits correspond in characters. Thus there are clingstone and freestone sorts of each. Both may have yellow, red or white flesh. The flowers of each may be large or small. Nectarine leaves, in one variety or another show all the variations in glands and serrations known to the peach and the stones of peach and nectarine are indistinguishable

FLOWERING AND FRUITING

The flowers in peach are perfect, solitary, sessile, in advance of foliage, pink in colour. The pistil is simple. Flowering starts in the first week of February and continues till end of February.

Under low temperature conditions, swelling buds are injured at – 6.5°C. Sites which are free from spring frost are more suitable as peaches bloom early in the season. The flowering can be delayed by application of GA_3 200 ppm before leaf fall or by application of ethephon, to avoid the risk of spring frost.

Peaches are pollinated through insects. The mode of pollination is through homogamy. The pollen of peach is highly viable. Commercial peach varieties are self-fruitful and set good crops without cross-pollination. J.L. Hale is perhaps the only variety which is self-unfruitful and requires to be pollinated by other varieties.

Fruit-setting starts in the beginning of March. The fruit of Flordasun peach took eleven weeks to reach the stage of harvest maturity from the time of setting. The growth in terms of length and diameter showed three rapid growth phases (*i*) upto 28 days (*ii*) between 35 and 56 days and (*iii*) 63 days and onwards and two slow growth phases, *i.e.* (*i*) between 28 and 35 days and (*ii*) between 56 and 63 days. The pattern of increase in the length, diameter and fruit weight followed a 'double sigmoid curve'.

Fruits are borne on one year-growth. A small proportion of the crop, however, is also borne on short-lived spurs. Peach is a drupe fruit and its edible portion is mesocarp and Epicarp. Endocarp in hard, stony that contain seed in it.

CLIMATE

In India, peach is mainly grown in midhills at a height ranging 1000-1600 metres above sea level and certain varieties are grown in sub-tropical areas which require only 250-300 hours of chilling during the year for proper flowering and fruiting. Peaches do well in wet and humid climate with cold winter and dry summer. It like mild climate. The varieties of superb quality and good taste do not grow well in plains, because their chilling requirements are not met with. They also require protection from hot desiccating wind. On the other hand peaches do not grow well where winter temperature falls to 10-15°F below the freezing point as it gets injured. Peach trees require chilling period below 7°C for breaking the dormancy and flowering. The chilling requirement varies from 200–850 hours depending upon the variety. The variety like Redhaven has a relatively high chilling requirement (800 – 850 hours) and should not be grown in areas experiencing mild winters.

Sub-tropical climate of Punjab is ideally suited for the cultivation of low chilling peaches. Availability of chilling temperature upto 300 hours during winter months is enough to break the dormancy of low chilling cultivars. After fruit setting from March to June, the climate is warm to hot (35 – 42°C). This is favourable for the development and maturity of fruits provided adequate water supply is available. The annual rainfall of 45 cm is sufficient for peach. Spring frost is more harmful for peach cultivation.

SOIL

The peach thrive well on light sandy soil. Deep fertile loam or sandy loam with lime content less than 10 per cent and having good drainage considered best for successful peach growing. The pH of the soil should be between 6 to 8. Fertile and heavy soils are hazardous as it makes heavy growth and hence results in winter injury. It does not tolerate imperfect drainge. Poorly drained soils resulted into spotty planting, short duration trees with low yield and high cost of production. Such soils should be rejected for peach cultivation.

CHOICE OF VARIETIES

Peaches are cultivated on commercial scale in Himachal Pradesh, Punjab, Uttarakhand. The varieties commonly grown in these areas are as follow :

1. Himachal Pradesh :

Early Varieties : Redhaven, Stark Red Gold, Early White Giant, World's Earliest, Snow Queen (Nectarine)

Mid Season Varieties. July Elberta, Sunhaven

Late Variety : J.H. Hale

2. Punjab :

Yellow Fleshed : Partap, Florda Prince, Shan-i-Punjab, Earli Grande

White Fleshed : Prabhat, Sharbhati, Khurmani

Nectarine : Punjab Nectarine

3. Uttarakhand and Uttar Pradesh :

Early Varieties : July Elberta, Saharanpur, Peshwari, Prabhat

Mid-season Varieties : Alexander, Crowford Early, July Elberta

Late-season Varieties : J.H. Hale, Parrot Delux.

4. Jammu and Kashmir : J.H. Hale, Alexander, Co Smith.

A number of high quality sub-tropical peaches evolved in the U.S.A., particularly in Florida and California, were introduced at PAU, Ludhiana during 1968. Some of these cultivars have recorded excellent performance under these sub-tropical conditions.

Redhaven : It is an early variety suitable for mid hills. Fruits are medium- sized, round, very lightly fuzzy, attractive and having yellow skin overlaid red to deep red. The flesh is firm, fine textured, melting and almost freestone when ripe. It has outstanding flavour but the skin tends to tear easily during harvest.

Alexander : It is an excellent early season cultivar which ripens in the last week of May to first week of June. Fruit is medium to large in size, round, skin is smooth and beet-root purple with some patches of pod green colour. The flesh is soft, greenish white, juicy, very sweet and aromatic. It is a free stone variety. However, its keeping quality is not good.

Elberta : The variety is used for canning. Fruit is large, round with smooth skin of pale yellow having red splash. The flesh is firm, juicy and very sweet. It is a free stone variety.

Stark Red Gold : It is an early variety and start ripening from last week of May. Fruits medium sized, moderately fuzzy. The skin colour is orange with a blush of red. The flesh is yellow and stone is semi cling. It is a high yielding variety.

Sunhaven : It starts ripening from the first week of July. Fruits medium-sized, round and skin is bright red. The flesh is yellow, fine, firm textured and has good flavour. It is freestone variety when fully ripe.

J.H. Hale : The fruits are medium in size, roundish ovate, skin colour red purple yellow and sub acidic in taste. It is free stone variety. It ripens in third week of July.

Partap : Tree is medium in vigour. Its fruits mature in the third week of April. Fruit weight is 65-70 *g*, almost round, and yellow with redover colour. The flesh is firm, yellow and freestone when fully ripe. The fruit contains TSS 12% and acidity 0.7%. Average yield is 70 kg fruits per tree.

Shan-i-Punjab : This is another early cultivar, maturing in the first week of May. Tree vigorous in growth. It produces large fruits of 5-5.5 cm diameter weighing about 90 gms each. The colour of the fruit is yellow with red blush, juicy and sweet, with excellent taste, flesh yellow and with completely free-stone. The fruit is quite firm in texture and can withstand transportation. In addition to its table use, this cultivar has also been found suitable for canning. Its TSS is 12% and acidity is 0.74%. The average yield is about 70 kg per tree.

Flordaprince : Tree is vigorous and the fruits mature in the fourth week of April. Fruit size medium (65-70 *g*), yellow with red blush at maturity, flesh firm, yellowish and stone at fully ripe stage. TSS is 12% and acidity 0.5%. Average yield is 100 kg fruits per tree.

Earli Grande : Tree is semi vigorous, high yielding and fruit maturity occurs in the first week of May. Fruit is large (90 *g*) and flesh firm, yellowish and free stone at full ripe stage. Keeping quality is good. Its TSS is 10.5% and acidity is 0.7%.

Sharbati : The tree is spreading and vigorous. Fruit medium to large, greenish yellow with rosy patches, very juicy, fleshwhite with excellent taste and flavour. Ripens in the first week of July. Average yield 100 to 120 kg per tree. TSS in 13% and acidity 0.33%. It is a Chingstone variety.

Prabhat : Tree is semi-vigorous. The fruits are medium in size, round with an attractive red blush, flesh white, juicy, sweet and free stone when fully ripe. TSS is 12 per cent and acidity 0.37 per cent. The average yield is 64 kg per tree. It mature in the third week of April.

Punjab Nectarine : Tree is vigorous and spreading. The fruits are large in size, fuzzless, weighing 90 g, round, attractive with 90 - 100 per cent red blush over yellow ground colour at maturity. The flesh is yellow, firm, melting and free stone at full ripe stage. TSS is 11.5 per cent, acidity 0.8 per cent. The average yield is about 40 kg per tree. It mature in second week of May.

Khurmani : The tree is medium and upright in growth. It blooms in early February and fruit ripens in first week of June. The fruit is large, weighing about 70 g and is attractive with red colouration. It is slightly pointed at the base. It is a clingstone cultivar with white, soft, juicy flesh. TSS is 13% and acidity 0.4%.

PLANTING AND AFTER CARE

Peach should be planted in the end of January when the plants are dormant. Planting should be done after digging 1 × 1 × 1 metre pits refilling them with fertile top soil, mixed 40 kg of well rotten farmyard manure per pit. Add 15 ml of chlorpyriphos 20 EC mixed in 2 kg soil to each pit to prevent the attack of white-ants.

Peach plants should be planted at the distance of 6.5 metres apart, thus accommodating 225 plants in square system and 259 plants in hexagonal system per hectare. In the hills, peaches are planted at a distance of 5 × 4 *m*. In the high density plantations the distance can be reduced to 3 × 3 *m*.

High density planting of peaches in sub-tropical climate of Punjab can be adopted with good success. Peach trees should be planted at spacing of 6 × 1.5 m with 'Y' system of training. This will ensures higher yield and better fruit quality than the traditional planting system.

After planting, the young peach plants need staking so as to make them grow upright and straight. The supports should be strong, preferably of bamboo or other wooden logs and should be well fixed in the soil. The young plants should be watered at frequent intervals. Modified basin method is best suited for young peach orchards. The stock sprouts should be removed carefully after every 10-15 days. The strings or tying materials tied at the bud or graft union may also be removed carefully so as to avoid constrictions. Training of young peach plants should be given utmost attention for developing proper framework and shape. If there is any indication of white ant attack, chlorphyriphos 2 ml per litre of water with irrigation should be given.

PROPAGATION AND ROOTSTOCKS

Peaches are commercially propagated by budding and grafting. Among budding methods, T-budding is commonly used. In case of grafting, the method employed depends upon the thickness of stock. If scion and stock are of the same size, tongue grafting is recommended. But when the stock is of more thickness, cleft or wedge grafting is done. Budding can be done from April to September and grafting is done during dormant season *i.e.*in December-January before the scion and stock start sprouting.

Raising of Rootstock : Rootstock for peaches is raised from the seeds of Desi peach trees. The seeds of Flordaguard and some commercial cultivars like Sharbati and Khurmani are also used to grow the rootstock for peach propagation. Peach plants can also be raised on peach almond hybrid, apricot, almond seedling, plum and Behmi. Procure ripe fruits of Flordaguard or Sharbati in June-July. Extract stones from pulp, wash and dry under shade for 4 – 5 days. Treat the stones with Ziram or Thiram or Captan @ 300 g/quintal of stones. Pack the stones in dry gunny/plastic bags and store them under cool dry place till these are used for stratification from November to January.

Flordaguard is recently recommended rootstock for peaches by PAU, Ludhiana. It is resistant to root knot nematodes. Its trees are spreading, self fertile and precocious having red leaves. Flowers produced in abundance, deep pink and showy. Fruits pubescent with dull red colour, yellow fleshed and free stone. It repens from end June to first week of July.

Peach seeds need certain chilling hours to germinate. The process of meeting the cold requirement of seeds is called stratification. The stratification of peach seeds can be done under natural conditions and under cold storage conditions at 10°C or below.

(*a*) **Stratification of seed under natural conditions :** The stratification under natural conditions can be done either in the wooden boxes or directly sowing the seeds in the nursery beds. The seeds in wooden boxes are placed, for stratification during middle of November in layers with alternate layers of sand at or below 7.2°C for 100–120 days till the seed dormancy is broken and germination starts. These boxes are watered from time to time to keep the seed in moist condition. The boxes used are usually 75 cm in length and 45 cm high. Four or five layers of sand and seeds can be accommodated in such boxes. When the seeds from the upper layer start germinating the stratification is thought to be completed. Then these layers of seed are separated one by one and are planted in the nursery beds. The seeds which have not germinated in boxes should also be sown in the beds as there is every possibility of its germination in the field.

The seeds are sown in lines 30 cm apart and a distance of 60 cm is left after every two rows. This will facilitate the budding process and cultural operations in the nursery beds. The seeds within a line are sown at a distance of 15 cm. The seeds in the boxes start germinating in the second or third week of January and are immediately transplanted in the nursery beds. The nursery beds should be prepared on well drained fertile soils. The sandy loam soil is considered the best for raising the peach nurseries. The field once used for raising the nursery should not be used again for the same purpose atleast for two years, as there is every possibility of attack of fungal diseases, nematodes and production of toxins by the peach roots. The land where the beds are to be prepared should be treated against fungal diseases and nematodes at least about 15 days before sowing the seed. For direct stratification, seeds are sown in lines in the nursery beds where they are to be budded or grafted. These nursery beds are irrigated from time to time to keep the soil in moist condition. The mulching of beds with Sarkanda is also recommended. This helps in better retention of moisture which gives more germination of peach seeds. The nursery beds should be kept free from weeds. The seedlings start coming out in third week of January and are allowed to grow at the same place where they have germinated.

The seeds before placing for stratification are soaked in water. Only those seeds are used for stratification which sink in water as they are thought to be viable. Treat the stones with Ziram or Thiram or Captan @ 300 *g* per quintal of stones. Peach seeds are collected in the month of July and are stored at a cool place till they are placed for stratification in the month of November. It is important that ripe fruit should be collected for extraction of seed. This will ensure better germination of seed. Seeds extracted form unriped dropped fruits do not germinate. So, only mature fruit should be collected for raising the peach rootstock.

(*b*) **Stratification in cold storage :** The wooden boxes containing seed and sand are placed in cold storage in December to meet the cold requirement of seed. The boxes are taken out from the cold storage in mid-January when the chilling required by the seed is met. Then these seeds are sown in the nursery beds to obtain the seedlings.

Grafting operations

Peach seedlings about 40 per cent from stratified seed planted in the nursery beds during January become fit for T-budding in first week of May, if they are grown in the fertile soil with full care. Budding of these seedlings continues upto September. The seedlings budded in May-June may attain saleable size upto next winter. But budding done in late season become saleable only in next to next winter. Peach seedlings budded during late September, do not spout but remain green and these green buds put vigorous growth in the coming spring. All the seedlings transplanted in January may not become buddable in the same year. In such case the seedlings left unbudded are grafted in the following winter. The grafting can be done when the seedlings are still in the nursery buds or these can be uprooted and brought at one place for grafting. This process of uprooting the seedlings and grafting them while sitting at one place is termed as bench grafting.

In middle of February, the scions produce new growth. Usually a scion may produce 3 – 4 shoots which may be allowed to grow upto April. In May, one of the vigorous shoots is retained and all others are removed. This practice produces vigorous nursery plants. Polythene tape around the graft union should be removed before it causes girdling. The young grafts should be properly staked to prevent breakage.

Stenting Technique : Peach plants can be propagated by stenting technique *i.e.* simultaneously grafting and rooting, in the first week of January by dipping the basal portion of cutting of Sharbati in 200 ppm IBA solution for two minutes. This technique will cut short the period of one year for propagation.

Care of young nursery plants

The nursery plants should be saved from fungal diseases like rhizocotonia. On seeing the attack of this fungus, the nursery beds should be applied with 10-12 kg of Brassicol per acre. For the rapid growth of nursery plants, regular irrigation at 7-10 days interval during summer months is required. A light dose of nitrogen (40 kg of CAN or Ammonium sulphate per acre) also helps in rapid growth of the budded plants. Irrigation immediately after budding in very essential for the better union of the buds.

ORCHARD CULTURAL PRACTICES

Irrigation

With the onset of spring, the trees put forth new growth flush. Consequently, they need much greater amounts of water than was being applied in winter. The young as well as the old peach trees should be irrigated regularly and more frequently. The need for irrigation is going to build up further as the weather becomes warmer. During April as the season gets quite hot, both newly planted young plants and bearing peach trees require frequent irrigations. Watering of the trees would depend upon-type of soil, age of plant, locality, etc. However, irrigation may be given at about 8-10 days interval. The newly set plants would require watering at still shorter intervals.

The fruit development period in peach fruit starts after fruit set in March and continues during April to June till maturity depending upon the variety. This is a critical period of irrigation for the trees. Peach trees should not suffer from any moisture stress particularly 25 – 30 days before maturity of fruit, because the maximum weight gain in fruits takes place during these days.

The critical period of irrigation for Partap and Florida Prince is end-March to third Week of April, for Shan-i-Punjab and Earli Grande is mid-April to first week of May and for Sharbati is from end-May to end June.

In plains for proper development of fruit size and quality, frequent irrigations should be given during April and May. In early maturing varieties, irrigation should be given during the first 3–4 weeks after fruit set at weekly intervals. Thereafter, from the second week of April to start of harvesting, the trees may be irrigated at 3–4 days interval. In the hills, atleast two irrigations during fruit development period are useful.

During November, the atmospheric temperature cools down considerably, irrigation to peach orchards should be given at longer intervals. The peach tree would become dormant and there will be less transpiration because of shedding of leaves. The irrigation at this time should be withheld, so that they enter into dormancy and become sufficiently hardened to withstand cool weather. By giving frequent irrigations at this time, the trees would continue to grow and become prone to winter injury.

Cultivation

Cultivation helps in better soil aeration, destruction of weeds, increased nitrification and destruction of pupae/grubs of hibernating insects. However, only shallow cultivation is recommended, as deep cultivation may do harm by damaging fibrous roots of the fruit tree, which are mostly in the upper soil.

Cultivation is most essential for getting a profitable crop of peach. Without good cultivation, the fruit will be inferior and the tree will get devitalized and fall a ready prey to pests and diseases. Ploughing should not be done deeper than 10 cm as otherwise, the root system may be severely injured. Cultivation should be started in winter and continued till April-May. A suitable cover crop may be sown in the rainy season after the fruit is picked and the same ploughed in during winter. This prove to be a very useful practice.

Peach as Filler Tree

In the orchards of mango, litchi and pear which came into bearing rather late peach may be planted as fillers. Peach came into bearing quite early and yield good income before the permanent trees start bearing commercial crops.

Weed Control

Weeds are common in peach orchards during spring and the rainy season. They can be kept under control by using the following doses of herbicides. Diuron 5 kg/ha or Glyphosate or Gramoxone at 4–5 *l/ha* are very effective in controlling the broad spectrum of weeds in peach orchard. Diuron should be used at the pre-emergence stage of weeds in the first week of March, whereas glyphosate or gramoxone should be used at the post-emergence stage of weeds when they grow 15–20 cm tall. Dissolve the required quantity of weedicide in 500 litres of water per ha and spray during calm days. The spray of post-emergence herbicides may be repeated as and when required particularly during the rainy season when the weeds are abundant.

Manuring and Fertilization

In peach, balance nutritional schedule is important in order to maintain tree health and productivity. Application of 60 kg FYM, 500 *g* N, 250 *g* P_2O_5 and 600 *g* K_2O per tree of 6 years of age has been recommended for growers of Himachal Pradesh. In sub-tropical climate of Punjab, a recommendation of 25 kg FYM, 500 *g* N, 120 *g* P_2O_5 and 500 *g* K_2O per tree to full grown tree of 5 years and above has been made. In Uttranchal for 6 years and above old peach trees, 10 kg FYM 300 *g* each N and K_2O and 500 *g* P_2O_5 is recommended.

To July Elberta peach, application of 600 g K_2O can be supplemented with two foliar sprays of 0.5 per cent potassium chloride for higher yield and quality fruits.

In Arunachal Pradesh to 7 years old trees and above , 50 kg FYM, 350 g N and 210 g P_2O_5 and K_2O each is applied.

Whole the quantity of farmyard manure along with phosphorus and potassium is given during December. Half of nitrogen should be given before flowering and the remaining half after the fruit-set. The manure or fertilizer should always be applied by evenly broadcasting in the tree basins which should be sufficiently large and should encompass the entire canopy of the tree. The manures should be thoroughly mixed with the soil by shallow hoeing done by Khurpa and spade. The trees should be watered immediately after the application of manures.

Iron deficiency : Peach trees planted on light textured and high pH soils often exhibit iron deficiency symptoms during summer and rainy season. Interveinal chlorosis of developing new leaves on the terminal part of shoots are the symptoms of deficiency. In severe case the new leaves may unfold without any green colour and later veins may turn green. Typical symptoms appear by the second fortnight of March and with the passage of time these progress and accentuate. Iron deficiency can be corrected by spraying peach trees with 0.3 per cent ferrous sulphate solution on spring flush in April, on summer flush in June and late summer flush in August September.

TRAINING AND PRUNING

The peach is trained to the 'Modified Leader System'. For admitting more sunlight for better colouration of the inside fruits, 'Open Centre System' may be favoured. But under sub-tropical conditions, where sunshine is plenty and there are strong winds during summer, this system is not suitable, in view of the weak frame-work and other obvious defects.

Training in first year : Plants should be headed back to a height of 90-100 cm at the time of planting in the field. All the branches on the plants are also cut back to two buds. After three to four weeks, plants develop many branches. Four to five laterals, which are well-oriented around the trunk, are selected as main scaffold branches and all other branches are removed. The lowest branch should not be below 40-50 cm from the ground level. The top most central branch in called leader.

Training in second year : Many new branches develop on the selected primary branches. The leader of the plant also grows in height and some side branches are developed on it. Select 3 – 4 more well placed branches on the central branch and remove all others. In the second year very little pruning is done. The branches which are crowding in the centre or interfering with each other are removed. The dominance of the central leader is maintained and no lateral is allowed to outgrow the other.

Training in third year : The leader in the third year should be suppressed by cutting it back to a suitable lateral. The leader is restricted in its vertical growth

Pruning of young and old trees

Peach fruits are borne on one-year growth. A small proportion of the crop, however, is also borne on short-lived spurs. Pruning should be done so as to produce 50 to 100 cm of growth in young trees and 30 to 70 cm in old trees, annually. About 40 per cent of one year old branches should be thinned out to ensure proper tree growth and improve fruit size and quality. Some thinning-out of branches is also done to allow adequate sunlight for the growth of fruits and the development of good colour. Pruning of peaches should be carried out in early January. Cuts thicker than 5 cm should be covered with Bordeaux paste followed by Bordeaux paint after one or two weeks.

THINNING OF FRUITS

To improve the prospectus of the developing peach industry, it is essential to improve the marketable size and quality of the fruits. There is generally excessive fruit-set in peach. If all the fruits are retained on the tree, their size as well as quality may not fetch good price in the market. Thinning is more desirable on mature trees making small annual growth than on young vigorous plants. Trees growing on light soils, deficient in moisture and nutrients, would also need for fruit thinning. The heavy bearing cultivars like Stark Red Gold, Pratap, Shan-i-Punjab, Flordaprince, Sharbati, and Early Grande need fruit thiuning to minimise the danger of limb breakage. Thinning may also be resorted when good-sized uniform fruits are needed for canning and fancy trade.

Early cultivar of peach, viz. Partap and Flordaprince has a much shorter fruit development period. In its case, hand thinning must be completed by the third week of March before the fruits show stone hardening. In mid-season cultivars, *e.g.* Shan-i-Punjab, this operation should be completed by the end of March. The late ripening cultivars like Sharbati should be thinned out by the third and fourth week of April, *i.e.* at the stone hardening stage. In July Elberta peaches, best flower thinning can be obtained with the spray application of 300 ppm ethephon. In Redhaven cultivar, ethephon @ 600 ppm 20–30 days after set when the fruitlets have attained the diameter of 20–25 cm, is recommended for thinning. While doing hand thinning, first shake the branches slightly in order to dislodge the fruits which are likely to drop off naturally. If there is still surplus fruit, then start thinning from top to the bootom of the branches. Hold the stem of the fruit to be removed between thumb and second finger and pull it off gently. The main point to be kept in mind while thinning is, to remove all the small, undersized and misshapen, insect or diseased attacked fruits.

Girdling + thinning done at full bloom or girdling alone done four weeks after full bloom advance fruit maturity by 7 – 12 days and improves fruit quality in Shan-i-Punjab.

The distance from fruit to fruit after thinning on the shoots should be between 10 and 15 cm and the average number of leaves per fruit should be 20 to 25.

HARVESTING AND HANDLING OF FRUITS

Peach fruits are harvested quickly when ready for harvest. It is a climacteric fruit. Fruits are picked when they are still hard as they ripen in storage or transit. The days taken from full bloom to maturity, change in ground colour, flesh firmness and fruit size are the reliable maturity indices for peach. The days from full bloom to maturity in different cultivars are Partap 76 days, Shan-1-Punjab 83 days, Alexander 86 days and Elberta 127 days.

The Pratap peach cvs. takes 11 weeks to reach the stage of harvest maturity from the time of fruit-setting. The peach comes into bearing within two years after planting in the field. The fruit of Pratap and Flordaprince cultivars starts maturing earlier of all *i.e.* by the end of April. The peak harvesting period of different peach cultivars in plains is from earth May to middle of June and in hills is from June to July. The pattern of increase in the length, diameter and fruit weight followed a 'Double Sigmoid Curve'. All peach fruits do not mature simultaneously. These may be harvested in 3–4 pickings at an interval of four days.

Field heat of the fruits can be effectively removed by giving them 10–15 minutes quick dip in cold water followed by surface drying the fruits in shed. This process slow down the ripening process of fruit and is helpful in extending the shelf life.

The peach fruit being perishable in nature needs to be handled quickly when it is ready for harvest. Even a few hours delay results in considerable economic loss to the grower. Fruits picked at the right stage of maturity, on ripening, give excellent taste and flavour, characteristic of a particular cultivar. For successful orcharding, harvesting the fruits at its proper stage of maturity is of utmost importance. For sending the fruit to distant market, they should be harvested when they are still hard-ripe. *i.e.* when the ground colour of fruit begins to change from green to yellow in yellow fleshed varieties and fruits yield to pressure very slightly in between cupped hands. For the local market, the fruits may be picked when nearly ripe. In white fleshed varieties, colour of the fruit changes from green to straw with pink blush on the sides.

The average yield of full grown tree of different varieties varies from 70 to 120 kg. Sharbati and Stark Red Gold are high yielding cultivars and produce 100 to 120 kg fruit per tree.

Grading and Packaging. Before packaging, remove the injured, damaged and undersized fruits from the lot and grade the fruits according to size and stage of maturity. Different grades of fruits are packed separately for better marketing. The commercially accepted fruit grades in peach and packaging size are as follow

Fruit Grade	Fruit size (mm)	Inner size of box (cm)	No. of Layers	No. of fruits per layer
Special	55–63 & above	37 × 16.5 × 16.5	3	28–32
Grade-I	46–55	37 × 16.5 × 16.5	4	35–38
Grade-II	Below 46	37 × 16.5 × 16.5	4	38–43

Generally 2 and 4 kg CFB boxes are used for packaging of fruits. These are better than wooden boxes.

The harvested fruits must be disposed off as expeditiously as possible. Peach fruits should be graded and then packed in wooden boxes or CFB cartons of suitable size.

Shelf life : Peach fruits harvested at optimum maturity can be kept in cold storage for about 2-4 weeks (0-3.3°C, temperature 85-90% R.H.) in perforated polythene bags. Precooled peaches can be stored for one month. The shelf life of peaches can be extended further by storing them in controlled atmosphere storage. Precooled peaches can be stored for 28-36 days. Peach cv. Shan-i-Punjab treated with 1-MCP (1000 ppb) can be stored for 4 weeks at 0–1°C and 90-95% RH.

Dipping of peach fruits cv. Shan-i-Punjab in calcium chloride @ 2 per cent for 5 minutes and kept at 0-1°C and 90-95 per cent RH and packing in CFB boxes can be stored for 30 days.

PLANT PROTECTION MEASURES

A. Insect-pests

Peach-leaf curl aphid (*Brachycaudus helichrysi* Kalt) : It is a polyphagous pest. The pest suck the cell sap from vegetative buds. Leaves infested with this aphis acquire a characteristic curly appearance generally from March to May in the plains and from April to June in the hills.

The pest can be controlled by spraying 800 ml of Rogor 30 FC (Dimethoate) in 500 litres of water immediately after the fruit-set. If necessary, spray should be repeated after 15 days.

Peach black aphid (*Pterochlorus persicae* Cholodkovsky) : They cause damage by sucking the sap from the bark of the stem, limbs and branches from April to June. The continuous drain of cell sap devatilizes the tree, which affect the fruit setting capacity as well as fruit size. To check this pest, spray 800 ml of Malathion 50 EC in 500 litres of water on the colonies on the stem and limbs as soon as the pest congregates on these parts. Spray should be done when the sun is high.

Chaffer and other Defoliating beetles (*Adoretus spp.*) : Adult beetles appear with break of monsoon and feed on leaves during night and hide during day. In case of severe attack, fruits are also scrapped near the apical end. Eggs are laid in the soil, grubs feed on roots and other organic matter and sometimes the grubs feeding on roots cause the death of tree. As soon as the damage starts, spray in the evening with one kg of Carbaryl (Sevin 50% WP) in 500 litres of water should be done. If the damage continues or the insecticidal deposit in washed away by rain, spray should be repeated after 5 or 6 days.

Peach fruit fly (*Bactocera dorsalis*) : Fruitfly is a serious pest of fruits. The incidence of this pest starts in early May in north India and continues till the crop is over. Fruits nearing maturity are punctured by the fruit-fly for egg laying. Its larvae feed and develop in the ripening fruit. The infested part of the fruit rots. A dirty-brown fluid oozes from the site of an egg puncture on pressing the infested fruits. The badly attacked fruits even drop. Isolated orchards are less infested by fruit fly.

Burry the infested fruits at 60 cm depth. Hoeing of orchard should be done in May and June to expose the pupae which are present mostly at 4-6 cm depth. Plant early maturing cultivars *i.e.* Partap, Prabhat, Earli Grande, Florda Price, Flordasun and Shan-i-Punjab. Spray 1250 ml (0.05%) Sumicidin 20 EC (fenvalerate) in 500 litres of water in mid May and repeat after one week if required. Fix fruit fly traps @ 16 traps/acre in the first week of May for the control of fruit flies. Recharge the traps if required.

Flat headed borer (*Sphenoptera dadkhani*) : It is a serious pest on peach. Adult beetals appear in middle of March and feed on foliage. Eggs are laid singly scattered all over the tree trunk and main branches. On hatching, young grubs feed below the bark making minute irregular gallaries. The bark gets loosened and splits. Full grown grubs bore into the wood. Outside on the bark, gum globules ooze out from the entrance holes. Leaves turn pale and the growth of the tree arrested. In severe infestation the entire tree may die.

Drench spray of 1000 ml chlorpyriphos 20 EC in 500 litres of water during June after the harvest of crop and in October.

B. Diseases

Shot hole (*Stigmina corpophila*) : Dark brown scattered lesions appear on leaves which enlarge rapidly. Abscission of the diseased leaves results in shot holes. The disease can be controlled by spraying with Captan, Ziram or Thiram (o.2%) at leaf fall or bud swelling stage.

Peach leaf-curl (*Taphrina deformans*) : This disease found in temperate and rarely in sub-tropical climate. The disease destroys new leaves in the spring and causes defoliation, thus reducing the vigour of the plant. Leaves become thickened, reddened, twisted and puckered. Young twiges become swollen and pale and may die back.

To check this disease, carry out the dormant spray with 0.2%. Ferbam (200 g in 100 litre of water). A single spray of copper oxychloride (0.3%), carbendazim 50 WP (0.05%) or of Captan 50 WP (0.3%) applied 3–4 weeks of bud-swell provides effective control of disease.

Powdery mildew (*Podosphaera leucotricha*) : Shoots and leaves become covered with a powdery or pearly-white coating during hot, dry weather. The tender buds in the axils of the mildewed leaves are also attacked. Ultimately, their skin becomes corky, rough and may crack.

To control this disease, diseased shoots should be pruned. Spray before the blossoms open, at petal fall, and again two weeks later with 0.1%. Morestan and Aureofungin (1 g per 10 litres of water) should be given. One spray of each during May-June should be given in addition.

Brown rot (*Sclerotinia fructicola* and *S. fructigena*) : Fungus causes wilting and killing of petals and young twigs. The leaves wither and drop. Canker develops on large limbs and the bark is killed, cracks open and excude gum. On fruit, light brown spots appear as small round areas which enlarge within a few days and the entire fruit rots, shrivels and becomes a hard, dry and wrinkled mummy, hanging on the tree or falling to the ground.

Collect and destroy the fruit mummies by burning or burying them in soil. The infected twigs and cankers should be cut out and burnt. Spray the trees with captan @ 0.2% (200 *g* in 100 litres of water) about 3 weeks before harvesting the fruits. If disease is severe repeat spray at fortnightly intervals after harvesting the fruits. Avoid injury during picking of fruits.

Peach leaf spot (***Phyllosticta cerasicola***) : Small, angular, ash coloured spots appear on the underside of the leaf which results in pre-mature defoliation.

To check the disease, spray mancozeb 1250 – 1500 g in 500 litres of water during growing season.

Viruses : Viruses usually found in temperature climate but rarely in sub-tropical climate. Symptoms appear as mosaic mottling, leaf-curling, puckering and reduction in the leaf size. There is excessive proliferation of buds. The severely affected tree in the orchard should be replaced with the progeny tested virus free nursery stock. Insect vectors and mites should be controlled with appropriate spray during the season to reduce the transmission of the virus. The use of graft wood or bud wood from infected mother tree should be avoided. The indexing of virus free mother trees prevents the further spread of viruses.

Crown Gall (***Agrobacterium tumefaciens***) : In recent years, the incidence of crown gall disease has been observed in peach nurseries and orchards. The disease in characterised by formation of tumors of varying sizes especially at the crown portion and sometimes on roots and other parts of the plant. For raising disease free plants in the orchard following points may be kept in view.

(*i*) Procure disease free plant-material from a reliable source.

(*ii*) Avoid injury to the roots and crown portion of the plant at the time of uprooting from nursery, replanting and performing other cultural practices in the orchard.

(*iii*) Keep the plants free from insects, nematodes and rodent injuries.

(*iv*) Discourage the exchange of plant material without knowing its sanitary condition.

(*v*) Uproot and destroy the diseased plant from nursery/orchards whenever noticed.

(*vi*) While planting, the diseased roots of the plant are pruned and remaining root system is dipped for one minute in 5% solution of bleaching powder and then planted in the orchard.

CHAPTER 29

Plum

Plum is temperate in nature and is a strong growing small tree. It is major fruit crop of hills but considered as important minor crop in north Indian plains. This fruit has found favour with the orchardists because of their phenomenal yield potential and high economic returns. The low chilling early ripening varieties of Japanese plum come into the market when the other fruits are scarce and thus had little competition in the market at that time. Being relatively a hardier tree, the establishing of plum orchard is little easier than the certain other fruit tree. In orchards of mango, litchi and pear, which come into bearing rather late, plum may be planted as filler tree. The Japanese plum (***Prunus salicina*** Lindl.) is grown in temperate and sub-tropical climate of India.

ORIGIN AND HISTORY

The Japanese plum is native to China where it was cultivated for thousands of years. Varieties of it were taken to Japan probably not earlier than 1500 A.D. Yet that are known in America as Japanese plums. The fruit tree of this species in America, the Kelsey variety was brought from Japan in 1870. Some of the **salicina** cultivars were later introduced into Europe from America. The plum first introduced in India by Mr. Alexander Coutts in his orchard at Mashobra (Shimla Hills). The European settlers and missionaries started its cultivation in about 1870 in Kulu Valley and the Shimla hills (HP), in Kumaon hills and Kashmir. Later on, number of varieties were imported from California, France and Italy on the advice of Prof. R.W. Hedgson and planted by Maharaja of Patiala at Kandaghat (H.P.). In Jammu and Kashmir many varieties of plum were introduced during 1910–20 by Mr. M. Pychard, a Frenchman. The Punjab Agricultural Department imported about 150 varieties of the temperate zone fruits including plum, in early thirties to lay out trials at Palampur.

Presently, plum is grown in all temperate climate countries in the world.

AREA AND PRODUCTION

The major plum producing countries are China, Serbia, Romania, Chile, Iran, USA, Turkey, Spain, India and Italy. China is the world's largest producer of plum.

In India plums are grown on a commercial scale in Jammu and Kashmir, Himachal Pradesh, Uttarakhand and Uttar Pradesh. They are also grown to some extent in the Nilgiri hills of South India. Low chilling Japanese plum is cultivated in Punjab, Haryana and some parts of Uttar Pradesh and Rajasthan.Plum in India occupies an area of 26000 ha with a total production of 72000 mt.

The total area under Japanesc plum in Punjab is 204 hectares which produce 3611 tonnes fruit annually. The districts of Ferozepur, Gurdaspur, Amritsar and Patiala are known for plum cultivation. The area under plum in Himachal Pradesh is 8530 hectares with annual production of 9842 mt.

IMPORTANCE AND USES

Besides being palatable and delicious, it has high nutritive value. It is one of the richest source of vitamin B_1 (Thiamine). Plum fruit is also rich in vitamin A and riboflavin. It is a good source of sugars, proteins, carbohydrates and minerals like calcium, phosphorus and iron.

The plum fruit is known for its cooling effect and is considered best to overcome the effect of jaundice. Plum is delicious fruit and generally taken fresh. The pleasantly blended pulp and juice of this fruit leaves a refreshing taste in the mouth. The plum fruit can be utilized profitably for the preparation of various kinds of products like jam, jelly ans chutney. The Plum fruit is used extensively for the preparation of juice and squash. The firm and ripe fruit can be canned in sugar syrup. Certain varieties of plums are consumed dried to make prunes.

Non alcoholic naturally carbonated beverage can be prepared from Satluj Purple and Kala Amritsari plum at small and large scale. It has three months shelf life and retains its original nutrients.

BOTANY

Plum belongs to the genus ***Prunus***, the sub-family Prunoidae and the family Rosaceae. The important species of plum are as follow :

1. ***Prunus domestica*** L : European Plum
2. ***Prunus salicina*** Lindl : Japanese plum
3. ***Prunus insititia*** L : Damson plum
4. ***Prunm cerasifera*** Ehrh : Cherry plum
5. ***Prunus americana*** : American plum

European plum is used for making prunes and various products.

Japanese plum is most common plum for fresh production. Damson plum is used for preparation of Jam, Jellies and preserve. It is also used as a rootstock for plums. Cherry plum is also used as a rootstock. American plum are wild small trees and produce small edible fruits which are used for preparation of various products.

The Japanese plum is strong small tree with glabrous parts, mostly with brown shinning twigs. The leaves are oblong-obovate or oblong-ovate, not prominently rugose, abruptly but prominently pointed, closely blunt serrate, dull, usually shinning above and glabrous beneath. The flowers are white, two or three from each bud but appearing clustered on the spurs. The flowering starts in the second week of February and the tree come to full bloom after 7-10 days of first flower appeared. The cyme with flowers is closely crowded on a very shorter peduncle and with pedicels of about equal length, hence, termed as cymose (Fascicle) inflorescence. The fruit-setting starts in the second week of March. It is a drupe or stone fruit and the exocarp is a thin skin. The mesocarp which is the edible portion is thick and fleshy. The hard stony endocarp contains seed.

CLIMATE

The cultivars of Japanese plum require comparatively less of winter chilling *i.e.* about 700 and 1000 hours below 7.2°C. Most of the Japanese plum cultivars are resistant to winter cold and thus can be grown in more northerly regions of the Northern Hemisphere. The bloom period of plum tends to get delayed on the northern slopes thus helping them to escape spring frost injury.

The Japanese plums do very well in the low and mid hill regions, ranging between 650 and 1650 metres above sea level. Plum require 100–125 cm of rainfall well distributed throughout the year for good growth and fruit production. A few varieties of Japanese plums with chilling requirement below 300 hours are also growing successfully in the sub-montane tracts of the Punjab and Haryana. Some varieties of plum can be grown successfully even in the warmer region of the plains. This region is marked by an extreme summer temperature reaching 45°C and very low relative humidity that is abruptly changed in first week of July by arrival of cool monsoon rains.

In winter, the night temperature may touch 0°C with occasional ground frosts. Plants get 250 to 300 chilling hours. Plum orchards are prone to damage by high wind velocity and must be protected by planting wind break trees.

Cool winter and warm summers are suitable for its successful cultivation. The location of a plantation on the road-side, where adequate transport facilities are available, prove advantageous both in establishing the orchard and in disposing of the crop.

SOIL

The Japanese plum can even do well on inferior soils having shallow water table and high pH. However, for good growth and longer life of the plants, well-drained medium to deep loam soil with pH between 5.5 to 6.5 is most suitable. Availability of ample good quality irrigation water is of primary importance while selecting site for plum plantation. Plum trees will fail to produce commercially acceptable crop if they suffer from water deficit. Plum propagated on peach rootstocks grow better on sandy loam soils whereas the heavy and wet soils are suitable for plants propagated on Kabul Green Gage rootstock of plum.

CHOICE OF VARIETIES

Plum varieties cultivated n Himachal Pradesh, Jammu and Kashmir, Uttarakhand and Punjab are given below on the basis of their fruit maturity.

State	Early Varieties	Mid-Season Varieties	Late-Season Varieties
Himachal Pradesh	Methley, Kelsey Sweet Early	Starking Delicious, Satsuma, Elephant Heart	Moriposa
(i) Mid-hills	Santa Rosa, Red Beaut, Beauty Early	Frontier, Kanto-5	Mariposa, Tarrol, Red Ace
(ii) Low-hills	Titron, Alucha Purple		
Jammu and Kashmir	Saharanpuri White, Ramgarh Maynard, Sharp Early, Subza	Formosa, Maynard, Burbank, Sant Rosa	Satsuma, Wickson, Grand Duke, Beauty
Uttarakhand	Jamuni, Titron, Settler, Ramgarh Maynard	Howe, Sharbati, Zardalu, Alubokhara Sharbati	Late Yellow, Kanto-5, Santa Rosa, Mariposa
Punjab	Satluj Purple	Titron, Kala-Amritsari, Kataru Chak	Alubokhara

Some of the important Japanese plum cultivars are briefly described here.

Santa Rosa : Trees are upright. The fruit is large purplish crimson in colour. The flesh is amber with red near the skin. It is self-fruitful and prolific bearer cultivar. The fruit is very juicy and gives characteristic flavour. it ripens in July.

Mariposa : An upright growing tree that requires cross-pollination for adequate fruit set. The fruit is heart shaped with greenish yellow fruit skin mottled with red. The flesh is red in colour of fair quality. The shelf life is also good.

Red Beaut : Trees are spreading. It can be grown even in low hills as its chilling requirement is 250 hours. Fruits medium sized with 80–90 per cent red and rest yellow in colour. The flesh is yellow with a mild sweet flavour. Pollens are sterile and requires a pollenzier which also has to be early flowering. It is an early maturing variety.

Frontier : Trees are vigorous, upright and high yielding. The variety is partially self unfruitful and bear good crop only if there is a provision of cross pollination. Fruits larger in size with external colour red purple.The flesh is red and firm, sweet and nice flavoured. It ripens 10–12 days after Santa Rosa. The yield of this variety will improve if Santa Rosa is planted as pollenizer.

Satluj Purple : It is cross between Open Pollinated Seedlings from cross of *Prunus salicina* from Tiwan × Methyley and 4 other plum cultivars grown in USA. The fruit of this variety is significantly superior to Kala Amritsar in terms of fruit weight and size. Its average yield is 40 kg per plant. It ripens a week earlier (around 10th May) than other sub-tropical plum varieties and takes 81 days to mature. The colour of fruit at maturity is bright crimson. It is sweet in taste and covered with white bloom. The fruit is medium large with average weight of 25–30 *g* and roundish in shape. Fruits are thick skinned with yellow orange firm flesh. TSS is 13–14% with 0.6–0.7% acidity and is suitable for table purpose. It is self unfruitful variety and requires Kala Amritsari as pollenizer. Satluj Purple and Kala Amritsari plants should be planted in the ratio of 85 : 25 in an acre.

Kala-Amritsari : The most widely grown cultivar in the plains of Punjab, 'Kala-Amritsari' is self-fruitful, the yield of which will imporve if pollinated with 'Titron'. The tree is low spreading but vigorous. The fruit is medium in size, round, oblate in shape, depressed on both ends and has brownish colour which turns into dark-brown at full maturity. The flesh is yellowish, moderately juicy with sub-acid taste and is excellent for a jam-making. Fruits are somewhat acidic with 15% TSS and 1.2 per acidity. It ripens in the second week of May. Bearing is heavily with an average yield of 40-50 kg fruit per tree.

Titron : The variety is self-fruitful but the yield will improve if 'Alucha Early Round' is planted as a pollenizer. The tree is spreading. Its fruit is small to medium in size, roundish with deep purple colour and thin skin. The flesh is yellow, moderately juicy and sub-acid in taste and is excellent for jam making.

Alu Bokhara : The tree is upright, tall and vigorous and self unfruitful. 'Howe' is a good pollenizer for this variety. The fruit is large having yellow skin tinted with red colour. Pulp is juicy and sweet. TSS is 15 per cent and acidity 0.7 percent.

PROPAGATION AND ROOTSTOCKS

Plums are generally propagated through hard-wood cuttings. In case rootstocks are to be used, budding and grafting method are employed for its propagation. Plum is raised on seedling root stock of wild apricot (Zardalu) and Myrobalan B ***(Prunus cerasifera)*** clonal rootstock. In Punjab, the cuttings of 'Kabul Green Gage' plum are used as rootstock for heavy and wet soils. The peach seedlings are recommended for sandy loam soils. Myrobalan B is mainly multiplied through mound layering. This rootstock can also multiplied through hard wood cuttings treated with 2500 ppm IBA for 10 seconds and planted in open field during January - February.

Raising of Rootstock

(*a*) Through Seed : In Himachal Pradesh, the seeds of wild apricot (Zardalu) are collected from fully ripe fruits. After drying, the seeds are treated with Bavistin @ 3 kg/kg and stored at temperature of 38 - 45°F and RH 20 per cent. In order to break dormancy, the seeds are stratified in moist sand for 45 - 50 days in 30 - 45 cm deep pits dug in cool and shady place in January. Water soaked seeds are put in 3 - 4 cm thick alternate layers of sand and kept moist during the period of stratification. The stratified seeds are sown in nursery beds at a depth of 6 - 10 cm in rows 25 - 30 cm a part with a distance of 10 - 15 cm from seed to seed. After sowing, beds are covered with 10 cm thick hay mulch to protect the germinating seedlings from direct sun, heavy rains and spring frost. Light irrigation is given after sowing to avoid desiccation of stratified seeds. When seedlings attain a height of about 5 cm hay mulch is removed. In one year about 90 per cent seedling become buddable.

In Punjab, the plum stones are extracted from the ripe fruits and stratified in the field or in the wooden boxes. For field stratification, the seeds are sown during November in rows 30 cm apart and distance of 60 cm is left after every two rows. The seeds within a row are sown at a distance of 10 cm. Stratification of seeds in the boxes is done in the beginning of December by keeping the seeds and moist sand in alternate layers. The sand should be kept moist without making it too wet or saturated. Stratification can also be done in shallow pits dug in the field. The seed in these can be placed in alternate layers with moist sand. The pits should always be prepared at a higher level, so as to avoid chances of accumulation of water which reduces the seed germination. Stratification is complete when the hard shell is broken and the plumule has emerged from the stone.

The stratified seed is sown during the end of January or first week of February in rows 30 cm apart with seed to seed distance of 10 cm. The light irrigation should be given immediately after sowing the seed.

(*b*) Through cuttings : Plum rootstock can be propagated from stem cuttings. For this purpose, cuttings of Kabul Green Gage plum are prepared during the first week of December and are kept for callusing for about a month. These are planted in the beds preferably during the first fortnight of January. The cuttings are planted at a distance of 15 cm in rows which are 30 cm apart. The rooted cuttings are budded in the following May-June or grafted in December-January.

(c) Clonal rootstock : Myrobalan B is multiplied through mound layering (stooling). The rooted layers of clone are planted in well prepared stool beds in December at a distance of 30 cms in rows and 60 cm apart. Numerous suckers come out from the layers are covered by 2 - 3 soil mounding before monsoon. Suckers are ringed near the base during rainy season and treated with 750 ppm IBA for quick and better root initiation. Rooted layers are separated in December and lined out in nursery buds for further grafting.

Vegetative Propagation

Hard wood cuttings : The rooted cuttings of Kala-Amritsari cultivar can be used directly without budding. The percentage of their successful establishment can be enhanced by dipping the basal portions (5-7.5 cm) of hard-wood cuttings for about 24 hours in 100 ppm solution of IBA. The cuttings taken from sub-apical portions, planted after dipping in IBA and callusing for about a month give higher percentage of success. The time of preparation of cutting is from end of December to end of January.

Budding and grafting : Budding by shield or T method is performed in April and July-August. The plants budded in April become saleable in January but those budded in July-August can only be sold after one and half year *i.e.* next January.

The propagation by cleft and tongue grafting is performed when the stock and scion are still dormant (December-January). Cleft grafting is generally performed when the stock is thicker than the scion. The rootstock which is left while budding during July-August can be grafted in the coming January which will be ready for sale in the next winter. In Himachal Pradesh, grafting is done in February. Chip budding done during mid-February also gives good success.

Simultaneous grafting/cuttings : The plum can be propagated simultaneously by grafting on unrooted cuttings of Kabul Green Gage by dipping the basal portion of cutting in 100 ppm solution of IBA for 24 hours during first fortnight of January. The plants from the cutting/grafts are available for planting after one year in the month of January.

PLANTING OPERATION

The plants do not need any earth ball and are lifted from the nursery with bare roots. They can be lifted with the help of a spade by digging deep trenches. The soil sticking to the roots should be removed by shaking the plants gently. Trimming of the exceptionally longer roots is done to avoid injury during transportation. These plants are then tied in bundles of suitable sizes for easy handling. Plants of one years' growth after propagation should be preferred, as fewer roots are injured in the processes of lifting and replanting and the desired framework can be attained by heading back the tree from required height. Trees older than two years should not be selected for planting.

Plums should be planted in January when the plants are in the dormant condition. The area is laid out and pits of 1 M × 1 M × 1 M are dug about a month before planting.

Pits are refilled with fertile top-soil mixed with 40 kg of well-rotten farmyard manure per pit. Add 15 ml of chlorpyriphos 20 EC mixed in 2 kg soil to each pit to prevent attack of white ants. Apply irrigation soon after setting the plants in the pits. The plum plants may be planted 6 metres apart from row to row and plant to plant in square system, thus accommodating 275 trees per hectare.

Plum is also planted as a filler trees is mango, litchi and pear orchards during the first fortnight of January. The plants of Kala Amritsari are also transplanted in the orchard of Satluj Purple as pollinizer in the ratio of 25 : 85 plants per acre. Alternate plants of pollinizer are planted in the every second row of Satluj Purple for effective pollination and improving fruit set in orchard.

High density planting. Satluj Purple plum trees can also be planted at 6 × 1.5 m distance with modified leader system and summer pinching (10 – 15 cm). This practice ensure high yield of better quality fruits.

Care of young plants : The newly planted young plants, being very tender, need lot of care and attention for their better survival and growth . They should be watered at frequent intervals. However, heavy irrigation should be avoided as stagnation of water in their basins may do more harm than good. The main stem should be cut back to the desired height for the scaffold branches to develop properly and to keep proper balance between the root-system and the growth of the stem. The young plants need staking so as to make them grow upright and straight. The supports should be of bamboo or other wooden logs and should be well fixed in the soil. The lower portion of their trunk should be white-washed to afford protection against sunburn. The provision of a thick row of tall trees alternating with small ones as effective windbreaks is very essential in order to check the adverse effect of strong winds.

FLOWERING AND FRUITING

The flowering in Japanese plum in Himachal Pradesh varied from 11-17 days which started on 5 March and ended on 21 March. In most of the plum varieties grown under sub-tropical conditions flowering starts in the second fortnight of February and last upto first week of March. Alu Bokhara is the late flowering varieties and bloom in the first fortnight of March. The presence of abnormal and imperfect type flowers do not materially affect the cropping as about 90 per cent of the flowers are hermaphrodite.

Pollen viability and germinability ranged from 30 to 90 per cent and 30 to 70 per cent respectively in different cultivars. The stigma become receptive one day before anthesis and remained so till three days after.

The growth pattern of plum followed a double sigmoid curve . The fruit weight continued to increase and specific gravity decreased from fruit set till maturity. As the picking season advanced an increase in the total soluble solids with a corresponding decrease in the acidity of the fruit was observed.

ORCHARD CULTURAL PRACTICES

Irrigation

The water requirement depends upon the age and size of the tree, type of soil, climatic conditions and cultural practices being followed. The young plum plants upto the age of 3–4 years need irrigation at 4–5 days interval during summer months starting from April to June. The irrigation should be avoided during flowering and fruit-setting stage. During April and May frequent irrigations at an interval of 4–5 days should be given for proper development of fruit size and quality. Irrigation should be stopped at the colour break stage to avoid heavy fruit drop. However, when there is rainless spell light waterings may be given. In Santa Rosa plum, irrigation at 50% field capacity at an interval of 12 days in May and 8–9 days in June is considered beneficial for better yield of high quality fruits. In mid-hills six irrigations in a season are sufficient for plum orchard.

Intercropping

Intercropping can be successfully practised during the non-bearing period of the trees and should not interfere with the fruit trees. Need-based manures and fertilizers, irrigation and plant protection measures should be given independently to the fruit trees and intercrops. The short-statured, shallow-rooted, leguminous crops like moong, mash, pear, gram, cluster been etc. can be sown as intercrops. Intercrops like wheat should not be sown in plum orchard as it need frequent irrigation during winter.

Weed Control

In plum orchard of Himachal Pradesh, several monocot weeds like ***Cyperus rotundus, Commelina nudiflora, Digitaria sanguinalis, Setaria glauca*** etc. and dicots like ***Amaranthus viridis, Chenopodium album, Medicago sp.*** etc. were recorded. Bromacil and atrazine at 2.5 to 7.5 kg/ha were found effective to reduce the weed population. Terbacil at 3 kg/ha and simazine at 4 kg/ha in plum orchards also found effective in checking weed. Both these herbicides also increased N, K and Ca content of leaf. In 12 year old Santa Rosa plum orchard diuron and atrazine at 4 kg/ha in April as pre-emergence and gramoxone at 2 l/ha or glyphosate at 800 ml/ha as post-emergence proved effective in controlling weeds.

Manuring and Fertilization

The plum trees must be manured and fertilized judiciously for vigorous and healthy growth and optimum yield of good quality. In Punjab, for one year old plum tree, 6 kg farmyard manure, 30 g N, 15 g P and 36 g K is recommended. Similar amount of farmyard manure and chemical fertilizers should be fed every year up to the age of 6 years. Thereafter, the quantity of farmyard manure, N, P and K should be kept constant at 36 kg, 180 g, 90 g and 216 g, respectively. Farmyard manure as well as phosphatic and potassic fertilizer should be applied in December. The nitrogenous fertilizer should be split into two equal parts. Apply half dose of nitrogen in spring before flowering and remaining half one month later after fruit set.

At Ferozepur (Punjab) 200 g N, 75 g P_2O_5 and 200 g K_2O resulted in largest and heaviest fruit in Kataru Chak cultivar.

In Himachal Pradesh, one year old plum is given 70 g nitrogen, 35 g phosphorus and 100 g potash besides 10 kg of FYM. Thereafter, the dosage are increased at the rate of 70 *g* N, 35 *g* P, 100 *g* K and 5 kg FYM for each complete year of plum trees in the orchard. The fertilizer dose are stabilized at the age of seven years and 40 kg FYM, 500 *g* N, 250 *g* P_2O_5 and 700 *g* K_2O is applied to per plant.

In Jammu and Kashmir, plum trees of 10 years age and above are applied 450 gN, 150 g P_2O_5 and 750 K_2O per plant.

Foliar application of urea @ 0.5-2.5 per cent for correcting nitrogen deficiency have been reported.

Zinc deficiency : The deficiency of zinc is frequently observed in plums growing in sandy soils during the summer month. Leaves on terminal parts of branches become narrow, small with interveinal chlorosis. On growing tips, leaves show rosette form. The deficiency cause dieback of twigs and fruits become hard and tough. It can be corrected by foliar sprays containing 3 kg zinc sulphate and 1.5 kg unslaked lime in 500 litres of water as and when the deficiency symptoms are observed on plants.

Boron deficiency : Due to boron deficiency fruits remain small and misshapen. Corky spots develop on fruits and they cracks. Leaves become dark green and boat like. Terminal buds fail to develop. Under severe deficiency, die back of shoots occur. The deficiency can be corrected by spraying 0.1% Boric acid in June.

TRAINING AND PRUNING

The plum plants are trained according to growth habit of varieties and vigour of the root stock. Generally, plum trees are trained to open centre system. In sub-tropical climate, the trees are trained according to ***modified leader system*** and the plant is headed back to the height of 90 cm ground the level after planting in the field. The plants sprout in February and produce numerous shoots during spring and summer months and continue growing until about the beginning of October. During the first dormancy of the plants in the field, select 4-5 laterals which are usually quite satisfactory but the one most favourably located around the main stem to make a proper framework. The remaining branches present on the central axis should be removed. At this stage, the central terminal branch is called the leader. The lowest branch on the stem should be about 45 cm from the ground. During second year, plant grows in height, produces secondary branches on the selected primary limbs and new branches above the first year extension. The training imparted to the third year old trees is designed to maintain the proper balance between the main scaffold limbs and secondary branches. The position of the laterals maintained during the previous growing season should not be disturbed during the third growing season. During this period water sprouts and undesirable twigs should also be removed. During fourth year, the leader should be headed back at a point where a suitable outgrowing lateral is present so as to check the height of the plant.

In **open centre system**, the top of the plant is headed back to 60 cm at the time of planting to stimulate the growth of lateral branches. During first summer 3 – 5 scaffold branches around the main stem are selected. The lowest scaffold should be about 30 cm above the ground level and the others scaffolds should be 15 cm apart in spiral order. In the first dormant pruning, the central leader is headed back and scaffold branches are allowed to grow whose about one-third growth is removed. In second dormant pruning 2 – 3 well spaced branches are selected on each primary scafford whose one-third to one-fourth portion are pinched off. In third year, training consists of heading back and thinning of unwanted branches. Training is completed in fourth year and only light pruning with heading back of branches is done.

Plum bears on one-year growth as well as on short spurs. To encourage fresh growth and to maintain a system of healthy spurs, light annual pruning should be done in January. It consists of the removal of thin and crowding twigs and branches within the tree. Criss-crossed, lengthy branches, dried and diseased branches should be thinned out to admit sunlight in the tree centre for the development of better colour of fruits. Besides, water sprouts or suckers arising from the crown part of the tree should also be cut regularly. After every 4-5 years of fruiting, heavy pruning of the tree is done by heading back the lengthy branches about half of their length.

In Himachal Pradesh, Santa Rosa plum require 25-30 cm annual extension growth for proper fruiting which consists of 25-30 per cent thinning alongwith 1/3 to 1/2 heading back of shoots.

THINNING OF FRUITS

To improve the prospects of the plum cultivation, it is essential to improve the marketable size and quality of the fruits. There is generally excessive fruit set in plum. If all the fruits are retained on the tree, their size as well as quality may deteriorate and such small sized and poor quality fruits may not fetch good price in the market.

Thinning is more desirable on mature trees making small annual growth than on young vigorous plants. Trees growing on light soils, deficient in moisture and nutrients, would also need for fruit thinning. The Heavy bearing cultivar of plum like Kala Amritsari normally need fruit thinning to minimise the danger of limb breakage. Thinning may also be resorted when good sized uniform fruits are needed for canning industry and fancy trade. Thinning should be done after natural fruit drop in April. This operation should be completed before the hardening of the stones within fruits.

Hand thinning is commonly practised. In this, first shake the branches slightly in order to disloge the fruits which are likely to drop off naturally. If there is still surplus fruit, then start thinning from top to the bottom of the branches. Hold the stem of the fruit to be removed between thumb and second finger and pull it off gently.

The main point to be kept in mind while thinning is to remove all the small, undersized, misshaped, insect or disease attacked fruits. For obtaining well coloured fruits of good size, the retained fruits should have a spacing of 5-8 cm apart depending upon variety.

Foliar spray of 200 ppm ethephon and 1000 ppm carbaryl at full bloom is very effective for blossom thinning.

POLLINATION AND FRUIT SETTING

The Japanese plum cultivars grown commercially require pollination to set satisfactory crops. Most Japanese plum cultivars are self-unfruitful and require cross-pollination. Some cultivars like the Santa Rosa and Beauty are partially self-fruitful and may bear heavier crops when planted among other cultivars. Self-fruitfulness is not a constantly stable character and may vary from year to year and area to area. The cultivar Santa Rosa is self-fruitful in India and in some areas of the USA, where it gives heavy yield when planted in solid blocks. However, in some northerly located areas of California, and Canada, Santa Rosa requires cross-pollination by bees from other cultivars.

Kala-Amritsari is the most widely grown plum cultivar in sub-tropical areas. It is a self-fruitful but in controlled pollination studies its yield improved up to 23 per cent when pollinated with Titron. Kataru Chak is partially self-fruitful cultivar but the yield improved up to 13 per cent if pollinated with Kala-Amritsari.

Fruit set by open pollination ranged between 15.3 per cent in Kataru Chak to 27.8 per cent in Kala Amritsari. Fruit set by self pollination is reported 11.6 per cent in Kala-Amritsari and 8.2 per cent in Kataru Chak.

PRE-HARVEST FRUIT DROP

The problem of pre-harvest fruit drop in Japanese plum reduce the fruit yield considerably and thus, is a great concern to the fruit growers. To check the fruit drop, two sprays of 10 ppm NAA in second and fourth week of April or one spray of 100 ppm ethrel in fourth week of March after pit hardening stage should be given to plum cv. Satluj Purple. It is important that early or late spray of ethrel may increase fruit drop. The fruit growth takes place at rapid rate, the trees should be irrigated frequently. There should not be any water stress in the orchard at the time of spray of growth regulators.

HARVESTING AND HANDLING OF FRUITS

Plum is a delicious fruit which ripens during summer months when other kinds of fruits are not available in plenty. It is a climacteric fruit and does not attain full ripe edible quality on the tree at harvest. Fruits should be picked at proper stage of maturity. It is precocious and starts yielding fruits within 2-3 years of planting. The fruit reaches ripe stage in 12 weeks after fruit-set. The peak season for plum harvest in sub-tropical climate is from first week of May to end of May in different varieties in Punjab and adjoining areas and June-July in Himachal Pradesh.

On the basis of days from full bloom (DFFB), picking dates of plum can be standardized. The optimum picking of cv. Santa Rosa is determined 94 ± 3 DFFB. The varieties like Beauty, Frontier and Alu Bokhara should be picked after 87 ± 2, 108 ± 2 and 102 ± 2 DFFB, respectively. Such predictions would be valid for areas with relatively constant summer temperature or for species in which very high summer temperatures do not hasten fruit maturity. Harvesting of Kala-Amritsari plum around 4th June i.e. after 84 days of fruit set under sub-tropical conditions of Abohar is suggested. At that time TSS should be around 13.0 per cent. The best indices for judging the maturity of plum are that specific gravity should be less than one with deep purple red colour of the fruits in Titron and Santa Rosa and light brown in Kala-Amritsar.

Plum fruits should be picked at ripe but firm stage from the tree for local consumption. However, for distant market, fruits are picked when these have developed 50% colour on the skin and should be firm. This keeps them in good condition during transportation and reach in the market in a firm and attractive condition.

The grown up tree of plum yield about 30–50 kg of fruits per tree in sub-tropical climate and 60-70 kg of fruits in mid-hills.

Plum fruits are picked with hand in several pickings, as the entire crop does not ripen uniformly at a time. While picking care should be taken that spurs are not damaged. Care should also be exercised not to tear the flesh of the fruit or to destroy the natural bloom. If the fruit is jerked in a direct pull from the spur, the fruit stalk may get torn out and the flesh may become ruptured. While picking the fruit give a gentle twist and let the stalk remain attached to it. Never permit threshing of branches with sticks for facilitating harvesting. Small baskets lined with Paper cloth or polythene should be used for placing the fruit during harvest.

The grading should be regularly practised for getting market value of the fruit. Before packing sorting should be done to remove under-ripe, under-sized, over-ripe and damaged fruits. Plum fruits are graded according to fruit size in 3 grades under Agmark system of grading.

Grade	Fruit size (mm)	Inner box size (cm)	No. of layers	No. of fruits (per layer)
Special	42 and above	36 × 16 × 16	3	28–32
Grade-I	36–42	36 × 16 × 16	4	38–42
Grade-II	Below 36	36 × 16 × 16	4	50–56

The fruits should be packed for sending to the distant market immediately after picking as plum fruits soften rapidly after picking. The fruits should be packed in 5 kg wooden boxes instead of, in bamboo baskets to avoid losses in transportation. To prevent the fruits from injury, interior of wooden box should be lined with newspaper sheets on all sides and paper strips as padding at the bottom. The fruits are placed in layers. After each layer make a partition of paper strips over lined with newspaper sheet. Top layer of the fruit is covered with a cushion of paper strips and newspaper sheet and finally the lid of the box is nailed.

Shelf life : The perishable nature of ripe plum fruit poses a serious problem for its storage, transport and marketing. The main reason for its limited cultivation in the subtropical areas is the poor keeping quality of its fruit. Storage in a fresh condition for extended period without loss in quality is, therefore, very pressing problem. Effective preservation in fresh condition is mainly governed by harvesting of fruits at right stage of maturity and post harvest treatments.

The ripe fruits of Kala-Amritsar plum could be stored for 4 days in paper bags at room temperature after treating with 3-6% wax-emulsion. The fruits remained in good conditions upto 30 days in the commercial cold storage (temperature 30-35°F with relative humidity of 85-90 per cent), when treated with 3-6 per cent wax-emulsion for 30 seconds and stored in perforated polythene bags of 100 gauge thickness.

Post-harvest dip in 4% $CaCl_2$ for 2 minutes increase the storability to Santa Rosa for 12 days at ambient temperature. Fruits of Kala-Amritsari plum can be stored for 55 days and of Satluj Purple for 30 days in the commercial cold storage (temp. 3.3°C and RH 85-90%) after treating with 10 ppm GA_3.

The Satluj Purple plum fruits harvested at colour break stage, followed by post-harvest treatment of calcium nitrate (2%) solution for 5 minutes, can be stored for 4 weeks in cold storage (0 to 1°C temp at 90 – 95% RH) with post storage shelf life of 2 days at ambient temperature.

INSECT-PESTS

1. Plum case worm (*Cramastopsychae pendula*) : It is a serious pest and causes damage by nibbing the bark of tender twigs, branches and stem. This can be controlled by spraying 1 kg Carbaryl (sevin 50 per cent WP) in 500 litres of water.

2. Hairy caterpillar (*Eupcrotis* sp) : It is sporadic pest and feed on the leaves. On hatching, the young caterpillars feed gregariously on leaf lamina, skeletonizing the same completely. Later, the caterpillars segregate and gnaw the leaves. In case of severe infestation, the entire tree may be defoliated. The affected outer coat of the young fruit becomes black and hard. For its control collect and destroy the egg masses and the gregariously feeding young caterpillars. Spray 1 kg Sevin 50 WP (Carbaryl) in 500 litres of water

3. Chaffer and defoliating beetles (*Adoretus* sp) : Extensive damage is caused by Chaffer and beetles by destroying the foliage and may also damage the developing fruits. To check these beetles, spray in the evening 1 kg of Carbaryl (sevin 50 per cent WP) in 500 litres of water as soon as the damage starts. Repeat the spraying after 5 or 6 days if the damage continues or the insecticidal deposit is washed away by rain.

4. Bark-eating caterpillars (*Indarbela quadrinotata*) : These are found commonly in old and neglected plum orchards. They cause damage by boring holes into the trunk and branches and by feeding on the bark. For control, apply karosene, after removing webbing, into the holes during September-October and again in January-February.

5. Plum fruit moth (*Laspeyresia pomonella*) : The attack of this pest has been observed in Shimla and Mandi districts especially on late maturing varieties. The larvae bore into the developing fruit and feed on the pulp. Affected fruits drop and rot. Spray carbaryl 0.1% about a month before the anticipated date of harvest. Collect and destroy the fallen fruits.

DISEASES

1. Bacterial canker and gummosis : The causal organism of this disease is ***Pseudomonas morsprunorum.*** The main trunk of the tree, branches, shoots, fruit spurs, blossoms, dormant buds, leaves and even fruits are attacked. The attacked bark becomes brown, gummy and sour-smelling. The attacked limbs are girdled when the infection is severe and the death of the limbs above the attacked point occurs occasionally. The disease can be controlled by applying Mashobra Paste after clearing the wound before the commencement of summer rains. The treatment should be repeated on the new lesions if any, in the following months. 5 kg of mashobra paste contains lanoline – 2.25 g, stearic acid – 425 g, marpholine – 150 g, streptocycline – 25 g dissloved in 5.5 litres of water.

2. Shot hole : The disease in caused by ***Stigmina carpophila.*** Dark-brown scattered lesions appear on leaves which enlarge rapidly. Abscission of the diseased area results in 'shot holes'. The disease can be controlled by spraying with Captan, Ziram or Thiram (0.2 per cent) at leaf fall or bud swelling stage.

CHAPTER 30

Almond

The almond (***Prunus amygdalus*** Batsch) is a favourite nut fruit in our country. It is a concentrated source of energy due to its high oil content. As production of almonds is very much limited in India, a bulk of the almonds are imported from foreign countries. Almond cultivation has been in progress to some extent in the hilly areas of Jammu and Kashmir and Himachal Pradesh.

ORIGIN AND HISTORY

The almond is native to hot arid region of Western Asia. It was probably carried to Greece, North Africa. Europe, Australia and America . In ancient times the species spread as far as the Mediterranean basin.

Almond is mainly cultivated between latitudes 36° and 45°N, although under certain mild climatic conditions, cultivation may extend further north. It is also found in South Africa, South America, Australia and India. In Mediterranean countries, the almond has been confined to marginal and non-irrigated lands, being considered a robust species. The cultivation of almond in USA between 1830 to 1930 was confined to marginal lands. After that the American growers began to plant almond in more fertile and irrigated areas.

USA, Spain, Italy, China, Iran, Greece, Tunisia, Turkey, Pakistan, Afghanistan, Algeria, Morocco, France, Persia and Syria are the important almond growing countries.

AREA AND PRODUCTION

The production of almonds in the world is about 2 million tonnes in 2011. USA is the largest producer which produces 80 per cent of the world production. Presently, the other leading almond producing countries are Spain, Iran, Morocco, Syria, Italy, Turkey, Afghanistan, Tunisia and Algeria.

The almond cultivation in India is restricted to selected hilly areas of Jammu and Kashmir and Himachal Pradesh. The total area under almond cultivation in India 23810 hectares producing 17230 tonnes almond anually. The productivity in India is 730 kg/ha as compound to 1500 kg/ha in the world.

The major almond growing area in India is the Kashmir Valley. The cool and dry areas of Himachal Pradesh especially Chini area bordering Tibet and Lahaul and Kinnaur have also been found suitable for the crop. The area under almond in this state is 5543 hectares yielding 1069 mt almonds. The productivity of almond is Kashmir is very low due to old and senile orchards.

The almond cultivation in Kashmir is concentrated in the districts of Srinagar, Anantnag and Baramula. There are vast stretches of almond plantation in this area and most of them are on high lands locally known as Krewas. The altitude of these areas ranges between 1500 to 1800 metres above sea level.

The interest in almond cultivation in Punjab was aroused by the efforts of a progressive grower in the village Pallian near Nawanshahar district. The plants of two varieties were propagated from old established trees in the villages Saloh (near Pallian) and Chhabewal near Hoshiarpur. The original solitary tree in Saloh was planted by a Muslim land owner about 50 years ago and its source of supply is not known. The second variety which was obtained from Chhabewal is said to have been introduced from some nursery in Saharanpur. The cultivation of peach × almond hybrid (locally known as Sloh) was earlier started by few growers on limited scale in Punjab. However, the quality of the nut from this cultivar is very inferior. Moreover, its kernels contain a toxic substance amygdalin.

IMPORTANCE AND USES

The almond is the most favoured nut as it is highly nourishing and has great medicinal value. Almond is a rich source of protein, minerals, fat and vitamin B_1. The kernel of almond is a very high energy source and results in 655 calories per 100 g fresh weight. It contains protein 20.8%, fat 58.9%, mineral matter 2.9%, fibre 1.7%, carbohydrate 10.5%, calcium 0.23%, phosphorus 0.49%, iron 3.5%, and vitamin B_1 240 mg per 100 g. Kernels of bitter almond were found to contain 55.6% lipids, 18.9% fat, 2.0% crude fibre, 2.3% ash, 7.9% total soluble sugars and 0.27% hydrocyanic acid. Kernels of almond contain rich amount of copper which is considrered good for human brain.

A very valuable oil called **badam roghan** is extracted from almond and it is considered to have a high medicinal value. The nuts are usually eaten when they are ripe. Kernels obtained after blanching, roasting, frying and salting are highly delicious and in great demand. Almond oil is used in confectionary and also for pharmaceutical and consmetic preparations. Green nuts can also be consumed. These are picked before the outer husk begins to lose its colour and harden. The nuts are then opened and the kernels eaten in the milky stage with lightly sugared cream cheese. Bitter almond kernels are used in perfume and pharmaceuticals.

BOTANY

Almond (***Prunus amygdalus***) belongs to the family Rosaceae, Genus **Prunus** and Subgenus **Amygdalus**. Morphologically and taxonomically, almond is very closely related to peach. The tree characters of peach and almond are very similar. The chief differences in the two are found in matured fruits. The fruit of peach is a delectable esculent, that of almond inedible. The flesh of peach is fleshy, juicy and soft, that of almond thin, tough and leathery. The pit of peach must be removed, while that of almond drops off naturally from hard flesh which splits at maturity. The pit of peach is deeply sculptured and of bone-like consistency, that of almond is nearly smooth and in some varieties thin and soft in texture. The buds of almonds are solitary and pointed, those of peach in triplets with the central bud being pointed and vegetative and the side buds rounded and floral.

Both almond and peach have low chilling requirement. Almond, in general, needs somewhat lesser chilling than peach as it sprouts earlier.

Botanically almond fruit is not a nut but a drupe. Exocarp is a thick, leathery, grey green in colour is called the hull. Inside the hull, hard woody shell is the endocarp. Inside the shell is the edible seed which is called a nut. Thus edible portion is cotyledons.

CLIMATE

Almonds can be grown successfully both in temperate and subtropical areas with low rainfall. Precipitation at the time of flowering and fruit maturity is injurious. The areas where almonds are being grown successfully in the world are located between 30° to 40° N or S. Elevation of prominent almond-growing areas ranges from above 700 to 2500 metres above sea level.

The altitude of almond growing areas in Kashmir ranges between 1500-1800 metres above sea level. Almonds can be grown successfully on lower elevations. The most tender stage is blossoming and development of young fruit is shortly after droping of the husk. The blossoms can often withstand temperature from – 2.0 to – 3.3°C for a short time. If low temperature continues for many hours they get damaged. As almond is known to have low chilling requirements, warmer aspects are preferable for its cultivation. Thus, it has more chances of success on the western and southern aspects of the hills as compared to the northern sides. Srinagar which is located in the midst of almond belt has an altitude of 1650 MSL. The place gets an annual rainfall of nearly 400 mm which is well distributed throughout the year. About one-third of the rains are received in spring months.

Almond requires a fairly large number of heat units for crop maturity and may not do well at places where summers are cool and foggy. At a place known as Dalwal in Jehlum district of West Pakistan, almonds are grown successfully under submontane and subtropical conditions.

The chilling requirements of almonds for proper growth and fruiting are rather low i.e. an exposure to low temperature of 250-500 hours below 7.2°C during winter is only needed. This requirement of about 200-350 hours of chilling temperature is usually available in the plains of Punjab.

SOIL

Almonds are not very fastidious in their soil requirements. However, good drainage is essential. In poorly drained soils, even well grown almond trees collapse suddenly whenever the soil remains saturated for 3 to 4 days.

Light loam soils are considered suitable for almond while heavy soils are not desirable. The ideal soil is the deep alluvial type. Shallow soils overlying a calcareous subsoil tend to dry out rapidly during summer unless frequently irrigated.

CHOICE OF VARIETIES

A lot of emphasis was laid on the almond cultivation in Kashmir valley in the past. All the old plantations as a rule, are of seedling type. The plantation of budded plants of known cultivars of good quality, mostly thin shelled and medium-shelled is now being encouraged.

A large collection of almond varieties, seedling selections and hybrids was made in orchard of PAU, Ludhiana during 1971 as a result of a survey of almond growing regions of Himachal Pradesh and Jammu and Kashmir. A considerable number of varieties were also procured from Australia, Greece, Itlaly, Spain and the USA. A brief description of promising varieties is given below :

Pethicks Wonder : Introduced for Australia.

Nut : Average weight 4.27 g. Length 3.25 cm. Breadth 2.1 cm. Thickness 1.49 cm. Size medium to large not uniform. Shape oblong, broad at basal end and tapering towads apex, fairly broad and slightly truncated on one side. Keel fairly prominent towards the apex in all cases and all along the length in some cases. Apex roundish to pointed. Basal end very prominent on account of peeling away of a part of the upper layer of the shell with the hull at the basal end. Pits not many, conspicous, deep. Colour brown with deep brownish tinge at odd places due to uneven hulling . Shell thick, soft, easily cracked with teeth. The outer layer of the shell is partially peeled off with the hull at places specially at both the ridges.

Kernel : Shrivelled, partially filling the shell. Average weight 1.66 g. Size medium. Length 2.4 cm. Breadth 1.25 cm. Thickness 0.78 cm. Shape oblong. Apex fairly pointed. The kernel is also truncated on one side. Colour brown to deep brown. Pellicle thick soft. Flavour and taste sweet fairly good in flavour, moderately rich in oil. Cotyledon whitish in colour. Kernel 38.8% of the nut.

California Paper Shell : Introduced from U.S.A.

Nut : Average weight 2.48 g. Length 3.22 cm. Breadth 1.98 cm. Thickness 1.55 cm. Size medium, uniform. Shape oblong, fairly broad, sword shape in most cases depressed at the back. Keel fairly distrinct all along the length. Basal end prominent. Pits numerous conspicuous, shallow to medium deep. Colour clear whitish brown. Shell is intact, thick, soft, cracks easily with teeth.

Kernel : Very shrivelled unattractive. Average weight 1.09 g. Size medium. Length 2.34 cm. Breadth 1.05 cm. Thickness 0.75 cm. Shape elongated, broad at the basal end and tapering towards the apex. Apex protruding and pointed. Colour dirty brown. Pellicle thin soft. Taste sweet. Flavour poor, appears moderately rich in oil. Cotyledon whitish in colour. Kernel 43.9% of the nut.

Non-Pareil : It is thin shelled nut variety with high percentage of kernels. The variety is regular in bearing and rated as best commercial variety. The nut is flattened, elongated and pointed at the apical end. The shell is white, papery and soft. The kernel is flat, light brown, sweet and having good flavour.

Ne-Plus-Ultra : The nut is big and its shells is attractive. It is valued as a good pollenizer for Non-Pareil. The nuts are frequently gummy when the soil becomes slightly water-logged. It is highly productive if not damaged by frost or disease.

White Brandis :

Nut : Small to medium in size. Cordate, papershelled. Moderately pored, open seal. Mature early in third week of June under mid hills.

Kernel : Small, medium dark brown. Moderately wrinkled. Shelling percentage 60 – 65. Sweet and good quality. More suitable for sale as kernels. Moderately high yielder.

Nauni Selection :

Nut : Small to medium in size. Cordate, papershelled. Moderately pored, open seal and poor cork retention. Mature early in third week of June under mid-hills.

Kernel : Small, medium brown. Moderatey wrinkled. Shelling percentage 50 – 60. Sweet and good quality. More suitable for sale as kernels owing to poor sealing of the nut.

Waris :

Nut : Medium and has soft shell. Shell colour moderately yellow with densely pored surface. Shell seal good. Mature in third to last week of August.

Kernel : Medium and plump. Colour is fair. Mid to late variety. Shell yield is 6 – 7 q/ha.

Hybrid-15 : Cross of Thin Shelled × Saloh (Peach × almond hybrid).

Nut : Average weight 1.73 g. Length 3.25 cm. Breadth 1.83 cm. Thickness 1.3 cm. Size medium, fairly uniform, shape oblong not very broad. Keel prominent towards the apex. Apex protruding and pointed, basal end roundish. Pits numerous and conspicuous, shallow to medium deep. Colour attractive-whitish brown. Shell medium thick, soft, easily cracked with teeth.

Kernel : Slightly shrivelled, not very plump. Average weight 0.89 g. Length 2.28 cm. Breadth 1.15 cm. Thickness 0.85 cm. Size medium uniform. Shape oblong sword shape, broad at the basal end and tapering towards the apex. Apex pointed. Colour brown with deep brownish tinge towards the apex. Pellicle thin, soft. Flavour poor and appears poor in oil content. Cotyledon creamish white in colour. Kernel 51.3% of the nut.

J & K Selection-55 :

Nut : Average weight 1.06 g. Length 2.53 cm. Breadth 1.41 cm. Thickness 1.12 cm. Size small, fairly uniform. Shape oblong. Keel present but not prominent. Colour whitish, shell easily cracked with teeth. Harvested on 8 June under Punjab condition i.e. earliest. Hulling is done in June before rains and can be stored well in time. In other cultivars harvesting is done during July (rain) and at the time of hulling chance of fungus is there. Average yield is 2.5 kg.

Kernel : Plump, not shrivelled. Average weight 0.5 g. Length 1.71 cm. Thickness 0.75 cm. Breadth 0.82 cm. Size small, uniform. Shape oblong. Colour light brown to brown. Flavour good. Shelling per cent 47.

Sloh : It is a hybrid between peach × almond. The quality of the nut from this cultivar is very inferior. Its kernel contains a toxic substance amygdalin (cyanoglucoside) the intake of which can produce ill effects in human beings. Size medium not uniform. Shape oblong. Keel not prominent. Apex sharply pointed, beaked. Basal end prominent. Pits grooved. Colour brown to deep brown. Shell thick, tough. Kernel is toxic and adhere to the shell.

Parbhat, Mukhdoom, Shalimar, IXL, Nikitskyi, Merced, Texas, Drake and Peerless are other varieties grown in temperate climate of India.

PROPAGATION AND ROOTSTOCKS

The old plantations in Kashmir valley have all been raised from seeds. Vegetative propagation by T-budding and Tongue or Cleft grafting is most successful.

Rootstocks : The most commonly used rootstocks for almond in Kashmir Valley are the seedlings raised from sweet or bitter almond. Wild peach is also used in certain areas of valley. Sweet almond seedlings are being favoured more because of the reason that if the budded sprout fails, at least the tree will yield sweet almonds.

In Australia, the Challeston variety has been a good source of seedling rootstocks. The variety California Paper Shell has proved as a good rootstock for poorly drained soils but the performance of almonds budded on plums has been highly variable.

Almond, peach and Marianna plum are the common rootstocks for almonds. The almond seedlings are the most satisfactory and widely used. In Himachal Pradesh, Behmi **Prunus mira** is also widely used as a rootstock for almonds. In a rootstock trial conducted at Solan, wild peach was observed a better rootstock than either bitter almond or Behmi. The wild peach rootstock was most vigorous and produced the maximum yield of green almonds, whereas the Behmi rootstock was the least vigorous and produced minimum fruit yield. At Dunda, Uttarkashi, bitter almond was considered as the best rootstock on the basis of different growth parameters, though the plants on local peach were more vigorous and those of Harsil peach were dwarf. Under the subtropical conditions of Punjab, the almond cultivars on Kabul Green Gage plum rootstock produced more flowers per spur and took significantly less time to mature the crop than those on Sloh rootstock. However, fruit set was significantly higher in trees grafted on Sloh than those of Kabul Green Gage rootstock.

Raising of Seedlings : The almond nuts are harvested from July to September and are stored in a cool and dry place till December. Stratification of nut is needed to break the rest period. The nuts are stratified in sand in boxes in the end of December. It consists in putting a layer of sand 3 cm thick at the bottom of the box and spreading almond nuts over it in 3 cm thick layer. They are covered over with a second sand layer of the same thickness and again a layer of nuts is put over it. In this way, 4-5 layers of seeds and sand are placed. By the middle of February, the hard shell of the seeds breaks open by absorbing moisture and the Kernels which begin to show signs of germination are exposed partly or wholly. When the shells have split partly, the nuts are taken out from the stratification box and sown in beds.

Seeds are sown 3-4 cm deep on well cultivated and manured beds in lines 30 cm apart. The seeds within a line are sown at a distance of 10 cm. A distance of 60 cm is left after every two rows which will facilitate the budding process and cultural operation in the nursery beds. Germination starts in 2 to 3 weeks.

For direct stratification, seeds are sown in lines in the nursery beds by the end of December. The seed received the required chilling in the field and starts germination as soon as the soil temperature is favourable. These nursery beds are irrigated from time to time to keep the soil in moist conditions. A fairly good germination is obtained by this method also.

The seedlings make vigorous growth and become fit for transplanting in their permanent places in the orchard after one year.

Vegetative Propagation : When the seedlings are of pencil thickness and have attained a height of 30 cm they are T-budded in June to August. The seedlings which do not make sufficient growth so as to become fit for T-buddings, are Tongue or cleft grafted in December-January. Tongue grafting is employed when stock and scion are of equal thickness.

Recently, mound layering, stooling etc. are also being tried for multiplication of almond plants.

PLANTING OPERATION

The land should be thorough prepared for almond planting. The pit should be dug 1 × 1 × 1 m size atleast fifteen days before actual planting. Depending upon the nature and fertility of the soil, almonds can be planted 6-7 m apart. The square system is easiest to plant and maintain. With the suggested planting distance 202-275 plants will be accommodated in one hectare. In Kashmir, budded plants are planted by square or hexagonal system at a distance of 5.4m-7.5 m depending upon the soil fertility, vigour of the tree and availability of irrigation. The planting should be made in autumn. Under Punjab conditions, the best time for plantation is the end of January. Almond sprouts very early and if plantation is delayed beyond January the rate of mortality may increase. Till sprouting starts, irrigation may be given at 10 day intervals, thereafter light irrigations should be given at weekly intervals.

The varieties of the almond are mostly self-unfruitful which is due to self incompatibility. It is, therefore, necessary that more than one variety of almond should be planted in an orchard. Ordinarily one variety will pollinate any other variety, provided their flowering periods overlap and when the pollens of the one veriety are produced while the pistils of the other are receptive. The varieties with long flowering periods are considered to be good pollenizers.

The best method to plant the different varieties together is to put 3 rows of the main variety and one row of the pollenizer variety. It is also useful to have 3-4 colonies of bees per hectare of orchard.

FLOWERING AND FRUITING

Almond is one of the first trees to blossom in spring and for this reason, it is very susceptible to spring frosts which make its cropping very uncertain from year to year. The bud differentiation in almond starts in August-September and continues upto February next. The most tender stage in blossoming and the development of the young fruit is shortly after the dropping of the clay or husk. The blossom becomes more and more tender as it opens. The blossom appear before the foliage develops and the first leaves appear about the time the last petals fall depending upon the variety and season. Flowering takes place in very early season occurring between January and April depending on the cultivar.

Flowers are hermaphrodite with white or pink petals, 5 sepals, a single and unicarpel pistil which usually contains 2 ovules in orthotropic position and 20-40 stamens.

The almond fruit is an egg-shaped drupe with a sigmoid growth pattern. Fruit development stops at 70-75 days after blooming. The pericarp (hull) is almost always thin and may be pubescent. In July it begins to split open freeing the endocarp. The endocarp contains one or two kernels varying in size weighing from 0.5- 1.5 g with brown integuments at maturity.

ORCHARD CULTURAL PRACTICES

Irrigation

Irrigation is the most important practice to improve the growth and yield of almond. In Kashmir, almond has proved as an exceptionally hardy tree, which can withstand drought as well as negligence remarkably. The almond orchards here are growing under rainfed conditions and are seldom irrigated. The trees should be given 3-4 irrigations during dry spell for achieving better yield and plump kernels.

Frequent dry summer irrigation is good for proper development of nuts and prevention of fruit drop besides laying foundation for the next year's crop. For successful growing and cropping of almond tree 65 cm or more annual rainfall is needed.

In case of established plants of almond, a 10 day interval of irrigation in summer and about 20-25 days during winter is sufficient. In the event of rainfall, irrigation may be suitably delayed and adjusted.

Manuring and Fertilization

Fertilization of the almond trees in Kashmir is rarely practised but some almond growers do apply nitrogenous fertilizers. Some apply diammonium phosphate which also provides phosphorus.

At Hariparbat, each tree is given 1 kg urea + 500 g potassic fertilizer.

The addition of nitrogenous fertilization to almond is important. Two to three kg ammonium sulphate and one kg superphosphate per tree annually are considered adequate doses.

It is reported that 200 kg P and K per hectare should be applied before planting. Subsequently 100-120 kg N, 50-60 kg each of P and K should be applied annually to maintain the fertility of the bearing orchards. Nitrogen should be given in three split doses i.e in February, March and April. The phosphorus and potash should be given in single dressing during December or January. In Kashmir for 10 years and above old almond trees, 450 *g* N, 65 *g* P_2O_5 and 600 *g* K_2O is recommended. Nitrogen may be split in 2-3 doses. First dose (half the quantity) should be applied alongwith phosphorus and potassium a fortnight before expected bloom, second dose (25% of total quantity) may be applied about three weeks after fruit set and third dose (25% of total quantity) should be applied in June-July.

It is also reported that full grown almond tree need 50 kg FYM, 500 gN, 250 g P_2O_5 and 700 g K_2O for better tree growth and yield of kernels.

Training and Pruning

At the time of planting, head back the tree to one metre above the ground level. Allow the lowest branch at 0.6 m from the ground. The plant should be trained to central modified leader system. Select 3 – 4 main scaffolds 15 – 20 cm apart spirally in order to produce a good framework of the tree. The crotch angles of the scaffold limbs should be 45 – 60°. In weak crotches, the branches should be tied by strong tying material with pegs.

The almond fruit is borne largely on short spurs. However, a small percentage is also borne on one-year old wood. The spur remain productive up to five years. In order to renew about one-fifth of fruiting wood every year it is a practice to stimulate new shoots by pruning. Amount of pruning depends on the previous crops, efficiency of pollination, kind of fertilization, cultivars, tree vigour and climate.

The young bearing trees should make an annual extension growth of 25-50 cm and older trees 20-30 cm. The almond should not be pruned severely, firstly because it never over bears and secondly its foliage is sparse enough to permit enough light to reach every part of the tree. The pruning consists most of thinning of branches rather than heading them back.

Reinvigorating pruning is carried out only when trees are old and unproductive but healthy. The main branches can be cut back and many new shoots will grow out to replace them in the spring.

POLLINATION AND FRUIT SETTING

Most almond varieties are self unfruitful and as such cross pollination is necessary. Generally any two varieties with over-lapping flowering period intercross and set good fruit if climatic conditions are favourable but certain cases of inter-sterility are also reported. A few such as Taxas and Languedoc, Non-pareil and I.X.L., California Paper Shell and I.X.L., Jordanalo and Harpareil are intersterile. Other varieties can cross-pollinate each other if their flowering period coincides.

On account of the acute problem of self-unfruitfulness, suitable pollenizers need to be provided right at the time of plantation. An efficient arrangement of the pollenizing varieties is to plant these at every third position in every third row. This means that no tree of the main variety is more than one tree away from the pollenizer tree. In some cases complete rows of the pollenizing variety are planted.

For obtaining proper fruit set, two or more cross compatible varieties should be planted in alternate rows. It is further evident that to obtain good fruit set and yields, the presence of honey bees is essential in the flowering season. Usually one or two colonies of honey bees per hectare, but four or five calonies will ensure good pollination even during less favourable seasons with lower temperatures, rain or wind.

HARVESTING AND HANDLING OF FRUITS

Almonds become ready for harvesting in the hills from July-September. In subtropical areas, the harvesting may be done in June. The thin leathery hull or husk in almond is non-edible. In Kashmir harvesting season starts by the end of July and lasts for 10-15 days. Dehulling of in-shell harvested almonds is done by engaging labour for the purpose. One labourer can dehull 10-12 kg of almond daily. Dehulled almonds are spread over mats for drying and they lose 20-50 percent weight in the drying process. The dry nuts are usually graded into two categories viz. thin-shelled and hard-shelled and sent to markets.

Normally, the harvesting should be started when the hulls split and before the nuts begins to fall. At harvest hull colour changes from green to yellow with cracks or splitting at suture starting from pedicel end. A sheet of cloth is spread under the tree and the nuts are made to fall by giving the branches a vigorous shaking or jarring. The more presistant nuts are knocked off by striking the branches with bamboo poles, taking care not to injure the bark of branches. The nuts are then dried in the sun for a short time. Hard-shelled varieties are bleached with sulphur fumes which makes the shells bright and improves their market value.

The nuts grown in Punjab have thin and papery shells. The yield of kernels from these nuts is about 60 per cent in Almond Hybrid-15, 72 per cent in H.P. Selection 10, 54 per cent in California Paper Shell and 46 per cent in Pathick's Wonder. The kernels are free from bitterness and are very tasty and rich in flavour.

The yield range 3 to 6 kg of nuts per plant. Usually, they are between 3 to 4 kg in varieties of good nut quality. In Kashmir, serveral trees yield 10-20 kg nuts each at Hariparbat, Tral, Noorpara, Zaboora, Khunmoh etc.

INSECT-PESTS

1. Aphids (*Hyalopterus amygdali* and *Hyalopterus pruni*) : Aphids appear on tiny shoots and cause damage by sucking sap in early spring. These aphids reduce plant growth and fruit set.

They can be controlled with spray of phosphoric esters and 1 kg carbaryl (Sevin 50% WP) in 500 litres of water in spring.

2. SanJose scale (*Quadraspidiotus perniciosus*) : SanJose Scale attacks the trees in early stage. It is a widespread and is very harmful pest. It can be controlled by spraying dimethoate (0.03%).

3. Twig borer (*Anarsia lineatella*) : The pest cause damage in some old plantations. It attacks buds, flowers, shoots and fruits.

It can be controlled by removing affected buds in spring or spraying the tree with 1 kg Sevin in 500 litres of water in summer. Mealy bugs are also reported to attack the roots of almond trees.

4. Almond weevil (*Myllocerus laetivirens*) : Adult weevils congregate on the ventral surface of leaves, nibble irregular holes and gradually eat away the entire leaf leaving only the midrib. It first consume the tender leaves and then move on to older ones.

Collection and destruction of beetles after sun set by shaking non-bearing trees can be very effective measure to control the weevils. Spray carbaryl 0.1 per cent or methyl parathion 0.05 per cent.

DISEASES

1. Gummosis : The disease is caused by ***Pseudomonas syringae.*** The bark and outer sapwood show symptoms of circular to elongated water-soaked lesions. The main symptom of infection is the appearance of a brownish watery ooze on the surface of the bark.

Spary Bordeaux mixture (2 : 2 : 250) or 50% copper oxychloride (0.3%) in the fall as well as in the spring to prevent infection. Mashobra paste in also found effective against this disease.

2. Shot hole : It is caused due to ***Wilsonomyces carpophilus.*** Dark-brown scattered lesions appear on leaves. The spots later on enlarge rapidly. Abscission of the diseased area in the leaf results in shot hole.

The disease can be controlled by spraying Captan, Ziram, or Thiram at the rate of 0.2 per cent at leaf fall or bud swelling stage.

3. Almond rust (*Tranzschelia discolor*) : Small, circular, yellowish brown to rusty coloured pustules appear on lower surface of leaves. Severe infection results in early defoliation.

To check the disease, give three sprays of mancozeb (250 *g* in 100 litres of water) at 15 days interval strating the spray at first disease appearance.

4. Crown gall : It is caused by ***Agrobacterium tumefaciens***. It occur worldwide and is the main bacterium to attack almond. Symptoms and control measures are suggested under peach diseases.

Among the diseases of foliage, leaf spot and leaf curl are quite common but these do not appear to cause much damage.

CHAPTER 31

Apricot

The apricot (***Prunus armeniaca*** **L.)** ranks second next to plum among the stone fruits in India in area, production and popularity. It is a drought resistant, salt tolerant, hardy plant being rather less susceptible to pests and diseases.

ORIGIN AND HISTORY

The centre of origin of apricot is north east China between the town Kan-Techeou and Russian border. The distribution of cultivated apricot, its wild forms and allied species is reported in temperate zone of Asia between 33° and 70° E longitude and 53° and 30°N latitude. Wild apricot (Zardalu) apears to be indigenous to India.

Apricot is known to Chinese since 2000-3000 BC. This delectable fruit moved westward from Central Asia through Iran and Transcaucasian region and reached Italy about 100 BC, to England in 13th Century and to North America by 1720. The specific name **armeniaca** indicates its introduction to Italy and Greece by Armenian traders.

Apricot is cultivated in China, Russia, Turkey, Italy, Spain, France, Greece, USA, Morocco, Syria and Romania.

AREA AND PRODUCTION

The leading apricot producing countries are Turkey, Iran, Uzbekistan, Algeria, Italy, Pakistan, Morocco, France, Ukraine and Japan. The world production of apricot is estimated 2.5 million metric tonnes half of which is located in Central Asian countries. Turkey is producing 27 per cent apricot fruits of the total world production. The other apricot producing countries are China, Greece, USA, Hungary, Egypt, Syria and Spain.

In India, apricot is cultivated chiefly in Himachal Pradesh, Jammu and Kashmir and Uttarakhand hills. The total production in the country is estimated 50120 mt annually out of 19000 hectares area. In Kashmir apricot occupy 6100 hectares and producing approx 16000 mt. The area under apricot in Himachal Pradesh in 3487 hectares and the production is about 3340 mt.

Some sporadic plantation of apricot exists in Amritsar and Patiala districts of Punjab.

IMPORTANCE AND USES

The apricot is an attractive, delicious and highly nutritious fruit. It is particularly a very rich source of vitamin A and contains more carbohydrates, protein, phosphorus and niacin than majority of other fruits. The percentage of different ingredients in the edible portion of fresh Indian apricot fruits have been recorded as protein 1.0%, fat 0.3%, fibre 1.1%, carbohydrates 11.6%, mineral matter 0.7%, calcium 20 mg, phosphorus 25 mg, iron 2.2 mg, vitamin A 3600 I.U., vitamin B_1 0.04 mg, vitamin B_2 0.13 mg and ascorbic acid 6 mg per 100 g fruit. The dry apricot contains protein 1.7%, mineral matter 2.8%, carbohydrates 72%, vitamin A 98 μ g/100 g, vitamin B_1 217 mg and vitamin B_2 2.2 mg/100g. The pulp of fresh apricot contains about 1% pectic substances as calcium pectate.

The ripe apricot is an excellent dessert fruit. The fruit is canned, candied, frozen and dried. The various products like jam, nectar and papad can be prepared. The beverage, apricot nectar is made by converting the ripe fruits into puree and mixing it with sugar syrup and citric acid. Apricot are commonly consumed as dry fruits. Its sweet kernels taste like almond and used as its substitute in pastes and confectionary and can be added to jam.

BOTANY

The cultivated apricot belongs to the family Rosaceae and species ***Prunus armeniaca.*** The other related species are either grown for fruits, rootstocks or ornamental purposes. These are ***P. ansu, P. brigantiaca, P. dasycarpa, P.davidiana, P. mandschurica, P.mume*** and ***P. sibirica.***

The cultivated apricot (***Prunus armeniaca***) is a small tree, 6-9 metres in height, with reddish bark and glabrous twigs. Leaves ovate to round ovate, sometimes subcordate, abruptly short-pointed, mostly obtusely serrate, glabrous above, pubescent on veins beneath, petioles with conspicuous glands. Flowers pinkish or nearly white, produced before the leaves. Fruit velvety when young, peach like in colour and shape, flesh yellowish orange. Stone smooth and flattened.

Apricot is drupe fruit and its edible portion is epicarp and mesocarp.

CLIMATE

Apricot is very much susceptible to frost due to early flowering. Flowers are liable to suffer from forsts or cold winds during the period early February or March. Temperature limit for flowering lies near about 27–31°F and for fruit setting is 30–32°F. The minimum temperature for fruit ripening varied from 15–19°C. The apricot is grown successfully at an altitude of 1200-1500 metres above sea level. Its variety St. Ambroise fruits better at higher altitude upto 1829 metres. White-fleshed, sweet kernelled apricots require cool climate and are grown in dry temperate region upto 3000 MSL. Yellow-fleshed, bitter kernelled apricots do best under the warm climate of mid hills ranging 900 – 1500 MSL and long cool winter, frost free and warm spring. They require 300 – 900 chilling hours below 7°C.

The long cool winter and uninterrupted warm spring are favourable for apricot fruiting. If the temperatures are hot for a long period during the dormancy, the flower bud may drop which is a serious problem in warmer climate. High humid conditions in summer increase the possibility of brown rot attack. An annual rainfall of about 100 cm is sufficient for obtaining a good apricot crop.

SOIL

Apricots are quite hardy to grow in most of the soils which are deep and well-drained. The soil should be about 3 metre deep. The pH of soil should range between 6 to 7. In Kinnaur region of Himachal Pradesh where apricots grow in large wild stands, the soils are sandy, well-drained but not very fertile. If the drainge is good, high lime content of the soil does not depress the tree growth.

CHOICE OF VARIETIES

The cultivars New Castle, Shipley Early, Shakarpara and Kaisha are grown in mid hills, while Moorpark, Turkey, Royal, St. Ambroise, Nugget and Charmagz in high hills. In cold arid zone comprising Kinnaur, Ladakh and higher ranges of Uttarakhand hills, Nari, Kaisi, Charmagz, Shakarpara, Halman, Moorpark, Turkey, Early Shipley, Chaubattia Madhu, Kesri and Rakcha Karpu cultivars are predominent. Brief description of important apricot varieties is given below:

New Castle : The fruits are medium-sized, roundish, highly coloured, orange yellow. Flesh in very sweet and juicy. It is an early cultivar ripening in the month of May. It is a popular dessert cultivar for warmer locations.

Shipley Early : The fruit medium sized and creamy white in colour. Flesh is sweet and juicy but kernel is bitter. It is a dessert cultivar. It is an early variety ripen in the middle of May.

Kaisha : Fruit medium-sized, round. Skin yellow with red cheeck. Flesh orange yellow with good flavour. Very prolific. Ripens in the middle of June. The kernel is bitter.

Charmagz : The fruit medium-sized, roundish flat. The skin is straw-yellow and the flesh is light yellow, very sweet and highly flavoured. The fruit is suitable for both dessert and drying purposes. The kernel is sweet. This is a self incompatible cultivar which gives good fruit set when the cultivar Turkey is used as pollenizer. It is a shy bearer variety.

Nugget : This is found one of the best cultivars for mid hills in respect of fruit quality, regularity in bearing and yield. It is the earliest cultivar to flower in the season. Fruits are medium to large in size and round in shape. Skin deep orange, glabrous. The flesh is deep yellow in colour, firm and juicy with fine texture. The fruit is ready to harvest in the last week of May or the first week of June.

Royal : Fruit large, roundish oval. Skin dull yellow, tinged with red. Flesh yellow, firm, juicy with high flavour when fully ripe. It is used for dessert, canning and drying purposes. Stone free to partially clinging. It ripens in the middle of June.

St. Ambroise : Fruit are large, oval and symmetrical. Skin is orange yellow. Flesh is also orange yellow, firm and tender. It is a freestore variety. It is a mid to late season cultivar ripening from the last week of June to the first week of July.

Moorpark : It is considered as best apricot cultivar when fully ripe but is shy in bearing . The fruits are roundish and large in size. The skin is light orange in colour with a light red blush. The flesh is juicy, sweet and excellent in flavour. The fruit ripens in the first week of June.

Nari : Fruit small to medium in size, oblong, depressed at both base and apex ends. The skin is smooth and pale yellow in colour. The flesh is light yellow with slight fibre having sweet pleasant aroma. The kernel is sweet like almond. The fruit ripens in the last week of May.

Shakarpara : Fruit small to medium in size, having creamy yellow skin with slight pink blush on the shoulders. The pale yellow flesh is sweet and has excellent aroma. The kernel is bold and sweet. Fruit ripens in third week of May. It is a shy bearing cultivar and requires high chilling.

Halman : It is an important dessert and drying cultivar of Ladakh. Fruit is medium sized and golden in colour. The flesh is very sweet but not very juicy. It is harvested in early August.

Rakcha Karpu : It is also important cultivar of Ladakh which also fruits well in mid hills. The kernel colour is white. It is dessert cultivar but kernel is used for oil extraction. It ripens in the last week of May in mid hills while in August in Ladakh.

Wanatcher, Tilton, Harcot, Vivagold, Harogem and Roksana are the other important varieties. Benazir variety is grown in Patiala region in the kitchen gardens.

PROPAGATION AND ROOTSTOCKS

Apricots are commercially raised by vegetative methods of propagation like budding and grafting.

Seed Propagation : Apricot seeds require stratification for a period of 72 days at 4°C. The stratification medium should have proper moisture retaining capacity and good aeration. The germination of seeds can be hastened by removal of kernel from shell, scarification and gibberellic acid or kinetin treatment. The seeds are soaked for 24 hours in 500 ppm GA_3 or 5 ppm kinetin solution before planting. Both the growth regulators also increase the seedling growth. The seeds should be sown carefully in 30 cm apart rows. Sufficient moisture in the nursery beds ensures good germination and seedling growth. Frequent watering and mulches helps in better germination. Application of terbacil at 2-3 kg/ha before weed emergence helps in weed control in the nursery. To make better growth of seedlings, small quantity of urea may be applied.

Rootstocks : Apricots are generally propagated on wild apricot (Zardalu), wild peach seedlings and plum. Apricot seedlings are the best rootstock as the graft union on this is good and the trees are more vigorous than on plum. Peach is also a satisfactory rootstock for apricot, but sometimes the graft union is enlarged or rough. In rainfed orchards, where drought conditions prevail, apricot on peach makes better growth than on apricot seedlings. Peach rootstock therefore, should be used in dry and light soils. Many apricot cultivars are not compatible with Myrobalan plum, but this rootstock is used when the trees are to be planted in heavy soils or under excessive soil moisture conditions. Marianna plum is also suitable under such conditions.

Vegetative Propagation : T-budding, chip-budding and tongue grafting are generally adopted for apricot multiplication. The seedlings which attain pencil thickness in the month of May-June are budded and the other seedlings are utilized for fall budding in September. The rootstock should be more than 0.6 cm in diameter with a bark separating readily from the wood. The stock may be budded at a height of about 10-25 cm above the ground level in a smooth bark surface. Some of the May-June budded plants become ready for planting in the dormant season while fall budded plants can only be utilized in the next dormant season. The seedlings which do not make enough growth for budding are usually grafted in the following dormant season January to mid February by tongue grafting. A high percentage of success is obtained in apricot both in budding and grafting.

PLANTING OPERATION

The pits of 1 × 1 × 1 m dimension are dug in winter season i.e. December-January and properly filled with a mixture of soil and well rotten farmyard manure. On the plain land planting is done according to the square or rectangular or triangle system but on hill slopes contour system is generally practiced. The spacing of plants varies with the soil, climate and vigour of the cultivar to be grown. The plants are generally planted at the distance of 6 × 6 m in square system, thus, accommodates 275 plants per hectare.

To derermine the miximum limit of planting density of 1110 to 8880 trees per hectare was followed in a trial adopting free spindle, Tatura and open centre training system. The highest cumulative 4-year yield was obtained with 2500-3333 trees per hectare.

Well grown plants of about one meter height should be planted. Water should be given immediately after planting to establish close contact between roots and soil.

FLOWERING AND FRUITING

In apricot, usually three flower buds develop in the axil of a leaf at each node on a shoot and spur. The central one is vegetative bud and the two side ones are floral buds. In Himachal

Pradesh, the flowering in apricot cultivars mostly occurs in the month of March. The duration of flowering varies with the cultivar and prevailing weather conditions. High temperature, low humidity and wind shorten the flowering duration by increasing the transpiration. The apricot suffer more due to spring frost because of earlier blooming than other temperate tree fruits. A delay in its flowering is, therefore, very much desired to reduce the frost damage.

The pattern of growth expressed by developing fruit of apricot cv. New Castle in respect of increase in length, diameter, weight and volume depicted double sigmoidal growth curve. The specific gravity of the young fruits, first showed an upward trend followed by a slight decline and thereafter, maintained more or less uniform trend, remaining slightly below unity. The approximate period of fruit development is 73, 82, 85, 88 and 96 days in case of Shipley, New Castle, Kaisha, Royal and Shakarpara cultivars.

ORCHARD CULTURAL PRACTICES

Irrigation

The apricot tree has shallow roots, therefore, good soil moisture is beneficial. The purpose of irrigation to apricot is to wet the entire area containing a major portion of the roots. Since apricot roots are mainly confined to about 2 metres from the surface, irrigation should aim at wetting the land up to a depth of 2 metres. Special attention to irrigating the apricot tree should be given during April-Mid June when the fruit is in developing and maturity stage. The apricot field should be irrigated at 10 days interval during May and weekly interval during June. In Himachal Pradesh, 8 irrigations in a season are sufficient for better fruit growth and quality. In the rainfed conditions mulching and water harvesting techniques should be practised but the cultivation of drought resistant cultivars is more desirable. Black polythene mulch in apricot orchard help in moisture conservation.

Weed Control

The weeds in apricot field are cleared with frequent light hoeing. The use of chemical weedicides has been tried successfully. Simazine or diuron each @ 4-6 kg per hectare as pre-emergence herbicides in 15 year old trees of cv. New Castle gave good control of emerging weeds for 90 days. The post-emergence herbicides glyphosate @ 800 ml/ha or gramoxone @ 2*l*/ha are also effective in checking the weed flora in apricot orchards. The cost of applying weedicides is much less than manual weeding.

Manuring and Fertilization

Nitrogen plays an important role in apricot nutrition as its deficiency adversely affects the leaf dry matter content, fruit set and number of mature fruits. The deficiency of phosphorus causes reduction in fruit set, fruit growth and calcium and magnesium contents of leaves. The potassium application increases the growth, flowering, fruit size and yield.

Highest yields were recorded on the trees receiving N at 100-200 kg, P at 80 kg and K at 100 kg per hectare with leaf NPK contents of 2.5-2.7, 0.17 - 0.18 and 3.3-3.5%, respectively. On poor sandy soils, application of organic manure along with inorganic fertilizers is necessary.

Application of 450 *g* N, 150 *g* P_2O_5 and 750 *g* K_2O per tree is recommended for 10 years old plants in Kashmir. Half dose of nitrogen and total quantity of phosphorus and potash should be applied two weeks before normal bloom. The second half of nitrogen should be applied three weeks after fruit set. In another study, for full grown tree of 7 years old, 40 kg FYM, 500 g nitrogen, 250 g phosphorus and 200 g potash in suggested. The phosphorus and potash alongwith FYM is applied in December. Half nitrogen is given a fortnight before flowering and half about one month after fruit-set.

TRAINING AND PRUNING

The apricot is trained according to modified leader system. The young plants are more branched. Thinning out and selection of 4-6 well spaced branches is very important aspect of training in the first year of growth.

Pruning of young trees : One year old trees of apricot usually have numerous lateral branches.

The main central axis is cut off 50-75 cm above the ground and all laterals are cut off if these are not properly spaced along the central axis. Pruning at the end of first growing season in winter consists in selection of 5-6 well placed laterals around the trunk. The lowest branch should be about 40-45 cm and all other laterals should be completely thinned out. All the selected laterals should be headed back to get the secondary branches on them. During the second year growth only 5-7 secondary scaffolds about breast height are retained and others are removed. At the end of third year, the pruning is confined to the thinning of branches which are either crossing or crowding each other for proper development of the framework and to admit sunlight in the tree cente to promote growth of spurs. The leader of the tree is modified after fourth year of its age by cutting it back to very close to a lateral branch.

Pruning of bearing trees : Most of the crop is borne on spurs which live for 4-5 years. A small portion of the crop is also borne on one year old shoots. To produce new spurs annually and to replace the older and unproductive ones, light to moderate thinning of branches and heading back of new laterals is essential annually.

In old trees when the growth becomes less the heavier pruning is done by way of cutting back of main primary limbs and thinning of undesirable secondary laterals.

THINNING OF FRUITS

The apricot tends to set heavily. To produce fruits of marketable size it must be thinned judiciously, otherwise the trees start alternate fruiting. Fruit to fruit spacing should be kept 4-8 cm when crop is heavy, when crop is light spacing may be done only upto 4-5 cm. Two to three fruits may be retained on each spur. Thinning should be done within 40 days after full bloom i.e. during the last week of April or first week of May, beacuse this is the effective period influencing fruit bud formation.

POLLINATION AND FRUIT SETTING

Most of the commercial apricot cultivars have been found self-fruitful in pollination and set fruits without pollenizers but open-pollination has always given better fruit set. The cultivars Charmagz and Perfection are self-incompatible. The failure of fruit set is mainly due to persistent rains. The pollination by honey bees prove superior over wind pollination. There is generally a good fruit set in apricot cultivars growing in appropriate climatic conditions. It was noted 45.6% in New Castle, Royal, Shipley Early and Kaisha cultivars of apricot. The highest fruit drop occurs in the second and third week after fruit set and ranges from 78.3 per cent in Kaisha to 61.4 per cent in New Castle. A spray of 10 ppm NAA or 50 ppm 2, 4, 5 T at the beginning of pit hardening reduced the preharvest drop.

HARVESTING AND HANDLING OF FRUITS

The fruits of apricot develop maximum flavour and are very delicious when ripen on the tree but such fruits cannot be transported to distant markets because of their perishable nature. Fruits harvested well in advance of ripening do not attain full taste. Therefore, the standardization of maturity and harvesting is essential for obtaining good return from the marketing of fresh fruits. The fruit colour, flesh colour, size, firmness, TSS, titratable acidity, dry matter content, days from bloom and accumulated heat units above 10°C are the main maturity indices. The best harvesting date of apricot is around 9th May i.e. 64 days after full bloom for the cultivar of New Castle under mid hill conditions. At this time, the fruit attained good size, barium yellow skin colour, amber yellow flesh colour, 10.03% TSS and 5.48% total sugars.

The apricot fruits are best harvested on the basis of days taken from full bloom to maturity. Charmagaz takes 70 – 75 days, Kaisha 72 – 77 days, Frogmore Early 80 – 87 days, Gilgati Sweet 120 – 124 days, Amba 127 – 130 days and Quetta 128 – 132 days from full bloom to maturity.

Early ripened better coloured fruits get a premium in the market. Ethrel @ 25-150 ppm two weeks before the expected harvest advance ripening by 2-5 days in the fruits of Kaisha cultivar.

Normally the fruits are picked when they changed colour from green to yellow and lose flesh firmness. Fully ripe fruits are harvested for freezing, canning and drying. The apricot plant starts bearing at the age of 4-5 years but attain full bearing age at about 8-10 years. The full grown apricot tree yields about 50-80 kg fruit. The productive life of a apricot tree is about 30-40 years.

Grading of Fruits : Apricot fruits are graded according to fruit size into three grades as follow :

1. Special : 42 mm and above	28 – 32 fruits in box
2. Grade-I : 36 – 42 mm	38 – 42 fruits in box
3. Grade-II : 36 mm	50 – 56 fruits in box

The fruits should be packed in 5 kg wooden box or CFB box (36 × 16 × 16 cm). Special grade fruits are packed in 3 layers and Grade-1 and Grade-2 in 4 layers in the box.

Storage of fruits : The apricot fruits harvested at optimum maturity can be stored for 7 days at 5°C temperature and 85 per cent relative humidity. The fruits kept at 0°C and 85 – 95 per cent RH can be stored for 1 – 2 weeks. Black mould rot can be effectively checked by treating the fruits with 1000 ppm Benlate.

INSECT-PESTS

1. Indian gypsy moth (*Lymantria obfuscata*) : The damage is caused by caterpillar which are gregarious and nocturnal in habit. In severe cases, the trees are completely defoliated.

The moth can be controlled by dusting with 5% Lindane in March-April. The egg masses having yellowish brown hairs should be located in August and March and destroyed. Pest can be checked by spraying fenvalerate (0.03%).

2. Leaf roller (*Archips micaceana*) : The leaves and petioles are cut and rolled up by caterpillar and then they feed inside the soft tissues. The caterpillar after puncturing the ripening fruits also eat up inner pulp.

It can be controlled by spraying 0.03 per cent fenvalerate. The rolled leaves and webbed flowers should be destroyed after collecting.

3. Peach stem borer (*Sphenoptera lafertei*) : The pest attack trunk and branches of apricot and sometimes the entire tree dries up. Infested inner bark becomes a powdery mass like sawdust which mixed with frass, oozes out from the splits on the surface.

Remove and burn heavily infested branches and trees. The adult beetles should be killed by clearing the holes and then insert 0.5 *g* paradichlorobenzene and plug the hole with mud or cotton wick soaked in petrol or methyl parathion 1 litre of water or dichlorovos 0.15% (2 ml Nuvan 78% EC in 1 litre of water).

4. Peach fruit fly (*Bactocera dorsalis*) : Fruit fly lay eggs on fruits and feed on pulp. The infested part of the fruit rots and even drop. The fruit become unfit for human consumption. Pupation takes place in soil under infected trees.

Burry the infested fruits at 60 cm depth. Hoeing of orchard should be done in May and June to expose the pupae which are present mostly at 4–6 cm depth. In case of severe infestation, spray 1250 ml (0.05%) Sumicidin 20 EC (fenvalerate) in 500 litres of water in mid May and repeat after one week if required.

DISEASES

1. Bacterial canker and gummosis : It is caused due to ***Pseudomonas syringae***. The bark and outer sapwood show symptoms of circular to elongated water-soaked lesions which later turn sour-smelling. Sunken black lesions are found on the infected fruits.

Spray Bordeaux mixture (2 : 2 : 250) or 50% copper oxychloride (0.3%) in the fall as well as in spring to prevent infection. Mashobra paste is also found effective against this disease. Mashobra paste includes stearic acid 25.5 g, morpholine 9 ml, water 340 ml, lanoline 136 g and non-sterile dihydrostreptomycin sulphate 3.1 g.

2. Powdery mildew : The disease is caused by fungus ***Sphaerotheca pannosa***. The young leaves and shoots are infected from the fungus. The young leaves get curled and narrowed as they expand. The growth of affected plant parts is ceased. The white powdery appearance is noted on the leaf surface. Spray 0.25 per cent wettable sulphur first before flowering, second at petal fall and third two weeks thereafter.

3. Brown rot : It is caused due to ***Monilinia laxa, M. fructigena, Sclerotina*** spp. Due to the attack of disease both flowers and fruits are affected. In severe infection, flowers turn brown and die. Within a few day, tiny brown spot enlarges to a large. The pathogens overwinter in fruit mumies, in twig cankers and in rotten fruits.

For effective control of disease, spray 0.3% Zineb in growing season and 0.1% benomyl during anthesis.

4. Coryneum blight or Shot hole : The disease is caused by ***Stigmina carpophila***. The disease attack leaves, twigs, fruits as well as unopened buds. Small, circular deep purple spot appearing on the fruit become raised and rough. Abscission of the diseased area results in shot hole.

Spray 50% copper oxychloride (0.3%) before leaf fall and bud swell stage.

5. Wilt : The causal organism of the disease is ***Verticillium albo-atrum***. The whole tree or part of it may be affected due to this disease. The leaves drop down from the affected limbs in early summer. The general stunting of tree is visible and trees remain unproductive for many years.

The pit soil should be sterilized with formalin before planting new sapling.

CHAPTER

32

Walnut

The walnut (***Juglans regia*** L.) is known by the name of akhrot in greater part of India. It is found in northern parts of the country in temperate zone. The only commercially important is the English or Persian walnut.

ORIGIN AND HISTORY

Walnut believed to have originated in the region from Persia to Kashmir. The army of Alexander the Great brought it to Europe. The other species of genus **Juglans** are native to the North and South America, Central China, Manchuria and Japan. The walnut moved from Italy to Spain, France, Portugal, Germany and to the Southern USSR and went to China from Tibet. It was introduced in England by 1562. In India, walnut remained confined to Kashmir and it appears that it has spread to Himachal Pradesh and Uttarakhand during the past century only.

AREA AND PRODUCTION

The major walnut growing countries are China, Iran, USA, Turkey, Ukraine, Mexico, France, India, Romania and Chile. The world production of walnut seed is 3.26 million metric tonnes. China is the largest producer of walnut seeds in the world.

The India, Jammu and Kashmir is principal walnut growing state. The area under walnut cultivation in this state is 83600 hectares yielding 2.25 lakh tonnes nut. It produces about 90 per cent of the total production in India with an average productivity of 2.69 mt per ha. The other walnut growing regions are Himachal Pradesh and Uttarakhand and Arunachal Pradesh. The total area under walnut in India is 1.5 lakh hectares with annual production of 2.84 lakh metric tonnes.

Export potential : The major importing countries of walnut from India are United Kingdom, Egypt, Netherlands, Germany, USA, China, Australia and Taiwan. India has exported 5295 mt walnut to different countries for the worth of Rs. 200 crores during 2012-13.

IMPORTANCE AND USES

The walnut is very rich in proteins, fats and minerals and is a concentrated source of energy. It contains good amount of vitamin B_6 among all the other nuts. Both immature fruits and green hulls of walnut are very rich sources of ascorbic acid containing about 2- 2.5% and

0.4 - 0.8% on fresh weight basis respectively. Walnut kernel contains 14.8 g protein, 64 g fat, 15.8 g carbohydrates, 2.1 g fibre, 1.9 g ash, 99 mg calcium, 380 mg phosphorus, 450 mg potassium per 100 g.

Immature fruits of walnut can be utilized for preparing various products like pickles, chutneys, marmalades, press juice and syrups. Walnut oil is used for edible purposes, artists oil colours, varnishes and soap making. The oil cake being rich in protein is fed to cattles.

The fruit has excellent flavour and is mainly consumed as a dry fruit being eaten for table purposes. Kernels are widely used in confectionary and bakery industries in the preparations like cake, pastries, chocolate, candy and ice-cream. Edible oil is extracted from the kernels. The nuts are processed by blanching, slicing, chopping, grinding into paste and butter and combining with other foods. The kernels are also taken as snacks between regular meals. Walnut shell flour is extensively used as an ingredient in plastic fillers, battery cases, moulding resin forms, industrial tile and as insecticide spreader. The tree yields valuable timber, which is most suitable for carving, making furniture and butts of guns.

BOTANY

Walnut belong to the family Juglandaceae and genus **Juglans.** The genus **Juglans** includes about 21 species among which ***Juglans regia*** (English or Persian walnut) is the most important being commercially cultivated in many countries. The other species are grown locally for timber and nuts. The somatic chromosome number (2 n) of Juglans is 32. The important species of genus Juglans are as follows :

(i) *Juglans californica* : **Southern California black walnut**
(ii) *Juglans hindsii* : **Northern California black walnut**
(iii) *Juglans jamaicensis* : **West Indian walnut**
(iv) *Juglans major* : **Arizona black walnut**
(v) *Juglans microcarpa* : **Texas black walnut**
(vi) *Juglans nigra* : **Eastern black walnut**
(vii) *Juglans ailantifolia* : **Japanese walnut**
(viii) *Juglans cathayensis* : **Chinese walnut**
(ix) *Juglans mandschurica* : **Manchurian walnut**
(x) *Juglans cinerea* : **The buttera nut**

Walnut is a deciduous tree. Leaves alternate, odd pinnate, large, aromatic, estipulate, leaflets opposite, serrate or entire. Flowers monoecious, the staminate flowers on last year's branchlets in lateral peduncles catkins, each consisting of a bract bearing 8-40 stamens, 2 bractlets and 1-4 calyx lobes. Pistillate flowers in few to many flowered terminal racemes with 4 calyx lobes and a 3-lobbed involucre consisting of a bract and 2 bractlets. Fruit a large indehiscent drupe. Nut thick walled, incompletely 2-4 celled, indehiscent or finally separating into 2 valves. Seed 2-4 lobed, remaining within the shell in germination. Flowers appear before or after the leaves. Edible portion is cotyledons.

CLIMATE

Walnut is found growing in all parts of the Himalayan region between the elevation of 1200 to 2100 metres above sea level. It requires a climate which is free from frost in spring and from extreme heat in summer. A temperature of even 2-3°C below freezing point (0°C) results in the killing of a large percentage of young walnut flowers if they are just starting to bloom.

If the summers are very hot, the nuts get sunburnt and such nuts usually become Blanks particularly if the temperature goes to about 37.8°C in the shade and humidity is low.

Sufficient chilling is needed for bud opening and blooming. The chilling requirement of different varieties ranges from 700 to 1500 hours. But, most cultivars needed 800 hours of winter temp. below 7°C for normal growth. Temperature of 29–32°C near harvest time result in well filled kernels. In cool summers, walnuts become excessively shrivelled.

The walnut is mostly grown in the mid-hills of Kashmir, Kulu Valley in Himachal Pradesh and Uttarakhand and Arunachal Pradesh. They grow well in areas with rainfall of about 76 cm or more.

In Kashmir, walnut cultivation is practised at an altitude of about 2000 m or more. A site, where frequent hailstorms are experienced or cold air settles down in low land making a frost pocket, is unsuitable for walnut. Higher northern sloping land is preferable to southern slopes and low lands as the plants growing there are less subjected to frost injury. The growth on northern slopes starts later because these are cooler than southern slopes. Evaporation on northern slope is considerably less as compared to southern slope.

SOIL

The soil most suitable for walnuts is a well drained, deep, silt loam containing an abundance of organic matter. Soil pH influences the availability of mineral nutrients and maturity of which are available to the plant in the pH range of 6-7. Soil should not have a fluctuating water level, hardpan, and sandy sub-soil. A soil 2-3 metres deep gives the best results because walnut roots penetrate upto a depth of about 3 metres. The sub soil should be free from solid rock, impervious clay or gravel layers which restrict root growth. The trees growing on shallow soil with less moisture content are liable to suffer more from sunburn than the trees growing on a deep silt soil. Alkaline soils and sandy sub-soils should be avoided for walnut growing.

CHOICE OF VARIETIES

All the walnut trees in India are of seedling origin except few seedlings locally named as cultivars. In Jammu and Kashmir, the survey of walnut growing areas was conducted and few promising varieties like Karan and Bulbul were released. Lake English, Drainovsky, Opex Caulchry, Hamdan and Suliman are other varieties grown in different parts of Kashmir. In Himachal Pradesh some promising selections are recommended to the growers are Gobind, Kandhaghat Selection, Tapan, Roopa, Eureka, Placenta, Wilson, Kashmir Budded, Franquette, Kotkhai Solution-1, Partap, Rattan, Kainthala Selection and Laxmi. From Garhwal hills of Uttarakhand, seedling selections such as Chakrata, 2, 4, 6 and 13 have been found promising. The followings are the important cultivars grown in Kashmir, Himachal Pradesh and Uttarakhand.

Payne : The trees are moderately vigorous. It can be grown in solid blocks because pollen and stigma mature simultaneously. Nut is medium to small and is well sealed. Paper shelled, medium sized kernels, good appearance and excellent in taste. It is a heavy yielder due to fruitfulness of lateral buds.

Franquette : The trees are large and upright. Nut is small and shell seal is good. Kernel 48 per cent, light coloured and good in quality. The variety mature late.

Lake English : The trees are medium in size. It is a semi hard shelled variety which yields medium sized nuts regularly. Nut is dull white with light brown kernel. Its separation from hull is easy. Filling and taste are very good.

Serr : The trees are vigorous but give average yield. The variety is well adapted to warm areas. Kernel 59 per cent, light coloured and good in quality. It is damaged by later spring frosts, codling moth and blight disease.

Eureka : The cracking quality of this variety is good. Nut is medium in size and shell seal is very good. Kernel 50 percent, light brown in colour and excellent in quality.

Placentia : The trees are small in size. It is an early maturing variety. Nut size is medium and shell seal is good. Kernel 48 per cent and whitish in colour.

Gobind : It ripens in the end of September under Kinnaur conditions. Nut size is medium, well filled and thin shelled. Kernel cremish in colour and good in quality.

Hamdan : It is precocious and dwarfing in nature. Nut weight is 14 g. Smooth shelled. Nut longer than breadth. Shelling percentage is 54.

Wilson : Nuts of this variety are somewhat flattened. The quality of nut is good. It matures in fall.

Partap : It is a selection from Kotkhai. Nut large, oblong, weight 24g, smooth surface with light amber colour. It is a semi thin shelled variety. Cracking and shelling quality excellent. Light coloured kernel with excellent taste. Heavy bearer variety

Hensen : It is a winter hardy variety and well adapted to a wide range of conditions. Self pollinating. Paper shelled with high kernel percentage.

Neilson, Blackmore, Kotkhai Selection-1, Solding Selection, Suliman, CITH walnut-6, 7 and 8, Tutle 16 and Tutle 31 are other important selections.

PROPAGATION AND ROOTSTOCKS

Walnut can be propagated either by seed or by vegetative methods. The seedlings are highly variable producing the nuts of inferior quality with an average shelling percentage of 30-35 per cent as compared to 50-60 per cent of good commercial cultivars.

Seed Propagation : The majority of trees in India are of seedling origin and as such they bear nuts of variable quality. The seedlings are usually raised for rootstock purpose but in this case hard-shelled nuts of inferior quality are sown. Although walnut germinates without stratification under some conditions, yet proper stratification is desirable for good germination and growth.

The walnuts should be collected from vigorous and high yielding trees. The desirable characters to look for in the selection of nuts are big size, bright brown colour and good cracking quality of the shell, bright yellow colour, good taste and flavour of the kernel. The moist nuts are placed in alternate layers with a suitable medium such as vermiculite, peat moss or sand in container and then subjected to cold treatment (3-5°C) for a period of 2-3 months. The nuts can also be sown directly in the nursery or field in fall, but the soil is to be kept just moist, neither dry not wet.

The walnuts ae stratified till December. If the soil is ready for sowing, the nuts are sown immediately in well prepared beds at a distance of 60 cm in row to row and 30 cm in seed to seed. The walnuts are sown 8-10 cm deep. The germination starts in the beginning of March. The seedlings do not attain good height in the first year but their root system is well developed. In the second year, the seedlings develop quickly and are ready for transplanting by the time the growth stops in the autumn. Seeds can also be sown **in situ** in December.

A large number of factors such as nut type, size, position of seed, planting depth, soil moisture and temperature and seed treatment influence the germination of seeds. The planting of large nuts at 7 cm depth in soil in vertical position gives better germination and seedling growth. The walnut of medium size (3-4 cm long) gave a germination of 90 per cent compared with only 71 per cent for smaller seeds and 85 per cent for larger ones. Higher germination of seeds sown in a vertical position was noticed than those placed flat in the soil. Treatment of nut with gibberellic acid at 750-1000 ppm increase the germination percentage and height of seedlings. Treating the seeds with ethrel at 100-1000 ppm was found to improve germination.

When the seedlings are to be left in place for about 2 years or more, a spacing of one metre between rows and 30 cm between seeds is a common practice. The mulch can be placed to conserve moisture and control the weeds which helps in better germination and growth of the seedlings. In order to ensure the establishment of grafts after transplanting, their taproot is cut off 20-25 cm below the ground level which should be done about a year before actual transplanting.

Rootstocks : The commercial walnut can be grown on a number of rootstocks such as seedlings of ***Juglans regia, Juglans hindsii, Juglans nigra, Juglans microcarpa, Juglans californica, Juglans sieboldiana*** **and** Paradox ***(J. hindsii*** × ***J. regia). Juglans regia*** is the most easily available rootstock in India and is the only one used whenever walnut trees are raised by budding or grafting. This rootstock has better compatibility and is particularly suitable for light soils. It is known for its resistance to crown rot disease. However, it is unsuitable for waterlogged, saline and nematode infected soils.

Vegetative Propagation : Walnut can be propagated vegetatively by grafting, budding and stooling. The per cent success in grafting and budding in walnut is lower than in pome and stone fruits. Better success in grafting by cleft, tongue and splice methods was obtained when grafting was either done in a greenhouse have temperature 28°C and relative humidity 80-100% or the grafts after preparation were placed in the incubator at 25 ± 1°C temperature with 75 ± 2% humidity.

The most common method of grafting practised in the case of this nut is cleft grafting. It gives higher success when incubated at 26°C and 90% relative humidity for 3 weeks before planting in the nursery. Better survival of grafts is obtained when grafting operation is carried out in the middle of January rather than in the last week of December or in the middle of February. Veneer grafting carried out in July gave more than 80% success followed by tongue grafting done in the late January with 50% success.

Patch budding is common among the budding method which give 30-35% success. Mid June is found an optimum time of budding. Removal of leaf blades 15 days before budding operation enhanced bud take. In Kashmir, the methods of patch budding and crown grafting have been found fairly successful. Walnut can also be propagated through annular budding and chip budding. Annular budding gives a very high percentage of bud take in walnut when performed during the month of July. Chip budding during May give good performance in walnut.

Stooling is an another method of vegetative propagation which can be performed in walnut. To obtain good rooting and better establishment of stool layers, the growth regulators like IBA, IAA and NAA can be used. The mother stools of the commerical cultivars will have to be raised by cuttings or layers in the first instance.

PLANTING OPERATION

Walnut when planted on flat land, square, quincunx and retangular system are followed but when it is to be planted on sloping land, contour and terrace system of layout are practised. Square system is commonly adopted in walnut. In India, walnut is usually grown on hill slopes. It is better to dig pits of one square metre dimension and then fill them with mixture of well rotten farmyard manure and soil 1 : 2 proportion in the month of November. The plants should be purchased well in advance of actual planting and be healed immediately on arrival after laying them in a trench and covering the root portion with moist soil which should never be allowed to go dry in the process.

The planting is done in late dormant season or early spring season. A walnut tree takes about 15-20 years to occupy the entire space alloted to it in conventional planting system leaving sufficient space unutilized in early stages. Therefore, a spacing of 6.6 × 6.6 m should be kept initially and should be adjusted 6.6 × 9.3 m finally by pruning and removal of temporary trees. In certain areas, the distance from row to row and plant to plant is kept 12 metres, which accommodates 70 plants per hectare. The planting can be kept 7.5 to 9.0 m depending upon the soil and climatic conditions.

The plant should be topped 40-50 cm above the graft union. Frequent watering is required in the first summer season. The trunks should be painted white to prevent sunburn.

FLOWERING AND FRUITING

The walnut seedlings take about 8-10 years to come into bearing but grafted begin fruiting early in about 4 or 5 years. Walnut is monoecious plant i.e. staminate and pistillate flowers are born separately on the same tree. The staminate flowers emerge laterally on the previous season's growth and hang in catkins. The pistillate flowers appear in pairs in the form of nutlets at the tip of current season's growth. Though the fruit bud formation of a pistillate flower is initiated during summer, yet its final development occurs shortly before anthesis in the following spring. Under Shimla conditions, peak flowering period of walnut is mid-April which is prolonged till the first week of May in late blooming cultivars.

The fruit growth begins and continues with the stimulation of pollination and fertilization. The nonpollinated pistillate flowers make some initial growth but ultimately drop down after about three weeks in absence of fertilization. The mesocarp started to form on 22-25 May, the testa on 3-8 June, the endocarp began to develop on 20-26 June and to harden on 5-10 August and the nuts matured on 15-25 September. Two rapid periods of walnut fruit growth are interspersed by a period of relatively slow growth. During the first growth period, the fruit gains size and weight. The fruit attains form and becomes richer in chemical constituents during the second growth period. In the developing walnut fruit, glucose, sucrose and fructose are the predominent sugars. Ethylene application hastens fruit abscission.

ORCHARD CULTURAL PRACTICES

Irrigation

Walnut trees are grown under rainfed conditions. However, whenever the rain is not sufficient and well distributed, irrigation is essential for walnut cultivation. Inadequate water supply to the trees results in slow growth, reduced yield and low nut quality, but excess of it retards orchard development and causes root and crown diseases. Where irrigation is available, it will be an advantage to apply casual irrigations to the trees. This will help them to put on better growth and start bearing early. To the bearing trees, irrigation from the time of fruit set till its maturity proves helpful in reducing the fruit drop and better filling of nuts. The water requirement decreases with the development of roots in adult trees. If irrigation facility is available it should be applied 2-4 weeks before expected harvest for obtaining plump kernals.

Manuring and Fertilization

Generally, no fertilizers are given to walnut trees in India. To avoid alternate bearing, it will be a good practice to manure the trees every year with nitrogenous and phosphatic fertilizers.

Nitrogen fertilization is essential for successful walnut cultivation. An application of 175-225 kg N per ha is sufficient to prevent the occurrence of nitrogen deficiency. Walnut do not respond to phosphorus application. To cope the need of potassium, a single application of 350 kg potassium sulphate per ha should be given.

For good growth of walnut trees 180 kg N, 180 kg P_2O_5 and 60 kg K_2O per hectare is considered optimum. For getting the highest yield and net profit, a general application of 60 kg/ha each of N, P and K is suggested. The bearing tree of walnut should be supplied with 50–100 kg of farmyard manure every year in the month of December. The fertilizer mixture should be applied during early spring before the start of new growth.

In Kashmir, 2 kg nitrogen, 500 g phosphorus and 1.5 kg potash is suggested to full grown tree of 20 years and above. Phosphorus, potash and half nitrogen is applied two weeks before expected bloom. Rest of the nitrogen should be split into two equal doses, one to be applied three weeks after fruit set and second during early July.

Zinc deficiency occur in walnut trees. It can be corrected with the foliar spray or 0.4 per cent zinc sulphate.

TRAINING AND PRUNING

Walnut bear fruits on one year old wood which is produced either terminally or both terminally and laterally. In this way walnut cultivars are of two types viz. terminal bearer and lateral bearer. The cultivars which bear terminally are thinned but not headed back. The lateral bearer cultivars are both thinned and headed back heavily in order to encourage shoot growth which get suppressed due to early fruit production.

Walnut trees are trained according to central leader or modified leader system. After the first year growth, the plant is headed back at the height of 2 m from ground level. All lateral are removed leaving one or two shoots at lower level on trunk. To avoid narrow crotches, all primary buds 1.3 m above the ground should be removed forcing the secondary buds to grow. Select 5 – 6 scaffold branches spirally spaced about 50 cm apart. After selecting the main scaffold limb 1.6m above the ground, the other primary scaffold limbs are selected to the various directions on the trunk. The distance between these should be kept 30 cm. All other vigorous branches should be removed where as small branches are left undisturbed for fruiting. All the selected limbs should be headed back on early fruiting cultivars but not on late fruiting ones. In later years, secondary scaffold limbs on primary scaffold ones are also allowed to grow by removing the extra vigorous branches. In early fruiting cultivars all scaffold limbs are headed back every year.

Pruning of young bearing trees : In the cultivars highly fruitful on lateral buds, the shoot growth is suppressed due to heavy crop load. Therefore, a large number of new shoots should be headed back on the periphery to reduce fruiting and increase vigorous shoot growth throughout the tree's periphery. The pruning in terminal bearing cultivars consists of heading back of selected framework branches and thinning out of competing limbs.

Pruning of mature trees : The main objective of pruning in mature trees is to obtain regular and high production of quality nuts. The overcrowding of branches, insufficient production of renewal wood and inadequate availability of sunlight reduced the yield and quality of nuts. The pruning of mature tree should be directed to control tree size and maintain vigour and fruitfulness of spurs. It should be done in such a way to develop renewal wood and to replace older and less productive branches. The weak, dead or interfering branches should be removed.

In mature trees shading is a problem as it reduces photosynthesis thereby weakens spur growth. Hence selective thinning out of limbs in the top and sides of the tree should be initiated well before overcrowding becomes serious. The pruning should be carried out in the dormant season or early spring.

TOP WORKING

In the hills a large number of young seedling trees produce inferior quality nuts. On the other hand, a high rate of mortality found in the transplanting of grafted or budded plants. The top working thus becomes very useful choice for walnut production. As the rootstock is already well established, the scion makes rapid growth and commences bearing earlier than the transplanted grafted trees. Top-working is usually carried out by modified cleft grafting or bark grafting late in the spring season or when new growth has taken place. The dormant scion wood should be cut from parent tree quite in advance and be stored in refrigerator after proper packing. Bleeding is a problem in top-grafting especially when it is done in early spring. This problem can be avoided by heading back the rootstock two weeks earlier of actual operation. After grafting, the open wound must be covered by grafting wax. The stem portion needs white washing to give protection against sunburning.

POLLINATION

The walnut is monoecious. The pollen is distributed by wind. The wind may carry the pollen upto 2 km but the effective range of distribution is 60 metres to 90 metres. The walnut is self fertile but pollination is not satisfactory in certain varieties mostly because these varieties fail to mature their pollen at time when the female flowers are receptive . The pollen of any variety is capable of fertilizing its own pistils or those of any variety. Snowfall or very cold weather at the time of flowering cause poor setting of the crop.

In certain regions, the varieties Payne, Eureka and Franquette shed their pollen before their pistillate flowers are receptive. In other places the varieties Placentia and others of Santa Barbara soft shell seedling group tend to shed their pollen after the pistillate flowers have ceased to be receptive. Hot spring weather somewhat hastens the development of catkins and makes them shed their pollen quickely. The pollination difficulties in established orchards can be solved temporarily by bringing catkins from the adjoining plantations and hanging them in the trees and permanently by top-working certain limbs with the desirable varieties. From pollination and marketing point of view, Waterloo and Eureka and Hartley and Payne are examples of desirable combinations.

Young trees just coming into bearing often do not produce enough catkins to supply pollen for all the pistillate flowers. The catkins on such trees have also a greater tendency to shed their pollen and drop before the pistillate flowers are receptive. More catkins are produced as the trees grow older and the pollen is shed over a long period thus making pollination more satisfactory. The new plantation of walnut if located near the existing bearing trees will come into bearing at an earlier age and yield more than if they are planted in isolation away from the bearing trees.

HARVESTING AND HANDLING OF FRUITS

Harvesting at proper maturity and subsequent handling of the nuts are of prime importance. Any delay in picking after maturity of kernels deteriorates the quality and increases the incidence of mould and pests. For determining the harvesting date of the walnut, two maturity indices are normally followed. The nuts are covered over with hulls which split at the time of maturity causing the fall of nut on the ground. When about 80% of the hulls have cracked exposing the nuts, it is the time for walnut picking. The harvesting is usually done after about two weeks of browning. If the harvesting is further delayed, the kernel turns darker. Ethephon at the rate of 200-500 ppm on kernel maturity advances harvesting by about 10 days.

The best time of harvesting the walnut is September-October. The nuts fall down on the ground are collected or they are made to drop on the ground by shaking the branches with hand or striking them with bamboo poles. The total harvest is done in two or three times at few days interval. The nuts are collected from the ground, cleaned, washed and dried by spreading them on a sheet or floor. Dipping of nuts in 1500 ppm ethephon while the hulls are still on, loosens the hull in 3–4 days. Sometimes in order to improve the appearance of nuts, these are bleached with either alkali or acid solution. The nuts which fall down with their husks intact are generally of second grade and after removal of the husks, cleaning and drying they should be stored and marketed separately to fetch higher rate of superior lot.

The nuts should be graded suitably according to the size, colour and variety. This practice can bring higher returns than marketing the whole lot mixed. The Indian walnuts are categorised into four categories viz. Paper shelled, Thin shelled, Medium shelled and Hard shelled.

Yield varies according to the age, size and variety of trees. Full commercial bearing commences after 18-20 years in seedling trees and after 8-10 years in grafted trees. A full grown big size tree may bear 150-175 kg nuts but an average yield is only around 40 kg.

Delay in drying causes rapid loss in nut quality and makes it susceptible to mould. Walnuts are dried to remove excess moisture from the shell and kernel. Drying of nuts stabilizes the product weight and prolongs storage life. The nuts are dried up to 8 per cent moisture level.

Walnuts are stored in gunny bags in small ventilated rooms free from excessive humidity. For export purpose, they are packed in double gunny bags. The boxes are lined with paper on all sides to avoid shaking and breaking of walnuts.

INSECT-PESTS

1. Codling moth (*Cydia pomonella*) : It is found in Ladakh region. Three generations of moth damage the fruits. Its first generation larvae enter the growing fruit through the blossom and cause dropping of immature fruits. The second and third generation of pest enter the nut through the side of the husk.

For its control, synthetic pheromone traps should be installed in May. Spray Diazinon or carbaryl (0.2%) for its control.

2. Indian gypsy moth (*Lymantria obfuscata*) : It hatched in the month of March. The caterpillars feed on buds and leaves. The pest hide during day under rocks, stones, soil and attacks the foliage after sunset which result into defoliation.

The pest can be effectively checked by applying fenvalerate (0.03%).

3. Walnut green aphid (*Chromaphis juglandicola*) : They suck sap from the underside of leaves and tender shoots during April to September. Due to severe infestation, leaves fall, kernels shrivel and sooty mould develops on honeydew.

The granules of disulfotan (5%) should be mixed thoroughly in the soil around the tree trunk to check the aphid attack. Spray dimethoate (0.03%) during and May to early June.

4. Walnut weevil (*Alcidodes porrectirostris*) : Its female lay eggs on the fruits. On hatching it feed by boring hole on kernels causing premature fruit drop. The adult weevils emerge from fruits and feed on petioles and tender shoots. The grub kill new shoots upto the old wood.

The pest can be checked by spraying twice carbaryl (0.2%) at 7 days interval. If feasible, spray the trees into quinalphos (0.04%).

5. Leopard moth (*Zeuzera spp.*) : The caterpillar bore into shoots and branches and pupate inside them. The attacked leaves and shoots wilt and die. The moth completes a single life cycle in about 2 years.

Insert cotton-wool soaked in carbon bisulphide, paradichlorobenzene or ethyl acetate in the hole. Seal the holes then with mud.

6. Walnut blister mite (*Eriophyes erineus*) : It is active from April to October. Suck the sap of leaves, yellow cavities on under surface and blister like swelling on the upper surface of leaves. Leaf size remain small in the nursery plants results stunted growth.

Spray the infested trees with dimethoate (0.02%) or Kalathene (0.05%) at bud swelling stage. Repeat the spray if need arises.

DISEASES

1. Anthracnose/Blotch : It is caused by fungus *Gnomonia leptostyla*. It is found in Kashmir Valley and symptoms are noted on leaves, young shoots and fruits. Initially small, circular light brown spots develop into large blotches involving a major part of lamina.

Collect and burn the fallen leaves. Spray Bordeaux mixture (4 : 4 : 50) or copper oxychloride (250–300 *g* in 100 litres of water) at the leaf unfolding stage, then after two weeks and at full leaf stage.

2. Die-back or Canker : The disease is caused by ***Glomerella cingulata***. The disease is prevalent in Jammu and Kashmir and Uttarakhand. Iregular dark brown spots appear on leaves which involve the entire leaf causing defoliation. Blighting of twigs is also common and young plant may die.

Spray Mancozeb or copper oxychloride (300 *g* in 100 litres of water) before rainy season. Repeat the spray if the disease is severe.

3. Walnut blight : Its causal organism is ***Xanthomonas arboricola*** pv. Juglandis.

The disease enters into the tree through stomata, wounds and insect puncture in the presence of free water. The bacteria attack all tissues of leaves, catkins and nuts. Brown and black spots with yellowish green perimeter develop on the leaves. Individual florets die in the distorted infected catkins. Nuts are dropped due to early infection but shrivelled and become discoloured due to late infection. Rainfall, fog and dew further aggravate the blight problem.

The first spray of Bordeaux mixture (2 : 2 : 250) is applied on the opening of first female flower. It should be followed by subsequent sprays of one to two weeks interval.

4. Black line disease (Viral) : It is reported in different walnut growing regions in India. The disease can be transmitted through infected pollens, seeds and scion wood.

For its control only virus-free scion wood should be used for grafting and budding.

5. Downy leafspot : It is caused by ***Microstroma juglandis***. The disease is serious in Kashmir. The white mould appear in geometric patches on the ventral side of leaves which may coalesce turning into large irregular shapes.

It can be controlled by spraying twice with bavistin 50 WP (0.03%) in June at an interval of 15 days.

6. Powdery mildew : The causal organism of this disease is ***Phyllactinia roboris.*** Greyish to white powdery spore mass appears on upper and lower surface of leaves.

Spray the trees wettable sulphur (300 *g* /100 litres of water) or carbendazim fungicide (50 *g* /100 litres of water). (*i*) during the late dormancy (*ii*) At bud swelling stage (*iii*) At petal fall and (*iv*) two weeks later.

CHAPTER 33

Cherry

Cherries occupy unique position among temperate fruits. The cultivated cherries are divided into two main groups i.e. sweet cherries (***Prunus avium*** L.) and sour cherries (***Prunus cerasus*** L.). The cultivation of sweet cherry has been taken up on a commercial scale in Kashmir Valley.

ORIGIN AND HISTORY

Cherries are considered natives of South East Europe and Asia Minor and as far east as northern India and China. The sweet cherry probably originated between the Black Sea and the Capsian Sea, but birds seem to have carried it into Europe in an ancient times. Diverse forms of sour cherry exist in eastern Europe and western region of earstwhile Soviet Union. On the basis of earliest records cherry was first domesticated in Greece around 300 B.C. It then spread to Italy and established as a fruit crop by 37 BC. By Christ's time it spread to England, Germany, Belgium and Portugal. Seeds of cherry were brought to North America by early settlers which eventually spread all over the northern parts and southern most parts of South America.

AREA AND PRODUCTION

The world production of cultivated cherry fruit is about 2.2 million tonnes. Europe produce 40 per cent of world production : Turkey, USA, Iran, Italy, Spain, Austria, Uzbekistan, Romania, Rusia, Ukraine etc. are the leading cherry producing countries.

Cherry cultivation in India is confined to Kashmir, Himachal Pradesh and hilly areas of Uttarakhand. Jammu and Kashmir is the mainly cherries growing state. The total area in this state is 3500 hectares with annual production of 10880 metric tonnes. This state produces 70 per cent of total cherry production in India. In Himachal Pradesh, area under cherry growing is 500 hectares producing 900 metric tonnes annually. The higher reaches of Shimla, Kullu, Mandi, Chamba, Kinnaur and Lahual-Spiti have emerged ideal for the cultivation of cherry.

IMPORTANCE AND USES

Cherries are rich in protein, sugars, carotene and folic acid. Its fruit is also rich in potassium, calcium, magnesium, iron and zinc. Cherries contains 83.7% water, 1.2% protein,

0.2% fat, 3.7% fructose, 4.9% glucose, 280 mg potassium, 30 mg calcium, 12 mg magnesium, 0.4 mg iron, 18 mg vitamin C and 747 I.U carotene per 100 g of edible fruit.

The sweet cherry is mainly used for table purposes and also in canned fruit cocktails, bakery, confectionary, ice-cream, juice making, fruit salads and distilling liquor.

The sour cherry is mainly used for processing purposes. The wine made from sour cherry is very popular. The fruits are largely preserved by canning, freezing and sun drying. Both fresh and frozen fruits are utilized for making cherry juice.

BOTANY

Cherries belong to the family Rosaceae, genus **Prunus** and subgenus **Cerasus.** ***Prunus avium*** and ***Prunus cerasus*** are the two most important commercial species.

Sweet Cherry : It is a tall tree with strong central leader, bark red-brown, scaling is transverse strips. Leaves usually oblong-ovate to oblong-obovate, gradually taper pointed, blade 10-15 cm long, soft in texture, hanging limp on the young growths, margins doubly acute-glandular-serrate at first but becoming more or less obtuse-serrate, the petiole usually bearing one or more large glands near top. Flowers white about 3 cm across, appearing with the first leaves from clusters of buds on lateral spurs, the inner glandular bud-scales large and persistent for a time, on glabrous pedicels about 3 cm long, calyx tube constricted near top, the lobes entire. Fruit globular or heart shaped, yellow or red with mostly sweet flesh.

On the basis of the texture of flesh, sweet cherries have been divided into two pomological groups i.e. Heart and Bigarreau. The Heart Cherry cultivars have soft and tender flesh and heart-shaped fruits. The fruit colour varies from dark with reddish juice to light coloured with colourless juice. The Bigarreau group are usually roundish, may be more or less heart-shaped. The colour of fruit and juice also varies from dark to light red. Cherry fruit is drupe and its edible portion is edicarp and mesocarp.

Sour Cherry : The tree is usually 6-9 m tall, open headed, round topped or spreading and often without a central leader. The branches are slender and more or less drooping. Fruit is 2 cm in diameter, roundish-oblate or cordate with slightly compressed sides. Leaves are much smaller and darker green in colour. The commonly grown cultivars are more hardy than sweet cherry.

CLIMATE

The sour cherry can tolerate more cold than sweet cherry. In the nursery stage sweet cherry suffered more bud damage at – 25 to – 33°C as compared to sour cherry. In the orchard also the sweet cherry suffer more from frost than sour cherry. Sour cherry requires 15°C mean temperature during the growing period and do not thrive well in warm climate. The sweet cherry is badly damaged at both severe cold and warm climate. Sweet cherries are well adapted to an elevation. 1500 – 2500 MSL. It require 1000 – 1500 hr. chilling period during winter. Climatic conditions of Kashmir and high hills of Himachal Pradesh are ideal for commercial growing of sweet cherry.

Always select frost free site for cherry as it is badly damaged by spring frosts. Hill slop is a preferable site where the cold air may drain down. The trees grown on the southern aspect on low elevations may suffer from drought in May-June. The southern aspect at higher elevations prove beneficial. An annual rainfall of 100 – 120 cm well distributed throughout the year is desirable. Heavy rains at the time of flowering and towards the ripening period cause heavy damage. Rain at flowering time results in blossom wilt as the spores of wilt enter through the stigma of the opened flowers. Fruit cracking is common due to rain at the time of fruit ripening. The fruits become under sized and shrivelled due to high transpiration rate.

SOIL

The cherry grow better on soil having high level of fertility. It give better performance on well-drained warm, deep, free-working and sandy loam soils. Soil should be able to hold sufficient water for 15-20 days during the period of high water requirement. Cherries do not tolerate wet feet, therefore, water-logged soils should be avoided. Planting of Cherris in clay soils should be avoided.

CHOICE OF VARIETIES

A large number of sweet cherry varieties have been tried out in the Shimla Hills, the Kulu Valley and the Kashmir Valley. The varieties of sweet cherry grown in Jammu and Kashmir, Himachal Pradesh and Uttarakhand are as follow :

Jammu and Kashmir : Black Heart, Early Purple Black Heart, Bigarreau Napolean, Guigne Noir, Gross Lucenta, Guigne Noir Hative and Bigarreau Noir Gross, White Bigarreau, Bigarreau de Schrecken.

Himachal Pradesh. Bing, Stella, White Heart, Early Rivers, Napolian White, Sam, Van, Lambert, Sue, Black Repulican, Emperor Francis, Black Tortarian.

Uttarakhand. Bedford Prolific, Black Heart, Governor Wood.

Brief description of important varieties is as follows :

Bedford Prolific : Its skin is black. Flesh of good taste and flavoured. Ripens by the middle of May. It is early flowering cultivar.

Early Rivers : This is the finest early cherry cultivar which ripens in the beginning of May. Fruits are large, black, oval with a small stone. The pink flesh is deliciously flavoured. The bearing is usually moderate but regular. It is resistant to cracking.

Bigarreau Napolean : Fruit very large and handsome with red skin. Flesh firm, sweet and juicy. It ripens by the end of June. It is late variety. The average yield is 19 kg fruit/plant.

Governor Wood : The fruits are large sized, heart shaped, light yellow with red cheek. The quality of white flesh is fair, soft and travels badly. It ripens during second week of May and needs to be picked green. It is regular prolific bearer variety. It is, however, very susceptible to brown rot.

Emperor Francis : The fruit is large and dark red in colour having good keeping quality. It flowers early but otherwise a late cultivar. The tree is a regular and good bearer.

White Bigarreau: The fruits are large in size with red skin. Flesh of very good taste. Ripens by the middle of May. Flowering mid-season.

Bigarreau de Schrecken : Fruit large-sized with black skin. Flesh sweet and of good quality and fine-flavoured. Ripens in the beginning of May. The fruit is susceptible to cracking in rain. Flowering mid-season.

Bing : The fruit is of the highest quality but cracks readily in rain. The tree is upright and spreading and bears moderate to heavy crop of large fruits. The blossom buds are susceptible to low temperatures.

Early Purple Black Heart. The tree is vigorous. Fruit is large, round and heart shaped. Skin is thick, fine red and blended with purple black. Pulp is fine and good. It ripens by the end of May and rated as good table variety.

Compact Lambert, Compact Stella, Salmo, Jubilee, Kristin, Van, Viscount, Montmorency, Meteor, North Star, English Morello, Early Richmond and CITH Cherry-1 and 2 are some leading new cultivars of cherry.

PROPAGATION AND ROOTSTOCKS

The cherries are propagated by stooling, cutting, budding and grafting. Budding or grafting is done on the seedlings or vegetatively propagated rootstocks. The cherries are mostly grafted on the seedlings of ***Prunus cerasoides*** or ***Prunus avium*** or ***Stockton morello* (*Prunus cerasus*)** .

Seed Propagation : The seeds of cherries need stratification for good percentage of seed germination. Stones of Waterloo and Misri cvs. are used for statification and better germination.

Stratification is done by placing the seed of cherries between the layers of moist sand, vermiculite and then storing in a cool place at 2-4°C temperature for a period of 80-120 days for Mahaleb and 120-150 days for Mazzard seeds. Before stratification, the seed should be soaked in GA_3 500 ppm for about 24 hours. Seeds are kept in the stratification medium until the embryonic root pushes out the seed covering. The seeds should be immediately planted after stratification is over. The sprouted seeds are transplanted 10 – 15 cm apart in rows spaced at 20 – 25 cm in nursery beds. The nursery beds should be mulched with 10 – 15 cm thick hay and light irrigation is applied. Mulch material is removed when seedlings attain 5 cm height. In case of high temperature the seeds may again enter into dormancy and fail to germinate.

Vegetative Propagation : The plants can be multiplied by stooling, cutting, suckers, budding and grafting.

Stooling : In Spring, the mother plant is cut back at the ground level before sprouting. When the shoots attain 25-30 cm length, their bases are covered with a mound of soil or sawdust building the mound to a height of 20-30 cm. Roots arise from the bases of the shoots and grow into the mound. Treating the ringid portion of F 12/1 rootstock with 7500 ppm IBA during summer, cent per cent rooting can be obtained. The mound is kept moist throughout the summer. The shoots normally become well-rooted by the winter and are transplanted in the nursery rows for a year to produce strong plants for budding or grafting. Suckers of **Prunus mahaleb** and **Prunus avium** are removed during winter. When the suckers attained thickness of 0.6 cm in diameter, then they can be grafted or budded during the next spring.

Cutting : Hardwood stem cuttings are made between late fall to early spring. The cuttings can be treated with 100 ppm IBA for 24 hours to obtain higher success. Semi hard wood cuttings are leafy and are usually taken during mid or late summer.

Colt rootstock is easy to root and can be easily multiplied through cuttings. Hard-wood cuttings are prepared in February and treated with IBA 2500 ppm for 10 seconds and planted in the nursery beds for rooting. These are grafted with desired scion variety in March.

Budding and grafting : Budding is done after the sap flow started i.e. from the last week of April to the last week of May. T-budding gives higher per cent success. For grafting, the scion wood is collected during the winter when the buds are dormant. Cleft grafting is considered the best method which is performed during February-March.

Rootstocks

The most common rootstock in Kashmir, Himachal Pradesh and Kumaon hills of Uttarakhand is Paja **(*Prunus cerasoides* var. Majestic)** seedlings. Colt (a semi dwarfing rootstock) ***Prunus avium* × *Prunus pseudocerasus*)** is used in Kashmir. The old plantations are found on Mazzard **(*Prunus avium*)** or Mahaleb **(*Prunus mahaleb*)** rootstocks. The wild cherry ***Prunus paddum* (bird cherry)** found growing wild in Shimla hills and adjoining areas is also sometimes used as a rootstock. The Paja rootstock has been observed to show delayed incompatibility with commercial cultivars of sweet cherry. The plants of cherry on Paja make good growth during the first 8-9 years, then start showing signs of illhealth, decline and completely decline or die after 14-15 years. In Himachal Pradesh, Paja rootstock has now been dispensed with and the clonal rootstock Colt and Mazzard F 12/1 are recommended. Colt is compatible with most of the sweet cherry varieties. It has good ancharge and resistant to gummosis and crown rot. Mazzard F12/1 is a semi-vigorous rootstock. The cherry performance on ***Prunus cornuta*** is also studied. It is a vigorous and deciduous species growing wild in the Himalayan ranges between elevation of 2140 and 3060 metres. The graft success of cherry cv. Emperor Francis was 93 per cent on ***Prunus cerasoides*** and 63 per cent on ***Prunus cornuta***. However, the average linear growth of the grafts was 95 cm on **Prunus cornuta** compared to 41 cm on ***Prunus cerasoides.***

PLANTING OPERATION

While planting, there should not be hard pan or big stone either below or on its sides which may restrict the development of the roots. The pit for cherry plantation should be 1 × 1 × 1 × m dimension. The pit may be filled with a mixture of top soil and farmyard manure in 1 : 1 ratio. All the broken or injured roots should be cut off and treat the cut portion with fungicide. In areas where winter is not too severe, planting may be done in early winter, so that the root system is well established before the opening of the buds in spring. The planting of cherries may be delayed to late winter in the areas having severe winter.

The distance between the trees should vary from 9-12 metres, in this way 75-123 plants per hectare will be accommodated. In vigorous rootstock F 12/1 and in Mazzard seedlings, the distance should be kept 12 metres. The distance in Mahaleb seedling should be 9 metres. The cherry tree remain in a profitable condition for over 60 years. It is also recommended that orchard of sweet cherry should be planted 6 × 6 m apart by square or hexagonal system in Kashmir Valley and Himachal Pradesh.

FLOWERING AND FRUITING

The sweet cherry grafted on vigorous rootstocks like F 12/1 take about eight years to come in commercial bearing. The flowers of cherry appear laterally on one year old spurs and shoots. The spur elongates in almost a straight line for several successive years because the terminal bud is a leaf bud. The flowers of sweet cherries are bisexual and hypogynous.

The growth of cherry fruits follows a double sigmoidal curve i.e. there are three stages of fruit development. In stage first, the epidermal fruit cells increase in number and size rapidly. In second stage, the growth slows down, and thereafter increases tremendously in the stage third.

ORCHARD CULTURAL PRACTICES

Irrigation

The water need of cherries is more during spring and early summer. During growth and development period of fruit, the plants need irrigation at weekly interval. The rains start from middle of June and continue up to mid September. Only one irrigation after the rainy season is sufficient. Overwatering in cherries is not desirable as the plant is very sensitive to wet feet. The provision of drainage of excess rain water should be made. The average yield in sweet cherry increased when it is irrigated before and during fruit ripening. Its tree produce 20 per cent higher yield when irrigated at 80-85 per cent soil moisture level.

Manuring and Fertilization

The application of 150 g Nitrogen for every 2.5 cm girth of the plant is recommended in Himachal Pradesh. The fertilizer should be applied in early spring at about 2-3 weeks before bloom in a 60 cm wide land under the canopy of the plant. As most of the roots are at depths of 11-40 cm, placement of fertilizer and tillage should be shallow. In Himachal Pradesh, 500 g nitrogen, 250 g phosphorus and 650 g potassium is added to a ten year old plant of cherry. FYM, phosphorus and potash should be applied in December. Half nitrogen is applied in spring before flowering and the other half one month later.

Application of 600 *g* N, 300 *g* P_2O_5 and 900 *g* K_2O is recommended for 15 years old plants of sweet cherry in Kashmir Valley. Total phosphorus and potassium and half nitrogen is applied 2 weeks before expected bloom and remaining half of nitrogen 3 weeks after fruit-set.

Zinc deficiency symptoms in cherries are noticed. Small, narrow, chlorotic leaves are produced which are at usually distorted or wavy. Foliar spray of zinc sulphate at 2.5 kg in 100 litres of water in early spring at 2-3 years interval may correct its deficiency.

Mulching and Weed Control

Clean basin management is a most common method of floor management in sweet cherry plantation in Himachal Pradesh. Most of the cherry orchards are maintained under permanent sod with a clean basin management. Mulching in the tree basins with 10-15 thick hay in April helps to conserve soil moisture and also control the weed growth. To improve the fertility level and soil texture, green manuring in the tree basins is very useful practice. The crops like bean, pea, red clover and white clover are good for green manuring. Pre-emergence herbicide Diuron @ 4 kg/ha or post-emergence herbicide paraquat @ 5*l*/ha can check for weed flora for 4-5 months in sweet cherry orchards.

TRAINING AND PRUNING

Training of young trees : Sweet cherry plants should be trained to central modified leader system. The plant is headed back at 90-100 cm at the time of planting. The wide angled scaffold branches should be kept 20-25 cm and located spirally around the main stem. While forming a well-shaped tree, the selected scaffold branches should be headed back minimum to have a good balance between them and the leader. During second year, the central leader is retained and all the other upright branches should be removed by cutting close to the trunk. At this time only 3-5 wide angled main branches at 20-25 cm distance and spirally around the tree are retained. The lower scaffold branches may be kept 50 cm above ground. During pre-bearing period, scaffold should be headed back only when they grow very long and willowy and when it is desirable to have secondary shoots. The leader is cut back when the trees grows larger just close to an suitable outward growing branch.

Pruning of bearing trees : Pruning in bearing trees is done with a view to remove week and unnecessary branches. The centre of bearing tree should be kept open. In sweet cherry, fruit is borne laterally on spur which arise on one year old shoots. The spurs grow less than 2.5 cm in a year with a terminal leaf bud. The productive life of the spurs is 10-12 years in sweet cherry. As compared to sour cherry, less renewal wood is needed in sweet cherry. As such 10 per cent of fruit bearing area should be removed annually.

In sour cherry, 10-20 cm long annual shoot growth is sufficient in full grown bearing trees. The fruit buds in this cherry are produced laterally on one year old terminal growth. The fruiting spurs are produced on 2-3 year old vigorous shoots. Most of the crop is borne on the periphery of the tree. Therefore, the pruning in some cherries should comprise thinning out of long branches.

Pruning in cherries should be done late in season after growth has started as the danger of infection by silver leaf disease is then minimised.

POLLINATION AND FRUIT-SETTING

A large number of cherries are self-unfruitful and thus do not set crops with their own pollen they need cross-pollination. The cherries are also cross-incompatible with some other commercial varieties. Thus, only the compatible varieties can be interplanted to get commercial crops. The compatible varieties to be grown should be those whose periods of flowering sufficiently overlap, to effect cross-pollination. Stella which is a self fruitful variety should preferably be used in the combinations of other varieties. The other donor varieties like Vista, Vic, Senecca and Vega can be planted with any variety to get good fruit set. It is important that their flowering period must overlaps with main varieties. Honey bee usually carry the pollen grains from the anthers of one cultivar to the stigma of another cultivar. In case of sour cherries, yield is increased to an average of 67.8 per cent by planting self-fertile cultivars compared with 13.4 per cent in self-incompatible cultivars.

Open pollination gives adequate fruit set for a commercial crop in cherries which ranges from 7-50 per cent depending upon cultivar, climate and management practices being followed. Frequent and high rainfall and low temperature during flowering often interfere pollination which can be overcome by increasing the number of bee-hives in cherry orchards. GA_3 200 ppm + DPU (diphenyl urea) 300 ppm + NOXA 50 ppm or NAA 10 ppm or 2, 4, 5 TP 10 ppm applied in spring increased fruit number in sweet cherry. Paclobutrazol @ 0.8 g in an area of 2 × 2 metre weed free soil under each tree of cv. Early River of sweet cherry in March increased fruit size and yield considerably.

HARVESTING AND HANDLING OF FRUITS

In cherries, the stage of maturity for harvesting is of great importance in maintaining consumer acceptance. The harvesting of cherries before maturity results in flat fruits and less yield as its fruit usually make rapid development during the last few days before full maturity is reached. The cherries should not be allowed to overripe on the trees which results in loss of weight and volume.

The colour development of fruit is the best guide, though it varies with the cultivar and the purpose for which the fruit will be used. Total soluble solids of fruit is an another reliable index of fruit maturity. The taste of fruit may also guide the time of picking. Fruits of sweet cherries picked earlier does not taste well. The fruit picked late may be either very sweet or inisipid. The fruit picked at right stage of maturity have better size, colour, general appearance, taste, flavour, firmness and sugar-acid blend.

Sweet cherry varieties can be picked on the basis of number of days taken from full bloom to maturity. The fruits of Black Heart requires 52-58 days, Guigne Noir Hative 54-60 days, Bigarreau Napolean 65-68 days and Bigarreau Noir Grossa 69-74 days from full bloom to maturity. The fruits of different varieties ripens from third week of May to second week of June in Kashmir.

The fruit of cherry is picked by hand for which labour is required. The sweet cherry is picked with the stems unless they are to be delivered for processing. Pulling the cherries from the supporting stems causes a slight wound. The fruit can be artificially ripened by spraying 400 ppm ethephon two weeks before harvesting. Sour cherry used for processing is picked by pulling or stripping the fruits from the stems leaving the latter on the trees. Ethrel is used by some growers to collect fruits by shaking the trees.

The yield of sweet cherry is extremely variable from year to year. Sweet cherry trees grow larger than sour cherry and bear heavily. A good yield of 6.3 to 9 tonnes or more per hectare is obtained from standard trees. The mean yield of high yielding cultivars is recorded as high as 13 to 21 tonnes per hectare (57-92 kg per tree). The average yield is 15-20 kg per fruits per tree. The fruits are packed in 5 kg CFB boxes for better marketing.

Storage : To reduce losses from rotting and poor quality, rapid cooling of fruits immediately after picking is recommended. A hydro-cooling can be used in the orchard. The shelf life of cherry fruits can be extended by spraying 30-50 ppm GA_3 in the orchard before harvesting. Postharvest dipping of fruits in 40 g per litre solution of calcium chloride for 2 hours at ambient temperature (20°C) maintained fruit firmnes after 30 days of storage. The storage life of sweet cherry is 18 days in normal temperature (0°C and 85% RH) and 30 days in controlled atmosphere (8% carbon dioxide + 5% oxygen). Some cherries can be stored for 15 days at 0-2°C and 24 days at 5% CO_2 + 3% O_2.

INSECT-PESTS

1. Black cherry aphid (*Myzus cerasi*) : Aphid attack the leaves as soon as the bud burst and they continue to feed as long as the growth remain succulent. Infested leaves of sweet cherry curl and cluster then they turn yellow and die. The aphid also feed on the fruit.

The pest can be controlled by spraying 1 m1 Rogor or metasystox per litre of water before or at bud-swell stage.

2. Flat headed stem borer (*Sphenoptera lafertei*) : The borer first appear serious pest during sixties in Himachal Pradesh.

It can be controlled by swabbing treatment of the stem and main trunk to a height of about 2 metre from ground level with 0.2% methyl parathion first in February-March and again with 0.25% insecticidal concentration of swabbs during May-June, August and October.

DISEASES

1. Bacterial canker : It is caused by ***Pseudomonas syringae***. It is serious in sweet cherries. The disease causes bare branches by extensive killing of leaves and flower buds and spurs on two year or older wood. The bacteria destory the conducting tissues just below the bark. Dark brown streak of dead tissue may extend up and down the branches for a considerable distance beyond a visible canker. Leaf and flower spurs or entire branches wilt and die. Leaf infection during spring develops as small purplish spot surrounded by a ring of light green tissues. These spots become irregular in shape and turn brown.

Application of Mashobra paste during dormancy on cleaned, localized wounds is recommended to control the disease.

2. Verticillium wilt : The diesase is caused by ***Verticillium albo-atrum*** and ***Verticillium dahliae***.

The disease causes defoliation and wilting in young trees of less than 10 years age especially in sweet cherries. The infected trees remain stunted and unproductive for several years. The symptoms consists in wilting of foliage and the leaves turn pale green or yellow and finally drop.

Always select desirable well-drained soil for planting cherry orchards to minimise soil-borne diseases. In the young non-bearing orchard do not intercrop potatoes, tomatoes, egg plants, peppers, strawberries and raspberries as they favour increase of fungus in the soil. The pits may be fumigated with 3% formalin before planting.

3. Brown rot : Causal organism of this disease is ***Monilinia fucticola***. It is important disease of sweet cherry. On the affected fruits, small round spots develop. It cause severe losses during hot and humid weather conditions at harvest.

The disease can be controlled by adopting sanitation practices.

4. Crown and root gall : It is caused by bacteria ***Agrobacterium tumefaciens***. The wart-like tumors or swellings appears at the crown or on the roots. The galls are at first light in colour and soft in texture but later turn black and become hard. The bacterium of this disease lives in the soil.

The plants may be dipped in a 0.4 per cent copper sulphate solution for one hour before planting. In case of infected plants apply Chaubattia paste after superficial heating of the localized lesions with blow lamp.

5. Leaf spot : The disease is caused by ***Cercospora circumscissa***. Numerous minute purple spots appear on the upper surface of the leaves. For its control, spray Captan 75 WP (200 *g* in 100 litres of water) after petal fall. Repeat the spray 20 days later and after harvest.

6. Viral diseases : Sweet cherries on ***Prunus mahaleb*** rootstock wilt and decline rapidly after infection. Mottle leaf causes yellowish mottling of the leaves.

DISORDER

Fruit Cracking

The different cultivars of sweet cherry differ in their susceptibility to cracking. The cultivars with a rapid rate of absorption and a low capacity for expansion crack readily while those with a slow rate of absorption and a high capacity for expansion tend to be immune. Any treatment that decreases the rate of water absorption or increases the capacity of the fruit tissues to stretch without rupturing reduces the amount of cracking.

A spray of calcium chloride at 300-350 g per 100 litre water applied at weekly interval before harvest checked the fruit cracking in Bing and Lambert cultivars. Spraying of GA_3 2000 ppm on Ekero cultivar 3 weeks before harvesting reduced the amount of fruit cracking caused by heavy rainfall following drought.

CHAPTER 34

Strawberry

The cultivated strawberry (***Fragaria*** × ***ananassa*** Duch.) is a result of hybridization of two American octoploid species ***F. chiloensis*** and ***F. virginiana*** (Virginian Strawberry). Strawberry is a fruit of temperate climate but its cultivation can be done successfully in sub-tropical climate. It is one of the most preferred fruit in different parts of the world. The growing of strawberry is restricted in semi-arid regions of India due to variable climatic conditions. The fruit of strawberry is different from other fruits as their seeds are produced on the outside of the fruit. Strawberry is a quick growing plant and is cherished in home gardens and in commercial land for its beautiful, nutritious and bright red coloured fruits. The fruit is highly perishable and yet grown on a small scale in India. It has tremendous scope for its cultivation near the towns, cities and processing units where the fruit can be utilized immediately after harvest. Plasticulture technique used in strawberry cultivation can play important role in the manipulation of microclimate favourable for its successful growing.

ORIGIN, HISTORY AND DISTRIBUTION

The cultivated strawberry (***Fragaria*** × ***ananassa***) originated in France in 17th Century. It is now grown commercially all over India. Its progenitors are native to the new world. ***F. chiloensis*** is found to occur in Chile and coastal areas of South America. ***F. virginiana*** is located in Canada and United States of America and introduced in Europe in 1624. Natural population of ***F. ananassa*** is restricted to coastal California, Oregan and Washington. ***F. versa*** is the most broadly distributed natural species which is found in North and South America, Europe, Asia and Hawaii. Pine Strawberries [hybrid of ***F. virginiana*** (Male) and ***F. chiloensis*** (Female)] culture spread to other European nations particularly England where the first cultivars were produced during the early 1800. In America, the strawberry cultivation was started in the beginning of 18th century. In India, many strawberry cultivars were introduced in early 1960. Strawberry is grown extensively throughout the Europe, Canada, South America and many other countries. The major producing centre are USA, Span, Japan, Mexico, Italy, Russia and Turkey. Now, it is also cultivated on large scale in China, Japan, Israel, Australia, Turkey and New Zealand. In India, it is mainly cultivated in Maharashtra, Himachal Pradesh, Jammu and Kashmir and Uttarakhand.

Strawberry is one of the most widely distributed fruit crop due to its genotypic diversity, highly heterozygous nature and broad range of environmental adaptations.

AREA AND PRODUCTION

Strawberries are produced in 73 countries in the world on 2.4 lakhs hectare area. The annual production of strawberry in the world is estimated 45.9 lakhs mt. The leading strawberry producing countries are USA, Turkey, Spain, Egypt, Mexico, Russia, Japan, South Korea, Poland and Germany. In USA, California and Florida are the chief strawberry producing states. In India, Maharashtra is the leading state in strawberry cultivation. Himachal Pradesh, Meghalaya, Uttarakhand, Jammu and Kashmir, Uttar Pradesh, West Bengal (Dareeling), Rajasthan, Punjab and Haryana are other strawberry growing states.

In India, Satara district (Mahabaleshwar and Panchgani) in Maharashtra is the major strawberry producing area. Nearly 880 hectares are under strawberry cultivation in Mahabaleshwar. The annual production of strawberry in this area is around 18000 tonnes. The other strawberry growing areas in the country are Bangalore, Ooty, Ratlam (Madhya Pradesh), Kunnoor (Karnataka) and Nilgiri hills.

India export strawberry mainly to Austria, Bangladesh, Germany, Jordan and USA. In 2006, some 600 tonnes strawberries were exported to France and Belgium among other countries. This is attracting growers to undertake strawberry cultivation.

IMPORTANCE AND USES

Strawberry fruit is a rich source of vitamins and minerals. It is a good source of vitamin C and contains 60 mg ascorbic acid per 100 g of pulp. The fruit contain 5 per cent total sugars, 0.9 – 1.8 per cent acidity in terms of maleic and citric acids, protein 0.7 g, carbohydrates 8.4 g, vitamin A 601U, Iron 1 g, calcium 21 mg, phosphorus 21 mg and potassium 164 mg per 100 g fruit.

The fruits are consumed mostly fresh. However, various products like jam, fruit juice, pies, syrup, candy, ice-creams, preserve etc. are prepared. The fruits of cultivated strawberry are considered for diarrhea, gout, stomachache and kidney stones. The fruits are used as astringents, diuretics and mild laxatives. Strawberries contain high quantities of ellagic acid which inhibit cancer and HIV onto cells and HIV enzyme activity on DNA and function as antioxidants and free-radical scavengers.

BOTANY

Fragaria × *ananassa* Duch. (Cultivated strawberry) is an octaploid ($2n = 8x = 56$) belongs to the family Rosaceae, sub-family Rosoideae. About 34 other species of *Fragaria* are found in Asia, North and South America and Europe. Wood strawberry (*F. vesca*) and Musky strawberry (*F. moschata*) were cultivated in Europe and Russia for centuries. Wood strawberries are small with both red and white coloured fruits. Musky strawberries bear light red to purple coloured fruits. *F. ananassa* is a hybrid of two species *F. chiloensis* and *F. virginiana*. Strawberries are perennial, stoliniferous herbs which spread via stolons or runners. The leaves have three leaflets and arise from the crown. The plants of *F. virginiana* are tall bear imperfect flowers. The fruits are small sized, light to deep red in colour, flesh soft with pleasant aroma. The plants are fertilie and both hermaphrodite and unisexual plants are produced. It yield large quantity of runners. The plants of *F. chiloensis* are spreading in nature with stout stolons. The leaves are thick, blunt and toothed, flowers are white and borne in small cultuster. The fruits are large sized. In this species, both hermaphrodite and unisexual male and female plants are found.

The strawberry is an aggregate fruit. The true fruits that contain the seeds of the strawberry are achenes. The achenes are the numerous, tiny, ellipsoid specks that cover the fruit surface. The edible portion of fruit is fleshy thalamus.

CLIMATE

Strawberry grow best in temperate climate but can be grown with good success in sub-tropical climate. It always thrives well under selected agro-climatic conditions. A long growth period with growing warm summer and mild antumn is desirable. The plant growth observed maximum at 22°C day temperature and 7 – 13°C night temperature. Flower bud formation need daylight period of twelve hours or moderate temperature. Strawberry prefer relatively low optimum temperature for growth and fruiting. The growth of the plants takes place better in short days and cool temperature. Being a short day plant, it requires exposure atleast for 10 days of about eight hours sunshine for initiation of flowering.

In winter, the plants remain dormant and thus helps in breaking dormancy of the plant. In spring, due to rise in temperature the days become longer, the plants resume growth and initiate flowering. The commercial varieties of strawberry develop flower buds only during the short light period.

The strawberries are sensitive to frost damage and winter injury in temperate climate. The fruit yield is considerably reduced. The centre of the open flower is damaged with frost, thus, causing symptioms of 'Black Eye'. Occurence of spring frost is also deteremental to strawberry plants.. Flower open in sequence on the trusses and plant have long flowering period (April to early May), as such frost pockets should be avoided for its cultivation.

Long days and warm temperature favour leaf and runner production. Exposure of plants to long day after transplanting is proved beneficial in advancing flowers, extending flowering period, advance fruit maturity, reduce harvest span and improved fruit quality. High light intensity promotes ripening of berries. The high velocity of wind cause discolouration of leaves and may reduce the fruit yield.

SOIL

Strawberries can be grown on wide variety of soil from sandy to loamy soils. However, it grows well in fertile, well drained soils, rich in organic matter with PH 5.5 – 6.5. Root formation is poor at high soil pH. On light soils, irrigation will be necessary to establish runners and maintain berry size and quality. Moisture should be adequate during dry season for obtaining high yields. The plants are sensitive to salinity and alkalinity conditions. Nematode infested soils should be avoided for strawberry cultivation. The soil erosion can be checked by growing cover crops. The soil rich in organic matter or light soils are considered better for runner formation.

CHOICE OF VARIETIES

A good number of strawberry varieties are grown in temperate and sub-tropical climate. A salient characteristics of some of the important varieties are as follows :

Chandler : The fruits are conical (ovate) to sometimes long flat, skin shinny, glossy and attractive. Flesh colour same as that of the skin and firm throughout. Plants semi erect, medium in runner production, self-fertile. It is resistant to damage caused by rain and highly resistant to viral diseases. The fruit is large with average weight of 15-20 g. Total soluble solids 8.0 per cent, acidity 0.85 per cent and vitamin C is 55 mg/100 of fruit.

Tioga : The fruits are large in size and flesh and skin firm. It is a good dessert variety and has good processing quality. Total soluble solids 7.0 per cent, acidity 0.7 per cent and TSS/acid ratio 9.97. It is tolerant to viruses. This variety is grown under long day lengths in autumn and moderate winter conditions.

Torrey : The fruits are large in size and flesh and stem firmness medium. It is a good dessert variety and has excellent quality. Total soluble solids 7.4 per cent, acidity 0.7 per cent and TSS/acid ratio 10.68. Ripening starts by the first week of April in temperate zone. It has good processing quality.

Senga Sengana : It is a hybrid between Markee × Sieger. Plants are healthy. Fruits are attractive with red skin. Flesh firmness medium. It has good freezing quality. Runners begin to form in late August. It grows under short day lengths in autumn and severe winter conditions.

Pazaro : It is resistant to plant viruses and grow well under summer conditions. The plants are susceptible to rain damage. Fruit weight is approx 7.5 g. Its sugar content is 5.5 per cent.

Srinagar, Dilpasand and Royal Sovereign are best varieties for hilly areas. Polka, Gilbert, Oso Grand, Cavalier, Arking, Bangalore, Belrubi, Pusa Early Dwarf and Sweet Charlie are other promising varieties.

PROPAGATION TECHNIQUES

Seed propagation in strawberry has little importance as the seedling do not come true-to-type. In vegetative method, strawberries are propagated by runners. Early formed runners are vigorous, have good root system and more productive. These runners should be preferred for planting. For nursery raising, sandy soils with irrigation facilities are preferred to produce quality runners. Heavy soils should be avoided for runner production. The soil should be rich in organic matter for better runner quality. The freshly dug runners should be best planted in nursery bed during early winter or spring. The runners are detached from mother plants after attaining proper size. These are severed at the stolon and used as propagules. The runners used for propagation should always be healthy, vigorous and free from virus and diseases. A single plant of strawberry usually produces 12 to 18 runners. Runner production can be stimulated by using IBA @ 100 ppm or morphactin @ 50 ppm about 10 days before flowering.

The ideal time for planting for cold stored runners is the month of July. The runners in dormant stage are kept in cold store. Runners are lifted in December - January. Runners of 'Pusa Early Dwarf' variety store at 32°F in cold store for 60 days survive far better after transplanting than fresh materials.

Micropropagation. Micro-propagation through tissue culture has emerged as the most widely used and viable technique for large scale production of planting material. Strawberry plants are often produced through tissue culture to have virus free material. The plants from meristem culture produce higher yield than multiplied through runners.

PLANTING OPERATIONS

Preparation of soil. Before planting, the soil should be prepared well and removal of all the weeds is essential. Strawberry plants do not produce deep roots. However, the land should be properly prepared by deep ploughing before planting. While preparing land, soil should not be in wet condition and making a fine tilth for good structure is important. There should be proper drainage for excess rain water. Application of desired quantity of manure and fertilizers be made and mixed well with the soil to make the nutrients easily available to the new runners. Roots of the newly planted strawberries need oxygen as well as soil moisture and warmth, therefore, soil should not be too compact or firm.

Planting should be done on well prepared raised beds, or flat beds, hill rows or matted rows during August-September. In hilly areas, transplanting is done in March-April and September-October. Staggered planting from mid-September to mid-October at bi-weekly/weekly interval can be made for longer period of availability of plants *i.e.* January to April. In semi-arid region of Punjab, strawberry given micro-irrigation planted in mid-September enhanced plant growth and resulted early flowering (77 days) and fruiting (33 days). Under sub-tropical conditions of Jammu, planting of strawberry on 9 October coupled with black polythene mulching was considered most favourable in terms of fruit size and yield.

Late planting results in reduction in yield during the first year. The beds made for planting should be sufficiently large to accommodate the roots. The soil around the roots should be pressed properly for better enchorage. In Kashmir Valley, runners can be planted during October-November and upto February-March provided soil and weather conditions are favourable. Planting in Mahabaleshwar is done on raised beds of 4 × 3 m or 4 × 4 m during November - December.

Systems of Planting

The strawberry plants are planted according to different systems as follow :

***(i)* Single hill beds :** In this system, the plants are to be planted 30 cm apart within the rows. Row to row distance is kept 90 cms.

***(ii)* Mid-hill planting :** The distance from plant to plant and row to row is kept 30 × 60 cm under this system. Spacing of 30 × 30 cm is also commonly followed which accommodate population of 55000 plants per hectare.

***(iii)* Double-row beds :** In this system, the double row plants are grown on each bed with a distance of 30 × 30 cm within the row and plant to plant. Distance from one bed to another bed is kept 105 to 120 cms.

Planting of runners at 25 × 25 cm spacing with four rows of plants per bed accommodates one lakh plants per hectare. The planting distance can be kept from plant to plant 45 cm and row to row 60 – 75 cm. In Shalimar Kashmir Valley, double row system of planting is considered most suitable for strawberry crop and distance of 30 × 40 × 60 cm within plants, rows and between beds yield maximum benefit. In another study, spacing of 30 – 50 cm in rows 100 cm apart allowing the pickers to work conveniently between rows.

FLOWERING AND FRUITING

The cultivated strawberry bear two types of flowers *i.e.* hermophrodite and pistillate flowers. The flowers occur in cluster and each flower contains five sepals and five petals. The inflorescence in strawberry is receme type. A flower contains 60 to 600 pistils and 20 to 35 stamens. Plants bloom in late winter or early spring depending upon the location and climatic conditions.

The strawberry fruits follow simple sigmoid growth pattern. An exponential increase in fruit size in the later stages was related to fruit softening. Three distinct phases of fruit development takes place. The first phase begins after pollination and is associated with the development of nucleus in the carpel. It ends about 10 days after pollination. The second phase is dependent on an actively growing cellular endosperm. The third phase starts after attainment of full size of embryo. This is termed as rapid enlargement of receptacle. This phase depend greatly on external application of growth substances. An increase in sugar content with corresponding decrease in acidity observed with the advancement of maturity.

Parthenocarpy : Parthenocarpy in fruits of strawberry can be induced with exogenous application of auxin *i.e.* 1AA. It is reported that contribution of fertilized achene in promoting fruit growth can be replaced with growth regulators. In male sterile varieties, induction of parthenocarpy is more successful.

Deblossoming : In June bearing strawberries, flowers are removed during the first growing season. This practice promotes runner development as well as helps in better root system and results in good crop in the following year. In day-neutral and everbearing strawberries, flowers should be removed until end June. After that, flowers are allowed to continue for setting fruit for summer/fall harvest.

ORCHARD CULTURAL PRACTICES

Irrigation

Regular watering to strawberry plants is very important for stable production over the years. It is a shallow-rooted plant that requires more frequent but less amount of water in each irrigation. Optimum irrigation improves size and general appearance of berries, enhance yield and extend harvesting period. Heavy watering leads to continuous growth of leaves and stolons and also enhance the incidence of *Botrytis* rot.

Early planting require more irrigation as runners are actively growing and will not withstand dry soil conditions. Late planting need lesser irrigations as they readily get established. The soil should always be just kept moist for good growth of the plant. During September - October, irrigation should be given twice a week. Irrigation interval should be kept weekly in November and fortnightly in December - January.

Irrigation is applied in furrows between the rows. Drip and sprinkler methods of irrigation are more suitable for strawberry plantation. Drip system should be run two or three times in a week and fertigation should be given fortnightly.

Weed Control

Weeds poses serious threat in strawberry production. They compete with the strawberry plants for nutrients and moisture results low yield of poor quality fruits. Motha is one of most serious weed in strawberry. Mulching with black polythene effectively suppresses weed growth. Oxyfluorfen + napropamide @ 0.60 + 5.0 kg a.*i*/ha check weed population effectively in strawberry plantation in Jammu region.

Simazine 3 kg/ha in spring is reported to control the weeds effectively. Stomp 5 l/ha also reduce weed flora in strawberry fields.

Mulching

Mulching the strawberry field is very useful practice as it helps in conservation of soil moisture, checks weed growth and avoids the direct contact of berries with soil. Both organic and inorganic mulches are used in cultivation of strawberries. Mulches reduces the percentage of spoiled fruits and prevents the infection due to fruit root. Before mulching, the soil should be dusted with insecticide for protection against insects.

Strawberry beds can be mulched with pine needles, grain straw or saw dust. Black polythene mulch increase temperature of the soil and also soil moisture during summer. In arid-irrigated zone of Punjab at Abohar under micro-irrigation conditions, strawberry mulched with black polythene produced higher yield than mulched with clear polythene and paddy straw.

Manuring and Fertilization

The healthy and vigorous growth and optimum fruit yield of good quality can be achieved only with proper application of manures and fertilizers to strawberry plants. Excessive fertilization cause profuse vegetative growth, reduce yield, attract foliar diseases and winter injury to the plants.

In Himachal Pradesh, 50 tonnes of farmyard manure alongwith 40 kg P_2O_5 and 40 kg K_2O per hectare is applied at the time of preparation of beds. Nitrogen @ 80 kg per hectare is applied in two split doses. Half the quantity is applied in the month of September or after the establishment of plants in September - October and half is given after blossoming. In another study, higher yield and better fruit quality was obtained with a fertilizer dose of 150 kg nitrogen and 75 kg, P_2O_5 per hectare.

In Kashmir, application of 50 - 70 tonnes of FYM alongwith 40 kg nitrogen and 80 kg K_2O per hectare is given for adequate cropping.

In Uttarakhand hills, 25 - 50 tonnes of FYM, 75 - 100 kg nitrogen, 80 - 120 kg P_2O_5 and 50 - 80 kg K_2O per hectare is applied. Half dose of nitrogen is given one month after planting and remaining half at the time of flowering. Whole phosphorus and half dose of potash is given at planting time. Remaining potash is applied at the time of flowering. Application of vermicompost to strawberry is very useful in improving plant growth and fruit yield. Vermicompost @ 10t/ha proved beneficial in increasing the yield and production of healthy fruits in Chandler variety.

Nutrient Deficiencies : Deficiencies of phosphorus, potassium, magnesium, iron and managenese are common in strawberry. Phosphorus deficiency results in poor growth of plants, early defoliation of older leaves with few crowns. Leaves remain dull green with a little purple tinge which increases as defoliation approaches. Potassium deficiency cause dark green leaves with scorched margins. Magnesium deficiency appears in older leaves. They turn bright yellow with red tints in centre and near the margins. Iron deficiency cause chlorotic leaves with visible vein pattern. Manganese deficiency results faint leaves with interveinal chlorosis beginning at margins.

PROTECTION FROM COLD

Both flowers and fruits are susceptible to frost injury after bud break. Thus protection from frost and cold winds is required during winter. Plastic covers on rows are deployed in autumn to protect the plants against frost damage. Sometimes, late occurrence of frost also prove more harmful. Plastic covers increase degree days, maintained required temperature and increase the fruit yield. These are removed in spring.

Straw mulch is commonly used during winter to protect the plants from frost. The thickness of straw mulch should be 10 cm for effective protection from cold. Use of plastic cover advanced flowering by about one week over use of conventional straw mulch. During winter, the plants should be protected from wind during night by putting up plastic tunnels over the beds with the help of wires. Light irrigation to plantation before frost occurrence also provide protection against freeze damage.

TRAINING SYSTEMS

Three training systems are followed in strawberry *i.e.* hill system, spaced row system and matted row system.

Hill System : Multiple rows are made in groups of 2, 3 or 4 plants with 60 cm path between each group of rows. Plants are set 30 cm apart in multiple rows. Runners are removed so that the available nutrients may be utilized by the mother plant. This system is the best for growing day-neutral and overbearing varieties. The cost of production is more in hill system. The yield is less but fruits are larger in size.

Spaced-row system : Runners are not removed. The number and spacing of new plant is regulated. The mother plants are set 30 to 75 cm apart in rows one meter apart. It helps in the increase of the size of the plant and fruit yield. Three to four plants may be allowed to develop from each runner.

Matted-row system : This system is commonly followed in India and considered best for June bearing cultivars. The mother plant may be spaced 30 cm × 90 cm apart in rows 120 to 150 cm apart. Runners allowed to develop so that the plants occupy a space of 90 – 120 cm. The yield depends on the number of plants and spacing between plants and rows. Leaves can be moved off after harvest to eliminate diseased foliage and facilitate weed control and mulching.

POLLINATION AND FRUIT-SETTING

In strawberry, cross pollination by insects is useful since stigmas become receptive before the anthers release pollen. However, fertilization of achene is possible through self-pollination. Honey bees are the main pollinating agent but some more insects are also involved in pollination process. *Apis mellifera* (Italian Honey bees) play important role in pollination of strawberries and the fruit produced are better in size and develop better marketable quality.

The receptacle swells after fertilization, becomes fleshy and develop into a berry. Poor fruit setting is associated with external factors which might be responsible for reduction in stamen abortion. Pollen fertility is reduced due to low temperature and short days. Frost occurrence, hot dry winds, insect-pests and diseases attack at flowering leads to poor fruit setting in strawberries. Nutrient status of soil also considered important in better flowering and fruit setting. Fruit-setting can be improved by spray application of plant growth regulators. GA_3 @ 50 ppm sprayed four days after flowering and maleic hydrazide @ 0.1 – 0.3 per cent sprayed after flowering improve the yield by 30 – 40 per cent. The fruit size can be improved by spraying morphactin @ 50 ppm.

PROTECTED CULTIVATION

The commercial production of strawberry using the plasticulture system is becoming popular with the growers. Protected cultivation of strawberry in plastic tunnels, green houses and glass house structure is meant for early production of fruits. The plants under these structures flower one to one and half month earlier than the unprotected plants and produce ripe fruits earlier than those available from open cultivation. Plastic films of 150 mm can be used and kept for two years. Ventilation is provided to avoid excessive heat and to avoid development of malformed fruits.

Chandler variety is most suitable for growing in protected structures and produced best quality fruits. In plasticulture system, the raised beds are formed each year, fumigated and covered with plastic to prevent weed growth and erosion. Plants are planted through holes punched in this covering.

Use of plastic tunnels in Chandler cultivar enhanced earliness in fruit ripening and produced higher yield. Low tunnels of 50 cm height with transparent polythene film of 50 micron with the help of G1 wires can be installed in winter months from December to February to protect the plants from cold. Tunnels should be opened during day time for maintaining high temperature inside for early flowering and better fruit yield.

HARVESTING AND HANDLING OF FRUITS

The strawberry plants starts fruiting after 3-4 months of planting. The fruit ripens from end February to April in the plains and during May and June at higher elevation like Kashmir, Nainital and Mahabaleshwar. Three successive crops can be taken but yield and quality deteriorate after two seasons.

The fruits are harvested alongwith the caps still attached and with their stalks when 50 percent of the surface has attained red colour. The fruits harvested at 75 per cent red colour, develop full red colour within 1-2 days at 21°C temperature. For sending to longer distant market, berries are harvested immediately after reaching full colour. For processing purpose, fruits are picked firm ripe with one to two third of the surface showing colour. For local markets, fruits are picked with cap and stem of about 12 mm length. Strawberries are allowed to ripen on the plant fully as they do not continue to ripen after harvest.

Strawberries do not mature uniformly, as such harvesting should be completed in many pickings. The fruits should be picked up daily in warm weather and 2-3 times a week under cold conditions. Picking operation should be completed before noon to avoid heating to berries. Picking should be done in the early hours to avoid spoilage during transportation and storage. After harvest, fruits should be kept under shade to avoid damage due to excessive heat in the open field. The strawberry fruits decay within 2-3 days of harvesting under natural conditions.

The taste of berry depends upon the sugar, acid and aroma which are associated with inherent characters and environment conditions. The berry is rich in vitamin C and its content increases as the ripening advanced. Sugar content increases and acidity decreases untill berry attain full ripe stage. Sugar/acid and tannin ratio is termed as a good index for judging stage of ripeness.

The strawberry is a non-climacteric fruit. The respiratory peaks is reached at full to overipe stage. Senga Sengana variety takes 30 to 40 days from full bloom to maturity. Different varieties of strawberry produced an average yield 50 - 60 q/ha but higher yield upto 8 q/ha can be achieved. Still higher yield upto 250 q/ha may be achieved by following standard practices and growing recommended cultivars.

Pre-cooling of fruits at 4°C immediately after harvesting is very useful practice in extending life in cold store. The fruits after pre-cooling should be transported in refrigerated van for sending to the markets. The fruits should be packed in perforated CFB cartons with paper cuttings as cashioning material.

The fruits can be stored upto 10 days in cold storage at 32°F. The shell life of Senga Sengana variety at 6°C was found to be 8 days with 20 per cent carbon dioxide. The fruits stored at 3°C in oxygen or at 5 – 20 per cent carbon dioxide remained is good condition for 10 days. All the concentration of carbon dioxide reduced rotting due to *Botrytis*.

PLANT PROTECTION MEASURES

A. Insect-Pests

White grubs and cut worms : These insects cut the roots and stems of young plants.

Drench the soil with chlorpyriphos 0.1 per cent (5 ml Durmet/Dursban 20 EC per litre water) during March. Give deep ploughing and treat the soil with insecticidal dust.

Hairy Caterpillars : These pests defoliate the plants during June-July. Spray malathion 0.05 per cent (200 ml cythion/malathion 50 EC in 200 *l* water) on the appearance of the insects. Harvest berries 7-10 days after Malathion spray.

Fruit borer (*Helicoverpa armigera*) : Larvae bore into the developing fruits and make them unfit for consumption.

Spray malathion 0.05 per cent (300 ml malathion in 200 *l* water) when the pest is noticed.

B. Diseases

Leaf spot (*Mycosphaerella fragariae*) : Deep, purple brown spots with white centre appear on leaflets. Elongated lesions develop on petioles and fruit stem. Entire leaflet may be killed, thus, affecting the yield.

Planting of strawberry should be done in well drained soil. Wider spacing can reduce the leaf spot injury. Check weeds in strawberry plantation. During growth period, give 2-3 sprays with Bordeaux mixture (copper sulphate 800 g + lime 800 g in 10 *l* water) at 10-15 days interval. In between these sprays, give one spray with carbendazim (100 g in 200 *l* water).

Leaf spot complex (***Phyllosticta fragaricola, Phyllosticta sp., Pestalotia sp., Robillarda sp., Hainesia lythri, Pestalotiopsis sp.***) : Spots of different shapes and sizes appear on the leaves during rainy season which results in drying and defoliation.

With the appearance of disease, give 2-3 sprays of hexaconazol (100 ml in 200 *l* water) or 5 sprays of carbendazim (100 g per 200 *l* water) at 21 days interval.

Gray mold or Fruit rot (*Botrytis cinerea*) : The fungus primarily starts as blossom infection by air borne spores or by contact with infected material. The infected fruits reduce to a soft mass covered with velvety grey dusty spores of the fungus. Fruit rot occur due to attack of this disease as fruit ripen.

Proper sanitation of strawberry field is needed as fungus survives in dead leaf material. Do not allow fruits to touch the soil. Apply black polythene or straw mulch before flowering. Spray carbendazim or thiophanate methyl @ 100 g or captan 50 WP @ 600 g in 200 *l* water just after the blossom open and repeat after 15 days.

Yellow leaf spot (*Dendrophoma abscurans*) : Minute, purplish spots appear scattered on the upper surface of leaf during July to September. The spots soon attain a characteristic halo with yellow brown center surrounded by a purplish zone. Later on spots become oblong or irrigular blotches. The affected area dies up and leaves become puckered or develop shot holes.

The disease can be controlled by spraying mancozeb @ 200 g/100 *l* water or carbendazim @ 50 g/100 *l* water.

Antrhacnose (*Colletotrichum gloeosporioides*) : Minute, dull, violet-black or black spots appear on leaf surrounded by yellow region. Spots coalesce forming bigger spots thus causing defoliation.

Plantation should be done in well-drained and weed free soils. Spray copper oxychloride (300 g in/100 *l* water) or carbendazim (50 g in 100 *l* water) at 10 – 15 days interval. Two or three sprays should be given repeatedly.

Leaf blight and dry stalk (*Rhizoctonia bataticola*) : Circular spots with ashy grey centre and purplish margins appear on leaves. Later on, spots become oval or irregular. Leaf puckering and curling takes place and defoliation occured. Runners and stalks turn dark brown or black with irregular lesions.

Disease free plant material should be planted. Water-logged and silk soils should be avoided for strawberry plantation. Spray mancozeb (300 g in 100 *l* water) or copper oxychloride (300 g in 100 *l* water) when disease is noticed. Sprays should be repeated twice-thrice at 15 days interval.

Black root rot complex (*Fusarium orthoceras, Pythium sp., Leptosphaeria coniothyrium, Corticium vagum*) : Uneven patches appear on plants due to dwarfing of affected plants, Roots develop brown areas. Small and fibrous rootlets are killed. Lesions extend and entire root is blackened. Leaves turn yellowish, remain small with short petioles. Old leaves wither. Berries remain small or wither before ripening.

Virus free plant material should be procured. Plantation on the same field should be avoided. Treat the soil before sowing with 40 per cent formaldehyde (40 ml per *l* water). Use 5 *l* solution per square metre area and cover with polythene sheet. These sheets are removed after 48 hours. Rake the soil before transplanting.

DISORDER

Albinism is a physiological disorder in the fruit of strawberry. Disorder occurred due to lack of fruit colour during ripening. Probably, this disorder is caused by certain climatic conditions and nutrition excess. Fruit remain white or irregularly pink and swollen in certain cases. The fruits become less firm and have acid taste. Such fruits often damaged during harvesting, become susceptible to *Botrytis* and decayed during storage.

References

BOOKS/BULLETINS/MANUALS/REPORTS/RESEARCH PAPERS/ WEBSITES CONSULTED

Anon, 1977. Papaya cultivation. I.I.H.R., Bangalore.

Anon, 1977. Pineapple cultivation. I.I.H.R., Bangalore.

Anon, 1979. Guava cultivation. I.I.H.R., Bangalore.

Anon, 2002. Package of Practices for Fruit Crops. SKUAST, Srinagar.

Anon, 2003. Package of Practices for Fruit Crops. YSPUHF, Solan

Anon, 2008. Strawberry cultivation in India. *www.scribed.com/doc/2297087/strawberry-cultivation.*

Anon, 2011. Fruits-Flowers-Vegetables-Production and Recommendations. CCS, HAU, Hisar.

Anon, 2012. Indian Horticulture Database, NHB

Anon, 2012. Agricultural Statistics at a Glance. Directorate of Economics and Statistics. Ministry of Agriculture, New Delhi.

Anon, 2012. Package of Practices for cultivation of Fruits. PAU, Ludhiana.

Anon, 2013. Apeda database. Ministry of Commerce and Industry, New Delhi.

Anon, 2013. Fruits area and production. Directorate of Horticulture, Punjab.

Atwal, A.S., and G.S. Dhaliwal, 2004. Agricultural Pests of South Asia and their Management. Kalyani Publishers, New Delhi.

Aulakh, P.S., V.K. Mehan, B.S. Chahil and J.S. Bal, 2011. Prospects and Problems of citrus in Punjab. PAU, Ludhiana.

Awasthi, R.P. and H.S. Verma, 1986. Apple cultivation in Himachal Pradesh. Dr. Y.S. Parmar University of Horticulture and Forestry, Solan.

Bajwa, B.S. and J.C. Bakshi, 1961. Date-palm in India. Ministry of Food and Agriculture, New Delhi.

Bajwa, G.S. and J.S. Bal, 1984. Citriculture manual. Department of Horticulture, P.A.U., Ludhiana.

Bajwa, M.S. and J.P. Nauriyal, 1972. Cultivation of Plum. P.A.U., Ludhiana.

Bal, J.S. 1985. The Horticultural Bulletin, Vol. 27 (1-12). The Punjab State Co-operative Fruit Development Federation Ltd., Patiala.

Bal, J.S. 2010. Horticulture News Letter, **6** (1 – 4).

Bal, J.S. 2013. The utilization of rootstocks in India jujube. *Acta Horticulturae*, 993 : 47-50.

Bal, J.S. and D.K Uppal, 1992. Ber Varieties. Associated Publishing Co., New Delhi.

Bal, J.S. and H. Singh, 2006. Practical Manual of Temperate Fruits. Department of Horticulture, P.A.U., Ludhiana.

Bal, J.S. and J.S. Randhawa, 2007 *Ber.* Punjab Agricultural University, Ludhiana.

Bal, J.S. and S. Singh, 2012. *Mulching in Ber Orchards.* LAMBERT Academic Publishing' GmbH and Co. K.G. Saarbrucken, Germany.

Bal, J.S. H.S. Rattanpal, N.K. Arora and J. Singh, 2008. Practical Manual of Work Experience in Specialized Skills in Horticulture. PAU, Ludhiana.

Bal, J.S., H.S. Dhaliwal and N.K. Arora, 2009. Practical Manual of Tropical and Sub-tropical Fruits. PAU, Ludhiana.

Barooah, S. 1995. Modern Fruit Culture. Kalyani Publishers, New Delhi.

Bose, T.K., S.K. Mitra and D. Sanyal, 2001. Fruits : Tropical and Subtropical Vol. I Naya Udyog, Calcutta.

Bose, T.K., S.K. Mitra and D. Sanyal, 2001. Fruits : Tropical and Sub-tropical. Vol. 2. Naya Udyog, Calcutta.

Brooke, J. 1951. Peaches, apricots and other stone fruit. London, Faber.

Chadha, K.L. and O.P. Pareek, 1993. Advances in Horticulture Vol. 2. Malhotra Publishing House, New Delhi.

Chadha, K.L. and O.P. Pareek, 1993. Advances in Horticulture. Vol. 4. Malhotra Publishing House, New Delhi.

Chadha, K.L. and R.P. Awashti, 2005. The Apple : Improvement, Production and Post-harvest Mangement. Malhotra Publishing House, New Delhi.

Chadha, T.R. 2001. Text Book of Temperate Fruits. ICAR, New Delhi.

Chanana, Y.R., J.S. Bal, V.K. Mehan, J.K. Sharma and M.I.S. Gill, 2005. 40 years of Research on Fruit Crops. PAU, Ludhiana.

Chandra, A. and I.C. Gupta, 1992. Date-palm research in Thar desert, Jodhpur.

Chattopadhyay, T.K. 1996. A Text Book on Pomology. Vol. II. Kalyani Publishers, New Delhi.

Chattopadhyay, T.K. 1997. A Text Book on Pomology. Vol. III. Kalyani Publishers, New Delhi.

Chattopadhyay, T.K. 1999. A Text Book on Pomology. Vol. IV. Kalyani Publishers, New Delhi.

Childers, N.F. 1973. Modern Fruit Science. Rutgers University, New Jersey.

Chundawat, B.S. and N.L. Sen, 2002. Principles of Fruit Culture. Agrotech Publishing, Co. Udaipur.

Gandhi, S.R. 1959. The mango in India. Farm Information Unit. Directorate of Extension, Ministry of Food and Agriculture, New Delhi.

Gandhi, S.R. 1964. The Chiku in India. ICAR, New Delhi.

Gardner, V.R., F.C. Bradford and H.D. Hooker, 1952. The fundamentals of Fruit production. McGraw Hill Book Co. Inc., USA.

Gill, G.S., A.S. Bindra and W.S. Dhillon, 1992. Viticulture in North West India. Deptt. of Horticulture, P.A.U., Ludhiana.

Gill, K.S., J.S. Kanwar and R. Singh, 1990. Citriculture in North-Western India P.A.U., Ludhiana.

Gill, S.S., J.S. Bal and A.S Sandhu, 1985. Raising Fruit Nursery. Kalyani Publishers, New Delhi.

Gourley, J.H. and F.S. Howlett, 1957. Modern Fruit Production. The MacMillan Co., New York.

Gupta, V.K. and S.K. Sharma, 2000. Diseases of Fruit Crops. Kalyani Publishers, New Delhi.

Hartmann, H.T., D.E. Kester and F.T. Davies, 1993. Plant Propagation, Principles and Practices. Prentice-Hall of India Pvt. Ltd., New Delhi.

Hayes, W.B. 1953. Fruit Growing in India. Kitabistan, Allahabad.

Jawanda, J.S. and K.L. Chadha, 1977. Grape cultivation in Punjab. P.A.U., Ludhiana.

Kannan, K.P. 1983. Cashew development in India : Potentialities and constraints. Agricole Publication, New Delhi.

Kanwar, J.S. and J.S. Bal, 2004. Practical Manual of Propagation and Nursery Management. Department of Horticulture, P.A.U., Ludhiana.

Madhava Rao, V.N. 1984. Banana. I.C.A.R., New Delhi.

Mitra, S.K., D.S. Rathore and T.K. Bose, 1991. Temperate Fruits. Naya Prokash, Calcutta.

Nagpal, R.L. 1964. Pomegranate cultivation in India. I.C.A.R., New Delhi.

Nauriyal, J.P. 1966. Apple cultivation in Punjab. P.A.U., Ludhiana.

Nijjar, G.S. 1972. Litchi cultivation, P.A.U., Ludhiana.

Nijjar, G.S. 1973. Citrus. P.A.U., Ludhiana.

Nijjar, G.S. 1985. Fruit Breeding in India. Oxford & IBH Publishing Co., New Delhi.

Nijjar, G.S. 1985. Nutrition of Fruit Trees. Kalyani Publishers, New Delhi.

Pandey, R.M. and S.N. Pandey, 1990. Grapes in India. I.C.A.R., New Delhi.

Pareek, O.P, 2001. Ber. International Centre for Underutilized Crops. Univ. of Southampton, Southampton (U.K.).

Pathak, R.K. 2009. Status Report on Genetic Resources of Indian Gooseberry - Aonla (*Emblica officinalis* Gaertn.) in South and Southeast Asia. NASC, New Delhi.

Philip, S. 2002. Fruit Crops Diseases in the Field and Storage. Kalyani Publishers, New Delhi.

Randhawa, G.S. and K.C. Srivastava, 1986. Citriculture in India. Hindustan Publication, Delhi.

Randhawa, G.S. and R.K.N. Singh, 1970. Loquat in India. I.C.A.R., New Delhi.

Ray, P.K. 2002. Breeding Tropical and Sub-tropical Fruits. Narosa Publishing House, New Delhi.

Rieger, M. 2006. *Introduction to Fruit Crops.* Food Products Press. NY, USA.

Sandhu, A.S., G.S. Dhaliwal and J.S. Bal, 2004. Laboratory Manual of Fruit Growing. PAU, Ludhiana.

Sharma, K.K. and M.S. Bajwa, 1983. Pear cultivation in the Punjab, P.A.U., Ludhiana.

Singh J. 2011 *Basic Horticulture*. Kalyani Publishers, New Delhi

Singh, A. 1990. Fruit Physiology and Production .Kalyani Publishers, New Delhi.

Singh, H.P. and S. Uma, 1997. Indian Hort.; **42** : 18-28.

Singh, K.K. and G.S. Nijjar, 1971. Cultivation of phalsa. P.A.U. Ludhiana.

Singh, L.B. 1968. The mango, botany, cultivation and utilization. Leonard Hill, London.

Singh, R. 1969. Fruits. National Book Trust, India.

Singh, R.N. 1990. Mango. I.C.A.R., New Delhi.

Singh, S. and J.S. Bal, 1988. Punjab vich nakhan di kashat. Ext. Bull. Deptt. of Horticulture, P.A.U., Ludhiana.

Singh, S., S. Krishnamurthi and S.L. Katyal, 1967. Fruit culture in India. I.C.A.R., New Delhi.

Singh, S.P. 1995. Commercial Fruits. Kalyani Publishers, New Delhi.

Wikipedia, 2013 and 2014. Area and Production of fruits. Wikipedia, the free encyclopedia. www.en.wikipedia. org/wiki/Fruit (Individual)

Zielinski, Q.B. 1955. Modern Systematic Pomology. W.M.C. Brown Company. Dubuque, Iowa.